SOUTHEASTERN
ALASKA

SCALE 1 INCH = APPROX. 60 MILES

N

PACIFIC OCEAN

ALEXANDER ARCHIPELAGO

CANADA
USA

STIKINE RIVER

KETCHIKAN

PRINCE OF WALES I.

ADMIRALTY I.

CHICHAGOF I.

Hoonah

Pelican

Mt. Edgecumbe

Sitka

Angoon

Killisnoo

Kake

Petersburg

Wrangell

Loring

Saxman

Metlakatla

Annette

Kasaan

Klawock

Craig

Hydaburg

Cape Addington

The State of Alaska

The State of

Random House

New York

ERNEST GRUENING

ALASKA

*To Dorothy, my beloved wife, and
to the wonderful sons she bore us,
Ernest, Jr., Huntington Sanders, and Peter Brown—
two of whom live on in cherished memory—and
to our grandchildren, Clark,
Bradford Ingalls, Winthrop Huntington,
Kimberley Louise and Peter Sather—
the last four born in Alaska.*

Alaska's past makes
the North Pacific archipelago of prime importance
in the history of man.
As the prehistoric gateway from Asia to America
it is both the *first frontier* in the New World
and a *last frontier*. It has the unique distinction of
being an *eastern frontier* and a *western frontier*.
It is both the *oldest frontier* and
the *newest frontier* of this continent.
That its prehistory and history deserve serious
research and writing is manifest.

Robert A. Frederick
June 10, 1967

Contents

Charts

Maps

Foreword

THE following study seeks to relate and interpret the history of a region which in the first half of its existence under the United States had less government and in the second half more government—but always less self-government—than any other American area since the founding of the Republic. The Russian period has been accorded only brief summary and comment, since it has been amply treated by Bancroft, Golder, Andrews, Tompkins, Okun, Hulley and others, and because, except for one transcendent contribution to history which is to be recorded—I believe for the first time—its subsequent influence on Alaska was slight and is today negligible. The American period is naturally of more concern to us, and but for Jeannette Paddock Nichols's scholarly work of thirty years ago, which takes the story only to 1912, no analysis of the relations of federal government and territory, and of the economic forces shaping the destiny of Alaska has been attempted.

Nevertheless I could not forbear to rewrite briefly what others have written about Bering, because Alaskan history begins with him, and there is a valid relation between the last great voyage of discovery on earth and the subsequent fate of the land he discovered. Similarly I have included Steller because his caliber and unique contributions make me feel that he should be enshrined in our thinking as an Alaskan figure, especially since, except for Stejneger's definitive biography, his memorable services seem not to have been accorded their due.

E. G.

Juneau, Alaska
August, 1954

Foreword to the Revised Edition

The State of Alaska was published in 1954. Its objective—to expose factually and objectively the unique neglect and downright discrimination which Alaska had endured under United States rule, as contrasted with other American territories, and to point out that statehood was essential as a remedial first step—was in part realized by the admission of Alaska as the forty-ninth state.

To complete the history of the event, it has seemed desirable to the author to record the final five years of the struggle for statehood, as well as to summarize the developments of the subsequent decade which bring the story of Alaska to the end of the first century under the American flag.

I think it may be affirmed, as suggested in the concluding sentence of the first edition, that the state of Alaska has gained appreciably because and since the State of Alaska came into being. Yet, it is evident that considerable vestiges of absentee controls, perpetuated in law and custom, particularly in government, persist. The heritage of stepchildhood and colonialism, manifested in distant bureaucratic domination, remains. Both "catching up" to recover from past omissions and further emancipation are required for Alaska's well-being. This is an essential part of the challenge confronting the citizens of the forty-ninth state as they enter the second century under the Stars and Stripes.

E. G.

Juneau, Alaska
June, 1968

DISCOVERY

1741-1867

Bering

I have fought a good fight, I have finished my course, I have kept the faith.
II TIMOTHY, 4: 7

BY THE end of the seventeenth century the shape of the earth's seas and continents was established except for parts of the circumpolar regions. The principal missing area was the North Pacific, which remained blank on world maps till well into the eighteenth century. The west coast of the American continent vanished abruptly just north of Cape Mendocino in the northern part of California. It was not known whether the converging continental masses of Asia and America were joined, whether they were separated by a narrow body of water, or by a large island mass, a possible sub-continent.

It was to this question primarily which Peter the Great and, after his death in 1725, his widow, the Empress Catherine I, sought an answer. It became available sixteen years later when Bering's two vessels sighted two widely separated portions of the American coast.

What had taken place was really the third discovery of America, assuming Leif Ericson's to be the first and Columbus's the second. It was also the first discovery of America from the west. Of course we mean *recorded* discovery. Asiatics, in the dim unknown reaches of prehistory, had discovered and settled the two Americas in migrations that presumably crossed Bering Strait and the Aleutian Islands stepping stones. Their descendants were occupying Alaska when Bering's discovery opened the way to an occupation of Russian America by the Czar's minions.

Bering's was the last great voyage of discovery on our planet. It completed the outlines of the habitable world. It marked the end of an epoch as well as the beginning of another. The discovery of Al-a-aska,[1] the "Great Land," as it was referred to in the language of the Aleuts, was also, considering all the difficulties, a worthy performance when measured in a retrospective view of mankind's epic. It raised a curtain on an important scene in the great act in history's drama in which Columbus, the Cabots, Cortez and others had been the principal actors and the Atlantic Ocean and its borders had been the stage, across which the westward course of empire had taken its way. Now, toward the end of the era of discovery, for the first time the course of empire moved eastward across the Pacific.

Besides exploration, imperial and national prestige and the ambition common to reigning dynasties in the seventeenth, eighteenth and nineteenth centuries to extend their dominions, the fur trade provided the basic economic motivation which led to the discovery of Alaska. This quest had carried the banners of the Czars across Siberia in the seventeenth century, subduing successively its varieties of semi-nomadic inhabitants. Siberia was a great storehouse of fur-bearing wild life. The sable, ermine and fox of its steppes adorned and kept warm the bodies of European Russians and furnished a lucrative income to those engaged in this traffic. But in those days "conservation" was a word and a practice undreamed of in the philosophy of the advancing pioneers. A newly penetrated region, abundant in fur-bearers, was soon depleted. More peltries must be found by pushing farther into new unexploited areas. By the early eighteenth century the explorers, fur seekers, traders, tribute gatherers and missionaries had reached the Pacific.

It was to Vitus Bering that Peter the Great had entrusted the mission of ascertaining what lay beyond. Bering, a Dane by birth, had been an officer in the Imperial Russian Navy since his twenty-third year. Considering the times and circumstances, his assignment was formidable. The materials and supplies for the ships he was ordered to build on the Pacific Coast had, but for the lumber, to be transported some six thousand miles across the largest continent at the point of its greatest width. It was a wilderness of forest, mountain, morass and steppe, without roads and without bridges over its great rivers, the crossing of which was a formidable undertaking. Over all were the rigors of the Siberian winters, two of which were to be endured from the departure from St. Petersburg, in February, 1725, to the arrival of the expedition on the shore of the Sea of Okhotsk.

Here ships had to be built to cross that sea to the Kamchatka Peninsula. They sailed on August 21, 1727. After a winter spent in cutting timbers and other preparations, construction of an ocean-going vessel was begun in April, 1728, and completed in July. The ship, the *St. Gabriel,* sailed on July 14th. It headed northward and on August 8th discovered a large island which, in honor of the day, Bering named St. Lawrence. The ship continued north to latitude 67° 18′, and at East Cape, on August 15th, turned about "because the coast did not extend further north" and no other land was near. Fearful of being unable to reach his Kamchatka quarters before winter set in on that bleak coast, Bering, with the approval of his officers and crew, turned back.

Though unencumbered by supplies, Bering's overland journey required a year and a half. He did not reach St. Petersburg until March 1, 1730. There his results were deemed inconclusive and unsatisfactory. He had discovered St. Lawrence Island (now part of Alaska). He had explored the east coast of Siberia to East Cape and had concluded that as the coast turned westward at that point, the separation of the Asiatic and American continents had been proved. But there was no certainty about what lay to the east. For Bering had not sighted the mainland beyond, which had been hidden by fog. Although he had sailed through the strait that was to bear his name, and which on a clear day permits easy visibility of both Asiatic and American shores, the American coast had remained obscured. He had not "discovered America." That still lay ahead.

A second expedition was ordered in St. Petersburg in 1732. The subsequent years of preparation again required the transportation of materials and supplies across Siberia. They were years in which Bering's efforts were harassed by political intrigue, official jealousies and bureaucratic interference, which, added to the physical obstacles to be overcome, made Bering, on the eve of his final undertaking, a tired and worn-out old man.

It was not till 1738 that Bering was able to approach the building of the two ships that were to constitute his command. The magnificent harbor in Avatcha Bay had been discovered since the first expedition and it was from there that Bering planned to sail. This had necessitated the construction of quarters, barracks, workshops, storehouses—in fact, of a small community. But transportation of materials to this remote port on the southeastern coast of eight-hundred-mile-long Kamchatka Peninsula—icebound for two-thirds of every year—presented new, difficult problems and caused further delays. Essential supplies were lost in transit. The ships, brig-rigged two-masters, were eighty feet long with a twenty-two-foot beam and a nine-foot draught. Bering christened them *St. Peter* and *St. Paul*, and named the harbor in Avatcha Bay Petropavlosk after them.

The expedition sailed on June 4, 1741. Bering commanded the *St. Peter* with a complement of seventy-seven men. The two ships lost sight of each other in the fog on June 20th, and were never to meet again. Perversities of fate beset the two vessels. The *St. Paul* sighted land first, and in a sense the glory of prior discovery belongs to its commander, Alexei Chirikov. However, through circumstances still shrouded in mystery, none of his men landed. One of the outer islands of the Alexander Archipelago (southeastern Alaska), a mountainous and forested coast near Cape Addington, was sighted on July 15th. No suitable landing place being visible, the ship turned northward. On the 18th a longboat with eleven armed men was sent ashore to get water and find an anchorage. They rounded a point and were not seen again. None of the *St. Paul's* signals was answered. The weather had been fair. But the anxious watchers on board concluded that the longboat had been damaged and could not return. After waiting for five days, the only remaining small boat with four men, including a carpenter and a calker and equipped with materials for repairing the larger boat, went ashore. It too disappeared and never returned. Two days later two boats, one large and one small, were seen coming around a point. At first, when they were thought to be the two missing boats, there was great cheer aboard. But as they drew near it became apparent that they were sharper prowed and were propelled by paddles, not oars. They did not come close. But men stood up in them, waved, shouted and returned to shore. The two canoes reappeared but could not be persuaded by the shouts and gestures of those on board to come closer. Then Chirikov became convinced that disaster had befallen both small boats and their crews, and on the eighth day, with heavy hearts, he and his shipmates sailed away.

Chirikov no longer had means of landing. His water supply was low and could be supplemented only by catching rain water. So there was every need of returning as speedily as possible. He reached Avatcha Bay on October 8th.

Chirikov and his men had "discovered America" and brought back the first news of it. But otherwise their voyage was singularly barren. The tragic mishap to the vessel's small boats and the consequent inability to land prevented their bringing back any appreciable information about the new land, although glimpses of a few of its inhabitants were obtained from the *St. Paul*, first in the Alexander Archipelago and later in the Aleutians.

On board the *St. Peter* July 16th was cloudy. There was a slight drizzle. The horizon was obscured. Suddenly the sun broke through the overcast, the clouds lifted, and there unfolded in all its glory a great snow-capped mountain range, high up in the sky. Its lofty central peak, towering 18,000 feet above the sea, Bering named St. Elias in honor of the day.

There was great rejoicing on board. But Bering, prematurely aged, tired, sick and apprehensive of the future, merely shrugged his shoulders and cast a damper on the congratulations with which his crew acclaimed him in what should have been the hour of his greatest triumph.

His mission of "discovering America" fulfilled, his mind lay on bringing his ship and crew home safely. He permitted landing on an island—later called Kayak Island—merely for the purpose of securing water. His apprehensions were not baseless. Scurvy was breaking out among his crew. In a few weeks the greater part of them were incapacitated by it. The first death occurred on August 30th. Storms, adverse winds and high seas battered and delayed the ship. On November 4th, land that was believed to be Kamchatka was sighted. A council of officers and crew met to decide whether they should land or attempt to return to the home port of Petropavlosk. Twelve of the crew had already died of scurvy, thirty-four were totally disabled, ten were able to get around only with the greatest difficulty and the remainder were not too fit. The water supply was low. It was decided to steer for shore. After two days of maneuvering a strong tide swept the *St. Peter* toward a reef. When the anchors failed to hold she escaped by a hair's breadth being ground to pieces, but finally slipped over the reef into calmer waters beyond.

Almost the entire crew was now prostrated by scurvy. The task of the few able to move, of transferring the sick and the supplies ashore, was almost superhuman. Winter, with its icy gales, was upon them. While plans to haul the *St. Peter* ashore to protect her for the winter were delayed because of the weakness of the crew, a storm broke the anchor cable and drove the vessel ashore, a wreck.

There was no wood on shore. The men had to improvise shelters by scooping out sand banks along a stream near the shore. In one of these makeshifts Captain Bering was housed and given such aid and comfort as was possible. He continued to sink steadily and died on December 8th.

Thirty-one of the crew of seventy-seven died before the abundant fresh meat of the island's wild life turned the scales and caused the remainder gradually to regain strength. By late March exploring parties were physically able to proceed along the shore sufficient distances to ascertain that the survivors were not on the mainland of Kamchatka but on an island. It was then decided to build a smaller vessel from the wreckage of the *St. Peter* and to attempt to return home. Building of the hooker *St. Peter* began on May 6th. She was launched August 9th, sailed the next day under command of Lieutenant Sven Waxel and reached Petropavlosk safely on September 5, 1742.

They had been given up as lost. They brought back news of the tragic death of Bering and thirty others. They also brought back some sea-otter skins, a circumstance which was shortly to lead to numerous expeditions in quest of the hitherto unknown, but henceforth coveted, fur. And they also brought back a treasury of information about the animal life of the newly discovered continent.

2

Steller

> And, indeed, what is a scientist? . . . We give the name scientist
> to the type of man who has felt experiment to be a means guiding
> him to search out the deep truth of life, to lift a veil from its fas-
> cinating secrets, and who, in this pursuit has felt arising within
> him a love for the mysteries of nature, so passionate as to annihilate
> the thought of himself.
> MARIA MONTESSORI, 1919

THE information brought back by the survivors of Bering's last voyage was to have far-reaching consequences. Its existence was due almost wholly to the most interesting, useful and vital personality
among the *St. Peter's* company. He was Georg Wilhelm Steller, a
German-born naturalist who had been detailed to accompany the expedition. His contribution has been enduring. It ranks with Bering's,
and in Steller's own field far exceeds it.

Born in a small Bavarian town, Windsheim, in 1709, Steller acquired
the thorough education available to students in Germany at that
time. He matriculated first as a student of theology at the University
of Wittenberg. Later, at the University of Halle where he studied
medicine, he was graduated as a physician. However, it was in natural
phenomena that his greatest interest lay. The nature of plants and animals was the object of his inquisitiveness in the placid Bavarian countryside of rolling hills, forest and meadow.

Botany in those days was not yet a science in its own right. It was
an adjunct to medicine. Plants were of interest chiefly because of the
drugs that could be derived from them. The only textbook available was that of a Greek physician, Dioscorides, who lived in the first
century A.D. Steller's knowledge of flowers, grasses and trees was self-
taught. Zoology was of interest, likewise, because of its value in the
study of human anatomy. It was in connection with his medical studies that Steller had the opportunity to dissect animals.

Steller began to teach botany at the age of twenty-three. But Germany at that time appeared to Steller to hold few opportunities for a
man of his roving spirit and intellectual curiosity. The past two cen-

turies of exploration, the tales of distant and romantic lands had fed
his deep-rooted appetite for adventure. Defoe's *Robinson Crusoe,*
translated into German, was having a great vogue. Steller's youth cor-
responded to the era when the great unknown field of natural science
beckoned invitingly to a man of his imagination and zest for knowledge. While his lectures attracted an increasing number of students
and were being widely acclaimed, they also aroused the envy of some
of his academic superiors. High-spirited, quick-tempered, ambitious,
with a growing confidence in his own abilities, and chafing at the
humdrum aspects of a young instructor's life, he went to Berlin in the
hope of securing a professorship in the field of his greatest interest.
But his hopes were unfulfilled, and while he waited, his resources
dwindled.

At that time the attention of the academic world was drawn to
Russia, which Peter the Great was transforming from a second-rate
semi-barbarous state to a first-class power in Western civilization. His
plan to establish an academy of sciences in St. Petersburg had been
carried out by his widow, Catherine I. It offered opportunities for
foreign scientists. Coincidentally came word that the second Kamchatka expedition, under Bering, was being organized. This combination of circumstances appealed to twenty-five-year-old Steller.

How to get to St. Petersburg and to achieve recognition were two
aspects of a problem. Steller's finances were at low ebb. However, the
free city of Danzig had, during the summer of 1734, been besieged by
the Russian Army in the final act of the War of the Polish Succession.
Losses had been heavy. The Russian Army, though modernized under Peter the Great's leadership, lacked surgeons and was welcoming
German medical students. Steller's medical training qualified him and
brought about his acceptance. Accompanying a transport of wounded
soldiers, he reached St. Petersburg late in 1734.

He knew no Russian and found himself in a strange land and without friends. But here his interest in botany favored his fortunes. Almost
his first act was to visit the apothecary garden of the naval hospital.
There he was able to converse with the German gardener in his
own language, and their common interest in plants proved a bond.
An inquiry at Steller's abode led to the admission of his straitened
circumstances. The gardener took him to the home of Archbishop
Theophan Prokopovitch who lived near by and who gave him shelter.

Theophan, Archbishop of Novogorod, a man of great learning and kindliness, was also one of the most powerful figures in Russian society. That Steller was a Lutheran proved no obstacle to the friendliness which the Patriarch of the Russian church showed him. Steller's facility in Latin, a part of the German university training of that day, enabled them to converse freely. The Archbishop was soon recommending Steller to the Academy of Sciences.

In the company of its scientific luminaries, French, Italian, Swiss, but mostly German, Steller found himself enthralled. But he lost no time augmenting his own qualifications. He botanized actively in the surrounding countryside. The first year was spent in assisting one of the academicians, the Swiss, Johann Ammam, to catalogue his herbarium, and in laying out a new botanical garden, a project of the academy. Concomitantly he was assisting another member in the study and dissection of some large animals that had died in the imperial menagerie. Steller's admission to membership in the academy followed.

Among the topics of discussion was the second Kamchatka expedition. Considering the times and the scope of the proposed project it has been fairly described as "the most gigantic geographic enterprise undertaken by any government at any time."[1] Its purpose was not only to settle the transcendent question of the physical relationship of Asia and America. It envisaged a mapping of the entire area of northern Asia, still largely unexplored, and of the American coast, and a charting of the adjacent Pacific and Arctic oceans. Moreover, the exploration was to be matched by elaborate studies in the sciences within these newly explored regions. Their anthropology, their mineralogy, their biology, were all to be thoroughly investigated and recorded. Overambitious in its attempt to capture all possible knowledge in every field of human experience, and obviously impossible of adequate fulfillment in one expedition, it marked the first attempted conjunction in history of geographic with other forms of exploration. That purpose remains a monument to the great Peter and his successors.

Over this multitude of interrelated enterprises, Captain Commander Vitus Bering was appointed chief. His heavy responsibilities were increased by various limitations on his authority, not the least fantastic of which was the necessity of having, even on board his vessels, to leave major decisions to a vote of the crew (a strange anachronism and paradox in the time and place of czarism!). It was the impossibility of this assignment, which lesser men would have abandoned, that aged Bering and hastened his death.

In 1737 Steller obtained permission to join the expedition as one "well versed in the fundamentals of botany and the other branches of natural history." He was elated. He departed on his long journey in January, 1738. Travel at that season was by sledge—in the familiar *troika*. But it was three years before he was to arrive at Okhotsk. It was an interval, however, consumed with studies of the Siberian flora and fauna. It was in this period that the true scientist began to emerge. His fellow academicians traveled with great equipment and in luxury. Their personal requirements added greatly to the transportation problem. But Steller would go hungry and thirsty in his pursuit of knowledge. The others were not too eager to endure the hardships that inevitably accompanied their tasks. Not so Steller. His ambition was to sail with Bering. When the latter requested his company Steller considered it the fulfillment of a lifelong hope. The scientist to sail with Chirikov was Louis de la Croyère. Even before his departure the academy considered him little qualified. The inability of the *St. Paul* to land anywhere of course limited his opportunities for observation. Moreover, he was taken ill with scurvy and died the day the vessel put into Petropavlosk. He left no record of what he had seen or experienced.

Steller's opportunities for observation were tantalizingly limited during the voyage. The first was compressed into some ten hours on Kayak Island, where Bering's men went ashore for water. Steller had to cajole and threaten for the chance to accompany them. Neither Bering, who was preoccupied with securing a safe return, nor his crew was sympathetic with any digression that might delay it. But in his few hours ashore, besides collecting plants not found in Asia and Europe, and artifacts revealing something of the native culture—whose living specimens fled on his approach—Steller took a number of unknown birds. One was a fairly large crested bird with a bright blue plumage. Steller recalled having seen a colored plate in an Englishman's recent *Natural History of the Carolinas and Florida* which had reached St. Petersburg's scientific circles before his departure. The close resemblance of the bird shot on Kayak Island and the Atlantic coast specimen led him to a brilliant deduction: "This bird proved to me that we were really in America!"

Steller was right. The eastern bluejay and the Alaskan or western bluejay, a sub-species of which was thereafter to bear Steller's name, differed only slightly. The Western Hemisphere was exclusively the habitat of both. Steller was the first white man to set foot in Alaska. He was the first to be able to affirm with an intuitive perception susceptible of proof that what Bering's expeditions had sought had been found.

Steller was ashore on but one more island—Kagai—during a landfall to get water, and where the first member of the expedition to die of scurvy, a sailor named Shumagin, was buried, giving his name to the whole group of islands. There again Steller was frustrated in his yearning for more time for thorough investigation. Despite his pleadings he was never able to set foot on the Alaskan mainland so often temptingly in view during the voyage. In his diary he bitterly contrasted the years spent in preparation for the expedition with the scant hours permitted him to carry out what to him were its major objectives.

When the *St. Peter* landed on November 6th—and was later wrecked—on a previously unknown island between America and Asia that was to bear the name of the company's ill-fated commander, the grim struggle for existence confronted those who had survived thus far. The island was treeless. Driftwood was scarce. The winter with its freezing blasts and torrential rains, soon turning to sleet and snow, was upon them. Shelter and warmth, two necessities for sustaining life, were hard to secure for men who were already sick, weak and drenched to the skin by salt water and rain and chilled to the marrow of their bones. The dead lay among the dying and the sick, the last too weak to remove the former or to minister to the latter—all subject to the attacks of the hordes of foxes who bit at the quick and the dead indiscriminately. It was a bitter experience which drove those who pulled through almost to the limits of human endurance. Steller, who had vainly tried to persuade the rest of the company at their previous landings to join him in the collection of anti-scorbutic plants which would have enabled them to survive and which kept him free from scurvy, was now able to make his knowledge count. Deaths continued until January 10th. By that time the fresh meat and pure water were bringing about the gradual recovery of the others.

For Steller the more than nine months on the island were an episode of undreamed-of opportunity. The island, previously uninhabited by man, teemed with strange animal life. The abundant sea otter was at first the principal source of food—and the medicine which finally routed the scurvy. When hundreds had been killed and others frightened beyond easy reach, the attention of the shipwrecked crew turned to a huge animal, in appearance a cross between a seal and a whale, which in large numbers was peacefully pasturing in the surrounding kelp beds. They called it a sea cow, a name which endured, though sea elephant might have been more appropriate, not merely because of its size—thirty or more feet long, twelve to fourteen feet thick—but because it was a marine descendant of elephantine ancestors. Not for months did the men regain the strength to kill and recover one of these easily accessible and inoffensive monsters. First attempts in May were failures. Not until the end of June was one of these marine mammoths successfully harpooned by five men in a small boat, with forty others—practically all the company being engaged in this task—pulling it to shore. Long before this, Steller had observed the sea cows' habits and noted them carefully. Now he completed his knowledge by dissecting a four-ton female. Its stomach, stuffed with seaweed and other marine plants, was six feet long and five feet wide; its heart weighed over thirty-six pounds. Probably no anatomist ever performed so great and unprecedented a professional task under such difficult circumstances. He performed a smilar operation on a "beachmaster," the large bull seal.

Steller did not live to enjoy fame. He never returned to Europe. The next years were spent in further investigations in Kamchatka and elsewhere in Siberia. Finally homeward bound, death from an undiagnosed fever and exposure overtook him in 1746.

In his great work, *De Bestiis Marinis*, based on his nine months on Bering Island and published in 1751, Steller gave the world its first account of four previously unknown marine mammals, the fur seal, the sea otter, the sea lion and the sea cow. The first two of these were to be of tremendous economic value. Their discovery brought the Russian fur hunters pouring eastward across the northern seas. It led the Czars from the path of the originally projected mere exploration to the more remunerative course of exploitation and permanent occupation.

It was characteristic of Steller's powers of shrewd observation and inference that he suggested that some of the sea otter be brought to

Russia and made tame; "They would multiply perhaps in a pond or
river, for they care but little for sea water, and I have seen that they
stay for several days in lakes and rivers, for the fun of it." [2]

What gives this proposal contemporary significance is that two centuries later, when the sea otter had been almost exterminated by
ruthless hunting and was placed under absolute protection by the
United States authorities attempting to restore its herds by the slow
process of natural reproduction, the Russians, under the Soviet regime,
were following Steller's counsel and transplanting the sea otter into
Siberian rivers and fresh waters with marked success.

The sea cow did not long survive. Though Steller found it present
at all seasons of the year in great numbers and in herds, it was exterminated within the short space of twenty-six years. The last one
succumbed in 1768 to the need and greed of the fur hunters who
slaughtered it for their food supply. Steller was the only naturalist—
no doubt the only trained and interested observer—who ever saw
one, and his fame rests in part on his having brought about its survival in the annals of zoology with a complete account of its appearance, structure and habits.

Steller likewise discovered and described in detail another animal
which has become extinct. This was the spectacled cormorant—a large
bird, weighing twelve to fourteen pounds—with its small wings almost flightless and an easy prey to hunters, who, Steller averred, found
it good eating. It lasted longer than the sea cow, but a hundred years
later it had joined the great auk and the passenger pigeon in the orni-
thological graveyard.

The most gorgeously caparisoned and the swiftest—although also
the smallest—of the four varieties of eider ducks was also discovered
and first described by Steller, and it bears his name.

Steller's part in the Bering epic revealed the true qualities of a
great scientist—intense intellectual curiosity, a dauntless determination to satisfy it exhibited in an unflagging industry, faithful accuracy
of observation—all these applied in the face of persistent frustration
and great physical hardships. He was, as his devoted and scholarly
biographer Leonhard Stejneger—who resurrected Steller's repute from
relative oblivion—has pointed out, the first to venture into the unexplored fields of natural science in the Pacific north of Japan and California, and "the pioneer of Alaskan natural history."

Aside from the immortality to which his contributions to science entitle him, it was not long after his death that his work made clear to the rulers of Russia that in the newly discovered animal kingdom beyond the Eurasian continent lay treasure that warranted the further extension of empire.

3

The Russian Occupation

> Standing here and looking far off into the northwest, I see the Russian as he busily occupies himself by establishing seaports and towns and fortifications, on the verge of this continent, as the outposts of St. Petersburg, and I can say, "Go on, and build up your outposts all along the coast and up even to the Arctic Ocean—they will yet become the outposts of my own country—monuments to the civilization of the United States in the northwest."
> WILLIAM HENRY SEWARD, SEPTEMBER 18, 1860

THE Russian sojourn on the North American continent lasted 126 years. The legacy of that century and a quarter of occupation is today negligible. It consists of a great number of place names; in the steadily attenuating strain of Slavic blood chiefly among the Aleuts—who themselves survive in greatly reduced numbers; in a few little-attended Greek Orthodox churches, among which the cathedral at Sitka preserves what is probably one of the best extant collection of ikons, since churches and church property have been confiscated and dispersed in Soviet Russia.

The real significance of the Russian-American regime in the pageant of history was that by it Alaska was transferred to the sovereignty of the United States. Russia's occupation began just in time to forestall Britain's. But for Russia, Alaska would today be a province of Canada. Captain James Cook's secret instructions from the Admiralty in 1776 were to take possession for the British crown of countries that were uninhabited even if previously visited and discovered by another European power.[1] Alaska's long coastline, extending far beyond the penetration of the *promyshleniki*—the Russian freebooting fur hunters—at the time of Cook's voyage in the ships *Resolution* and *Discovery* in 1778, lent itself admirably to those orders. And Cook followed them by setting up marks and inscriptions and depositing bottles with the names of the ships, the date of the "discovery" and contemporary British coins—including even one on Kayak Island, Bering's first landfall and the scene of Steller's sensational identification of it as America.

But at the time of Cook's voyage along the northwest coast of America, the limits of Russia's dominion in America were not defined. No permanent settlement had been attempted anywhere. For some forty years after Bering's discovery the American shores were visited only by buccaneering enterprisers who slaughtered the fur-bearers, plundered the Aleuts, and killed those who resisted. In the earlier days a single voyage made its promoter rich. But in twoscore years reckless slaughter had quite depleted the Aleutians, and the Siberian fur dealers, who had financed many such expeditions, became alarmed. It was deemed necessary, in order to maintain the fur catch, to extend the hunt farther east. That would require longer and costlier journeys. A settlement as a base of operations would no doubt pay for itself. This plan coincided with a growing view in court circles that the reckless competition between the *promyshleniki* was of no advantage to the crown, and that the lack of any establishment on land would encourage the invasion of foreign traders; they would inevitably follow in the wake of British, Spanish and French explorers. There was concern too for the aborigines whose reported ill-treatment was displeasing to the imperial household which desired the conversion of these new subjects to the Christianity of the Eastern Church.

These considerations led the most aggressive of the merchants engaged in the American fur trade, Gregory Shelikov, to found a settlement on Kodiak Island in 1784. He used that achievement as an argument for seeking at the imperial court a charter that would secure him a monopoly of the American business. The successive Czars and Czarinas had not, except for the indifferently collected tribute from the Aleuts, participated in the Russian-American enterprises as they had in the Siberian. For a time they were reluctant to bestow monopolies. Matters dragged on. Shelikov died. His widow, brothers-in-law and his daughter, who had married the dashing Count Nicolai Rezanov, took over the business. Largely because of his influence a charter was granted by Czar Paul I in 1799 for twenty years, giving exclusive rights as far south as the fifty-fifth parallel. In the newly formed Russian-American Company the imperial family, the Shelikov interests and various competitors each received a third of the stock.

For the next sixty-eight years the Russian-American Company was not only the exclusive commercial enterprise in Russian America but also exercised the governing power. The grant brought into

prominence Alexander Baranov, who had been manager of the Shelikov interests since 1791, with headquarters at Kodiak. He soon conceived the idea of founding a new trading post much farther east. In
1800 he established a fort six miles north of an Indian village where
Sitka is now situated. Two years later its occupants were massacred
by the Indians—only a few escaping—and the post destroyed. With
the aid of a Russian naval vessel the hostile Tlingits were subdued
and a new settlement, New Archangel, later known as Sitka,
was founded. Baranov established his headquarters there, and it became the capital of Russian America. Baranov continued as General
Manager of the company and as such Russia's first governor of the
colony for nineteen years—until 1818. Thus Russia established its
dominion over a vast area that was being pressed from the south and
the east by advancing fur seekers owing allegiance to a rival imperialism—that of Great Britain.

However, considerations of greater importance elsewhere prevented
a collision in this field between the two imperial powers and a quarter
of a century later, in 1825, Britain and Russia signed a convention
defining their boundaries in northwestern America and agreeing that
neither should trespass on the other's domain. Russia's southern
boundary in America was fixed at 54° 40', a latitude that was to have
historic import.

That convention was soon circumvented by the greatest power in
the fur trade on the North American continent, the Hudson's Bay
Company. As in Russian America where the Russian-American Company was the agent of the Czar and the instrument of his government
as well as a commercial company dealing principally in furs, so in
Rupert's Land "The Governor and Company of Adventurers of Eng
land Trading into Hudson's Bay," as it was officially designated in the
charter granted in 1670 by King Charles II, was the ruling power until confederation of the scattered British provinces on July 1, 1867,
formed the Dominion of Canada. But it was ever far more potent
than its Russian rival. It was older by 129 years. It had been able
from the start to exploit a much larger territory, over which it had
virtually absolute power, and had, from the days of its first Governor,
Prince Rupert, cousin of King Charles II, returned rich dividends to
him and to the other "seventeen nobles and gentlemen" who were its
original stockholders.[2]

"The Company," as it had long been known in Canada, where it had established its forts not merely from Atlantic to Pacific but from the Arctic Ocean as far south as the Sacramento and Columbia rivers, saw a further opportunity in the clause of the Anglo-Russian Treaty of 1825 which permitted the British free navigation of streams that crossed Russian territory. In 1833 it was making plans to establish a trading post on the Stikhine River. A company vessel arrived from the company's post, Fort Vancouver, to supply it. The Russian Governor, Baron Ferdinand von Wrangell, apprised of these plans, erected a fort —Redoubt St. Dionysius—at an Indian village (later to be named Wrangell) near the mouth of the river, and sent two Russian warships which opened fire on the brig *Dryad*. She was ordered out of Russian-American waters. Demand for damages of 20,000 pounds sterling was made and backed by Britain. A settlement agreed upon in 1839 waived the damage claim in consideration of a ten-year lease by the Russian-American Company to the Hudson's Bay Company of the mainland of southeastern Alaska—for a rental of two thousand land-otter skins annually. The lease was renewed three times, bringing its last term to June 1867—the year of the transfer of Alaska to the United States. Thus the British had maneuvered a three-hundred-mile commercial beachhead in Russian America and held it profitably for more than a quarter of a century thereafter.

Meanwhile, in the far north the Hudson's Bay Company had by direct action invaded Russian America and secured a lucrative trade. In 1847 it had sent a party down the Porcupine River and at its junction with the Yukon on the Arctic Circle, nearly a hundred miles inside Russian territory, established a trading post, Fort Yukon. It was later alleged that in those unsurveyed wilderness regions it was difficult to know just where the 141st meridian—the boundary fixed by treaty—was. This no doubt inadvertent error did not, however, quite explain the annual trading mission, immediately after the spring breakup, of "the enterprising and energetic Scotchmen of the station," [3] some three hundred miles down the river to a place called Nuclucayette, where they bought the assembled Indians' winter catch of furs before the Russians could make the longer and more difficult upstream voyage from their nearest trading post at Nulato.

The war with Britain in the Crimea had made the Russians fearful that they might not, in the event of renewed hostilities, be able to hold their American colony. The Russian interest now lay more greatly in a southward penetration along the Amur. Besides, the

Russian-American Company, in the eighteen sixties, was doing poorly. The price envisioned in the event of a sale would enable that company to liquidate without loss. Friendship between Russia and the United States was also a factor: the United States as the future possessor of Russia's American holdings and a near neighbor was preferred to all others.

The Treaty of Cession in 1867 halted the British-Canadian westward advance. It ended their occupancy of the mainland of southeastern Alaska which they had leased. Two years later Captain Charles P. Raymond journeyed up the Yukon to request the Hudson's Bay Company to remove its post beyond the boundary.

The boundary between Canada and Alaska continued to be a matter of acute controversy and considerable hard feeling even after it was finally settled by an international tribunal in 1903. The disputes arose over the conflicting interpretations of the wording of the Anglo-Russian Treaty of 1825 by which the boundary of southeastern Alaska was to follow the summits of the mountains parallel to the coast, but not more than ten marine leagues from it. The Canadian contention was that the ten leagues should be measured from the mouths of the bays—the American contention that it was from the heads of the bays. The American position was largely, if not wholly, sustained, and there was much resultant bitterness in Canada.

Toward the end of the nineteenth century, Lord Strathcona and Mount Royal, then, and for ten years previously, the Governor of the Hudson's Bay Company, wrote revealingly in an introduction to a history of the company:

> It is not too much to say that the fur traders were the pioneers of civilization in the far West . . . These fur traders penetrated to the Rocky Mountains and beyond, into what is now known as British Columbia, and even to the far north and northwest in connection with the extension of trade, and the establishment of the famous "H.B.C." posts and forts which were the leading features of the maps of the country until comparatively recent times. . . .
>
> The American and Russian companies which were seeking trade on the Pacific Coast, in the early days of the present century, were not able to withstand the activity and enterprise of their British rivals, but for whose discoveries and work even British Columbia might not have remained British territory. For

many years the only civilized occupants of both banks of the Columbia River were the fur traders, and it is not their fault that
the region between it and the international boundary does not
now belong to Canada. Alaska was also leased by the Hudson's
Bay Company from Russia, and one cannot help thinking that if
that country had been secured by Great Britain, we should probably never have heard of the Boundary Question, or of disputes
over the Seal Fisheries.[4]

Obviously not, because there would then have been no international boundary between Alaska and Canada over which to dispute,
and the seal fisheries would have been wholly British. And no doubt
Britain—and then Canada—would have "secured" Alaska had it not
been for Peter the Great and Catherine I and their successors. It is not
within the purview of this study to speculate in what ways British—
and later, Canadian—rule would have affected the subsequent history of the territory. The question is academic in any event. What is
salient is that Russia's occupation of Alaska determined that territory's
permanent incorporation in the United States.

Russian America
Becomes Alaska

Human experience has shown throughout the ages, that utterly
erroneous ideas outlive the plain truth.
WILLIAM E. WOODWARD

ON MARCH 29, 1867, Secretary of State William H. Seward and
Baron Edouard Stoeckel, Russian Minister to the United States, after
some three weeks of negotiation, completed the draft of a Treaty of
Cession of Russian America to the United States. The next day,
March 30th, at four in the morning, the treaty was signed (15 Stat.
539).

The adjournment of Congress had been fixed for noon on that
very day, only eight hours after the signing of the treaty. But Seward
was determined to secure the Senate's ratification before adjournment. Early that forenoon he hastened to the Capitol and took several
influential senators into his confidence. He was able to persuade them
that an executive session was necessary. What was said in the course
of it for and against the treaty has never been recorded. It is known,
however, that there was substantial opposition and that the chances
of the two-thirds vote of approval were slight. Had a vote been taken
immediately, the purchase would doubtless have been defeated. Senator Sumner, in an effort to gain time, moved that the treaty be referred to the Committee on Foreign Relations, of which he was
chairman. Meanwhile Seward summoned all his logic and personal persuasion, in which he was assisted by a small section of the press. Seward's strongest reliance, however, was on the national feeling of
amity toward Russia. Russia's attitude during the Civil War, in contrast to that of Britain and France, had been friendly to the North.
The argument that a rejection of the treaty would be deemed an act
of base ingratitude and a rebuff to the Union's great friend, Czar
Alexander II, successor to Nicholas I, carried weight.

Sumner, who in principle was opposed to the acquisition of further territory without the clear consent of its inhabitants, had at first been lukewarm toward the treaty. However, he was persuaded to espouse it. Aided by industrious research, he was able to deliver a three-hour speech on April 9th in the Senate's special session covering this hitherto unknown territory as thoroughly as if it had been the interest of his lifetime. It was a summary of everything that was then known about Russian America; and it was Sumner who proposed that, under its new sovereignty, its name be "Alaska."

The Senate then numbered forty-five. Thirty votes would be the necessary two-thirds for ratification if all were present. When the vote was taken twenty-seven were in favor and twelve opposed—with six absent, a sufficiency, but only one more than needed. By so narrow a margin was this momentous decision made. It was then proposed to make the vote unanimous. This was almost, but not quite, achieved, the official record being thirty-seven to two.

All the speeches but Sumner's have been lost to posterity. His has become a classic in the literature of Alaska. News of the ratification without the details of the roll call and without the price to be paid was released to the press on April 12th.

Congratulations "upon this brilliant achievement which adds so vast a territory to our Union; whose ports, whose mines, whose waters, whose furs, whose fisheries, are of untold value," came by letter from Cassius M. Clay, United States Minister to Russia. Alaska, he further stated, would in time become "the seat of a hearty white population," was worth at least fifty millions of dollars and hereafter the wonder would be "that we ever got it at all." [1]

Similar plaudits came from others who either had first-hand information, or access to it, about the newly acquired territory. Samuel C. Jackson, acting State Librarian of Massachusetts, communicated the gist of a conversation with a member of the Massachusetts legislature, a former whaling captain familiar with Alaskan waters, who stressed the immense importance of their fisheries and added his view that the $7,000,000 purchase price was "nothing" in comparison to the area's true value.[2]

Major Perry McDonough Collins, who had been active in the uncompleted Western Union enterprise of stringing telegraph lines across Alaska and Siberia, wrote in refutation of "the many erroneous statements in the press of the day" in regard to Russian America. He considered the fisheries alone worth more than the whole cost of the country. Timber for building purposes he declared to be abundant and forecast that sawmills would soon make the lumber trade a source of profit not only for domestic use but for export.[3]

Wrote Jared I. Kirtland from Cleveland to Seward, based on reports of his grandson, Lt. Charles Pease, who had been a member of the overland telegraph expedition and had brought home Robert Kennicott's, its commander's, body when the latter died in Nulato on the Yukon, on May 13, 1866:

"Its [Alaska's] fur trade, fisheries and probable minerals are of immense value. . . . A want of knowledge of its resources can account only for any opposition to the ratification of the treaty." [4]

These optimistic evaluations, however sound they were to be proved, represented a minority view in the court of public opinion of that day.

The ceremonies attending the formal transfer of Russian America to the United States took place on October 18, 1867. Sitka Harbor, beautiful with its backdrop of steep, forested mountains, was crowded with shipping which had ridden patiently at anchor for ten days. On the morning of the 18th, the U.S.S. *Ossipee* arrived with Brigadier General Lovell H. Rousseau, United States Commissioner, aboard. At mid-afternoon of a "bright and beautiful" day[5] the Russian troops, numbering a hundred, formed in front of the house of the Governor, Prince Maksoutoff. At the same time launches belonging to the Army transport *John L. Stevens*, bearing the Commanding General, Jefferson C. Davis, his staff and men, and from the warships *Jamestown*, *Resaca* and *Ossipee*, and the revenue cutter *Lincoln* headed for shore. Soldiers, marines and sailors numbering nearly two hundred, some sixty American civilians and the principal Russian officials formed around the ninety-foot flagpole. Few Russian civilians attended; they regarded the event with sorrow. After the two commissioners, Captain Alexei Petchouroff and General Rousseau, had uttered the appropriate words, amid the booming salute of guns, alternately from Russian and American men-of-war, the double-eagle ensign of Imperial Russia was lowered and the Stars and Stripes of the United States raised in its place.

"The Russian eagle has now given place to the American," wrote the correspondent of San Francisco's newspaper, *Alta California*, "and the national colors floated over a new widespread territory. Our dominion now borders on a new ocean and almost touches the old continent—Asia. Democratic institutions now extend over an area hitherto the possession of a despotic government. The occasion inspired the soul of every American present, and as the officers retired, three mighty cheers were given and we all rejoiced that we now stood on American soil." [6]

When the second session of the Fortieth Congress reassembled, it received on July 6th from President Johnson a special message enclosing a copy of the Treaty of Cession and calling attention to the need of an appropriation to pay for the purchase. No action was taken at that session. Upon Congress's convening for the third session in November, Representative Cadwalader C. Washburn, R., of Wisconsin, secured adoption of a resolution opposing further purchases of territory. The purchase of St. Thomas in the Danish West Indies had been under active consideration. In response to objection Mr. Washburn made it clear that his resolution was not intended to apply to what he termed "Walrussia." But no immediate action on the appropriation bill was contemplated. Congressmen were more deeply interested in the pending impeachment proceedings against the President. They delayed action on the purchase until the summer of 1868. Debate on the appropriation bill began in the House of Representatives on June 30th. There appeared to be substantial opposition to the measure.

The day-and-night sessions during the heat of a Washington summer were marked by the unextinguished bitterness against an administration charged by its critics with usurpation and arbitrariness, whose chief executive had escaped impeachment by the margin of one vote. Indeed the attacks of the opposition were primarily directed at the haste, secrecy and alleged illegality surrounding the negotiation of the treaty with Russia, thereby reopening the very points at issue in the impeachment proceedings. Speaker after speaker pointed to the constitutional provision that appropriation measures must originate in the House. That the treaty, signed in the small hours of the morning on March 30th of the previous year and ratified by the Senate after a secret session, was then presented to the House as an accomplished fact was deemed an affront by its opposing members. They argued, with extensive citations, that a treaty requiring an appropriation should have secured the prior consent of the House; they likewise objected to the provision admitting the inhabitants of the territory to citizenship[7] without the consent of Congress—meaning both houses; and they amended the bill to reassert the House's prerogatives. The opposition seemed more formidable than it actually was. The fact that the United States had taken possession of Alaska eight months previously weakened the case of those who did not wish to pay. It became clear to the sponsors of the bill that they had sufficient strength to pass it. Except for the presentation by Nathaniel P. Banks, R., of Massachusetts, Chairman of the House Foreign Relations Committee, the content of which followed the favorable report of the committee's majority, and a few others, the measure's supporters apparently felt excessive defense thereof unnecessary. It passed the House on July 14th, with a comfortable margin of a 113 yeas, forty-three nays and forty-four not voting. It was then passed back and forth between Senate and House until the amendatory language in modified form was approved by both (15 Stat. 198). No division along sectional, party or other lines was clearly defined. The Western states predominantly favored the bill and all but three of the Democrats voted for it, while the Republicans were divided.

Of lasting consequence, however, was the buttressing of a substantial number—though actually a minority—of the arguments in opposition by gravely adverse commentaries on the *value* of the acquisition. In addition to the treaty's being "an outrage on the Constitution"[8] Alaska was declared by a variety of speakers to be "worthless." Then and there arose the myth which has persisted to this day that Alaska is a desolate and uninhabitable waste.

The section of the press critical of the transaction had already coined the enduring appellation, "Seward's Folly." Other epithets applied to Alaska were "Icebergia," "Polaria," "Seward's Icebox," and, as already noted, "Walrussia." The New York *World* declared, "Russia has sold us a sucked orange,"[9] and to the New York *Herald* Alaska was ". . . an ice house, a worthless desert with which to enable the Secretary of State to cover up the mortification and defeats he has suffered with the shipwrecked Southern policy of Andrew Johnson . . ."[10]

The minority report of the House Committee on Foreign Relations had, several weeks earlier, made a sweepingly unfavorable report based on its "conclusion that the possession of the country is of no value . . . to the United States . . . that it will be a source of weakness instead of power, and a constant annual expense for which there will be no adequate return . . . no capacity as an agricultural country . . . no value as a mineral country . . . its timber . . . generally of a poor quality and growing upon inaccessible mountains . . . its fur trade . . . of insignificant value and will speedily come to an end . . . the fisheries of doubtful value" and, finally, "that the right to govern a nation . . . of savages in a climate unfit for the habitation of civilized men was not worthy of purchase." [11]

In the debate on the floor of the House, opponents of the appropriation bill rang all the changes on this adverse verdict.

"The territory is intrinsically and virtually valueless," affirmed Representative John A. Peters, R., of Bangor, Maine. He declared that the press of the country was opposed to the purchase and that the proposition had met with ridicule and opposition except where there had been some special interest or motive for a contrary course.[12]

Representative Dennis McCarthy, R., of Syracuse, New York, having heard "reports that every foot of the soil of Alaska is frozen from five to six feet in depth" ventured that his colleagues would soon "hear that Greenland and Iceland are on the market." [13]

Representative Hiram Price, R., of Davenport, Iowa, deplored the willingness of members of Congress to vote millions "for the purchase of the icebergs of Alaska" when they hesitated to appropriate "a few thousand dollars to remove the obstructions in the Mississippi, the grandest river upon the globe and inhabited by a loyal, intelligent and energetic people." [14]

Representative Benjamin F. Loan, Radical, of St. Louis, Missouri, averred that "the acquisition of this inhospitable and barren waste would never add a dollar to the wealth of our country or furnish any homes to our people." Alaska, he said, was "utterly worthless," and that "to suppose that anyone would leave the United States . . . to seek a home . . . in the regions of perpetual snow, is simply to suppose such a person insane." [15]

Representative Orange Ferris, R., of Glens Falls, New York, labeling the transaction a "swindle," asked, "Of what possible commercial importance can the territory be to us?" and asserted that "Alaska, a barren, unproductive region, covered with ice and snow . . . will never be populated by an enterprising people." [16]

And Representative Benjamin F. Butler, R., of Lowell, Massachusetts, vouchsafed that $7,200,000 would be a small price to pay for

Russia's friendship "if we could only get rid of the land, or ice, rather, which we are to get by paying it." [17]

A promising beginning had been made to assure Alaska its place as the nation's ugly duckling.

THE ERA OF
TOTAL NEGLECT

1867 - 1884

The Seventeen Years
of No Government

> Her [Russia's] government there [in Alaska] is little more than a
> name or a shadow. It is not even a skeleton. It is hardly visible. Its
> only representative is a fur company. The immense country is with-
> out form and without light; without activity and without progress.
> Distant from the imperial capital, and separated from the huge
> bulk of Russian empire, it does not share the vitality of a common
> country. Its life is solitary and feeble. Its settlements are only en-
> campments and lodges.
> SENATOR CHARLES SUMNER OF MASSACHUSETTS,
> APRIL 9, 1867

> When the American people get hold of a country there is some-
> thing about them which quickens, vitalizes and energizes it. . . .
> Let American enterprise go there, and as if by electricity all that
> country will waken into life and possess value.
> REPRESENTATIVE WILLIAM HIGBY OF CALIFORNIA,
> JULY 7, 1868

PRESIDENT JOHNSON'S message of transmittal of the treaty to
the House of Representatives on July 6, 1867, was remarkable for its
brevity. It consisted of three sentences. The last of these read:

> The attention of Congress is invited to the subject of an ap-
> propriation for this payment, and also to that of proper legis-
> lation for the occupation and government of the territory as part
> of the dominion of the United States.[1]

That part of the message dealing with the appropriation was
referred to the Committee on Appropriations, with the result previously recorded; and that part dealing with occupation and government, to the Committee on Territories.

Meantime Alaska was to be made a military district, and posts were
established at Sitka and Wrangell. This was considered to be merely
a transitional step.

"It is presumed that the transfer of this country will be followed by an organized territorial civil government with the extension over it of the general laws of the United States," wrote Major General H. W. Halleck, commanding the Military Division of the Pacific at San Francisco, to the Adjutant General's office in Washington.[2]

Indeed it was also presumed by others that with Old Glory waving over the new domain, settlement such as was taking place in those other outposts of promise, the western territories, would follow. The prairies, the Rockies, the Coast—and now Alaska! The days of '49 in California would be repeated in the days of '69 in the still farther west and north! To it flocked men of all sorts, businessmen who had preceded or accompanied the commissioners with a view to "getting in on the ground floor," frontiersmen who had roamed the West, squatters, aspirants for public office—all the traditional American followers of "the main chance." A wilderness empire of unparalleled beauty and mystery had unfolded itself to them on their way. Their journey northwestward along the coast had led them through protected waterways, past deep fjords, through long inlets from whose cold clear waters the mountains, densely forested, rose steeply to great heights. At Sitka the newcomers looked across a great bay studded with islands and landwards to the encircling peaks. They breathed an invigorating air that was fresh with the tang of sea and the fragrance of spruce and hemlock. They found the prospect pleasing. Deer, waterfowl, salmon were available for everyone's larder for the taking. Timber, fish, furs abounded, and no doubt much else. It was a virgin country, a land of opportunity.

Before the first sunset gun was fired stakes dotted the ground, plotting out this and that homestead; within a few days the framework of shanties had begun to arise, new stores were under construction, a new restaurant opened its doors, and the budding enterprises included two tenpin alleys and, of course, saloons. Moreover, nearly a thousand of the widely scattered employees of the Russian-American Company had been assembled in Sitka from all over the territory, incidental to winding up the company's affairs. They had three years in which to choose between returning to the mother country, or, as the treaty provided, being admitted "to the enjoyment of all the rights, advantages and immunities of citizens of the United States." It was an attractive alternative and many proposed to stay. Trade was brisk and the outlook rosy. Soon a newspaper, the Sitka *Times*, was started and a city government was organized.

These happy days were not to last long. The keen hopes for the settlement of Alaska and the aspirations of Americans heading thither in true pioneer spirit were destined to be long deferred.[3]

Indeed scarcely a week after the inspiring ceremony of transferral the bad news was on its way that any attempts by citizens or others to acquire land in the newly annexed dominion were illegal, and that they might even be forcibly ejected therefrom.[4]

For the Fortieth Congress (1867-69) passed only a Customs Act (15 Stat. 240), creating Alaska a customs district which meant merely that foreign goods were subject to the same duties in Alaska as elsewhere in the United States, extending to Alaska the laws regarding commerce and navigation and prohibiting the importation and sale of distilled liquors.[5] Violators were made subject to prosecution in any of the neighboring United States District Courts—in Oregon or California. A collector would be in charge of collection and enforcement. In 1873 this act was amended to forbid the sale of liquor to Indians.[6] The Forty-first Congress likewise by-passed the needs of government or settlement. It made the Pribilof Islands a reservation and enacted into law a twenty-year exclusive concession of their seal fisheries to a private company in San Francisco from which the federal treasury was to receive an annual fixed rental plus a royalty on each of the 100,000 sealskins to be taken.[7] The successful contenders were organized under the name of the Alaska Commercial Company.

These two acts comprised the only legislation for Alaska that was to be enacted by the Congress for seventeen years. Throughout those years the citizens of Alaska would be forwarding petitions reminding Congress of its obligations. Officials stationed in Alaska would add their pleas. All went unheeded. Measures were introduced in the national legislature from time to time to establish some measure of law and civil government, but adjournment found them still reposing in committee. Within those seventeen years eight successive Congresses did precisely nothing as far as Alaska was concerned and the four corresponding presidential administrations passed without any action.

During that period in Alaska no hopeful settler could acquire a title to land; no pioneer could clear a bit of the forested wilderness and count on the fruits of his toil, or build a log cabin with the assurance that it was his; no prospector could stake a mining claim with security for his enterprise; property could not be deeded or transferred; no will was valid; marriage could not be celebrated; no injured party could secure redress for grievances except through his own acts; crime could not be punished.

Such semblance of government as there was was exercised without legal authority by the commanding general of the troops stationed in Sitka.[8] It was to be so for a decade. The ten-year military rule was not acclaimed as a success by anyone, least of all by the responsible elements of the community, official or civilian. There was repeated complaint buttressed by specific example, which to this day remains uncontradicted, that the soldiery was drunk and disorderly, officers as well as men, that they debauched the Indians, greatly intensified the evils wrought by the relatively moderate use of their ancient home-brew made of spruce bark and berries, by inculcating the distillation of a more potent "hoochenoo" made of molasses and sugar;[9] and that the military, instead of being guardians of law and order, were responsible for much of the crime and violence among the aborigines, and for creating a menace in the Indians' relation with the whites which would otherwise not have existed.

So when the troops were withdrawn in 1877 to help put down an uprising of the Nez Percé tribe in Idaho, and even their shadowy authority and potency ceased to exist, it was not surprising that there should be alarm lest a similar uprising take place in Alaska.[10]

The evacuation took place from Sitka on June 14th and from Wrangell two days later. It left the collector of customs, M. P. Berry, as the sole federal official with any legal authority in charge of Alaska's destinies. However Berry was taken very ill, and left Sitka for medical advice in Victoria, B. C. Possibly a contributory factor to his illness was revealed in his dispatch of July 13th to the Treasury Department that unless a vessel were dispatched at a very early day to Sitka its people would "have been handed over bodily for slaughter to the Indians." [11]

This view was supported by the Treasury's special agent, then at Port Townsend, Washington, William G. Morris, who on July 23rd telegraphed the content of Berry's letter from Sitka of ten days earlier to the department, adding that the captain and officers of the mail steamer *California* (which brought a copy of Berry's letter), just arrived from Sitka, were "much alarmed" and anticipated "immediate trouble" and that "all reports" were "confirmatory of danger." He followed this on the same day with a letter to John Sherman, Secretary of the Treasury, in which, after detailing more fully the information brought by the *California's* captain, he declared that the outlook in Alaska was "exceedingly dangerous and alarming." He informed his chief that "all concurrent testimony" pointed to "a speedy outbreak and resultant bloodshed by the warlike tribes, unless restrained by the strong arm of the government" and that "an armed vessel" was "absolutely needed in the Sitka Archipelago without delay." [12]

Although Berry was the ranking official of the Treasury Department in Alaska, and Morris had been assigned a special mission to investigate and report on Alaskan affairs, and as such were presumably entitled to credence, their superiors in Washington seemed inclined to discount their views.[13] On July 25th Assistant Secretary of the Treasury R. C. McCormick wired the collector at Port Townsend, Washington, asking whether he had heard "any reliable information about trouble in Sitka." [14]

Meanwhile, on his own authority, Morris sought to persuade the commander of the revenue cutter *Wolcott*, stationed at Port Townsend, to proceed to Alaskan waters, but her captain, J. M. Selden, replied that he considered her entirely unfitted for the kind of service which would be expected of her, and that in any event she could not be readied for sailing before September 1st.

This prompted Morris to write the department telling of his futile efforts to get the *Wolcott* to Sitka, declaring that he no longer considered a revenue cutter sufficient. The situation had changed and while "for mere intimidation the *Wolcott* would be an admirable scarecrow," a vessel of a different class was now needed. It was his firm conviction that the department did not realize the situation, and the sooner it recognized fully the importance, condition and responsibility of the legacy bequeathed it by the War Department, the sooner would the Treasury become convinced of doing something and that speedily. "Some sort of government must be had," he concluded, and as the Treasury seemed to him the most proper bureau for the task of administration, it "should at once enter on the task and evolve some kind of order out of this impending and present chaos." [15]

The Treasury Department proceeded to do nothing of the kind. In fact it gave serious thought to abandoning the responsibilities which had been conferred upon it legally, Secretary Sherman recommending in his annual report at the beginning of 1878 that the Alaska Customs District be abolished.[16] The reason for this proposed abdication was that the customs receipts for the district had been less than the cost of administration. This circumstance, however, was patently due to a lack of enforcement machinery, beginning with an almost total absence of revenue cutters to prevent the extensive smuggling from Canada along the long boundary, with its multitude of bays and inlets.[17]

One deterrent to the sending of cutters, besides inadequate appropriations, was "the want of reliable charts," which made navigation in Alaskan waters extremely hazardous.[18]

Apart from its failure to provide vessels to carry out the only legally established functions of government in Alaska, namely, the collection of customs duties and the prevention of liquor importation, the Treasury was not answering its correspondence from Alaska.

Letters addressed to the Secretary asking for instructions relative to the situation created in the liquor traffic by the withdrawal of the troops; for advice concerning the problem posed by the shipping in a three months' period of 4,889 gallons of molasses into Sitka and 1,635 gallons into Wrangell for the manufacture of "hoochenoo"; for expression of policy on the extensive importation into Alaska of "root bitters," presumably a medicine, and of high alcoholic content—all these went unanswered.[19]

Under the circumstances it is understandable that Special Agent Morris should communicate to his department his ideas of what a collector's qualifications—in Alaska—should be, for nowhere else under the flag, he felt were "more essential requisites" called for. In addition to being well versed in the whole organic law of the land, as well as in the laws and regulations for the collection of revenue, he must be "of sound and discreet judgment, willing whenever the necessities of the case demand, to assume responsibility; in fine he must be a man equal to the occasion, neither a moral nor a physical coward." Morris added what must have already been known to his chief, that since the customs district had been established in 1868—ten years earlier—not fewer than seven different collectors had held office.

One reason, doubtless, for the rapid turnover, was that the collector's five assistants, the deputy collectors at Sitka, Wrangell, Tongass,

Unalaska and Kodiak, had received no pay for periods varying between thirteen and twenty-two months, while the acting collector at Sitka, Edward H. Francis, who had assumed office nearly a year earlier, when his predecessor, Henry C. De Ahna, failed of Senate confirmation, had received no pay whatsoever for his 358 days' service in that post. When paid, the salaries of the deputies were $1,200 a year, excepting at Wrangell, where the salary was $1,500. The collector himself was entitled to $2,500 per annum plus fees which might not exceed $1,500.[20]

Meanwhile, receiving no assurance that their pleas for a war vessel of some sort to be stationed in Alaskan waters to ward off trouble would be heeded by their own government, the Sitkans finally appealed to the British.

"We have made application to our government for protection and aid, and thus far it has taken no notice of our supplication," they wrote.[21] The appeal, carried by mail steamer, was addressed "to the captain of any one of Her Majesty's ships at Esquimault" [22] (on Vancouver Island). The cry for help was responded to in good-neighborly fashion by Captain H. Holmes A'Court, who without waiting for instructions, proceeded northward on the vessel under his command, H.M.S. *Osprey*. He arrived at Sitka on March 1, 1879, and reported finding "the inhabitants in a great state of anxiety and alarm" which his arrival dispelled when he announced that he would remain until an American vessel relieved him.[23]

On March 22nd the revenue cutter *Oliver Wolcott* arrived. Its captain, J. M. Selden, A'Court and Collector Ball conferred and agreed that the *Wolcott* could not guarantee sufficient protection, and A'Court offered to remain until a U. S. warship arrived. The U.S.S. *Alaska* arrived on April 3rd and the *Osprey* returned to British Columbia, having performed a service unique in American annals. A few days later the *Wolcott* also departed. As the *Alaska's* skipper, Captain Brown, had no orders for a prolonged stay, another petition "in behalf of three hundred residents of Sitka" asking for permanent protection was dispatched to the President of the United States by H.M.S. *Osprey*. On June 14th the *Alaska* was relieved by the U.S.S. *Jamestown* under Commander L. A. Beardslee in whose "wisdom, capacity and discretion"—pending action, which Secretary of the Navy, R. W. Thompson, "believed" would take place at the next session of Congress, to establish civil authority in Alaska—the Navy Department had "full confidence . . . to dispose of such matters" as might "require" his "intervention." [24]

Thus ended what has been known as the rule of the Treasury Department in Alaska, which had lasted exactly two years.

The two successive "administrations," if they may be called by so flattering a name, had scarcely fulfilled the hopeful dictum, twenty-one years previously, of Representative William Higby. Six months earlier Special Treasury Agent Morris had reported that the commerce of the port of Sitka had dwindled to almost nothing. "No stately ships now ride in that beautiful harbor," and save the monthly visit of the mail steamer, and an occasional other visiting vessel, the quiet of the place was undisturbed. "The decline in trade has been gradual but sure since the purchase by the United States." [25]

Sitka's population, estimated as twenty-five hundred at the time of the purchase, had shrunk to about a third of that number. Most of the Russians had departed, unappreciative of the value of American citizenship as they had seen it. Early American enterprisers had likewise folded their tents and returned to the States. Sitka indeed was beginning to present, as Morris put it, the appearance of "Goldsmith's deserted village."

For the next five years, the successive commanders of naval vessels stationed at Sitka were, *de facto*, the rulers of Alaska.

Beardslee, the first of these to grapple—without legal authority—with Alaska's problems, turned his attention immediately to the tense situation purportedly endangering the population of Sitka. His conclusion was that the community had "narrowly escaped a massacre," and that that escape had been due "to the influence of certain friendly Indians of superior intelligence." [26] As had others before him, Beardslee concluded that "hoochenoo" was at the bottom of the trouble.[27]

Immediately upon his arrival Commander Beardslee had been asked by Collector Ball to assist in the prevention of liquor smuggling, as the latter had learned that upon the arrival of the monthly mail steamer its crew were engaged therein. Beardslee assented and assigned an officer and four men, who, sworn in as deputies to the collector, confiscated such whisky as they found. But a few weeks later the naval commander declined to continue this assistance, because aside from his apprehension that he was not acting lawfully, he felt it "simply ridiculous to take strong measures to stop a little whisky and protect at the same time tons of molasses, a gallon of which will do as much harm as a barrel of the former." [28] He then raised the question whether in the furtherance of the congressional prohibition against the sale of liquor to the Indians and against distilleries, this problem could not be attacked at the source by cutting off the supply of the ingredients. But the decision of Attorney General Charles Devens was adverse.[29] Not only were molasses and sugar sacrosanct, but the commander's decision to refrain from assisting in the search and seizure of imported liquor further encouraged and increased the traffic.[30] The collector's means of enforcement were negligible.

Possibly abuse of liquor was for some of the local citizens an attempt to escape from their frustrations, and its sale, no doubt, a source of income in a legislatively restricted economy. But their real wants were scarcely satisfied thereby. They besieged their new overlord with requests to present to still higher authority their necessity for acquiring homes. He requested advice from the Navy Department as to how this might be done. "There are a number of miners, mining engineers, and others who are desirous of settling in Sitka and bringing their families," he reported. "If they could pre-empt land or purchase land or houses from the government, the place would take a step forward." [31] The reply from Washington was negative. It "must depend upon what Congress may do" was Navy Secretary Thompson's response.[32]

Meanwhile attempts at organizing provisional local government were as unsuccessful as were the efforts of the citizenry to establish claims to lands and to the buildings they sought to erect on them, by homemade attempts at filing claims, posting signs, and fencing what they hoped might become their property. The naval commander felt obliged to order these practices discontinued:

"I make this report with reluctance, for my sympathies are with those who are thus trying to obtain homes in Sitka," Beardslee wrote the Secretary of the Navy, deploring "the helpless condition of the citizens of the United States who have sought Alaska for homes." [33]

Nevertheless, the population was beginning to grow slowly. Citizens from the States imbued with hopefulness and oblivious of the difficulties they would encounter were coming north. Prospectors, attracted by reports of gold strikes, were heading for Alaska. Missionaries of the Presbyterian Church, apprised of a field of useful activity, had come in. They established the first permanent schools—1877 in Wrangell and 1878 in Sitka—with funds supplied partly by the home mission, partly by local subscription.[34] Concomitantly, growing more and more restive, the Sitkans sought increasingly to bring their plight to the attention of a distant government; when news came that Congress was considering some legislation designed to afford relief, they sensed the need of having someone with first-hand information present their case. They urged Collector Ball to go. Permission from the Treasury Department secured, he went, early in 1880, leaving, as Beardslee reported, "the entire management of affairs, afloat and ashore, in my hands." After a five months' absence, Ball returned empty-handed. Back in Washington four thousand miles away, the bills had not gotten beyond discussion in committee.

Commander Beardslee's tour of duty was drawing to a close. He had surveyed and charted Sitka Harbor and its approaches. He had established a police system among the Indians by appointing their leaders and making them responsible, and had won their confidence and friendship. He had done his best, though in vain, to assist the citizens of Alaska to make their needs known in Washington through the channels available. Although Beardslee received high commendation from the Navy Department, he reported that his various duties, alien to his inclinations as a seafarer, "were irksome and uninteresting, and the responsibility great, inasmuch as it was frequently necessary . . . that acts be performed by us which could not be justified by any law except the natural law by which might becomes right." [35]

Commander Beardslee was succeeded in September of 1880 by Commander Henry Glass, who after five months, reported that "open violation of law had grown to such proportions that some prompt and decided action was necessary to avoid future disorders in the territory," particularly in view of the probable speedy increase in the population, and on May 2, 1881, proclaimed that he would govern by military law.[36] When under these self-ordained powers he arrested three civilians charged with an attempted murder and asked for instructions, the Secretary of the Navy authorized him to "keep these men in confinement as long as, in your judgment, the interests of peace and good order . . . may require. . . ." [37]

Glass on the *Jamestown* was succeeded by Commander Edward P. Lull on the *Wachusett*. Unless he had "strong reason for other action" he was ordered to "maintain the order of things which Commander Glass . . . saw fit to establish in Alaska." [38]

Naval rule continued until September 15, 1884. Its last representative, Lieutenant Commander H. E. Nichols, of the U.S.S. *Pinta*, was not pleased at the turn of events which ended his sovereignty. When asked by the first U. S. District Judge for Alaska, Ward McAllister, Jr., to keep a prisoner committed to jail in default of bail, pending trial, in the naval guardhouse—since no moneys had been made available to carry out the provision of Congress to repair the Sitka jail as a penitentiary for the succeeding civil administration—Nichols refused, writing in reply: "I must distinctly state that I decline in every particular to be the pivot on which the success of this new civil government of Alaska will swing." [39]

THE ERA OF
FLAGRANT
NEGLECT

1884 - 1898

The First Organic Act

'Tis the story of a strange and picturesque people and of a strange and picturesque country, governed at long range by men, who, because they lacked firsthand knowledge were compelled to act upon information furnished by those who had an axe to grind—'twas so under the Russian Czars—'tis still so under the American Congress.

J. A. HELLENTHAL, 1936

IN THE fifteen years that followed the purchase, some twenty-five bills had been introduced into the Congress providing civil government for Alaska. They had not been deemed worthy of debate on the floor. They remained buried in committee. But in Alaska the people were waxing more and more indignant over congressional inaction. Friction between the naval command and the miners flocking into the Harrisburg mining district—later to be renamed and become the cities of Juneau and Douglas—aroused their tempers still further. They determined to exercise, as best they might, the traditional American rights of assembly and petition for redress of grievances. Public meetings were held in various communities of southeastern Alaska. A resulting convention at Juneau, August 16, 1881, with representatives elected from Sitka, Juneau, Wrangell, Klawock and Killisnoo, drafted a memorial to the President and Congress and determined on the election of a delegate to Congress. Inevitably the electoral contest would be between men with established responsibilities and with the maximum familiarity with the intricacies of a government long conspicuous by its absence—the collectors of customs, past and present. On what might be deemed a date historic in Alaska's long struggle for self-government, September, 5, 1881, the collector in office, Mottrom D. Ball, defeated his predecessor, M. P. Berry, who, recovered from a serious illness superinduced by the difficulties of his office, had returned to Sitka and had hopefully hung out his shingle as attorney at law.

Ball was to have another chance to present Alaska's case to Congress. Besides his certificate of election, duly certified to by the deputy collector of customs, "under his hand and customs seal," there being no other authority in the district authorized to administer oaths, Ball carried with him the memorial adopted by the convention. In restrained language it called attention to the failure of "the proprietary government" to prescribe any rule of action or civil code by which the rights of the residents of its "property" might be determined and protected, and their consequent inability "lawfully to arraign the perpetrator of wrong or demand the vindication of right"; that for want of such government southeastern Alaska had been "a useless piece of territory to the United States while with its development its civilization and value would be rapidly advanced"; and, that in order to establish such government a proper understanding of their wants was necessary, and "to prevent the misrepresentation" [1] which obstructed the enjoyment of their rights, they asked that their delegate be seated.[2]

This memorial was the precursor of a long line of similar pleas to the federal authorities through which, for the next three-quarters of a century, Alaskans would be asking for recognition of what they deemed their rights as American citizens.

In Washington a new attitude toward Alaska was gaining ground "on the hill." The five successive promptings of Presidents Hayes and Garfield had contributed.[3] Citing the provisions of the third article of the Treaty of Cession, Hayes urged that "both the obligations of the treaty and the necessities of the people require that some organized form of government over the Territory of Alaska be adopted." [4]

The debates on a variety of bills for civil government in Alaska in the Forty-seventh Congress (1881-1883) revealed an acute consciousness on the part of many members of past legislative dereliction.[5]

The Forty-seventh Congress was notable for a bill which enjoyed a favorable report of the Senate Committee on Territories.[6] Presented as a substitute for another bill, which the committee disapproved because of its unusual provision of uniting the executive and judicial power in one person, the substitute bill established all *three* branches of government. It provided for a governor, a secretary who would be ex-officio treasurer of the territory, a supreme court with four inferior courts to consist of one chief justice and four lower-court judges, a marshal and four deputies, to be located at Sitka, the capital, Juneau, Wrangell and Unalaska. The territory was to be constituted as a surveying and land district, a surveyor general was to be appointed who would also act as register and receiver, his duties to be similar to those exercised in the other territories. All the laws then in force for the survey, sale and disposal of the public lands of the United States were to apply in the territory. The governor, secretary, chief justice, marshal and surveyor general were to be appointed by the President for four-year terms with the advice and consent of the Senate. These five, without the secretary, but with the collector of customs in his stead, were to constitute a legislative council, which was to provide necessary legislation, collect taxes and license fees, appoint the four inferior-court justices and other necessary officials not otherwise provided for. They were also to divide the territory into counties, provide for the listing and registration of voters and the proper apportionment of representation. Once this was done, a delegate to Congress was to be elected every two years, the date of the first election to be fixed by the governor.

It is idle to speculate on what might have happened to Alaska if this granting a very large measure of territorial government had become law, and to what extent the development of Alaska might have been advanced, for the bill's approval by the Senate committee was the high-water mark in its brief existence. The Forty-seventh Congress adjourned without any action on this or other Alaskan measures; and it would be twenty years more before the nation's land laws were made available to Alaska, twenty-three years before Congress granted representation in the limited form of a voteless delegate in the House (for Ball was not seated) and twenty-nine years before a legislative branch of government was permitted Alaskans.

Instead the Forty-eighth Congress passed Senate Bill 153, drafted and sponsored by Senator Benjamin Harrison, R., of Indiana. By it Alaska was constituted "a civil and judicial district" with a "temporary" seat of government at Sitka, and provided with a governor, a district judge, a district attorney, a clerk of court and four lesser-court judges to be stationed at Sitka, Juneau, Wrangell and Unalaska, a marshal and four deputies. The mining laws of the United States were put into effect, but the general land laws were specifically excluded. The act likewise prohibited a legislative assembly and a delegate to Congress. The Secretary of the Interior was to make provision for the education of children of school age and $25,000 was appropriated therefor. The general laws of the state of Oregon then in force were to be declared to be the law of the district so far as they might be applicable, and not in conflict with the provisions of the act or with the laws of the United States.

In the effort to be economical, although the government's annual net revenues of some $307,000 from the seal concession amounted to about ten times the estimated costs of the proposed civil administration, various supplementary functions were assigned to the newly created officials. The clerk of court, in addition to his prescribed duties, was to be receiver of fines and moneys derived from forfeitures under the Customs Act, recorder of certificates of location of mining claims, and register of wills.

Although none of the land laws of the United States was to be applicable to the District of Alaska, it was nevertheless created a land district and a United States land office established at Sitka, with the various functions relating to land apportioned among the newly created officials. Thus the clerk of the court was to be the recorder of deeds and mortgages and of other contracts relating to real estate. The commissioner residing in Sitka was to be ex-officio register of the land office. The marshal was to be surveyor general of the district.

Other provisions relating to lands were that the Indians or other persons were not to be disturbed in the possession of any lands actually in their use and occupation or then claimed by them, but the terms under which such persons might acquire title to such lands was reserved for future legislation by Congress. Lands not exceeding 640 acres, then occupied as missionary stations among the Indian tribes, together with the improvements thereon, were to be continued in the occupancy of the various religious societies to which the stations belonged, until further action by Congress.

The lower-court judges, called commissioners, were to exercise all the duties and powers, civil and criminal, then conferred upon justices of the peace in Oregon—the power to grant writs of habeas corpus, jurisdiction in testamentary and probate matters, the powers of notaries public—and were charged with keeping records of all deeds and instruments acknowledged before them and relating to the title or transfer of property within the district. The deputy marshals were to exercise the powers and duties of deputy marshals of the United States as well as those of Oregon constables in force in 1884.

The act continued the existing prohibition against the importation, manufacture and sale of intoxicating liquors. Public buildings not required for the customs service or military purposes were to be used for courtrooms and offices of the civil government. The act provided for the appointment by the President, with the advice and consent of the

Senate, of the governor, judge, commissioners, clerk, attorney and marshal, all for four-year terms, and fixed their emoluments. The governor and judge would receive $3,000 annually; the clerk, attorney and marshal $2,500. The commissioners were to receive the usual fees of United States commissioners and such fees for recording instruments as were then allowed by the laws of Oregon for similar services, and a salary of $1,000. The deputy marshals, in addition to the usual fees of constables in Oregon, were to receive $750 annually.

The act provided for no taxes to be raised within the district for the purposes of government. Federal revenues, other than from the seal islands, were to be collected in the district, but except for incidental expenses of the District Court were not to be disbursed there.

The act was notable in several respects. It was specific in its limitations and prohibitions, indefinite and equivocal in its grants. No legislature, no delegate, no general land laws. But the provisions concerning the general laws and the administration of justice—establishing the Oregon code, as it *then* was, as the law of Alaska, signifying that no subsequent modification or improvement of Oregonian statutes would apply to Alaska—were valid only "so far as they may be applicable," and also "not in conflict with the provisions of this act or the laws of the United States." These ambiguities were to haunt and confuse the attempts to administer justice and other aspects of civil administration for a generation.

The act was negative in its land provisions: It prescribed numerous functions relating to land and entrusted their execution to various officials, ex-officio, but it failed to provide any legislative authority under which they could perform.

The carelessness of the draftsmanship, which in turn reflected the casualness of the content, was manifest in the provision that the governor should from time to time inquire into the operations of the "Alaska Seal and Fur Company," and should annually report to Congress the result of such inquiries and on any and all violations of the agreement between the United States and said company. There was, of course, no company by that name. It was the "Alaska Commercial Company" into whose affairs the governor was to inquire.

The lack of any serious endeavor to erect a suitable body of law for Alaska was revealed in response to the question of Senator James B. Beck, D., of Kentucky why the laws of the state of Oregon, laws a good deal more complicated than those of Washington Territory, which lay nearer to Alaska, had been selected in preference to those of Washington. Replied Senator Harrison: "Not because the committee had made any careful study of the laws either of the state of Oregon or of the territory of Washington, but because it was supposed that the Oregon code was in a more mature and satisfactory shape." [7]

It was likewise an economical act, or niggardly, depending on the point of view, as shown not merely by the salary scale and the multiplication of functions assigned to the few officials named to administer so vast a territory, in the meager appropriation for education of a population of thirty thousand people, in the failure to make any provision for transportation for a governor who was expected not merely to inform himself and report about conditions on the Pribilof Islands, some fifteen hundred miles from the capital, but was charged with the interests of the federal government in a district one-fifth as large as the United States, was to see that the laws enacted for it were enforced, and was to report annually not merely his "official acts and doings," but on the condition of said district, its resources, industries and population.

Alaska's first organic act (23 Stat. 24) became law on May 17, 1884. Even while it was being debated several months earlier, its proponents were apologizing for it. Replying to Senator George F. Hoar, R., of Massachusetts, who had urged an appropriation of $40,000 for education, instead of the $25,000 which the bill provided, its sponsor, Chairman Benjamin Harrison, of the Senate Committee on Territories, declared:

> I agree that the appropriation is inadequate; indeed, I am willing to confess upon the challenge of almost any Senator that all the provisions of the bill are inadequate. It is a mere shift; it is a mere expedient; it is a mere beginning in what we believe to be the right direction toward giving a civil government and education to Alaska. I hope more will follow, but the committee in considering this matter adjudged what they believed to be the probable limit of the generosity of the Senate.[8]

Alaska as a District:

Governor Swineford

The laws of a country should be related to its physical character, to its climate, whether warm, cold, or temperate; to the quality of its soil, to its location, to its size, to the kind of life led by its people, whether farmers, hunters or laborers.
CHARLES LOUIS DE SECONDAT MONTESQUIEU, 1748

IF THE Congress had declined to make Alaska a territory, either organized or unorganized, it had at least made Alaska several kinds of a district. In addition to its seventeen-year status as a customs district, its vanished ten-year phase as a military district, it was now, by virtue of the act of 1884, a civil district, a judicial district and a land district.

However, Alaska was a civil district in which the civil administration was authorized only to inspect, enforce the laws, and report, yet denied the means either to inspect or enforce.

Alaska was a judicial district, but Congress had so confused its mandate that no judge could be certain what the law was, and the marshal and his deputies often lacked the wherewithal to enforce a court order or sentence when there was one. The Oregon code had frequent reference to county and town functions and prescribed duties for their respective officials; but as Alaska had neither counties nor towns, and no power to create them, these provisions were meaningless, and left the corresponding functions for Alaska nonexistent.

Alaska was a land district, but without land laws.

The act's benefits were that by extension of the mining laws to Alaska it made mining possible;[1] that it gave public education an entering, if thin, wedge;[2] and that it afforded the governor at least a voice, if he chose to utilize it through his annual report or otherwise. During the next four administrations of four successive governors their voices were in varying degree crying in the wilderness.

Alaska's first governor, John Henry Kinkead, a former Governor of Nevada, appointed July 4, 1884, had also been one of the first arrivals in Sitka.[3] He served during the remaining months of the Arthur administration. His solitary report was made twenty-six days after his arrival in the district. But his familiarity with Alaska was sufficient to forewarn his successors of the obstacles they would encounter. He noted that all government officials, himself included, were embarrassed by the lack of any instructions. Nor had the Attorney General of the United States yet supplied the governor, judge, attorney, commissioners, clerk and marshal, as required by the organic act, with so much of the general laws of the United States and of Oregon as would be applicable to their duties. In the absence of such clarification these officials could scarcely function. Kinkead reported also that all public buildings were "in a sad state of disrepair." The civil government was even worse off than appeared, since under the act it was entitled only to such buildings as were not required by the Navy and customs service. Neither of these was eager to relinquish what it had.

In his recommendations Kinkead called attention to the impossibility of administering an area of the size and diversity of Alaska without transportation and personnel. Successful civil administration, he urged, must rest upon the support and aid of the federal government. But Congress, having given Alaska an act, was uninterested in supplying either the support or the aid that would make civil government other than an empty gesture.

The appointment, May 7, 1885, by President Grover Cleveland, of Alfred P. Swineford, Michigan newspaper editor, to the governorship, brought to Alaska a man of energy, courage and vision. His four annual reports may be considered classics in the literature of protest.

Swineford was convinced by the time of his first report that Alaska had vast natural resources and that no territory of the Union had at so early a period of its history presented nearly as many possibilities. Conversely, he contended that no American territory had suffered such discriminatory treatment. Its inability to progress he ascribed to lack of a form of government which would enable the people to legislate for themselves on local matters, and to the further failure of Congress to provide the means by which even the totally inadequate existing form of civil government could be made to work.

Swineford hammered away at various issues which were all related to his general theme. First was the unworkability of the *form* of civil government established by the act of 1884. It was wrong, he iterated and reiterated, in principle. He could not conscientiously "refrain" from calling attention "to the unjust withholding from Alaska of political rights never before denied to any section of territory or any fraction of the American people since the adoption of the Federal Constitution."[4] Alaska had neither a legislature of its own, nor any voice in any legislative body anywhere; no laws of its own making, and practically none that were adapted to its wants—with no one to advocate its cause or defend its rights in the national legislature.[5] In his final report he declared that the civil government of Alaska was "little, if any, better than a burlesque both in form and substance," and that aside from the preparation of the annual report "there is really no duty enjoined upon the governor, the performance of which is possible, no power he can exercise, no authority that he can assert." [6]

The governor was assisted in the propagation of his views by the publication in Sitka, beginning November 7, 1885, of a well-printed, ably edited weekly, the *Alaskan,* which reflected his thinking. It was for many years to be a useful, if minor, agent for presenting Alaska's case.

The civil government was unworkable, among other causes, because, with all the great distances, adequate transportation was unavailable. The monthly mail service from the States, from Port Townsend, Washington Territory, serving only Wrangell, Killisnoo, Juneau and Sitka, should, Swineford contended, be semimonthly, and extended monthly to Kodiak and Unalaska. Transportation between them and the capital, Sitka, was by way of San Francisco through a steamer connecting at Port Townsend with the Pacific Coast Steamship Company's monthly vessel to southeastern Alaska. With that service it was impossible to communicate with the authorities in the national capital and have a reply in less than three months.

The Post Office Department in Washington was not co-operative. When in April, 1886, the agents for the line rendering the only regular service to any part of Alaska announced their intention of running steamers fortnightly, "during the excursion months," May to October, inclusive, and suggested that mail be carried on every voyage, the department deemed it "inadvisable to increase the service." [7]

Even when the captain of the vessel offered to carry the mail on the alternate steamers free of charge as an accommodation to Alaskans, the postmaster at Port Townsend refused to allow the accumulated mail to be taken aboard—to the indignation of the Sitkans.[8]

A yeaı later, in May, 1887, an appeal to Postmaster General William F. Vilas called attention to the inadequacy of the mail service, pointed out that the white population of Alaska had more than doubled, and asked for weekly deliveries. It was signed by Governor Swineford, the District Judge, Lafayette Dawson, District Attorney M. D. Ball, Arthur K. Delaney, Collector of Customs and others.[9] No reply was received, but instead the monthly mail steamer *Idaho* missed the mail completely on her October trip. For the mail contract had expired. Its nonrenewal and sequent interruption of service were ascribed to the Postmaster General's absence from Washington.[10]

As far as "the westward" (as those parts of Alaska lying west of southeastern Alaska are known to Alaskans) was concerned, two years after the establishment of civil government, the *Alaskan's* special correspondent from Kodiak, reporting fishing and canning activities at Karluk on Kodiak Island, and Kasilof on the Kenai Peninsula, and the arrival of prospectors en route to Cook's Inlet, commented:

"It seems strange to us that this central region of Alaska, with a creole[11] population of several thousand and many white men, has been totally overlooked in that voluminous document, the 'Organic Act.' Up to this time we have had no ocular proof of the existence of the District Government." [12]

From still farther westward came the resignation of U. S. Deputy Marshal Isaac Anderson of Unalaska, saying that after seventeen months' service he found his salary of $750 per annum too small to "justify any man living in such an out of the way corner of the world," where the mail arrived and left only during six months out of the twelve. A 250- to 300-ton mail steamer between Sitka and the westward ports could, he pointed out, operate profitably with only a small mail subsidy by serving the points in between, and connect at Sitka with the Pacific Coast Steamship Company's steamer.[13]

Swineford had been vainly urging the same thing, and pleaded, as even more necessary, for some vessel at his disposal—even an ocean-going tug—to enable him to carry out his duties prescribed in the act of 1884. He had hoped to get transportation on naval vessels. But the senior naval officer in Alaskan waters was unco-operative.[14]

How could he report on the seal fisheries on the Pribilof Islands, fifteen hundred miles from Sitka, without means of getting there, Swineford asked persistently. There were no roads and trails in Alaska; all transportation had to be by water. Alaska's coastline was longer than the Atlantic, Gulf and Pacific coastlines of the United States, combined.

"To hold a term of court at Wrangell, which may not in itself consume more than a single day's time, a full month is required, with corresponding expense to the government," wrote Swineford.[15] The civil officials were charged with the responsibility of enforcing the laws and yet furnished no means for doing so. Unless that were rectified civil government would be "little better than a ridiculous farce." [16]

The means were not furnished. Not until the closing months of his fourth and last year did Swineford secure transportation on a naval vessel. But the conclusion of the decade of the eighties saw only monthly mail service to Alaska, although the steamers were, by that time, running a regular bimonthly and occasionally a weekly service.[17]

There was the judicial confusion. When the Attorney General issued his compilation of United States and Oregon laws he made it clear that he could not decide on their applicability.[18] And four years later Swineford reported that while frequent complaints came to him of "open and flagrant violations of the law" both he and his law officers were powerless to afford relief: "Several murders have been committed since the inauguration of civil government and the murderers are still at large and likely to remain so," he reported, since the authorities had no ways and means for making arrests.[19]

Distances, great or small, were among the impediments, in view of the lack of transportation. When Marshal Barton Atkins at Sitka received word from Deputy Marshal Thomas at Wrangell that he had warrants against three men at Klawock for burglary, and that he was being urged to go there and arrest them, the marshal had to reply that he had no means of transportation at his command, and no means to pay the expenses of arrest and transportation by others, Klawock being eighty miles distant from the nearest point the mail steamer touched on her route.[20]

Then there were the prohibition laws, the enforcement of which was "practically inoperative." With the extensive coastline and no revenue cutters, the customs officials were helpless.[21] Swineford related the impaneling of a grand jury, and the indictment and conviction of a number of persons charged with selling intoxicating liquor, but the case, appealed on a writ of error, was reposing in the circuit court in Oregon.[22] Meanwhile the flow of liquor continued, and Swineford began to doubt whether even a revenue cutter could stop it. He urged that the law be repealed and that a stringent licensing system be adopted so the traffic could at least be controlled and substantial revenue obtained which could cover a large part of the expenses of the civil government.

"The only effect of the law had been to flood the Territory with liquors the most vile and poisonous, to the enrichment of the few who have been engaged in their illegal importation," [23] wrote Swineford. And two years later in his final accounting, Swineford regretted to say that the law was "practically a dead letter." [24] Public sentiment in the district was averse to it; grand juries would not indict and petit juries would not convict persons charged with violation. "In the case of Alaska," he concluded, "prohibition does not prohibit," and he repeated that a stringent license law would enable the courts to close up half the saloons and put an end to the whisky smuggler's vocation, "by taking away the enormous profits which the law offers as an inducement to its own violation." [25]

Actually juries were not legal in Alaska and the lawyers knew it. A large part of the failures to uphold convictions in appeals to the circuit courts arose from that defect. The Oregon code required that to be a member of grand or petit jury in a civil or criminal case one had to be a taxpayer, and Congress had not seen fit to levy any taxes in Alaska.[26]

As for education, the $25,000 appropriated for children regardless of race, plus a further $15,000 for Indians, was not nearly sufficient. The matter could be handled easily if the people of Alaska could legislate for themselves on questions of purely local character.[27] Reviewing the entire educational program exhaustively, and commenting on the schools then being conducted by the Friends Society, the Catholic Sisters of Charity and the seventeen schools being then continued by the Russian Government through its established church, Swineford felt it "not altogether creditable to us, that the despotic government of Russia expends annually more money for the education and christianization of the native people of Alaska than does the professedly more free, liberal and enlightened one to whose care and protection they were transferred twenty years ago." [28]

The organic act obstructed local control of education. When the people of Sitka desired to constitute that town into a separate and distinct school district, so that they might elect a school board and have some voice in the management of the public school, they found that the common-school law of Oregon, under which they were obliged to operate, made this impossible. It provided that county superintendents alone had the power to create school districts, and in Alaska there were no counties, and hence no county superintendents.[29]

In addition to being inadequate, the appropriations for education were not made in time to be applied in the year for which they were intended, illustrating early in Alaska's rule by the United States a failure on the part of Congress, oft repeated through the years, to make the necessary allowances for the *time* as well as the *space* factors when dealing with Alaska.

However great the handicaps, they were to be vigorously attacked during the next generation by one who brought to his gigantic task an apostolic fervor which never permitted difficulties to dampen his ardor or diminish his determination—Sheldon Jackson.

There were two provisions concerning education in Alaska under the act of 1884. It appropriated $25,000 for the education of children without regard to race. It authorized a commission consisting of the governor and two others to examine into the condition of the Indians and to determine what should be done for their education. Secretary of the Interior Henry M. Teller, to whom Congress had delegated those responsibilities, passed them on to Commissioner of Education John Eaton.

Eaton came to the conclusion that $25,000 was a very small appropriation, and that with Alaska's nearest school some four thousand miles from Washington, a general agent resident in Alaska, at Sitka, should be named. For this post he reported that none was so well qualified as Sheldon Jackson, who had repeatedly visited Alaska, had written a book about it, had already established Presbyterian missionary schools there, and worked hard to secure the entry of other denominations. Jackson was recommended by all the private organizations interested in education in Alaska. His salary was fixed at $1,200 a year.

When the congressional appropriation for the school year, 1886-87, was not made till August, 1886, after all the vessels for western Alaska had sailed, Sheldon Jackson chartered a schooner as the only means by which teachers and supplies could reach their new destinations. The journey, beset by equinoctial storms through largely uncharted waters, required 104 days. Once the schooner was stranded on reefs, but the schools' inauguration, while delayed, took place.[30]

Sheldon Jackson lost no time, both through his reports and through personal contact, in bringing home the facts of life in Alaska to Washington officialdom.

For Alaskan distances were, clearly, something to which Congress and the federal bureaucracy were oblivious. Among the rules and regulations for the conduct of public schools and education in the Territory of Alaska, prescribed by Secretary of the Interior L. Q. C. Lamar, Section 4 provided that the General Agent for Education "shall visit each school district and each school in the district of Sitka once a year." [31] (Southeastern Alaska was the Sitka district, and the rest of Alaska, the western district.)

"This is a physical impossibility," General Agent Sheldon Jackson promptly reported to his superior, the U. S. Commissioner of Education: With the means of transportation available no one could visit each school in Alaska once a year. If one visited the schools of southeastern Alaska in one year, he would have to forego those of western Alaska, and vice-versa.[32]

In a voluminous report to the Commissioner of Indian Affairs he reiterated a still earlier exposition of the transportation difficulties in Alaska. Secretary of the Interior Lamar transmitted it to the United States Senate, which had asked for information on education in Alaska and, upon its receipt, ordered it printed.[33]

If the General Agent for Education for Alaska, with headquarters at Sitka, wished to visit a school on the Yukon, the Senate learned, his nearest way was to take the monthly mail steamer from Sitka to Juneau, a distance of 166 miles, then hire a canoe and have natives take him, together with blankets and provisions, to the head of Dyya Inlet (also spelled Taiya), at the upper end of the Inside Passage, another hundred miles. There he left the water and hired a fresh crew of natives to carry his supplies on foot twenty-five miles over a dangerous mountain trail to the upper waters of the Yukon River. There they would have to construct a raft and float downstream fifteen hundred miles to Nulato, where there was a school, and an additional 250 miles to Anvik, where there was another. This trip would require two months, and would be possible only between late May and early October because the Yukon was frozen at other times. An alternative method was to take the mail steamer from Sitka to San Francisco, some sixteen hundred miles, then "a chance steamer" to St. Michaels (near the mouth of the Yukon) 3,264 miles, then a small river steamer to Nulato, 769 miles, a total distance of 5,633 miles. To make the trip and return in the same year would require close connections. Three schools, at St. Michaels, Anvik and Nulato, would have been visited.

If the General Agent wanted to visit the school at Bethel, on the lower Kuskokwim River, he would take a mail steamer to San Francisco, sixteen hundred miles, wait until some vessel sailed for Unalaska, 2,418 miles, to which there were no scheduled departures, then wait again until some trading vessel had occasion to visit the mouth of the Kuskokwim, 461 miles, and go thence the rest of the way in a *bidarka* (a large sea-lion skin canoe)—a total distance of 4,629 miles. The teachers' annual mail followed the same tedious route.[34]

With federal funds scant, Sheldon Jackson enlisted the co-operation of missionary groups which had already sensed Alaska's possibilities. By the winter of 1887-1888 there was the slender beginning of a far-flung school system in Alaska. In southeastern Alaska sixteen schools were functioning. Sitka had three, one for whites and creoles, one for natives, with emphasis on industrial training, and a Russian church school. Juneau had a similar arrangement, but instead of the Greek Orthodox Church school there was one conducted by Roman Catholics. There were public schools at Haines, Wrangell, Killisnoo, Howkan, Klawock. A school at Douglas had been established by the Society of Friends, the Presbyterians had one at Hoonah on Chichagof Island, and the Swedish mission had founded a school at Yakutat. At the lower end of the "Panhandle" (an alternative designation for southeastern Alaska) was a school conducted by the Reverend William Duncan, an Anglican missionary who had broken with his superiors of the Church of England in British Columbia, and had secured from Congress permission to bring his flock of Tsimshean Indians into Alaska and establish them on a reservation on Annette Island, where he named his settlement "New Metlakatla."

To the westward, besides the Russian mission schools, and the two schools on the Pribilof Islands of St. Paul and St. George, stipulated in the government contract with the Alaska Commercial Company, were public schools on Kodiak and Afognak Islands, and at Unga on the Shumagins. With the sanction of contracts with the Bureau of Education, the Moravians had come into the lower Kuskokwim and were conducting schools at Bethel and at Carmel on the Nushagak River flowing into Bristol Bay. The Swedish mission had started a school at Unalakleet on Norton Sound on the Bering Sea. The Episcopalians had moved into the Yukon with schools at St. Michael near the river's mouth and at Anvik and would soon take over a Church of England mission farther up the Yukon originating in Canada. The Catholics had established a school in Nulato and shortly thereafter opened two more schools on the lower Yukon, at Holy Cross and Tununuk. Within a year the Methodists would begin their educational work at Unalaska. Other schools run by still other denominations, Baptists, Congregationalists and Friends, were to follow closely.

The various religious denominations made possible the establishment of so many schools in so short a time. They supplied such funds as Congress did not furnish.

The missionary zeal may likewise have been sufficiently contagious so that the public-school teachers contributed to relieve the financial stringency by consenting to a reduction in their salaries. Perhaps they did so "cheerfully" as the Commissioner of Education of the United States reported after his summer visit to Alaska in 1887.[35] But a year later a further reduction ordered by the District Board of Education, consisting of the Governor, District Judge and General Agent, aroused sufficient rebellion that public and press entered into the matter.[36] The pertinent issue of Alaska's higher living costs was raised then, as it would be again and again.

Governor Swineford was concerned about the health of the native population: the Indians, Aleuts and Eskimos. A hospital for their care was not only needed, but indispensable. He had seen them "dying almost daily" for want of the medical care and attention which it seemed to him "a humane government" ought not to hesitate to provide.[37]

The population of Alaska was of course predominantly native, and therefore a fitting subject for the governor's concern. A census of sorts had been taken between 1880 and 1882. In August of the latter year Superintendent of the Census Charles W. Seaton received from Special Agent Ivan Petroff the report he had been asked to make some twenty-seven months earlier, to ascertain "as far as possible" the number of inhabitants of the Alaska District and whatever else might be learned about their occupations, subsistence and mode of life. Petroff, working alone, spent the better part of the next two years traveling through the Alaskan wilderness, saw much at first hand, inquired assiduously of others, collected what data he could and (but for W. H. Dall's work of a decade earlier) published the first general account of Alaska's topography, ethnology, fauna and other visible natural resources. His population census was, however, sharply disputed, and with some justification, since not only was accurate enumeration impossible, but as he was shipwrecked on his way south, he was unable to visit southeastern Alaska.

The census taking of that most developed part of Alaska he delegated to another. Petroff's figures gave Alaska a total population of 33,426, of whom 430 were white, 1,756 creole, and the remainder natives divided into Eskimo, 17,617, Aleut, 2,145 and Indian, 11,478. The Indians were further subdivided into Athabascan, 3,927, Tlingit, 6,763 and Haida, 788.[38] The allegedly small number of whites was to prove an obstacle to Alaskans' hope for extending self-government, as it would be again repeatedly through the next half-century or more, no matter how their number increased. But Petroff's figures were emphatically challenged, and contradictory statements by him elsewhere in his report cited as evidence of error. Governor Swineford, among others, called attention to Petroff's reporting that the gold discoveries in the Juneau-Douglas area since 1880 had "attracted several thousand miners and their followers." [39]

Swineford in 1885 estimated the white population of southeastern Alaska, alone, at 1,900, and three years later gave the following as his "conservative estimate" of Alaska's total population: "Whites, 6,500; Creoles (practically white) 1,900; Aleuts, 2,950; Natives (partially educated and who have adopted civilized ways of living) 3,500. Natives wholly uncivilized, 35,000. Total 49,850."

Failure to apply the land laws to Alaska, indeed to pass any land laws such as would permit the establishment of town sites, was retarding the development of Alaska, Swineford repeatedly reported. People seeking homes in a new country would not be inclined to go where they could not enjoy the same rights accorded settlers on public domain elsewhere.[40]

A mass meeting of the citizens of Sitka, March 3, 1886, addressed a memorial to the President, asking him to declare a reservation for town-site purposes, and to order the survey and plotting of the same, to the end that full and absolute titles in fee simple might be brought within the reach of their then occupants and claimants, as well as intending purchasers, and the improvement of streets, sidewalks and public grounds thereby secured.[41] The memorial went unanswered.

Another obstacle to growth and development was the prohibition to cut timber from public lands—and all lands in Alaska were public lands—with the exception of timber cut from mineral lands by bona-fide residents for their own use in building, mining, or other domestic purposes. To supply these there were only six sawmills in all Alaska. But the lumbermen were unable to comply with the stringent regulations of the Department of the Interior for cutting timber, and, being forbidden to export it, found supplying only the domestic users unprofitable. So even the home builders had difficulty in securing cut lumber. In Juneau there was complaint that but for these restrictions much more building would be going on there. Alaska's virgin forests even at that early day were filled with overripe trees dying on the stump, but a distant bureaucracy inhibited their use. A salmon cannery at Klawock which had established its own sawmill was forbidden to ship out its fish product in barrels and boxes manufactured from local timber, and ordered to import them.[42]

The lumber import was of course lucrative for the lumbermen of the Northwest, and there was no urgency on the part of its spokesmen in Congress to yield any part of the business to the residents of the District of Alaska.[43]

The lumber import was also beneficial to the Pacific Coast Steamship Company which was charging $10 a thousand for freighting it, and making the cost to Alaskans higher than if they had been permitted to patronize their local sawmills, whose owners likewise chafed at their inability to supply this local and growing market.[44] What was particularly tantalizing to them was to read in Secretary of the Interior John W. Noble's annual report that "the immense forests of Alaska, consisting mainly of spruce, hemlock and red cedar, are of excellent quality for economic purposes." [45] The secretary added that the existing timber law caused much embarrassment. Alaskans had stronger words to describe their feelings on the subject.

Failure to pass any tax laws, to secure a return on the profits from the raw materials extracted from Alaska, was likewise hindering Alaska's development, Swineford contended. Fifteen million dollars, he estimated, would be a fair value of the mining developments in the district from which revenue could be obtained. As for the fisheries, which by then were supporting seventeen canneries and an equal number of salteries, with many more in contemplation—the lack of land legislation through which they could acquire title to their locations, and of tax measures based on their operations, meant a great loss of revenue. It also produced abuses such as the seizing of salmon streams by the first come who held them against all others.[46]

"As a consequence," Swineford concluded, "the fisheries are being absorbed by corporations, who occupy public lands without let or hindrance, and who, under the existing political status pay no taxes for any purpose whatever." He pointed out that he was not averse to the occupation of the fishing grounds, but that lack of governmental action was preventing men of limited means from engaging in these pursuits. As it was, immense profits would be made which would flow out of the territory without any corresponding influx of either capital or population. Without a single exception the canneries were owned and operated by nonresident corporations whose operators came in the spring, bringing with them all the cheap Chinese and other labor they required, few if any of their employees becoming actual residents. But for the mining, "Alaska would be to the country at large nothing more than a national fat goose left unprotected and to be annually plucked of its valuable plumage by nonresident corporations." [47]

"Is it desired that the undeveloped resources of Alaska shall be developed? If so it lies with Congress to inaugurate a substantial beginning in that direction. It is only necessary that the shackles which fetter the progress of a great empire in embryo be removed. . . ." [48]

Congress was removing no shackles, was passing no legislation whatever for Alaska. Bills were introduced annually, but got nowhere. The question arose in Swineford's mind, as in that of other spectators of congressional torpor, how such prolonged indifference, such protracted inaction, could be explained.

It was a question that could well puzzle its contemporary observers —and victims—as well as future historians. Having acquired an area one fifth as large as the United States, the federal authorities, legislative and executive, might have been expected to display some curiosity, some interest. What resources did this vast land contain? How could they be developed? What were its people's needs and desires? There was no such curiosity or interest. The national census of 1870 did not include Alaska.[49] And ten years later, Petroff's mission was at best an informal and irregular venture, a product of parsimony, with its delegation to one man of the impossible task of making the first decennial census, without any attempt to establish safeguards and checks as to accuracy, for an area as vast as Alaska, still largely unexplored.

The fact seems to have been that the majority of federal officials, executive and legislative, continued to think of Alaska as a bad bargain, a worthless waste, further expenditure on which would be still more waste.[50] Its only value in their eyes appeared to lie in the slightly over $300,000 annual payment for the lease of the seal islands and the royalty on sealskins, which by the middle eighties had repaid to the Treasury more than half of the purchase price.

The annual budgets of the period revealed the focus of the governance's interest. In the estimates for the fiscal year 1887, the total appropriation for the operation of the civil government in Alaska, exclusive of education, was $25,500. But for government operation in connection with the seal islands $43,350 was budgeted.[51]

Indeed when Senator Benjamin Harrison extenuated the inadequacy of the act of 1884 with his view that it went to the probable limit of the Senate's generosity, he was not far wrong. In the same debate, Senator John J. Ingalls, R., of Kansas, a statesman of considerable stature, re-echoed the adverse views expressed seventeen years earlier in the House debate on the payment for Alaska, by declaring it "the most worthless territorial acquisition with which any government was ever afflicted," and that he was "yet without information" on "what compensation" other than the gratification of extending the American idea on the continent, we had received.[52]

Why were Senator Ingalls and other members of that senior deliberative body without such information?

There was, and had been, prior to and since the purchase, an intense and special interest in certain of Alaska's economic potentialities, particularly in fur and fisheries, manifested by men of great power on the Washington scene—men from the far West. The first of these was Senator William McK. Gwin, D., of California. In December, 1859, during the closing days of President Buchanan's administration, he had had more than one interview with the Russian minister looking toward the acquisition of the assets of the Russian-American Company. His negotiations, however, which were arranged through the State Department, fell through.

In 1866 the California Fur Company was organized with a capital stock of $5,000,000 to take over from the Russian-American Company the lease to the mainland of southeastern Alaska. Its president was

General John F. Miller, Collector of the Port of San Francisco, later to become United States Senator, and numbered among its stockholders some of the most powerful financial leaders in the state. The legal work of obtaining the lease was entrusted to another prominent Californian, Cornelius Cole, likewise shortly to become Senator Cole.

Another San Francisco firm, Hutchinson and Co., later Hutchinson, Kohl & Co., was likewise interested in Alaska fur resources. One of its representatives, "a Mr. Schloss," [53] reported Hiram Ketchum, Jr., the second Collector of the Customs District of Alaska, from San Francisco, on October 26, 1868, "will probably leave here for Washington next week, where he will remain all winter endeavoring to procure legislation in favor of his interests." The "third house," also known as the "lobby," was already at work in Washington for its "interests" in Alaska. It had powerful friends in Congress. "His right bower," wrote Collector Ketchum, referring to Hutchinson & Co.'s representative, Sloss, "is Hon. William M. Stewart, Senator from Nevada." [54] Procuring—and preventing—legislation concerning Alaska was to play a decisive, if not always a visible, part in Alaska's subsequent history.

For the stakes were big, and the game was played ruthlessly in the field, more suavely in the national capital. Writing in 1870, Dall reported that he had "obtained abundance of evidence that during 1868 great abuses were prevalent in the new territory. One trading company in particular, hoping by its large capital and connections with the officers of the defunct Russian company to crush all small concerns, had not hesitated at force, fraud and corruption to attain these ends." [55]

There were thirteen bidders for the Pribilof Islands lease based on a permitted annual take of 100,000 seals. The presumption was that the highest bid would be accepted. When the bids were opened in Washington, July 20, 1870, the lowest of the thirteen bids proved to be that of the Alaska Commercial Company. However, the lease was awarded to it, but on the terms offered by another bidder. Just how this result was achieved was not explained at the time. It has been plausibly conjectured that the influence of Senator Cornelius Cole, R., former attorney of the principal stockholders, who had been elected to the Senate in 1867, may have had something to do with it.[56]

So it was the Alaska Commercial Company that by purchase, influence or otherwise survived all its competitors and became the concessionaire for the Alaska sealskin trade for a period of twenty years.[57]

As early as 1878 William G. Morris, Special Agent of the Treasury Department, after two years' study of Alaska, had written Secretary of the Treasury John Sherman:

"I am not prepared at present to charge directly any persons with a deliberate intent to undervalue the natural wealth of Alaska, and to prevent its settlement and civilization, but that there is an undercurrent at work to belittle the purchase and decry the acquisition from Russia as worthless and a desert watery waste is patent to all those who have the good weal and interest of the Territory at heart . . . and who are cognizant there lie in Alaska immense fields of undeveloped mineral wealth, which only require the fostering care of the Government to make more valuable to mankind." [58]

Before a Senate subcommittee considering Senator Matthew Calbraith Butler's bill to give a substantial measure of territorial government to Alaska (S.1153), G. C. Hanus, a master from the U.S.S. *Jamestown*, just returned from Alaskan waters, testified in 1882 to the widespread belief in Alaska that the Alaska Commercial Company did "not want any government for Alaska at all; that they would rather have Alaska left alone." He referred to a man who was writing newspaper articles to the effect that Alaska was worthless but for its furs and was carrying that message around Washington.[59]

Marcus Baker, of the Coast Survey, testifying subsequently, identified the individual in question as Henry W. Elliott. Elliott, formerly a special agent for the Treasury Department, had taken employ with the company, and was spending his winters in Washington where he testified freely—and adversely—to Alaska's potentialities before Senate and House committees.

Baker expressed the feelings of Americans who had come to Alaska when he said: "There should be someone here who would be charged with looking to the general interests of all the people there as opposed to the interests of any company. I believe the people of Alaska are entitled to their rights as we promised them, and I cannot understand why all the bills introduced for the purpose of securing those rights should fail, unless it is to somebody's interest to have them fail." [60]

Earlier in the hearings, Sheldon Jackson, then representing in Alaska the Board of Home Missions of the Presbyterian Church, had testified that in addition to the seal-monopoly lease for which the

Alaska Commercial Company was paying the government some $317,-500 a year, it was heavily engaged in the fur trade in the interior with some eighteen posts on the Yukon, along the Alaska Peninsula and in the Aleutians. He estimated the company was making $1,000,000 a year and was paying the government nothing whatever on this revenue.[61]

Governor Swineford was convinced that the Alaska Commercial Company's lobbying in Washington through Elliott and others was responsible for the lack of effective government in Alaska and the defeat of every legislative attempt to improve the situation. In his first report he condemned the "paid agents" to whose "either ignorant or willful misstatements" Congress looked for information on which to base any and all legislation, "affecting the rights, privileges and interests of Alaska and its people."

The following year he cited Elliott's admission before the House Committee on Territories that he was "a paid lobbyist" of the Alaska Commercial Company, whom he declared "ready to bob up and give wholly disinterested (?) information to the honorable Senators and members" and he concluded his fifty-three-page second report with the pessimistic assertion that he had little hope until Congress should conclude to give ear to the respectful pleadings of Alaska's people, in preference "to the willful misrepresentations of the hired assassins of her progress and welfare who infest the national capital during its every session."

Elliott was not only appearing before congressional committees where he was instilling the always welcome thought that expenditures for Alaska were needless, and the extension of anything but the minimal governmental services there unnecessary,[62] but he was also propagating this idea in newspaper and magazine.[63]

In Governor Swineford's third report he held the monopoly responsible for "defeating nearly every proposed act of legislation calculated to insure the settlement and development of Alaska."

"Ever since the transfer," wrote Swineford, "a studied and determined effort has been made to imbue the general public, as well as the government, with the belief that there is nothing of value in Alaska save its fur-bearing animals. Agents of the government, sent out to examine and report upon its resources, instead of honestly performing the service for which they were paid, have, in the interest of a corporation into whose service they have drifted . . . broadcast statements concerning the climate and undeveloped resources of Alaska which they knew were utterly false, but which, according with a preconceived public opinion born of ignorance, were generally accepted as true."

Later in the same report he gave what he saw as the basis for the Alaska Commercial Company's opposition to territorial government —its attempt to control the entire fur trade of Alaska.[64]

And in his valedictory Governor Swineford pointed out that a territorial form of government would bring with it a system of local taxation, which was opposed by a corporation which had not only monopolized all there was of material value in the fur trade, but indirectly "through 'corporations within a corporation'" was doing its utmost "to secure possession of all the best salmon fisheries as well."[65]

Alaska After Twenty-five Years of United States Rule

There can be no question that a petition, in whatever form it may come, from the people within a geographical area, wherever it may lie, which is under the American flag, should be answered, and answered on its merits. The citizens of the United States are guaranteed by their basic structure of government, the American Constitution, the right of petition. The right to inquire, without the right to answer, is nothing. The right to petition, without the right to have the petition properly considered and acted upon, is an idle gesture and is of the essence of futility.

SENATOR GUY CORDON OF OREGON,
FEBRUARY 26, 1952

IN THE presidential election of 1888 Benjamin Harrison defeated Grover Cleveland. With the change of administration, Lyman E. Knapp of Vermont, Civil War veteran, editor and lawyer, succeeded Swineford as Governor of Alaska. During his four-year term Knapp transmitted to Washington pleas and plaints almost identical with those voiced by his predecessor. The tone of his earlier reports had the sweet reasonableness of confident hope that needs so obvious and demands so clearly valid could not but be recognized by the federal authorities. He differed with Swineford at first in only one major respect: He did not see how the machinery for electing a legislature could be established. Apart from that he made the same requests for a delegate, for clarification—and means for enforcement—of laws, for adequate transportation and mail service, for more appropriations for basic public necessities, especially schools. His later messages, including reference to full territorial government, revealed in their more passionate pleading the frustration resulting from an almost total lack of response to his efforts.

Although Congress continued to ignore the district's most elementary needs, some changes were taking place in Alaska.

Mail service that would link southeastern and western Alaska, but without postmasters at the receiving stations, was established on a part-year basis in 1891.[1] But there was keen disappointment that the mail boat could carry no passengers.[2] The North American Commercial Co., which had succeeded the Alaska Commercial Co. as the Seal Islands lessee and had secured the mail contract, was charged with intent to keep settlers out and to maintain thereby a monopoly of western Alaska.[3]

The fur trade, now a seasoned and well-established traffic, was, to a limited degree, opening up the Yukon and Kuskokwim valleys, whose navigable rivers and their tributaries offered the only means of transportation to Alaska's vast interior. The Alaska Commercial Company's near-monopoly of the earlier years had ended. A newly organized rival, the North American Commercial Company, had outbid it and succeeded to the twenty-year lease of the seal islands,[4] and along the coast and in the interior the fur business was being aggressively sought by more than a score of competitors. Their trading posts in coastal villages, and throughout the interior, usually established within or close to Indian and Eskimo settlements, were becoming rendezvous for natives with furs to sell. These posts became the nuclei of future communities, still almost wholly native, that would introduce the white man's economy into the primitive villages. The trader, in many remote and long-isolated areas of Alaska, was the forerunner and representative of an order that spelled the beginning of a gradual economic change.

Financially, and in terms of employment, the fur trade was still Alaska's mainstay. The furs had a brisk sale value, although credit at the store, rather than cash, was invariably the prevailing method of compensation. Thus the purely subsistence economy of the aborigines was converted into a trade economy, in which "store clothes" and "white man's food" replaced the skin garments and, in part, the food derived from the hunt and the trap line.

The eighteen eighties in Alaska produced more pelts in every category than any previous decade: Fur seal, sea otter, land otter, muskrat, beaver, marten, lynx, black, red, cross and blue fox, and deerskin. But with deadlier weapons and the strongly acquisitive drive of the newcomers, the most valuable of the furs were becoming seriously depleted. The fur seal suffered severe inroads from pelagic sealing—the taking of seals on the high seas—on their way to the Pribilof rookeries. And the near-extermination of the valuable sea otter was being hastened by enterprising white hunters, mostly Norwegians and Swedes, who cheerfully accommodated themselves to the governmental regulation that none but natives could hunt otter by hunting up and marrying the comelier native women, thus combining love and business to the benefit of all concerned—except the sea otter—but likewise to the detriment, before long, of a region whose economy depended on it.[5] The evasion of the regulation by this means was sanctioned by the Secretary of the Treasury.[6]

Miners in small numbers had drifted into Alaska in the seventies. Their strikes around Sitka had looked promising but failed to pan out. They were active on the gravel bars of the upper Yukon and nearby creeks, and, along with the fur traders and missions, helped support the summer stern-wheelers' traffic up from St. Michaels on the Bering Sea coast. Starting up the swift silt-laden waters of the Yukon as soon as the ice went out in May, they carried some three thousand tons at an average price of $50 a ton in the early nineties. They were fueled with wood, and cutting it assisted the economy of the primitive river settlements.

The complete absence of government authority in the interior was compensated for by the establishment of a frontier democracy embodied in a miners' code. Each camp or diggings organized itself, decided matters of common concern by a majority vote, functioning with only one elected official, a recorder, and meted out justice with punishment to fit the crime. Murder was punished by hanging; offenses of the next gravity, such as theft or assault, by banishment or whipping; lesser offenses by fines. With men of all races and creeds mingling on a basis of absolute equality, these pioneers established a simple and workable self-government suited to the time and place.

The first important mining strike was in 1880, when Joseph Juneau and Richard Harris found gold up a creek emptying into one of the narrow salt-water channels near the upper end of the Inside Passage. The news brought a rush of miners, and further nearby discoveries on the mainland and across the narrow waterway on Douglas Island increased the stampede. The miners organized, plotted a town site and created a mining district which was successively called Pilzburg, Fliptown, Rockwell, Harrisburg and Juneau City. During the first four years, claims there and in the vicinity were held by a mixture of force and "miners' law." But the application of the nation's mining laws to Alaska in the act of 1884 gave that industry a substantial impetus.

More than five hundred claims were staked, more than a third of them patented, and both quartz and placer mining began along the Gastineau Channel. Some $800,000 was invested in the Treadwell property on Douglas Island for the establishment of a 240-stamp mill, one of the largest of its time, which by the end of the decade had yielded over three million dollars worth of gold. Other adjacent properties were destined to be consolidated in the famous Alaska-Juneau mine which made Juneau the center of hard-rock gold mining in Alaska for the next sixty years.

Juneau was a bustling frontier mining town. As the eighteen nineties opened it boasted nine general-merchandise stores, three hotels and a lodging house, nine saloons (although the importation of liquor was forbidden by act of Congress), two breweries, two drug stores, two cigar factories, two hardware stores, a photo studio, a confectionery store, a steam laundry, a millinery shop, three schools, churches, a hospital—St. Ann's, established in 1886—and miscellaneous undertakings. It had a theatre, proudly called the "opera house," and a weekly newspaper, the Juneau City *Mining Record*. Its population was 1,253, of whom 671 were whites, who dwelt, according to the 1890 census report, in "many neat residences." [7]

The salmon fisheries of Alaska had attracted American enterprise to establish the first two canneries in 1878—near Sitka and at Klawock on Prince of Wales Island at the lower end of the Alexander Archipelago, as the islands of southeastern Alaska are named. From an initial pack in that year of 14,854 cases valued at $59,416, which did not vary greatly in the next three years, it rose to 696,732 cases in 1889 with an estimated value of $2,786,929. Thirty-seven canneries were operating that year of which twelve were in southeastern Alaska, twenty-one in central Alaska, which included the Yakutat, Prince William Sound, Cook Inlet and Kodiak areas, and four in western Alaska—in the area, with its rivers, known as Bristol Bay. A few salteries also packed and exported salmon in barrels.

The salmon cannery was generally to persist as an isolated factory for the processing of fish brought there from nearby waters, a scene of feverish activity for a few weeks before and during the "runs"; then, but for a watchman, to be deserted till the following spring reactivation. Occasionally it was abandoned because of nearby competition or for a better location. But sometimes it was destined to be the kernel from which a community would spring. A store to supply the workers, as well as the nearby native fishermen, and to run a side line in the fur trade or in native curios—baskets, wooden implements, moccasins, silver and ivory handicrafts—was invariably the first step in such expansion. It invited settlement near by if the terrain was favorable. Thus Kichikan, a tiny native hamlet on the banks of an abundant salmon stream emptying into Tongass Narrows, was the site of an early salmon cannery. It was destroyed by fire in 1889 and for a time abandoned. But the salmon stream was a powerful magnet to re-attract the enterprise. Moreover, the site was on the principal channel of the Alaskan steamers. In time Ketchikan would become "the world's salmon capital," processing more salmon than any other community on earth.

The most important fishing center was Karluk on Kodiak Island. On a gravel spit near the mouth of the Karluk River, one of the most bounteous of red-salmon streams, five canneries equipped with the most up-to-date machinery had been established by California capitalists. In 1890, with the aid of a bonus system to fishermen, more than three million fish were caught, and the summer population reached eleven hundred.

But even before the industry had become fully established, reckless overfishing was bringing on a decline. In pursuit of big catches and quick profits in a frequently venturesome and uncertain undertaking, barricades were erected in salmon streams, netting a huge catch—801,400 cases in 1891—but diminishing the prospects for future years. Congress, roused momentarily when prodded by constituents from the northwestern states, passed in 1889 an act declaring unlawful the erection of barricades in Alaskan rivers to prevent the ascent of fish to their spawning grounds.[8] But no means were provided for its enforcement. Varyingly, such enforcement, prescribed by Congress and delegated to a federal agency, but unprovided with adequate funds, would, for the next sixty years, be the story of the alternating rise and fall of what congressional oratory described as "a great national resource."

A conscientious attempt at an accurate estimate of Alaska's population had been made—under substantial difficulties—by the census of 1890. Its total was given as 32,052, of whom 4,298 were white, 1,823 mixed, 23,531 native, with others constituting the remainder.[9] The white population had not quite attained Swineford's estimate, but it was nearly ten times Petroff's controversial figure of ten years earlier. As always along American frontiers, the males among the whites exceeded the females in Alaska—at this time, in a ratio of nine to one.

It is reasonable to assume from all the data available that Alaska's population remained stationary in the first quarter of a century of United States dominion. The gain of some four thousand in the number of whites in the eighteen eighties, but of whom only one-half were listed as permanent white inhabitants and the other half as temporary,[10] was in all probability offset by a dwindling indigenous population weakened by the invasion of the white man's liquor, and of tuberculosis, diphtheria, measles and influenza, diseases, often of epidemic proportions, to which the natives were little resistant.

During that same period every state in the Union and every territory increased substantially in population. The 1870 census showed a population for the entire country of 38,558,271. The 1890 census brought the figure up to 62,947,714. Alaska, alone among American areas, remained static during a period of dynamic growth everywhere else. Its unique stasis reflected its unique treatment at the hands of a distant and uninterested government.

Some slight stirrings of interest in Alaska there were. They were exhibited in a genteel tourist trade, given a start by an initial excursion party led by General Nelson A. Miles in 1882. Weekly summer sailings to southeastern Alaska, with a few hours in ports while the freight was unloaded, gave tourists a chance to admire the matchless scenery and to bargain for the natives' curios. Beginning in 1883 the visitors were truly regaled by a side trip to Glacier Bay, a scenic wonderland, discovered by John Muir and the Reverend S. Hall Young in 1879, or to the Taku Glacier, south of Juneau.[11]

There was the initiation on a small scale of coast surveys, stimulated by the marine underwriters, following a high toll of vessels wrecked on uncharted rocks. Even the important approaches to the Yukon and Kuskokwim rivers, the only two arteries of travel to the interior of Alaska, and the dangerous coast between them were not yet charted. There was the publication of Schwatka's book on the Yukon. There were reports on the fauna and flora by scientists aboard the revenue cutter *Corwin* making an annual summer cruise to the Bering Sea and Arctic Ocean; the studies of the Eskimo by ethnologists of the Smithsonian accompanying Lieutenant P. H. Ray, U.S.A., who headed the international polar expedition to Barrow in 1881; the explorations by Revenue Marine officers, Lt. George M. Stoney and Lt. John C. Cantwell, of the Kobuk and Noatak rivers; the remarkably extensive explorations of Lt. Henry T. Allen, U.S.A., in 1885 of the Copper, Tanana and Koyukuk valleys.[12]

Much of Alaska was still unexplored. "What the country north of Cook Inlet is like no civilized man can tell," wrote the anonymous scribe of the *Eleventh Census Report.* "The Indians tell us . . . stories of mountains of immense altitude visible for hundreds of miles . . . which may be accepted until reliable explorers are enabled to penetrate this region." It would be six more years until W. A. Dickey, a prospector, in 1896 discovered, named and correctly estimated the height of Mount McKinley visible from the shores of Cook Inlet on a clear day. Neither government nor private enterprise had in twenty-five years developed any great urge to explore and chart its long-derided acquisition.

In fact governmental hamstringing of what might well have been evolutionary growth in keeping with the traditional westward march of settlement was instead establishing the forms of transiency which would long pattern Alaska.

"The homestead and pre-emption laws having been withheld from this territory, the most desirable class of settlers have been barred out." [13]

"The vast sums paid out every season by the salmon canning companies" were falling "almost entirely into the hands of nonresidents of the territory, both white and Chinese." [14]

"The number of native laborers employed in any of the fishing establishments" was "insignificant compared to that of imported laborers." [15]

"Few of the fishermen, packers and sailors engaged in the work have become permanent residents of the country, which is being rapidly drained of its principal resources without getting even a partial return in wages paid for labor." [16]

These were the flat assertions made in so dispassionate and unbiased a document as the *Eleventh Census Report.*

"There is no encouragement for anyone to make improvements of which he has no assurance that he will have the enjoyment," wrote Governor Knapp in his second annual report in 1890. He was referring again to the refusal of Congress to make any land acquisition in Alaska possible.

The Nineties

In the carving out of the Territories belonging to our Union since the beginning of its history, legislators never had so fine an opportunity to mold for happy destinies a great domain, as is now given them in Alaska. Free and unincumbered, with only a few almost unintelligible records upon its clean and uncut pages, this magnificent empire of the north is awaiting the artist touch which shall make it a mighty volume dedicated to the genius of American progress. To which one of our national representatives shall belong the honor and glory of standing sponsor for this stalwart child by adoption? It was welcomed into our family circle by the great statesmen of the Lincoln epoch. Is there not at this time an oasis of brains in the desert of nonentity at the Nation's capital? Is there not one man of either political party who can command a winning following, broad enough, patriotic enough, to arise in his place, and demand a just recognition of Alaska's just and imperative claims? The Government of the United States, since the acquisition of this Territory, instead of lighting the torch of freedom and keeping it brightly burning on these far-off shores, has by restriction— which is often worse than actual oppression—so retarded the growth and impeded the development of its material resources as to make the memory of the Russian autocratic *regime* appear a blessed thing by comparison with that which has come to it under our free institutions.

HENRY E. HAYDON, SEPTEMBER 3, 1890

IN NONE of his messages during his four years in office had President Grover Cleveland made any allusion to Alaska and the needs and problems of its inhabitants. (Except references to fur seals and the necessity of a boundary survey.)

But now Benjamin Harrison had become President of the United States. As Senator Harrison, sponsor of the act of 1884, he had confessed to the inadequacy of all its provisions, declared it to be a mere expedient, a mere beginning, and expressed the hope that more would follow. As Chairman of the Senate Committee on Territories he had had four years to learn of the unworkability of the act and to receive the steady flow of protest and the repeated demands for a greater measure of home rule, for a delegate who could informedly present Alaska's requirements, for change in the general laws, for land legislation, for repeal of prohibition, for transportation to enable government to function, for adequate appropriations for courts, schools and needed public buildings.

Hope that with the change of administration would come a change also for the better was expressed in the Alaska press, which reflected in that respect prevailing Alaska sentiment. Again was pointed out the contrast between the treatment of Alaska and the other territories, which with a single exception, it was stated, had less population than Alaska, while Alaska contributed more revenue than any other territory to the national treasury.[1] But there was no great optimism. Alaskans had already experienced the disheartening effects of "hope deferred." Moreover they were fully aware that it was President Harrison, who, as senator, had withheld from Alaska the varieties of legislation which all other American territories had enjoyed.

President Harrison's message to Congress was deeply disappointing to Alaskans. He recommended provisions for the locating of town sites and for obtaining title to town lots within them, and "perhaps for the organization of several sub-districts with a small municipal council of limited powers." He was opposed to any other application of land laws. The great distances and smallness of the population he considered obstacles to territorial government. He suggested since the people had not power to levy taxes and were wholly dependent on the general government to whose revenues the seal fisheries made a large annual contribution, "an appropriation for education should neither be overlooked nor stinted." He also asked Congress to provide more customs facilities.[2]

The Fifty-first Congress which President Harrison addressed, like its immediate predecessors, had its grist of Alaskan bills. They would have given Alaskans their hearts' desires: Territorial government, a delegate in Congress, homestead and general land legislation, prohibition repeal, revision of the laws, funds for a government vessel for the use of Alaska's civil administration—all were included somewhere. But they were never able to muster enough support to get out of the committees to which they were referred.

As for the presidential suggestion that the appropriation for education be not stinted, the Congress, which had before it a request for $75,000 for the ensuing fiscal year, cut the appropriation from the previous $50,000 to $45,000.

An effort to assist Congress by electing delegates to national political conventions who would endeavor to mobilize their party's backing for Alaska's needs resulted in two delegates journeying to the Democratic National Convention of 1888 where they were seated —the first political recognition to be accorded Alaska. The Republicans sent no delegates to the 1888 national convention, but a year later held a convention of representatives from southeastern Alaska and elected a Republican national committeeman from Alaska, Miner W. Bruce, who together with another emissary, a Juneau mining engineer, George W. Garside, went to Washington in the hope of securing legislation. For added measure, public meetings in southeastern Alaska culminated in a Non-Partisan Convention which by unanimous vote elected a delegate who, it was hoped, would be able to impress the Congress of the urgency of Alaska's needs. He was popular James Carroll, who had commanded passenger vessels of the Pacific Coast Steamship Company on their Alaska runs for a decade, knew and was known by nearly everyone on the route.[3] All their joint efforts failed to secure the passage of an Alaska measure. But on the last day of its second session the Fifty-first Congress incorporated some of President Harrison's suggestions as a rider to a general measure known as "An act to repeal timber-culture laws, and for other purposes." [4]

The act provided for the establishment of town sites and of the survey and sale of plots therein under rules and regulations to be prescribed by the Secretary of the Interior. It provided for the sale elsewhere of sites, not to exceed 160 acres, at $2.50 an acre, for purposes of trade and manufacturing only. It set aside Annette Island as a reservation for the Reverend William Duncan's flock of Tsimshean Indians whom he had brought there from British Columbia four years earlier.

The title to the act was an ironic paradox for Alaskans because it did *not* repeal the restrictions on cutting timber on public lands. The act brought disillusionment to Alaskans. At first they were inclined to view it, if not as half a loaf, at least as a substantial crumb. But they objected bitterly that only businesses could acquire title to land outside of town sites; that no individual, no pioneer, no would-be homesteader could, as in all other territories, carve even a tiny sliver for his own use out of Alaska's 375,000,000 acres. They had also still to learn of the obstacles that could and would be concealed in the phrase "under the rules and regulations to be prescribed by the Secretary of the Interior."

A public meeting called in Sitka to ascertain the best and least expensive method of applying the law, for the citizens were compelled to advance the cost of the survey, greeted with applause the recommendations of the principal speaker that they take no action to comply with its costly and cumbersome procedures so that they could insist that the next Congress enact a better measure.[5]

Two years were required before Juneau's town site became a reality. But Sitkans were still wrestling with its complexities.

Finally, the act conveyed no authority to establish municipal government. It created no power to levy local taxes which would provide for municipal services—policing, lighting, water supply, sewage disposal, street paving.

In the ensuing years the attitude of Alaskans took a new turn. For twenty-five years they had failed to understand the inaction of Congress. With faith in the processes of democratic government, they had assumed that once Congress could be apprised of the facts, action was bound to follow. They were encouraged by the visits of senators and representatives, arriving in Alaska either singly or in committees, who appeared generally sympathetic with Alaskans' pleas and left them with the hope that something would soon be done. And so they continued to be buoyed up by the introduction at each session of bills which promised relief, whose progress they watched as expectantly as the bimonthly mail service would permit. As each session adjourned without action they pinned their faith on the next one, extracting such comfort as they might from the extent of a measure's legislative progress short of enactment.

But as the eighteen nineties began to roll by without effective action, Alaskans, while increasingly impatient of their legislators but obviously impotent to register their feelings effectively, turned, instead, on the visible representatives of the distant powers that ruled Alaska, the appointed federal officials.

It was relatively early that the Alaskans' frustration at their inability to impress their far-off rulers led to a demand for "Alaskans" to fill the appointive federal offices in the territory—and all offices were federal and appointive—and to the designation of the new incumbents arriving from "below" as "carpetbaggers." It might seem odd that within less than a decade of Juneau's coming into existence, before it even enjoyed the form or stability of town government, when all whites were newcomers and, in the current and well-liked term, "pioneers," this feeling would manifest itself. But it did, and it continued to do so. It was explicable in that it was the Alaskans' only outlet for their deepening resentments.

"From the outset, Alaska has served political purposes in a variety of ways," wrote Jeannette Paddock Nichols, author of the authoritative study of Alaska's political history during its first forty-five years after the transfer. "In 1884, she became a political preserve for the payment of small debts owed by big politicians to little ones. In this role, at which her people were destined to protest with rising voice, Alaska experienced the maladministrations of various appointees." [6]

It is not within the purview of this study to examine into the validity of the allegation of local maladministration or the extent thereof. That Alaska, under the system of political spoilsmanship which has existed varyingly through the eighty-seven years of possession by the United States, has had its share of incompetents, misfits, mediocrities and, occasionally, dishonest public officials, is undoubted. That there were—no less—able, upright and conscientious public servants, who left Alaska better than they found it, seems equally demonstrable. To the extent that the inadequacy of the federal officialdom in Alaska during the forty-five years during which it was wholly appointive justified the often caustic attitude of many Alaskans toward their government which has become a well-recognized territorial characteristic, it is understandable. What has not been so clear, perhaps, is that the conditions created by distant government embodied in the Congress and the Washington bureaucracy inevitably fostered such an attitude on the part of Alaskans.

Alaska's first governor, Kinkead, who owed his post to Senator John P. Jones of Nevada, did not serve in Alaska long enough to earn the paeans of supporters or to draw the fire of opponents. But as the former governor of a "sovereign state," Nevada, a western state whose sparseness of population bore the closest analogy to Alaska's, who moreover had spent the first three years after the transfer in Alaska, his appointment could scarcely be considered other than praiseworthy. In fact, Kinkead was probably unique in his combination of qualifications.

Alfred P. Swineford was a man of high principle and ability. Although a stranger to Alaska, he became sufficiently interested to settle there after his term of office and, as a newspaper editor, to devote the remainder of his life trying to secure for Alaska what he considered its due. His outspokenness earned him numerous enemies among those whose abuses he attacked. They sought to prevent his confirmation. But the Senate Committee on Territories, which heard all the charges, voted unanimously for his confirmation, which was followed by a like vote in the whole Senate. Yet the opposition engendered by his fearless espousal of what he deemed in the public interest was sufficient, despite petitions from Alaskans in his behalf, to prevent his reappointment when Cleveland again became President in 1893.

Lyman E. Knapp of Vermont had worked his way through college, graduating with honors, enlisted in the Union Army and finished his military service as colonel in command of the Seventeenth Vermont Infantry. At the close of the Civil War he became the editor and later also the proprietor of the Middlebury *Register*. During that time he studied law, served as county probate judge, and was a practicing attorney when appointed by President Harrison to the governorship of Alaska.

It was he who was to receive the opening gun and later a barrage of opposition on the ground that he came from what Alaskans refer to as "outside."

"First, last, and all the time," declared the Juneau City *Mining Record* in its issue of April 11, 1889, before the gubernatorial appointment had been announced, it was "in favor of all appointments for Alaska to be made from among the residents."

Two weeks later it saluted the appointment of "a Mr. Knapp of Vermont" as "one well recommended, with no blemishes on his private and political record," while expressing regret that the choice was not made "from the residents of the territory."

Governor Knapp was enjoying a brief political honeymoon.

However, the other federal officials, judges, attorneys, marshals, commissioners and collectors—particularly the last two—came in for the most frequent attacks. The first judge, Ward McAllister, Jr., of California, was removed from office for bibulousness. His successor, E. J. Dawne of Oregon, was found to have embezzled funds before his appointment and left Alaska hastily after a sojourn of less than two months.[7] The third judge, Lafayette Dawson, of Missouri, who had failed by a narrow margin to secure a congressional nomination in his home district, proved more satisfactory.

As many of the federal appointees came from Oregon, that state, viewed as a symbol of some of Alaska's difficulties, became a journalistic target:

"Aside from the laws of Oregon being forced upon us, and it must be kept in mind that Oregon is an agricultural and fruit-growing section, while Alaska is simply a mining and fishing country," editorialized the Juneau City *Mining Record*. "Alaska is flooded with carpetbaggers to fill the federal offices." [8] As the situation continued the editorial attacks became more virulent:

"Alaska has been made the dumping ground for the political offal of the state of Oregon. Out of the half-dozen or more carpetbag appointments now in Alaska, not one of them have the necessary qualifications to fill the positions they occupy." [9]

As the Harrison administration drew to a close dissatisfaction with it in Alaska increased; and a new note of rebelliousness was sounded:

"What Alaska wants," wrote Frank F. Myers, the *Mining Record's* editor, "is representation in Congress and a bill of divorce from Oregon, and Oregon's political children sent back to Mitchell and Dolph's suckling establishment. Alaska is for Alaskans. Give us our rights as American citizens and as guaranteed by the constitution." [10]

Oregon's two senators, Joseph N. Dolph, who served from 1883 to 1895, and John N. Mitchell, from 1885 to 1897, and who enjoyed most of the Alaska patronage, came in for considerable mention, especially Dolph, who visited Alaska several times during his senatorial service:

"Last summer, Senator Dolph made a flying trip to Alaska on an excursion steamer," commented the *Mining Record*, "and while in Juneau he came ashore and remained long enough to take a bath, and upon arriving at Sitka he remained there the usual twenty-four hours." [11]

Upon his return to the States Dolph declared; "The country is developing very slowly. The condition of the district is peculiar and calls for different treatment from that of other territories." [12]

This comment that Alaska was "peculiar," "anomalous," which had begun to be a form of stock excuse for congressional inaction, made Alaskans' hackles rise.[13]

"Imagine, if you can," retorted one, "when Louisiana, and Florida and Texas stood knocking for legislation and admission . . . that some member of either House had cried out, 'Don't let them in! Don't grant them the legislation they demand! Their condition is anomalous!' It is the Congressmen who are 'anomalous', not Alaska, not its people." [14]

Some senatorial committees, as Alaskans began to learn, came to Alaska and discovered the obvious—or what to the local residents had long appeared obvious.[15] But on the senators' return to Washington the findings of the obvious in the field were not translated into the obviously needed corrective action. Alaskans were to learn that, too.

A dim view of the value of senatorial visits, as he had observed them, was taken retrospectively by Alfred P. Swineford, after he had left the governorship. "Two committees were sent to Alaska during my administration," he was quoted as saying in a press interview, "but they did nothing but play poker and view the sights. They took no interest in the country, and days when they were supposed to be gathering material for a good report . . . to be presented to the Senate, they were engaged in the pleasant pastime of playing a $25-limit game." [16]

Securing no legislation for their needs, Alaskans increasingly placed the blame on those who were felt to have their own special interests to serve—the businessmen of California and Oregon. Thus an organization called the Alaska Pioneers Business Association was held responsible for deleting, from a Senate bill, then awaiting only favorable action in the House, all but the limited land-acquisition provisions that would be included in the act of 1891. That act, which was to become known in Alaska as the Trade and Manufacturing Sites Act, was beneficial almost exclusively to the salmon canneries (at that time chiefly financed by California capital) while withholding land for other purposes from resident individuals.

"The A.P.B.A. . . . has been organized in the sole interest of San Francisco businessmen, who do not intend to contribute a cent to the material welfare of the Territory," asserted the Sitka *Alaskan*, "bringing, as they do, all the supplies they need with them, and engaging the help they require below, to return there when their services are no longer wanted." [17]

The Alaska Commercial Company, although now subject to increasing competition in the fur trade, was still held responsible for the failures of Congress:

"The people of Alaska have asked for . . . the enactment of laws beneficial . . . to this section, such as the extension of land laws, representation in Congress, a judicial code, suitable to our conditions, etc., but whenever anything for the benefit of Alaska is brought before Congress, this monopoly, through its agents in Washington interposes an objection . . . and Alaska receives nothing. . . . Such has been the condition of things since the first settlement of Alaska." Thus the Juneau City *Mining Record* voiced a general belief of Alaskans.[18] And nearly two years later the editor wondered why the Pacific Coast senators should be so concerned about the monopolies in Alaska, and so little interested in its general prosperity, that they could influence a majority of the members of Congress to oppose any bills introduced for Alaska's benefit.[19]

The fieriness of the Juneau editor's utterances led the Seattle *Press-Times* to view them, with his motto "Alaska for Alaskans," as an attempt to rebel against the United States to which he replied, "That would be impossible as there are grave doubts whether we belong to it or not." [20]

Possibly the newly admitted state of Washington could help! The former territory's admission to statehood in 1889 was hailed as providing a competitor to Oregon.[21]

Alaska's wrongs were an ever-present topic of discussion. The Fourth of July oration in Juneau delivered by the District Judge, John S. Bugbee, enumerated them, adding a few new ones: No government hospital for the sick, no prison for the felons, no asylum for the insane . . . public buildings at the capital acquired from the Russian government allowed to go to decay . . . but one wagon road in the whole territory over two miles in length and that built by private enterprise . . . no banks and no insurance companies because of Alaska's inability to offer the security of real estate. He termed Alaska "the Cinderella of the nation." [22]

"When we realize that the only legislation we have been able to obtain from Congress in seven years, having anything like a general application," confessed Governor Knapp, in a mood of depression, "was the town-site and land bill, and consider that this bill aims rather to meet the wants of business firms than the requirements of individual settlers, a sense of hopelessness as to success in the patchwork business comes over us." [23]

But while public sentiment in Alaska reflected the view that President Harrison "has let us down," his gubernatorial appointee grew more impassioned as the administration drew to a close. As a variant from his personal presentations, Knapp transmitted some carefully drawn recommendations by the district judge and the district attorney for reform in the judicial code and enumerated fifteen items of "legislation needed," appealing in his final report to Congress for relief, "in behalf of the people, in the name of justice and obligation, in the interest of civilization, for the honor of our nation. . . ."

But the President and the Congress were much more deeply concerned about another issue, Alaskan in a special sense, yet remote both geographically and in point of interest from the thinking of those who had come to Alaska in an endeavor to make their way there. It was the same issue that had had priority in the concern of senators and representatives since the purchase. The decade and a half, 1882-1897, in which Republican and Democratic administrations alternately succeeded each other, would demonstrate that fur seals were still their principal, if not almost their sole, Alaskan concern.[24]

The fur seals, which for twenty-five years had been, and for another quarter of a century would continue to be, of intense concern to the federal authorities, have their breeding grounds on the two small fog-bound islands of St. Paul and St. George, which with two smaller adjacent islands in the southern Bering Sea constitute the Pribilofs. Thither every summer the fur seals migrate from the west coast of the United States, and in the fall, when their young have been born, return. These are distinct from other fur seals which exist in smaller numbers in the Southern Hemisphere, and wholly different from the relatively valueless and widely distributed hair seal. *Callorhinus ursinus*, the fur seal made American by the purchase, constitutes four-fifths of the world's fur-seal population. Its island rookeries were unknown even to the aborigines and were uninhabited when discovered by Gerassim Pribilof in 1786; Aleuts were brought in from the Aleutian Islands to help kill and skin these valuable fur-bearers. In the earlier days of Russian rule they were slaughtered recklessly until the herd was nearly exterminated. This taught the Russians the need of conservation. In 1835 they suspended all killing for some years, and thereafter safeguarded the cows, taking only the young, unprocreative bachelors, which at the age of three or four years have the most desirable pelts, leaving the propagation to the old bulls each of which enjoys a "harem." These practices had built back the herd to some three million seals when Russian rule ended, and, after the lease, were resumed for a time.

In the months after the purchase American enterprisers were busily engaged in killing seals, taking some 350,000 in the Seal Islands—as the Pribilofs were more commonly known—until the Leasing Act made it unlawful to kill any females, any seals less than one year old, or to kill any of them in the waters. The twenty-year lease with the Alaska Commercial Company in 1870 embodied these conditions, gave the company the exclusive right to the seals to the number of 100,000 annually in return for an annual rental of $55,000, plus a tax of $2.62½ on each skin taken, and 55 cents a gallon for seal oil extracted. The company was also to do whatever the Secretary of the Treasury required for the "comfort, maintenance, education and protection" of their employees, the natives on the islands, which, the lease specified, was to include 25,000 dried salmon as food, sixty cords of firewood, etc., and to maintain a school on each island.

In the late eighteen seventies a few vessels found it profitable to hunt seals while they were on their way to the rookeries. While lucrative, it was highly wasteful of seals. When surfacing to breathe, the seals would be shot with rifle or shotgun. A seal if wounded would elude capture, and if killed outright, would sink immediately and be lost unless the body could be promptly gaffed. More seals were killed than were retrieved. More detrimental, however, was the loss of female seals. It was impossible to determine the sex of the seal swimming in the water, nor did the hunters care. Most of the cows were with pup, and the mother's death doubled the loss. In addition, the female seals after giving birth to their pups on the islands, and while again pregnant, would go to sea in quest of food, sometimes traveling a hundred miles. If the mother was killed while on this foraging journey, the pup on the island starved to death, because each mother seal nurses only her own offspring. The killing of a cow would therefore often mean a threefold loss, the mother, the nursing seal on the shore and the embryo. Pelagic sealing increased rapidly. From an average of one vessel a year in the late eighteen seventies, the number jumped to sixteen in 1880, to thirty-four in 1886, to sixty-eight in 1889, to over a hundred in 1894.

As the leasing law of 1870 forbade the killing of fur seals at sea and provided for the seizure of vessels engaging in this practice, the Alaska Commercial Company appealed to the Treasury Department, as the lessor, to protect the company's monopoly. Appropriate orders were given. In 1886 the Treasury Department instructed the revenue cutters to seize all vessels engaged in what was termed marauding, poaching and piracy.[25] A substantial number of the captured vessels were Canadian, and international complications ensued.

The United States' contention was that since these seals originated on American shores and bred on the American Pribilofs, they were wholly American. The British invoked the "freedom of the seas" under international law: Outside the three-mile limit the seals were anybody's who took them!

Alaska's waters were for the first time alive with American warships and revenue cutters—sixteen of them in 1892—all but one obsolete gunboat stationed at Sitka, dedicated to the preservation of the seals and the prevention of British plunder, the flagship being, appropriately, the U.S.S. *Yorktown*. It was commanded by Robley D. Evans, the "Fighting Bob" Evans of later, Spanish War, fame.

A number of the seized Canadian vessels were brought into Sitka, where their captains were tried before the District Judge, Lafayette Dawson, thus giving this court a previously undreamed-of importance. In the case of the United States *vs.* the British schooners, *Dolphin*, *Anna*, *Beck* and *Ada*, seized by the revenue cutter *Rush*, the judge overruled the demurrer filed by the Queen's Counsel of British Columbia that the United States had no jurisdiction outside of the three-mile limit. And so the court ordered a judgment of forfeiture against each of the vessels seized, together with their cargoes and tackle.[26]

Unfortunately for the American case, wholly new legal questions arose from the fact that seals traveling from one part of the United States to another had to traverse two thousand miles of open sea. The British at first seemed disposed to yield, but their resistance was stiffened by the determination of the Canadian sealing interests and the Canadian authorities not to give an inch.[27] After a fruitless interchange of notes the matter was referred to arbitration. A tribunal, meeting in Paris, composed in addition to two United States and two British representatives, of one each from France, Italy and Scandinavia, upheld the British position. It ordered the seized vessels returned and their owners indemnified. It did, however, establish a *modus vivendi*, with new regulations under which pelagic sealing was not to take place within sixty miles of the Pribilof Islands nor anywhere during certain months, was to be carried on only in sailing vessels and without the use of firearms.[28]

The arrangement proved a failure. The pelagic take increased, the seal herd diminished, its depletion hastened also by the Seal Islands lessees' departure from established regulations.[29]

The Alaska Commercial Company had averaged 92,811 sealskins annually during its lease which netted its fourteen stockholders eighteen million dollars in the twenty years.[30] As the lease neared expiration they were aware that the seal herd was seriously depleted. The yield in the lease's final year, 1889, of 102,617 pelts, had been achieved only by taking 40,000 undersize skins. "The contrast between the present condition of seal life and that of the first decade of lease is so marked that the most inexpert can not fail to notice it," wrote H. H. McIntyre, the company's general agent, in a confidential letter to his principals.[31] It was apparent, he pointed out, that for the next two or three years the lessees must be content with very small catches.

Nevertheless the company bid again, and, as twenty years earlier, was the lowest bidder among eight. This time, however, the award went to the highest bidder, another California group organized under the name of the North American Commercial Company of San Francisco.[32] The new lessees soon discovered that they had leased a lot of trouble, and that the Alaska Commercial Company, their predecessors, had skimmed the cream of the Pribilof seal monopoly.[33]

The new twenty-year lease provided for payment to the government of a higher rental, a higher price per pelt, reduced to 60,000 sealskins the quota for the first year, further providing that it was subject to change by the Treasury.[34] But the first year's quota was never approached in the next twenty years. It was only 25,152 in the first year, dropped to 13,473 the next and was only 7,554 and 7,402 the years 1892 and 1893. The maximum number, 30,004, was taken in 1896.[35]

Before the 1890 season was far under way, the Treasury's agent-in-charge reported that the time had suddenly come "when . . . imagination must cease and the truth be told," and the depletion in the herd was so great that he recommended "there be no killing of fur seals . . . for an indefinite number of years." [36]

More truth was to be told. For twenty years Treasury agents had been painting rosy pictures of the Pribilof islanders' well-being. Now it developed that not only the seal but the human population had been declining, that the excess of deaths over births had been steady, and that but for the influx of people from nearby Aleutian islands, the native residents would have been extinct.[37]

Fifteen years earlier Henry W. Elliott had reported the condition of the Seal Islands natives "wonderfully improved" by the action of the lessee, and that they were now "comfortably clad, fed and housed." [38] Their physical and moral condition had advanced under American rule and was slowly but steadily improving, Agent in Charge Harrison G. Otis reported in 1879,[39] while Special Agent T. F. Ryan in 1885 felt that the natives "were not only treated well, but in a measure spoiled." [40]

Now however, a new assistant agent found "the total absence of water closets . . . a disgrace" and, with the domestic water supply a well into which the drainage of half the village flowed, beyond all question the cause of the natives' disease and death. That such a state of things had been "allowed to exist for twenty years" he termed "a disgrace to our civilization." [41]

The schools which the company was under its contract to maintain had been reported by an earlier Treasury agent "well taught," and the progress of the pupils "not discreditable." [42]

Now it was discovered that children who had been to school for seven years on St. George Island did "not know how to speak or read a sentence in the English language," [43] and that but little advancement had been made by the natives of St. Paul Island "toward an intelligent American citizenship." [44]

The contrast between the schools on the Seal Islands and the mission school at Unalaska was pictured by Assistant Treasury Agent Murray in the 1893 report. Six orphan girls sent there in 1890 taken from among "the poorest, lowest, dirtiest and most ignorant . . . who could not speak a word of English," had after a term of two years all been able to write English as well as the average white school child of similar age.[45] He recommended that the government make itself, and not the company, responsible for the islands' schools. The recommendation was not followed.

Similar reports came from other agents during the following years with recommendations for improvement. The eighty-ton coal supply to be furnished by the company for heating the natives' houses, specified in the lease, was deemed insufficient. Despite the drastically reduced income resulting from fewer sealskins, additional demands were made on the company. Orders came that the natives should be treated better, a belated recognition of conditions to which the government had previously given no attention.[46] Agents were ordered to check prices at the company's stores and determine whether the natives were being charged more than a fair price. The company was found charging the natives $33.60 a ton for coal and government representatives only $15.[47] The company was required to make such repairs to the natives' houses as would make them comfortable.

The company urged that the decreased seal quota warranted a reduction in the annual rental. The Treasury declined. The case was taken to court, and ultimately the United States Supreme Court upheld the company's contention that the rental should be adjusted to the proportion of seals taken.[48]

The reduced seal take spelled a corresponding reduction in the natives' income, since they were paid by piecework—at the rate of 50 cents a skin. The government was therefore obliged, beginning in 1893, to appropriate increasing amounts to supplement their income. In fact the second Seal Islands lease was to prove even less profitable to the government than to the lessees. What with the costs of the revenue cutters and Navy patrol and of the Paris tribunal, the indemnities paid to the seized Canadian pelagic sealers, the support of the islands' natives, the salaries to agents, the cost of various investigating commissions, the Treasury Department was to report a net loss to Uncle Sam in the first twelve years of about one and a half million dollars.[49]

From 1867 until 1898 the hundred square miles of Pribilofs and their seals received many times more governmental attention than did the rest of Alaska's 586,000 square miles and its people. In the last decade and a half of the nineteenth century and the first decade thereafter the economy of this unique resource unleashed a vast amount of energy at high federal levels. Nearly every presidential message dealt with it. Hearing after hearing was held by committees of the Congress. Violent tempers flared. Witnesses denounced each other in unbridled terms. Charges of corruption, of perjury, of political influence in procuring or stopping legislation were freely made. International tension was high. When the second twenty-year lease expired in 1909, the fur-seal herd that had numbered at least three million at the beginning of United States rule was reduced to a scant hundred thousand. The lease to private lessees was not renewed. Instead Congress ordered the Department of Commerce and Labor (which had succeeded the Treasury in 1903 in the management of fisheries and fur seals) to take over the business and endeavor to build it back. With the herd close to extinction, the evils of pelagic sealing were sufficiently clear so that it was abolished by international treaty in 1911, ratified by the United States Senate in 1912 (37 Stat. 499). Under it the United States and Russia, the two nations having seal herds, agreed that in exchange for abstention from pelagic sealing, Great Britain and Japan should receive annually 15 per cent of the United States product of the land sealing. The management of the Pribilof seal herd was henceforth to be wholly by the United States Government. The processing of the Pribilof sealskins, previously in London, was transferred to St. Louis, Missouri.

In contrast, the depletion of two other marine resources and the disastrous consequences to a considerable portion of Alaska's inhabitants aroused no congressional interest. Whaling in the North Pacific had, in the earlier and middle decades of the nineteenth century, been followed by hundreds of vessels captained by sturdy men from New Bedford, Nantucket and other New England ports. The Civil War seriously crippled the whalers owing to the destruction of their sailing vessels by the Confederate cruiser *Shenandoah*. But after the purchase whaling was resumed, with San Francisco increasingly the home port. In the earlier days whale oil was in demand for lighting and "whalebone" for the corset stays which feminine fashion decreed. In the eighteen eighties steamships began to replace sailboats and the killing of whales and walrus went on more rapidly and extended farther and farther north.

With the displacement of whale oil by kerosene, the baleen alone was taken and the whale carcasses with their tons of valuable content jettisoned. Walrus were hunted only for their ivory tusks, and their carcasses, weighing from one to two tons, likewise discarded. These wasteful activities gravely imperiled the Eskimo's way of life, since he depended on the whale for both food and fuel, and on the walrus for food—both for man and sled dog—for some articles of clothing, for the hide to cover his *oomiak* or skin boat, and for the ivory for a variety of uses, including carvings, which provided his only cash income. An estimated hundred thousand walrus were killed in the eighteen seventies and the herds were nearing extinction. Whales became scarcer and scarcer. Starvation menaced the Eskimo coastal villages.

Their plight attracted the sympathetic attention of Dr. Sheldon Jackson, the General Agent for Education in Alaska. In 1890 aboard the U.S. revenue cutter *Bear*, he was making his first trip into the Bering Sea and Arctic Ocean for the purpose of founding schools on their shores. Three schools, all principally supported by private endeavor, resulted. On Cape Prince of Wales, the westernmost point on the continent, a school in charge of the American Missionary Association of the Congregational Church, financed by the Congregational Church of Southport, Connecticut, was established. Next, on Point Hope—a village on the tip of a long spit of land extending northwestward into the Arctic Ocean—the mission society of the Protestant Episcopal Church was the new school's "angel." Finally at Barrow, on the northernmost tip of Alaska, the government contract was given to the Board of Home Missions of the Presbyterian Church.

At each of these villages and at other points of call, Sheldon Jackson learned of the diminished yield from the Eskimos' whaling and walrus hunting and the consequent shortage. On the same cruise the *Bear* made several landings on the Siberian coast, where Dr. Jackson was impressed with the well-being of the natives, Chukchees and Koraks, who were deriving their livelihood from large herds of domesticated reindeer. The animals supplied nearly all the material wants of these partly civilized, semi-nomadic people. Contrasting their condition with that of the Eskimos Jackson thought that the importation of reindeer would go far to relieve the distress that he had witnessed under the American flag.

In his report to the Commissioner of Education, General Agent Jackson proposed that reindeer be purchased from their Siberian owners, brought to Alaska on revenue cutters, and the Eskimos trained in this new form of animal husbandry. He stressed the value of the reindeer in the economy of eastern Siberia in corresponding latitudes and climate and among similar people. In arctic Lapland and Scandinavia, he pointed out, thousands of people were not only supporting themselves largely from reindeer but also paying a tax to the government on the enterprise. He urged that instead of being fed by the government and pauperized, as was being done in the States with the destitute Indian, the Eskimos should be given this opportunity to support themselves.

The Interior Department approved this sound and constructive project. The Congress was asked to extend to Alaska an act which it had passed in 1887 for agricultural-experiment stations in connection with colleges established in the States. The plan was to make the importation, propagation and management of the reindeer part of industrial education in the Eskimo country. A joint resolution was introduced in the House by Representative Louis E. McComas, R., of Maryland in December, 1890, and referred to the Committee on Education, which reported it favorably. The House, however, did not act. As the session neared its end in March, 1891, Senator Henry M. Teller, R., of Colorado, who had been Secretary of the Interior in President Arthur's cabinet, moved to amend the sundry civil bill by making an appropriation of $15,000 for the introduction of domestic reindeer in Alaska, which carried. The House conferees, however, refused to concur and the Fifty-first Congress (1889-1891) adjourned without any action to help the starving Eskimos and to introduce a new element into Alaska's economy. The $15,000 would have meant a congressional largess of one dollar per Eskimo.

Conscious of the urgency of the situation, and undeterred by the congressional failure to act, Jackson appealed to the public with letters to daily newspapers in Washington, Philadelphia, New York, Boston and Chicago and to the religious press. Contributions of more than $2,000 were promptly received. With this fund Jackson returned to the Siberian coast in the summer of 1891 and with the co-operation of Captain Healy and the crew of the *Bear*, overcame numerous obstacles and acquired sixteen reindeer which were landed in good condition in Alaska.

In the first session of the Fifty-second Congress, 1891-1893, bills to appropriate $15,000 for the introduction and maintenance of domestic reindeer were again introduced. Teller's Senate bill was referred to the Committee on Forestry and Agriculture from which it was reported favorably and was passed. But the companion bill in the House, despite a favorable committee report, failed to pass.

Jackson, however, proceeded again with private funds. In the summer of 1892 he was able to add 171 head to the small Alaska herd, and to superintend the erection of the necessary structures for his dreamed-of industrial school, on a spit of land in the protected waters of Port Clarence. He named it the Teller Reindeer Station and Teller became a village with a post office in what in an earlier day had been the Eskimo settlement of Nookmute.

Public interest had now been aroused by this unprecedented

experiment, sufficient at least to induce Congress in 1893 to appropriate $6,000 for it. The reindeer meanwhile, unmindful of congressional procrastination, had begun to procreate. Seventy-nine fawns were born on American soil that spring and 127 more Siberian reindeer were naturalized. To insure the success of the experiment and to give the Eskimo the proper training in reindeer husbandry, several Lapp herders were brought from Lapland, this expense being again defrayed by private contributions. In 1894 Congress increased its appropriation to $7,500. Despite many difficulties the reindeer herds developed from a total of 1,280 head imported, in time were widely spread over western Alaska, and for many years contributed substantially to its economy and to the welfare of the Eskimo.

The Alaska press welcomed the defeat of Harrison in 1892 and the re-election of Cleveland. The only thing that mattered, the Juneau *Mining Record* pointed out, was the pledge contained in the Democratic platform that Alaska should have "home rule," and called on the President-elect to fulfill the pledge.[50]

President Cleveland on June 28, 1893, appointed James Sheakley Governor. Sheakley had been a resident of Alaska six years, having served as commissioner at Wrangell, and also as assistant superintendent of education. He had served from Pennsylvania in the Forty-fourth Congress, 1875-1877. His appointment was considered a fulfillment of the aspiration to appoint a resident. He was not, by any means, as fervent as his two predecessors in pleading for all the legislation they had considered essential. There is evidence that he considered such efforts fruitless. His annual reports were short and perfunctory.

Sheakley concentrated chiefly on more aid to education, legislation to permit the incorporation of municipalities, abolition of prohibition, provision for care of the insane, enforcement of regulations to preserve salmon.

But twenty-nine government schools were operating in 1895, he reported, and in several places where there were schoolhouses, the appropriation for education was insufficient to permit the hiring of teachers. To meet the demand for more teachers and more school buildings he asked that the annual appropriation be increased to $60,-000.[51]

Congress should make provision for the incorporation of municipalities, he urged. Juneau was a seaport and mining town which now had two thousand inhabitants, schools, churches, "three well and ably conducted newspapers," waterworks, an electric-light plant, two good and substantial wharves, large mercantile houses, good hotels, paved streets, fire and hose companies. The legal and medical professions were well represented. Yet it had no municipal government and could obtain no corporate existence either under the laws of the United States or Oregon.[52]

The salmon in Alaska were decreasing because of incessant fishing, and the illegal obstructions of streams. That therefore the laws relating to salmon fishing needed to be made more stringent, a rigid closed season be provided, and inspectors appointed to enforce the law was the recommendation of Assistant Secretary of the Treasury Charles S. Hamlin, who visited Alaska in connection with the fur-seal situation in the summer of 1894. He also recommended that a small tax be imposed upon each case of salmon canned in the territory so that "some part of the expense of maintaining the Territorial government will be borne by those who take from it annually a rich harvest and contribute nothing in return." [53]

He also learned that in Sitka many people were confined in jail because of offenses against the prohibition law and to his "great surprise" that some had been imprisoned for over fourteen months, awaiting trial for offenses for which on conviction not over six months' imprisonment could be imposed. The reason for this was that there had been no term of court during that period, a situation resulting from insufficient appropriation.[54]

Finally he asserted his belief that a large immigration would set in as soon as Congress by legislation made it possible for settlers to acquire ownership to land which was only possible to occupiers of town sites, the owners of mines and canneries and persons engaged in manufacture.

Two years later the Fifty-fourth Congress, 1895-1897, adopted a small part of Hamlin's recommendations. While it omitted the small tax on each case of salmon canned, it amended the act of 1889 prohibiting obstruction of salmon streams by giving the Secretary of the Treasury discretion to close any of them, to establish closed seasons—such powers to be exercised only after hearing those interested—and provided for the appointment of an inspector of fisheries at $1,800 and two assistants at $1,600 per annum.[55]

However, the inspectors were furnished no means of transportation over the vast distances between the isolated canneries and the even more numerous streams which required safeguarding. The inspector, arriving at the nearest port by mail steamer, would be obliged to hire a canoe and travel over distances impossible to achieve within the fishing season. Or more usually he would perforce accept transportation on a tender belonging to the cannery whose practices he was supposed to regulate. The inspection had been "a farce," reported Governor Brady.[56] No wonder, he commented, that not a single prosecution had taken place on evidence furnished by an inspector. Meanwhile stream robbing and other practices destructive of the salmon supply continued unabated.

The livelihood of the Indians, dependent chiefly on the fisheries, was also being seriously impaired.

In the 1896 presidential campaign both major party platforms promised Alaska a delegate in Congress. Following the inauguration of President McKinley, he appointed John Green Brady Governor of Alaska. Brady was on every count an "Alaskan." He had been in the district for nineteen years, arriving first as a missionary, engaging thereafter in mercantile business, and serving as U.S. commissioner at Sitka.

Brady's first report was comprehensive and followed trails blazed by his predecessors. Nothing, he declared, had so retarded the true and substantial growth of Alaska as its people's helplessness to obtain titles to their homes.[57] The marshals and their deputies were unable to enforce court orders because they had no means of transportation except the regular bimonthly mail steamers which touched only at a few ports. He renewed the plea for a small steam vessel for the civil government's needs. He requested funds for public buildings, for the dredging of a channel north of Juneau, for provision for care of the insane, for a code of laws suitable to Alaska.

But the President who had appointed Brady was, like his predecessors, more engrossed, as far as Alaska was concerned, in the fur-seal issue. Except for one general reference in his first message to the need of changes in the laws of Alaska and the desirability of encouraging its development and settlement, that message and the second annual message to the Congress and several special messages dealt in detail with fur seals. And while the Congress was regularly receiving, discussing, reporting on various bills for the improvement of conditions in Alaska, it was advancing none of them to final passage.

On the eve of unforeseen events which would jolt Congress out of its thirty-year lethargy, "Seward's Folly" had through the fur-seal lease repaid into the United States treasury more than the cost of the purchase, and despite the legal restrictions on its development had contributed over one hundred million dollars' worth of products to the national wealth.

THE ERA OF MILD BUT UNENLIGHTENED INTEREST

1898-1912

The Third Discovery of Alaska:
The Gold Rush

The Klondike rush has made very effective propaganda for Alaska.
HENRY VILLARD, 1899

THE "days of '49" had started the rush across the continent. In its
wake the eternal lure of gold caused the adventurous to roam throughout the West. The strikes in the Cassiar, in British Columbia, in the
sixties, brought prospectors into higher latitudes. From there they
wandered down the Stikhine or the Lewes into Alaska and found
"pay" in a score of places—along the coast and the upper Yukon. But
except for the Gastineau Channel area after Juneau and Harris had
discovered Gold Creek, few had struck it rich. The few included the
California and British owners of the Treadwell, which in the late nineties, with 880 stamps, was running the biggest gold mill in the world.
For a decade and a half it had served as a sort of magnet drawing the
prospector northward.

George Washington Carmack was born in California a few years
too late to be a "forty-niner." He was attracted to Alaska by the strikes
in Juneau. From there he wandered into the upper Yukon country
over the boundary into Canada's Yukon Territory, prospecting, fishing and trading furs. Like many white prospectors of that time and
place he had married an Indian girl and had "gone Siwash," living
with the tribe. Carmack and her two brothers, Skookum Jim and
Tagish Charlie, found gold on Rabbit, later renamed Bonanza Creek,
which flowed into the Klondike River, a tributary of the Yukon. It
was late July, 1896. They staked out their claims according to custom.
The news spread to the camps on the Sixty Mile and Forty Mile and
down to Eagle and Circle City. Before summer's end much of the
ground around the creeks that flowed into the Klondike and Indian
rivers was staked out. There was lots of gold in "them cricks." At
the junction of the Yukon and the Klondike a tent camp mushroomed
into a frontier city—Dawson.

As a national and international sensation "the Klondike" did not break onto the front pages till midsummer, 1897. When the ships returned from St. Michaels at the mouth of the Yukon they had aboard the first and luckiest of the prospectors. "A ton of gold" was what the *Portland* brought with her. That news, flashed around the globe, ushered in a new era for Alaska.

The "rush" was on. From every state of the Union and from abroad they came. Some sixty thousand headed north. Nearly all went through Alaska. There were two principal routes. One was by boat from Seattle, Portland or San Francisco, up the Inside Passage. At the upper end of its long terminal fiord, Lynn Canal, two trails led to the Klondike: the Chilkoot from Dyea, and the White Pass from Skagua (which later became Skagway). The other way was across the Gulf of Alaska and through Bering Sea to St. Michaels and then up the Yukon. The first was more arduous; the second longer. Both were costly. Some rushers never got all the way. The weaker perished. Few panned out. Some struck it as rich, or even richer, by setting themselves up in business to supply the miners. Within three years new strikes at Nome and in the Tanana Valley had spread the gold-seekers all over Alaska, and converted "the Klondike" into an Alaskan episode. It was the first big "break" for Alaska. Its consequences for the territory were to be considerable.

For, kindled by the gold fever, a great new optimism about Alaska's riches surged through the land. Gold, of course—in abundance. Only the merest surface had been scratched! But also silver, copper, platinum, coal, furs, timber—a land of infinite potentialities! But how to reach these inland treasures? Docks, roads, railways would have to be built to get the pioneers inland, to supply them and get their stuff out. Back in the states Alaska was a stock promoters' paradise. It attracted the great capitalists as well as the fly-by-night. It brought Alaska for the first time to the ken of millions of Americans. The gold rush was reported in thousands of newspaper columns, in a multitude of magazine articles, and was more permanently recorded in not fewer than three hundred bound volumes of personal experiences as well as fuller compendia. Not least notable was the fiction of Jack London, Rex Beach and others. They wrote a new chapter, a postscript, to the great American romance of "the West."

It was in fact the third discovery of Alaska, if Vitus Bering's is considered the first, William H. Seward's the second. After each, Alaska had lapsed into oblivion. Both St. Petersburg and Washington were too far away. Alaska was beyond the sustained vision of those who occupied the seats of power.

But now they stirred in those seats. Congress, if not fully awakened, was, at least, disturbed by the sound of rushing feet. They were the feet of home folks, constituents, voters.[1] Their opinions and their desires really mattered. While the Fifty-fourth Congress, 1895-1897, laid the usual legislative goose egg for Alaska, and the first session of the Fifty-fifth, in the spring and early summer of '97, was similarly uneventful,[2] the largest number of bills and resolutions relating to Alaska ever introduced, some fifty in all, in the second and third sessions, betokened a new interest.

Two major pieces of Alaska legislation were passed by the Fifty-fifth Congress, 1897-1899, but only one before the end of 1898. It was entitled "An Act Extending the Homestead Laws and Providing for Right of Way for Railroads in the District of Alaska."[3] It extended homestead laws to Alaska, but reduced the acreage to eighty, and provided that no entry should extend more than eighty rods along any navigable waters and that there should be a shore-space reserve of equal width between each entry. It permitted homesteaders the use of soldiers' scrip. It set forth in great detail the provisions under which applicants could file for permission to traverse the public domain and construct a road, a trolley line or a railway. It reduced the area of the trade and manufacturing sites permitted under the act of 1891 from 160 to eighty acres, giving preference to those who could show prior use or occupancy. It provided that native-born citizens of Canada would be accorded the same mining rights as American citizens in the Dominion, and that goods could be transported without payment of duty between Alaskan ports and Canadian points if Canadians granted reciprocal arrangements.

The problems which beset this first serious legislative attempt to satisfy Alaska's necessities were revealed in the prolonged debates which preceded enactment. The bill was rewritten and amended repeatedly. The principal obstacle was the evident lack of information concerning Alaska of many senators and representatives taking active part in the discussion. Another difficulty was their desire to square the congressional conscience with the pressure of constituents, or to accommodate diverging interests between them. Their ventures in dock sites, wharves, railway propositions and mining claims were generally made known to their representatives in Congress. The act's detailed emphasis on the rights of way over public domain reflected the eagerness of the maritime companies and of various enterprisers to provide something better than shank's mare transportation over the rugged passes into Alaska's interior.

"I feel that those people who are constituents of mine and have large interests in Alaska should have some protection," was the reasonably expressed position of Senator John L. Wilson, R., of Washington.[4]

If homesteads were located on lands running to tidewater they might interfere with the granting of franchises for wharves and docks was the view of Senator George C. Perkins, R., of California, of the Pacific Coast Steamship Company.[5] The shore-space reservation met that objection.

Senators Frye and Hale of Maine, and Hoar and Lodge of Massachusetts wished to tack on a proviso protecting the rights of New England fishermen in Canadian ports, in exchange for advantages to be given Canadian miners in Alaska. Their rider, which threatened the defeat of the whole bill, was finally eliminated when it went back to the House for concurrence. But it delayed action on the bill for two months.

After an early enthusiasm aroused by the magic word "homestead," where securing one had for so long been a mirage, Alaskans became disillusioned with the act's provisions, and even more with the prospects for its successful administration. Its regulations were invariably "as prescribed by the Secretary of the Interior," to whom the act made not fewer than twenty-four references. There were no surveyed lands in Alaska and no system of surveys had been provided. The homesteader would have to survey his land at his own expense, and remain uncertain whether it would be acceptable to the Commissioner of the General Land Office. Alaskans' skepticism on this score was based on their experience with the Trade and Manufacturing Sites Act of 1891, under which applications made out in conformity with regulations had in only two instances been granted in the first ten years after enactment.[6] Funds advanced by the applicants in their unsuccessful effort to secure title had not been returned. The act's reduction of the usual 160-acre-sized homestead to eighty acres was viewed as a discrimination. "A feeble attempt to extend homestead rights to Alaska" was Governor Brady's comment.[7]

In their unchanged adoption except by reduced acreage, the United States homestead laws would prove inappropriate, as Alaskans later discovered. In the many days' debate on the bill, only one senator had pointed out this basic defect.

"We are trying," said Senator John L. Wilson of Washington, "to deal with Alaska as if it were an agricultural district, which is far removed from the fact. . . . If a man settles on a piece of land in Alaska under the homestead law and is required to inhabit it, cultivate it . . . and improve it, under such rules and regulations as the Secretary of the Interior may prescribe, he will have an exceedingly difficult task in obtaining title." [8]

Wilson instead advocated a provision permitting the would-be homesteader to buy the land. Unfortunately his view did not prevail. Fifty-six years later the homestead laws in Alaska, little changed in the interval, had demonstrated his prophetic wisdom.

That this unsatisfactory homestead bill was the only major measure for Alaska passed as the second session adjourned in July, 1898, when a code of laws, a delegate and much else had been anticipated, deepened the Alaskans' disappointment.

The plank in the Republican platform was recalled to the Secretary of the Interior's attention:

> We believe the citizens of Alaska should have representation in the Congress of the United States, to the end that needful legislation may be intelligently enacted.

Quoting it, Governor Brady added: "The people of Alaska now call upon the Republicans in Congress to keep this promise. . . . If the reasons for Alaska having a delegate in . . . Congress in June, 1896, were good, they are emphatically strong now in the closing months of 1898." [9]

He voiced the Alaskan opinion that the administration had failed to produce either the "needful" or the "intelligently enacted" legislation pledged during the campaign.

Alaskans would go through that experience again.

The other piece of major legislation emerging before the close of the century was a bill "to define and punish crime in the District of Alaska and to provide a code of criminal procedure." [10] It was prepared by a code commission under instructions to codify the laws of Alaska, which in effect meant codifying the laws of Oregon to that

date, with such modifications as would make them appropriate to
Alaska. When the Fifty-fifth Congress had concluded its third and
final session it had amended the proposed Oregonesque Alaska code
with numerous provisions adapted from the codes of the amenders'
states. By extraordinary parliamentary legerdemain the legislators
also wrote in the first taxation levied in the district[11] and repealed
Alaska's thirty-two-year-old prohibition.

Representative William Henry Moody, R., of Massachusetts, who
opened the debate, considered the measure important "because we
are beginning to practice now upon the government of the colonies." [12]

Most of the controversy raged about the retention or elimination of
prohibition, and the views of all of Alaska's governors, including those
of teetotaler Brady, were cited in behalf of a change to high license.
The House found the issue so thorny that 172 members did not vote
at all, thirteen answered "present" and repeal won by the scant margin
of ninety-four to seventy-five.[13] In the Senate the prohibitionists were
overwhelmed forty to eleven with thirty not voting.[14]

The revenues to be derived from the proposed high liquor licenses
suggested the desirability also of other licenses as revenue measures to
defray the costs of territorial government. The forty-odd occupations
to engage in which Alaskans would have to obtain a license from the
District Court provided a novel method of taxation. The list, with
their fees per annum, from: Abstract offices, $50; banks, $250; boarding houses having accommodations for ten or more guests, $25; brok-
ers (money, bill, note and stock) $100; billiard rooms, $25 per table;
bowling alleys, $25; breweries, $500; bottling works, $200; cigar man-
ufacturers, $25; cigar store or stand, $25; drug stores, $50; through
the alphabet to tobacconists, tramways, transfer companies, taxider-
mists, theatres and waterworks—retain more than an antiquarian interest. The formula was to persist with only minor modifications for
over half a century. Particularly was this to be important in the fisheries, salmon canneries being taxed at 4 cents per case. Mercantile establishments paid on a sliding scale—$10 from those doing an annual
business of under $4,000, to $500 a year for a $100,000 volume. Rail-
roads were taxed at a hundred dollars per mile per annum on each
mile operated.[15]

In the Senate the congestion attendant on the closing days threatened defeat. "In Alaska they have needed a code for years now; it has

been a scandal that they have not had one," the venerable George Frisbie Hoar admonished his colleagues,[16] when with a great press of measures and the appropriation bills not acted upon there were only two weeks to go.

Senator Eugene Hale, R., of Maine, opined that there were matters of more importance. "This is legislation for a far-distant people, in a sense alien to the United States," he declared.[17]

Senator Benjamin R. Tillman, D., of South Carolina, could not see why if the people of Alaska had been without a code so long, the senators "should get into a sweat" and press the measure "in the expiring hours of Congress." [18]

Senator Hale again objected to taking up a bill of nearly seven hundred pages "on a subject nobody knows anything about." [19]

Senator Thomas H. Carter of Montana, active in promoting legislation for Alaska, proceeded to demonstrate the contrary. It was a serious matter that a legal jury could not be impaneled in Alaska, he insisted. The laws of Oregon required that to be eligible to serve on either a grand or a petit jury one had to be a taxpayer. There was no law applicable to Alaska by which a tax could be levied. Consequently there could not be nor had there been in the past a legal jury in the district. Yet people had been tried, convicted and executed.[20]

Senate and House conferees met on the last night, March 3rd, and issued a conference report. Representative Sereno E. Payne, R., of New York, said it was evident that the report gave the House "no light on the subject," [21] and insisted on a statement. Unanimous consent was asked that Representative Vespasian Warner, R., of Illinois, of the House conferees, be permitted to make a statement from the floor instead of a written statement as required by the rules. Mr. Warner explained that he had not had time to write a statement since the enrolling clerks must have the bill within thirty minutes if it was to become law in that session. Representative Charles H. Grosvenor, R., of Ohio, concluded the debate by saying:

"Notwithstanding the crudities and the errors in the code of Alaska, I think, in view of the fact that there can be no intelligent legislation upon any question in this House at this time, it is better 'to take the evils we have than to fly to others that we know not of.' " [22] Amid cries of "Vote! Vote!" the conference report was adopted.

The high license introduced a form of local option. Before a liquor license could be granted by the District Court it would have to be shown that a majority of the white residents over eighteen years of age within a radius of two miles consented.

Some wholly Alaskan touches had found their way into the bill. "Intoxicating liquors" included not merely the standard varieties, but also "hoochenoo." The section setting up penalties for horse thievery included reindeer among domestic animals.

The reform of Alaska's civil government passed the Senate in the Fifty-fifth Congress but did not secure final action in the House. The administration of the Homestead and Rights of Way Act and of the Criminal Code Act was therefore further delayed for want of administrative machinery.

In Alaska opinion began to be diversified. There was the conflict between Sitka, which apprehended the danger of losing the capital, and Juneau, which wanted it. In back of this was the long seething conflict between the Presbyterian missionary groups represented by Sheldon Jackson whose headquarters were in Sitka, and who supported prohibition—although Governor Brady, of their number, had swung over to support high license—and the business elements in Juneau and Skagway which supported licensing. There was the divergency of interest, as well as lack of close contact between the miners in the interior and southeastern Alaska. There was diversity of interests—fisheries, furs, mining, steamship, railroads, mercantile—each intent on grinding their own axes. Their representatives were active in Washington—which was Alaska's real capital—each and everyone purportedly representing the true needs of Alaska. They were adding to the already existing confusion in Congress as to what was best to do for Alaska and how to do it.

Although there was some satisfaction in southeastern Alaska at the attention that Alaska was beginning to receive, the cry for representation was given added volume by the new taxation. It was estimated by the Congress to produce $200,000 a year, while the expenses of government would not exceed $50,000. The balance would go into the federal treasury.[23]

To this Alaskans objected. It was taxation without representation. In the Senate this view had been vainly championed by Senator Teller who declared that the Government of the United States had, for the first time, exacted revenues from a territory for the payment of officials. It would, he said, impose a burden on the people of Alaska not imposed on any other people.[24]

In its final form the civil-government bill (31 Stat. 321) illustrated the various difficulties that had plagued and would continue to plague Congress in legislating for Alaska—foremost of which was lack of information. As Senator Orville H. Platt, R., of Connecticut, remarked in the course of the debate:

"The trouble with the senators who do not know anything about this matter is that they have to vote." [25]

Another difficulty, or perhaps another aspect of the same difficulty, was the persistence of the legend of Alaska's worthlessness, its reiteration, and the consequently prejudiced opposition to the adoption of measures needed and always overdue. It had been and would continue to be a hardy perennial in almost every debate on Alaska. One of its proponents in the period when the nationwide interest of numerous constituencies was, for the first time, galvanizing Congress into action, was Senator George C. Vest, D., of Missouri. A former member of the Confederate Congress, his election to the United States Senate in 1878 and his re-election for four terms gave his words the weight of seniority. He was against the creation of three judicial divisions.[26] If the homestead laws were extended to Alaska, there would be the cost of surveys—for there could be no homesteads without surveys—and to that expenditure he was opposed. There was not a farm in all Alaska, he declared. The potatoes were full of water. So were the lettuce, cabbages and cauliflower. If ever there was a purchase made recklessly and heedlessly by any government on earth it was the purchase of Alaska.[27]

A second difficulty was insufficient interest and the resulting tendency to choose the easiest and quickest legislative formula—of preserving something already there. In this case the new civil structure was to be erected on "the lack of local government" for which earlier Congresses had been responsible. It was clear to the bill's sponsor, Senator Carter of Montana, "that no provision could be made for the execution of the laws through a governor who was not provided with any revenue or any legislative assembly to enact laws." Carter had ruled out the legislature because the cost of an election would "certainly be very great." Further, what with the great rush to the interior, to hold an election "during the gold excitement would be something like holding a general election at a circus." By the same logic there could be no delegate.[28]

So "the present unsatisfactory government seemed better suited to the situation" than any other which the Congress could devise. Hence the Governor was left practically as he had been under the act of 1884 with few duties and no powers.[29]

The surveyor general of the district was made ex-officio secretary thereof. He was to be the keeper of the district seal, receive the $10 fees from the notaries public and otherwise perform the duties performed by the secretary of a territory insofar as applicable in the district.

The new act provided for the appointment by the President with the advice and consent of the Senate of the governor, surveyor general, judges, attorneys and marshals for terms of four years during which they were removable only for cause. It increased their salaries. The Governor and judges were given $5,000, the surveyor general and the marshal, $4,000, and the attorneys $3,000.

The capital of the district was to be Juneau—but the transfer from Sitka postponed until suitable government buildings could be secured. With the new act came a civil code and a code of civil procedure.

One change, obviously well-intentioned and seemingly unimportant, was to haunt the administration of justice in Alaska for the next half century and more. The commissioners—in effect, lower-court judges—formerly appointed by the President, at a salary of $1,000 a year plus the fees they collected for their services,[30] were henceforth to be appointed by the district judges and to subsist on the fees only. With new mining discoveries and the consequent new settlements obviously needing a commissioner it seemed undesirable to wait the slow process previously in vogue of congressional authorization and enactment for the new post. Hence appointment by the judge at no salary was substituted.

"This commissioner," Senator Carter explained, "would not necessarily give his entire time to the work of the commissioner's office, but the country merchant or tavern keeper or any citizen . . . could be appointed." [31] It was also a very economical move and established a new method of "living off the country."

Recognition of the inability of one judge to serve the vast district and of the new litigation pending in the interior led to the establishment of three judicial divisions within the district, with a judge, attorney, marshal and clerk in each (June 13, 1902. 32 Stat. 385). The new courts were to be located at Juneau for two terms of court and an equal number at Skagway; at St. Michaels in Bering Sea; and at Eagle City on the upper Yukon. The judges were given permission to hold court at any places they might deem expedient, a recognition of the fluid state of the interior white population. As soon as practicable the judges were to meet and divide the District of Alaska into three recording divisions, and later to subdivide these divisions into recording districts of each of which a commissioner would be ex-officio recorder. The new legislation for Alaska greatly increased the power and functions of the judicial branch; it kept the executive branch, the Governor, in *statu quo*, namely a figurehead; while the legislative branch was still more than a decade away.

Incorporation of towns, long delayed, was provided. Sixty residents of any community numbering over three hundred could apply to the district judge setting forth the proposed boundaries. The judge, after a hearing, could decide whether or not to grant incorporation. If he approved he would set a date for an election at which the voters would ratify or reject incorporation and elect a city council of seven members. The council was empowered to collect a tax on electors, that is, a poll tax, taxes on dogs, on real and personal property, which, however, must not exceed 1 per cent of the assessed valuation, and such license taxes on business as it deemed proper. An elected school board of three would have exclusive jurisdiction of schools within the municipality. Fifty per cent of the license moneys levied by the clerk of court under the previously enacted Criminal Code Act were to be turned over to the municipality for school purposes. An amendment adopted a year later provided that if all these funds were not required for school purposes, the district judge could authorize the expenditure of the surplus for other municipal purposes. Also license moneys derived from businesses outside of incorporated towns could in the discretion of the Secretary of the Interior be expended for schools outside the towns.[32]

As further amended, three years later, as a result of protests,[33] the municipal license taxes were eliminated as a duplication of the federal, and *all* the federal license taxes collected within a community would go to it. The property-tax ceiling was raised to 2 per cent. The poll tax was to be not less than $2 or more than $4 a year and to be levied on males between the ages of twenty-one and fifty, who were not active members, serving without pay, of a volunteer fire company in the town. The judge's powers were increased to permit him not only to reject incorporation but if he granted it to alter the boundaries which the petitioners had proposed.[34]

Nome was for a time to be the goal of the turn-of-the-century Argonauts. Late in '98 a strike on Anvil Creek on the tundra, a few miles inland, by John Brynteson, Erick Lindblom and Jafet Linde-berg increased the rush westward from the Klondike and north from the States. With the creeks rapidly staked by the first come through the "power of attorney" the thousands of disappointed later rushers were electrified by a new discovery. In January, 1899, the magic "colors" denoting gold were found in the sands along the shore. Before long fifteen miles of beach were covered with tents and with men working plots twenty feet square with their rockers—the early miners' simple device for separating the heavier gold from sand and gravel.

In addition Nome experienced the furor of a notorious claim-jumping case, made possible by the dishonesty of the judge appointed to the newly created Second Judicial Division. The subsequent conviction of Judge Arthur H. Noyes by the U. S. Circuit Court at San Francisco, the conviction and imprisonment of the District Attorney Joseph K. Wood and of the judge's confederate, Alexander McKenzie, who had fraudulently taken over and was working the original and best gold claims in the guise of a "receiver," constituted a cause célèbre. It was widely publicized through Rex Beach's novel The Spoilers, which to the outside world gave Nome added glamor. In Alaska, the fear that similar corruption might interfere with the legitimate efforts of other miners was quickly dispelled when Judge James Wickersham was temporarily transferred from the Third Division and promptly restored confidence in the integrity of the judiciary.

Nome and its hinterland, the Seward Peninsula, had brought new wealth to the nation. In 1899, the year after the discoveries there, this farthest western area produced $2,800,000 worth of gold. Production jumped to over $4,000,000 in 1900, and maintained that figure for each of the next six years. Southeastern Alaska's gold production, principally from the Juneau-Douglas mines, was $2,152,000 in 1899. But mining in southeastern Alaska had begun in 1880 and in the twenty years to the end of the nineteenth century had yielded $17,276,000.

Both areas' gold production would continue to rise in the first decade of the twentieth century.

In Washington while Congress was legislating and belatedly providing a minimum of civil government for Alaska, the executive departments were also showing a new interest. "The Department of Alaska" was re-established by the War Department. Its headquarters were at St. Michaels, the transfer point for the booming Yukon River traffic, under command of Brigadier General George M. Randall. Military camps, somewhat pretentiously, but in the western Indian warfare habit, called "forts," were established along the prospectors' routes of travel: Fort Davis, to furnish protection to the thousands of gold diggers on the beach at Nome and on the surrounding tundra; Fort Gibbon, at the junction of the Tanana and Yukon, where important trading posts had sprung up; Fort Egbert, at Eagle on the Yukon, near the Canadian boundary; Fort Liscum, at Valdez, where a new trail had been blazed northward to the placers along the Tanana and Yukon; Fort Seward, near Haines, where the Chilcat Trail led by the shortest route to the American side of the Yukon country. Fort Seward also provided detachments for neighboring Dyea and Skagway where the rush over the Chilkoot and White passes into the Klondike had begun.

Telegraphic communication between these far-flung outposts was essential. The chief signal officer, Major General Adolphus W. Greely, had found in William Mitchell an invaluable lieutenant to drive through to completion the monumental task which called for unbounded determination and resourcefulness. The Canadian authorities, consistently more alert to frontier opportunities than the American, had already built a telegraph line as far as Dawson, largely over the route surveyed in 1864 by the Western Union Telegraph Company, which permitted overland connection with the states in June, 1903. What was to become the Alaska Communication System would two years later be linked by cable.

As the wire, equipment and supplies were being pushed through the trackless wilderness that Alaska was then, a system of trails came into being. Further explorations by Army officers, Captain W. R. Abercrombie, Captain E. F. Glenn, and their lieutenants, increased the almost nonexistent information about large areas of interior Alaska.

The gold strikes in Juneau and elsewhere in Alaska in the eighties and nineties had been made without benefit of geology. Not until 1895 did Congress appropriate for a study of Alaska's gold and coal resources the sum of $5,000. The study continued the next year, but could not proceed in 1897 owing to passage of the appropriation bill too late to apply the funds to Alaska.[35] After the Klondike discoveries, Interior Secretary David R. Francis requested $25,000, which Congress pared down to $20,000.[36] With this, systematic geologic studies began in 1898.[37] They were not sufficient to meet the demand for topographic surveys and for information concerning mineral prospects. A decade after the Geological Survey began its work in Alaska, reconnaissance surveys had been effected in but one-fifth of the territory, leaving large areas still practically unexplored.[38]

Shipping multiplied. Five American companies and a few independent one-vessel enterprises were competing for the Yukon River traffic.[39] Between them, in addition to their seagoing vessels, they operated in 1900, forty-one sizable steamers, fifteen smaller vessels and thirty-nine barges.[40] The steamers had to be especially designed for the river. Some were built on the West Coast and risked the perils of towage across the open ocean. More than half of these were lost or seriously damaged en route. To avert these losses shipyards were built on Unalaska Island and St. Michaels and shallow draft vessels constructed there.

The coal-land laws were extended to Alaska in 1900 to help provide fuel for the river traffic.[41] But they were to prove inoperative because of the regulations and lack of surveys.

The rapidly expanding maritime transportation both up the Inside Passage to Skagway and to the Bering Sea, with a high loss due to wrecks along a still largely uncharted coast, brought the demand for lighthouses. The Fifty-sixth Congress, 1899-1901, made the first appropriations for that purpose, and two lighthouses were completed by 1902. But construction lagged far behind need and in 1901 Governor Brady began what was to be an insistently repeated demand for making Alaska into a lighthouse district.[42] A magnetic observatory to study the deflection of ships' compasses due to the nearness of the magnetic pole, came into being at Sitka under the direction of the Coast and Geodetic Survey.

There was great interest in the United States in the construction of railroads in Alaska as a better method of connecting the coast with the interior. A score of such projects were to attain various stages of promotion and initiation. But the only one to achieve success was the British-financed White Pass and Yukon Railroad from Skagway to Whitehorse Rapids on the Yukon, where the town of Whitehorse came into being. While only the first twenty miles were in Alaska and the remaining ninety-two in British Columbia and Yukon Territory, the British-Canadian financiers had gotten the jump on all others. The first to file under an act of an American Congress, they completed the only railroad that in the next twenty-four years would give access to the interior. The W.P. & Y.R.R. (referred to by the humorously inclined as the "Wait patiently and you'll ride") was a great feat of engineering, and was timed so well that it was exceedingly profitable. The connecting Canadian river boats out of Whitehorse were able, because of the much shorter over-all distance, to maintain high rates into the upper Yukon and still undercut the tariffs of the American stern-wheelers. The Dominion authorities were quick to co-operate by removing obstacles to navigation in the Yukon within Canadian territory, and by building roads from the camps to the nearest point of navigation—a contrast with United States governmental performance which was repeatedly called to the attention of members of Congress. These circumstances led increasingly to agitation for an "all-American" route into Alaska. But a quarter of a century would pass before its achievement. It would take more than a decade to push through the first wagon road.

Agricultural possibilities in Alaska were to be investigated. An initial appropriation of $5,000 in 1898 led to a favorable report, requesting $15,000 for the establishment and maintenance of agricultural-experiment stations, which was voted. Within five years stations were established at Sitka, at Kenai on the Kenai Peninsula, at Copper Center in the Copper River Valley, 105 miles north of Valdez, at Kodiak, and at Rampart on the Yukon. The appropriations were small and some of the centers would after a few years be discontinued. Farming, no matter what experimentation revealed its potentialities to be, could scarcely flourish when farm land, given the lack of surveys, could not be acquired by would-be farmers.

There was a rush also of distinguished visitors. Edward H. Harriman of the Union Pacific chartered a steamship and brought with him a galaxy of scientists whose studies along the coast would be preserved in a fourteen-volume opus of enduring value. Others to visit

Alaska were John D. Rockefeller, Henry Villard of the Northern Pacific, numerous senators and representatives, including important committee chairmen, among them Senator Charles Warren Fairbanks of Indiana, soon to become Vice President of the United States.

The conflict with Canada over the boundary of southeastern Alaska was settled in October, 1903. The issue stemmed from the treaty between Russia and Great Britain in 1825, when the boundary of Russian America was defined as being ten marine leagues from the coast. The controversy had not been acute until the gold strikes in the Klondike, when the terrain in question became valuable, and Canada, also, aspired to a port in southeastern Alaska. Considerable friction between American and Canadian prospectors arose in areas previously accepted as American, but in which the Canadian authorities were for the first time exercising jurisdiction. The Canadian contention was that measurement should begin at the mouth rather than at the head of bays, which would have placed Haines, Dyea and Skagway in Canada, and have given the Dominion the shore approaches to the Chilcat, Chilkoot and White passes. It would likewise have separated southeastern from western Alaska. A tribunal established by treaty, consisting of three American, two Canadian and one British representative, voted four to two to uphold the United States position in its essentials, the British member, Lord Chief Justice Alverstone, accepting the American view.

It was getting time for Congress to take a first-hand and a searching look. Following a resolution adopted at a special session of the Senate of the Fifty-eighth Congress in March of 1903 the Chairman of the Committee on Territories, Senator Albert J. Beveridge of Indiana, appointed a subcommittee which spent two months in Alaska the following summer. While committees of Congress and individual senators and representatives had visited Alaska before, this was the first thorough and serious congressional investigation. Its members were William P. Dillingham, R., of Vermont, Thomas M. Patterson, D., of Colorado, Henry E. Burnham, R., of New Hampshire and Knute Nelson, R., of Minnesota.

The subcommittee reported that since the cession Alaska had yielded the national treasury one million dollars above all the expenses of the federal government, and in addition had enriched the nation by $52,000,000 in furs, $50,000,000 in fisheries and $31,000,-000 in gold. While Congress had now provided a government for the district it had done nothing to aid its development. The report italicized the senators' shock that there was *"not to be found a single wagon road over which vehicles can be drawn summer or winter,"* and concluded: "The inaction of our government is manifest."

Said government, of which the committeemen were an important part, they reported to their fellow-senators, had neither built roads nor provided other means of transportation for "the hardy and adventurous citizens" who had "sought the wealth hidden in the Valley of the Yukon, the Koyukuk and Seward Peninsula" amid unbelievable obstacles. A great obligation, the senators affirmed, rested upon the United States to adopt a system of wagon roads: the first link should be one from Valdez on the Pacific to connect with the waters of the Yukon at Eagle—a distance of about four hundred miles.[43]

The senators observed that the Treasury regulation requiring the canneries to plant ten salmon fry for every salmon caught had not been enforced, recommended that the hatcheries be conducted by the federal government, and suggested that the revenues of the district might be increased by a higher rate of taxation on the fishing industries.[44]

The committee reported that everywhere there was protest against individuals staking out an indefinite number of mining claims under powers of attorney and thus depriving later arrivals of legitimate opportunities, recommended that no one be allowed to stake out more than one claim, that every claimant be required to do a certain amount of "assessment work" before the claim could be recorded[45] and that the amount of such work be increased.

The committee recommended improvements to provide harborless Nome with a roadstead, as well as a life-saving station; improvement of the waterway from St. Michael to the mouth of the Yukon; the creation of a fourth judicial division to take care of the long coastal area of the Pacific west of southeastern Alaska. It found sentiment for a delegate universal and recommended that Congress provide one either by appointment or election; but that opinion in Alaska on the immediate advisability of a legislature was divided, and took the position that the time for it had not yet come.

The real emphasis of the committee was on the need to have the federal government promote Alaska's development, particularly by the construction of a highway system.

Despite the new turn-of-the-century legislation, problems which it aimed to resolve remained. The extension to Alaska in 1900 of the public-land laws applicable to coal lands was "in fact inoperative" as Senate and House Committees reported three years later.[46] Amendatory legislation introduced in the Fifty-seventh Congress was finally adopted in the Fifty-eighth.[47] It aimed to make possible the securing of title to coal mines on which money, effort and labor had been expended. It would continue to prove inoperative.

One obvious reason why some of the legislation adopted for Alaska by Congress was inoperative was that it was not implemented by the necessary appropriations. Congress, finally, in 1903, extended to Alaska the public-land laws of the United States applicable to homesteads, at the same time increasing the size of these homesteads to 320 acres.[48] But lack of surveys nullified the congressional intent. Not an acre of homestead land had been surveyed by the end of 1904 and the regulations issued by the General Land Office beset homesteading with insuperable difficulties.

In the extensive placer-mining areas throughout the interior the prospectors were encountering a new obstacle, the filing of claims by power of attorney. One person could stake as many claims as he desired, ostensibly for others—who were not even in Alaska, and hold them for speculation. Some of these "pencil miners," as the frustrated prospectors called them, staked over a hundred claims. Newly arrived prospectors would find at the end of their long journey every creek in a region "located," and that the "assessment work" required by United States laws to permit holding a claim was deferable till the end of the next year. This issue became paramount from the Canadian boundary to the Bering Sea. The individual prospector, the small miner, could talk of almost nothing else. Its reform became his chief need; failure to obtain it, his principal grievance against a distant government. In hearings in Washington the attention of House and Senate committees on Public Lands and on Mines and Mining had as early as 1900 been called to this abuse.[49] Senator Dillingham's subcommittee on territories had heard it denounced by "almost every person they came in contact with" in Alaska three years later; agreed that the plaints were just and recommended amendments to the mining laws that would provide a cure.[50] Bills to that end were introduced in the Fifty-fifth (1897-1899), Fifty-sixth and subsequent Congresses. But it was not until twelve years later that Congress would enact legislation designed to effect that simple and manifestly desirable reform.[51] Meanwhile many prospectors had given up and gotten out.

The twelfth census in 1900 showed a population of 63,592. It had been approximately doubled by the gold rush. The increase was wholly in the white population, which was now slightly greater than the native—the latter being 29,536. The flow of population into Alaska continued in the years immediately following the taking of the census.

After thirty-five years under the flag a form of civil government had been set up *for* the people of Alaska. But except in the municipalities, it was not in any sense a government *of* or *by* the people of Alaska.

There was virtual unanimity among Alaskans that they wanted, at the very least, the degree of representation that a delegate in Congress would provide. There was division among Alaskans as to the desirability of a legislature. The fishing and larger mining interests were opposed, in part on the ground of expense, which they felt might be reflected in higher tax rates. These interests were well represented in the Chambers of Commerce of the various Alaska towns and were able to dominate their course of action. In Washington these interests continued to oppose any increase in self-government for Alaska, even to the extent of a delegate.

But as the shortcomings of and delays incident to long-range legislation became increasingly clear, sentiment for more and more self-government was voiced in Alaska. It was voiced most vigorously to the Senate Subcommittee on Territories when it visited Ketchikan in July of 1903, by the city's mayor, George Irving, an attorney:

"We are the same men that you are. We are Americans and should be treated the same as you. We have the money, the mines, the timber and many other resources, and why the devil shouldn't we have our own government? Put the burden on us. You talk about self-government for the Philippines, for Hawaii, and Puerto Rico, but you don't say a word about it for Alaska." [52]

That same question, without the change of a syllable, would be pertinent half a century later.

The Last Frontier

> Most forms of governmental pathology are exemplified in the history of Alaska. . . . The primary difficulty is neglect. . . . What is everybody's business is nobody's, and what happens in Alaska is generally nobody's business. No concentration of power, no adequate legislation, no sufficient appropriation—on these forms of neglect our failure chiefly rests.
>
> DAVID STARR JORDAN, 1898

AFTER Theodore Roosevelt succeeded to the Presidency in 1901 his first message to Congress made no mention of Alaska. He discussed in detail the needs of the Philippines, Puerto Rico, Hawaii and even Cuba.[1]

But in his message, a year later, to the second session of the Fifty-seventh Congress he devoted a paragraph to Alaska.[2] It was not to the nation's credit, he said, that after thirty-five years, Alaska still had so poor a system of laws. Land laws that would encourage permanent settlement and the building of homes were needed. He urged that Congress give Alaska a delegate.

The next year, 1903, the mention was likewise brief, but it again stressed the need of "proper" land laws, and of beginning the survey of public lands immediately.[3] Coal-land laws should be provided so that patent could be procured.

But a year later, his message dealt with Alaska extensively.[4] From a very small beginning its products had grown until they were a steady and material contribution to the wealth of the nation. Owing to Alaska's vast size and location private enterprise could not alone provide the many things essential to its growth and to the happiness and comfort of its people, and reasonable aid from the government should be provided. Its present laws were inadequate. Many administrative functions that should be vested in the Governor were now handled by the courts. The Governor had "nothing specific to do except to make annual reports, issue Thanksgiving Day proclamations and appoint Indian policemen and notaries public."

The President urged that the salaries of judges and district attorneys be increased to make them equal to those received by corresponding officers in the United States with allowance for the difference in the cost of living, and that another judicial division be created with another judge so that the oppressive delays be diminished.

But above all the President inveighed against the "discredited fee system" for the United States commissioners, and requested that they be paid a salary. He urged that a mounted constabulary be created to police the territory outside of the incorporated towns, a vast section "wholly without police protection." He urged the establishment of hospitals and an educational system that would enable the Indians to meet changing conditions. He urged federal aid for roads and for an all-American railroad route from the Gulf of Alaska to the Yukon River. He renewed his previous recommendation for a delegate.

In Alaska heroic efforts were being made to bring new life to the "last frontier." The "sourdoughs" were ranging the vast country in search of gold, traveling up the Koyukuk into the Arctic and down the Tanana, where a new strike in 1903 gave birth to the town called Fairbanks. But they were handicapped by lack of transportation. Away from the long and costly Yukon River route only a few trails penetrated the wilderness. Getting supplies to the mining camps involved staggering costs and effort. From Valdez to the Yukon by horse or dog team the cost was from $5 to $6 a ton-mile in summer; half as much in winter. Winter travel with all its exposures was cheaper, as travel over the frozen ground was faster, and the numerous river crossings could be made on the ice. In summer, horses and men would for stretches sink deep into soggy meadow bottoms. Crossing the swift, swollen silt-laden rivers required rafts, flat-bottom boats, not always available, and occasionally the assistance of an overhead cable. Freighting heavy machinery presented almost insuperable obstacles, and at any season the task was beset with body-breaking hardships. Even machinery transported several thousand miles at high cost from the States by the Yukon River route could not be carried to the creeks twenty or thirty miles away and had to be abandoned on the river's banks, where it was soon ruined by rust.[5]

Congress had become sufficiently apprised of that situation since the late nineties to legislate by mid-decade. In January, 1905, the third session of the Fifty-eighth Congress passed a triple-purpose bill which became known as the Nelson Act.[6] It created out of the liquor and trade licenses received outside of incorporated towns the "Alaska fund." One-fourth of the fund was to go to the establishment and maintenance of schools outside of towns for the education of white children and children of mixed blood "who lead a civilized life." The education of the Indians and Eskimos, not included in the above provisions, was turned over to the Secretary of the Interior, to be met by annual appropriations. The Governor was made ex-officio commissioner of education.

Five per cent of the fund was to be devoted to the care of the insane of the district.

The remainder of the fund—70 per cent—was to be devoted to the construction and maintenance of wagon roads, bridges and trails. A board of three road commissioners appointed by the Secretary of War was to be in charge, one of them an engineer officer and the other two Army officers stationed in the district. No more money was to be expended by this board than was available in the fund. Alaskans were to pay the full cost of their roads, bridges and trails.

However, this was an improvement of the previously existent condition by which the license funds collected from them went into the treasury of the United States without benefit to Alaska. In fact it was this injustice, as well as his understanding of the need for roads, which prompted Senator Knute Nelson to sponsor the bill, and to get the Senate and House Committees on Territories to support it.[7]

But, as had so often occurred in congressional decisions affecting Alaska, and would again, this action, if not "too little and too late," to pre-empt a phrase that would have wide currency in a later day, was little, and because of its littleness would also become increasingly late in achievement. The board provided by the act came into being early in 1905, with Major Wilds P. Richardson as its president. It was greeted with enthusiasm throughout Alaska and with an overwhelming number of demands for road and trail construction. Sentiment was expressed for expending in each judicial division the funds collected by the clerks of court in that division. "The amount ($28,000) received so far from the Treasury," reported Major Richardson at the end of the first season "is not sufficient to make the question at present of any importance."[8]

The board, he reported further, was "considerably surprised and disappointed" at the smallness of available funds, and the engineer officer of the board, Lieutenant G. B. Pillsbury, reported that the lack of funds had "militated against satisfactory work during the past season." [9]

The extent of the insufficiency was made manifest by a survey the previous year of the project deemed of paramount importance, that of a wagon road from Fort Liscum (Valdez) to Fort Egbert (Eagle), to provide the "all-American" route to connect the Pacific coast of Alaska with the Yukon. The Corps of Engineers had reported the probable cost of the road, 430 miles long, at $3,500 a mile, or a million and a half dollars. And the miners in the Seward Peninsula, in the Koyukuk, the Kantishna, and elsewhere, were clamoring at least for trails.

So a demand arose for a special appropriation—a million dollars, for roads, trails and bridges in Alaska! It was requested by the Secretary of War for the year 1906. No action followed that year, but in 1907 Congress made a special appropriation of $150,000. That would insure the construction of at least one-tenth of the "all-American" route, and leave the road and trail construction in the rest of Alaska to the 70 per cent of the license taxes in the Alaska fund, which, happily, was increasing. It rose to $80,500 in 1906, and to $128,584 in 1907. Congress moreover not only repeated its appropriation in 1908 but raised it to $175,000.

The important new gold strikes in the Tanana Valley, where, after Felix Pedro struck gold in 1903, placer mining spread rapidly to all the neighboring creeks, furnished Congress with a new incentive, especially since capital in the States was asking for a way to bring larger equipment into the field and to replace the primitive rocker and pan of the earlier sourdoughs[10] with dredges and hydraulic machinery. By 1905 the new gold belt, with Fairbanks on the Chena Slough as its budding metropolis, had topped all other Alaska gold production with more than a third of the Alaska total—$5,765,100 out of an estimated over-all production of $14,925,600. By 1906 this area had increased its yield by 3,850,000 ounces while the Seward Peninsula's increase was 2,700,000 ounces. These two areas lifted Alaska's gold production to second place in the nation. Alaska was pressing Colorado closely, and the two were producing nearly one-half of the nation's gold.[11]

This promising gold production was destined to drop off, however. It had in 1906 reached its all-time high in Alaska. Lack of cheap fuel and lack of transportation were to erect difficult barriers to the great interior of Alaska which could not be reached by sea, or at best through the long and costly journey via St. Michael and up the Yukon for those communities and those camps that lay close to that mighty river and its tributaries.

In the absence of roads—and the potential wagon roads which were promised, but did not exist, were ineffective arteries of transportation—strenuous efforts were made to reach the interior by railway. None of these enterprises, which were begun and constructed some miles inland, was destined to succeed. Coal development was inseparable from successful railroad operation and Congress would not make the changes in the coal-land laws and appropriate for the surveys that would have made possible the mining of Alaska's rich coal deposits.

"Legislation is urgently needed to enable the development of the coal lands," reported Governor Wilford B. Hoggatt, who succeeded Governor Brady in 1906.[12] Hoggatt was a successful mining man. The coal lands had assumed greater importance because of the scarcity of fuel on the Pacific Coast. Railroads were building toward them—toward the Matanuska and Bering coal fields. If only title could be secured so that their coal could be mined, Alaska would be able to supply the deficiency in coal and the railroads would have a chance of success.

"Considering the quantity of fuel consumed in Alaska and by steamers plying between the ports of the Pacific states and the territory, the tardy development of what are known to be excellent coal beds in Alaska is somewhat remarkable." Thus, the 1906 report of the Geological Survey on the mineral resources of Alaska. In that year Alaska had produced 5,541 tons valued at $17,974. It was importing twenty times that amount and had been since 1903—over 120,000 tons annually at a value of nearly half a million dollars.

Five producers had mined Alaska's coal in 1906. In 1907 there were four, and the survey repeated its "somewhat remarkable" comment of the previous year.[13] By 1910 there were none.[14] Coal importations had risen to 151,465 tons with a value of $662,589.

All Alaskan mining showed a distinct decline in 1908. In part this was the result of the nationwide financial panic of 1907. But in Alaska, wrote Alfred H. Brooks in the survey's annual report, there was also the continuing lack of provision in the public-land laws by which placer ground was acquired and held—the power-of-attorney practice, and the "delays in obtaining title to coal lands," which had discouraged railway construction. Up to the close of 1908 not a single patent for coal lands had been issued. Nor had one been issued by 1910. Nor for some years thereafter.

Nature had provided two major gateways through the towering mountain ramparts that rose steeply from the Pacific shores of Alaska. In both cases it had likewise provided natural harbors, ice-free the year round. One route was up the Copper River Valley, and could be reached through either of two bays in Prince William Sound. One was Orca Inlet where an Indian settlement named Eyak had yielded its name to the Spanish appellation Cordova. The other bay lay to the northwestward and was called Port Valdez. The second route to the interior began two hundred miles to the westward and led up the broad valley of the Susitna. For it, Resurrection Bay, on the southeast of the Kenai Peninsula, provided a harbor that was long, wide and deep.

These two portals were early occupied by groups of railroad builders. The easterly Copper River route was to reach Eagle on the Yukon, close to the Canadian boundary, a distance of 525 miles, with a twenty-five-mile spur contemplated from the lower end of the road to the Bering River coal fields. The westerly route was to tap the Matanuska coal fields, 190 miles inland, and extend to the Chena–Fairbanks district on the Tanana, a total distance of about 460 miles.

In the optimism about Alaska of the century's first few years, these two routes were not deemed in competition with each other. Both were considered necessary to open up rich and different sections of Alaska. In further contemplation was a nine-hundred-mile westward railway extension from Fairbanks into the Seward Peninsula.

Over the westerly route a group of northwestern capitalists had founded the town of Seward at the head of Resurrection Bay and had begun constructing the "Alaska Central Railroad" in 1903. Former Senator George Turner of Washington was a director and stockholder and represented the enterprise in the national capital. By 1905 fifty miles had been constructed at a cost of $2,500,000, and the entire 463 miles to Fairbanks had been surveyed.

Several groups were competing for the Copper River route, either from Valdez or Cordova. Top-flight Philadelphia and New York banking and bond houses were promoting an Alaska railroad. Associated with them were experienced railroad men, the President of the Chicago and Alton and the Chairman of the Board of the Wisconsin Central. They planned to reach Eagle on the Yukon by way of Mentasta Pass, and extend branches to the mining camps along the Chitina and Tanana rivers, with a spur to the Kayak or Bering coal fields.

Another group with less impressive backing called itself the Alaska Pacific Railroad and Terminal Company. It was represented in Washington by former Senator James K. Jones of Arkansas. Another was the Valdez-Yukon Railroad. There were other lesser contenders.

Most of these found that they had underestimated both the difficulties and the costs of construction, and therefore found it impossible to comply with the provision in the Homestead and Right of Way Act of 1898 which compelled them to complete the projected road within four years or forfeit their rights to the uncompleted part. Repeatedly they were obliged to appeal to Congress for special acts granting them extensions of time, several of which were enacted. Another difficulty was the $100 a mile annual tax on completed portions of the railroad. Soon these enterprises were asking for aid from the Congress in the form of legislation guaranteeing the interest on the railroad bonds—to enable them to secure additional financing—as had been done in 1905 in behalf of railroads constructed in the Philippines. The Alaskan railroad proponents argued with logic that Alaska should have the same moderate form of assistance and pointed also to the huge land grants, which, a couple of generations earlier, had permitted American railroads to finance their spanning of the continent.

Bills providing that type of aid for Alaskan railroads to the extent of a total of a thousand miles were introduced in the Fifty-eighth, Fifty-ninth, Sixtieth and Sixty-first Congresses. Repeated hearings were held at which the difficulties of railroad construction in Alaska were fully expounded. Secretary of War Taft appeared at some hearings and seemed favorably inclined. His road board president in Alaska, Major Wilds P. Richardson, urged such a course. There was President Roosevelt's encouraging recommendation in his 1904 message that it was especially important to aid in such a manner as seemed "just and feasible" in the construction of a trunk-line railway to connect the Gulf of Alaska with the Yukon River through American territory. But Congress took no action. Investors in the States lost many millions of dollars. The Alaska Central Railroad went into receivership, and its uncompleted construction was taken over by another group which called it the Alaska Northern Railway. By 1911 it had pushed on to a total of seventy-two miles before giving up.

The larger plans of private enterprise to connect the Gulf of Alaska with the Yukon were destined to fail. However, in the Tanana Valley, twenty-six miles of narrow gauge connected Fairbanks and Chena with the placer creeks.

In the Seward Peninsula, also, were several small railroads. Some twenty miles of narrow gauge connected Nome with the camps on the upper Nome River and was being extended farther. The Solomon River and Council City Railroad, a standard gauge, was connecting the southern coast with the mining camps along the river, and from Council City eight more miles extended to Ophir Creek. These were mining railroads only, and served no other purpose.

Unlike the unfinished railroad up the Kenai Peninsula, the enterprise which prevailed over the Copper River route, while it did not penetrate far into the interior, as planned, proved a highly successful mining road. In 1906 the internationally known banking house of J. P. Morgan & Co., in association with the Guggenheim brothers, formed the Alaska Syndicate. They had acquired at a cost of $3,000,-000 the Bonanza copper mine in the Chitina Valley, which with some adjacent properties became known as the Kennecott mines. They had secured one of the richest copper deposits, and moved in 1907 to complete a railroad already begun up the Copper River Valley from Cordova to the junction of the Copper and Chitina rivers and then on into the Chitina Valley. The railroad, two hundred miles in length, was a magnificent feat of engineering and cost some $20,000,000. At the same time the syndicate acquired a dominant interest in the Northwestern Commercial Company which owned the Alaska Steamship Company. The steamship line was used to carry the copper ore southbound and general commercial cargo northbound. The enterprise was highly profitable because of the richness of the copper deposits, which were worked for a quarter of a century, when the deposits were exhausted. The syndicate also acquired twelve canneries which were producing about one-eighth of the Alaska salmon pack.

At the end of the century's first decade, the decade which followed Alaska's first coal-land legislation, coal mining had been negligible. The act of 1900 had proved a nullity. Its revision in 1904 was similarly ineffective because it limited the tracts that could be acquired to 160 acres. No one experienced in coal mining considered feasible opening a coal field on so small an area. Legislation was again sought and measures, presumably remedial, were adopted by Congress in 1908. This new law (35 Stat. 424) permitted the consolidation of claims staked previous to November 12, 1906, in tracts of 2,560 acres. But another clause in the law invalidated the title if any individual or corporation at any time in the future owned any interest, directly or indirectly, in more than one tract. While intended to guard against monopolization of the coal fields this legislation effectively blocked further coal mining. On top of all this, President Roosevelt had by executive order on November 12, 1906, withdrawn all coal lands on the public domain from location and entry, thus double-locking this resource.[15] Restriction was carried still further by his creation between 1904 and 1907 of extensive forest reserves which included all southeastern Alaska and the coast surrounding Prince William Sound, thereby adding one further layer of impenetrability for the would-be homesteader, coal operator or miner.

These two actions were part of a nationwide conservation program, which under the inspiration of Gifford Pinchot was established in the administrations of Theodore Roosevelt, and has become accepted in principle as national policy ever since. Its *application* as distinct from its purpose has often been, and continues to be, a matter of controversy. We are here concerned only with the effect of these far-reaching withdrawals on Alaska. There they proved a further impediment to development and settlement. For Alaska had not even remotely approached the point where its natural resources—with the exception of the salmon fisheries and sea otter—were in danger of depletion. They had neither been wasted nor, except for fur seals, monopolized. Congressional inaction or misaction and bureaucratic obstruction had thus far prevented their utilization and concomitant settlement. What had been wasted was much human effort and substance.

In the forty-eight states there was much coal land that was not in public domain. Some two-thirds of it was privately owned and operated. But in Alaska all was public domain. In the blanket application to Alaska of a national policy conceived wholly in stateside requirements, Alaska encountered, as it would again, the damaging effects of legislation unsuited to its needs. The execution, in practice, of these conservation policies and their timing, as distinct from their beneficence in theory or for conditions elsewhere, was peculiarly disastrous in Alaska. The newly created Chugach National Forest, originally some eleven million acres surrounding Prince William Sound and including the Kenai Peninsula, was at the very best too marginal an area to be reserved as a national forest. Half a century later no important forestry use had been made of it by the U. S. Forest Service, while other utilization had been precluded. Parts of it—the very parts which contained the most valuable coal deposits—were virtually timberless. Included in its original boundaries were twenty-one out of thirty-three of the Cunningham claims underlying the famous Ballinger-Pinchot controversy which led to the Bull Moose secession from the Republican Party in 1912 and the consequent election of Woodrow Wilson. In a subsequent extension of the Chugach Forest all the Cunningham claims were included! The sorely needed coal deposits could, however, have been made as readily available under Roosevelt's proposed leasing and royalty system, whatever the opposition of those who would have preferred patent and private ownership. But Congress acted no more to implement the new conservation policies than the old. Its paralysis as far as Alaska was concerned was recurrent.

The retarding effects on Alaska of federal inaction are disclosed in the annual reports of Governor Wilford B. Hoggatt, 1906-1909. Hoggatt was an Alaskan gold-lode owner, politically a conservative, and representative of that group of property owners and business interests who were opposed to territorial government.[16]

The population of Alaska had not increased during the past year, he reported successively in 1907, 1908 and 1909. Legislation was "urgently needed" to enable the development of the coal lands, he reported in 1907. "No titles having been secured to any coal lands in Alaska," he reported in 1909, developments of the deposits had not been made. Once title had been given, development would follow, but unless a way was found to open up the coal fields of Alaska the population would decrease and the resources of the country remain undiscovered for an indefinite period.

The laws affecting placer mining were most unsatisfactory and it was practically impossible for a great majority of the miners to conform to them, since Department of the Interior regulations made "location"—the filing of claims—dependent on surveys, and most miners were either not equipped to make surveys or were remote from a surveyor, Hoggatt reported in 1907. Government surveyors, of course, were few and far between, and next to no surveying had been done due to lack of appropriations. The desire on the part of the people of Alaska to take up lands under the homestead or other land laws, Hoggatt further reported, depended on the establishment of survey base lines, and this had not been done. He urged also that the law be amended to permit surveys to be made at per diem compensation, as reliable surveyors would not submit bids at existing rates.

Large areas of placer ground were being held for speculative purposes through unlimited staking by power of attorney, Hoggatt reported the next year, 1908, and thereby "kept closed to any army of prospectors," who, if given an opportunity, would work the placer fields. Congress, he urged, should enact corrective legislation. Hoggatt echoed this plea in his 1909 report, as did his successor, Walter E. Clark (1909-1913). This was an old story by now. Governor Brady had first called attention to this defect in the mining laws back in 1899, and had continued to stress it annually. Dr. Alfred H. Brooks, whose mission was geological exploration, had been citing the discouraging effects on bona-fide miners and prospectors of the pre-emption of large tracts of land by mere speculators who would hold them for a year, and sometimes for nearly two without doing any development work. Senator Dillingham's subcommittee on territories had fully recognized the abuse during its visit to Alaska in 1903, and prescribed the needed legislative remedies. But Congress would not fill out the prescription until ten years later—in 1912. By then thousands of prospectors had left Alaska, disillusioned and disgusted.

The effect of congressional and executive action and inaction on another aspect of Alaskan development was clearly set forth by Alfred H. Brooks in the Geological Survey's report for 1910: "As in previous years, the lack of cheap fuel is the greatest hindrance to the advancement of the mining industry in Alaska." Railway construction, he pointed out, would be active only when cheap fuel for operating was available. With the nondevelopment of the coal fields the Alaskan railways were at a double disadvantage. They were paying $11 to $12 a ton for coal used in operating when high-grade coal superior to the imported product should have been made available near by at a cost of only $2.50 to $3.50 a ton. Moreover the coal tonnage needed to help support the railways was nonexistent.

And reviewing the decade two years later when all the railway undertakings under private enterprise had failed,[17] Brooks summed up Alaska's plight as follows:

"The development of the coal fields still awaits the establishment of a definite policy in regard to the disposition of the public coal lands. The delay in securing cheap fuel for the Territory has now for many years caused a stagnation in many industries.[18] These enterprises include not only coal-mining ventures but railway construction . . ." [19]

Nor had a change of administration brought any relief. For President Taft by executive order on July 2, 1910, had "ratified, confirmed and continued in full force and effect" his predecessor's action in withdrawing "from settlement, location, sale or entry" all public lands and lands in forests in the District of Alaska in which workable coal was known to occur.

Before long exasperated Alaskans would take unusual steps to bring their plight to the attention of the nation and its authorities. On May 5, 1911, the Associated Press carried to all corners of the globe the story of the Cordova Coal Party. It was presented to residents of Seattle by their morning newspaper, the Seattle *Post-Intelligencer*, as follows:

ALASKAN CITIZENS THROW CANADIAN COAL OVERBOARD

Emulating Boston Tea Party, 300 Men Take Possession of Alaska Steamship Company's Wharf at Cordova and Dump Fuel into Harbor—Federal Officers Are Powerless to Act—Long-Expected Struggle Precipitated

---

U. S. TROOPS WILL BE ASKED FOR TO PREVENT BLOODSHED

Seattle Officials, Advised of Attack, Believe Situation Is Growing More Serious Hourly—Plans for Demonstration Made Saturday—Government Denounced for Refusal to Open Coal Fields—Pinchot Burned in Effigy

---

By Cable to the Associated Press.

CORDOVA, May 4 —The excitement caused by the government's failure to hurry action on the Alaska coal land cases reached a climax here today, when 300 businessmen and citizens formed in a body and, armed with shovels, marched to the ocean wharf of the Alaska Steamship Company, where they proceeded to throw several hundred tons of British Columbia coal into the bay.

Incensed at the thought of no reply to the many appeals cabled to President Taft to urge early action looking to the opening of the Alaska coal fields, the citizens of Cordova decided to follow the example set by the Boston "tea party" and thus express the serious crisis that has been reached in the Alaska coal situation.

OUTBURST FOLLOWS MEETING

For several days the sentiment in favor of some public outburst has been quietly growing. At a secret meeting held recently cooler heads endeavored to prevent an outbreak, but shovels kept collecting, one by one, in the rear of the Alaska Transfer Company's property, owned by Mayor Austin E. Lathrop.

When cable dispatches from Washington, received today, brought no news of President Taft's having ever acknowledged the receipt of the appeals from Alaska the angry feeling increased and the call to arms, which in this instance meant a call to shovels, was sounded, word being passed around to assemble at 3 o'clock this afternoon.

CITY IS IN TURMOIL

Just who instigated the raid has not been determined. The city is still in a turmoil and those who participated in the raid on the coal wharf will not disclose the names of the agitators.

Among those who participated in the "coal party" were A. J. Adams, President of the Chamber of Commerce; former Mayor W. H. Chase and Councilmen James Flynn and Charles Ross.

The time selected for the movement was opportune, for by some chance United States Marshal Sam Brightwell was three miles away at the Orca cannery, where he had gone on business connected with his office. United States Commissioner O. A. Tucker could not be found and Chief of Police George Dooley was not found until several tons of coal had been disposed of and the "party" was in full swing.

"GIVE US ALASKA COAL"

Richard J. Barry, general agent of the Alaska Steamship Company and the Copper River railroad, was in his office on the wharf and was taken by complete surprise when the men swooped onto the property. He demanded that the shoveling cease, but the crowd's only answer was "Give us Alaska coal," and continued dumping the fuel into the bay.

Barry was armed, but friends persuaded him not to fire, but to telephone to the mayor and marshal for assistance. The workmen in the railroad shops were sent for and arrived with Supt. Van Cleave at the same time that Chief of Police Dooley put in an appearance.

Dooley ordered the crowd to disperse, but President Adams, of the Chamber of Commerce, shouted: "Shovel away, boys. We want only Alaska coal."

Newspaper comment throughout the United States was inclined to be sympathetic. The Seattle *Times* compared the affray with the Boston Tea Party to the latter's disadvantage, since the Bostonians had gone "in dead of night . . . and disguised as Indians," while the Cordovans had acted unashamedly in broad daylight. The San Francisco *Chronicle* held the government's neglect of Alaska responsible for "a very serious situation." The Philadelphia *Bulletin* called it "a demonstration of a not unreasonable impatience with the dilatory federal policy relating to the development of Alaskan resources." The Washington *Post* felt that "a great American principle" was involved in the Alaskan controversy.

However, Secretary of the Interior Walter L. Fisher declared it to be an act of lawlessness which view was likewise expressed by Governor Walter E. Clark who at the time was visiting friends in Willimantic, Connecticut.

There were, however, no consequences. No one was arrested and prosecuted. No troops were called. No further coal parties took place. No action by Congress or the executive departments followed.

In Katalla, the budding port of entry for the Bering coal fields, Pinchot was burned in effigy. Printed posters displayed about the town expressed local sentiment:

PINCHOT, MY POLICY
No patents to coal lands!
All timber in forest reserves!
Bottle up Alaska!
Save Alaska for all time to come!

A copy of the presidential proclamation withdrawing the coal lands from entry was likewise consigned to a bonfire.

Indeed Washington's unconcern was revealed by Dr. Brooks in the next annual administrative report of the Geological Survey:

"In 1912 the appropriation for the continuation of the investigations of the mineral resources of Alaska was not made until August 24th, and was reduced from $100,000 to $90,000. As a consequence of this delay but little could be accomplished and the projects undertaken could be carried out only at relatively heavy expense." [20]

In the report on general conditions in Alaska's mining industry Dr. Brooks reiterated, much as he had for the past six years:

"Railway construction and to a certain extent railway operation have stopped and many mining enterprises have been hampered if not entirely abandoned on account of the unsatisfactory condition of the fuel problem." [21]

More lighthouses—and a separate lighthouse district for Alaska with its twenty-six thousand-mile coast, longer than the total shore of the United States, a coastline still almost uncharted, its perils aggravated by strong tide rips and the second highest tides in the world—had been requested in every governor's report since 1898. Even prior to that Governor Knapp in 1890 had recorded ten shipwrecks the preceding year, and in 1891 listed ten more vessels that were total losses, besides others variously damaged. Governor Hoggatt reiterated Brady's annual requests in 1906, 1907 and 1908, as did Governor Clark, who, in his first report in 1910, buttressed his plea by calling attention to the high marine-insurance rates, and that these in turn made for high freight rates. And the next year he recorded that seven steamers of large tonnage had been wrecked in the first nine months of 1911 on the routes between Puget Sound and Alaska and urged that the current $100,000 appropriation for lighthouse construction and maintenance for Alaska be quadrupled for the ensuing year.

"We are graduates from the school of patience," Governor Brady had written in his 1904 report, referring to Alaska's continually deferred delegateship.

Bills to give Alaska a delegate had been introduced at various times since the purchase. The matter was actively discussed in relation to proposed legislation which eventuated in the organic act of 1884, and a bill for an elected delegate received at least a strong minority report from the House Committee on Territories in the Forty-seventh Congress.[22] In subsequent Congresses such bills were again introduced but remained buried in committees.

In the Fiftieth Congress a bill for territorial government, including a delegate, received a favorable report from the House Committee on

Territories, which asserted that had a form of civil government such as the committee was recommending been adopted immediately after the acquisition of Alaska, there was little reason to doubt that the district might by then have a population, nearly, if not quite large enough to warrant its admission as a state.[23]

Bills providing a delegate failed to get action in the Fifty-first and Fifty-second Congresses. From the Fifty-fourth Congress on they began to receive favorable committee reports, but could not muster the strength for final passage of both houses. In the Fifty-fourth Congress the House Committee on Territories report inserted a table showing the white and total population of twelve of the states and of the Territory of Arizona as the census nearest the date of their organization as territories.[24] The table was as follows:

	DATE OF ORGANIZATION	POPULATION BY CENSUS NEAREST DATE OF ORGANIZATION		
		Census	White	Total
Arizona	Feb. 24, 1863	1870	9,581	9,658
Dakota, N. & S.	Mar. 2, 1861	1860	2,576	4,837
Idaho	Mar. 3, 1863	1870	10,618	14,999
Illinois	Feb. 3, 1809	1810	11,501	12,282
Indiana	May 7, 1800	1800	2,402	2,517
Michigan	Jan. 11, 1805	1810	4,618	4,762
Minnesota	Mar. 2, 1849	1850	6,938	6,977
Mississippi	Apr. 7, 1798	1800	4,446	7,600
Montana	May 26, 1864	1870	18,306	20,595
Nevada	Mar. 2, 1863	1860	6,812	6,857
Utah	Sept. 9, 1850	1850	11,330	11,380
Washington	Mar. 2, 1853	1860	11,138	11,594
Wyoming	July 18, 1868	1870	8,726	9,118
Alaska		1890	4,298	32,052
		1896*	10,000	37,000

The committee added the comment that in many of these territories the enumeration was made several years after representation by delegate was accorded and that the influx of population was very rapid after their organization. It was probable that their average white pop-

* Estimated

ulation at the time of their becoming territories with delegates in Congress was not over three thousand, while Alaska's was already over ten thousand.

The comparison—or rather contrast—with the treatment accorded Alaska and other territories was frequently stressed in debate. In arguing for his bill for territorial government, Representative William Sulzer of New York cited the case of Nebraska. When it was made a territory in 1854, embracing all the country between the Missouri River and the Rocky Mountains and extending from the fortieth parallel to the Canadian boundary, it had a population "too insignificant to be mentioned . . . in the preceding census, if indeed it were ascertainable." [25] Even six years later it had attained a population of only 28,841, less than half that of Alaska in 1900.[26] The story of Dakota Territory was similarly cited.

In the Fifty-fifth, Fifty-sixth and Fifty-seventh Congresses delegate bills got further than ever before—but not quite far enough. While the Fifty-sixth Congress was in session—1899-1901—the gold rush had already taken place, and senators and representatives were trying, with scant knowledge, to enact legislation to meet the wishes of some fifty thousand or more constituents who had gone to Alaska to seek their fortunes. Sentiment in Alaska was universal for someone with first-hand knowledge of conditions who could speak officially for Alaska in Washington. Sentiment was not lacking for full territorial government, with a delegate of course included.[27]

In the Fifty-seventh Congress a delegate bill, while passing the House, failed in the Senate. In the Fifty-eighth Congress the favorable House report reprinted the table of comparative population in the territories at the time of their organization, calling attention to Alaska's newly recorded 1900 census population of 63,592.[28] It added to the long list of reasons for a delegate, another, namely that most of the relations of the territory were with the general government. Again the bill passed the House.

At the other end of the capitol Senator Charles H. Dietrich, R., of Nebraska, declared: "It is impossible for Congress to give adequate time to Alaska's needs, and the conflicting opinions advanced by the volunteer representatives at Washington tend to confuse the minds of legislators." [29]

Senator Knute Nelson, chief congressional sponsor of Alaska legislation, expressed trust that the Senate would afford the people of Alaska "the poor privilege of sending a delegate to Congress." [30]

Despite a favorable Senate committee report the poor privilege was not afforded.

The bill was blocked again in the Senate by the continuing opposition of veteran Senator Orville H. Platt of Connecticut, serving his fifth term, whose ear the "taxable interests" in Alaska had secured, and whose seniority and standing in the Republican majority gave him great influence.

Finally in the Fifty-ninth Congress both Houses passed a bill—Senator Platt having passed away—providing for the election of a delegate for the short term—the balance of the Fifty-ninth Congress—and one for the full session of the Sixtieth. The bill also provided that Alaska should be referred to as the "Territory of Alaska" instead of the "District of Alaska," as it had been officially designated hitherto, thus conferring a promotion without the expense of territorial government or the self-governmental features inherent in territorial status. At the election on August 14, 1906, Frank II. Waskey was elected for the short term and Thomas Cale to the long term. Waskey was sworn in December 3, 1906, and his presentation at the bar of the House by Representative Francis W. Cushman, R., of Washington, was greeted with the applause of the voting members.

Delegate Waskey was entitled to applause—at least as a symbol. Despite presidential recommendations, and the repeated pleas of Alaska's governors representing a united Alaskan sentiment, it had required nineteen Congresses, dcliberating thirty-eight years, to extend to Alaska that minimum of representation which had almost automatically been accorded every other territory. Hawaii and Puerto Rico had been given representation in the national capital in 1900—two years after they had come under the flag. In the case of Alaska seven consecutive Congresses—from the Fifty-third to the Fifty-ninth inclusive—had found it necessary to discuss intensively, through fourteen years, the enormous concession of one voteless delegate in the lower house.

At the end of the century's first decade there was still virtually no land transportation in Alaska. The Valdez-Fairbanks route had had a total of $650,000 expended upon it over a period of seven years, or about $1,700 a mile. It was a low-grade wagon road, not constructed with a view to heavy traffic in summer, and was not recommended foɪ automobiles. The smaller streams had been bridged; the larger ones were crossed by "captive" ferries.

The roads and trails thus far constructed, Major Richardson wrote
in his 1910 report, were with few exceptions of a pioneer character,
and their value should be measured against the conditions of a few
years previous, which still existed in the greater part of the territory,
rather than in comparison with what were known as "good" roads in
the States.

For the construction of the "all-American" road from the Gulf of
Alaska to the water route of the Yukon, and for all other roads,
bridges and trails in a wilderness one-fifth as large as the United
States, the Alaska Road Commission had received only some $250,000
annually, derived from the slightly more than $100,000 annual
70 per cent from the Alaska fund and the average $150,000 which
Congress appropriated in the closing years of the first decade. In the
rest of Alaska construction consisted principally of "winter trails" over
which mail could be safely transported by dog team or single-horse
sled in winter, and by foot passengers or pack animals in summer,
with bridging of dangerous streams and impassable swamps. A few
branch roads had been improved beyond that point to permit double or four-horse sleds for freight traffic in winter or light-wheeled
traffic in summer. Given the seasonal freezing and thawing, the spring
and early-summer rampages of glacier streams, road maintenance after
construction presented a problem with which available funds could
cope only most inadequately.

Twelve years after the Klondike, the congressional flurry of interest
in Alaska, never excessive, had begun to wane. President Roosevelt's
belatedly aroused interest had also dwindled. A short paragraph in
his 1906 message declared that Alaska's needs had been partially met,
but that a complete reorganization of the governmental system was
needed. "Properly developed" it would in large degree become "a
land of homes." [31] But Congress was not furnishing the wherewithal
to develop Alaska properly. In President Roosevelt's final message to
Congress in December, 1908, he made no mention of Alaska, but
discussed the problems and needs of Hawaii, the Philippines, Puerto
Rico and even Cuba.[32] Those recent accessions presented new and al-
luring arenas of interest. What was of direct concern to Alaska was
the presidential declaration that all coal lands on the public domain
would henceforth be open only to lease, and his actions in the closing
months of his second term, under the stimulation of Gifford Pinchot,

of withdrawing into forest reserves virtually all the timbered areas of Alaska.

Government aid to economic development that could have manifested itself through a real highway program or sufficient assistance to build at least one of the railroads over an "all-American" route had not been forthcoming. Such wealth as had been found in Alaska had been taken almost wholly through the unaided efforts of the pioneers in the face of distantly man-made obstacles without precedent in American history.

The thirteenth census in 1910 gave Alaska a population of 64,356. It was an increase of only 764 or 1.3 per cent over the 1900 figure. In the same decade the population of the United States had grown by nearly sixteen million, from 75,994,575 in 1900 to 91,972,266 in 1910, or 21 per cent. The population of Alaska gained in the years immediately after the twelfth census was taken in 1900 and declined somewhat after the middle of the decade. The impulse given Alaska by the gold rushes had petered out, despite a new and important strike in the Innoko-Iditarod region in 1909. While the population of every state of the Union and of the territories of New Mexico and Arizona had increased, Alaska's had remained virtually stationary. National policy had thwarted in Alaska the evolutionary development that had previously built up every American territory and was registering tremendous increases in population in the West.[33]

That national policy was reflected in the attitude and actions of the people of Alaska. In reply to the question asked by the Chairman of the Senate Committee on Territories, two years later, as to whether as a whole they were "discouraged and leaving," or whether they were "hopeful and sticking by the ship" the governor of Alaska replied:

"The people are not hopeful. There is a great feeling of disappointment. . . . Of course, most people who go to a frontier country like Alaska expect hardships, and as a general rule they are optimistic, but . . . there has been quite a spread of a hopeless feeling in the Territory on account of the coal-land situation and the railroad situation. The population is absolutely stationary, if not decreasing." [34]

Toward Self-Government, Limited

A Delegate can do but little. He is no more than a legalized lobby-ist, and the average Senator or Congressman is just as liable to be guided by the unlegalized lobbyist as by the Delegate. These great special interests are able to engage as lobbyists men high in Civil and Army life, who have opportunities to present their schemes in the most innocent way to those in power and thus to secure advantage of position which not even a dozen delegates can obtain. Under the promise of developing the great territory, they secure its resources and possession of its natural strategic points, and thus deny others an equal opportunity; and having secured these natural advantages they are in a position to control not only the material development of the Territory, but even its government.

DELEGATE JAMES WICKERSHAM,
AUGUST 21, 1911

THE conservation issue throughout the nation, coupled with the entry of the Morgan-Guggenheim Syndicate and of other mining and railroad enterprises into Alaska, was to have unexpected and unforeseen effects on the future of the territory. On the one hand, the conservationist efforts were to frustrate and indefinitely delay the exploitation and hence the development of Alaska's land resources. On the other hand, they set in motion a train of events that was to give Alaska the limited benefits of an abbreviated form of territorial government.

While President Taft had been the political heir to the mantle of Theodore Roosevelt, and the presumed guardian of his policies, the conservationism of T. R. was, in his eyes and those of his followers, turned into conservatism by William Howard Taft. The century's first decade had ushered in an era of political ferment based on new economic and social concepts. It was the day of the muckrakers, of the trust busters, of the reformers, of T. R.'s "square deal." The second decade marked the Progressive revolt, the rise of LaFollette, Norris, Borah and of Woodrow Wilson's "new freedom." The Ballinger-Pinchot controversy not only dramatized the rift between the "stand-patters" and the insurgents, but focused attention on Alaska. For the conservatives Alaska was a region of great potentialities whose development was being thwarted by addlepated reformers. For the reformers Alaska was likewise a great frontier of potential settlement which must be rescued from the tentacles of the corporate octopus. For once Alaska was to receive a sort of double-barreled sympathy in the halls of Congress. Both schools of thought had their supporters in Alaska. This conflict was to underlie Alaskan politics and economics for the next half century. Alaska would become a battleground between the contending forces, and its people the victims of clashing theory and practice.

Alaskans were not long in discovering that the "representation" afforded by a voteless delegate provided no solution for their problems. Nevertheless they had, in their third delegate, James Wickersham, elected in 1908, a lusty and resourceful battler who was able to make the most of the turbulent political situation that was developing. Wickersham had been an able and upright judge. Appointed by President McKinley in 1900, he had the enthusiastic support of President Roosevelt. His confirmation blocked repeatedly by Senator Nelson, who was personally interested in a mining case which Wickersham had decided adversely to the Senator's interest, Wickersham nevertheless kept his judgeship for seven years by repeated presidential recess appointments.

The elections for delegate in 1906 had dispelled any lingering doubts in the minds of many Alaskans about the feasibility of electing a legislature. Previously, the holding of elections in so vast a territory, so lacking in means of transportation, with a widely scattered population, had seemed to present a grave obstacle; at least so the opponents of territorialism maintained. The delegate elections dissolved that obstacle. Both Waskey and Cale strongly supported territorial government with an elected legislature, and Wickersham, previously opposed, but never troubled by the hobgoblin of inconsistency, swung swiftly to that side. His conversion synchronized with his bitter opposition to "the Guggenheims" which became his battle cry. By 1910 sentiment for territorial government in Alaska was numerically overwhelming although still opposed by the fishing and larger mining interests.

A splinter of self-government having been implanted into Alaska with the long-delayed right to elect a delegate, political activity was automatically bound to follow the accumulated frustrations of the years. It was likewise almost inevitable that a man as energetic, determined and combative as Wickersham would voice the multitude of dissatisfactions that existed in Alaska. In addition to his oratorical ability and versatility, Wickersham had acquired a vast acquaintance from holding court in both the Second and Third Judicial Divisions. His election brought out some of the differences that would continue to exist in Alaska's public life. Though not wholly clear-cut at the time, and confused by personalities as well as by Wickersham's changed stand on various issues, broadly they resolved themselves into a struggle for increased self-government and conflict with the interests that opposed it. At that time that meant an all-out fight against "the Guggenheims." In common with the other larger mining, fishery and transportation interests "the Guggenheims" were opposed to any extension of home rule in the belief that it would increase taxes and lessen their control which they had been able to exercise successfully in a distant and uninterested Congress. Their attitude was reflected in the chambers of commerce, early formed in every Alaskan community, where their and kindred interests were well represented through resident attorneys and other beneficiaries. Their view was strongly supported by Governor Hoggatt, part owner in the Jualin gold mine, located some fifty miles north of Juneau.

The extension of territorial government, with a legislature, to the newly acquired Territory of Hawaii two years after its annexation again pointed to the contrastingly generous treatment accorded by Congress to this more recent ward in the national family. At the same time the classification of the new possessions, and of Alaska by the Supreme Court of the United States in the so-called "insular cases" had substantially boosted Alaska's stock in the Congress. These cases dealt with various problems which raised the issue of the constitutional status of areas under the American flag outside of the forty-eight states. In the case of Rasmussen vs. United States (197 U.S. 516) the Court decided on April 10, 1905, that Alaska had been incorporated into the United States because of the action of *both* houses of Congress in ratifying the Treaty of Cession in 1867, plus its subsequent acts in extending to Alaska the laws relating to customs, commerce and navigation, and establishing a collection district therein. While Alaska was still an *unorganized* territory, since it had no legislature, or at least a partially *organized* territory because of the act of 1884, it took precedence over all other non-contiguous areas as an unquestionably *incorporated* territory. Although legislatively Alaska had been denominated merely as a district, judicially it had been recognized as of the highest category among the nation's wards. The decision in the insular cases regarding Alaska, while, for immediately practical purposes, merely a highly flattering designation as contrasted with unincorporated territories or mere "possessions," held out the pledge of inalienability of the territory and the prospect of future statehood. It rendered the transformation of Alaska with the constitutional status of being "incorporated" into an "organized" territory—the latter an administrative and political promotion—appear to be a logical and appropriate step. However, it required seven years after the insular cases had been decided for Congress to take that step in Alaska.

The aspiration of Alaskans toward territorial government was given a dash of cold water when President Taft in an eagerly anticipated address at the Alaska-Yukon-Pacific Exposition at Seattle in the fall of 1909 came out in opposition to territorial government. In his message to Congress a few weeks later he reaffirmed his view that what Alaska needed was only an executive council appointed by the President, which should have the necessary legislative powers. He deprecated legislation looking toward the election of a legislature. The small number of people in Alaska and the lack of permanence of residence of many of them made the popular election of a legislative body, in his view, altogether unfitting.[1]

A year later Taft repeated his recommendation to Congress with even greater emphasis.[2] He was convinced that the migratory character of the population, its unequal distribution, its smallness of number, which the new census showed "to be about 50,000" (he had under-stated it by some 14,000) made it "altogether impracticable" to give them the power to elect a legislature. An appointed commission, he said, had worked well in the Philippines and would work well in Alaska. He likewise said he had decided against the extension of government credit to the railroads in Alaska, reversing the stand he had taken in his Seattle speech, and now expressed the belief that the capital already invested in these enterprises in Alaska would attract more capital sufficient to complete the railroads already building, if laws were passed providing for the proper development of Alaska.

This was hardly realistic, because Congress was not passing the proper laws and the railroad projects in Alaska—except those wholly devoted to mining—had folded up while awaiting federal action.

In Alaska the reaction to Taft's proposed government on the Philippine model was decidedly adverse.[3] In the United States increasingly progressive public opinion was creating a climate more favorable to the aspirations of the territorialists. In the congressional elections of 1910 various Republican stalwarts in the Senate, including Albert J. Beveridge, Chairman of the Committee on Territories, were defeated, and the House became Democratic for the first time in sixteen years.

President Taft in 1909 appointed Walter E. Clark of Connecticut as Governor of Alaska to succeed Hoggatt. Clark was a newspaperman, a Washington correspondent for various West Coast papers. He had mined near Nome in 1900 and subsequently traveled through Alaska in 1903 and 1906. His journalistic criticisms of President Roosevelt had angered the President who had forbidden him entrée to the White House. He considered Clark's appointment to the governorship of Alaska something of an affront. It was an incident in the growing rift between Roosevelt and Taft.

Taft's appointment of Clark in a sense reflected his own conservatism, particularly in regard to Alaska. So it was not surprising that his appointive governor should be opposed to territorial government. Clark believed that there were some ten important matters which Congress could correct by legislation; that if that were done there would be no need for a territorial legislature, and that the government in Alaska should continue as it had been.

These were (1) legislation to open up the coal lands; (2) the promotion of railroad construction; (3) amendment of the mining laws; (4) legislation to regulate and protect the fisheries; (5) increased appropriations for aids to navigation and for the construction of roads and trails; (6) revision of Alaska's civil and criminal codes. The other requests dealt with specific legislative measures; for the registration of vital statistics, to permit incorporated towns to extend their limits, for a banking code, for compulsory school attendance, for sanitation and public health legislation and provision for relief of the indigent.

If Congress would take care of these matters, there would, Clark urged, be no need of territorial government and a legislature. His opposition was based on the smallness of the white population, some 36,556. While composed of fine people of excellent character, he felt it was an unstable and shifting population. Many had quit the territory either because they had made a competence, or discouraged by lack of success in making one. Very few people had taken up homesteading. The lack of transportation facilities in Alaska formed one of the chief obstacles to the establishment of an elected territorial legislature. Territorial government would cost too much. Clark in his estimates of increased cost included the operation of courts and law enforcement, the protection of game, the care of the insane, relief of destitution. He stated that many people in Alaska favored territorial government, but that much of this feeling arose from the fact that Congress had not provided needed legislation and that if it would do so, much of the agitation would cease. On the other hand others opposed it strongly and among those were "the larger property owners, sometimes the representatives of large corporations." At these, he said, had been leveled the charge, "just, in some instances no doubt, that self-interest, and not the public interest" was responsible for their attitude. The subject had been debated with much bitterness, and, added Clark, had been "involved with selfish political ambitions." [4]

As for him, he did not want "to get the cart before the horse. What we want is people, and before we get too much government we had better get a good many more people than we have now." [5]

The presentation of Governor Clark's views after several years in the governorship early in the second decade is significant because it embodies the entire ideology of the conflict between those who then and thereafter sought increased self-government for the people of Alaska, and those who wished to maintain the status quo. That conflict would continue after limited self-government was established in 1912 and form the basis of the difference of opinion on the subject of statehood thirty-five years later and thereafter. So these differences at that earlier period merit analysis.

If Congress would just do these things . . . said Governor Clark.

First, open up the coal lands. But the federal government had been confronted with that urgent need for twelve years, since the first coal-lands law for Alaska had been adopted in 1900 (not counting the previous thirty-three years under United States rule) and, in the face of ever mounting demands had done nothing. For more than a decade this man-made paralysis of remote origin had continued and would continue.[6]

Second, urged Clark, promote railroad construction: Successful railroad construction and operation by private enterprise, as had already been amply demonstrated, depended on opening up the coal fields. But additional ways of assisting the railroads in Alaska had been proposed and received substantial endorsements. Yet in 1910, after a decade of failure, President Taft was still opposed to any government assistance, and it would not be undertaken during his administration.

Third, urged Clark, amend the mining laws. The two greatest evils were staking by power of attorney and the association claim, by which one man with the power of attorney could with seven of those powers stake eight times twenty acres—160 acres—and do only $100 worth of assessment work annually, as if it were an individual claim. Congress had been hearing about this since 1898, but, although rectification was easy, had done nothing about it.[7]

Fourth, urged Clark, regulate and protect the fisheries. This related, first, to the evident need of preventing the depletion of the fisheries by overfishing and other practices long complained of, and variously restricted by acts of Congress, but ineffectively so through lack of means for enforcement. It related, second, to taxation of the fisheries. The business license taxes enacted in 1899 had fixed the tax on salmon canneries at 4 cents a case. Clark declared this to be too low as well as "unscientific," that there was a great difference in the value of different types of salmon, that red salmon was more valuable than pink, that the taxes should be modified accordingly, and the more valuable salmon taxed at at least 10 cents a case. He cited one cannery's profit of $250,000 the preceding season, on which the taxes paid were only $5,000. There was also the evasion of these license taxes through misapplication of an act passed in 1906, by which cannery men were permitted to hatch and liberate salmon fry and in proportion to the number liberated to secure a rebate on their license taxes. Clark pointed out that in the absence of adequate government supervision there was no way of knowing whether the reports were accurate but that the Alaska fund was being impaired by the resulting decrease in the case tax.[8]

Fifth, increase appropriations for aids to navigation and for the construction of roads and trails, urged Clark. Not a lighthouse was built on the coast of Alaska during the first thirty-five years of United States rule. Road construction in Alaska was not authorized till thirty-seven years had passed. Thereafter appropriations for these purposes lagged far behind needs. When Clark was testifying as to their need in his last year in office, 1912, he could recall that in his two previous annual reports he had pleaded for them in vain, as had Hoggatt and Brady before him.[9]

The other legislative needs that Clark had stressed in his 1910 and 1911 reports, before congressional committees in these years and in 1912, had been urged by previous governors and, since 1906, by Alaska's delegates in Congress. "The singular lack of certain laws applicable to Alaska—all or nearly all of which laws have been enacted for or extended to every other Territory under the jurisdiction of the United States," Clark wrote in 1911, "is a matter which should be neglected no longer." [10] And he discussed them convincingly in detail. Practically all of them could have been provided by a territorial legislature endowed with the powers previously bestowed by Congress in other territories, and enjoyed by Hawaii and Puerto Rico since 1900, two years after their coming under the flag.[11]

Clark's sincere conservatism on the subject of territorial government was a defiance of the facts that he himself cited about congressional inaction and of the Alaskan needs which in the face of his pleas and those of others before him went unfulfilled. His apprehensions of the inability of Alaska to support territorial government would soon be refuted by events.

The commission bill desired by President Taft had been introduced in the second session of the Sixty-first Congress, 1909-1911, by Senator Beveridge. It provided for the appointment by the President of a governor, an attorney general, a commissioner of the interior, a commissioner of education and health, and a commissioner of mines who together with four others also to be appointed by the President, one from each judicial division, should constitute a legislative council. The bill provided that one or more of the offices created by this act could be filled by officers of the United States Army.

Wickersham opposed the proposal vigorously. When Senator Robert L. Owen, D., of Oklahoma, a member of the Territories Committee, asked the delegate whether he had presented his views to the President, Wickersham revealed that Taft had refused to see him, as his mind was made up and there was no use discussing the matter.[12] That they were both of the same political faith did not secure for

Alaska's delegate an entrée to the White House to discuss the most vital matter affecting Alaska. Despite the delegate's opposition the committee reported the bill favorably. But it died on the Senate's calendar after an extended debate which indicated that the bill had no chance of passage.

By the spring of 1911 the political climate had generated a new warmth for Alaskan home rule. The Democrats, who had captured control of the House in 1910, were critical of the Republicans for their disregard of Alaskans' pleas. The House Committee on Territories, under the chairmanship of Henry D. Flood, D., of Virginia, promptly held extensive hearings on Wickersham's bill, H.R. 38, introduced on April 14th, and reported it favorably. By the second session of the Sixty-second Congress which lasted into the late summer of that turbulent campaign year, its passage was reasonably assured, reinforced by the Democratic platform plank with its vigorous "demand" for the people of Alaska of "the full enjoyment of the rights and privileges of a territorial form of government."

The long-standing neglect of Alaska was further emphasized by a special message to Congress from President Taft on February 2, 1912. It dealt principally with Alaska and opened with the challenging statement that there was no branch of the federal jurisdiction which called "more imperatively for immediate legislation" than that which concerned the public domain "and especially the part of that domain which is in Alaska." [13] While the President again alluded to his recommendation for a form of commission government his emphasis was on "the imperative necessity" for Congress to take action "to permit the beginning of the development of Alaska and the opening of her resources." And he summed up the previous forty-five years by declaring:

"There is nothing in the history of the United States which affords such just reason for criticism as the failure of the federal government to extend the benefit of its fostering care to the Territory of Alaska."

Debate, which began in the House on April 17, 1912, lasted several hours. It brought out that since the purchase the expenses of the federal government had been only slightly in excess of thirty-five million dollars whereas Alaska had contributed in taxes and in the value of its products nearly four hundred and fifty million dollars, leaving Alaska as the nation's creditor by the difference, and, according to Representative Flood, "enriching many of our citizens, and adding to the prosperity and wealth of the Pacific Coast states, if it has not at times saved that section from bankruptcy." [14]

In addition to numerous statistics comparing Alaska favorably with other territories, and eloquent expatiation on its resources, beauty and grandeur as well as tribute to the sturdy qualities of its citizenry, the debate was embellished by much poetic quotation from Robert Service and others.[15]

But while Congress was to grant Alaska a legislature, the interests opposing territorial government were sufficiently powerful to restrict its scope.

"The bill recommended for passage carefully limits the power of the legislature and provides more than the usual safeguards against unwise or vicious legislation," stated the report of the House Committee on Territories. There were, it added "many limitations on the legislative power"; then the Governor was given the veto; and finally power was "specially reserved by Congress to repeal any act of the territorial legislature." And while many provisions in the bill were copies of previous enactments for other territories, they were, the committee report made clear, "more carefully limited." [16]

The legislature was forbidden to alter, amend or repeal any laws passed by Congress establishing the executive and judicial departments. That meant that the territory could not establish its own judiciary and had to keep the existing administrative powers of the judges and clerks of court undiminished, with the unpaid-commissioner system, and law enforcement by the marshals and their deputies.

The legislature was forbidden to pass any law interfering with the primary disposal of the soil, thus preventing it from doing anything about the land laws which were already proving unworkable.

The legislature was forbidden to alter, amend, modify or repeal any laws then in force relating to the customs, internal revenue, postal or any general laws of the United States—an understandable restriction—but further than that was not to touch the game, fish and fur-seal laws, or laws relating to fur-bearing animals; thereby retaining federal control and management of Alaska's principal resource.

The legislature was forbidden to alter the system of license taxes on business and trade imposed by Congress in the Alaska Criminal Code Act of 1899. The legislature was forbidden to alter the Nelson Act of January, 1905, with its subsequent amendments, which provided for the allocation of the revenues from the above business and trade license taxes, for roads, schools and the care of the insane.

The legislature was specifically forbidden to contravene an act of Congress passed twenty-six years earlier (July 30, 1866)—when nine continental areas subsequently to become states were still territories— prohibiting territorial legislatures from passing any "local or special laws" in some twenty-four categories: These included "the management of common schools"; "regulating the rate of interest on money," "incorporating cities, towns or villages, or changing or amending the charter of any town, city or village"; "for the assessment and collection of taxes for territorial township, or road purposes; granting divorces; granting to any corporation, association or individual any special or exclusive privilege, immunity or franchise," or "the right to lay down railroad tracks, or amending existing charters for such purpose."

Alaska's fiscal opportunities were strictly confined. The territory and its municipalities were forbidden to create or assume any bonded indebtedness whatever. No change was to be made in the legislation creating the Alaska fund or in the license fees provided therein. No tax was to be levied for territorial purposes in excess of 1 per cent upon the assessed value of property, or over 2 per cent within municipalities.

The territory was, however, given a limited power to tax. It had managed to save the right to tax the fisheries, over the last-ditch opposition of the canned-salmon interests, which had successfully contrived to keep the regulation and management of the fisheries under federal control.

The legislature was forbidden to provide a county form of government until such proposals should have been submitted to Congress for its prior approval. The legislature was to consist of eight senators and sixteen representatives, with two and four, respectively, elected from each judicial division. By this provision Congress imposed upon Alaska an unprecedented form of representation, in which the members of both upper and lower house represented exactly the same constituency, the only distinction between senators and representatives being that the former served for four years, the latter for two. This was a lazy way, practiced before by the Congress in dealing with Alaska, of "taking what there was" and making it do. The judicial divisions had grown out of the exigencies of enabling a district judge to get around Alaska's vast distances to try cases, chiefly dealing with conflicting mining claims, once a year, utilizing maritime transportation along the coast all year round; and in the interior, the rivers in summer and the dog sled in winter. The judicial division had no political basis, no population base, and *disproportional* representation was thereby established. A certain "divisional" interest had, to be sure, been created by the extra-judicial functions of the various judges and clerks of court.

The new organic act was the result of various compromises with the forces that had consistently opposed any and all extensions of self-government for forty-five years. Under the act of 1912, which replaced in part and in part continued the unworkable act of 1884, the powers of the executive except for a veto over legislative enactments were as limited as ever. The legislative power was greatly restricted. The judicial power was wholly retained by the federal government. A much more limited authority had been granted to Alaska than had been given to the older territories, which with the admission of New Mexico and Arizona to statehood in the same year had ceased to exist. It was a much more limited self-government than had been granted to the only other incorporated and organized territory, Hawaii, twelve years earlier.

Still, Alaska in 1912 had, after forty-five years, become an organized territory and attained a substantially increased, even though a limited, measure of self-government.

THE ERA OF
INDIFFERENCE
AND UNCONCERN

1912-1933

The Second Organic Act:
The First Territorial Legislatures

A Territorial legislature with limited jurisdiction has been created for the Territory and will undoubtedly give its attention to many measures of local relief, for which bills were drafted in this Department and urged upon the last session of Congress, but were not passed. . . . The local legislative body, however . . . has but restricted powers and cannot be expected to solve the main problems of Alaska. These must necessarily be dealt with by Congress alone.
SECRETARY OF THE INTERIOR WALTER L. FISHER,
DECEMBER 2, 1912

ALASKA'S second organic act (37 Stat. 512) was signed by President Taft on August 24, 1912. It provided for the election of eight senators and sixteen representatives to the Territorial Legislature on the first Tuesday following the first Monday, the following November—the national election day. Time was short. But Alaskans promptly busied themselves with what the Cordova *Daily Alaskan* termed "the novel occupation of really electing Alaskans to office." There was not too much optimism about the new act which had created that novelty. Preponderant opinion was inclined to view it as a step forward, but only a short step. Sentiment was divided between the adherents of Wickersham who pronounced his securing of territorial government as a substantial, if long-delayed, achievement, and those who viewed it varyingly from legislation far short of what it should have been to a "sellout."

The act is notable chiefly "for what the territorial legislators cannot do, rather than for what they can do," commented the Valdez *Prospector*.[1]

Wickersham had been elected delegate for the third time, eleven days earlier, on August 13th, running as a "Bull Moose" Progressive in a field of five, being opposed by a Republican, two Democratic and a Socialist candidates, and receiving 3,335 out of a total of 8,784 votes cast.

Wickersham's defeated Republican opponent, William A. Gilmore, voiced the totally adverse view in saying: "If ever there was a bill passed in favor of special interests that is one, and the whole common people of Alaska will find it out when the so-called legislature convenes at Juneau in March. The big questions and all big interests are reserved from the people to Congress. Such questions as railroads, game laws, fishing industry, establishment of schools, building of roads, poll tax, modifying licenses on business and trade, and most everything else is taken from the people." [2]

A tendency to eschew party partisanship and to nominate and elect "the best men" on a non-partisan basis to the legislature soon gathered strength. This trend primarily reflected territorial conditions, although in the nation established party lines were more than usually fluid in 1912 with the secession from the Republican Party of the "Bull Moose" Progressives under the leadership of Theodore Roosevelt and Hiram Johnson.

The only elections—other than municipal—in which Alaskans had been permitted to take part had disregarded conventional party lines. The first delegates, Cale and Waskey, in 1906, owed their elections to industrial rather than to political line-ups in which the miners' vote played the determining part. In 1908, Wickersham, a late entrant into a field of five candidates, had won largely on his personality, his wide acquaintance, and his anti-Guggenheim campaign. In 1910 Wickersham had been re-elected in a three-cornered race as an "insurgent" Republican against a "regular" Republican and a laborite, while the Democrats put no candidate in the field. Party alignment therefore had no roots or precedents of importance at the time of the first election to the territorial legislature. Despite some moves toward party affiliation, Alaskans voted for the individual they liked most or identified with their own interests or what they conceived to be the territorial interest. Or they voted against the man whom they disliked for corresponding reasons. With the emergence of Wickersham as a political figure of prestige and driving power, Alaskans, in that tumultuous era, divided more into pro- or anti-Wickersham than into any other classifications. In back of this personal support or opposition were the issues that would from time to time arise again in Alaska, accompanied by the same personal adherences or rejections.

In the elections to the First Territorial Legislature the prevailing Alaskans' mood was well expressed at a Non-Partisan convention held in Juneau on October 9th by Charles E. Ingersoll of Ketchikan, nominated by it for the House of Representatives, and later elected. He urged that "in this, our initial step into the introdden field," Alaskans should "sink all personal grievances, obliterate all quarrels . . . forget all animosities, refuse to align ourselves with any of the political parties . . . and fight the battle of Alaska and the people as a whole." [3]

In the First Division—southeastern Alaska—two such Non-Partisan conventions placed a ticket in the field, and a Progressive convention another. Both slates adopted platforms which endorsed woman suffrage, an eight-hour day, abolition of fish traps, simplification of the acquisition of titles to land. The platforms included other planks, like the last two, expressing aspirations which were beyond the scope of permitted territorial legislation. In the First Division the Non-Partisan slate captured the two senatorships and the four seats in the House.

In the Second Division the Nome *Nugget* editorially urged "Elect Good Men," [4] and announced in an eight-column headline "PARTIES WILL COMBINE FOR PROPER REPRESENTATION." [5] Conrad Freeding, Nome storekeeper and miner, declared:

"I believe in a combination of the Republicans, Democrats and Progressives so that Nome will not be made ashamed of the election of men who are not fitted." [6] However, non-partisanship was only partly achieved along the Bering and Arctic coasts. In a field of five for the Senate, Elwood Bruner, refusing to accept any party designation, and Freeding, running as a Democrat, were elected, while two Socialists and an Independent were defeated. Out of fourteen candidates for the House, Thomas Gaffney, the only candidate running as a Democrat, Frank A. Aldrich and Charles D. Jones, running as Independents, and J. C. Kennedy, without party designation, were elected. Of the thirteen unsuccessful candidates for both houses none had filed as a Republican, and the others appeared variously as Independent, Progressive, Socialist or without any label.

In the Third Division the Non-Partisan ticket elected its two senators and three representatives. The "Home Rule" ticket elected one House member.

In the Fourth Division a coalition of Republicans and Democrats held a Non-Partisan meeting and nominated a slate which was opposed by the Socialists. The latter's ticket was endorsed by the Fairbanks *News-Miner* under the editorship of W. F. ("Wrong Font") Thompson who was strongly opposed to Wickersham and labeled the coalition ticket as composed of his supporters, which in fact it was. It elected all six of its candidates.

It was, in the view of their contemporaries, a judgment not modified by the passage of time, a representative, able and high-minded body of men who assembled in Juneau the following March 3rd for Alaskans' first exercise in self-government. It was a mature group. The average age in the Senate was fifty-two; in the House, forty-two; the oldest member was sixty-three, the youngest thirty-three. They represented both vocational and geographic diversity. Mining predominated heavily, but its ten representatives were variously mine operators and miners—or both—and mining engineers. Five were merchants, four, lawyers—two of them graduates of the Harvard Law School; one was engaged in shipping and wharfage; one in fisheries and transportation; one was a fisherman. The eight senators came from seven different communities; the sixteen representatives from twelve. Of the twenty-four legislators eighteen were born in the United States, six had their birthplaces respectively in Canada, England, Ireland, Norway, Sweden and Switzerland. But in its roster of members the House proudly listed the number of years each had been a bona-fide resident of Alaska, and the average was fifteen years: only three had reached Alaska after the turn of the century.[7]

Some difficulties, owing to ambiguities in the organic act, had been anticipated. No appropriation, authorization or other arrangement for the employment of any legal adviser had been made. The legislators would have trouble in discovering whether they were "acting within the law or not when passing bills," editorialized the Nome *Nugget*, raising the question of whom they should look to for an official interpretation of the act, adding:

"The law seems to be so hazy and the power of the body so restricted that even attorneys might well be nonplussed as to how they can begin, what they can begin on, and what they can do after beginning." [8]

On convening, the two houses of the legislature were called into joint session to hear the Governor's message. Although the administration of Woodrow Wilson was inaugurated the next day, Taft's appointee remained in office during the sixty days of the legislature.

"We are on the threshold of limited self-government, through the acts of a local legislature, the powers of which are somewhat severely, though not in all respects clearly, curtailed by the provisions of the creative act of Congress," Governor Clark's message began. Although he had consistently opposed territorial government, now that it had become a reality, he viewed it as "unfortunate" that "a rather larger scope of authority" had not been granted to the first legislature; but perhaps the total measure of its power was not disproportionate to the ability of Alaskans to pay the expenses of their own government, since while the dormant natural resources of the territory were very large, the developed resources, those capable of being taxed, were comparatively small.

Since the basis of all government was revenue and there was no territorial treasury, Governor Clark urged that the matter of taxation be taken up early in the session, recommended that it be light and mentioned "two sources only" because they had been widely discussed:

"The salmon-cannery business does not now bear its full share of taxation," said Governor Clark, adding, "any taxes imposed on the product of the fish canneries should be in addition to the flat rate of 4 cents per case on canned salmon [the federally imposed tax of the "Alaska fund"], and should be graduated according to the kind and value of the fish, so that the total taxes will range from 4 cents on the lowest grades to about 10 cents on the highest." The other source recommended was a moderate tax on foreign corporations doing business in the territory.

Legislation in many fields was needed, for, said the Governor: "There are wanting in Alaska several elementary provisions of law which are afforded in some form probably in every other civilized territory in the world. . . . Some of these were passed by the United States Senate last year but were not acted upon by the House of Representatives." Revision of existing laws, as far as lay within the legislature's permitted powers, was needed, for the codes, enacted by Congress more than a decade ago, were "not based on the best models" and "somewhat hastily prepared without a full knowledge of the needs of the district," and, said Governor Clark in conclusion:

"It is an unwelcome reminder of our present condition of comparative neglect and lack of fostering care by government that the body of law and regulation applicable to Alaska appear, when considered as a whole, a patchwork of inequalities and conflicts, incapable of being economically or harmoniously administered. Some of the worst faults are found in the school system, and in the game, fishery and fur laws; and it is unfortunate that the legislative assembly is expressly inhibited from applying proper remedies by amending those laws." [9]

The first legislature made a substantial beginning of a framework of territorial legislation to the extent permitted it. Of eighty-four acts passed within the sixty days' session, thirty-eight specifically amended the criminal and civil codes passed by Congress over a decade earlier. Others supplied legislation which, in the absence of any local legislative body, Congress should have passed, but had not. Some of the new legislation was enlightened and not only abreast, but ahead of the times. The first act of the legislature extended the franchise to women and thus became Chapter I of the First Alaska Assembly, having received a unanimous vote in both houses. It was signed by Governor Clark on March 21st. ("He signed the *equivox* bill on the equinox," declared a legislative wit.)

The legislature passed considerable labor legislation—a reflection of current aspirations. It established an eight-hour working day; an act "to prevent employees from being oppressed by reason of an employer compelling them to board at a particular boarding house, or to purchase goods or supplies at a particular store," such practices being declared misdemeanors; an act for liens on mines in favor of laborers and material men; an act specifically regulating the conditions of labor in mining; an act penalizing the solicitation of workers under false pretenses; another fixing the liability of employers for personal injuries sustained by employees; still another providing for arbitration of industrial disputes. Most of these measures were sponsored by Senator Henry Roden, attorney and miner, of the Fourth Division.

The legislature provided for the compulsory education of children. It created juvenile courts by assigning the function of juvenile-court judge to United States commissioners, and created Boards of Children's Guardians, consisting in each judicial division of the federal judge, the United States marshal, and a woman to be appointed by the Governor. It passed an act penalizing cruelty to animals.

It set up a territorial health structure by making the governor ex-officio commissioner of health, providing for his appointment of four physicians, one in each judicial division, as assistant commissioners, defining their duties, and provided for health districts to coincide with the school districts and incorporated towns, to be headed by local boards of health. It passed other acts to regulate respectively the practices of medicine, dentistry and pharmacy through boards appointed by the Governor. It passed an anti-pollution act.

It took steps to provide a home for aged and indigent prospectors, and passed another act for the relief of destitution and appropriated therefor.

The preponderance of mining men in the legislature—and the general interest in mining—was reflected in the legislation. A mine-safety code was enacted: mine inspection was provided; the office of mine inspector was created. The taking of ore or amalgam with intent to defraud was made a felony. The purchasing of ore was regulated. The legislature supplemented the United States mining laws to try to remove the evils of unlimited powers-of- attorney claim-staking and to protect the true prospector and miner. There was some question as to the validity of the legislature's attempt to effect the reforms which had been vainly sought from the Congress.

The First Territorial Legislature passed acts regulating banks and banking; concerning the formation of corporations; concerning bills of lading; warehousing; negotiable instruments; wills; escheats; the estates of persons who had disappeared; for the registration of lobbyists. It revised the municipal codes; provided for the incorporation of smaller communities. There was much else.

Finally it established, on a modest basis, the beginnings of a revenue system for the territory. It created the office of treasurer. The legislation was prudent in its financial commitments. It sought to economize by assigning nearly all the newly created functions to existing officials without extra costs, thereby running, subsequently, into some legal difficulties.

In revenue measures the legislators adopted the simple formula of business and trade licenses to which they had become accustomed through the fourteen years since Congress had enacted them; the organic act forbade their modifying those taxes, but had stated that "this provision shall not operate to prevent the legislature from imposing other and additional taxes and licenses."

So Chapter 52, the principal revenue act, followed Governor Clark's recommendation to levy a license tax on the pack of salmon canneries—in addition to the flat 4 cents per case tax levied by the federal government and assigned by it to the Alaska fund. And since there was, and is, a wide difference in the commercial value of the different species of salmon, the legislators placed a 7 cents a case tax on the two more valuable species, namely, chinook or king salmon, and sock-eye or red salmon; and ½ cent a case on the three less valuable species, coho or silver salmon, humpback or pink salmon, chum or dog salmon. One half of the amount collected under this tax was to be turned over to the United States Bureau of Fisheries for the propagation of salmon and other fish in Alaska. This unusual provision by a territorial legislature to assist the federal government was a striking illustration of the concern already felt for the insufficient appropriation made for the protection of Alaska's fisheries.

Other license taxes for reasonable sums were levied on occupations not included in the existing federal list: Cold-storage plants, on a sliding scale, depending on the volume of business, from $10 to $500 annually; laundries doing a business of more than $5,000 annually, $25; furs, one half of one per cent of the gross value of furs exported; telephone companies, one half of one per cent of gross business above $2,400 per annum; mining, one half of one per cent of net income above $5,000 annually; insurance companies, one per cent of premiums payable on risks in Alaska; express companies, one per cent of business done in Alaska; lighterage and transportation companies, 10 cents per ton of freight handled.

Chapter 54 took another leaf from the federal book by providing a poll tax of $4 upon every male person between the ages of twenty-one and fifty. An identical tax at the rate of $2 a person had been provided by Congress in an amendment (March 2, 1903) to the Civil Code of June 6, 1900, and gave authority to municipal councils in Alaska to levy it. While called a poll tax, it had nothing to do with voting, but was in reality a head tax. In Alaska it came to be referred to as a school tax, since a later legislature (1919) earmarked it exclusively for schools.

But when they reached the considerable and vital fields in which the organic act forbade their legislating, the Alaskan lawmakers memorialized the Congress praying for legislative action by it. All these pleas were directed at the larger objective of developing Alaska, of making settlement easier—indeed possible. In regard to land there were not fewer than six memorials—evidence of the importance which Alaskans attached to that basic issue.[10] They asked that the homestead laws be revised to make them workable in Alaska; that an act passed for the states three years earlier "to provide agricultural entries on coal lands," be extended to Alaska; that Congress appropriate for surveys—without which Alaskan homesteaders would have to continue to do the surveying at their own expense, with the validity of such surveys doubtful; that Congress appropriate so that qualified land officials could be appointed;[11] that the eighty-rod shore-space reservations between claims be repealed; the memorial pointed out that these, purportedly intended at their inception to prevent the acquisition of an entire valuable shoreline by a single interest to the exclusion of others, were being held out of use indefinitely by the federal government; finally the legislators asked for an end to reservations and withdrawals, and that, instead, the land "be thrown open for the general use of the prospector, miner and settler." [12]

Other memorials protested against the inadequate protection given the Alaska salmon by the U. S. Bureau of Fisheries;[13] urged payment of salaries to U. S. commissioners in place of the existing fee system;[14] sought funds for road construction and specifically proposed that the proceeds of the seal fisheries and from the sale of public lands in Alaska be set aside for that purpose;[15] asked that federal appropriations for roads be increased.[16] Another protested against the locking-up of the coal deposits, at the anomaly of Alaskans being stopped from mining their own coal and obliged to pay huge prices for coal imported from British Columbia, and called attention to the disparity between U. S. Government expenditures in Alaska and in the more recent territorial acquisitions.[17]

Not long after the adjournment on May 3, 1913, of the First Territorial Legislature, the people of Alaska were to become aware of a new set of problems and of new obstacles to the territory's progress. Licenses whose fees would be productive of the principal territorial revenue were either not applied for, or, if secured, were not followed by payment to the territorial treasury of the moneys due.

Chapter 52, the licensing act and the territory's chief dependence for revenue, provided that the licenses should be secured from and issued by the clerks of court who were handling the similar federal license taxes.

Chapter 54 assigned the collection of the poll taxes to the United States commissioners and compensated them with 15 per cent of the amount collected.

The validity of these provisions—the use of federal officials to assist in a territorial function—was promptly challenged. Court action was threatened by the canned-salmon companies' refusal to pay the taxes and representations were made to the Attorney General of the United States. On November 17th Attorney General James C. McReynolds ruled that these arrangements contravened the provision in the organic act of 1912 that "no person holding a commission or appointment under the United States . . . shall hold any office under the government of said Territory."

The immediate result, Governor John F. A. Strong, who had succeeded Governor Clark, reported, "was the drying up of the chief sources of revenue. . . . A few salmon canneries paid the taxes upon their products for the year 1913, the taxes thus paid having come from the smaller concerns doing business in the territory. None of the larger corporations paid the tax, nor did any evince any disposition to do so." [18] And he promptly wired territorial Senator Elwood Bruner who had gone to Washington, D. C., that the stopping of revenue "practically puts the territory out of business." [19]

Governor Strong had come to Alaska in 1897, and had been a miner and newspaper editor in the territory. His appointment was well received, and was considered a fulfillment of the Democratic platform pledge of 1912 that "the officials appointed to administer the government of all our territories and the District of Columbia, should be qualified by previous bona-fide residence." Now he faced a dilemma. If he called the legislature back, the fifteen days to which the organic act limited such a special session would be insufficient to devise an entirely new system of tax collection. An alternative was to ask Congress to validate the use of federal officialdom for territorial tax collection. Delegate Wickersham thereupon introduced a bill (H.R. 11740) "to validate Chapters 52 and 54 of the acts of the Alaskan legislature." Section 1 of the bill validated the two acts; Section 2 made all federal officials in Alaska available, when not inconsistent with their regular duties, for the enforcement of territorial laws.

The bill was vigorously opposed by the canned-salmon industry. At hearings begun in Washington before the House Committee on Territories, Representative Charles F. Curry, R., of California, stated that he had had some communications from the Alaska Packers' Association of San Francisco and others who were "very much opposed" to the bill.[20] Alexander Britton, Washington, D. C., attorney representing the association, testified that not only his clients but others, including delegations from Seattle and Portland, desired to appear in opposition not merely to the tax on salmon levied in Chapter 52, but to the lighterage and tonnage taxes as well.[21]

Protests were also made by the Alaska-Portland Packers Association and several other Portland salmon-canning companies, the Portland Chamber of Commerce, the New Seattle Chamber of Commerce. The canners were represented at the hearings by their attorneys, in addition to Britton, Charles W. Dorr representing the Association of Alaska Salmon Packers of Seattle, E. S. McCord, representing Pacific-American Fisheries, and John S. Webb, representing the Northwestern Fisheries of Seattle. They argued that the territorial license taxes were "prohibitive," [22] that they were "already taxed to death" [23] and that moreover under the organic act the territory had no right to tax the fisheries.

The controversy hinged on the allegedly contradictory clauses of Section 3 of the organic act "that except as herein provided all laws now in force in Alaska shall continue in full force and effect until altered, amended or repealed by act of Congress or by the legislature; provided, That the authority herein granted to the legislature to alter, amend, modify and repeal laws in force in Alaska shall not extend to the customs, internal revenue, postal or other general laws of the United States, or to the game, fish and fur-seal laws and laws relating to fur-bearing animals of the United States applicable to Alaska, or to the laws of the United States providing for taxes on business and trade, or to the Act entitled 'An Act to provide for the construction and maintenance of roads, the establishment and maintenance of schools, and the care and support of insane persons in the District of Alaska, and for other purposes,' approved January twenty-seventh, nineteen hundred and five, and the several acts amendatory thereof: Provided further, that this provision shall not operate to prevent the legislature from imposing other and additional taxes or licenses."

The representatives of the canned-salmon industry argued that the act of June 26, 1906, amending the previous fisheries legislation for Alaska, confirmed the earlier license tax of 4 cents a case on canned salmon but had provided that this tax was to be "in lieu of all other license fees and taxes therefor and thereon," [24] and that the legislature had no authority to alter, amend or repeal any part of that law since it dealt with fish.[25]

Evans Browne of the firm of Britton and Gray, Washington counsel for the Alaska Packers' Association, protested also against the taxes imposed by the legislature in Chapter 52 of 10 cents a ton on fish shipped out of the territory and of 10 cents a ton on freight handled by the lighterage companies, asserting that this was a tax on interstate commerce and was likewise in violation of the provisions of the Organic Act.[26]

Territorial Senator Elwood Bruner, of Nome, testified to his surprise at the canners' opposition. He stated that they had been represented throughout the session of the First Territorial Legislature at Juneau by Mr. J. R. Heckman of Ketchikan, who had expressed no dissent from the licensing legislation as passed. Nor had another representative of the canners, a Mr. G. A. Teal, who had been present during the entire session. Bruner pointed out that red salmon had been bringing $5.40 a case, and pink salmon from $1.75 to $1.80 a case, and that therefore the taxes appeared equitable.[27]

A majority of the House committee decided that the question of the equitableness of the tax was the responsibility of the territorial legislature, and that its legality would be under consideration in connection with other bills with provisions seeking to establish their illegality (one introduced by Senator Wesley L. Jones of Washington in the Sixty-third Congress) and that the only question before the committee was the question of validating the employment of federal officials in territorial tax collection. The committee therefore deleted Section 1 of Wickersham's H.R. 11740 and approved Section 2, and in that form the bill became on August 29, 1914, the first amendment to the organic act of 1912.

This signified that Chapters 52 and 54 were not valid until reenacted by the next session of the territorial legislature. Unless the Governor called a special session the territorial treasury would have to wait till the regular session the following March, seven months later. A call for a special session was, however, made next to impossible since the appropriation act for the fiscal year 1915, approved the previous July 16, 1914, contained a new provision that "hereafter the estimates for expenses of government in the territories shall be submitted through and be subject to revision by the Department of the Interior." [28] Of course that appropriation act contained no provision in the Interior Department's item "government in the territories" for a special session of the Alaska legislature.

Actually the battle between the salmon canneries and the territorial interests, which was to continue to the present day, was already being waged on the territorial as well as the congressional front. In the legislature Mr. J. R. Heckman had succeeded in securing the modification of Senate Joint Memorial 26. The memorial was introduced by territorial Senator Dan Sutherland immediately following the defeat of his bill to abolish fish traps by a four to three vote not because the territorial Senate sentiment did not favor the measure but that it seemed reasonably certain that the act would, if passed, be held void in view of its interference with the power retained in the organic act for federal regulation of the fisheries. (A similar House bill introduced by Representative A. J. Svindseth of Wrangell, which had been advanced by an eleven to three vote, was later withdrawn for the same reason.)

In Sutherland's memorial draft, following the "whereases," Section 1 recommended to Congress: "That all mechanical contrivances known as traps or weirs be abolished from Alaskan waters; our attitude on this matter being so clearly and distinctly expressed by Dr. David Starr Jordan in his report of the Alaska salmon commission in 1904, on page 29, that we hereby quote—

" 'That problem of the use of traps in the large streams and their estuaries is a most difficult one. If we consider the ultimate interests of Alaska and the permanence of her salmon fisheries, no traps should be allowed anywhere . . .' " [29]

The memorial was referred to the territorial Senate Committee on Fisheries, Fish, Game and Agriculture. It returned an amplified substitute, which passed the Senate eight to zero. The territorial House, however, modified the request for abolition of fish traps to the abolition of "the contrivance known as a jigger," the limitation of "leads" on fish traps to a total length of six hundred feet, and that no fish traps be allowed within a mile of a salmon stream.

The Senate refused to concur; the House insisted on its amendments; and so conference committees were appointed, and the House modification prevailed.[30]

Thus—around this implement—there early developed one sector of the conflict between the canned-salmon and opposing interests, the question of retaining or abolishing fish traps.

At this point it is desirable to describe a "fish trap" as known in Alaska. No object in the life of Alaska has been so much in controversy and conflict, from its first installations in the early days of the salmon industry to the present. The fish trap or "pound net" is a stationary mechanical device for catching the Pacific salmon. It consists of a rectangular wooden structure, some one hundred by fifty feet, fixed on piles or floating, whose bottom is sealed by netting, and which is attached to the land by a "lead" several hundred or several thousand feet long, extending at a right angle from the shore. The "lead," whether attached to piles or floating buoys, is a webbing which extends from the surface of the water to the bottom, and consequently presents a barrier to the passage of migrating fish. It is placed in waterways where it is known the salmon will pass on their way to the streams in which they will spawn. As these salmon encounter the "lead" and are unable to advance to their destination, they turn outward—since they would encounter the shore if they were to turn inward—and traveling along the "lead" are led into an outer V-shaped "heart," the opening of which is wider than an inner exit which leads into a second or inner, also V-shaped, "heart," from which in turn they are guided by its converging sides into the "pot," and then through narrow web-enclosed tunnels into the "spiller." There they are irrevocably captive and swim around in close confinement until the trap is "brailed," or emptied, by the lifting of its rope web floor and its content of fish dumped into a scow in which they are conveyed to the cannery. The "jigger" is a lateral extension of the trap, curved or hooked, extending away from the wall of the outer "heart" into the direction from which the salmon come. It makes avoidance of the trap toward which at that point the salmon are heading almost impossible. The fish trap is the most efficient of the various types of gear used in catching salmon, judged by the number it takes, because it is situated in a location proved by experience, and because, once erected, it is capable of fishing without interruption, night and day.

In this respect the trap is generally considered superior to the purse seine, the gill net and trolling gear which are operated from boats by fishermen whose hours are limited by human necessities, although in the controversy those favoring traps occasionally denounce purse seines as equally efficient—that is, in terms of conservation, equally destructive.

The trap is a valuable commercial asset to its owner. Its economic and social aspects have been under unceasing attack by virtually all fishermen, by cannery men who do not own or control traps and have to depend on other types of gear for their salmon, and by the Alaskan public generally. The opponents maintain that traps are destructive of the supply and cannot be effectively regulated. The officials of the federal regulatory agencies deny this and have consistently defended and endorsed the use of traps. One important aspect of the controversy is that the trap owner by virtue of custom has an exclusive right to the fishing in its immediate area, a right which he consistently has sought both to maintain and to strengthen by legislation.[31]

A collateral controversy had been in the making since the act of June 26, 1906, had exempted canneries—if they operated hatcheries —from payment of the 4-cent-a-case license tax to the extent of the tax on every ten cases (40 cents) for every thousand red or king salmon fry liberated. The exemption originated in a Treasury regulation of May 2, 1900, that every company engaged in taking salmon should establish a hatchery and propagate and release four red-salmon fry for every fish taken. The ratio was increased to ten to one in 1902, and the regulation continued after the Department of Commerce and Labor took charge of the fisheries in 1903. This regulation was ignored by the canneries, except in the case of four which had already established hatcheries, and the Government made no attempt to enforce the regulation. Now, however, by the act of 1906, a tax-exemption incentive was to be offered for compliance. This provision, proposed by Mr. Charles W. Dorr of the Alaska Packers' Association, was designed to be a stimulus to the conservation of the salmon supply, and was welcomed by the Bureau of Fisheries because of the difficulty of getting appropriations for government hatcheries in Alaska.[32] But it decreased the amount paid into the Alaska fund, and thus became a sore point with those who were interested in schools and roads—naturally a large proportion of the public. Passage of this proviso in Congress was ascribed to Mr. David H. Jarvis, for some years prominent in Alaska in the employ of the Treasury Department. As a lieutenant in the revenue-cutter service he had headed a successful expedition for the relief of the whalers stranded at Point Barrow in 1898, and subsequently became the principal collector of customs for the district. Next he took employment with the Northwest Fisheries Company, which was affiliated with the Alaska Syndicate. He proved an effective lobbyist.

Senator Knute Nelson, who took a paternal pride in his bill creating the Alaska fund, and shared the popular objection to its diminution, also charged that the canneries escaped taxation by that means.[33]

The Alaska Packers' Association had operated a hatchery at Karluk on Kodiak Island since 1896, and at Loring on Revillagigedo Island since 1901. Northwest Fisheries had established one at Quadra and there were hatcheries at Hetta and Klawock, all in southeastern Alaska.[34] The action of Congress in rebating their taxes in proportion to the fry liberated was generally viewed as merely paying these packers out of Alaska's revenues for what they had been previously doing at their own expense.

In the eight years, 1908-1915 inclusive, the rebates from the five hatcheries amounted to $241,949.24 for the packers who operated them, the cash license payments for the entire industry during that same period amounting to $931,510.70.[35]

By the end of that period the fisheries officials of the Department of Commerce had reached the conclusion that salmon propagation should be carried on wholly by the government, which was operating two salmon hatcheries in Alaska, and sought legislation—though unsuccessfully—to that end. The arrangement had also not been popular with the cannery men who did not operate hatcheries and therefore secured no rebates.[36]

Spokesmen for those who had operated the hatcheries expressed a preference for continuing the arrangement although they asserted they lost money by it.[37] The value, from the standpoint of conservation, of the manner in which this method of propagation was carried on was later doubted by the bureau's and privately employed fisheries' scientists, and both the government and industry hatcheries in Alaska were discontinued some years later. But whatever may have been the benefits to the propagation of salmon by private interests, or the financial advantages or disadvantages to the few canneries which secured the rebates, there is little question that the effect on the public relations of the whole canned-salmon industry in Alaska was decidedly adverse.

Those relations were not improved by the revelation that after the passage of H.R. 11740 by the Congress, making possible the validation of Chapters 52 and 54 of the First Territorial Legislature, the canned-salmon industry would still refuse to pay its license taxes to the territory, would continue to contest Alaska's right to levy them in the courts, and would renew the fight in the Congress.

When the Second Territorial Legislature opened on March 2, 1915, Governor Strong expressed his view that the legislative powers conferred on the territory should be enlarged, that they did not equal those conferred on other territories, nor those currently enjoyed by the legislatures of Hawaii, Puerto Rico or the Philippines, and referred to President Wilson's recommendation to the Congress to grant Alaska a "full territorial form of government."

He urged the enactment of an adequate system of taxation and revenue. "The fisheries of Alaska," he gave as his opinion, "do not pay a sufficient amount of taxes. The tax laid upon the salmon canneries by the federal government is far from burdensome . . . Practically all of these fisheries are owned outside the territory, and they should pay a fair tax for the privileges they enjoy." His views in this respect coincided with those of his Republican predecessor, Governor Clark.

The school system required serious attention, the Governor pointed out. There were three classes of schools, those within incorporated towns supported in part by federal licenses and local taxes; those outside incorporated communities, supported by moneys from the Alaska fund; and the schools for natives under the United States Bureau of Education supported by congressional appropriations. The first two categories particularly needed help. Since under existing law enacted by Congress towns could not bond themselves for any purpose without previous specific congressional legislation, raising additional money speedily was next to impossible. While the schools outside the towns were nominally under the direction of the Governor, as ex-officio superintendent of schools, the school districts were created by the clerks of court, and under the laws, once a school district had been created it could not be divided no matter what the necessities of the situation. The school law passed by Congress provided that there could be no rural school unless the district contained twenty white children of school age. This was unfair to communities with fewer than twenty youngsters, but the law was inflexible. There should be, urged Governor Strong, a territorial board of education, a board of examiners, the appointment of superintendents, and sufficient funds to pay adequate salaries and defray expenses. Under the existing system each teacher determined the course of study, which was generally that of the state from which he or she came.

The legislature responded with an act to provide a uniform system of schools, a board of education, consisting of the Governor, the Treasurer of the Territory and the Assistant Superintendent of Public Instruction, who was to be a trained schoolman appointed by the Governor, and would, in effect, be the executive in charge of primary and secondary education.

The 1915 Territorial Legislature enacted what appears to have been the first old-age pension system in the United States. Under it indigents of sixty-five who did not desire to go to the Pioneers' Home provided by the first legislature, could, if qualified, receive a monthly pension of $12.50. The provision was made available also to women.

The legislature created four road districts in the territory, corresponding to the four judicial divisions, and provided for the election of road commissioners, and for their disbursal of 75 per cent of the funds coming to the territory from receipts of the Tongass and Chugach National Forests.[38] It passed several acts improving the banking in the territory. It established a bounty on wolves at the rate of $10 per wolf pelt. It created the office of attorney general and provided for his election by the voters for a four-year term.

It passed several acts relating to Indians, providing a means by which they could become citizens: they were obliged to demonstrate that they had given up their tribal ways and had adopted "the ways and habits of a civilized life." It likewise passed an act providing self-government for native villages whose inhabitants were members or descendants of Tlingit, Tsimshean or Haida Indian tribes (all in southeastern Alaska) where there were forty or more adults. It passed a workmen's-compensation act on a voluntary basis.

It passed an act to punish family desertion and to compel support of dependents. It provided two referenda on issues of the day, one on the eight-hour working day, the other on prohibition for the territory, to be held at the 1916 elections.

It validated all bills passed by the 1913 legislature utilizing the services of federal officials in Alaska for territorial purposes, now legalized by the Congress.

The increasing influence in the legislature of the canned-salmon interests was manifest. Mr. J. R. Heckman, a man of attractive personality and good standing in his community, Ketchikan, who had served as the industry's lobbyist during the first legislature, had been elected to the House. The defeat, in the second legislature, of two revenue bills designed to produce something more effective than the license taxes, may be credited to him.

House Bill 107, "to provide for the taxation of real and personal property, and to provide for the levy, assessment and collection thereof," was brought out by the Committee on Ways and Means, consisting, out of the House's sixteen members, of seven, of whom Heckman was one. It was referred to the Committee of the Whole which, after consideration, ordered it placed on the calendar. After it was read a second time, section by section, it was made a special order of business for the next morning. It was read again, amended slightly. A motion to recommit, for the purpose of rewriting one section, carried. When the bill came up again with the section rewritten, two motions were made to recommit for the purpose of rewriting two sections. Mr. Heckman then moved that House Bill 107 be laid on the table. The motion carried, nine to seven. Four of the seven members of the Ways and Means Committee, which had sponsored the bill, had been persuaded to vote to lay it on the table.

The maximum property-tax levy permitted under the Organic Act was 1 per cent—not an oppressive rate. (Within incorporated towns a 2 per cent rate for municipal purposes was allowed.) But in the Second Territorial Legislature the idea was propagated that with so low a rate the cost of collection would be prohibitive in proportion to the total revenue obtainable. That idea was nourished in succeeding legislatures when such legislation was mentioned until it became widely accepted as an insuperable obstacle to the enactment of a general property tax.

Senate Bill 45, "An act to provide a license tax upon the fishing industry . . . and repealing certain provisions of Chapter 52 of 1913" was introduced by Senator J. M. Tanner of Skagway, who had drawn the four-year term in 1913. It was reported by the Committee on Taxation and Revenue, and by the Committee of the Whole, passed the Senate eight to zero, which by the same unanimity added the emergency clause—meaning that the bill would become effective immediately upon the Governor's signature and not have to wait ninety days. In the House the bill was laid on the table. No roll call of the House vote appeared in the House journal.

It was not till the defeat of the property-tax measure on the evening of the fifty-eighth day on motion of Representative J. R. Heckman, that on Mr. Heckman's further motion the speaker was asked to appoint a committee of five—one from each division and the speaker—which would bring in a license-tax measure by eleven the next morning. The speaker's four appointees included three who had voted to shelve Senator Tanner's fishing-industry-license tax bill.

The committee therefore on the fifty-ninth day brought forth a revision of the 1913 license revenue measure. It listed a few additional occupations at nominal sums: Attorneys at law, doctors and dentists, $10 per annum; automobiles, $5; bakeries, $15; electric light and power plants, ½ of 1% of gross revenues in excess of $2,500. The fisheries licenses were amended: 4 cents a case on kings and reds; 2 cents a case on medium reds (another term for cohoes or silver salmon); 1 cent went on other varieties. Fish traps were taxed at $100 per annum.

The memorials again expressed the legislators' aspirations in the areas where they were forbidden to act. They asked Congress for full territorial government;[39] for the transfer of the fisheries to territorial control;[40] the same for the control of game;[41] for the repeal of the shore-space reservations;[42] for more deputy marshals to control crime;[43] that the sending of Alaska insane under a contract system to Morningside Sanitarium at Portland—the basis of serious criticism—be replaced by an asylum built within Alaska;[44] for the disbursal of the Alaska fund by Alaskans;[45] for the extension of the postal savings-bank system enjoyed by the states and other territories to Alaska;[46] for the extension of the parcel post to Alaska.[47]

An Administration
Faces a Duty

> The statement that the people of Alaska have borne more handicaps than any other people who have pioneered new, undeveloped territory, at least on the North American continent, has been made so often that it has become trite. Nevertheless it is true.
> SECRETARY OF THE INTERIOR FRANKLIN K. LANE,
> NOVEMBER 27, 1917

"A DUTY faces us with regard to Alaska which seems to me very pressing and very imperative; perhaps I should say a double duty, for it concerns both the political and the material development of the territory," declared President Woodrow Wilson in his first State of the Union Message to Congress, and proceeded to outline that double duty clearly:

"The people of Alaska should be given the full territorial form of government, and Alaska, as a storehouse, should be unlocked. One key to it is a system of railways. These the Government should itself build and administer, and the ports and terminals it should itself control in the interest of all who wish to use them for the service and development of the country and its people.[1]

"But the construction of railways is only the first step," continued the President, "is only thrusting in the key to the storehouse and throwing back the lock and opening the door. . . . We must use the resources of the country, not lock them up." He would, he added, call to the attention of Congress from time to time, how this should be done, for the policy would have to "be worked out by well-considered stages, not upon theory, but upon lines of practical expediency."

An important factor in the belated realization of the need to open the Alaska coal fields and to transport coal to tidewater was the high cost of meeting the needs of the United States Navy in the Pacific. Its annual peacetime requirement of between 160,000 and 300,000 tons had to be supplied by the long journey from Newport News around Cape Horn at a transportation cost of $5 to $8 a ton, which, with other government requirements on the Pacific Coast, amounted to well over a million dollars annually. In the event of war the Navy estimated the coal consumption would be greatly increased—probably to 2,000,000 tons a month—and the difficulties incidental to the long haul seriously detrimental to adequate operation. The Panama Canal, while under construction, was not yet ready for traffic. Matanuska coal had undergone the Navy's tests and was found to meet its every requirement.

For over a decade American private enterprise had attempted to construct railways from the coast of Alaska to the interior. None had succeeded. Not merely had there been a lack of governmental cooperation such as had aided the transcontinental lines in an earlier day, but specific federal executive action and congressional inaction had combined to erect unsurmountable barriers to corresponding achievement in Alaska. Their removal seemed increasingly unlikely. Two successive Republican administrations, those of Theodore Roosevelt and William Howard Taft, while differing widely in fundamental outlook, had maintained the withdrawal of the essential coal lands by executive order. Now, the only alternative, apparently, if "a system of railways" was to be built in Alaska, was to have the federal government do it.

Bills authorizing the government to construct a railway to the Matanuska coal field were introduced in the Sixty-second Congress, but the only legislation to emerge was a provision creating a railroad commission which was to report on "the best and most available routes for railroads in Alaska which would develop the country and its resources." To insure its enactment it was tacked on as a rider to the bill giving Alaska its second organic act, and thus became law on August 24, 1912.

A competent commission—consisting of Major Jay J. Morrow of the Army Engineers as chairman, Dr. Alfred H. Brooks of the U. S. Geological Survey, as vice-chairman, Leonard M. Cox, Navy engineer, and Colin M. Ingersoll, a consulting railway engineer—was appointed by President Taft. It produced a comprehensive report in less than five months (January 20, 1913). It recommended the construction of two railroads: One from Cordova up the Copper River to the Tanana River and Fairbanks, the other from Seward to the

Matanuska coal field, the Susitna Valley and thence to the Kuskokwim River—thus uniting the Pacific seaboard with the two great river
systems of the interior, and tapping the principal coal and agricultural areas. The commission avoided recommendations as to whether
these railroads should be built by private ownership with or without
government assistance or by the government, leaving that decision to
Congress.

In transmitting the report on February 6th, less than a month before his retirement, President Taft quoted the commission's unanimous conclusion that the development should be "undertaken at
once and prosecuted with vigor," and that it could be achieved only
if the railroads recommended were provided under a system
that would "insure low transportation charges and the consequent
rapid settlement of this new land and the utilization of its great resources."

The necessary inference from the report, Taft wrote, was that its
recommendations could be carried out only if the government built
or guaranteed the construction cost of the railroads. If the government were to guarantee the principal and interest on the construction bonds, it was clear to him that it should own the roads, which,
in effect, it would. And while he was "very much opposed to government operation," he believed that "government ownership with private operation under a lease was the proper solution." [2]

The Wilson administration had already indicated its support for a
government railroad. Intensive hearings were promptly undertaken
in the Sixty-third Congress before both Senate and House Committees on Territories. The opposition to a government railroad came
chiefly from representatives of existing and incompleted railway enterprises in Alaska. They presented the understandable view that the
federal government should, instead of building the railroad, remove
the obstacles to private construction and operation, including the license tax of $100 on each mile of railroad in operation, and by mak-
ing coal operation possible permit the railways both to have tonnage
and get their fuel from a nearby and abundant supply at a reasonable
rate. Mr. Falcon Joslin of Fairbanks, President of the Tanana Valley
Railway, which connected Fairbanks with the placer-mining operations in that valley, testified that in the preceding year, 1912, nearly
three thousand miles of new railway had been built in the United
States; that nearly every state and territory had some, but Alaska had

none; that in Canada some 2,200 miles of new railroad had been built in 1912, nearly, if not all, with substantial government aid, and he listed the obstacles which private railroad construction and operation in Alaska had faced and were continuing to face. He contrasted the government's treatment of private enterprise in railroading in Alaska with the grants of 6,400 acres of land per mile of construction to the Union Pacific and Central Pacific Railroads, plus loans averaging $23,000 a mile—the land grants totaling 24,500,000 acres and loans $5,000,000. In the case of the Northern Pacific Railroad the land grants amounted to 30,472,000 acres.[3]

Mr. Francis G. Jemmett, Treasurer of the Alaska Northern Railway, which had taken over the Alaska Central Railroad, and had also failed after seventy-one miles had been built north from Seward, gave what appeared to him the essence of the case for government construction:

"We have had people here advocating government construction and advocating it sincerely to the extent of their ability, but when you get back of their argument, the argument in effect . . . is the condition of things in Alaska. We have been trying for years and years to get Alaska opened up and its resources developed. We come down here to Congress and tell them the facts year after year and go away and nothing is done. It is quite clear that under the conditions as they exist private capital will not build railroads in Alaska; therefore they say, let us get the government to build these roads and the government having spent $35,000,000 to $50,000,000 in Alaska cannot haul anything or carry on business until the resources are let loose; that then the government will get busy and let loose those resources." [4]

Mr. Jemmett's summary of the arguments made by Alaskans in favor of government construction was correct. The people of Alaska, having despaired of action from the federal executive and Congress that would make private railroad construction in Alaska possible, had grasped at the proposal that Uncle Sam do it.

Approval of the legislation was received from Secretary of the Interior Franklin K. Lane. Prolonged hearings before the Senate Committee on Territories in May, 1913, resulted in a unanimously favorable report on June 17th, of the bill (S. 48) sponsored by Senator George Earle Chamberlain, D., of Oregon, which authorized the

President "to cause to be located main lines for railways from points on tidewater to the interior as will in his judgment best promote the settlement of Alaska, develop its resources, and provide adequate and suitable transportation for coal for the Army, Navy and other government services . . . and when located, to cause to be constructed, completed, equipped and operated thereon . . . a railroad or railroads with the necessary equipment, docks, wharves and terminal facilities." [5] The Secretary of the Treasury was authorized to borrow $40,000,000 for the purpose.

In reporting the bill Senator Chamberlain declared: "Alaska . . . has practically been bottled up from development by the Congress of the United States and by the executive by the creation of different sorts of reserves, so that private capital has not been invested in Alaska as it ought to be." [6]

To the opponents of the government's undertaking the railroad's construction, Senator William E. Borah, R., of Idaho, replied:

"Alaska has been tied up for a number of years through executive orders. . . . So thoroughly have the resources of Alaska been locked up . . . that capital has ceased to be interested in the development of the territory, and it would be many years, even if the situation were relieved in that respect, before capital would go there to develop the country. . . . The only alternative is that the railroads be constructed by the government itself." [7]

Senator Thomas J. Walsh, D., of Montana, supporting the measure, gave his view that the original withdrawal of coal land merited "unqualified commendation" but that "to have kept that great wealth locked up . . . for a period of eight years" approached "in gravity to a crime." [8]

Senator William S. Kenyon, R., of Iowa, declared the bill "a great piece of constructive legislation; a step forward in the economic policies of this country; a declaration of courage on the part of Congress . . . an attempt to do justice to a great possession." [9]

"For long years men have toiled against the obstacles in Alaska," said Senator Key Pittman, D., of Nevada, Chairman of the Committee on Territories, who had first-hand familiarity with Alaska dating from the rush to Nome, "and waited in poverty with a splendid patience for their government to do something that would indicate that they realized that they own a great territory, greater than the

Hawaiian Islands, over which our government takes such a paternal interest; greater than the Philippine Islands in which our government has expended millions." [10]

The opponents of the bill, including the two remaining members of the Committee on Territories who had visited Alaska in 1903, William P. Dillingham of Vermont and Knute Nelson of Minnesota, objected to government ownership and argued that Alaska needed roads more than a railroad, and Senator John Sharp Williams, D., of Mississippi, pointed out that feeder roads would have to supplement the railroads if settlement were to be promoted. Senator Dillingham felt that the time was "not ripe . . . to enter into a scheme as large" as the bill involved and: "I never expect to see the time when the supplies for Alaska will not in a large measure be carried upon the navigable streams of that district." [11]

Senator Theodore E. Burton, R., of Ohio, speaking in opposition, declared, "What Alaska needs is a policy, not an appropriation." [12]

Senator Frank B. Brandegee, R., of Connecticut, said he did not know why the government was "under any obligation to develop the Territory of Alaska," and if it did "not offer opportunities and inducements enough for people who rose superior to the obstacles here in the United States to enter it and develop it," saw no reason "why it should not lie idle." [13]

Most of the opposition was directed at the idea of the government's undertaking the unprecedented step of constructing a railroad. Senator Porter J. McCumber, R., of North Dakota, said he was "not prepared as yet to raise the socialistic flag," and the bill was "the beginning of the paternalistic or socialistic idea of complete ownership of all public utilities," and a step from which there was "no receding." [14]

To him and others who had voiced similar objection Senator Albert B. Cummins, R., of Iowa replied:

"If I may be permitted to speak to my fellow-Republicans . . . especially to those who are shrinking from the proposal that the Government shall build a railroad in Alaska, I would say that our party believes it is . . . at least one of the functions of the government to do what it can to give work to the people of the United States, to enlarge the field of their energy, and to broaden the possibilities that open out to the American capitalist and laborer. Our party does not believe in the theory . . . advanced by Herbert Spencer . . . that government should be a mere policeman. Some of the argument against this bill upon this side of the Chamber has proceeded upon the theory that the Government of the United States has nothing more to do for the welfare of the people than to keep the peace—that is, to maintain order. I have a different conception regarding the functions of government. I am not willing to advance to the other extreme and adopt the views of Karl Marx, who believed that the government should be a universal parent, absorbing all the energies of the people and distributing among its subjects in just proportions the results of labor; but somewhere between the policeman of Herbert Spencer and the universal parent of Karl Marx there is to be drawn the line which divides governmental and altruistic activity from individual and selfish activity." [15]

"The fact is," interjected Senator Borah, "that we have discovered the midway point between the policeman and the universal father so far as Alaska is concerned, and that is the stepfather." [16]

A number of senators made clear that they supported the railroad bill only on the assumption that other legislation to unlock Alaska's resources and to promote settlement would follow. Unless legislation "giving opportunity not only for the ascertainment but for the acquisition and development of the resources of Alaska" would follow, the railroad effort would be useless, was the view of Senator Charles S. Thomas, D., of Colorado. "The two must go together, and I believe the one will follow the other. If I did not so believe, then I would not under any circumstances support this bill." [17]

Senator John D. Works, R., of California, felt that the railroad was only one step toward opening Alaska's resources, and unless fair and just laws were enacted to that end, money spent on the railway would be wasted.[18]

A vigorous plea for the measure came from Senator Furnifold McL. Simmons, D., of North Carolina:

"The United States Government has not only not helped the people of Alaska to build needed transportation requisite to the development of that country, as to all new countries, and to develop their industries, but it has literally fettered and gagged the people of that Territory in their effort to develop it. . . . We have practically prohibited railroad building.

"How have we done this? By the most outrageous system of discriminatory legislation that any great country ever followed toward one of its territories or colonies. . . . We imposed an annual license tax of $100 a mile upon every mile of railway. . . . We have withdrawn from entry all the coal and oil lands in Alaska. . . . We have deliberately denied to the railroads that have been constructed there, and we deliberately deny to any railroad that may hereafter be constructed in Alaska, the use of these two great natural resources for the purpose of operating their lines."

Senator Simmons added that a further impediment was the application to the railroads of Alaska of the commodity clause of the interstate-commerce law which prohibited the ownership by any railway of coal, oil or timber, and contrasted the policies of Canada in her western provinces with United States policy in Alaska.[19]

The bill passed the Senate on January 24, 1914, by a vote of forty-six to sixteen with thirty-three not voting. Thirty-one Democrats and fifteen Republicans voted for it; four Democrats and twelve Republicans voted against.

A similar bill had been reported out after hearings during July, 1913, by the House Committee on Territories. Two of its nineteen members dissented and brought in a minority report.[20]

"The purpose of the bill," said committee chairman William C. Houston, D., of Tennessee, in opening the debate, "is to develop the Territory of Alaska . . . to open up the interior . . . to settlement and to home builders." If Congress allowed this vast area of wealth belonging to the people to lie idle and undeveloped, he urged, it would be unfaithful to its trust, and sluggard in meeting a responsibility that naturally devolved upon its members. The bill proposed to do something for the people of Alaska which they could not do for themselves without such assistance. It was merely the extension of the hand of government to aid in creating conditions that would enable our own people to gain a foothold.[21]

In addition to the arguments for and against the bill voiced in the Senate the time-honored theme of Alaska as "worthless" and an "arctic waste" constantly recurred.

Representative Martin Dies, D., of Texas, opposing the bill, said: "We have owned this colossal chunk of frozen earth for more than fifty years, and with great labor and expense have succeeded in thawing out only two or three thousand acres sufficient for the growth of quickly maturing crops." [22]

Representative Edward Watts Saunders, D., of Virginia, likewise in opposition, declared that Alaska was "a frozen wilderness for the greater part of the year, and a fly-plagued sweat-bath for the balance of the time" and that otherwise it was "just as it came from the hands of the Creator." [23]

Representative Martin B. Madden, R., of Illinois, felt the fact that only 153 homesteads had been patented in Alaska was an indictment of the territory as an agricultural region and that the vast sum of $35,000,000 ought not to be expended for a railroad there.[24]

Representative Thomas W. Hardwick, D., of Georgia, asked "Why spend it at the North Pole? Why not spend it at home? Have we so much money, are we so rich, that we would rather send it to the North Pole than send it to the people of our districts? Are we so rich that we can afford to develop Alaska while America languishes?" [25]

Representative Walter Elder, D., of Louisiana, stated that in the region to be served by the railroad there was a killing frost every month in the year and that the ground was frozen to a depth of fifty to two hundred feet.[26]

Representative Charles G. Edwards, D., of Georgia, felt it would be "an unwise and wasteful thing" for the government to "dump its millions . . . in that frozen and unproductive section . . . for the thirty-five thousand white people in Alaska." He felt that if money were to be spent it should be in sections of the country, like his, where drainage and other improvements were needed.[27]

Representative Frank Mondell, R., of Wyoming, opposing the measure, made the interesting point that agriculture in the interior would be more benefited if there were no railroad to bring in produce because then the Alaska communities would have to pay the local farmers' high prices for home-grown vegetables.[28]

Representative William J. Fields, D., of Kentucky, felt that "before going to Alaska to break the Ice Trust by building a railroad through it" Congress could find better ways of spending $40,000,000 to better advantage in the continental United States.[29]

Countering these views, Representative Henry T. Rainey, D., of Illinois, cited the adverse judgments of former Senators Daniel Webster of Massachusetts, John C. Calhoun and George McDuffie of South Carolina on the characteristics of Oregon Territory.[30]

Representative James M. Graham, D., of Illinois, took issue with those who opposed the railroad on account of the small number of homesteaders, and small population generally, saying:

"The great cost of making surveys and the great expenses of traveling back and forth to Juneau prevent homesteading; and so it goes through the whole ridiculous round. Indeed it seems as if the territorial laws could not be made more effectual if the purpose was to prevent the development of the country. The laws in force are calculated to drive out those who are there and offer no inducement to others to take their places. Is it candid under these well-known conditions to charge the diminishing population to a lack of natural advantages in the country? Is it frank or fair to argue that because under these wretched and disheartening conditions the population does not increase, is it useless to give Alaska a chance? . . . Alaska is starving for the want of railroads and for necessary legislation. Because it is starved it is not growing, and because it is not growing they say what is the use of helping it." [31]

In opposition to the numerous arguments against government ownership and possible operation of the railroad, Representative Elsworth R. Bathrick, D., of Ohio, declared that such action was "a proper expression of government"; that it did not go to the people and "hand them a disquisition upon government philosophy in place of material help" and that he hoped that when the railroad was in operation the people would discover it as something more than a mere statement by the government: " 'We will give you the right to work out your own salvation.' " [32]

Responding to the charge that the railroad would not pay, Representative Thetus W. Sims, D., of Tennessee, said: "I do not care whether the road, as an investment, pays or not. I do not care whether, regarding it as an independent enterprise, the freight and passenger traffic maintains it; but if opening up the whole of Alaska, being government-owned property, is benefited to the extent of the value of the railroad and its maintenance, then it is good business to do it. . . ." [33]

"The government has a much greater and higher interest in Alaskan development than mere profit on an investment. It is a nation builder," said Representative Horace Mann Towner, R., of Iowa. "It is not limited to an inquiry as to how much per acre it can sell its land, or how much per bushel it can obtain as rental or royalty for its coal. . . . It holds these resources in trust for its people; primarily for those of its citizens who shall locate in the particular territory, and secondarily for the people of the nation, who must protect it and develop it as a part of the nation's domain. Whatever shall further these larger interests is justified and a duty." [34]

Representative Frank E. Guernsey, R., of Maine, said: "Public confidence in the Taft administration began to crumble early in its existence due in no small part to the fact that the public lost faith in its Alaska policy as early as the fall of 1909. . . . The public wants something done toward the development, for the public benefit of the great Alaskan domain and its resources. . . . In Alaska we will build a railroad over government land, and thereby enhance the value of public property along that road. . . . Unless it is undertaken, the country is destined to continue to be locked up for the next half century, as it has during our ownership going on fifty years." [35]

The bill passed the House on February 18th by a vote of 232 to 86.[36] Differences between Senate and House drafts were settled in conference and the bill was signed by President Wilson on March 12th (38 Stat. 305).

In its final form it authorized the expenditure of $35,000,000, of which $1,000,000 was appropriated for immediate use, and empowered the President to construct one thousand miles of one or more railroads to connect one or more of the Pacific ports of Alaska with the navigable rivers of the interior, to build or acquire docks and terminal facilities, including the purchase of existing rail lines, and the construction of necessary telephone and telegraph lines. The President was granted discretion to have the government operate the lines or lease them.

Having provided for a government railroad, the Congress repealed the $100-a-mile tax on each mile of railway in operation, replacing it with a 1 per cent tax on a road's gross income.

It was an extraordinary example of congressional response to executive leadership. In the relative magnitude, in that day, of the undertaking, the concern shown for its objectives, and the speed of its enactment, it was also an unprecedented event in federal legislation for Alaska.

As Delegate Wickersham stated in the course of the debate: "The plan proposed in the bill for the location and construction of a railroad in Alaska is a Democratic administration plan; it is strictly within the pledges of the Progressive platform and has the support of that party and of republican majorities," [37] and further, "there never was the slightest sympathy for the Territory of Alaska until Woodrow Wilson became President." [38]

There followed shortly the Alaska coal-lands bill, "intended" as its manager in the House, Representative Scott Ferris, D., of Oklahoma, declared, "to go as a companion bill to the Alaska railroad bill, so that the Alaska coal fields may be opened."

"It is one of the most amazing things," said he in the opening debate, "that Alaska with all her coal, could never get enough coal to put in a cook stove as the laws now stand." [39]

Representative Frank Mondell, R., of Wyoming, expressed the prevailing feeling in saying: "We have waited so long, conditions have become so unbearable, that we might better legislate somewhat unwisely than not to legislate at all." [40]

Despite objections against the abolition of fee-simple titles for Alaska coal lands, assertions that its provisions were unfair to Alaskans, that the bill's intent to prevent coal monopolization would not prevent it,[41] and that giving unlimited discretion to the Secretary of the Interior to administer the act could lead to abuse and bureaucratic tyranny, the bill passed both houses by a voice vote and was signed by President Wilson on October 20, 1914.

The act provided that coal lands on the public domain and in the forest reservations in Alaska could be leased in tracts not to exceed 2,560 acres at a minimum royalty of 2 cents a ton plus a rental of 25 cents an acre for the first year, 50 cents for the second to fifth years, and $1 per acre thereafter. Some twelve thousand acres were reserved for the government. All applications and claims pending before the Department of the Interior, the act provided, would have to be disposed of within one year. At the time of the passage of the act 566 applications out of a total of 1,162 entries were still pending. Only two claims totaling some two hundred acres had ever gone to patent. But the Land Office still held over $400,000 of the entrymen's money, some of which they had paid to it over ten years previously.[42]

The Sixty-third Congress also approved a bill which set aside two sections, numbers 16 and 36, in every Alaska township for the benefit of schools, a provision which Delegate Wickersham pointed out had been granted every territory at the time of its organization. The act in addition granted the territory three sections just west of Fairbanks as a site for an Agricultural College and School of Mines, when the Alaska legislature should take the necessary steps to establish it, and likewise reserved Section 33 in each of the eighty townships in the great Tanana Valley, amounting to slightly over fifty thousand acres, for the support of such an institution. At the same time it fixed the future location of the institution by making the land grant conditional on the use of the Fairbanks site.

Objection was made by Representative Patrick D. Norton, R., of North Dakota, who felt it unfair for Congress to make that decision. Why not grant the land without conditions as to locality and leave that to be determined at some future time by the people of Alaska? he asked.

Representative James R. Mann, R., of Illinois, the minority floor leader, explained that the land granted was that occupied by one of the four federal agricultural-experiment stations, and that "we want to get rid of an expensive proposition that we have up there." The station near Fairbanks, he said, was "very costly," did not raise enough to pay its expenses, and, in his view, never would. (Its average cost in the eighteen years since the agricultural-experiment stations had been established in 1898 was about $5,000 annually.)

On the objection of Representative Norton, the bill being on the unanimous-consent calendar, the bill was passed over. By the next unanimous-consent calendar, a week later, Wickersham, who favored the Fairbanks location, had sought and secured a telegram from Juneau, where the legislature was convening, signed by the Governor and nineteen out of the twenty-four legislators, expressing their approval of the bill.

Representative Norton was satisfied, but this time Representative Jacob A. Falconer, Prog., of Washington, objected on the ground there were only thirty-five thousand people in Alaska; that if an Agricultural College were established in one place, within five, ten or twenty years, it might be proposed to establish a university at another place in Alaska, and that many states had "experienced a logrolling proposition" for the maintenance of such institutions. He offered to withdraw his objection to the bill, and leave the sections for the support of schools if the college were deleted. He wanted to obviate the possible logrolling in Alaska's future, and moreover believed that "now was not the time to put an educational institution into the territory."

His objection would not only have again postponed action on the bill, but have killed it in the Sixty-third Congress since this action took place on the last day. But Delegate Wickersham took the step—unprecedented for a voteless delegate and startling in that it proved successful—of moving for a suspension of the rules. The required two-thirds majority approved and passed the bill. It had already passed the Senate, and the next day, March 4, 1915, became law with the President's signature.[48]

But Not a Double Duty

> When the United States acquires extensive dominion over extensive tracts of territory, the duty devolves upon it not so much to exploit the natural resources for the benefit of the people of the States as to build there a civilization, to induce immigration and settlement . . . that homes may spring up and that that territory may contribute to the general strength and happiness of the whole Union.
>
> REPRESENTATIVE HALVOR STEENERSON OF MINNESOTA,
> FEBRUARY 5, 1915

THE three measures—to construct a railroad or railroads, to make possible coal mining through a federal leasing system, and the granting of land for educational purposes—enacted by the Sixty-third Congress (March 4, 1913—March 3, 1915), the first of the several Democratic Congresses during the eight-year Presidency of Woodrow Wilson, were the only significant legislative achievements in behalf of Alaska during that period that had been ushered in so promisingly. The coal-leasing bill, as the record indicates, was a long-belated effort to relieve a paralysis imposed on Alaska by federal executive action and congressional inaction. The Alaska land grant repeated, also belatedly, in behalf of schools and a college, merely what Congress had previously done, often more generously, for other American territories.

The first duty which Woodrow Wilson had specified as "very pressing and very imperative"—to give the people of Alaska the full territorial form of government—was not performed. Nor were the other steps, of which the construction of railways was declared to be "only the first," to be taken during his administrations.

Delegate Wickersham's bill providing for full territorial government (H.R. 6887) was introduced early in the first session of the Sixty-fourth Congress. It was referred to the Committee on Territories, but never acted upon. To understand the circumstances of this renege it is necessary to go back to the forces which were consistently opposing the increase of any self-government for Alaska whenever this was sought.

It will be recalled that when the First Territorial Legislature, in quest of a modest amount of revenue for territorial public services, had placed a small license tax on various occupations, and had sought to utilize the clerks of court, who were issuing the federal licenses and collecting the tax therefrom, similarly, the canned-salmon industry—upon which one of these license taxes had been levied—initiated action to have the measure declared invalid, and had, for the greater part, refused to pay the tax. When the Congress validated the use of the clerks of court and of other federal officials to assist in the administration and enforcement of territorial legislation, the canned-salmon industry still refused to pay the tax and sought action on two fronts—judicial and legislative.

In order to collect the tax the territory had to go to court and meet the canners' challenge. There were several such actions: Two against Alaska-Pacific Fisheries, another against the Alaska Salmon Company; still another against the Hoonah Packing Company. The territory's right to levy the license taxes on canned salmon, on fish traps and other gear, which had been re-imposed in somewhat modified form by the Second Territorial Legislature, was sustained in the United States District Court of Alaska's First Judicial Division by Judge Robert W. Jennings. On appeal to the Ninth Circuit Court at San Francisco the District Court's decision was affirmed.[1] Attempts to appeal the decisions further to the Supreme Court of the United States failed when the highest tribunal refused to grant the industry *certiorari*,[2] and subsequently denied a writ of error.[3]

Meanwhile in anticipation of adverse court findings, bills were introduced in Congress to deprive the territory of its right to tax the fisheries. One, H.R. 9527, was entitled "A Bill to Repeal the Law Allowing the Territory of Alaska to tax fisheries." It sought to amend the organic act by the insertion in section 3, after the provision permitting the legislature to impose "other and additional licenses and taxes," of the clause "except that no other and additional taxes or licenses shall be imposed upon the fisheries of Alaska or appliances used therein or any business or trade connected therewith." [4]

Another bill, H.R. 9528, entitled "A Bill for the Protection, Regulation and Conservation of the Fisheries of Alaska," provided new regulations for the Alaska fisheries. Its general provisions had been under consideration during the previous four sessions of Congress and had been sought by the Bureau of Fisheries in the interest of better control of the Alaska fisheries resources. In the Sixty-third Congress the draft, for the first time, contained a clause denying to Alaska any revenue from the fisheries for general purposes, and further provided that henceforth the territory could not impose "any license fees or taxes" upon the fisheries, "nor upon the output thereof, nor upon any property, real or personal, used in said business in said Territory, and any such existing statutes heretofore enacted by the Territory of Alaska are hereby expressly disapproved." [5] Both bills had been introduced early in the first session of the Sixty-fourth Congress —on January 20, 1916—upon request of the Department of Commerce, by Representative Joshua W. Alexander, D., of Missouri, Chairman of the Committee on Merchant Marine and Fisheries. This bill was referred to that committee.

The bill therefore proposed to take away not only the previously granted right to levy license taxes on the canned salmon and the gear, but would also have rescinded—on the fisheries exclusively—the property tax for general territorial purposes which the organic act had limited to 1 per cent. On top of that the bill was retroactive and would have canceled the indebtedness to the territory of the canned-salmon industry, which amounted to some $250,000 for the first legislative biennium, 1913–1915, and approximately half as much more for the current year.

The bills had the support of the Department of Commerce. Secretary William C. Redfield, the Solicitor of the Department, Albert Lee Thurman, Commissioner Hugh M. Smith of the Bureau of Fisheries, Ward T. Bower, chief agent of the bureau's Alaska Service, testified that the action of the Alaska legislature in taxing the fisheries constituted "double taxation" and established an objectionable "dual control" over the industry.

The hearings brought out how the bills—and earlier drafts with similar objectives in preceding Congresses—had been drawn.

Secretary Redfield testified that the legislation was "framed in the department . . . as a result of conferences . . . with the parties concerned," and that it had "the substantially unanimous . . . support of the persons upon whom these taxes are to be imposed." [6]

Solicitor Thurman, who had testified that he had prepared H.R. 9527 on orders from Secretary Redfield, and naturally so, he felt, because "I do not know who is going to prepare department bills unless it is the legal adviser of the department," nevertheless did not know who had prepared H.R. 2598 and other similar bills presented in the preceding Congress.[7]

"If you will allow me to give the department's connection with the bill," said Mr. Thurman, "I was telephoned one morning—I knew nothing of the bill—by Dr. Smith asking me for a meeting with himself and Mr. Bower on the bill, and some gentlemen engaged in the Alaskan fisheries, asking me if I would go over the bill with them, which they had agreed upon as being a good bill: the Bureau of Fisheries feeling . . . that the general fish laws of Alaska should be revised." [8] Present at the meeting besides Smith and Bower were Mr. Alexander Britton and Mr. Frank M. Warren, representing the industry.[9]

Mr. Alexander Britton, representing the Alaska Packers' Association testified: ". . . we were invited by the Department of Commerce to come in and see if we could not agree on some sort of legislation, and a great deal of time and labor was spent on this bill [H.R. 9528], which is fairly satisfactory to the people interested in the business. . . . We are here to give any information that the committee may want by way of explanation or otherwise." [10]

Asked by Delegate Wickersham how many canneries in Alaska the Alaska Packers' Association had, Mr. Britton replied:

"I really could not tell you. I am not here to testify to facts relating to the company's business, but I am here to represent them in the matter of assisting, if possible, in the passage of the bill that they agreed upon as being a proper bill." [11]

Delegate Wickersham presented a confidential committee print of a corresponding Senate bill introduced in the Sixty-second Congress which was marked, "Tentative draft of the bill suggested by United States Bureau of Fisheries and the representatives of the various Alaskan fisheries which has been agreed upon and prepared by them jointly after numerous conferences." [12]

Secretary Redfield's conception of "the parties concerned" with the legislation did not include Alaska's delegate in Congress. Wickersham had been invited to none of the meetings nor had he seen the bills before their introduction. Representative Charles C. Kearns, R., of Ohio, asked why:

"Judge Wickersham represents Alaska. . . . It seems here is a bill . . . affecting Alaska alone, and the thing that is in my mind is why all these bills do not come from the delegate up there; he is the man directly interested. . . . It seems to me if you are going to have a bill affecting my district and my district alone, and some man introduced a bill without consulting me, I would feel angry." [13]

Voteless delegates, as Delegate Wickersham and his successors would discover, could scarcely afford the luxury of anger at being slighted. They would learn that it was all part of being a delegate.

The hearings brought out, as subsequent hearings would again and again, certain basic conflicts involving the federal government, the people of Alaska and the fisheries, with their several component parts.

The Department of Commerce representatives made clear that they felt they could protect, regulate and conserve the fisheries better than the territorial authorities—a position fully supported then and thereafter by the canned-salmon industry. At the same time the federal officials bore witness to the inadequacy of their means to perform the task. Secretary Redfield testified that the annual appropriation to supervise the Alaskan fisheries, the annual value of whose product was over $21,000,000, was only $60,000—less than one third of one per cent. "The situation has been very humiliating for the government," he said. "For example, it has been our unfortunate necessity to call upon the canneries to loan us the boats with which to transport our officers, who were to do the supervising of those same canneries, and it is true that the government has not, up to the last two or three years, certainly, taken this task as seriously as it should, and certainly has not as adequately equipped itself as it should." But he was confident that that day had gone by.[14]

Commissioner Hugh Smith testified that the total expenditures for regulation and conservation during the past ten years had been $325,124.98—an average of less than $33,000 a year—and to enforce the law would require a much larger force than Congress had provided.[15]

E. Lester Jones, Superintendent of the Coast and Geodetic Survey and former Deputy Commissioner of Fisheries, who had completed an extensive inspection tour of Alaska, testified on May 25th that the difficulty in protecting the salmon and enforcing the law was due to the fact that adequate funds had not been provided for vessels and wardens.[16] Answering a question of Representative Rufus Hardy, D., of Texas, how much opportunity there would be to catch one of the canneries in a violation of the law, if—as Jones had testified—the

warden had to take one of the cannery boats to look into the matter.
Jones replied:

"There is none at all. Under the present conditions it is considered
a joke in many localities on account of the manner in which government officials try to enforce the law." [17]

Testifying two weeks later, after the appropriations for the coming fiscal year had been reported, Jones said:

"One vessel . . . for southeastern Alaska is about as foolish as trying to have one submarine protect all of our coastline. . . . I made
an appeal last year before the Committee on Appropriations, emphasizing the fact that the laws of Alaska pertaining to the fisheries, if
they were not observed, was not the fault of the bureau, but because
they had not the ships, and still not a dollar was appropriated. This
year in the sundry civil bill . . . just reported, they have given two
$5,000 launches, instead of giving two or three vessels of sufficient
size to accommodate the officers and crew and making it possible to
go into all waters, rough or smooth. . . . They have not provided a
vessel for central Alaska or western Alaska and that is the way it is going on and on. . . ." [18]

Governor Strong, testifying to the financial needs of the terrritory,
especially of its schools, said that no more than $3,000 had been paid
of the fisheries' taxes and that the total due from that source, of
about $250,000, depended on the outcome of the court action.[19]
Some $90,000 had been received from mining taxes, and the larger
mining companies—except Kennecott—had not paid their taxes
either. The Treadwell and affiliated companies had likewise taken
the position—though for wholly different reasons—that the one-half
of one per cent territorial license tax on the net profits of mining,
with an exemption of the first $5,000, was not valid.[20]

In the Governor's view the territorial taxes levied on the fisheries
were equitable. He felt that the fisheries could be better controlled
and administered by the territory than by the federal government,
because, "the people of Alaska have a vital interest in the fisheries of
the territory. They are deeply concerned in the conservation of the
fisheries, and they are on the ground. They are thoroughly familiar
with all the conditions." [21]

In the meantime Delegate Wickersham had early in the Sixty-
fourth Congress introduced a bill, H.R. 6887, for full territorial government for Alaska. It supplied the features, available to other ter-

ritories, which the organic act of 1912 had denied to Alaska—the right to its own judiciary and territorial law enforcement; the right to create counties and elect county officials; control over the fisheries and game. The bill was referred to the Committee on Territories.

It has been customary in Congress to ask the opinion of the various executive departments on proposed legislation which affects them, or in which they have a special interest. A letter to the Department of Commerce drew an unfavorable response in the form of a reply by Solicitor Thurman enclosing a memorandum from Commissioner Hugh Smith of the Bureau of Fisheries. The reasons for the opposition were stated in part as follows:

"The taking over the control of the fisheries by the territory would undoubtedly mean the appointment of local men to enforce the law and administer all of the duties pertaining to the industry. It has been thought by some that the appointment of men who are more or less identified and linked with local interests is not as conducive to an impartial handling of the situation as is the case when men are brought in from the outside." An added objection was the smallness and transient character of Alaska's population.

No reports from other departments were received. Franklin K. Lane, Secretary of the Department of the Interior, which had general jurisdiction over Alaska, as well as direct responsibility for several of its most important federal agencies, and had expressed great concern for Alaska in his annual reports, was silent.

Wickersham's bill for full territorial government as well as other bills introduced by him to transfer the fisheries to territorial control ran directly counter to the efforts of the canned-salmon industry to deprive Alaska of its right to tax. The result proved a stand-off. The provisions depriving Alaska of the power to tax the fisheries were ultimately to be deleted from the legislation. The impasse arose from the fact that while the industry and the bureau were in agreement on not giving Alaska control of its fisheries or the right to tax them, industry and bureau could not agree on conservation measures, and so no legislation on any aspect of this issue was enacted for another eight years. By that time Alaska's taxation of fisheries had gone on so long that it had become an established practice. Alaska's delegates, moreover, were on hand at every hearing to make a last-ditch fight against the withdrawal of that right.

But neither did the territory gain an inch in the direction of full territorial government. If the opponents of increased home rule did not succeed in turning the clock back, they at least managed to keep its hands motionless.

In a comprehensive review of the struggle for more autonomy for Alaska, delivered in the House, July 25, 1916, Wickersham quoted the plank in the platform of the Democratic territorial convention of the preceding May 24th asking that the right to legislate concerning fish and game be transferred to the territorial legislature. He pointed out that the presidential appointee to the governorship had strongly endorsed the transfer of the fisheries and full territorial government, but that these expressions no longer registered with the national Democratic administration. He pointed out that the House Committee on Territories which declined to report his bill out was composed of ten Democrats and six Republicans; that Secretary of Commerce Redfield was a subordinate of the President, and that both of these would have been expected to follow declared administration policy. Wickersham reported that the President had refused, a year earlier, to assist him in getting legislation to transfer control of the fisheries to Alaska.[22] And with evident bitterness the Delegate offered "this word of warning and advice to Alaskans," born, as he said of his experience with the "full territorial government" bill:

"Full territorial government for Alaska will never be accomplished as long as the Bureau and the Alaska Fish Trust can prevent it." [23]

Wickersham added: "The power thus sought for the people will be obtained by statehood more certainly than in any other way." He realized that statehood would probably be even more difficult to achieve than "full territorial government." Nevertheless he introduced a statehood bill—on March 30, 1916, "the forty-ninth anniversary of the signing of the Treaty of the Purchase of Alaska," his diary records. It was the first Alaska statehood bill, the forerunner of many that were to come.

The Bureaus Move In

The most civilized country in the world cannot give satisfactory government to a distant people, because their interests and aims are not identical. No satisfactory administration . . . can ever be made by a bureau located two thousand miles away. What seems to be justice to the agent appears to be tyranny to the citizen. A bureau obsessed with the importance of its work is always endeavoring to extend the field of its operation and to enlarge its force. It is continually grasping for more power.

SENATOR JOHN C. SHAFROTH OF COLORADO,
SEPTEMBER 22, 1914

FRANKLIN K. LANE, Secretary of the Interior in Woodrow Wilson's cabinet, was deeply concerned about Alaska.

"We have committed ourselves to a new policy of development in Alaska," he declared, citing President Wilson's first message to Congress. Secretary Lane's first annual report dealt extensively and sympathetically with the need and with ways of carrying out that policy. Upon consideration he felt that new machinery was needed. Within a few months he set forth his program in a special publication, entitled "Red Tape in the Government of Alaska," which analyzed the problem as he saw it and proposed a remedy.[1]

Instead of one government in Alaska, Lane wrote, "we have a number, interlocked, overlapped, cumbersome and confusing." There was "a government of the forests, a government of the fisheries, one of the reindeer and natives, another of the cables and telegraphs." There was a government "for certain public lands and forests," and another "for other lands and forests."

Each of these governments was "intent upon its own particular business, jealous of its own success and prerogatives." In their zeal for their particular assignments these "long-distance representatives of bureaus located in Washington," more or less unrelated and independent in their operation, were apt to lose sight of the fact that they all represented the same interest and purpose.

Secretary Lane's broadside cited chapter and verse:

A citizen who wanted to lease an island for fox farming sought for several months—vainly—by correspondence with three different federal departments to ascertain which had the jurisdiction and authority to make the lease. It finally developed that none of them had.

The fact was that certain islands could be leased for fur farming by the Department of Commerce; other adjoining islands could not be leased, but could be acquired under certain conditions from the Department of the Interior after complying with the requirements of the general land laws; still other islands reserved for special purposes were under the control of the Department of Agriculture.

The land laws were so encumbered with red tape that citizens would struggle for years to get a patent to a homestead. The cost of surveying had to be borne by the homesteader on top of his effort and investment in improvements. At times, after unaccountable delays, action could be secured only by hiring an attorney whose fees were added to the homesteader's costs. These difficulties were encountered in simple, undisputed claims. If there was a conflict with another claimant or with a government withdrawal, the difficulties and delays were still further increased. Homesteads in the extensive national forest areas were further complicated by the necessity of securing clearances successively from two federal agencies, the General Land Office of the Department of the Interior and the Forest Service of the Department of Agriculture—with their various sub-agencies. The sub-agencies had to be satisfied that the land sought did not contain coal, mineral or petroleum deposits, that the land was not valuable for forest purposes on the one hand, and good for agriculture on the other. Varieties of affidavits had to be secured. In some cases the papers made so many trips back and forth to Washington that it was impossible to trace their journeys, and before securing the patent, if an error had been made somewhere the papers might be found scattered between various departments. Town sites, presumably available under the land laws to the extent of 640 acres upon application of a community numbering two hundred people, required from three to ten years to be processed. The people of Valdez made application in 1899 but did not receive their patent until 1912, after thirteen years of effort.

The game laws—important because wild life as a food supply was essential to prospectors and homesteaders as well as furnishing a livelihood to fur hunters and trappers—were in Lane's words "badly mixed." Brown bears were classified as game animals—and therefore protected—and under the Department of Agriculture. Black bears, on the other hand, were classed as fur-bearing animals and under the jurisdiction of the Department of Commerce. The vicious brown bear and grizzly, dangerous to human life and destructive of cattle, were safeguarded, while the harmless black bear was not. The situation was further complicated for Alaskans in that black bear litters often contain a brown cub, a color phase of the species. The question would then arise, whether such was merely *a* brown bear, or *the* brown bear, meaning the larger species, popularly known as the Kodiak bear and prized by big-game hunters, although this largest of carnivores was found not only on Kodiak Island but was widely distributed throughout Alaska. A few years later the situation was further complicated, when after the setting aside of Mt. McKinley National Park and Katmai National Monument, the bears within them, both brown and black, and both fully protected, came under the jurisdiction of the Department of the Interior.[2]

The remedy Lane proposed was the consolidation of the greater part of the federal functions in Alaska under a development board. And so a bill (S. 4318) was introduced by Senator George Earle Chamberlain of Oregon providing for the appointment of three men by the President subject to Senate confirmation to whom should be transferred the care, use and disposition in Alaska of all reserved and unreserved lands, including forests and water resources therein, fish and fisheries, reindeer, mines and minerals, Indians, Eskimos, roads and "all other matters or things now subject or which may be made subject to national ownership, care, disposition, control or regulation." The board, whose members were to reside in Alaska, was to be under supervision of the Secretary of the Interior.

In stating the bill's purpose Senator Chamberlain declared:

"One of the great obstacles in the way of the development of Alaska has been that it takes so long to accomplish anything . . . that it has practically amounted to a denial of justice to would-be settlers." Illustrating his point, he added that it sometimes took about eight months to secure action for a right of way through a forest for a prospector or other person, and the object of the bill was to obviate these difficulties.[3]

However, this legislation and its similarly intentioned successors would be before Congress more than eight *years* and then be unable to secure action for a right of way through the forest of bureaucratic opposition.

The board bill got nowhere during the remaining seven years of the Wilson administration, while the Sixty-third, Sixty-fourth, Sixty-fifth and Sixty-sixth Congresses came and went. But as the Harding administration took over, a similar version (H.R. 5694) was introduced in the first session of the Sixty-seventh Congress by Representative Charles F. Curry of California, now Chairman of the House Committee on Territories. Its chief value was to lie in producing another extensive record of the red tape against which Secretary Lane had inveighed seven years before. Said tape had, if anything, become more tangled in the interval.

The hearings opened with an unexceptionable—but by this time not wholly unfamiliar—declaration of purpose:

"We have possessed this great territory for fifty-three years," said Chairman Curry. "There has been small effort to settle it with people who will make it their home. There has been no broad, helpful policy. There has been neglect, reservation, hindrance, obstruction. . . . Numberless administrations have urged the necessity of 'doing something' for Alaska, of 'developing the territory,' but nothing has been done. The time for action has arrived. Words will not develop the territory." [4]

Representative Albert Johnson of Washington, the ranking Republican member of the committee, commented:

". . . From 1906 to 1920 we had not only inflicted on Alaska, our last frontier, a policy of restriction and reservation absolutely prohibitive to its development, but, as if to make up for our lack of interest and action, we more extravagantly and unwisely inflicted upon her a multiplicity of governmental agencies without any centralized responsible head, which, administered from Washington at a distance of from four thousand to six thousand miles by different departments, bureaus and divisions, caused jealousy and confusion and resulted in inefficiency and waste." [5]

The hearings disclosed that thirty-eight federal bureaus were operating in Alaska "overlapping each other, and often in conflict with each other in jurisdiction." [6] They revealed that the difficulties in securing title to land were undiminished. The case of one would-be settler was cited who had been trying since 1907 to get a patent on his homestead, and in 1921, fourteen years later, had not yet succeeded.[7] Representative Albert Johnson stated that claimants whose unsettled appeals had been reposing in the Department of the Interior for years, were "dying off on account of old age." [8]

Delay, duplication and waste were illustrated by the practice of one bureau, the Forest Service, of sending a surveying party from its district office in Portland to survey a prospective homestead, when the surveying party of another bureau, the General Land Office, was on the ground, surveying an adjacent applicant's tract. The expense of these surveying parties, it was pointed out, was heavy, because after leaving their steamer they nearly always had to charter a private vessel to get to the place nearest the area to be surveyed.[9]

On Kodiak Island the cattle and sheep being raised by the experiment station of the States Relations Service of the Department of Agriculture were being regularly killed off by the brown bear, which were under the protection of the Biological Survey, another bureau of the same department.[10] The two bureaus reflected the differences that existed between their respective charges. The question was asked how the individual cattle raiser, without benefit of government support, could meet such a situation. Protests from two successive governors, John F.A. Strong and Thomas Riggs, Jr., against the protection of the brown bear were read into the record.[11]

The failure of executive agencies to function, as well as the obstacles imposed by legislation, were jointly illustrated in the applications for power development sought for local sawmills, homesteads or urban development. O.C. Merrill, Executive Secretary of the Federal Power Commission, testified that the commission was composed of the Secretaries of War, Interior and Agriculture. The bill creating it had provided that the work of the commission should be performed through those three departments "as far as possible." But these last four words were stricken before the bill's final passage, and the Comptroller of the Treasury had ruled that the commission could employ no personnel of its own but had to borrow it from the departments concerned. To pass on an application in the national forests of Alaska—within which practically all the power sites applied for were located—the commission was dependent on reports from the Forest Service of the Department of Agriculture and the Geological Survey of the Department of the Interior. Out of twenty-two applications from Alaska, nineteen had been completed as far as the commission could go, and had been duly advertised, but although reports had been requested of the Department of Agriculture and of the Department of the Interior, none had been received. Meanwhile the powerless applicants waited.[12]

Whether the proposed legislation transferring most of the federal agencies in Alaska to a board would have improved a situation that obviously required remedial action would never be determined. A number of witnesses felt that the people of Alaska should participate in the management of agencies whose activities played so important a part in the Alaskans' lives.

Charles Sheldon, naturalist, big-game hunter and author of various books on the wild life of Alaska and the Yukon, testified to his belief that "the fundamental principle in protecting Alaskan game consists in a law which has the approval and the backing of the Alaskan people themselves." [13] Delegate Dan Sutherland believed, as had his predecessor Wickersham, that the territorial authorities should have control of their wild life as well as of their fisheries.

E. Lester Jones, a former Deputy Commissioner of Fisheries, and currently Director of the United States Coast and Geodetic Survey and an International Boundary Commissioner, wanted the legislation to assure that the governor and legislators of Alaska would not be mere figureheads and that it would be laying the foundation of their future handling of their own affairs.[14] This approach was not in line with the thinking of the committee chairman who declared that "this bill and this board cannot have anything to do with the local government of Alaska," [15] and had long been strongly on record against the transfer of the fisheries to Alaska, as well as against the legislature's right to tax the fisheries.[16]

The development-board legislation failed, however, perhaps because in the words of Representative Albert Johnson, "the cabinet officers or their representatives rarely can agree to the loosening up of anything they control. . . . It is hard to pry it from one cabinet place to another." [17]

The testimony of the cabinet officers and their representatives bore out Representative Johnson's dictum. Henry C. Wallace, Secretary of Agriculture in President Harding's cabinet, wrote the committee at length saying:

"We have in Alaska the opportunity to create a second Norway. Under intelligent management these forests can be made to produce for all time to come a quantity of paper equivalent to one-third of the present annual requirements of the United States," and he concluded that that prospect and much else would be jeopardized by the proposed legislation.[18]

To this Chairman Curry replied that the opportunity to make a second Norway had been "within our grasp" for the past fifty-three years, but that bureau control had depopulated Alaska for the past twenty years.[19]

The Assistant Secretary of Commerce, C. H. Huston, speaking for his department, declared that "the present condition of the Alaskan fisheries" which he termed "critical" could not be handled by a development board, and that instead remedial legislation was needed to do away with the "obsolete law, limited authority and inadequate funds," under which the Bureau of Fisheries was functioning.[20]

Defense by the bureaus was in fact interspersed with counterattack. Edward W. Nelson, Chief of the Biological Survey, one of the bureaus proposed for transfer, felt that Alaska's interests under bureau management were as well cared for as was possible "under the handicap of obsolete legislation and the lack of funds" for proper administration.

"Most of the difficulties relating to federal administration in Alaska," declared Nelson, "are not due to inefficiency but . . . to the inadequate laws . . . and to the utterly inadequate appropriations," and added, "the final responsibility comes back to Congress which makes the laws and the appropriations." [21]

A similar view, expressed more mildly by E. Lester Jones of the Coast and Geodetic Survey, was that Alaska's condition was "not altogether due to mismanagement on the part of the federal bureaus," but that it was "partly due to the failure to make proper appropriations to carry on the work there and also the failure to protect the Alaskan's interests with proper laws." [22]

Support for this view came from a committee member. "Would it not be true to state," asked Representative Albert Johnson of Washington, "that a dead hand lies on Alaska largely because of congressional action of a kind that had prevented capital from going there . . . and that while Alaska is suffering for the want of development, the various bureaus . . . in Alaska have done the best that could be done with the limited appropriations?" [23]

But Chairman Curry countered the counterattack with vigor. To the statement of Ward T. Bower, Chief Agent of the Alaska Service of the Bureau of Fisheries, that if the bureau hadn't functioned properly it was "due to a lack of money . . . and inadequate laws" and that "the responsibility is on Congress," Curry retorted:[24]

"Not always. I have seen Congress try to legislate year after year, and . . . prevented from carrying out its will by the bureaus. . . . I do not believe I should sit quiet as a member of Congress and hear it said that the lack of necessary legislation is due to the inactivity of Congress. It is due to the bureaus themselves. . . . They are jealous of their prerogatives and of each other and . . . I have seen many good bills that passed the House killed in the Senate, and many good bills that passed the Senate killed in the House by the direct influence of the bureaus. The bureaus have no strict party politics; they may be either Republicans or Democrats, but they are always bureaucrats. All they want to do is to get right with the people in office at the time." [25]

Apparently this conflict—as far as Alaska was concerned—was a draw, for the bill did not pass. Congress for the next twenty years was to continue to legislate and appropriate for Alaska much as it had, and the bureaus were to continue in Alaska much as they had been. Representative Curry, however, claimed that the mere introduction of his bill, and the threat of transfer of functions, had had some beneficial effect, saying:

"Now the Forestry Service in Alaska has not been good, and I do not think it is good now. It has been improved probably since the bill was introduced, but before that it had no representative in Alaska." [26] Earlier in the hearings he had pointed out that on January 1, 1921, the Forest Service had established an Alaska division with headquarters at Juneau.

Alaska After a Half-Century of United States Rule

We are likely to think that all these outlying and thinly peopled places are wastes. I suspect that they contribute more to the race than we think. I am glad that there are still some places of mystery, some reaches of hope, some things far beyond us, some spaces to conjure up dreams. . . . They add much to the ambition of the race; they make for strength, for courage, and for renewal.

LIBERTY HYDE BAILEY, 1915

THERE was hope in the Alaskan air at the century's second mid-decade. The promises of Woodrow Wilson's "new freedom" had been specifically extended to Alaska. Work on a railroad that would link the Pacific Coast with the interior had actually begun after fifteen years of disappointments. This time the Government of the United States, by undertaking its construction, guaranteed its certain and speedy completion. A coal-leasing law had been enacted which, it was anticipated, would release Alaska's long-imprisoned fuel resources, and thereby stimulate mining and other development in the vast interior. These, too, Washington had announced, were only the first steps. Others would follow.

Alaska had its own legislature which, despite the widely recognized limitations on its authority, was providing locally needed and long-overdue legislation and, pending the full territorial government promised by the national administration, could, through memorials and resolutions, present the aspirations and needs of Alaskans to Congress. The territorial legislature had already made a vigorous start in making them known. With a declaredly friendly and sympathetic administration these pleas would be heeded!

Mining, which had declined in 1913—the second successive year in which the work of the U. S. Geological Survey in Alaska, on which the industry increasingly relied, had been drastically curtailed because of late appropriations—took an upward swing in 1914.[1] A noteworthy feature of that year was the large number of investigations by private investors in search of properties warranting development on a large scale—a result of the railroad and coal legislation. The early establishment of copper smelters in Alaska's coastal districts was confidently forecast by Alfred H. Brooks, as well as the utilization of some of Alaska's iron ores at possibly no distant date.[2]

An all-time Alaska peak in mining in 1915 was attained with a value of $32,854,229, a bonanza chiefly attributable to the great copper production at high prices—some 86,509,375 pounds worth $15,139,581 —the high price a consequence of World War I demand. Thirteen copper mines, contrasted with four in 1914, were operating, six in the Ketchikan district, although the bulk of the production came from the Kennecott properties of the Alaska Syndicate in the Chitina district.

The next year, 1916, eclipsed all previous records, with a total mineral production for Alaska valued at $48,632,138—an increase of almost 50 per cent over the previous banner year. Again this was chiefly due to copper, with eighteen mines producing the enormous output of 119,602,028 pounds valued at $29,484,291. Again the greater part of this came from the Kennecott mines, but had the nine smaller mines along the coast in the Ketchikan district been able to secure transportation and smelting facilities for their ore, their output and the total production would have been larger.

Gold production also reached its highest point in quantity and value since 1909, with a total of 834,068 ounces worth $17,241,713—figures exceeded only in the peak years of 1906 to 1909. Alaska gold mining was beginning to show signs of a transition. Some $11,140,000 worth came from the placers, but nearly a fourth of this was recovered by the thirty-four dredges in operation that year, a sign that the primitive tools of the pioneers—the rocker, cradle and pan—were being replaced by modern machinery, and that the industry was increasingly becoming big business. It was already so in the twenty-nine gold-lode or hard-rock mines which, principally in the Juneau district, but also in the interior, in 1906 produced over a third of Alaska's gold. Mining in the Juneau area suffered a severe setback in 1917 with the Treadwell disaster—the caving in and flooding by the salt waters of the Gastineau Channel of two of the mines on Douglas Island which were never reopened. Some of the lode operators in the

Fairbanks area were awaiting the cheapening of transportation which the railroad would bring.

Containing much promise were the discoveries and increased output of other minerals, albeit in small quantities. The first antimony had been shipped out of Alaska in 1915. Tungsten ore was discovered in the same year in the Fairbanks district and by the end of 1916 some forty-seven tons were sold for which the operators received $103,300. Tin production, which had been proceeding on a minor scale for a decade and a half on the Seward Peninsula, reached a new high with the production of 139 tons of metallic tin, valued at $121,000. Lead, likewise previously mined in insignificant totals, also reached a new peak with 820 tons, valued at $109,120. Prospecting was done on chrome deposits in the Kenai Peninsula. Molybdenite was found in various places. Nickel and cobalt were reported on Chichagof Island, and the Geological Survey indicated that sufficient platinum had been found in widely separated localities in the gold placers to justify a special search for it.[3] Mining in Alaska employed somewhat more than eight thousand men in the years 1911 to 1914, 9,110 in 1915, the high point being reached the next year, 1916, with a total, in all forms of productive mining, of 9,840. There was decline thereafter—to 7,990 in 1917, and then a sharp drop, to 6,010 in 1918, 4,710 in 1919, to 4,570 in 1920.[4]

Mining in Alaska was given federal assistance by the establishment of a mine-experiment station in Fairbanks in 1917. This was one of eight such stations authorized by Congress in 1915 for the mining states, the total number being increased four years later to ten. One of the important services that it began to render was the identification of mineral specimens submitted to it by prospectors, and of making assays of samples of ore to establish their mineral content and their value. A technical library was also at the disposal of the public.

In these years, great as were the gains in mineral production, the fisheries were destined to surpass them in value. The Alaska salmon pack, which had exceeded a million cases in 1899, two million in 1901, and had hovered around that figure for a dozen years, now began to soar. It reached an all-time high of 2,820,963 cases in 1911, leaped to 4,060,129 in 1912, receded slightly to 3,756,433 in 1913, and then rose again, reaching a new peak in production every year for the next five years, 4,167,832 cases in 1914, 4,489,002 in 1915, 4,919,589 in

1916, 5,922,320 in 1917, and culminating in 1918 at the dizzy height of 6,677,369 cases as Alaska swung into its second half-century under the American flag. Prices on the whole kept close pace with quantity. Prior to 1910 the pack had never reached ten million dollars in annual value. The values of the successive packs thereafter were: 1911, $14,-532,188; 1912, $16,291,917; 1913—a recession year—$13,531,604; 1914, $18,920,589; 1915, $18,653,015; 1916, $23,269,429; 1917, $46,-304,090; 1918, $51,041,949.[5] The pack had quintupled in value in a decade.

The number of canneries, and of those employed in fishing and fish processing, increased substantially. The salmon canneries tripled in the ten years from 1909 to 1918, inclusive, from forty-five to 135.[6] They represented, with their boats and equipment, in 1918, an investment of $63,901,397 out of a total in all Alaskan fisheries of $73,764,-289. The salmon were caught by 552 traps and by fishermen operating 838 seines, 4,367 gill nets and trolling. Altogether the canned-salmon industry in that year employed 31,213 persons—an all-time high in dollars, plants, gear and employees.[7] Profits were fabulous. In 1916 only three Alaska companies failed to make a profit, an extraordinary showing since thirteen new canneries were established that year. Twenty-one companies made less than 15 per cent; thirty-one made between 15 and 50 per cent; eleven made between 50 and 100 per cent; and eleven made over 100 per cent.[8] Nineteen eighteen was still bigger, with an all-time record value of the pack of $51,041,949, although seventeen new canneries helped divide this bonanza. Salmon —other than canned—mild cured, pickled, smoked, frozen and fresh —added about two and a quarter million dollars' worth of products. A few warning voices were raised against overfishing, but both the industry, which was enjoying a heyday, and the Bureau of Fisheries, were unperturbed.[9]

The products of other fisheries—halibut, herring, cod, whales, clams, crabs, shrimp and miscellaneous fish, with a combined investment of $9,863,432—totaled in 1918 the handsome sum of $5,629,-947.[10] Altogether these were flush years for those who sought a livelihood from the sea. A relatively small part of this opulence, however, remained in Alaska. Not only was the ownership predominantly "outside," where it bought the bulk of its supplies, but of the 31,231 people employed by the salmon canners, only one-sixth, 5,251, were classed as natives and twelve-months-out-of-the-year residents. The greater number, of whom 17,693 were classed as whites, and the remaining 8,269 Chinese, Japanese, Filipino, Mexican and miscellaneous, for the most part brought up from "down below," received their pay at the end of the season after returning to their ports of embarkation—Seattle, Portland or San Francisco.[11]

Yet while Alaska's marine cornucopia was pouring out its superabundance—with unimpaired and inexhaustible fecundity, according to all the best current authorities, industrial and governmental—the third Alaska legislature, in 1917, set aside what for it in those days was a substantial sum, $80,000, for fish hatcheries. To provide them it created a Board of Fish Commissioners with the additional duties of directing "the protection and care of natural spawning grounds in such streams and lakes as in the opinion of the board require such care and protection." [12] While the federal regulatory agency which Congress had endowed with all the power and responsibility of conserving Alaska's salmon was proceeding on the happy assumption that there were as many fish in the sea as had ever been caught, the territorial authorities thought otherwise. And, unlike the parental legislative body in Washington, they were enacting legislation to do something about it.

That third legislature, incidentally, meeting in the semicentennial year of Alaska's coming under the flag, enacted some other legislation not free from symbolism. In addition to the accepted American holidays it established as holidays March 30th, commemorating the signing of the Treaty of Purchase, to be called Seward's Day, and the 18th of October, when the Stars and Stripes were raised over the newly acquired terrain, to be called Alaska Day. And it designated as the territorial flower the forget-me-not.

Furs to a value of $1,143,601 were exported from Alaska in 1916 and $1,338,599 in 1917. These figures included $211,330 and $274,200 respectively of fur-seal pelts from the Pribilofs, where the depleted herds, now under government management, were being slowly restored, although the Alaskan economy derived no direct benefits from that resource. The other furs, in the order of quantity, were muskrat, lynx (1916 and 1917 being years of the height of a rabbit cycle on which the lynx thrive), mink, the several varieties of foxes, and in financial value, lynx were first, fur seal second, red fox third, white fox fourth, cross fox fifth and mink sixth.

The 1,280 reindeer imported from Siberia had by 1917 multiplied to an estimated ninety-five thousand, supplying in addition to food and materials a cash income of $91,430 for the Eskimo population and helping to stabilize their economy. This growing meat supply was catching the eye of local commercial interests which visualized a profitable export business in reindeer venison, and soon would attempt it.

Farming, despite great handicaps, had made some slender beginnings. Four agricultural-experiment stations conducted with modest appropriations by the States Relations Service of the United States Department of Agriculture had been operating variously since the turn of the century at Sitka, Kodiak, Fairbanks and Rampart, testing the possibilities of these widely separated regions' differing soils and diverse climates. They had demonstrated the feasibility of Alaskan agriculture. Dr. C. C. Georgeson, a Dane by birth, a competent and enthusiastic agronomist, had had overall responsibility from the beginning. A fifth station at Copper Center had been abandoned because of poor soil in that area, but a new station in the Matanuska Valley had been authorized. At the end of the century's second decade nearly four hundred families were deriving a livelihood, wholly or in part, from agricultural pursuits. The majority were in the Tanana, Susitna and Matanuska valleys. Two score were scattered around the shores of Cook Inlet, an equal number in southeastern Alaska. A dairy on the outskirts of nearly every incorporated town was supplying limited but increasing quantities of fresh milk and cream and competing with the already traditional condensed-milk can of the earlier days. While the markets for dairy products and other produce were of necessity local, homesteaders in the Susitna and Matanuska valleys in the summer of 1917 produced several hundred tons of potatoes, some of which were for the first time shipped by boat to other Alaskan towns, competing successfully with the outside product, and large quantities of other vegetables and three hundred tons of a new variety of turnip were exported to Puget Sound. These sold at from 1 to 1½ cents higher than the local product.[13]

Root vegetables had also been shipped south annually since 1911 from the Chilkat and Eagle River valleys of southeastern Alaska, and in 1918 fifty tons of turnips sold in the Seattle market for $2 a sack of from eighty-five to ninety pounds each, at a price from 50 to 100 per cent higher than the Washington turnips.[14]

The handicaps—besides those attendant upon venturing into a virgin field—against which the farmers had to contend were lack of markets, lack of roads, lack of financing while they were clearing their land, high transportation rates and difficulties in getting titles to their lands, the cost of whose surveys they also had to pay.

Alaska was continuing to import most of its lumber. Its value exceeded a million dollars in 1916, rising to $1,343,336 in 1917, to $1,817,328 in 1918 and receding only slightly to $1,604,508 in 1919.[15] Although the only merchantable timber in the forest reserves was overripe and much of it was dying on the stump, the Forest Service, which controlled it, was permitting only a very limited use of this resource.[16] Within the restrictions imposed, some fifty small sawmills and shingle mills were cutting, for local use, over forty million board feet annually in the last three years of the second decade, to a value in 1917 of nearly $60,000.[17]

In 1917 Alaska's commerce (virtually all with the United States) for the first time passed the $100,000,000 mark. Imports to Alaska from the states totaled $38,427,618 and Alaska's exports $76,228,858. Imports had risen steadily in all but one of the five previous years: $18,809,270 in 1912; $20,179,547 in 1913; $21,929,460 in 1914; $20,792,609 in 1915; $26,502,311 in 1916. The principal items dollarwise were, first, hardware and machinery; second, provisions; third, lumber. The great increase in 1917 could be ascribed to war-increased prices rather than to increased consumption. The large hardware and machinery items were attributable to the great increase in the number of canneries, to mining, and to the government railroad construction.

Exports also increased markedly except in the years 1913 and 1914. They were $39,088,533 in 1912; $38,721,583 in 1913; $33,920,884 in 1914; $42,651,742 in 1915; $65,921,074 in 1916. The principal exports in value were first, canned salmon, next gold—except in 1916 and 1917 when copper surpassed them both—but was otherwise third, fish products, other than canned salmon, fourth, and furs fifth.

Alaska–U.S. trade, with higher price levels, soared still further in 1918, imports reaching $44,280,075 and exports $84,723,829.

The foundations of a comprehensive public-school system were laid in 1917—fifty years after Alaska had come under the American flag. The first legislature in 1913 had passed an act (Chapter 44) making school attendance compulsory for children between the ages of eight and sixteen, making the parents responsible and levying fines upon them for any unjustified absences of their children. But as the act provided that the complaints of the school boards in truancy cases were to be laid before the United States commissioner, it was invalid until validated by the passage by Congress in 1914 of Wickersham's bill, H.R. 11740, which became the first amendment to the organic act, permitting the utilization, for the execution of territorial laws, of federal officials stationed in Alaska. The Second Territorial Legislature therefore repassed the compulsory-attendance act.

The second legislature, also, bent on establishing "a general and uniform" school system throughout the territory, passed two acts which established a territorial board of education. It consisted of the Governor, the Treasurer, and an assistant superintendent of public instruction, who was to be appointed by the Governor. The assistant superintendent was to be a qualified educator and his minimal qualifications were stated in the law. He was to establish a territorial curriculum and its educational standards. The number of children required to establish a school district was reduced from twenty to ten. These changes contravened the so-called Nelson Act, which had established the larger number and made the Governor the superintendent of public instruction, ex-officio, a position for which he might seldom be expected to have the requisite professional training. The new territorial acts made some minor changes in the election of schools boards. But as the organic act of 1912 specifically prohibited the Alaska legislature from altering, amending or modifying "the Act entitled 'An Act to Provide for the Maintenance of Roads, the Establishment and Maintenance of Schools, and the Care and Support of Insane Persons in the District of Alaska and for other Purposes' approved January 27, 1905, and all Acts Amendatory Thereof," the new school legislation was ruled void by the Solicitor of the Department of the Interior. The legislature had obviously anticipated the situation, for in a House Joint Memorial (No. 12) it requested Congress to turn over to the territory the responsibility for the education of its "white children and children of mixed blood who lead a civilized life," which, the memorial pointed out, was wholly paid for by taxes on territorial activities. Wickersham's bill, limited to annulment of the interdiction to alter the school provisions of the Nelson Act, passed in the closing days of the Sixty-fourth Congress. The absurdity of the original provision was too evident to justify congressional opposition.

Armed with this dispensation, the third legislature, in 1917, completely revised all previous school legislation. One act authorized the creation of school districts outside of incorporated towns where there was a population of one hundred or more, upon the petition to the district judge of fifty or more citizens outlining the boundaries of the proposed district.[18] The judge would then order an election, and if ratified by a majority of the electors dwelling within it, the proposed district would come into existence. The authorities of the district, elected by popular vote, were empowered to levy real- and personal-property taxes, not to exceed 1 per cent of the assessed valuation, for school purposes. Thus an entirely new source of revenue for schools was created.

Another act provided that the territory would refund to each incorporated town 75 per cent of the cost of operation and maintenance of its schools.[19] Construction of school buildings remained the town's school-district responsibility—every incorporated town being constituted also as a school district, with a popularly elected school board.

A third act created a new Territorial Board of Education, composed of the Governor as chairman and the four senior senators—one from each division—which selected a commissioner of education, who must be a thoroughly qualified educator.[20] These acts would be revised from time to time in their details: the composition of the board would be altered to one without the Governor as a member, but appointed by him and subject to confirmation by the legislature. The proportion of refund to the towns would be modified in proportion to their enrollments. But a system of public education was established which was to be unwaveringly cherished by the people of Alaska, and would measure well up to standards by which any American public-school system might be judged. The territory had made itself wholly responsible for the conduct of the rural schools; it would furnish the greater part of the support of the schools in the municipalities. For the next thirty-five years primary and secondary education would be the principal item in every territorial budget, incurring its maximum biennial expenditure; and no request by the board for the education of Alaska's children would be denied or curtailed by any of the twenty-one legislatures which succeeded each other. Schools would repeatedly be the beneficiaries of earmarking of funds, as with the so-called poll tax in 1919, and of new levies. Moreover high pecuniary standards of recognition of the worth and importance of the teacher would be set and maintained in Alaska, contrasting with the widely underpaid teaching profession prevalent in the States. Thus there was early established a striking example of what the people of Alaska could do in an important field in which they had authority and responsibility.

In the school year, 1917-18, there were schools in the territory's fifteen incorporated towns—Cordova, Douglas, Eagle, Fairbanks, Haines, Iditarod, Juneau, Ketchikan, Nome, Petersburg, Seward, Skagway, Tanana, Valdez and Wrangell—and in forty schools outside the towns. The school enrollment in the towns was 1,778, with sixty-eight teachers; outside the towns, 1,364, with fifty teachers. The next year, 1918-19, nine new districts had been organized and there were twenty-three more teachers, although the school enrollment had increased only by the negligible number of twenty-four pupils, evidences of the flexibility of the new school legislation.

Juneau in 1916 issued bonds for $75,000 to construct an adequate school building. Specific legislation had to be sought from the Congress—as required by the organic act of 1912 whenever the territory or a municipality desired to borrow money—and was obtained. Other Alaska towns would follow suit.

Evidence of the desire on the part of Alaskans to consider Alaska as a place of permanent residence was that 56.9 per cent of the school children were born in Alaska.

The territorial school system provided education for "white children and those of mixed blood leading a civilized life." In the Indian and Eskimo villages another school system supported by the federal government and conducted by the Bureau of Education of the Department of the Interior had been developing since its establishment by Sheldon Jackson under the authority of the organic act of 1884. In 1918 it operated sixty-five schools with a total enrollment of 3,600, individual school enrollments ranging from twelve to 169. Its appropriation, that year, was $215,000.

A native medical service for Alaska was initiated in 1916—the health work among the Eskimos and Indians having been previously performed by the Bureau of Education, which was operating small hospitals for natives only in Juneau, at Kanakanak on Bristol Bay and at Nulato on the Yukon. The original appropriation for the new medical service was $25,000, which in 1917 was doubled.

By 1917 the Alaska Road Commission of the Army, which had been functioning since 1905, had built 980 miles of wagon road, 549 miles of sled road, and 2,291 miles of trail. It had expended $4,097,611, of which $2,335,966 had been appropriated by Congress to the War Department and $1,805,646 had been contributed by Alaska through the Alaska fund.[21] The principal wagon road, 371 miles long, finally connected Valdez, on the Pacific Ocean, with Fairbanks. The other roads were scattered, relatively short, stretches from towns into their environs, to mines, or from navigable waters to mines. They were practically nonexistent in southeastern Alaska, where because of the land being almost totally a national forest, highway construction was under the Bureau of Public Roads of the Department of Agriculture. In 1916, Congress had passed the Federal Aid Act, but had excluded Alaska from its benefits except for a limited participation under the section providing for construction in the national forests.[22] Alaska's financial obligation, under the matching formula of the Federal Aid Highway Act, which in 1921 amended and amplified the earlier measure, would have been far less than the approximately 44 per cent it had been contributing to the Alaska Road Commission— probably close to one-third of that percentage—or, for the same contribution, would have produced nearly three times the highway mileage.[23] Now there was at least a prospect of applying some funds to the roadless forest areas. The 1917 legislature had also made a substantial beginning by appropriating $400,000 for road construction and maintenance, and these funds would be available for co-operative agreements with the federal road-building agencies.

A dozen daily newspapers were being published in Alaska in 1917. Juneau, Fairbanks and Nome had two, Ketchikan, Skagway, Valdez, Cordova, Seward and the new town of Anchorage, established as the headquarters of the Alaska Railroad, had one. Weeklies were also published in some of these cities and in Chitina, Douglas, Nenana on the railroad, likewise a new town, and the prospective head of navigation for the Tanana and Yukon rivers, Petersburg, a fishing town founded chiefly with an attracted group of sturdy Norwegians, Ruby, a village on the Yukon and the shipping point for a placer-mining district, and Wrangell.

In President Wilson's second State of the Union Message to the Congress on December 8, 1914 he made another reference to Alaska. Urging adequate provisions for the survey and charting of our coasts, he stated that it was "immediately pressing and exigent in connection with the immense coastline of Alaska . . ." adding "ships will not ply thither if those coasts and their many hidden dangers are not thoroughly surveyed and charted. The work is incomplete at almost every point. Ships and lives have been lost in threading what were supposed to be well-known main channels."

This was already an ancient saga to Alaskans, perhaps more ancient than many of them knew, for the need and the peril had been pointed out officially within a few days after the transfer.

"There should be a lighthouse establishment here," wrote William Sumner Dodge, the first collector of customs, and the highest legally constituted government official in Alaska, to his chief, Secretary of the Treasury Hugh McCulloch, on November 10, 1867. It was Dodge's first communication, reporting his arrival on October 18th, and making various recommendations. "The entrance to the harbor is perilous and . . . its necessity is apparent. Previous to the federal occupation of this soil the Russian Governor had maintained a light for the assistance of navigators . . . but since our possession the light has not been kept." Dodge explained that in a tower on the Russian governor's house "situate on a bold bluff of the harbor" on stands were four cups in which seal oil had been burned, and back of these lights was a circular reflector three feet in diameter. The light could be seen six miles. While it was impossible any longer to secure seal oil "as the Russian company are out," Dodge and General Davis had examined the matter and had concluded "that at little expense twelve kerosene lamps, small, can be set in the cups of the present lights and that consumption will not exceed one gallon per night." General Davis would detail a soldier to be lighthouse keeper if Dodge would pay him 46 cents a day, the ordinary amount paid by the government for extra duty. "Thus the expense will be small while property and life may be saved. If therefore the department deems it proper to designate me as superintendent of lights and authorize the necessary expenses incident to it I will so act with pleasure. . . . Meantime considering the necessities of the case I will endeavor to arrange and perfect the lights and maintain them trusting that the department will appreciate the circumstances under which it is done and audit the account of disbursements. Otherwise I shall be the personal loser." [24]

Apparently Dodge was the personal loser for his devoted efforts. No light was permanently established. He was succeeded in a few months by Hiram Ketchum, Jr. On November 24, 1868, Collector Ketchum wrote Secretary of the Treasury McCulloch that his predecessor, Collector Dodge, was "in a very necessitous condition owing to his not having received his pay." On top of his outlays for the light, and the nonreceipt of his own pay as collector of customs, Dodge had, out of his pocket, advanced to Lieutenant Moore of the Revenue Service stationed at Wrangell a part of Moore's pay, which Moore likewise had not received. Ketchum explained that Dodge had exceeded his authority in order to relieve Moore "from the pressure of actual want." [25]

A decade later, in 1878, Special Treasury Agent Morris reported the total lack of lights and of reliable charts, citing the loss of two United States warships, the *Suwanee* and the *Saranac*, in Alaskan waters, and of other craft mostly "on rocks that are not laid down in the charts." [26]

Governor Knapp began listing the annual wrecks off the Alaska coast in his 1890 report, pointing out that the coast was dangerous because of unaccountable currents and sunken rocks, and that these marine disasters were likely to occur with greater frequency unless new and accurate surveys were made. The following year, 1891, he recorded a longer toll of lost vessels, and concluded with the comment that marine underwriters were questioning the advisability of taking risks on vessels going into Alaskan waters until better surveys were made.

Governor Brady resumed the practice of listing the shipwrecks, and in his second report in 1898 called attention to the related need of making Alaska a lighthouse district, a plea which he repeated with increased emphasis in subsequent reports. "In all our vast extent of coast there is not a single lighthouse," he wrote in 1900.[27]

Even before the first appropriation for lights and aids to navigation in Alaska by the first session of the Fifty-sixth Congress in 1900, the United States Lighthouse Board had recommended a separate district for Alaska. Alaska formed part of the Thirteenth Lighthouse District, which also included Washington and Oregon. The board's 1899 report recommended that this vast area be divided "so as to make two districts, one to include Alaskan waters only, with headquarters at Sitka." [28]

On January 9, 1900, Lyman J. Gage, Secretary of the Treasury in President McKinley's cabinet, wrote the Speaker of the House citing the previously expressed view of the Lighthouse Board—repeated at its meeting of the previous day—and enclosing the draft of a proposed bill to raise the statutory number of lighthouse districts from sixteen to seventeen in order to make Alaska the new district.[29]

No action was taken by the Congress despite its newfound gold-rush interest in Alaska, and in 1902 Leslie M. Shaw, Secretary of the Treasury in President Theodore Roosevelt's cabinet, raised the request to two additional districts to include Puerto Rico, adding its weight to Alaska's. Quoting from the board's thrice-repeated recommendations concerning Alaska, Shaw wrote the Speaker of the House:

"The great distance between Alaskan aids to navigation and the offices of the lighthouse inspector and engineer at Portland, Oregon, renders it impossible to maintain Alaskan aids to navigation which the reliability of the service demands . . . the department therefore invites the attention of the Congress and suggests immediate action, especially as what is asked can be done without increase of the appropriations for maintenance of the United States lighthouse establishment." [30]

Even with this concluding clincher Congress did not accept the invitation or comply with the suggestion.

In 1903 Congress transferred the Lighthouse Board from the Treasury Department to the newly created Department of Commerce and Labor which continued to repeat the requests for the two additional lighthouse districts—in 1905, 1906 and 1907. In 1908 it threw Hawaii into the scales, requesting three additional districts.

This triple array, with the added appeal of Uncle Sam's newer acquisitions, was persuasive, although their navigational perils were, admittedly, not comparable to Alaska's: the law was amended to provide nineteen lighthouse districts; and in 1910 Alaska finally became one, with headquarters at Ketchikan.[31]

This was only part of the problem which had long concerned Alaskans and to which President Wilson made alllusion in 1914. The report of the Secretary of Commerce for 1914 devoted forty printed pages to the work of the Coast and Geodetic Survey, to the inadequate appropriations for it, described in dramatic detail the worthlessness of the ships at its disposal, gave a partial list of wrecks in Alaska, illustrated it with photographs of some of these, and presented the need of wire-dragging Alaska coastal waters to locate the submerged rock pinnacles which made these waters uniquely perilous. Ironically the recent wrecks included the government-owned *Armeria*, a new vessel constructed for the Bureau of Lighthouses and assigned to the

Alaska service, and the *Tahoma* of the U. S. Revenue Cutter Service, both of which became total losses when they struck uncharted rock pinnacles.

In the House, Representative William E. Humphrey, R., of Seattle, denounced the refusal of the previous session of Congress to appropriate $40,000 for wire-dragging in Alaska. A small expenditure the previous year for working a wire-drag in one of the main channels between Seattle and Alaska through which two thousand ships carrying forty-three thousand passengers had passed in one season had uncovered fourteen dangerous pinnacles not known before. These rocks rose abruptly from depths of forty to six hundred feet. In six cases they were less than eight feet from the surface, and in no case more than thirty feet. Humphrey cited the recent sinking of the steamer *State of California*, with a loss of thirty-one lives, which had made sixteen previous trips over the same course and had struck a rock where the chart showed a depth of twelve and one-half fathoms. He read into the *Record* a list of 260 wrecks in Alaskan waters since the acquisition of Alaska, a list he termed incomplete, resulting in the loss of 449 lives.

"It is a gruesome list," said Humphrey. "It is a long list of disaster, destruction and death. I hope it may burn its way into the memory of every member of this House so deeply that all the speeches and selfish and ignorant cries about economy that may hereafter be made against these appropriations will not dim it. . . . For this present criminal neglect Congress alone is responsible." [32]

In his address at the centennial celebration of the U. S. Coast and Geodetic Survey, in 1916, Secretary of Commerce William C. Redfield declared:

"We have paid in Alaska twice the whole price of Alaska since we got it, in wrecked vessels not counting the lives of the people on board as worth anything at all. . . We have had very peculiar habits of surveying up there. We have found many rocks by running merchant ships upon them and have had the regular habit of naming the rocks after ships which struck them. You may go along that coast now and pick up rock after rock bearing the names of the ships that were wrecked upon them." [33]

By 1917, fifty years after the acquisition of Alaska, only 9 per cent of Alaska's ocean waterways had been surveyed. But in the nineteen years since the Philippine Islands had been a dependency of the United States, 64 per cent of their coasts had been surveyed. [34] Despite the revelation that the work of surveying Alaska waterways and providing the necessary aids to navigation was "still in an initial stage," [35] the total appropriation for the Coast and Geodetic Survey, which had varied between a low of $204,419 and a high of $261,824 in the six years between 1913 and 1918, was cut to $100,000 for 1917, a figure lower than any annual appropriation since 1906, and to $49,716 in 1919, a figure lower than any appropriation since 1897.[36] A revised and up-to-date list in 1918 by the Alaska Bureau of the Seattle Chamber of Commerce raised the total of ships lost in Alaskan waters to 426, with a loss of 862 lives, not counting ninety vessels which met with total or partial loss on which complete data were lacking.[37] Four years later, E. Lester Jones, Director of the U. S. Coast and Geodetic Survey, testified that at the rate at which the charting of Alaska's coast was proceeding, it would take from forty to sixty years to complete.[38]

As a consequence the high cost of marine insurance, twice the rate or higher to Alaskan ports than was paid to other Pacific ports, and amounting to approximately 10 per cent of the gross operating revenue of the steamship lines serving Alaska, was reflected in increased transportation costs.[39]

Geologically, 80 per cent of Alaska was unsurveyed—including even the accessible oil fields lying near the coast—at the end of the century's second decade. "The present annual appropriation for investigating the mineral resources of Alaska is but $75,000," Dr. Brooks testified by way of explanation.[40]

The bill to construct the Alaska railroad had become law on October 20, 1914. President Wilson promptly appointed a commission to recommend a route. This commission, known as the Alaska Engineering Commission, was composed of William C. Edes, who for twenty-five years had been engaged in locating railways for the Southern Pacific, Central Pacific and Santa Fe Railroads, Lieutenant Frederick Mears, U.S.A., who had had charge of building the Panama Railroad which paralleled the canal, and Thomas Riggs, Jr., engineer, who had surveyed the international boundary between Alaska and Canada, and having come to Alaska in 1897, was familiar with its conditions.

On April 10, 1915, President Wilson announced that what was known as the Susitna route had been selected. This route, starting at the ocean terminus of Seward on Resurrection Bay west of Prince William Sound, was preferred to the one possible alternative, the route east of Prince William Sound, north from Cordova or Valdez. Had the latter route been chosen it would probably have involved the purchase of the Copper River and Northwestern Railroad, and the extension of that road from Chitina to Fairbanks. It would have been somewhat shorter than the Susitna route, but would have crossed no coal fields and fewer promising agricultural areas. The Susitna route had the advantage of passing through more territory, including, first, the Kenai Peninsula. It tapped the Matanuska coal fields, whose fuel had been approved by the Navy, as well as the Nenana coal fields two hundred miles farther north. It passed through the potentially good agricultural areas of the Matanuska and Susitna valleys.

While there was some disappointment among the residents of Cordova and Valdez and those who had interests there that the westerly route had been chosen, the choice was generally approved. With the determination of that route it became clear that the administration would not go to the full extent authorized by the railway bill: it would build *a* railroad, and not railroads; the construction would connect only one, and not "one or more of the open Pacific harbors" with the interior, and the permitted aggregate of a thousand miles would be approximately halved. Incidental to the undertaking, the government purchased the existing seventy-one-mile construction of the Alaska Northern and the thirty-nine miles of the Tanana Valley railroads.

The construction of the railroad, so long awaited, was fated to proceed slowly. When the first requested appropriation of $2,000,000 came up in the House in 1915, it met with resistance. Those who had opposed the project in the first instance now centered their fight on this issue of supplying the authorized funds.

"There is no reason for haste in making this appropriation now. The time is not propitious to begin the construction," declared Representative Samuel J. Tribble, D., of Georgia, and urged that the item be stricken entirely.[41] He was strongly supported by Representative Frederick H. Gillett, R., of Massachusetts.

Representative James S. Davenport, D., of Oklahoma, moved that the appropriation be reduced to $1,000,000.[42] The amendment was debated at length and finally defeated. The attempt was, however, a foretaste of things to come. The next year the $2,000,000 was deducted by the House Appropriations Committee from the $8,471,620 requested by the Engineering Commission. Uncertainty as to the amounts available each year, reduction in the sums requested, and the lateness of the appropriations—four in July, well after the beginning of the construction season—added greatly and needlessly to the cost of the undertaking, and retarded its progress. These costly delays and the rapidly rising prices of materials and labor made legislation requesting an additional $17,000,000 in 1919 necessary.[43] Congress voted the amount reluctantly, as well as another $4,000,000 in 1921, chiefly because an unfinished railroad would have represented total waste.[44]

Congressional foot-dragging was typified in the expression by Representative Frank W. Mondell, R., of Wyoming, consistently against the railroad project, and now, with the return in 1920 of the Republicans to the helm, a power in the House:

"I trust the gentlemen will not be influenced in voting on this bill by any idea that the Committee on Appropriations will include in the first appropriation bill the sum necessary to complete the Alaskan Railroad. I should hope, at least, that the committee would not do that. Our duty is to determine whether the Alaskan Railroad shall be completed; and if so to determine the sum we shall eventually authorize for its completion, leaving with the Appropriations Committee to determine when the appropriation shall be made and the rapidity with which the development and completion of the road shall be carried on." [45]

The Alaska Railroad was finally completed in the summer of 1923 —nine years after its authorization.

But not long thereafter it was revealed that the road was not really completed when President Harding drove the golden spike on July 15th, and would require considerable reconstruction to make it safe.[46]

Mount McKinley National Park, an area of 2,100 square miles (subsequently enlarged to 3,030) was established by act of Congress, February 26, 1917 (39 Stat. 938). Its principal attraction was that it contained the loftiest peak on the North American continent, 20,300 feet high, reputed also to have the greatest *visible* vertical dimension of any mountain on earth. Its Indian name was Denali, signifying "home of the sun." It was rechristened in the summer of 1896 by its discoverer, a prospector named W. A. Dickey, an enthusiastic Republican, after the Republican nominee of that year for the presidency.

The next loftiest peak in the park, and the third highest in Alaska, some 2,500 taller than any in the forty-eight states, was Foraker, 17,000 feet, also named after an Ohio Republican, a United States Senator whose only notable relation to Alaska was opposing and aiding in the defeat of a bill to grant Alaska a delegate.[47]

The third highest peak in the park, Hunter, 14,850 feet, and also higher than any mountain in the forty-eight states, was named after a Miss A. F. Hunter of Newport by Dr. Frederick A. Cook, whose claim to the first ascent of Mount McKinley was given no more credence than his claim to have been the first to reach the North Pole.[48]

The park also included an excellent variety and abundance of Alaska big game—grizzlies, moose, caribou, mountain sheep and wolves. The Alaska Railroad would touch the eastern boundary of the park, some ninety miles east of the mountain, which was not visible at that point, and a highway extending westward would be required to enable visitors to see "the mountain" at reasonably close range.

Katmai National Monument, of 4,215 square miles—and larger than any national park or monument in the States—was created by presidential proclamation September 24, 1918. It enclosed the crater of Mount Katmai, which erupted in June, 1912, as well as the Valley of Ten Thousand Smokes, named by the National Geographic Society, which sent four expeditions there.

The delay in completing the railroad was a severe setback to the economy of interior Alaska and to the protracted anticipations of its people. Nor did the coal-leasing law, finally passed in 1914, fulfill the hopes of speedy development. The Alaska Engineering Commission had begun mining coal for the railroad in the Matanuska Valley at Eska and Chicaloon in 1916, and in the next five years produced an average of 52,644 tons, with 61,111 in 1920.[49] This was the first considerable coal production in Alaska, and gave an encouraging prospect of future coal-resource development.

But private development under the leasing system did not flourish comparably to the government's which had an immediate use and outlet for the coal it mined. One lease was made in 1917 and two more in 1918, covering a total of 5,940 acres. None of the leased properties had reached a productive stage by 1921. There were also some fourteen coal-mining permits chiefly for lignitic coal covering some 140 acres for local use.[50]

The fact was that with the long delays and consequent passage of time Alaska coal had lost a large part of its potential market, which a decade earlier had been properly visualized as supplying not only Alaska's needs but those of the west coast of the United States. The Panama Canal, in full operation in 1915, had greatly shortened the haul of eastern coal to the West Coast, and lessened its cost there. Substantial quantities of coal were still being shipped in the early nineteen twenties by that less costly—though still wasteful—route, chiefly for the Navy.[51] But California petroleum had undergone a great development in the previous decade, and was furnishing a new and increasingly sizable competition to coal as a fuel. The Navy would shortly abandon coal altogether and convert to oil. These factors, together with the uncertainties that still surrounded the administration of the coal-leasing law in Alaska, were not encouraging to private capital.[52] Had Alaska coal resources been available twenty years, or even a decade earlier, there is little doubt that a substantial coal industry would have been flourishing in Alaska, reflected in metalliferous mining and related activities and stimulating an entire economy. The episode demonstrated, as subsequent events would again, that in government the power to delay may be the power to destroy.

The land laws—and their administration—constituted obstacles to settlement. At the end of 1913 only 162 homesteaders had received titles to their tracts.[53] By the end of 1917 this number had increased slightly though it represented a small proportion of those seeking patents. Long delays in securing action had discouraged many would-be settlers. The cost of the survey, ranging from $200 to $1,000, imposed a heavy burden on the would-be homesteader.[54] Owing to lack of appropriations, the amount of land surveyed was negligible. It amounted to 39,000 acres in township surveys for all Alaska in 1912,[55] slightly above one ten-thousandth part of Alaska's area. Not until 1914 was any surveyed public land available for the homesteader.[56]

Not a few homesteaders were unable to comply with the cultivation and other requirements of the laws which had been drawn up half a century earlier for the Western public lands, were not appropriate to Alaska, and became even less so by subsequent amendments never made with Alaska's conditions in view. There was a different procedure for entrants on surveyed and unsurveyed lands. The General Land Office requirements in Alaska at that time for a 160-acre homestead (this figure having been re-established in 1916) was that ten acres had to be under cultivation in the second year, twenty in the third, and every year thereafter until final proof. This involved first clearing the land, removing the timber and stumps by hand—for the fuel-driven machinery of a later day was not available to the homesteader, who was of necessity also engaged in providing himself with food and shelter, the erection of "a habitable home" being also a Land Office requirement. Difficult as were these physical tasks, and unachievable by some, others managed to win the battle with nature imposed by law and regulations only to be defeated by the baffling intricacies of paper requirements. At the end of the second decade the Land Office reported 96,518 acres of homesteads,[57] which suggests more than three hundred individual established homesteaders. But statistics on this subject for this time do not accurately reflect the conditions of settlement, since not a few homesteaders had abandoned their homesteads and returned to the States, leaving, incidentally, a problem of land held out of use which would trouble Alaska two generations later.

The 1920 census showed Alaska with a population of 55,036. This was a decrease of 14.7 per cent from the 1910 figure of 64,356. During that decade the population of the United States had risen from 91,972,266 to 105,710,620, an increase of 14.9 per cent.

In the twenty-year period since 1900, when the lure of the Klondike and other gold discoveries had approximately doubled Alaska's previously stationary population and awakened a transient interest in the Congress and federal executive departments, Alaska's population had diminished by 11.9 per cent. In the same score of years the population of the forty-eight states had increased by 38 per cent. Not only had all the states' populations increased in varying degree—even those which were not augmented by immigration, but merely registered the normal increase of births over deaths—but all the other territories and possessions which had come under federal guardianship at that time and remained under it during that period, the Philippines, Hawaii, Puerto Rico and Samoa, showed marked and continuous growth. In that twenty years the population of Hawaii, the only other incorporated territory, rose from 154,000 to 255,912, a gain of 66.1 per cent.[58]

World War I was not the cause of Alaska's shrinkage in population.

Men were called to the colors from every state and territory. Others from every state were attracted to munitions plants, shipyards and other industrial establishments by high wages. But Alaska alone suffered the striking decrease in population in a nation that was burgeoning everywhere.

President Wilson's interest in Alaska had ceased to manifest itself. It had ceased long before the entry of the United States into the World War, in April, 1917, naturally preoccupied him to the exclusion of many other lesser concerns. His second, and last, reference to Alaska in his messages to Congress, concerning Coast Survey appropriations, was in December of 1914. He would, he had said in his first message, referring to the nation's "double duty" to achieve "both the political and material development of the territory," call the attention of Congress from time to time to how the resources of the country might be exploited—the railroad being "only the first step." But no further calls to the attention of Congress emanated from the White House. No second step, or other step, was taken. And the pledge of full territorial government was honored in the breach through the resolute opposition of a responsible cabinet member, who controlled the only federal agency a part of which would be taken from him by full territorial government.

Secretary of the Interior Franklin K. Lane had written with great fervor and realism about Alaska in his first annual report in 1913. "The largest body of unused and neglected land in the United States is Alaska" was his salutatory comment. And shortly thereafter he issued a long and factual indictment against the red tape wound around Alaska by the federal bureaus. This, he felt, should be unwound by the consolidation and co-ordination of the federal agencies dealing with Alaska under a "development board." But as we have seen, while the bureau chiefs and their subordinates admitted that there was undoubtedly room for improvement, it was mostly in some other bureau. Nor were *their* chiefs, the cabinet officers, eager to lose any parts of their bureaus—especially the Alaska parts—to a board under the control of the Secretary of the Interior. As for the participation of Alaskans in a program to solve *their* problems, to secure *their* cooperation in the unwinding of the red tape which bound *them*—that was not dreamt of in the philosophy of either the bureaus or Congress.

Yet Secretary Lane had a number of agencies operating in Alaska in his own Interior Department—more, actually, than any other cabinet officer. He required no legislation or the approval of any other cabinet officer or of anyone else to deal with them. Of these none was more important to the objective of developing Alaska than the General Land Office.

In his first annual report in 1918, Governor Riggs, appointed to succeed Governor Strong on the recommendation of Secretary Lane, wrote that much could be gained by the reorganization of the Land Office's service in Alaska. That bureau was then operating in the territory through a surveyor general, an assistant supervisor of surveys, a chief of field division, and three local offices, at Juneau, Nome and Fairbanks, each of which was presided over by a register and receiver. "All of these branches," wrote Governor Riggs, "are independent of one another and deal directly with the General Land Office in Washington, frequently about the same matter, without the other being aware of what is taking place." The consolidation of all these under one head, apart from the economies effected and the keeping of one set of records instead of four, would increase efficiency through responsible local control: "The people of the territory are far away from Washington, and their problems are so distinct from those in the States that they are entitled to a single officer with whom they can deal, who can speak authoritatively for the General Land Office, instead of the present divided authority, which makes every land claim the subject of consideration by four different branches of that bureau."

Under the heading "Native Land Titles a Problem" Secretary Lane had written in his article on red tape:

"Under the law natives and other original settlers are guaranteed undisturbed occupancy of their lands. No provision is made, however, for granting titles to these lands, and nothing has been done toward a solution of this problem, which is constantly growing more vexatious."

But the General Land Office and the Indian Bureau, and the Bureau of Education, which dealt specifically with the natives in Alaska, were under the Interior Department. And as the law had established the fact of occupancy of original settlers and natives, only department regulation and administration would have been required to achieve a solution of this constantly more vexatious problem. Yet nothing was done about it in the seven years of Secretary Lane's stewardship of the Interior Department.

There was apparently intradepartmental as well as interdepartmental red tape in the federal administration of Alaska.

"For the last fifteen years the people who have been living in Alaska have been living in hopes that there would be a change each year. I have seen pioneers each year leaving their localities. Year after year I have seen such centers as Fairbanks decline until today there is only a skeleton of the population that was there six or seven years ago. That is true of a majority of the other older Alaskan communities."

This was the testimony of J. L. McPherson, a civil engineer engaged almost continuously in Alaska from 1898 to 1914. In 1911 with others he organized the Alaska Bureau of the Seattle Chamber of Commerce, with the objective of aiding Alaska in securing legislation that would aid in its rational development. Representative Curry had asked him to compile and organize the information preparatory to the hearings on his bill, H.R. 5694, in the Sixty-seventh Congress, designed to co-ordinate the federal agencies in Alaska under a board.

Contrasting Canada's successful policy in the frontier provinces, McPherson said:

"It is all based on a policy of encouragement and aid. They make the homesteader feel that he is the one of importance, that they are as interested in his success as he is himself, and without that interest there cannot be any development." [59]

People were leaving Alaska *after* the summons of war had ceased. "Last summer," Edward W. Nelson, chief of the Biological Survey, testified in the spring of 1921, "I saw many men who had lived there for years and desired to continue to live in Alaska but were forced by the unfortunate business conditions to dispose of their homes for trifling sums. They sold houses there all the way from $50 to $150 and similar sums in order to get out of the territory simply because there was no work they could do to earn a living. They often expressed their regret at being forced to leave and their hope that conditions would improve so they could return." [60]

"Unless the government pursues a more liberal policy in connection with the development of Alaska," wrote Governor Riggs, in concluding his second annual report in 1919, "the territory can never reach that stage of productiveness for which there is every possibility and so become one of the great sources of revenue now so greatly needed in this period of national adjustment.

"We hold out our hands to Washington, not as supplicants for bounty but in petition to be allowed to develop as were the greatest western territories, now the great western states."

That plea had been made before, and would be again.

But fewer Alaskans were making it as the territory passed into its second half-century under the rule of the United States. Nearly ten thousand of them had gone back there.

The Judicial Branch
Establishes a Fact

> We are under a Constitution, but the Constitution is what the judges say it is. . . .
>
> CHARLES EVANS HUGHES, MAY 3, 1907

> But there is a higher law than the Constitution, which regulates our authority over the domain. . . . The Territory is a part, no inconsiderable part, of the common heritage of mankind, bestowed upon them by the Creator of the Universe. We are His stewards, and must so discharge our trust as to secure in the highest attainable degree their happiness.
>
> WILLIAM HENRY SEWARD, MARCH 11, 1850

WHATEVER may have been the limitations upon the powers of self-government granted the people of Alaska by the second organic act, it at least gave them a voice. It permitted them to express, through their elected representatives, their hopes, their desires and their needs, all, of course, in fields which they were forbidden to enter. During the nearly half-century of United States rule that had preceded, the people had had during the first seventeen years no method of registering their views. Thereafter, for twenty-two years, their spokesmen were appointed governors whose enlistment in the causes dear to most Alaskans depended upon the executive's sympathies and outlook. After 1906 a delegate was the authorized spokesman, but he, too, though elected as such, was limited to a degree by his associations and his inclinations. From 1913 on, the legislatures, elected every two years, and representing collectively the greatest possible Alaskan geographic, political and economic diversity, were able through the years to record in continuity and seek—if only by petition—what Alaskans felt was their due.

The composition of the Alaska legislatures changed appreciably from biennium to biennium. In the first five sessions—the first decade of the legislature—seventy-six different members served. While senators were all elected for two terms (except in the first legislature where four, drawn by lot, were elected for only one term) the turnover brought into those five first sessions a great diversity of opinion and variety of party affiliation, although party partisanship was relatively negligible in the early assemblies. Not one legislator served through all five sessions, two served in four (Dan Sutherland and Earnest B. Collins), eight in three, nineteen in two, and forty-seven in one. Some of these would serve again in later legislatures. With each assembly composed of twenty-four members, there were therefore three wholly different sets of legislators in the first ten years. Yet they agreed on their basic desires as subsequent legislatures would again and again.

The subjects that most concerned the legislators were the fisheries, transportation and the land laws. Every legislature pleaded for better conservation of the fisheries, or made proposals to further it, and steadily requested their transfer to territorial control as a means to attain the desired end. Not a legislature failed to memorialize on the subject of roads, with the ever-recurring plea to be included in the Federal Aid Highway Act. The land laws were approached again and again from a half-dozen angles. Adapt them to Alaska's needs, repeal their restrictive provisions, simplify the procedures, put an end to reservations and withdrawals! Give us better law enforcement! (This was a field, which, along with the judicial system, the federal government had pre-empted.) Pay the United States commissioners a salary —a living wage; put an end to the fee system! Do not farm out our insane under the undesirable contract system to Morningside—a Portland, Oregon, institution, a thousand miles from Alaska's nearest community; establish a hospital and asylum for the mentally ill in Alaska where their families have a better chance to visit them occasionally and their prospect for improvement is greater. Full territorial government was a chronic objective which encompassed other pleas.

It would be anticipating the course of history—and of this narrative —to indicate, at this point, to what extent these repeated pleas were to be wholly or partially heeded through the years, and the aspirations they embodied attained—up to the present. Some of them, certainly, were not even controversial; but whether controversial or not, they represented and would represent through changing times the unwavering wishes of the people of Alaska for more than two generations, and to this day.

There was much else. There was the reiterated opposition to the game laws, their lack of appropriateness to Alaska's widely varied conditions, and, in consequence, the request for the transfer of that resource and its administration by local authority.

There was the continuingly inadequate mail service, subject of at least one, generally several memorial protests per legislative session.

There were the mining laws. Alaska was bound to the United States mining laws, and its legislative powers to modify them almost totally precluded because more than 99 per cent of its land was in public domain.

Under the United States laws $100 worth of labor—for improvement—was required annually on every unpatented mining claim. The first legislature pointed out, and subsequent legislatures repeated, that on many claims such labor could not be usefully performed, and proposed as an alternative that the owner at his option contribute $100 to the road fund—since roads were so essential to mining development.[1] This sensible request, demonstrative of owner interest and responsibility, and sparing the government the problem of inspection, was ignored.

There was the conflict of laws and administrative rulings from Washington. There was the need for clarification and the uncertainties derived therefrom. Rights of way for irrigation ditches, for flumes and pipe lines, for power lines essential to mining operations, sawmills or canneries could not be granted across public domain, according to the Secretary of the Interior, but could across national-forest reserves, according to the Secretary of Agriculture. A conduit of one of these varieties which was partly in public domain and partly in national forest was in trouble. The Congress was asked to legislate out the conflict.[2]

With the coming of dredging and hydraulicking, a substantial group of claims had to be secured by one owner before the expense of importing and installing this costly modern machinery could be incurred. No development work on each claim was needed or of any value after the claim had been prospected. But the Department of the Interior had ruled that the claims would not be accepted for patent proceedings unless development work in extracting minerals from each claim had been performed. This interpretation of the law had deterred owners from applying for patent, resulting in loss of funds to the government and continuingly unsettled title to much mining ground.³

The legislation finally enacted by Congress in 1912 to limit the abuse of unlimited claim-staking by power of attorney created new problems. Since it had taken fourteen years to get such legislation in an attempt to remedy that abuse, further corrective action by the Congress would obviously not be secured quickly. "The act of Congress of August 1, 1912 covers subject matter upon which your memorialists are best advised as to the needs of Alaska." And so the Alaskan legislators asked repeal of that act and that legislation by the territorial legislature in conflict with the congressional act be permitted to prevail.⁴

But toward the close of the second decade one chronic ailment—as Alaskans viewed it—flared into acute trouble, with lasting impairment of Alaska's body economic. "The great outstanding problem of Alaska is that of transportation," wrote Governor Riggs in his final report in 1920. Drastically increased rates, poor and uncertain service, discrimination against certain shippers were the factors in an upheaval that would extend from the territorial legislature to Congress.

In the absence of railroads or highways connecting Alaska with its source of supplies, complaint against maritime transportation, "Alaska's lifeline," was an ancient story. The uncharted coast with its perils of hidden rock pinnacles, "weather," the savage rips of the second highest tides on earth—to these natural obstacles were added Alaska's seasonality: great activity in mining, fisheries and construction during the six months embracing the summer, followed by six months of economic hibernation; one-way cargoes; the large number of small ports to be served. These factors were constantly and understandably stressed by steamship operators justifying their demands for higher rates and in defending themselves against unfavorable criticism.

Still, the history of maritime transportation in Alaska appears to be a sequence of monopoly, alternating with periods of competition in which before long the competitors sank their differences and made common cause, with consequently adverse effects in Alaska and corresponding reactions on Alaskan public opinion.

"It is not surprising that the people of Alaska find fault with the Pacific Coast Steamship Company, and look upon it as a grinding monopoly, and pray for the day when competition will afford some relief," editorialized the Sitka *Alaskan* in the early years of the first regular steamship service to southeastern Alaska ports. "If a strike would rectify matters there would be one in which every man who has business relations with that company would most heartily join. Possibly by this criticism we are laying ourselves open to the wrath of this company and may be deprived of material with which to run this little paper. But . . . there is no denying that the charges of that company are simply outrageous. We know of a man who shipped from Portland an ordinary-sized table, 5 x 3, the cost of which, at Portland, was $7, and the freight on that table was $20." After citing other examples, the paper asked Messrs. Goodall, Perkins & Co., the line's agents, to reduce somewhat "such extortion." [5]

In Juneau another complaint was added. Under the heading "A Detriment to Alaska," the *Mining Record* wrote: "The people of Alaska have been and are now being imposed upon by not only the exorbitant freight rates of the P.C.SS. Co., but by the wharf companies as well. Shippers could save money by lightering their goods from vessels to the beach, if the officers of the steamship company would permit them to receive their freight at ship's tackle, but . . . this will not be allowed . . . the steamship company acts in conjunction with the wharf companies, and the wharf bill is added to the freight bill before the freight passes over it.

"In the shipment of cattle to Juneau when they have been driven overboard and made to swim ashore, without a hoof touching the wharf, wharfage has been charged; also where small boats have been shipped as freight and lifted from the steamer's deck and dropped in the water, the same rates have been charged as though they had been landed on the dock." [6]

Stating that "this grasping monopoly" was exacting "a larger freight rate than is charged by any common carrier in the world," and that on many articles shipped to Alaska the freight exceeded the original cost price,[7] the future capital's newspaper continued its criticism, contrasting the rates between Juneau and Port Townsend as six times higher than between the comparable distance between Port Townsend and San Francisco. "It can readily be seen that the people of Alaska have a right to complain of unjust treatment at the hands of the steamship company," asserted an editorial three years later. "These rates do not materially affect the merchant as he adds these high freight rates to the price of his goods and wares to the consumer who is the one who suffers." [8]

Similar comments would continue to be made by Alaskans through the years concerning the maritime carriers.

Toward the end of the twentieth century's second decade steamship rates to and from Alaska were generally condemned as excessive.[9] "The cost of this water transportation . . . is . . . now so high as to prove a serious deterrent to pioneer effort. This condition must be remedied if Alaska is to progress," testified J. L. McPherson, executive officer of the Seattle Chamber of Commerce.[10]

Alaska's post-war grievances were emphasized by discriminatory rates and discrimination in service. The Alaska Line—then owned by the Morgan-Guggenheim Syndicate—was carrying its own ore southward at a low rate, a rate far lower than was afforded other commodities. From their mines at Latouche, on Prince William Sound, ore was shipped to their smelter at Tacoma at $4 a ton. Four miles away a herring-packing plant shipping out on the same vessel was obliged to pay $8.50 a ton.[11] Cement paid $9 a ton; general merchandise, $13.50.[12] Smaller copper miners in the Ketchikan area were unable to arrange for any cargo space, and also because of high costs and labor shortages forced to suspend operations.[13]

During the winter of 1917-18 hearings were held before the United States Shipping Board upon the request of the American carriers, the Alaska Steamship Company and the Pacific Steamship Company, which were asking for rate increases. The companies were not without their grievances. Operating costs had risen sharply; the federal government had commandeered a number of the Alaska Steamship Company's vessels and had withheld the agreed charter price of $407,000.[14] The companies presented their case so convincingly that the board noted that "there was a significant absence of protests from the important commercial interests and localities directly affected" by the proposed increase in rates. Representatives of substantial commercial interests in southeastern Alaska stated that while they did not invite increases in rates, they would acquiesce if the carriers showed insufficient earnings. Others testified that they felt the carriers were not earning what they might in other trades. A representative of an Alaska labor union at Juneau withdrew the protest of that organization.[15]

Once in effect, the increases however worked great hardship; particularly burdensome were the advances on heavy commodities, mine and mill equipment and supplies, fuel, oil, hay, oats and coal—which was being imported in large quantities even by the government, although it was mining coal in the Matanuska Valley.[16] There were further rate boosts in 1919—resulting in 300 per cent increases since April, 1916, on some commodities.[17] Owing to the inability of government and steamship companies to agree, no mail contracts had been entered into since August 1, 1918. The services of mail clerks on the vessels had been discontinued. Incalculable confusion resulted in all Alaska.

Governor Riggs did not view these increases with the equanimity with which others had apparently greeted their initiation: "Based on war-time valuation of ships," he reported, "the capital stock of the steamship companies was increased, necessitating a ruinous increase in tariffs to provide high dividends, after income taxation had been deducted." [18]

The territory's difficult economic situation, the loss of population, the lack of constructive measures in the national capital, the influenza epidemic in the fall and winter of 1918-19 which hit Alaska hard, disastrous floods and fires severely crippling some of Alaska's towns, induced a mood of depression when the Fourth Alaska Legislature convened on March 3, 1919. Governor Riggs's message, his first to a legislature, did not deal with shipping. But on March 19th still another increase in freight rates was announced. A week later the Governor sent a special message to the legislature suggesting that it establish a territorial shipping service. The legislature enacted "An Act authorizing the Territory of Alaska and Incorporated Cities therein to Engage in Maritime and River Commerce, and Creating the Alaska Territorial Shipping Board" (Chapter 32). The act departed from custom in beginning with a preamble:

"Whereas freight and passenger rates of the steamship companies engaged in transportation to the ports of Alaska have become, by reason of recent increases, a burden on the people of Alaska, and are excessive and exorbitant, and based upon the unreasonable hypothesis of paying a large percentage on inflated and watered capitalization; and

"Whereas, such burden is a tax upon the very existence of the Territory, and a grave and ever increasing menace to its development, and the people are unanimously demanding relief . . ."

The act created a shipping board consisting of the Governor, Attorney General and Treasurer of the Territory with authority to appoint a territorial shipping commissioner. It provided that the board should have full authority to carry on a steamship freight-and-passenger business with power to charter, purchase or contract for the construction of vessels, with the understanding, however, that this authority was not mandatory, but an alternative to relief through the courts, the Interstate Commerce Commission, the United States Shipping Board or by any other proper means. The sum of $300,000 was appropriated, and the Attorney General was instructed to have a bill prepared and introduced in the Congress permitting the territory to bond itself to the extent of $5,000,000, the proceeds from the sale of bonds to be used for the purchase and charter of vessels.

In Congress, S. 4012, "A Bill to Provide for the Improvement of Transportation by Water to and from and within the Territory of Alaska" was introduced by Senator Chamberlain of Oregon at the request of Governor Riggs and the two shipping experts whom he had retained for the territory. The bill departed radically from the legislature's proposal—principally because it became clear that Congress would not approve. It made no provision for bonding the territory. It provided that every vessel of more than twenty tons carrying passengers or cargo in Alaskan waters would be obliged to secure a license for which it would pay $3 a ton annually on the vessel's net tonnage. The money thus collected was to be used "only for the betterment of water transportation and transportation conditions, including the improvement of harbors and river-boat landings," but no portion of the moneys was to be used directly and indirectly in the purchase, construction, charter or operation of any vessels.[19]

This provision elicited a letter to Senator Chamberlain from Secretary of the Interior John Barton Payne pointing to the decrease in Alaska's population and saying in part: "Unless something can be done to arouse interest in Alaska to take people there and start enterprise moving within the territory, the building of the railroad will have been a colossal failure. . . . It seems to me that we must have an independent line of steamships operating direct with low fares, even though it cost the government considerable money to establish and maintain it." [20]

Richard Semmes, who had been retained by the territory as a shipping expert, replied that the act's purpose was to make contracts for smaller vessels to serve the lesser ports and to subsidize them when

necessary to insure continuous service. At that time, in addition to
the two American carriers, two Canadian lines, the Canadian Pacific
Steamship Company and the Grand Trunk Pacific Steamship Company, were operating out of Vancouver to Prince Rupert, now the Pacific terminus of a new transcontinental rail line, to the southeastern
Alaska ports, and connecting at Skagway with the White Pass and Yukon Railroad which for three more years would still furnish the only
rail and water connection with the interior of Alaska, and whose boats
were operating on the Yukon. The proponents of territorial steamship
operation felt that the existing lines between Alaska and "the outside" were sufficient for the larger ports but not in the service they
had been rendering to the numerous smaller communities. The additional traffic to be developed for the principal carriers by transship-
ment to the smaller feeder vessels was viewed as fully justifying the
proposed tonnage license tax.

The legislation had no chance of favorable action in the Congress
any more than the legislature's original proposal. It was openly opposed
by the canned-salmon interests. The larger companies were operating
their own vessels which took up their crews and supplies from the
West Coast in the spring and returned them with the canned salmon
in the fall. They pointed out that they used their own vessels because
adequate service from the common carriers was not available to them,
and certainly not at comparable costs. They could see no reason why
they should pay a tonnage tax on their vessels, which made only a few
trips a season. They took their protests directly to Senator Wesley L.
Jones, who had shipping provisions in mind which would be beneficial to his constituency, and, by virtue of his potent position
as Chairman of the Senate Commerce Committee, likely to have
them prevail.

For that committee had other maritime legislation under consideration, which with its endorsement had no difficulty in securing congressional approval. The Maritime Act of June 5, 1920 (41 Stat. 999),
which became known as the Jones Act after its senatorial sponsor,
contained a special reference to the Alaska situation, but scarcely one
that Alaskans anticipated. In Section 27 an exception was made to
previously existing shipping legislation to permit shipments of freight
across the continent by either American or Canadian carriers and
permitted them to carry such cargo across the Atlantic if eastbound,
or, if westbound, across the Pacific or southward along the Pacific

Coast in either United States or Canadian vessels. But in the heart of that section were found the words "excluding Alaska," which meant that from Puget Sound north, and from Alaska south, cargo could be shipped only in American bottoms.

The Fifth Territorial Legislature, meeting in March, 1921, declared its view that this discrimination violated the commerce clause of the Constitution that "no preference shall be given by any regulation of commerce or revenue to the ports of one state over those of another," and instructed the Attorney General to fight the new law.[21]

The legislature adopted two other memorials praying that the President and Congress take note of the emergency that existed in Alaska and, as quickly as possible, supply it with adequate and dependable ocean transportation.[22] As a result of greatly decreased efficiency and increased expense to the traveling and shipping public, the memorials stated, the territory's industries had become paralyzed and were faced with extinction; in consequence a large part of the population had been driven out of the territory; and for these reasons the financial resources of the territory had so diminished that it was impossible for the legislature to raise the funds to supply the needs of better transportation.[23] There was nothing to do but repeal the Territorial Shipping Act and pray to the President and Congress.

But the Congress had already decided the issue, and had denied Alaska the benefits it was offering to the states, to the other offshore territories and to foreign nations in making available both United States and Canadian transportation facilities. Alaska's only remedy— if any—lay in the courts.

The case came to the Supreme Court of the United States, on appeal from a decree of the U. S. District Court dismissing the suit brought by the territory and the Juneau Hardware Company to restrain the Alaska collector of customs, Mr. John W. Troy, from confiscating merchandise ordered, or to be ordered shipped, by the hardware company and others in Alaska from points in the United States over Canadian railroads to Canadian ports and thence to Alaska by Canadian vessels, or merchandise to be shipped from Alaska in like manner to the United States.

Alaska's Attorney General, John Rustgard, argued that the provisions in Article III in the Treaty of Cession with Russia granted the inhabitants of the ceded territory "the enjoyment of all the rights, advantages and immunities of citizens of the United States," and that moreover the Constitution had been specifically extended to Alaska in Section 3 of the organic act of 1912.

For the federal government the Solicitor General of the United States, James M. Beck, argued: "It is an economic and political question . . . the immunity from discrimination is a reserved right on the part of the constituent states. . . . The clear distinction of governmental power between states and territories must be constantly borne in mind. As to the state, there was only a limited delegation of power, subject to many reservations and qualifications. As to the territory, there was a plenary power to deal with it as the property of the United States to the extent even of disposing of it at the pleasure of the federal government." And Beck concluded:

"If the Fathers had anticipated the control of the United States over the far-distant Philippine Islands, would they, whose concern was the reserved rights of the states, have considered for a moment, a project that any special privilege which the interests of the United States might require for the ports of entry of the several states should by compulsion be extended to the ports of entry of the colonial dependencies, living in a different civilization and having economic interests which might be wrecked by the application of the rule of equality?"

Mr. Justice McReynolds, rendering the opinion of the court declared: "The act does give preference to ports of the states over those of the territory . . ." but that the court could "find nothing in the Constitution itself or its history which impels the conclusion that it was intended to deprive Congress of the power so to act." [24]

In sum, the Merchant Marine Act of 1920 did discriminate against Alaska, said the court of last resort, but Congress can discriminate against a territory. That fact was now officially established. Alaskans had for fifty-five years had experience with the executive and legislative branches of the federal government. They had now had their first important encounter with the judicial branch.

The unfavorable effects of the new maritime legislation, designed, in its exclusion of Alaska from the benefits specifically extended to all other parts of the world, in order to give the existing Puget Sound carriers a monopoly of the Alaska trade, were felt immediately in Alaska even before the finding of the Supreme Court made the new policy irrevocable.

A Juneau resident had established a mill for Alaskan Sitka spruce and was developing a market for its use in airplane manufacture for which it was and is peculiarly adapted. He was shipping it through Vancouver where it cost him $5 a thousand to place it on the cars destined for its purchasers in the Middle West. After passage of the Jones Act he was obliged to ship by way of Seattle where he was charged $11 a thousand, or $6 more to load his produce on the railway cars, which was more than his profit. As a consequence his mill was shut down, and a promising industry utilizing an abundant, but little used, Alaskan resource and giving employment in Alaska was nipped in the bud.[25]

The direct effect of the Jones Act was to more than triple the costs of handling Alaska freight in Seattle on Seattle purchases as compared with locally bought Hawaiian or Asia-bound cargoes. Delegate Sutherland testified that Seattle terminal charges on local shipments to the Hawaiian Islands or to the Orient were 30 cents a ton, and all handling charges were absorbed by the steamship lines. Seattle terminal charges on local shipments to Alaska, on the other hand, were 60 cents a ton plus 50 cents a ton wharfage. Thus Alaskans paid $1.10 a ton for what cost Hawaiians and Asiatics 30 cents a ton.

On shipments made from the east of the United States through Seattle consigned to the Hawaiian Islands or to Oriental ports the total handling charges were 30 cents a ton wharfage, and all other costs were absorbed by railroad and steamship lines. But for the same type of shipments consigned to Alaska, there was an unloading charge of 65 cents a ton, a wharfage charge of 50 cents a ton, and handling charge from wharf to ship of 60 cents a ton. These charges, which in the aggregate were over five times the cost to Hawaiian or Oriental consignees or shippers, had to be paid by the Alaska consignee or shipper.[26] Delegate Sutherland's testimony was uncontradicted and unrefuted in that hearing or in subsequent supplemental hearings although delivered in the presence of a representative of the Seattle Chamber of Commerce.

"At the threshold of Alaskan development is the subject of transportation. Adequate steamship service with reasonable rates for passengers and freight from the Pacific Coast to Alaska is imperative," Secretary of the Interior John Barton Payne had written in his 1920 report.

Were Alaska's interest, and its development—allegedly, at intervals, the concern of national administrations—sacrificed "to build up the American merchant marine," a phrase to be heard repeatedly when

Alaskans would wonder why they were estopped from utilizing fully the partly paralleling services of Canadian carriers? Were the American carriers in such straits that they needed to be rescued at Alaskans' expense?

In a communication to Governor Scott C. Bone, President Harding's appointee to succeed Governor Riggs, Attorney General Rustgard presented an analysis he had made of the financial position of the two American carriers operating to Alaska. It disclosed that the Alaska Steamship Company in the six years, 1915 to 1920, had reported to its stockholders an annual average profit on its investment of 38.69 per cent, but that other factors, which he detailed, had revealed an actual annual earning of 53.29 per cent.

As for the Pacific Steamship Company, it was a subsidiary formed in 1916 of two other companies of similar names—the Pacific Coast Steamship Company and the Pacific Alaska Navigation Company—with the same officers, from which it chartered ships. A series of complex financial transactions followed between the various interlocking companies. Rustgard after detailed analysis came to the conclusion that in the six years since the formation of the company a profit of 535.20 per cent had been earned on the original capital investment, or approximately 89 per cent annually.[27] This presentation was likewise unrefuted by the carriers.

A new administration was ushered in on March 4, 1921. Its gubernatorial appointee for Alaska was Scott C. Bone.

"Vital and urgent is the problem of transportation," began his discussion of the subject in his first annual report. "That the situation calls for remedy and relief no one will seriously deny. Industry in Alaska cannot thrive under existing conditions. That is as clear as day." And, after some further discussion, he concluded: "And so no progress has been made toward the solution of Alaska's transportation problem, either through federal or territorial agencies."

Governor Bone, by nature a kindly optimist, had been guilty of understatement. As with Alaska's population, so with its transportation. There had not only been "no progress." There had been regress.

Salmon in Jeopardy

The marvelous abundance of several species of salmon in Alaskan waters has been long known, but in consequence of the remoteness of this region and its inaccessibility, the abundant supply in rivers nearer markets, and a disposition on the part of buyers to under-rate Alaskan products, its fishery resources have not been laid under contribution for market supply until within a few years, during which we have seen, as the result of reckless and improvident fishing, the practical destruction of the salmon fisheries of the Sacramento and the reduction of the take on the Columbia to hardly one-third of what it was in the early history of the salmon-canning industry in that river. At present the streams of Alaska furnish the larger proportion of the canned salmon which find their way to the markets.

Whether these fisheries shall continue to furnish the opportunity for profitable enterprise and investment depends upon the policy to be inaugurated and maintained by the Government. Under judicious regulation and restraint these fisheries may be made a continuing source of wealth to the inhabitants of the Territory and an important food resource to the nation; without such regulation and restraint we shall have repeated in Alaskan rivers the story of the Sacramento and the Columbia; and the destruction in Alaska will be more rapid because of the small size of the rivers and the ease with which salmon can be prevented from ascending them. For a few years there will be wanton waste of that marvelous abundance, which the fishermen—concerned only for immediate profit and utterly improvident of the future—declare to be inexhaustible. The season of prosperity will be followed by a rapid decline in the value and production of these fisheries, and a point will be eventually reached where the salmon-canning industry will be no longer profitable.

TARLETON H. BEAN, 1889[1]

SALMON and Alaska have been as closely intertwined as cotton and the South. Before the coming of the white man this abundant fish furnished the principal food supply for the Indians along the coast and inland along the rivers. With the discovery of its commercial value and the establishment of the first canneries in 1878, extension and expansion into Alaska of the activities of the northwestern salmon entrepreneurs followed. Half a century later Alaska had become the world's principal salmon producer; its salmon fisheries were surpassing mining as Alaska's major industry, representing there the largest investment of capital, the biggest annual financial yield, the greatest employment, direct and indirect, of labor, the largest single source of territorial revenue, and the dominant factor in Alaska's political, economic and social life.

The industry presents certain characteristics. The five species of Pacific salmon—king or chinook, red or sockeye, pink or humpback, silver or coho, chum or dog—differ somewhat in their life cycle and habits. In common they are born in the rivers and tributary lakes, migrate from them to the sea, generally returning as mature fish to the rivers of their birth to spawn and—unlike the Atlantic salmon—to die after spawning. Kings and reds generally return in four or five years, cohos in three to four years, pinks in two years, chums in two to four years. Spawning consists of the female laying her roe on the bottom of the stream's shallow waters, where the eggs are then fertilized by the male salmon's milt. The industry in salmon consists in catching these fish as they return during the summer months from their sojourn in the sea, and processing them promptly. Therefore canneries have to be established within easy transportation of the fishing grounds and require intensive labor during the salmon runs. The industry incurs the hazards incidental to the uncertainty as to the times and size of the runs, and, once the processing is completed, marketing factors; the various species differ in commercial value, kings and reds bringing the highest prices. Kings, though far larger than the other species, averaging twenty-two pounds, are far less numerous, and though also canned, are chiefly reserved for other forms of processing and are caught principally by trolling, as are also in part the cohos. Besides the plant, seasonal equipment—in boats, fishing apparatus, cans, fuel, etc.—and an assurable labor supply, require a heavy investment which presages a correspondingly heavy profit or loss depending on the supply of fish. The conservation of that supply has thus always been presumed of basic concern to all interested parties—fishermen, canners, the public and the governments, federal and territorial. The essence of conservation—it has been universally assumed—has been in permitting adequate escapement, that is, allowing salmon to get back to the spawning grounds in numbers sufficient to insure an adequate reproduction of their species and to perpetuate the supply of that stream or lake.

Conservation was totally ignored in the industry's earlier days. The first legislation for Alaska enacted, on the next to last day of the Fiftieth Congress, merely provided that " the erection of dams, barricades or other obstructions in any of the rivers of Alaska, with the purpose of preventing or impeding the ascent of salmon . . . to their spawning grounds" was unlawful, and provided a penalty of a fine of $250 a day for such violation.[2] The Secretary of the Treasury—who then had charge of fisheries—was authorized to establish the necessary surveillance to see the law was enforced. But Congress made no appropriation for the enforcement. The same act authorized the Commissioner of Fish and Fisheries to investigate the habits of the Alaska salmon as well as the conditions and methods of the fisheries with a view to recommending to Congress "such additional legislation as may be necessary to prevent the impairment or exhaustion of these valuable fisheries . . ."

Congress likewise made no special appropriation for this investigation. However, the Commissioner, M. McDonald, took it upon himself to transfer the needed funds from the general appropriation for the conduct of his office and Tarleton H. Bean's exhaustive study followed. It contained the afore-quoted warning of the dangers of depletion.

There were other such warnings but they were unheeded.[3]

In 1889, when the first regulatory legislation for Alaska was enacted, the Alaska salmon pack far surpassed the other Pacific Coast salmon fisheries, with 719,196 cases against a total of 477,659 for the California, Oregon and Washington canners. The temporarily diminished Alaska pack in the immediately subsequent years, of an average of 651,543 cases for the six years, 1890-1895, inclusive, was due in part to market conditions. These conditions and their relation to demand, and to over- and under-supply, due to shortages from exhaustion of streams, competition, and from other causes, were an ever-recurring factor in the trade.[4]

The visit to Alaska in 1894 of Assistant Secretary of the Treasury Charles S. Hamlin, accompanied by Joseph Murray, Inspector of Salmon Fisheries, and an unfavorable report on their condition, led to further legislation for the regulation and preservation of the salmon supply.[5]

In addition to repeating the previous interdiction to barricade streams, the new act forbade the taking of salmon above tidewater in any creek or river less than five hundred feet wide, or to lay any net or seine across the tidewaters of any river for more than one-third the width of such stream, or within one hundred feet of any other net or seine, provided a closed period each week from midnight Friday to 6 A.M. Sunday, in which it was forbidden to fish for salmon except in Cook Inlet, Prince William Sound, Bering Sea and the water tributary thereto, or to take salmon between six in the evening and six in the morning in any stream less than a hundred yards in width. (These restrictions did not apply to fishing with a pole, hand line, or spear.) The act further permitted the Secretary of the Treasury at his discretion to set aside any stream as spawning ground and forbid all fishing therein when in his judgment the results of fishing operations indicated that the number of fish taken from that stream exceeded its capacity to produce, to establish weekly closed seasons, or to prohibit fishing entirely. However, these powers could be exercised only after due notice to all interested, and after public hearings. Fines of a thousand dollars or imprisonment for ninety days, or both, were provided as penalty for violations. For enforcement the act authorized the Secretary to appoint one inspector of fisheries at $1,800 per annum and two assistant inspectors at $1,600, plus necessary expenses for their travel.[6]

While the act gave the regulatory agency increased and very considerable authority, the means whereby that responsibility could be applied intelligently and effectively were virtually lacking. Three inspectors could scarcely, in the few weeks of the fishing season, discover violations and report on conditions requiring correction in an area of thousands of square miles containing hundreds of salmon streams.

After listing in detail an inspector's itinerary in Alaska, Governor Brady set forth his dilemma somewhat quizzically:

"Now, here are 4,735 miles an agent must travel to reach the different canneries. But that is only half the story, for each cannery is supplied with fish from a number of streams, some of them more than 150 miles from the place of packing. . . . An agent is appointed . . . told to proceed to Alaska . . . and finding a folder of the Pacific Coast Steamship Company wrestles with the Alaska route until he believes he understands it. Finally he arrives at Sitka. . . . He inquires how far is the nearest cannery, and how he can get there. It is forty miles, and there is no regular boat running there. The only way to get there is to hire a canoe or wait until the cannery steamer, the *Wig-wam*, happens to pass by. There is no boat of any kind belonging to the fish inspector, nor has the collector a boat he can loan; so all he can do is wait and take the next mail steamer for Karluk, seven hundred miles west of Sitka. When he reaches there the cannery people will show him every courtesy and see that he has a boat to get around in. Can anything be more humiliating to a government officer appointed to carry out an important duty?" [7]

The provisions of the act of 1896 were incorporated in the Alaska Criminal Code of March 3, 1899. In 1903 the seal and salmon fisheries were transferred from the Treasury Department to the newly created Department of Commerce and Labor (32 Stat. 828).

The Bureau of Fisheries of the Department of Commerce and Labor considered the act of 1896 inadequate and sought amendatory legislation in the Fifty-eighth and Fifty-ninth Congresses. Its draft was disapproved by the Alaska fishery interests; the bill was withdrawn and rewritten.[8] As passed by the Fifty-ninth Congress it incorporated previous legislation, including the 4-cents-per-case tax of the Criminal Code, and provided that it should be "in lieu of all other license fees and taxes." It arranged for rebates on this tax for canneries operating hatcheries. It forbade the wanton waste and destruction of salmon—a practice which had occasionally been engaged in in the course of heated rivalry between canners who had preferred to destroy fish they could not use in preference to letting a competitor have them; or throwing away less valuable species such as pinks or chums to process only reds; or holding salmon in traps too long and then dumping them.[9] The only substantial new fishing restriction was to forbid the placing of any barricade or trap in any waters where the distance from shore to shore was less than five hundred feet, or within five hundred yards of the mouth of any red-salmon stream which was less than five hundred feet in width.[10]

Attempts to secure better protection of this valuable resource were to be protracted for eighteen more years. A vast amount of legislation was introduced. But the net result, for eight Congresses, could be summed up in Delegate Wickersham's pithy comment: "All Alaska gets is a volume of hearings and never any laws for protection." [11] There would be many volumes.

S. 5856, "A Bill to Amend an Act for the Protection and Regulation of the Fisheries of Alaska," was introduced in the second session of the

Sixty-second Congress and referred to the Committee on Fisheries, of which Senator Wesley L. Jones of Washington was chairman.

It provided a new and higher scale of taxation for the fisheries. It departed from the flat 4-cents-per-case rate, increased and varied it in accord with the differences in the values of various salmon species. Kings and reds were taxed at 11 cents, medium reds at 7 cents; pinks and chums at 5 cents. It placed a tax on gear; fish traps at $100 per annum; purse seines at 30 cents per fathom per year; all other forms of gear at 1 cent a fathom.

It provided for the continuation of the tax rebate on privately operated hatcheries, with the new proviso that these had to measure up to certain standards of efficiency and productiveness before securing the rebate.

It increased the distance from the mouth of a stream where a trap or barricade could be erected from five hundred to six hundred yards, and provided that this regulation apply to "any salmon stream." The previous act applied the restriction only to red-salmon streams.

It established a method of applying to the Department of Commerce for a fish-trap license, and gave preferential rights to owners of existing fish traps as long as they continued to operate them, but provided that such fish traps could not be transferred or assigned unless the licensee was engaged in canning and wanted to transfer it to another canner. It limited the length of the lead to four thousand feet and ruled out the jigger. It provided, besides fine or imprisonment, for cancellation of the license for violations of the law.

It provided a closed period for all fishing from 6 P.M. Saturday to 6 A.M. Monday in all waters except Bering Sea. Existing legislation had also excepted Cook Inlet and Prince William Sound.

It enlarged the powers of the Secretary of Commerce to prohibit fishing within such distance of the mouth of a stream as he deemed necessary.

The provisions of the bill were explained by Dr. Barton W. Evermann, chief of the Division of Alaska Fisheries. Their purpose was conservation. The taxes, more realistic than the original case tax, imposed at a 4-cent rate regardless of the value of the species, had been increased because salmon prices had greatly increased since 1906, but the new tax figures were far less proportionately than the rise in the value of the product.[12] The tax on gear was not only for revenue but for better control.[13]

The proposed changes in the new legislation were emphatically opposed by the representatives of the canned-salmon industry. All objected to increasing the federal license fees.

Mr. Charles W. Dorr of Seattle, representing twelve salmon-packing companies operating fifteen canneries in Alaska, which had produced about one-fourth of the Alaska pack, objected to the prohibition to fish within six hundred yards of the mouth of "any salmon stream." Existing legislation limited to "red-salmon streams" went far enough. The inclusion of pink-salmon streams, he said, "would eliminate a great fishing field" without corresponding benefits to the perpetuation of the species.[14]

Dr. Evermann replied that the pink-salmon runs had diminished and that every stream which carried commercial fish should be safeguarded. [15] Mr. Dorr felt that this provision would cut out the Ketchikan fishery entirely.[16]

Mr. Dorr, while approving of the proposed trap provisions giving an exclusive right to the previous occupant of a site, objected to the restriction on selling trap locations. He did not think it right "that this species of property" should be prohibited from any kind of sale.[17] He objected also to the penalty of forfeiture of the trap franchise in case of conviction for operating it illegally, which he thought "too severe." [18]

Mr. Dorr wanted it understood "as being at all times, with all the force we have, objecting to the abolishment of the jigger." [19] He returned to the subject: "The trap is constructed for the purpose of catching fish. I do not believe it should be crippled while it is permitted to fish." [20]

Mr. Dorr objected to applying the week-end closing to Cook Inlet and Prince William Sound. Of Cook Inlet he said: "We all know from practical experience that the great mass of fish go up in spite of anything the fishermen can do to intercept them. There never has been any sign of diminution of fish there, and we think it absolutely impossible to catch enough fish in Cook Inlet to interfere with the natural replenishment." [21]

Mr. Dorr objected to giving the Secretary of Commerce the power to set aside streams and lakes as spawning areas, and urged that Congress should not delegate such powers. He believed that "the true function of the Bureau of Fisheries . . . and certainly a most important one" should be "in the line of fish culture—the scientific and biological end of the work." It should not, he thought, "be burdened with or charged with the duty of acting as a police force." [22]

Mr. Dorr concluded that nothing had developed in the hearings to indicate that there was any new situation that needed to be met.[23] He said that the figures did not show any diminution in the output of fish in Alaska.[24]

Another witness was Jefferson F. Moser, a retired naval officer, who for six years had commanded the *Albatross,* the U. S. Fish Commission vessel, which had made regular Alaska cruises between 1896 and 1901 with scientists studying the marine resources. Moser had himself made extensive reports on the fisheries and was considered an expert on the subject. In 1904 Captain Moser had taken employment with the Alaska Packers' Association of San Francisco, whom he represented at the hearings. This was the largest of the canned-salmon companies, operating at the time fourteen canneries in Alaska and three in Puget Sound, and a fleet of twenty-four large sailing vessels and some sixty steamers and launches.[25] Its Alaska pack, since the association's formation in 1893, slightly exceeded that of all other Alaska packers, 16,620,514 cases as compared with the rest of the pack in that period of 16,076,774.[26] It was in a way a descendant of the Alaska Commercial Company, since the owners in that dissolved fur-trading corporation and members of their families were among the principal and controlling stockholders in the Alaska Packers' Association.[27]

Captain Moser testified that "the law now in existence," adopted in 1906, on the advice of "a special board of fishery experts . . . in conjunction with the commercial interests . . . was quite sufficient, possibly with certain small amendments, to control the Alaska salmon interests at the present time." The only feature of the proposed bill that he favored was that "making some provision for the control and ownership of trap sites," but that other than that "there should be very little done to disturb present conditions." [28]

Specifically Captain Moser objected to the elimination of the "jigger." Traps, he said, "are built of course to catch fish. In taking off the jigger you take away part of the machinery for catching fish. Necessarily all parts of the trap are arranged so that they will catch fish." [29]

Captain Moser objected to the change in the bill from "red-salmon streams" to "any salmon streams." [30]

He was opposed to giving the Secretary of Commerce discretionary power to close salmon streams and whole fishing districts.[31] Moser considered it unnecessary in the interest of conservation.[32] In spite of the number of salmon taken from Alaskan waters, he said, the canners were putting up "quite as large a pack as ever and increasing year by year with no great signs of diminution." [33] Failure of certain streams, he felt, was due to causes other than overfishing. He did, however, believe that the number of canneries should be restricted and none allowed to operate without a permit, a provision recommended by Secretary of the Treasury Lyman J. Gage, fourteen years previously, and urged, earlier in the hearings, by Governor Clark.[34]

While the hearings were still under way the representatives of the companies, Dorr, Moser, John S. Webb and Aldis B. Browne, had decided that they had better present a bill of their own, "if," Mr. Dorr said, "the committee concludes any legislation is necessary." [35]

Dr. Evermann, summing up for the Bureau of Fisheries, and urging that despite the opposition the conservation measures in the bill be retained and enacted, said that he could present the matter fairly by quoting from "the very careful and comprehensive investigations of the Alaska fisheries" made between 1897 and 1901 by Captain Moser, the results of which were "embodied in two splendid reports published in the bulletin of the U. S. Fish Commission." Fourteen years earlier, in his 1898 report, Captain Moser had written:

"When a person interested in a cannery is questioned regarding the decrease of salmon in Alaskan waters he is likely to assure you at once that there are just as many salmon in the streams as there ever were . . . but any disinterested authority on the subject will say that the streams of Alaska are becoming depleted. While it can hardly be said that the streams will fail entirely within a few years there is no doubt that the average runs show fewer fish year by year, and if the laws are not amended and enforced the time will come in the not very distant future when the canneries must suffer through their own actions. It is a difficult matter to furnish convincing proofs to those who do not wish to be convinced, and any argument may fail with those who are interested commercially." [36]

Dr. Evermann cited at length passages which Moser had written to sustain his judgment of Alaskan stream depletion, concluding with the drastic recommendation that "the only fishing apparatus allowed should be gill nets and drag seines; no exceptions should be made," and concluding his quotations from Moser's 1900-1901 report:

"With the large accessions of canneries in Alaska the struggle in the fisheries is sure to increase, and every means will be employed for the capture of fish regardless of the law, unless the government enforces it by an efficient and intelligent inspection. The future, even more than the past, requires efficient inspection, which, however, cannot be realized under the present conditions." [37]

Captain Moser replied that after "eight years' experience in commercial life with the canned-salmon industry" his views were in some respects modified;[38] that his work in Alaska had changed the conditions he had found there, and that due to his efforts, streams once threatened with depletion were now showing "splendid results." He considered his contemporary testimony "more mature" than his earlier judgments. He now believed that the pending legislation was "premature," and that, of the entire bill, only the section dealing with trap regulation was justified.[39]

In conclusion, Captain Moser protested against the allocation of salmon-license taxes "to build roads in which these fisheries have no interest," and asked "by all the power I may invoke, to take the salmon tax out of the Alaska fund, and the clamor for more drastic Alaska salmon legislation will surely cease." [40]

This parting shot aroused Delegate Wickersham, who though attendant at the hearings, had up to the moment taken an unusually passive part in them. His chief legislative preoccupation at the time (June 10, 1912) was, of course, with the passage of Alaska's organic act which was then before the Congress, with some of its provisions still in controversy.

"Mr. Chairman," began Wickersham, "the last sentence of Captain Moser's testimony . . . states the objection that I have to the Alaska Packers' Association. It exhibits as plainly as the English language can be made to exhibit it their desire to get everything they can out of Alaska and give absolutely nothing in return. They resent the suggestion that Alaska or the people of Alaska have any right or interest in the salmon or the fisheries of that country. They are non-residents themselves; they do nothing toward the upbuilding of the territory; and they resent it when it is suggested that they pay some little portion of the tax for the building of roads or the development of the country." [41]

Delegate Wickersham then outlined the prevailing Alaska view—critical of both the industry and the Bureau of Fisheries—urging better protection for the salmon fisheries, advancing the belief that the people of Alaska should have some voice in their management, and opposing the "beginning of a permanent right" to fish-trap ownership as provided in the bill. He cited numerous petitions and read into the record a letter from Forest J. Hunt, a well-known merchant of Ketchikan (and later a territorial senator) expressing these sentiments:

". . . There is nothing of more vital necessity to southeastern Alaska than protective laws that will conserve the fish supply. The high price of canned salmon has created a mania for the canning business, and while it is helping business conditions here now, unless laws are enacted at once to protect the present and conserve the future supply it will be a matter of but a few years until our waters are denuded of one of Alaska's great resources. The fish traps should be abolished or very much restricted, and the drawing of seines in the mouths of fresh-water streams prohibited. There should be a greater force of government officials stationed in Alaska to enforce protective laws, provided with means of transportation without being compelled, as at present, to rely upon the boats of the canning companies whom they are supposed to prosecute for infractions of the laws. At present prices of canned salmon and normal conditions, a cannery can be built and equipped and paid for from the proceeds of the first season's pack and a nice margin of profit realized by the investors. Of course the abolishing of the fish traps would reduce this enormous margin of profit, but it would leave an attractive profit still, and to supply the necessary amount of fish would give employment to many more fishermen and be a factor toward increasing Alaska's population. . . ." [42]

The hearings concluded, no action on S. 5856, "A Bill to Amend an Act for the Protection and Regulation of the Fisheries of Alaska," was taken by the committee. It was the successor and forerunner of a score of bills with similar objectives introduced in the Senate and House over a period of eighteen years. Each would uncover the same conflict of interest. And so conservation of the Alaska salmon resource waited, because, apparently, the opponents of its further protection and regulation were powerful enough to prevail.

Was the federal agency entrusted with responsibility for the Alaska fisheries more than mildly interested in securing the legislation it sought? The question is suggested by the non-appearance at the hearings of any of its top officials. Neither the Secretary of Commerce and Labor, Charles Nagel, nor any of the assistant secretaries, nor the solicitor of the department, nor the Commissioner of Fisheries, nor the Deputy Commissioner, appeared even once at the eleven sessions of the hearings extending from April 11th to June 10th. Dr. Evermann and the Assistant Agent of the Division of Alaska Fisheries, Ward T. Bower, alone represented the federal government.

Alaska's deep interest, although vigorously expressed by its delegate, and from 1913 on by the biennial memorials of the Alaska legislature, was not a factor.

And yet while the territory's interest in the fisheries received no consideration, Alaska, as a new, if unsuccessful, contender for recognition, was to exercise an inadvertent influence on legislation in the national capital, and on the course of events back home.

The great concern of the Department of Commerce in behalf of legislation which would withdraw from Alaska the right to tax the fisheries, let alone regulate them, has been previously discussed in another context, the striving for self-government. The issue arises again in connection with the conservation of Alaska's fisheries. In Washington it mobilized all the departmental "brass." It brought the Secretary of Commerce, William C. Redfield, as a principal witness to the congressional committee rooms. It brought the department's solicitor, the Commissioner of Fisheries, a former Deputy Commissioner, as well as the lesser officialdom previously considered adequate for such hearings. It caused the cabinet officer to speak with an emphasis unwonted in him, in his predecessors entrusted with like responsibilities, and at no time characteristic of his subordinates when addressing themselves to the vital problem of Alaska's fisheries conservation.

Testifying as the opening witness on May 25, 1916, on H.R. 9528, "A Bill for the Protection, Regulation, and Conservation of the Fisheries of Alaska," Secretary Redfield devoted himself to the problem of Alaska's intromission into the realm of Alaska fisheries. Referring to the license taxes levied on the fisheries by the territorial legislature three years previously and re-enacted two years later, the Secretary of Commerce quoted from his previous annual report:

"Not even the possibility of such a situation, much less the situation itself, should be allowed to exist." This pronouncement he amplified fully. When he had concluded, the Chairman of the

Committee, Representative Joshua W. Alexander, D., of Missouri, asked a pertinent question:

"Well, what is the necessity for this legislation? What is there in the industry in Alaska that demands legislation?"

Secretary Redfield was unable to give the proper response: "You ask a question, Mr. Chairman, which will be answered more fully by the Commissioner of Fisheries than I am able to answer."

However, to the Chairman's question, it will be recalled, as to whether the bill was "framed in the department," Redfield replied that it was, "as a result of conferences . . . with . . . the experts of the department and with the parties concerned" and that it had "the substantially unanimous . . . support of the persons upon whom these taxes are to be imposed." [43]

Commissioner Hugh Smith testified briefly, gave the history of past attempts to secure legislation and stated that the bill's essential purpose was the preservation of Alaska's fisheries.

E. Lester Jones, former Deputy Commissioner of Fisheries, stressed the need of providing money for vessels for the bureau's inspectors. At present the bureau had only one small slow boat to cover the entire territory. That was "the primary reason for lack of enforcement of the law," and the wardens "simply were helpless." [44]

Asked by the Chairman whether there was "any depletion of the fish supply appreciable now," Jones replied: "The season varies, but I should say not . . . And I did not find that anybody, comparatively speaking, thought the future supply was in jeopardy." [45]

Mr. Ward T. Bower, now Agent of the Alaska Fisheries Service of the Bureau of Fisheries, after expressing his belief that "by intelligent regulation and conservation the fisheries of Alaska can be made to continue not only at their present high level of importance, but may be increased materially," [46] added that it had been "said by some that the fishery has become depleted seriously, but the department does not regard such as the case." [47] He then presented the bill, section by section.

There was a new scale of license fees. They differed from those proposed by the Bureau of Fisheries in S. 5856. Every establishment processing fish and every piece of gear was to be licensed at nominal figures. For the first time the fisherman's catch was taxed. On the other hand the license tax on canned salmon established in 1899, which in the department's drafts of earlier bills had been increased in view of higher salmon prices, was reduced—kings, reds and medium reds remaining at 4 cents, pinks and chums being lowered to 3 cents.[48]

There was a new method of distributing the license-tax revenue. One-half only was to go to the territory instead of all, as formerly. The other half was to be applied to the administration of the fisheries.[49]

There were substantial changes in the legislation concerning traps. The license would constitute notice that the location was owned by the licensee, that he would thereafter have exclusive right to it and that this right would go to his "heirs, administrators, executors, successors and assigns," and that he or they could mortgage, transfer or sell such. To hold it the licensee was not obligated to operate the trap every year, as provided in S. 5856, but only once in three years.

The length of the lead was limited to three thousand feet—there had been no limit previously—the lateral distance between traps was increased from the existing eighteen hundred to twenty-four hundred feet, and the end-to-end distance from three hundred to six hundred feet. The jigger was permitted, its length not to exceed three hundred feet.

Fishing was forbidden within five hundred yards from the mouth of "any" stream, or within any waters where the distance from shore to shore was less than three hundred feet.

A weekly closed period of thirty-six hours was provided, excluding the Arctic Ocean, Bering Sea, Cook Inlet and the Copper River Delta.

The Secretary of Commerce was permitted in his discretion to limit or stop fishing in rivers and lakes at a distance not to exceed five hundred yards from the mouth of a stream, but such power to be exercised only after a hearing for which due notice must be given not less than sixty days previously.

Dams had to be provided with fishways to be approved by the Secretary of Commerce. Pollution of waters was forbidden.

Privately owned hatcheries were to be purchased by the government, payment to be made by rebating their license taxes to the extent of the hatchery's value. Territorial taxation of the fisheries in any form, including both license and real- and personal-property taxes, was prohibited and the license taxes already enacted by the legislature were repealed.

The bill disclosed a marked contrast to that presented by the Bureau of Fisheries four years previously, S. 5856. The only significant conservation measure in the new bill, advocated earlier, was the prohibition to fish within five hundred yards of the mouth of "any" salmon stream—and not merely red-salmon streams—but the six hundred yards distance requested four years earlier was back at five hundred. The fixing of lead lengths and the widened distance between traps was a slight change toward conservation.

Perpetual trap ownership was definitely provided, thus conveying exclusive privileges on those who had the means to secure the sites.

Four years previously Dr. Evermann, testifying to the need of abolishing the jigger, which the departmental draft of S. 5856 had done, had stated: "A trap with a jigger becomes virtually a barricade and gives the fish little or no chance at all." [50]

After the protests in those 1912 hearings of the canned-salmon industry's representatives, Messrs. Dorr and Moser, against abolishing the jigger, Mr. Bower had ventured that if the committee decided "to allow jiggers on traps there ought to be a limit placed on the length of the jigger," and the following colloquy took place:

"THE CHAIRMAN: 'What limit would you suggest?'

"MR. BOWER: 'Well, conditions vary; but I should say that one hundred feet would be ample.'

"THE CHAIRMAN: 'That is, that the jigger should not extend out more than one hundred feet from the trap proper?'

"MR. BOWER: 'Yes, sir; and perhaps that is too much.' " [51]

In 1916 Mr. Bower was sanctioning a three-hundred-foot jigger without wincing.

The department's regulatory powers were sharply reduced. The previous draft had given the Secretary the power to close *any* area, if he considered it necessary in the interest of conservation. The new bill limited these powers to within five hundred yards of a stream. The previous bill had required a hearing on thirty days' notice before such action could be taken. The new bill required sixty days' notice, thus completely nullifying the power, since the possibilities of permitting escapement in an impaired stream would long since have passed after that length of time.

The previous draft provided a weekly thirty-six-hour closed period for all areas except Bering Sea. The new bill perpetuated the exception for Cook Inlet and the Copper River Delta in the Prince William Sound area.

The previous draft had forbidden the use of "aprons" to close traps during these weekly non-fishing periods—the apron being an easily removable web, which facilitated week-end trap-fishing violations. The new bill permitted the use of the apron.

The previous draft had provided for revocation of fish-trap licenses in case of conviction of their illegal use. The new bill omitted such penalty.

Delegate Wickersham denounced the bill unsparingly. If enacted it would "give the Fish Trust title to all these trap sites." [52] He cited the state of Washington's fisheries-code provision that it was unlawful for anyone to fish in its waters unless for twelve months previous he had been a resident of the state, saying:

"I have called this to your attention for the reason that I have been trying to get some laws passed here for seven years in order that we might have a fishing population in the Territory of Alaska; that we might have fishing hamlets and towns; that we might get something out of these fisheries with which to build homes, churches, schools and establish civilization there. But, on the contrary, the whole policy of these fish trusts is to take everything out of the territory and permit nothing to come into it. . . . They are robbing the territory." [53]

Wickersham attacked the canners' refusal to pay the territorial taxes and their efforts to get the territory's right to tax them repealed. He introduced numerous protests from Alaska. They included the memorial of the first legislature (S.J.M. 26), three years earlier, whose recommendations on conservation measures had acquired a new pertinence. They sought the "abolishment of the contrivance known as a jigger, the limiting of all leads on all fish traps to a length of six hundred feet, that no fish traps . . . be allowed within a distance of one mile from any salmon stream nor in any bay, estuary, inlet or channel . . . less than a mile in width, and that traps now established within such limits be removed." The memorialists further prayed that no law be enacted by Congress whereby any right or title to the tidelands or waters now occupied by fishing appliances could be acquired for fish-trap sites, nor any areas of tideland or water in any way reserved for the operation of any certain kind of fishing-gear contrivances to the exclusion of other fishing gear.[54]

The representatives of the canned-salmon interests, including Mr. Alexander Britton, representing the Alaska Packers' Association, had no criticism of the bill's provisions. They were well pleased with it. Only when possible modification by the House Committee of the section forbidding Alaska to levy any taxes whatever on the fisheries, to permit the territory to impose property taxes, was discussed, did Mr. Frank M. Warren, representing the Alaska-Portland Packers' Association, object.

"When we went over this measure," he said, "that is when I say 'we' I mean when the company I represent went over it, we considered that as long as the . . . taxation schedule of this bill should be in lieu of all other license fees and taxes . . . we were satisfied that the rate was equitable, but if the suggestion . . . is adopted that the territory be still permitted to levy on real and personal property, then we consider that the tax schedule provided is too high." [55]

Despite the 385 pages of printed hearings the bill never got out of committee. The canned-salmon interests, while satisfied with the bill, were even more content with the status quo, when it became clear that Wickersham's determined opposition would at least delete the section taking away Alaska's right to tax the fisheries. Under the status quo they had the fish traps—equipped with jigger of any length they pleased, with leads of unlimited lengths—not even an inch of closed area at the mouths of pink-salmon streams, in fact only the negligible restrictions of the 1906 law; and, what was new, a demonstratedly complaisant regulatory agency. As for the Bureau of Fisheries, it had, what was also new, an overriding preoccupation, greater even than the conservation of Alaska's fisheries. It was to conserve those fisheries for the bureau.

The industry and the bureau now had a common cause, which overshadowed all possible differences—to keep the territory from regulating and controlling the fisheries. For each a vital vested interest was at stake. Inevitably, while that common danger threatened, industry and the bureau would see eye to eye.

In consequence salmon fishing continued at an accelerated rate and by the end of the decade depletion was sufficiently evident that it was generally admitted.[56]

Bills to amend the 1906 act continued to be introduced regularly at every session of Congress, and hearings held on them with no result. By 1920 Commissioner Hugh M. Smith publicly expressed the view that the department's jurisdiction extending only five hundred yards from the stream mouth was "wholly inadequate." [57]

"Up until the present instance, I have never known cannery men operating in Alaska to come forward in any numbers publicly and state that Alaska was being overfished and that the salmon supply was in danger," testified Dr. C. H. Gilbert of Stanford University in 1921. He had been a consultant for the Bureau of Fisheries for twenty-one years and had visited Alaska eight times in the course of his investigations. "You can go along the entire coast of Alaska and talk with those engaged in fishing in past years, and you will not find any man . . . who does not admit the salmon supply has been seriously impaired and that the end of the industry is in sight . . . unless some strenuous measures are taken. . . . The packers themselves admit it. They have never done it heretofore, but they do it now and they know it is true. They are frightened about it, and are willing to have some remedial measures which heretofore they have been unwilling to have taken." [58]

How willing were they now? The hearings on H.R. 2394, the measure introduced in the first session of the newly installed Republican Congress, which became known as the White bill, throws light on their attitude. Mr. E. S. McCord of Seattle, representing Pacific American Fisheries, Libby, McNeill and Libby, the Fidalgo Island Packing Company and the Hoonah Packing Company, and Mr. Frank M. Warren, representing the Alaska-Portland Packers' Association, were on hand to protest that the measure did not go far enough! This, McCord further stated, was the view of all the salmon packers but one. Now they were preparing a substitute bill to present to the committee. [59]

In what way did the White bill not go far enough? Mr. McCord made clear that its provision to extend to three miles the existing distance of five hundred yards from the mouths of streams within which fishing was to be prohibited would eliminate numerous fish-trap locations. [60]

Instead Mr. McCord proposed to give the Secretary of Commerce unlimited power to stop fishing anywhere and everywhere—and not merely within three miles of the mouths of salmon streams. And, as had happened before, the bill before the committee was withdrawn and a substitute bill was under consideration.

"I prepared the first draft of the bill on Monday after I arrived in Washington," testified Mr. McCord, referring to the substitute bill. "I turned it over to the Solicitor of the department and had an interview with Mr. Hoover. He made certain suggestions as to it and turned it over to the Solicitor, and this is the result of his amendments to the original draft which I prepared on the part of the canners." [61]

Unlimited power—which the industry had so long resisted—would have an attractiveness to any bureau, especially in the emergency which Secretary Herbert Hoover declared now existed. And so Commerce's new chief favored the proposal. But he had detected and balked at a proposal in Mr. McCord's draft "that possessory rights of occupancy" should not be lost by nonuse caused by the closing or limiting of fishing. "The department," wrote Secretary Hoover to Committee Chairman William S. Greene, "would be opposed to a provision in any bill that would serve to create possessory rights in perpetuity, and if the language suggested would have that effect this department would not support it." [62]

The people of Alaska, who had already, through the Board of Fish Commissioners, gone on record as favoring the White bill, had likewise detected what seemed to them a "joker" in the substitute proposal and deluged Delegate Sutherland with protests. And he presented the opposition of the people of Alaska to what they, like Secretary Hoover, considered the creation of possessory rights in perpetuity in the fisheries.[63]

So, despite the admitted urgency of the situation, again no bill to protect the Alaska fisheries passed the Sixty-seventh Congress. The canners had turned thumbs down on the White bill; and their substitute, given Secretary Hoover's objection to what they considered its very essence, was rendered valueless. Another bill, H.R. 10427, containing Sutherland's limitation on traps in waters of less than certain widths, received a favorable committee report, but got no further.

The Harding administration was persuaded that the emergency called for extraordinary measures. It extended the Aleutian Islands reservation, established by President Taft eleven years earlier, for birds and fur-bearers, to apply to the fish in the surrounding waters, and eight months later created a Southwestern Alaska Fisheries Reservation, which included the Bristol Bay and Kodiak areas. The two reservations took in about 40 per cent of the fishing grounds, accounting for about one-third of the previous pack.

The Alaska reaction was unfavorable. The Sixth Territorial Legislature, meeting in March of 1923, made its first House Joint Memorial a vigorous protest. Although it was based primarily on principle and so couched, Alaskans' fears of the *administration* of the reserve were contained in the memorial's contention that "irrespective of the good intentions of present officials, the privileges upon a reserve must, in the very nature of things, go to those who maintain the strongest lobby. It cannot be presumed that before the Bureau of Fisheries . . . a claimant who can neither appear in person or by counsel can possibly have an even chance with one who is constantly represented by men specially skilled in presenting facts."

There were numerous other protests, based on the assumption in Alaska that this was a move inspired by the canned-salmon interests, and that administration of the reserves would favor them to the detriment of local fishermen—a situation which the protestors considered amply proved during the 1923 fishing season.

With the convening of the Sixty-eighth Congress in December of 1923 efforts were made to give legal justification to the executive orders creating the reservations, which had been challenged, while the arduous process of securing the legislation which Congress had been unable to achieve for more than a decade and a half was again undertaken. Representative Wallace H. White, Jr., R., of Maine, introduced H.R. 2714, which gave the President the power to declare fishery reservations pending action by Congress. Senator Wesley L. Jones introduced an identical measure, S. 486, which was known as the Jones bill. Delegate Sutherland, eager to get rid of the two reservations and to forestall others introduced a bill, H.R. 4826, giving the Secretary of Commerce full powers but providing "the right of fishing in areas where fishing is permitted shall not be denied to any citizen of the United States"—in other words, barring exclusive fishing rights by the granting of permanent trap privileges—and further forbidding the use of fixed or floating traps in any bay, inlet or estuary less than three miles wide, or within a mile of the mouth of any salmon stream.[64]

Supporting the legislation confirming the reservation policy was the new Commissioner, Mr. Henry O'Malley. He testified that not a single fishing district was capable of producing even approximately the number of salmon it had formerly furnished, and some were so seriously menaced that it would be wise to close them for a term of years: "The salmon packers," he said, "are always the last to acknowledge that overfishing is having its inevitable result, but as regards Alaska, they also have joined the ranks of those who agree that immediate action is imperative." [65]

Delegate Sutherland charged that the cannery interests had

brought about the reservation orders, because they felt they could control the Department of Commerce if there were no law but only its regulations. He cited the depletion of the Copper River, once a great red-salmon stream, despite the protests for years of the residents of that region against the establishment of canneries one hundred miles up the stream. But, said Sutherland, the reason it was not closed is because the cannery representatives were stronger than the Department of Commerce.[66]

Delegate Sutherland introduced voluminous evidence to show that as the reservations had been administered during the previous season, the larger companies had controlled who could and who could not fish.[67] He introduced a copy of a recommendation from the Alaska Packers' Association to the Bureau of Fisheries for a division of the fishing areas which had been followed almost to the letter by the bureau.[68] He cited examples of legitimate requests for fishing permits which had been refused. He read into the record a telegram from the Seattle Chamber of Commerce to various chambers in Alaska urging them to support the bill validating the reservations.[69]

Sutherland introduced a letter signed by seventy-seven residents of Yakutat urging no fish reserve be established there. It "would be most disastrous to us fishermen," they wrote, "as it would give practical monopoly to the Libby, McNeill and Libby Co. here. This in turn would force us to sell our fish to this mentioned company for little or nothing. Threats of lockout and starvation have often been resorted to in the past by this company to hold fish prices down, but at times fear of competition, and actually encountering such, has caused the Libby people to loosen up a little. . . .

"We took this matter of reserve up with Fish Commissioner O'Malley, Senator Jones and Representative Hadley on their visit here.[70] But we are doubtful as to the result. Mr. David Branch, Libby, McNeill and Libby manager of Seattle, was here at the time. He sought to bring pressure on us to go on record in favor of a reserve. But we could not betray our best interests. On the other hand, we pleaded with these representatives of our Government not to create a reserve. However, we suspect Mr. Branch had greater influence over them than we. . . ."[71]

Stephen B. Davis, Solicitor of the Department of Commerce, testified that the only penalties for violations that could be legally imposed in the reservations were the light ones provided by the act of 1906, thus furnishing further understanding of the advocacy of the fisheries reservations.[72]

Secretary Hoover had written the committee, "This method of protection works many inequities and a tendency to establish monopolies and is only in public interest as a temporary emergency method." [73] He repeated this in a fuller letter, February 7, 1924, concluding with: "We need constructive legislation . . . or another of our national heritages will be destroyed, and no interest, whether canners, fishermen, personal or partisan, has any right to oppose such constructive action . . . by Congress." [74]

President Coolidge added his voice by writing to Congress: "If our Alaskan fisheries are to be saved from destruction there must be further legislation declaring a general policy and delegating the authority to make rules and regulations to an administrative body." [75]

All this, the furor over the administration of the reservations, the obvious crisis, combined to favor action on a new White bill, H.R. 8143, which gave the Secretary of Commerce unrestricted powers.

In debate, Representative Ewin L. Davis, D., of Tennessee, stated that the bill represented "somewhat of a compromise," that it went further than some of those interested thought it should but not as far as others wanted, but that it gave the Secretary of Commerce such powers that if the salmon runs were not fully protected and permitted to multiply, "the responsibility will rest alone upon and the blame can be traceable to the Secretary of Commerce and the Bureau of Fisheries." [76]

Representative John Rankin, D., of Mississippi, observed that the bill did not prohibit traps and that they "not only destroy the supply of salmon but . . . deprive the individual of making his living by fishing. . . . It seems to me that if we are going to try to encourage people to go to Alaska and make it their home, these traps ought to be taken out and destroyed. . . ." [77]

Representative Wallace H. White, Jr., asked whether under the power given the Department of Commerce by the bill traps could not be prohibited.

"Yes," replied Delegate Sutherland, "but judging from the past, they never will." [78] And he introduced his amendment forbidding the use of traps in the narrower inside waters. The debate thereafter dealt largely with the amendment.

Representative Lindley H. Hadley, R., of Washington, leading off in opposition, declared purse seines were more deadly than traps, and trap fishing was "the most sanitary, most efficient, most economical, and the least difficult to control and supervise." [79]

Representative White felt that the bill, with the mandatory provision for 50 per cent escapement, went as far as necessary and feared the amendment would jeopardize the legislation.[80]

Representative John Franklin Miller, R., of Washington, a nephew of the California senator of the same name who had played so important a part in Alaska fur-seal matters in the early days of the district, opposed the amendment. Purse seines and gill nets, he felt, were as destructive of salmon as traps.[81]

Representative William S. Greene, R., of Massachusetts, Chairman of the Committee on Merchant Marine and Fisheries, said he had been a member of it for twenty-five years and in all that time, except for the law of 1906, it had been impossible to get agreement on Alaska-fisheries legislation. It was time to vote the bill.[82]

The Sutherland amendment carried fifty-one to forty-eight. Representative Greene called for tellers. On the recount the ayes were seventy-four, the noes sixty-three. Representative Greene noted the absence of a quorum and asked for a roll call. The amendment was adopted 182 to 139.

Representative Hadley then moved to amend the bill to eliminate the weekly closed period for Bering Sea and the waters tributary thereto—the Bristol Bay red-salmon area. He urged that the fishing there was only for thirty days and that four week-end one-and-a-half-day closing periods would leave only twenty-four days for fishing.[83]

Representative Davis said that the committee had considered the matter carefully and that if the men had twenty-four days, the fish should have four or five to produce fish of the future.[84] The amendment was defeated. The bill then passed by a voice vote.

Because of the continuing efforts of the canned-salmon industry to challenge the territorial legislature's right to tax the fisheries—the last attempt as recent as 1923 and in the courts on appeal at this time—Delegate Sutherland had requested that the bill reassert that right, and its final section did so.

In the Senate the White bill was referred to the Committee on Commerce. In committee the words "purse seines" were inserted into the paragraph containing the Sutherland amendment. On the floor

Senator Wesley L. Jones, the committee chairman, moved that the whole paragraph limiting both fish traps and purse seines be stricken. To eliminate both fish traps and purse seines would be "a very great injury and detriment," he said.[85] Without debate the amendment was agreed to.

The only dissenting voice in the upper house was that of Senator William H. King, D., of Utah, who said he "would prefer to trust the people of Alaska to handle the problem than . . . trust an unrestrained bureaucracy." [86]

The House refused to concur in the Senate amendment. The Senate insisted upon it and requested a conference. Out of the conference committee the bill was reported with Senator Jones's modification, that is, without the Sutherland amendment. It became law June 26, 1924 (43 Stat. 464).

The White Act was widely considered a milestone in the long effort to perpetuate Alaska's salmon fisheries. It was promptly hailed as insuring their permanence by the fisheries industry's trade journal.[87] Even fifteen years later it was acclaimed as having "become a landmark in conservation philosophy and technique." [88] Its greatest novelty was the declaration of congressional "intent and policy" that there be an escapement of not less than 50 per cent. The only question that seemed to remain was whether congressional appropriations would be adequate to enforce regulations which the Secretary of Commerce and the Bureau of Fisheries were free to make, and, in Alaska, whether the virtually absolute regulatory powers conferred by the act would be exercised wisely.

The appropriations had been improving, though, in the view of the bureau, still far from sufficient. Commissioner O'Malley testified that in 1923 around $125,000 had been expended, and that eight vessels and fifty stream watchmen had guarded the Alaska fisheries, while British Columbia, with a much shorter coastline and a much smaller fishery, was spending $325,000 a year.[89] But in 1924, after the passage of the White Act, the bureau operated ten vessels, which with crews, 103 stream guards and sixteen statutory employees made a total of 146 government employees in the Alaska fisheries.[90]

The Twilit Twenties

Civilization needs continuity of effort in place.
ISAIAH BOWMAN, 1931

ALASKA was going backward.

"She's on the skids right now," was the testimony of the Director of the United States Coast and Geodetic Survey—a competent and well-informed witness—at one of the numerous inquests held by those who retained the responsibility for Alaska to discover what they ought to do about "her." [1]

For the United States the nineteen twenties were confident, lusty, expansive and rambunctious years. Only a fool or a knave would "sell America short." That was the widespread assumption, at least, till late October, 1929. But in Alaska it was a period in which words replaced deeds at governmental levels. Constructive endeavor, seldom conspicuous, and as often offset by destructive legislation and paralyzing restraint, was now to be succeeded by a phase in which action in re Alaska was a shrug. In the territory, the realization that, in Wickersham's words, "Alaska is only a red-headed stepchild and the other children want its estate," [2] had been translated into a general exodus. In Washington, on the other hand, Alaska was viewed as a more or less hopeless problem child.

It was not always admitted. "Alaska is going ahead," was Governor Bone's salutatory.[3] Scott C. Bone of New York was President Harding's appointee. He had been a newspaper man in various cities, editor of the Seattle *Post-Intelligencer*, and in charge of publicity for the Republican National Committee during the 1920 campaign. His appointment did not carry out the 1916 platform pledge which, "reaffirming the attitude long maintained by the Republican Party," held that "officials appointed to administer the government of any territory should be bona-fide residents." But then neither had been the previous Republican gubernatorial appointee, Walter E. Clark. Alaskans, through circumstance devoid of their customary starch, and having met and liked friendly and personable Bone when he accompanied a Seattle Chamber of Commerce tour to Alaska some years earlier, were inclined to make a jest of the matter. "Well, if he's not *bona* fide, at least he's Bone!" Besides, the 1920 Republican platform had said nothing whatever about Alaska.

"Inherently Alaska is all right," wrote Governor Bone a year later.[4] By nature an optimist, he was no doubt following the current vogue of Emile Coué, a famous French physician, whose cult of cure was embodied in the therapeutic phrase, "Every day, in every way, I'm getting better and better." Fundamentally, Alaska was sound!

A usual concomitant of such hopeful expression was denunciation of governmental sins of omission and commission in respect to Alaska:

"Of the inefficiency of federal administration in Alaska, through innumerable agencies constituting a bureaucratic form of government, official testimony, based on experience, is in full accord," wrote Bone.[5]

Dr. Hubert Work of Colorado, who had succeeded Albert B. Fall of New Mexico as Secretary of the Interior in the Harding cabinet, officially pronounced: "Alaska is rapidly becoming a lost province."[6] In a widely publicized magazine article entitled, "What Future Has Alaska?" Secretary Work answered his own question:

"Alaska, our last frontier, is a territory with its resources and national wealth undeveloped. Without the inspiration of self-government and freedom, essential to natural expansion, the country is now being retarded by unnecessary activity of government bureaus, whose officials have been made hesitant by limited local authority and confused by far distant direction."[7]

"If the Finns owned Alaska," declared President Harding in a public address in Seattle after his visit to the territory, "they would in three generations make it one of the foremost states in modern times."[8]

Alaska was more and more resembling the weather which everyone talks about but nobody does anything about.

Dr. Work was not without a prescription: "The situation calls for prompt sympathetic study by Congress. . . . The suggestion that all of the government's activities in Alaska be merged into one department should have the immediate consideration of Congress."[9]

That department would, of course, be Interior. Such a plan had been worked at since 1914, eleven years earlier, and had gotten no-

where. Nor had any evidence been adduced that it would improve
matters.

Then there was the "darkest-before-dawn" motif. "Indifferent and
inefficient systems of administration" which had been "imposed for
fifty-five years" had "been a heavy handicap to settlement and industry," declared Governor Bone in his dedicatory address at the
Alaska Agricultural College and School of Mines on September 13,
1922. "But a measure of co-ordination is coming about and constructive policies are now assured. No longer can it be said that the
government at Washington is neglectful and unconcerned. An awakened public interest in Alaska's welfare is speeding a better era. Material advancement has been marked during the year and every prospect is today most heartening." [10]

And two and a half years later Governor Bone declared: "The biennium has not marked an appreciable growth in population or development of industry, but it has witnessed a steady progress." [11]

In mid-decade President Calvin Coolidge turned his attention
briefly to Alaska. He had earlier communicated to Congress the need
for legislating for the conservation of Alaska's fisheries. Now he
animadverted on the high cost of the territory.

"The time has come for careful investigation of the expenditures
and success of the laws by which we have undertaken to administer
our outlying possessions. A very large amount of money is being expended for administration in Alaska. It appears so far out of proportion to the number of inhabitants and the amount of production as to
indicate cause for thorough investigation." [12]

The President's message struck a receptive chord in Congress.
Representative Allen T. Treadway, R., of Massachusetts, said that
altogether too much money was being spent in Alaska: Eleven million dollars annually for a mere twenty thousand white people. The
smallness of Alaska's population—and it seemed generally that
"white" population alone was considered—became a reason for retrenchment. Some Congressmen were re-enacting—not too unhap-
pily—the days of 1868. There was nothing in Alaska to justify anyone's living there. The fact that so many people had left proved it.

The operating deficiency for the Alaska Railroad furnished a fruit-
ful theme for oratory. Scrapping the railroad was seriously recommended. When Representative John W. Summers, R., of
Washington, suggested that we had spent large sums of money on the

Panama Canal, Treadway retorted that that was different; the Panama Canal was self-supporting. "Alaska is not and never will be." [13] His program was that the use of the Alaska Railroad be very materially curtailed, road and trail building stopped, government positions vacated, and the whole management of the territory placed under the Interior Department.

Representative Edward T. Taylor, D., of Colorado, agreed that no one could "accomplish anything with all this labyrinth of bureaucracy up there." He would stop "all this meddling" and put everything in Alaska under one bureau.[14]

No reduction of the bureaucracy followed, but appropriations which would benefit Alaskans or help develop Alaska were cut back all along the line.

The railroad, to be sure, was not making its operating expenses and the first year's deficit, $1,739,000, provoked a congressional storm. But some of the reasons for it were clear. Apart from the long delay in its inauguration and its inadequate construction, no effort whatever had been made in the Interior Department, whose responsibility it was, to develop any traffic, an endeavor which should have begun with the determination of the route in 1915. The need to do this was specifically called to Secretary Lane's attention.[15] In 1920 the Senate by resolution inquired of the department what steps had been taken to develop and settle the country through which the railroad would be built, what organization had been created for that purpose, and what measures had been adopted to develop traffic.[16]

The reply was that no organization had been created and no steps taken because the department did not deem itself authorized to do so under the act for the railroad's construction.[17] There the matter rested. Neither did the Congress, which initiated the inquiry, provide the legislation for this obviously necessary supplementary task, nor did the Interior Department display any initiative in seeking such authority or proceeding without it, which could have been done without specific legislative authorization. Nor had the Alaska Road Commission, whose chief, Wilds P. Richardson, was antagonistic to the railroad project, done anything about constructing the feeder roads, which, as had been pointed out in the debates preceding the railroad legislation, were essential adjuncts to the undertaking.

At the same time road appropriations were far, far short of need. In 1920 a ten-year road program to cost ten million dollars had been prepared by the Alaska Road Commission, which had the approval of President Harding, the Interdepartmental Board, an advisory body dealing with Alaska established by the Secretary of the Interior, with representation of the other departments, approval of the Territorial Board of Road Commissioners and all other federal and territorial officials concerned. But in each of the first five years congressional appropriations were less than half the estimates and the program had to be greatly reduced, three-quarters of the funds having to go for maintenance.

By the end of the decade, in 1930, when the Alaska Road Commission had completed a quarter-century of service, it had, in that period, expended on the construction of wagon roads and trails and on their maintenance just under fifteen million dollars. Of the total, $10,965,437 was appropriated by Congress, $3,566,870 came from the Alaska fund, and $1,453,212 from territorial appropriations. Thus nearly one-third of the funds had come from the territory, a higher proportion than was contributed to road construction under the Federal Aid Highway Act of 1916 by a number of the Western states, and twice what would have been Alaska's percentage had the benefits of the act been extended to it. Federal road moneys for Alaska were therefore not only short of need, but short of equity.

Actually, the railroad, while delayed in fulfilling its mission, would substantially contribute to "opening up" interior Alaska, which had suffered greater economic deterioration than the coastal areas. The middle twenties saw the increasing transformation of much individual and small-scale placer mining into the big business of hydraulicking and dredging—by 1929, 71 per cent of Alaska's placer gold was extracted by dredges—and the heavy machinery for it was in part transported on the railroad with substantial savings for the consignees. At about the same time was developed the process of thawing out, by the use of water and steam, sections of placer ground underlaid by permafrost. These factors facilitated the establishment of the Fairbanks Exploration Company, a subsidiary of the powerful United States Smelting, Refining & Mining Company of Boston, which in 1928 assembled three dredges in the Fairbanks area, and with operations in Nome was to become the principal gold-mining enterprise in the interior of Alaska. By the acquisition of the claims of many smaller operators and prospectors—and conditions in Alaska made it a good buyer's market—and by intensive development work, it would be the dominant economic factor in the North for the next twenty-five years. It was likewise to be a considerable political factor. It was almost continuously represented in the legislature in both the Fourth and Second Division delegations.

Other undertakings assisted by the railroad were those headed by Austin E. Lathrop, a self-made captain of industry, who acquired by government lease the only mine in the Nenana coal fields that was operated from the early twenties, and added to his holdings a great variety of profitable enterprises—motion-picture theatres, banks, general-merchandise stores, apartment houses, newspapers, the Alaska distributorship for a well-known beer, and, later, radio stations. Fairbanks was the headquarters of his economic empire.

But just as the railroad, after seven years of operation, was barely beginning to fulfill its purpose, a change of federal policy threatened to jeopardize its usefulness and for a time did so. Irked by the continuing operating deficits, the Seventy-first Congress (1929-1931) ordered an investigation.[18] A select committee of the Senate composed of Senators Robert B. Howell, R., of Nebraska, as Chairman, John Thomas, R., of Idaho, and John B. Kendrick, D., of Wyoming, visited Alaska and recommended a drastic increase in the already high passenger and freight rates. Passenger rates were to be raised from 6 cents to 10 cents a mile, freight rates to provide at least 50 per cent more revenue.[19] The Howell committee's recommendation was in effect a mandate to the Interior Department; the congressional alternative was shutting down the railroad completely, and the increases went into effect on April 1, 1931. Freight from Seattle to Fairbanks, which had previously been $78.20 a ton, now cost $119.00. Business slumped and the voice of protest from central Alaska was emphatic.

President Bunnell, attempting with slender means to conduct the Alaska Agricultural College and School of Mines on the line of the railroad a few miles west of Fairbanks, detailed by letter to the Congress the hardship which these rate increases imposed not only on that institution, but on the whole interior community. Recalling the declared purpose of the earlier Congress to construct the railroad that it might aid in the development of the agricultural and mineral resources of Alaska and the settlement of its public lands, he wrote: "An instrumentality calculated to be of service to the people of the United States is perfunctorily resolved into a mechanism of extortion to wrest from the people served by the railroad the last farthing they are humanly able to pay." [20]

In Washington, Delegate Wickersham vainly attempted to combat the recommendations of the Howell report and to prevent the rate increases. While without the railroad "we would be lost," he insisted that until it was "frankly operated on the theory that its main purpose is the development of the territory, we are not much better off with it than we would be without it." He contrasted the railroad grants in the Western states and concluded:

"We feel that a million dollars a year spent on the Alaskan road is a small outlay in comparison with the tremendous wealth that has flowed into the United States from a section of the country which is being treated as a stepchild." [21]

The Howell committee had also cited, as adversely affecting the railroad, the competition of automobiles and trucks over the wagon road connecting Valdez and Fairbanks which had been christened the "Richardson Highway." But the drastic rail-rate increases merely stimulated and increased this competitive traffic with consequent loss of passengers and tonnage to the railroad. The Seventy-second Congress sought to meet this aggravation of what it deemed the railroad's problem by transferring the Alaska Road Commission from the War Department to the Interior Department, and in the same act of June 30, 1932 (47 Stat. 446) authorizing the Secretary of the Interior in his discretion to levy and collect tolls. In consequence a toll of $9 a ton was imposed on freight trucked over the Richardson Highway. The toll, designed "to help the railroad," did not help either the railroad or the people living along these now costlier arteries of transportation. The net result of these congressional and departmental measures was to hinder the development of the interior and to increase the unpopularity in Alaska of the Department of the Interior. Against these tolls Alaska's delegate would for nearly a decade protest in vain. [22]

Settlement was further postponed by the elimination by Congress of funds for triangulation. the basis of land surveys.

"It is unfortunate that the triangulation undertaken several years ago in the interior of Alaska had to be abandoned for lack of funds," wrote Governor Parks in his 1926 report. [23] George Alexander Parks had come to Alaska in 1907. From 1908 to 1917 he was mineral examiner for the General Land Office, served as chief of its field Division from 1920 to 1923, and as assistant supervisor of surveys and public lands until his appointment by President Coolidge as governor, June 16, 1925. After explaining in detail how this work was essential to getting land into private ownership, Governor Parks added: "It is to be hoped that this work will be included in the program during the next year." But it wasn't. "Discontinued for the present," was his report the following year. Nor was it resumed during the remainder of his administration, which ended in 1933.

The appropriation for the mine-experiment station at Fairbanks, which had been established in 1917, was deleted from the departmental budget in 1925 and the station closed. Alaska's was the only one of the ten stations conducted by the United States Bureau of Mines that was discontinued. It had rendered valuable assistance to prospectors and miners. The assay work was, however, taken over by the Alaska Agricultural College and School of Mines, and the bureau continued to pay the salary of the mineral analyst.

Prospecting and mining were likewise not advanced by the reduction of the appropriations for the investigation of the mineral resources in Alaska by the United States Geological Survey, which had reached an annual figure of $100,000 during the years 1914 to 1918 inclusive. Thereafter for the next seven years it was reduced to $75,-000, an amount smaller than at any time since 1904; to $72,000 in 1926; to $50,000 in 1927. It was $60,000 in 1928; $67,500 in 1929 and 1930.

Indeed the entire Alaska appropriation for the Geological Survey narrowly escaped elimination in the closing days of the Hoover administration. (This was in the last of the so-called "lame-duck" sessions abolished by the Twentieth Amendment to the Constitution sponsored by Senator George W. Norris, R., of Nebraska.) Although the previous year Secretary Wilbur had stressed that less than 45 per cent of Alaska had been mapped "even in a reconnaissance way and reported from the point of view of its mineral resources," [24] the item was wholly deleted in the House from the Interior Department appropriation bill for the fiscal year 1934. Delegate Wickersham attempted to get the departmental request for $60,000 which had been appropriated the previous year reinserted on the floor of the House, but unsuccessfully. However he got the Senate to insert it, and in amputated form it survived the conference between upper and lower house,[25] being cut to $30,000, a figure lower than in any year since 1900.

While the effort to have appropriation items deleted by one house restored in the other was not limited to Alaska's delegates, and was, of necessity, indulged in by senators and representatives, to no other member of Congress did the task fall so often and beset with such difficulties, in view of the delegate's votelessness and lack of power to reciprocate a legislative favor by the process known as "logrolling." The requirement to represent Alaska not merely in the House but in the Senate on such occasions, and before the multitude of bureaus, to render services that even in the states of smallest population were shared by not fewer than three members of Congress—two senators and a representative, all with a vote—made the task of the Alaska delegate the most arduous and difficult assignment among the 531 elected members.

Mining itself declined steadily in the twenties. The first year of the decade was the highest in mineral production, to a value of $23,-330,586, though less than half what it had been in the peak year, 1916. With fluctuations it was down to $18,220,692 by mid-decade, in 1925, dropped to $13,812,000 in 1930, and, as the nationwide depression deepened, sank to $12,278,000 in 1931, to $11,638,000 in 1932 and to $10,366,000 in 1933—the lowest point since 1904, thirty years earlier.

Alaska's agricultural-experiment stations were totally eliminated from the Department of Agriculture budget in 1931. Various proposals to keep them alive were entertained. Colonel Otto F. Ohlson, General Manager of the Alaska Railroad, in the belief that abolition of the two stations on the line of the railroad, in the Matanuska Valley and in the Tanana Valley near Fairbanks, would be detrimental to traffic in its further discouragement of possible farm settlers, offered to maintain these two stations "on a modified scale," [26] and the Interior Department's Budget Officer, Mr. E. K. Burlew, assured the chairman of the Senate Appropriations Committee, Senator Wesley L. Jones, that the railroad could do this "without the appropriation of additional funds." [27] All that was needed was new language in the appropriation item for the Alaska Railroad, permitting such use of funds, which was provided.

The station at Rampart had been closed in 1925. The Sitka and

Kodiak stations were now also abandoned. The Fairbanks and Matanuska Valley stations were nominally kept alive for a year under railroad management. However, the next year they were transferred to
the care of the land-grant Alaska Agricultural College and School of
Mines. The saving of these two experiment stations was achieved
through the efforts of Charles Ernest Bunnell, former schoolteacher
and federal district judge in Alaska, who had become the first president of the college and would continue to serve for a quarter of a century. It became the University of Alaska in 1935.

In 1929 he had persuaded the Department of Agriculture to support the extension to Alaska of legislation known as the Hatch Act
(24 Stat. 440) approved March 2, 1887, to establish agricultural-
experiment stations in connection with land-grant colleges. The
act authorized an annual appropriation of $15,000 for such college.
The act extending the Hatch Act to Alaska (45 Stat. 1256) limited
the number of stations that could be maintained under it to two.
The appropriation would scarcely have permitted more. The stations'
lands and buildings were turned over to the college. Dr. Bunnell
likewise persuaded the Congress to make an additional grant of 100,-
000 acres to it. The only difficulty was that the act (45 Stat. 1091)
specified that the acreage be in "vacant non-mineral surveyed and
unreserved lands" and no money or means for surveying such land,
or of determining its non-mineral character was provided. Thus the
university was unable to benefit by the potential revenues from the
grant.

Congress had through the years enacted other acts further endow-
ing agricultural research and agricultural-extension work in connection with land-grant colleges. Despite the earnest efforts of Dr.
Bunnell and Alaska's delegates, these acts would not be made available to Alaska for some years and then the appropriations would be
reduced from the amounts authorized by law and enjoyed by the
states.

The educational field which the federal government had pre-
empted—that of the natives who constituted approximately half of
Alaska's population—was likewise severely stinted.

"The appropriation made by Congress is not large enough," Secretary Work stated in his 1924 report. Of the total native population
of 25,508, as reported in the previous census, fewer than half—11,-
158—were served.[28]

"Every phase of the work of the Bureau of Education," wrote Governor Parks four years later, "is hampered by lack of funds. There are large villages without school facilities; some of them have more than fifty children of school age; many sections are without medical attention of any kind; the hospitals are the best the limited appropriations will provide, but they are woefully inadequate." [29]

The military establishment in Alaska, with the exception of Fort Seward, near Haines, more generally known as Chilkoot Barracks, was abandoned in the twenties, beginning with Fort Davis, near Nome, in 1921.[30] Fort Egbert at Eagle, Fort Gibbon at Tanana, Fort St. Michael on Norton Sound and Fort Liscum at Valdez were abandoned in 1925.[31] The purpose for which these outposts had been established—to maintain law and order during the gold-rush days in the absence of any civil government equipped to do so—had ceased to exist. The idea of establishing in Alaska an outpost for national defense was not entertained. There is no evidence that it even occurred to the military or congressional authorities of that time.

Suggested care of Alaska's insane in some of the abandoned Army structures led to a request by Congress that the Secretary of the Interior, to whom they were turned over, investigate such a possibility. The arrangement, in existence since 1904, by which the Interior Department was paying the Sanitarium Company at Portland, Oregon, so much annually per patient—$624 in 1926—had come under constant criticism in Alaska. Though the military buildings were found unsuitable, Governor Parks, whose views Secretary Work had requested, recommended that the existing contract system be abolished and that "steps be taken to provide a suitable institution under government control." In a detailed report he estimated the cost of construction of a suitable institution in Alaska at $575,000 and the cost of maintenance at $500 per patient per annum. Opposition to a change in the existing arrangement was expressed by Representative Maurice E. Crumpacker, R., of Portland, Oregon. Secretary Work transmitted to Congress without recommendation Governor Parks's report as well as that of a department inspector who likewise recommended non-renewal of the contract with the owners of the Morningside Hospital at Portland when it expired in 1930.[32] Congress took no action toward constructing an institution in Alaska and the contract was renewed by Secretary Work's successor, Secre-

tary Ray Lyman Wilbur, as, despite Alaskan pleas, it would continue to be by his successors for the next twenty-four years.

The profits from the custody of Alaska's insane during the half century of federal control have been a vested Oregon interest. Invariably
the Secretary of the Interior would accommodate the state's legislators by preserving that pecuniary perquisite for their home institution.
The increasingly indicated requirements of modern psychiatric therapy and the meliorating factors of familiar surroundings and access-
ibility to relatives and friends, for these doubly underprivileged—
the mentally ill of the Territory—would be subordinated to other
considerations.

Moreover the proceeding by which these unfortunates are committed is barbarously antiquated. Upon a written complaint "by any
adult person," the local United States commissioner impanels a jury
of six adults to determine the mental condition of the individual
"charged" with being insane. Before the "trial" the commissioner
appoints "some suitable person" to appear for the person complained
of as insane. If so found by the commissioner and jury, he is turned
over to the custody of the United States marshal, who delivers him—
precisely as one convicted of a crime—to the mental institution designated by the Secretary of the Interior. If a physician is available in
the community the commissioner shall call upon him for an opinion,
but if there is not—which is the case in the greater part of Alaska—
the taking of medical testimony is discretionary with the commissioner.

Alaskans are powerless to remove this relic of medievalism since the
Organic Act of 1912 specifically forbids the Territorial legislature "to
alter and amend, modify and repeal" the federal code dealing with
Alaska's insane, legislation which, enacted half a century ago, ante-
dated modern mental therapy. That so crass an anachronism persists
may be ascribed in part to the general congressional uninterestedness
in Alaskan matters, but more particularly to the apprehension of those
who are not disinterested that a suitable reform, once undertaken
conscientiously, would likewise abolish the absentee contract system.

Except for the White Act of 1924 to conserve Alaska's salmon,
no legislation of importance for Alaska took place in the successive
administrations of Harding, Coolidge and Hoover. Mention should
be made of another conservation law, to protect the likewise depleted
northern Pacific halibut fishery, enacted June 7, 1924 (43 Stat. 648),

followed by an exchange of ratifications of a convention for that purpose between Great Britain and the United States, proclaimed October 22, 1924 (43 Stat. 1841).

Noted likewise should be an act of January 13, 1925 (43 Stat. 739), ending the divided control by Commerce and Agriculture of Alaska's wild-life by centering the management of all the territory's game and fur-bearers in the Biological Survey of the Department of Agriculture. The new act created the Alaska Game Commission, to be composed of four Alaskans, one from each judicial division, and the executive officer, a federal official, all five to be appointed by the Secretary of Agriculture. The commission was to make recommendations to him as to game regulations. While the act constituted a substantial improvement of the previously inadequate Alaska game laws which had been the object of almost unrelieved criticism since the first enactment of June 7, 1902, it still fell far short of Alaskans' expressed desires to manage their wild-life resources. Governor Parks, a year and a half later, reported that it had "not proved to be as satisfactory as was anticipated when the law was enacted." [33] These three acts, while necessary, were in fact merely corrective of previous defective legislation.[34]

Noted also should be the establishment, by presidential proclamation, February 27, 1925, of Glacier Bay National Monument of some 1,164,800 acres, subsequently enlarged to 2,297,734, which, with McKinley National Park and Katmai National Monument, constituted a total park area in Alaska larger than the combined areas of three small states, Connecticut, Delaware and Rhode Island. No appropriations would be made, however, for a quarter of a century for the two monuments, and the park appropriations were delayed and, when made, meager.[35] The first park appropriation was for the fiscal year 1922—to the extent of $8,000. It permitted of the employment of a park superintendent and one ranger.[36] There were no roads in the park, but in 1923 an arrangement would be made between the Alaska Road Commission and the National Park Service by which the trail to the Kantishna mining district leading ninety miles westward through the park area would be improved and in time converted into a wagon road.

The visit of President Harding to Alaska in the summer of 1923, the first time a chief executive of the nation had set foot in the territory, with the accompanying three cabinet members, Hoover, Work and Wallace, and various congressmen, was described as a "shot in the arm" to Alaskans' spirits. But with his death, the loss of that powerful "friend at court," who had "been there" and had "seen it," the obvious lack of interest in Alaska in the national capital, the persistent ignoring by Congress of every vital request repeatedly sought in legislative memorials, the declining population—all this had its effect on the Alaskans' morale. They began, many of them, to subscribe to the view that there was really nothing much in Alaska, or if there was, the federal government made it too difficult to get. An increasing number, while doing well in some retail enterprise, began to think of Alaska as merely a temporary abode. "Get in, get it and get out," became their motto, and not a few pursued such a course successfully. That attitude did not in turn stimulate or maintain concern for the building up of the territory. "Why pay taxes to support schools? We'll be 'outside' by the time the youngsters are ready for high school. Why be taxed for civic improvements when we won't be here to enjoy them? Why build a good home here? We'll build it 'down below.' Let's get along in this shack or 'wannigan.' Why put a hook in the wall? A nail will do." And so the profits of many an enterprise were sent "down below" to be invested there—principally in Seattle real estate. Not all, by any means, so thought and acted. But enough to create doubt, instability, and the contagion of disparagement.

The same underlying conditions and the public's reactions registered with their elected representatives. A decade had shown Alaska's legislators that they could not legislate on matters most vital to them. Their efforts had been repeatedly frustrated. Congress had shut the door on their attempts to secure lower steamship rates and better service. The Supreme Court had locked the door securely and told the Alaskans that they were territorial colonials. By the White Act Congress had foreclosed Alaskans' principal aspiration—control of their fisheries. And while under its administration the salmon supply had apparently been fully restored and even reaching new heights, the social and economic effects on the residents of Alaska were not correspondingly beneficial.

With an annual pack of some five million cases the Alaskan fisheries were employing some 5,960 independent fishermen, while British Columbia with a pack of only a million and a quarter cases was using the services of 7,312 fishermen. So Delegate Dan Sutherland informed the Congress, saying that with the same proportion Alaska would have a resident population of eighteen thousand fishermen.[37] Since the inauguration of the White Act the number of traps considered by fishermen to be in competition with them had increased. It was 442 the year before enactment; 458 in 1924; 546 in 1925; 639 in 1926 and 799 in 1927. Purse seines had increased in the same period only from 510 in 1923 to 593 in 1927; gill nets had diminished somewhat from 3,473 to 3,037. In 1926 the industry reached an all-time peak of 6,653,882 cases, and prices were also high. But the employment was predominantly of those brought up from the States and paid off there after their return from the fishing and canning season. The industry's heads maintained that they could not get sufficient competent labor in Alaska, which allegation in turn was denied by its residents.[38]

So with a basic framework of local government erected in the first few sessions and no matters of great importance any longer to legislate about, the legislature's chief need was for revenue—to support schools, to extend the almost nonexistent health service, to augment the inadequate amounts available for the all-essential roads, to make harbor and water-front improvements, to get into this new airport construction. But a dwindling population and a stationary economy made for timidity. This attitude was abetted by the larger fishing and mining interests which were paying extremely slight taxes under the existing license system and, understandably—being almost all either temporary residents or nonresidents—wanting to keep them so.[39] "Do not affright outside capital," was their plausible and comprehensible counsel of caution.

Actually, the taxes they paid were exceedingly moderate—and it was long before the day of high federal personal income and corporation levies. Frugality, and not prodigality, was characteristic of Alaskan legislatures. The mining companies for the first decade were paying the negligible 1 per cent (increased from ½ per cent imposed by the first legislature) on the net proceeds of mining with a $5,000 exemption. In 1923, the mining lobby succeeded in having the exemption raised to $10,000, but as a compensatory gesture agreed that 1.5 per cent would be paid on the net profits in excess of $500,000, and 1.75 per cent on all in excess of $1,000,000. "Jim" Fozzard, the big, plausible lobbyist for Kennecott, accomplished that, working from his lavishly liquor-stocked room in the Gastineau Hotel. The word "net" of course permitted every form of deduction—depletion, federal taxes, lobbying expenses, etc.—to such an extent that it came to be known as a "nit" tax.

The canned-salmon industry, the greater part of the fisheries, beginning in 1915, were paying 4 cents a case on kings and reds; 2 cents on cohos; 1 cent on pinks and chums—a case consisting of forty-eight one-pound cans. This was less than 1 per cent on kings and reds at current prices; less than one-half of one per cent on the others, though, to be sure, on the market price per case, and not, as with the mining industry, on the "net." In 1917 salmon prices had doubled for some species, tripled for others, but the third legislature in that year raised the tax by only half a cent on three species, one cent on the two others. By 1919 reds and kings were selling at $13 a case, cohos at $11, pinks and chums at $6. The fourth legislature in that year, while raising the per-case tax slightly, provided a new departure—an additional tax of 1 per cent on the net income of canneries. And the sixth legislature in 1923 provided a graduated pack tax on the product of any one cannery. The industry refused to pay these levies and again challenged the territory's right to tax it. An action by Pacific-American Fisheries brought in the United States District Court at Juneau to restrain the territorial treasurer from enforcing the provisions applicable to the canneries was dismissed by the court. In a subsequent suit by the territory against the company to recover the amount due, judgment was rendered against the company with penalty for nonpayment and accrued interest added (February 9, 1924, 7 Alaska 160). On appeal to the Ninth Circuit Court at San Francisco the District Court's judgment for the territory was affirmed (October 20, 1924, 2 Fed. 9) and an appeal for a rehearing denied. The case went to the United States Supreme Court on *certiorari*, which on December 7, 1925, likewise upheld the lower court's decision (269 U.S. 269). In delivering the opinion for the court, Justice Oliver Wendell Holmes pointed out that the latest revision of the Alaska fisheries law, namely the White Act of June 6, 1924, enacted after the judgment of the District Court had been rendered, specifically affirmed the power of the legislature to tax the fisheries.

Actually the industry missed the opportunity to co-operate with the legislature in drafting revenue measures that would vary with the value of the pack rather than on its number of cases. When salmon prices dropped, taxes had been fixed for the biennium. But even when the war-inflated prices diminished they remained far above pre-war levels, and but for the depression years of the early nineteen thirties, would show a steadily rising curve for the next quarter of a century. Costs of operation, of course, were also increasing for the industry—and the government. So the legislative struggles resolved themselves in the twenties and thereafter into the securing of adequate revenues for territorial needs, which was countered by the mining and fishing industries' strategy of "keeping her down," that is, in decrying the needs. To discredit any item of expenditure concerning which doubt could be aroused became the assignment of the lobbyists and such legislators as they could influence or control. It was this motivation that killed the appropriation for the Agricultural College and School of Mines in the 1919 legislature and postponed the college's opening two years, as it would continue to keep the college, and later, the university, appropriations at the lowest levels of parsimony. Primary and secondary education they dared not attack, but "higher" education could be portrayed as a luxury. Wouldn't it be cheaper, it was suggested, to send those youngsters who must have a college education, "outside"? Such propaganda, and "Where is the money coming from?", a rhetorical pseudo-query inculcated by the lobbyists, found fertile soil in a growing legislative conservatism, inconsistent with the traditionally enterprising spirit of the frontier, but logically consequent to a dwindling population and a stationary or declining economy.[40] In the territorial legislatures the twenties and early thirties were sterile years. Territorial vision and hope were in twilight.

One legislative reaction was the endeavor to vest such autonomy as the legislature might dispense in the people of Alaska. It crystallized in the effort to enact what became known as the Comptroller Bill. Discussed during several previous sessions, it was Senate Bill No. 1 in the eighth legislature in 1927. It transferred all the functions conferred upon the Governor by previous legislatures to the Attorney General, an elective official. It would, in effect, have created two executives in Alaska, the federal governor, with only the limited functions provided by the organic act of 1912, and a territorial comptroller with all the powers and duties that the legislature would see fit to convey to an elected official. The motivations for this legislation were mixed. In addition to its recapture of granted powers it furnished a method of expressing opposition to the chief federal appointee. In 1927 it passed the House by a nine to seven vote, but failed of passage in the Senate by a tie vote—four to four. The measure would reappear in subsequent assemblies whenever one or more legislators were displeased with the governor.

Unable to achieve this larger objective, the legislators in the next session, in 1929, made every possible territorial office elective. They created the office of auditor, which was not really endowed with auditing functions, but to which were transferred various duties which through the years had been assigned to the secretary, leaving that federal official with little else than being keeper of the seal and serving as governor during the Governor's absence from the territory (Chapt. 118). The same act made the office of treasurer elective. The legislature also created the office of highway engineer and made it elective (Chapt. 114).

These new territorial offices tended to revive slightly—but only slightly—the general interest in public affairs, which had waned since the tense conflicts for the delegateship in the century's second decade. Popular interest had diminished in the twenties because offices available to Alaskans by election seemed to offer little opportunity for useful service, and hence were regarded as unimportant by a large portion of the public. Legislative performance in turn reflected public apathy. That apathy was maintained by the public's difficulty in ascertaining what really went on behind the legislative scenes in Juneau. No journalistic spotlight was turned on these biennial assemblies. Press coverage was inadequate, generally reflecting the newspaper ownership's political bias or personal interest. The lobbyists were the chief beneficiaries of these conditions. Their principals —the larger mining and canning interests—were increasingly able to dominate legislative performance, to keep meaningful action at a minimum and to perpetuate inaction. "It has been the most disappointing legislature in our history," Wickersham confided in his diary of the 1927 session; "the non-public interests and their subsidized newspapers have controlled it in everything in which they were interested." [41] The 1927 legislature was not exceptional in this respect and similar performance was more nearly the rule than otherwise in succeeding years.

In the 1914 election Wickersham, running as an independent, "supporting the policies of Woodrow Wilson," had defeated Democratic and Republican opponents. In 1916—the Wilsonian promises having failed to materialize, and with the Bull Moose Progressives back in the Republican fold—Wickersham ran as a Republican. His Democratic opponent, miner and territorial senator, was Charles Sulzer of Sulzer, site of his copper mine on Prince of Wales Island, and a brother of William Sulzer, representative from New York and later state governor. After an exceedingly bitter campaign the canvassing board—established by the 1906 act of Congress creating the office of delegate—composed of the Governor, the Secretary of the Territory and the Collector of customs, counted the ballots and found Wickersham elected by thirty-one votes. But the territorial Attorney General, George B. Grigsby, invalidated the votes of several remote communities in which the regular ballots had not been received by election day and makeshift ballots substituted, and appealed the board's canvass to the United States District Court at Juneau. There Judge Robert W. Jennings ruled in favor of Sulzer to whom was issued a certificate of election. Wickersham promptly contested the verdict, and the House of Representatives, after prolonged hearings, declared him legally elected, but not until the Sixty-fourth Congress had expired.

The affair revealed a trend which persisted in Alaska. Governor Strong and Secretary Charles E. Davidson were Democrats. Their count of ballots had determined the election adversely to the candidate of their party. Grigsby and Judge Jennings were likewise Democrats—the latter having been an unsuccessful candidate for delegate against Wickersham in 1912. But the two sets of Democrats belonged to different wings of the party and the ideological split had been evidenced in the 1912 election when another Democrat, Martin Harrais, had been one of the five contenders. The Committee on Elections of the House, which voted unanimously to seat Wickersham, and the House itself, which seated him by a vote of 224 to 64, were Democratic—conclusive evidence of the validity of his case.

While waiting the final decision of the House, both Wickersham and Sulzer filed again. Again the election was hairbreadth close. Sulzer died unexpectedly on April 16, 1919, before the canvassing board had announced its count—the delay due to the slowness in receiving the ballots from remote precincts. Two days after Sulzer's death, the canvassing board, on which Governor Riggs had succeeded Governor Strong, declared Sulzer elected by thirty-three votes. Riggs then called a special election to determine Sulzer's successor, in which Attorney General Grigsby, nominated by a party convention, filed as the Democratic aspirant. A Labor candidate also filed. But Wickersham declined to file, declaring himself elected. He rejected the canvassing board's verdict because of the illegality of the vote of soldiers in the various Army forts, who, it had been shown in the hearings on the previous election, had voted solidly for Sulzer, a preference ascribed to the antagonism between Wickersham and Colonel Wilds P. Richardson. Again, after prolonged hearings, Wickersham was seated, but not till February 28, 1921, three days before the expiration of the Sixty-fifth Congress.

The case was unique in that in two successive electoral contests for the House between the same opponents the winner was twice deprived of the right to serve. More pertinent to Alaska's history was the evidence in both contests that conventional party lines were overshadowed by economic allegiances, although Wickersham himself had obviously never been a faithful party adherent. The larger interests—fishery and mining—were bitterly opposed to Wickersham and supported Sulzer, contributing heavily to his two campaigns, and would subsequently, in other elections, follow a similar course. What Wickersham labeled the "bipartisan press," that is, the newspapers, which, regardless of their purported party affiliation, favored the conservative position, would, by and large, continue to rise above party, except when party and special interest coincided.

Wickersham decided to retire from public life. He had been elected delegate six times, but deprived of four years of service in Congress to which he had been legally entitled. The two contests had been wearing and costly—though both he and his opponents were granted their congressional pay. He resumed in Juneau the practice of law which he had followed in Tacoma prior to his judicial career in Alaska. He had also been long at work on a bibliography of Alaskan literature, and in collecting a library of Alaskana which he purposed to leave to the university-to-be—both monuments to the breadth and quality of his interest in Alaska. The college published his 635-page bibliography in 1927.

Dan Sutherland, miner, and four times a territorial senator, succeeded him in Congress, serving five terms, and, as a Republican, successively defeating four Democratic opponents, and in 1928 an independent representing a coalition of conservative Democrats and conservative Republicans. When Sutherland declared his intention not to run again, Wickersham, hale and hearty at seventy-three, re-entered the arena, securing the Republican nomination in a close primary contest against Attorney-General John Rustgard, and defeating Grigsby—who had been twice defeated by Sutherland—in the 1930 general election. But in 1932 Wickersham was swept under by the Democratic landslide and was succeeded as delegate by Anthony J. Dimond, attorney and territorial legislator. Wickersham resumed the practice of law in Juneau until his death in 1939.

It was after the first session of the Seventy-second Congress that Wickersham, returning to Juneau in the late summer of 1932, enunciated a classic. He was met at the dock by a group of his cronies, who after the warm preliminary greetings to them and other bystanders—for a return from the States is always an "occasion"—whisked him off for conversation and refreshment. When conviviality had begun, one of their number, with a mingling of friendly provocativeness and mock solemnity, addressed their leader:

"Tell us, Jim," he said, "now tell us; *what* did you accomplish for Alaska in this last session of Congress?"

Wickersham beamed happily at the opening thus afforded him. "What did I accomplish for Alaska in this last session of Congress?" His grin broadened in pleasant anticipation of the witticism he was formulating, born of the mellowing experience of long years in Washington. "It isn't what I accomplished!" He paused to give his words effectiveness. "It's what I prevented from happening! That's what you boys have got to be grateful for."

It was in a sense his political epitaph. A few months later he would be returning to his last session as the elected delegate to Congress. Though he had accomplished much, through ability, doggedness and tireless devotion to the cause of his people—the qualities that made him, and would make his successors, memorable—he had epitomized the mission and ordeal of an Alaska delegate.

The principal subject of congressional legislation dealing with Alaska in the twenties were the authorizations granted, upon their request, to Alaska's incorporated towns to bond themselves to provide school buildings and other improvements. Juneau had begun it in 1916 with a request for $75,000 for a school. Seward, in 1918, followed in asking for $25,000 to control a rampaging stream, Lowell Creek. Petersburg, in 1919, sought and obtained $75,000 for a municipal light and power plant and a school building, which was amended to double the amount the following year. Ketchikan in 1920 secured $100,000 for schools, amended four years later to $150,-000. Wrangell, in the same year, 1920, bonded itself for $80,000 for a water supply, sewer system, city dock and a school, and came back seven years later for $80,000 more for further improvements. Sitka in 1925 got $25,000 for a school, and Juneau $60,000 to improve its sewer system. In 1927 it obtained another $100,000 for a high-school building, and Fairbanks a like amount for a light and power plant, a telephone system and repairs to its water front on the Chena Slough. Seward and Anchorage came along in 1928 with $50,000 and $100,000 respectively for schools. Cordova in 1930 floated $50,000 worth of securities for a sewer system and bulkhead. The most important undertaking of this nature was Ketchikan's investment of a million dollars in 1930 to purchase the properties of the Foshay Company and the establishment therefrom of one of the finest municipal utility systems in the United States. For the next generation Ketchikan enjoyed as low a light and power rate as any American city. The municipalities, which had achieved a high degree of local self-government, fared relatively better than did Alaska as a whole, although subject of course to the prevailing over-all economic trends.

The twenties were also the years in which Alaskans laid the groundwork for an undreamed-of developmental resource. While the little noted flight of the Wright brothers on December 17, 1903, near Kitty Hawk, North Carolina, was to have worldwide consequences, no area on the globe was to be so vitally and beneficially affected as Alaska. Its lack of the other established means of transportation made aviation a heaven-sent gift. Alaskans took to the air with ease and enthusiasm. From the start they were flying thirty to forty times as much as other Americans measured per capita in number of flights or passenger miles.

Alaskan bush pilots were blazing new sky trails. Their landing fields were sand bars in rivers, beaches, small clearings anywhere, lakes, rivers and coastal waterways for planes on floats; the snow-covered tundra with planes on skis in winter. Of aids to aviation there were none: a moistened finger was held up to the breeze and the pilot took off. Alaska's roadless vastnesses were to yield to this new means of transportation. Alaskans' pioneer spirit responded automatically to the latest form of transportation. "The flyingest people under the American flag and probably . . . in the world," a chronicler of that early flying epoch correctly called them.[42] Everything that could be was squeezed into a plane—from cows to live young walrus. Mining machinery was flown to remote parts. The prospector on his isolated creek was supplied by air. Nearly every Alaskan was an aviation enthusiast. When Anchorage built its first airport in May, 1923, the whole town turned out to help—men with horses and tractors, women and children with rakes, clearing sixteen acres of stumps and undergrowth in a day.[43] Similar community help was forthcoming throughout Alaska.

The 1925 legislature took note of the need. It authorized the expenditure of road moneys for landing fields (Chap. 46). That year the first commercial flight between Fairbanks and Nome took place. That Bering Sea town had always been isolated after the departure of the last southbound boat in the fall, until the arrival of the first steamer after the pack-ice breakup in late spring.

The 1927 legislature enacted a law (Chap. 57) and made an appropriation to subsidize air travel between Seward Peninsula points and the Alaska Railroad. By 1927, forty-four landing fields had been built and three transportation companies were operating commercially. The enterprises were wholly Alaskan both as to financing and personnel.

The 1930 census showed Alaska with a virtually static population. There had been a slight increase—4,242, or 7.7 per cent—since 1920, bringing Alaska's population to 59,278, but still below the 1910 and 1900 figures. By contrast every state in the Union and every other territory had grown markedly, the total population of the United States having risen over 16 per cent from 105,710,620 in 1920 to 122,775,046 in 1930. The significant comparison, however, was with the census figures of thirty years earlier and the contrast with what had happened everywhere else under the flag in the twentieth century. For it was then that Alaska had been "discovered" by a large segment of the American public, and that Congress had, for the first time, given Alaska a measure of attention, igniting a spark which after 1906 had been kept aglow with much effort by a succession of voteless delegates seeking to press Alaska's needs before a generally uninterested Congress. In their quarter-century of service they had presented bills for full territorial government, for transfer of the fisheries, for participation in the Federal Aid Highway Act, for surveys and reform of the land laws, for payment of salaries to United States commissioners, for granting, in simple justice, a few elementary demands made in behalf of the people of Alaska by their legislators, whose memorials were duly printed in the *Congressional Record*, for inclusion of Alaska in various measures provided by voting senators and representatives for their forty-eight states.

Were all the members of Congress oblivious to Alaska's pleas and to the obvious solution of its difficulties? By no means. Back in the middle twenties a pertinent exchange of comments took place on the floor of the House of Representatives.

Said Representative Charles Lee Underhill, R., of Massachusetts: "If we give the pioneer a gambler's chance, with a free rein, we need not bother ourselves with the development of the future of Alaska. Those hardy, courageous individuals, if given a square deal and a fair chance, will take advantage of it; but they are not going to endure the hardships and the chances of failure which come usually to a pioneer industry unless the government is willing to give at least a 50-50 break, and the government does not do it at the present time."

"Does not the gentleman think," responded Representative John Rankin, D., of Mississippi, "that if we could give the people of Alaska more voice in the supervision of their own resources it would tend to encourage development there, and encourage people to come there and live, and encourage those who are there to remain?"

"Absolutely," responded Representative Underhill. "That is the solution of the problem."

That solution desired by Alaskans, which had not been tried by either Republican or Democratic administrations, was to find a warm supporter in the next Governor, appointed by President Franklin D. Roosevelt, John Weir Troy. He was a newspaper man, the owner and editor of dailies in Skagway and Juneau. During the Woodrow Wilson administration he had been collector of customs for Alaska.

"My few months' experience as Governor of Alaska," he wrote in his first report on September 29, 1933, "has confirmed a lifelong conviction that wherever possible, Alaska should govern herself. Her laws should be made by her own legislature and executed by her own officials."

The country had experienced the worst depression in the memory of living men. Alaska with no backlog of prosperity, either real or fancied, during the twenties, had suffered its share of the disaster. However, a "new deal" was in the offing for the nation. Would it apply also to Alaska?

THE ERA OF GROWING AWARENESS

1933 - 1954

The New Deal

The people of Alaska are not now and never have been responsible for the policies in force and effect which seek to conserve its coal, oil and forests for future generations and which have blanketed the territory with a patchwork of reserves. Had the same policies been adopted with reference to its territories in the early years of the Union it is doubtful if the frontier line of the United States would have yet reached the eastern slope of the Rocky Mountains.
CHARLES ERNEST BUNNELL, DECEMBER 11, 1931

We are almost at a dead standstill in Alaska at the present time. The population is not increasing any, has not for thirty years. . . . I wonder if we could not adopt some basic change that would be beneficial to our country.
REPRESENTATIVE EDWARD THOMAS TAYLOR OF COLORADO,
DECEMBER 23, 1931

AGAIN there was hope in the air of Alaska in March of 1933 as the administration of Franklin Delano Roosevelt took office.

"Hope supports prospectors and miners—who are always rich—in anticipation, if no other way," Wickersham had written in his diary some eight years earlier.[1]

This aphorism was applicable to Alaskans in general, not merely because the mining psychology was widely prevalent among them. It applied no less to the even more numerous Alaskan toilers of the sea, who, whatever their fisherman's luck in this year, looked forward to the next season as bound to be better. Indeed all Alaskans were—and are—prospectors in a larger sense, whether for gold or fish, for other opportunity a fluid frontier society affords, or for the freedom of wide open spaces and the beauty of its unspoiled wilderness. The prospector, apart from the specific definition of his calling, is one with a prospect, and to him, a pleasing prospect. The marked seasonality of Alaskan life, the alternation of intense activity with quiescence, with its leisure for hopeful anticipation, intensify the optimism characteristic of the frontier.

And so despite the stagnation of the twenties, which Alaska alone experienced, and the deepening depression of the early thirties,

which Alaska shared with the rest of the nation, there was hope in
the far North. It found encouragement, first, in the golden voice of
the fireside chats—now audible to Alaskans through the innovation
of radio—bidding Americans to lift up their hearts and to banish
fear. It found, next, actual fulfillment through the rapid-fire action
in Washington.

The first action that benefitted Alaska most particularly was the
presidential order in September of 1933 increasing the price of gold
from $20.67 to $35 an ounce, though increased production did not
appear for two years. The value of Alaska's gold had been $9,701,000
in 1933. It leaped to $16,007,000 in 1934 and rose to $26,178,000
by 1940, the greatest value for Alaska's gold output in history. Quantity rose also, although not proportionately, from 469,286 ounces in
1933 to 749,943 ounces in 1940. Actually gold mining, which in a
sense is a depression industry, had not suffered as much relatively as
other pursuits. While the price of other minerals, of fish and furs had
dropped to ruinous levels and there was little purchasing power for
them even then, the price of gold had long been fixed, and the depression actually lowered the cost of operation for the industry. The
number of dredges remained approximately constant through the
twenties and through the three and a half depression years, averaging
twenty-eight in Alaska. However, the increased price of gold brought
their number to forty-eight in 1940.

General measures taken by the Roosevelt administration, which
started the wheels of industry humming anew, gave stimulation to
Alaskan mining other than gold—although gold remained far ahead
as Alaska's mineral staple. Coal, which had averaged about 100,000
tons during the latter twenties, reached a new high of 136,600 tons
in 1936 and 173,970 in 1940. Its value in that year was $695,000,
the highest figure in Alaska's history. It was being produced by two
mines, one in the Nenana, the other in the Matanuska, field, and
was supplying local needs. Importation of coal had dwindled to a
mere 22,407 tons in that year, not only as Alaska's coal production
had increased but as the use of petroleum products was replacing
coal as fuel, the importation that year totaling 728,726,489 gallons.
And other mineral products, including platinum, quicksilver, antimony and gypsum, which had never before reached half a million
dollars in value returned over a million dollars annually in the last
three years of the nineteen thirties.

Next came the famous Matanuska colonization project. President Roosevelt saw in it a threefold opportunity: First, to take Americans from stricken agricultural areas, who were "down and out" often through no fault of theirs, and give them a chance to start life anew; second, to stimulate population growth in Alaska; third, to demonstrate the agricultural potentialities of Alaska. The Matanuska Valley was chosen after consultation with Alaskans as the site of this adventure. Its execution was entrusted to the Federal Emergency Relief Administration, which had the responsibility for those on the relief rolls, from among whom the colonists would be chosen, and, not being tied to a budget as were the old-line established government agencies, could make funds promptly available.

Even when the project had only been rumored, letters of application began pouring into Washington—totaling fifteen thousand after plans were announced. Some errors were committed in the execution. Better planning was sacrificed to speed. The applicants, whose number was to be limited to two hundred, with their dependents presumably a thousand persons, were to be chosen from three states only, Michigan, Wisconsin and Minnesota, on the assumption that their climates would best predispose the settlers to life in Alaska. That approach was reasonable, but qualified applicants from other states should have been considered. Selection from among the eager thousands who wanted to go, careful screening to determine farming experience and mental and physical fitness, would have improved the chances of successful colonization. Instead not a few of the social workers considered the project an opportunity to get rid of their problem cases. Instead of making election a prize worth seeking—an easy objective in view of the many applicants—all the unsolicited applications were disregarded and prospective colonists actually solicited and urged to go. In the process, generous promises as to the facilities that would be bestowed led the prospective settlers to the belief that they were conferring a favor on the government by accepting its offer. That impression was heightened by the fanfare surrounding their journey on special trains, one by way of San Francisco, the other through Seattle, where the population feted the colonists as heroes, and they began to think of themselves as such. The misfits were promptly weeded out and returned to the States. Their places were soon filled, and the succeeding settlers, who received less generous treatment, proved themselves worthier of the unique opportunity which their government had afforded them.

Whatever the initial errors of execution—including the original forty-acre land limitation—the undertaking, characteristic of the imaginative concepts and enterprise of the New Deal, was destined to be a success and achieve its principal purposes. It implanted in Alaska the nucleus of a farm population which in a few years, after its beginning in May of 1935, had become rooted in the Matanuska Valley and grew steadily. It publicized Alaska in a way that was needed after the two decades of decline, and led other Americans to look again to the Northland as a possible realm of opportunity and to try their fortunes there. It added an element of stability which a farm population can supply.

The economy of Alaska everywhere was quickened by projects, large and small, of the Public Works and Work Projects Administrations. They not only gave employment to the numerous previously unemployed, but erected projects of enduring worth—schools, fire stations, waterworks, paved streets, playgrounds. They provided a great steel bridge across Gastineau Channel connecting Juneau on the mainland with Douglas on Douglas Island. They included a hotel at the entrance of Mount McKinley Park, intended as the first unit in a plan to make the park available to visitors and to stimulate one little-developed Alaska potential, the tourist industry. The Civilian Conservation Corps put hundreds of jobless young men to work building forest trails and shelter cabins and creating improvements of lasting value. One unique project which resulted from these various efforts was the restoration and relocation of a great number of totem poles, monuments of the culture of the northwest Indians, which would otherwise have disintegrated and been lost. And a group of painters from the W.P.A. art project recorded some of the scenic beauties of Alaska for posterity. Of great practical value were the harbor improvements, breakwaters, and small-boat harbors, some of them earlier examined and approved by the U. S. Army Engineers, and now carried to completion.

An administration conscious of the *national* need for rehabilitation and sympathetic with it, geared for emergency action and therefore able to assist promptly thus extended a helping hand. When fire destroyed the greater part of Nome in September, 1934, emergency relief funds were available. In 1937 the national social-security program was extended to Alaska, Governor Troy, upon request of the federal authorities, having called a special session of the legislature to adopt the necessary enabling legislation. The benefits of the Federal Housing Administration were extended to Alaska. Through it homes, the building of which would otherwise have been impossible, were financed.

Despite these favorable factors which gave Alaska its first slight impetus since the gold-rush days, a third of a century earlier, no solution of the territory's basic problems was achieved or even attempted. The continuing memorials of successive legislatures, pleading, as they had for nearly three decades—for increased road construction with extension to Alaska of the Federal Aid Highway Act, for measures to improve maritime transportation, for revision of the land laws, with a cessation of reservations and withdrawals, for better law enforcement, with salaries for United States commissioners, for transfer of the fisheries and wild life to territorial control, for full territorial government—were ignored by the Congress and the bureaus despite the earnest pleas of Alaska's delegate Anthony J. Dimond, and his repeated introduction of bills to achieve the ends that required legislation.[2]

Highway construction, perhaps the most important single element in development, was curtailed. New projects to extend Alaska's limited wagon-road mileage, proposed by the Alaska Road Commission, since June, 1932, under the Interior Department, were pretty well deleted in the course of their gantlet-running through the department, the Bureau of the Budget, and the House and Senate approprations committees. With slight exceptions, money for maintenance only trickled forth in the nineteen thirties.[3] For not only was Alaska steadily denied inclusion in the general provisions of the Federal Aid Highway Act, although Hawaii, Puerto Rico and the District of Columbia had been included,[4] but even the limited participation granted to Alaska in its national-forest areas was drastically reduced.

Under the formula prescribed by the Federal Aid Act of 1916 and its amended successor, the Federal Aid Highway Act of 1921, the section dealing with roads and trails in national forests—which alone applied to Alaska—established Alaska's participation at 9.5 per cent of the total appropriation. The formula was based on forest area, value of timber, relative fire danger, existing transportation facilities and other factors. In the second session of the Seventy-first Congress (December 5, 1932–March 3, 1933), the last "lame-duck" session,

a member of the appropriations committee, on its agricultural subcommittee dealing with forest roads and trails, Representative Robert G. Simmons, R., of Nebraska (himself a "lame duck" as he had
been defeated for re-election in November, 1932), proposed a limitation of $350,000 on the appropriation for forest highways in
Alaska.[5] The committee accepted the proposal and it became an established custom, being reaffirmed in successive appropriation acts
for over a decade.

The amount of which Alaska was thus deprived in the nineteen
thirties was approximately $7,000,000. The total appropriation avail-
able for distribution varied from year to year. Confronted with this
reduction, first accomplished prior to his delegateship, Delegate Dimond pleaded annually for restoration of the funds provided by the
legally established formula. By 1937 he urged that if the funds to
which Alaska was lawfully entitled were not restored in full, that at
least they be increased above $350,000 to provide not merely for
bare maintenance but for replacement of twenty-one wooden bridges
which the Bureau of Public Roads had declared unsafe. Alaska's
rightful share for the coming fiscal year, he pointed out was approximately $1,330,000.[6] This, like his previous and succeeding pleas, was
ignored.

The motive for these repeated discriminatory actions by the
House appropriations subcommittees—each year ratified by House
and Senate—was not economy. The federal treasury was not the
gainer by these slashes in Alaska's national forest highway funds.
The money due Alaska was distributed among various states whose
representatives in Congress had the votes to accomplish the objective.[7]

Actually few, if any, national forest reserves in the states were relatively as much in need of road construction as Alaska's. The national
forests in the states when set aside were for the most part wilderness
areas and remained sparsely inhabited. The economies of the states
in which they were located were not thereby impeded. But when the
Tongass and Chugach National Forests were set aside by proclamation of President Theodore Roosevelt, they blanketed two vital
coastal areas, both from the standpoint of population and of the
territorial economy. Although the approximately 16,000,000 acres in
the Tongass and 4,800,000 in the Chugach, areas respectively as large
as West Virginia and New Jersey, occupied only some 6 per cent of

Alaska's total area, they contained, with the towns adjacent, over a third of Alaska's population. They included Juneau and Ketchikan, two of the territory's four principal cities, as well as nearly all the towns next in order of population, Sitka, Wrangell, Petersburg, Cordova and Seward. Not one of these enjoyed an appreciable road system, but merely short stretches of highway that stopped short a few miles out. The total highway mileage in the Tongass was 130, in the Chugach, 120.

Juneau, with forty-three miles of road extending from it, at the end of the fourth decade of the century led all southeastern Alaska towns in highway mileage. Ketchikan came next with only twenty. The next three cities in size, Sitka, Petersburg and Wrangell, had less than twenty miles for all three. Yet probably nowhere in the world was so much use made of so little highway mileage. Juneau, with a city population of 5,729 in 1939, and an area population of 7,311, had 963 automobiles, or one for every 7.5 persons in the area, or twenty-two cars for every mile of highway. Ketchikan, with a city population of 4,695 and an area population of 5,290, had 583 automobiles, one for every nine inhabitants, or twenty-seven cars for every mile of highway.

Assistance to aviation—emergency landing fields, radio-range stations, beacons—authorized for the nation by the Air Commerce Act of May 20, 1926 (44 Stat. 568), was also not forthcoming for Alaska although the territories were included in the legislation. Such fields as existed were due wholly to territorial efforts and appropriations and local assistance. Governor Troy in 1935 had compiled a minimal list of needed avigational aids, the cost of which totaled $2,900,000. In his appeal for this appropriation two years later Delegate Dimond cited impressive figures to show the growth of aviation in Alaska and its needs. There were at that time in Alaska ninety-four airfields "of a kind"—many of them hazardous. Seventy-nine planes were in regular service. In the preceding eight years—1929 to 1936—the number of passengers carried had increased from 2,171 to 16,982; the number of plane miles from 33,591 to 2,130,929; the number of passenger miles from 272,990 to 3,035,018, and the poundage of mail and freight carried from 118,951 to 2,418,616.[8] No appropriation was made.

Commercial air transportation, while already substantially developed *within* Alaska, and there wholly by local enterprise, did not

connect Alaska with the United States, although American carriers
had already established commercial routes to South America and
the Orient.[9] Thus air transportation—in the virtual absence of highways and, but for the single-track 470-mile Alaska Railroad, of railways—of inestimable value to Alaska, was likewise slighted by the
powers in Washington that ruled Alaska's destiny.

These were not the only discriminations. The *threat* of them
existed in nearly every piece of beneficent legislation. Was Alaska included? To answer that question Alaska's delegate would have to
scan every measure of nationwide import upon its introduction, with
a battle, sometimes successful, sometimes not, to secure equal treatment, if, as not infrequently, Alaska was omitted. A similar prospect
faced Alaska in appropriations.

Testifying on December 20, 1933, at his first appearance before
the House Subcommittee on Appropriations for the Interior Department, Delegate Dimond pointed out that the Indians in Alaska had
been receiving only one-third as much "federal aid of any kind" as
the Indians in the United States.

"I do not know why this discrimination occurred unless it was because they did not make war on the whites and kill off the settlers,"
declared the Delegate.[10]

Appropriations for operation, maintenance and repair of school
buildings by the Office of Indian Affairs were substantially lower per
unit in Alaska than in the states. A detailed comparison was inserted
into the record of the appropriations committee hearings by Delegate
Dimond.[11] "And it costs a whole lot more up there to repair
the schools than it does in the States," volunteered the subcommittee chairman, Representative Edward T. Taylor of Colorado. But the
committee recommended no change in the figures, and none was
made.

Illustrative of these discriminations—not the quirk of a single session but re-enacted through the years—were the allocations to Alaska
under the Adams and Purnell Acts. The Adams Act of March 16,
1906 (34 Stat. 63), fathered by Representative Henry Cullen Adams, R., of Wisconsin, was an act further to endow agricultural-
experiment stations beyond the provisions of the Hatch Act. Under
the Adams Act each state and territory was entitled to receive $15,-
000 annually. Nearly twenty years later these endowments were further amplified by the Purnell Act of February 24, 1925 (43 Stat.

970), sponsored by Representative Fred S. Purnell, R., of Indiana, which authorized appropriations for agricultural experiment stations in annually increasing sums but fixed $60,000 as the amount beginning with the year 1930. Alaska was denied inclusion in these acts until 1936 and lost their benefits for six years. However, the full amounts authorized for each state and territory were not, and in the case of the Purnell Act have not been to this day, appropriated for Alaska. The Adams Act appropriation was arbitrarily cut in half, and, for the next fourteen years, 1937 to 1951, Alaska received $7,500. Only in 1951 was the full amount restored. Alaska's loss of Adams Act funds was $195,000.

Instead of the $60,000 authorized under the Purnell Act, no appropriations whatever were made in the first two years after the act had been extended to Alaska. But in 1938 the Congress allowed all of $1,250, which munificence—2.08 per cent of the amount authorized and appropriated for every state—was repeated the next year. For the next three years Congress doubled the subvention with $2,500 annually, then allotted $15,000 for two years, $20,000 each for the next six, in 1952 raised the amount to $35,000 and finally in 1953 to $47,500—still $12,500 short of what every state had received. Thus during the twenty-three years that the Purnell Act had been law each state received $1,380,000 and Alaska, $242,500, a difference of $1,137,500. The total deficiency for Alaska under these two acts since 1930 was $1,332,500.[12]

Agricultural research for Alaska, the foundation of any successful farming there, which had been maintained on a subsistence basis by the federal government till the late twenties and then abolished, was resumed in a serious way only in the late forties. Its resumption with moderate, and by no means lavish, federal support, was due to word of the intensive efforts and great strides of Soviet agriculture in corresponding latitudes in Siberia. The real credit for this belated concern about one of Alaska's potentials—one evidence of which was Alaska's achievement of appropriational parity in the Adams Act, and almost, if not quite, in the Purnell Act—belonged to a gentleman from Georgia, neither a United States Senator nor a Representative. His name was Joseph Stalin. With a similar concern for its outlying provinces, our nation might, eighteen years earlier, have made a promising start in developing Alaska's agricultural potential through the slow but sure process of experiment and research if Congress had sustained the provisions of its own acts with respect to Alaska. It might then have also provided some suitable farm credit, farm-price support, farm clearing, or other legislation adapted to Alaska such as flows easily to the constituencies in the states where the farmers have votes.[13]

Despite these adverse factors, the preponderance of the favorable over the unfavorable produced the first substantial increase in Alaska's population since the gold rush. The sixteenth United States census, taken in Alaska on October 1, 1939, showed a total population of 72,524. It was an increase of 22.3 per cent from the 1929 figure of 59,278. Percentages do not mean so much when the figures are relatively small, but in this instance they carried with them some reasonably significant implications. Only two states, New Mexico and Florida, exceeded Alaska's growth percentagewise. The national population had in the fourth decade increased by 7.2 per cent, the first time, except in 1900, that the national growth percentage was less than Alaska's. Alaska's population at the end of the century's fourth decade was the largest it had ever been. It had overcome the losses of the second and third decades. The growth had been territory-wide, was shared by each judicial division. Both white and native populations had increased, the former from 28,640 in 1929 to 39,170 in 1930; the latter from 29,983 in 1929 to 32,458 in 1939. For the first time the white population was substantially larger than the native, due both to new arrivals and an increase of births over deaths, the latter alone responsible for the growth of the native population.

The over-all increase was normal and evolutionary. Except for the thousand persons brought into the Matanuska Valley in 1935, no artificial factor had stimulated it. Military construction had not begun. The Sixteenth Census offered suggestive evidence that given even the least diminution in federal obstruction, or the slightest encouragement, Alaska would grow.

War Rediscovers Alaska

Through to this day Alaska has never received the attention in national defense planning that it deserves . . .

Alaska had always been and no matter what happened in any theater of war, always remained, to me privately, a high priority. But we were never able to get the money or allocations for the air force that we really needed there to give us the kind of bases we required then—and need more than ever now.

GENERAL OF THE AIR FORCE HENRY HARLEY ARNOLD, 1949

ALASKA'S has been a history of remote control. During the Russian occupation the saying, "Heaven is high and the Czar is far away" embodied the philosophy of the Russian-American Company's employees and government officials. Under the rule of the United States, Washington was far away, and its long-range government accounted largely for what happened and did not happen in and to Alaska.

The great events that have shaped Alaska's destiny, that have made the sharp turns in the road that Alaskans have trod, have also been of remote origin. They have been unplanned, unanticipated and with unforeseeable consequences.

The acts of Czars, living two centuries ago, whose very names are unknown to most Americans, preserved Alaska for United States dominion.

After thirty years of oblivion, the accidental discovery of gold in northwestern Canada called Alaska for the first time to the notice of the American people and gave it the first modicum of congressional and executive attention.

Over forty years later, the madness of a German guttersnipe risen to absolute power and the folly of a military clique in Tokyo brought war to the United States, and to Alaska much of what three-quarters of a century of peaceful civil endeavor had failed to secure. And when the peril of those two totalitarianisms had been disposed of by victory on the field of battle, no less a menace, in the communist imperialism directed from Moscow, was bringing to Alaska a continuing solicitude of sorts, which, as a dependent area of potentiality and promise, it should properly have had without foreign threat, but could never have secured of and by itself.

The Second World War and the "Cold War" which followed brought Alaska its first defenses. At the close of the twentieth century's fourth decade, two years before Pearl Harbor, the only military establishment was Chilkoot Barracks. Fort Seward, its official name, was an infantry post dating from the gold-rush days. It was snugly ensconced at the upper end of the Inside Passage where it could observe the pack-toting traffic bound inland or back over the three historic trails—the Chilcat, Chilkoot and White passes. The post had a complement of two hundred men, equipped with Springfield rifles. It did not at that time boast even an anti-aircraft gun. Even this minuscule detachment would have been relatively immobile in the event of hostilities. No road then connected Haines, where the post was located, with the interior. The company's only means of mobilization was a fifty-two-year-old harbor tug, the *Fornance*. Her engines were so feeble, that in December, 1939, returning from Juneau with the commanding officer aboard, and encountering a thirty-knot headwind blowing down Lynn Canal, she was unable to advance and had to be rescued by the Coast Guard. The fact is that Fort Seward was never intended for the repelling of foreign aggression.

No military establishment for national defense existed in Alaska and none ever had.

Nor any naval establishment! With a coastline longer than the Atlantic, Pacific and Gulf Coasts of the forty-eight states, with its terrain extending—uniquely under the flag—across the meridians of longitude into the Eastern Hemisphere and through the parallels of latitude into the Arctic, America's "first line of defense" had never received a taxpayer's dollar to fulfill its historic mission in these waters. As in the case of the Army, occasional policing had been the Navy's only employment in Alaska.

It need not have been so. As early as 1904 the Navy Department had set aside Kiska Island near the western end of the Aleutian chain of islands as a naval reservation. The Navy planned to make it an important coaling station and to give it the necessary defenses that its adjacency to Asia connoted. It might have become a Gibraltar of the North Pacific.

The Navy Department, reported Governor Brady in 1904, had "de-termined . . . to make it one of our great strategic points in the possible complications that may arise between ourselves and the Orient."

"No doubt the general sense of the country will approve such action," commented Governor Brady.

No doubt. But the sense of the Congress was otherwise. Even national defense in Alaska was to follow the pattern early established by the federal authorities for that remote province.

"Plans for the construction of a coaling station have been prepared" (in Kiska Harbor in the Aleutian Islands), reported Secretary of the Navy Paul Morton two years later. And in his 1907 report, the year following, it was the same:

"Kiska Harbor, Aleutian Islands. No funds have yet been appropriated for building a coal depot at this island."

And so through the next thirty-five years till in 1942 the first navy to occupy Kiska Harbor was not Uncle Sam's but the Mikado's.

For the first eighteen years it had been an error of omission. But in 1922 *not* defending the Aleutians was established as national policy. By the five-power treaty on the limitation of armaments of February 6, 1922, the United States agreed not to fortify the Aleutians. Alaska was the only area in the Western Hemisphere in which the United States agreed to abdicate a portion of its right to self-defense. However, Japan denounced the treaty in December, 1934.

It was as early as March 5, 1934, less than a year after he had begun what would be a twelve-year service in the House of Representatives, that Delegate Anthony J. Dimond arose to plead for defenses for Alaska:

"Establish bases at Anchorage or Fairbanks, also in the Aleutians. . . . I say to you, 'Defend the United States by defending Alaska!' " urged Dimond.

He pointed out what was not widely appreciated at that time, that the shortest distance between the United States and the Orient lay over the Great Circle Route, which, while two thousand miles north of well-defended Hawaii, was only 276 miles south of the Aleutians. From San Francisco to Yokohama the shortest route was 5,233 miles; from Seattle the distance was only 4,924 miles. But the distance from Yokohama, by way of Hawaii, to the nearest point on the western coast of the United States was 6,316 miles.

"Is it not obvious," asked Delegate Dimond, returning to the battle on the floor, "that an enemy moving across the Pacific . . . would rather first . . . invade . . . Alaska?" [2] And he introduced a bill authorizing the appropriation of some $10,000,000 for an air base in Alaska.

"I am assuming in all this," continued Alaska's delegate, "that the fortifications already installed at Honolulu are justified. There is hardly a person in the United States who does not feel that they are more than justified. . . . I am not asking that any part of the defensive armament of Honolulu should be transferred to Alaska . . . the point is, however, that if the defensive works at Honolulu are justified and justifiable, then in the same degree, considering the strategic position of Alaska with respect to the continental United States, similar installations in Alaska are required." [3]

Dimond's bill for an Alaskan air base and another bill for a naval base were referred to the House Military and Naval Affairs Committees, respectively, and died there.

However, early in the Seventy-fourth Congress provision was made to expand the air defenses of the United States. The law of August 12, 1935 (49 Stat. 610), named six strategic areas in each of which there would be an Army Air Corps base, and provided for intermediate stations. Alaska was to be one of these areas.

Hearings before the House Committee on Military Affairs brought out unvarying military support of such a base in Alaska. There was never any question about the other air bases projected for the various areas within the States. Their representatives came to the hearings merely to register their approval of such projected location. In the case of Alaska, regular Army and Army Air Corps officers pointed out that a base there was needed for two reasons, first, for defensive-offensive purposes, and second, to provide training in cold-weather aviation which American military fliers totally lacked.

Brigadier General Charles E. Kilbourne and Colonel Walter Krueger, both on the General Staff and attached to the War Plans Division, recommended such an Alaskan base. [4]

Brigadier General Frank M. Andrews testified: "Alaska with its tremendous and almost untouched resources should not be left defenseless. A base in Alaska is therefore required to deter any enemy desirous of seizing and utilizing its resources and geographic location against our west coast." [5]

The hearings, however, derived their lasting significance because of the testimony, on February 13, 1935, of Brigadier General William Mitchell. It was virtually his last public appearance before his death a year later. He testified at length and with great forcefulness on the theme which was to give him immortality—the importance and value of air power in war. But there was also a corollary to those passionately held and unflinchingly maintained beliefs which time would completely vindicate—namely, the strategic importance of Alaska in the coming era of air power whose prophet he was:

"Japan is our dangerous enemy in the Pacific," Mitchell declared. "They won't attack Panama. They will come right here to Alaska. Alaska is the most central place in the world for aircraft, and that is true either of Europe, Asia or North America. I believe in the future he who holds Alaska will hold the world, and I think it is the most important strategic place in the world." [6]

With such support, and given the increasingly tense international situation, early construction of the Alaskan base would have seemed assured. But the act provided authorization only. Appropriation, as Alaskans had learned before, and would again, was another matter.

An interested attendant at these hearings was Representative Wesley Lloyd, D., of Tacoma, Washington.

"Let me ask the distinguished gentleman who was formerly a member of this committee," Chairman John J. McSwain, D., of North Carolina, asked Lloyd, "what his idea of the priority should be as between an air base in Alaska and an air base in the northwest corner of the United States, as, for instance, in the state of Washington?"

"Should it ever come to a question of priority, Mr. Chairman," responded Representative Lloyd, "I hope it never comes to that because Alaska needs protection—but should it ever come to a question of priority, I would say that the state of Washington must have first consideration, because within that state are those infinitely great cities, that infinitely rich territory. An enemy intrenched in Alaska would still to all intents and purposes be removed from the United States. An enemy intrenched on the Pacific slope of the continental United States would be able, as I have suggested, to harass our cities." [7]

"Remember that if the coast of Alaska falls into the possession of a foreign power," retorted Delegate Dimond, "you have the airplanes . . . within 750 miles of Seattle. . . . How long will it take to cover that and bring all this destruction and devastation which was so fully pointed out by Mr. Lloyd of Washington? Alaska is undefended, and we know from past experience that we are not going to be met across the Pacific with any declaration of war. We know what happened when there was a contest in which Russia was involved some years ago, when the stroke came first and the declaration afterward. So if we have any difficulties there, the first thing that is going to happen is that we will find the hostile power in possession of the coast of Alaska." [8]

The second session of the Seventy-fourth Congress passed with no appropriation for Alaska's base, despite Delegate Dimond's efforts to introduce an amendment in the Army appropriation bill for that purpose. Again in the first session of the Seventy-fifth Congress he sought to secure an amendment appropriating $2,000,000 to begin construction of the Alaska base, the site of which had been tentatively designated by the War Department as near Fairbanks. Dimond spoke eloquently for the amendment, pointing out that at the very least American fliers needed the type of cold-weather aviation training which could not be secured in the forty-eight states.[9]

Representative John F. Dockweiler, D., of California, speaking in opposition to Dimond's amendment, expressed sympathy. "However, these things have to be taken up in regular order. It was thought . . . more important at this juncture . . . to establish an air base in the northwest of the United States . . . so you will find the committee recommendation . . . for . . . an air base . . . near Tacoma, Washington." [10]

So, as the *Congressional Record* recorded:

"The amendment was rejected." [11]

Delegate Dimond fought for Alaska bases in committees as well as on the floor.

"It seems to be that it is the part of wisdom to have a strong defensive naval station in Alaska, and to install immediately without delay the Army air station that has already been located for the interior of Alaska," Dimond urged on January 26, 1938. "The time to install defense works in Alaska is now, and not tomorrow or next year." And he repeated his earlier prophecy: "Recent events indicate that hereafter the fighting will start before war is declared." [12]

Three weeks later Dimond was pleading before the Subcommittee on the War Department of the House Appropriations Committee that Alaska was the one part of the nation without any defenses whatever, and that while that was important, of course, to its residents, it was equally important to the people of the entire United States because it was obvious "that any hostile foreign power in possession of the coast of Alaska could inflict untold damage upon the Pacific Coast states and cities before any corresponding defensive force could be brought in to stop them." [13]

"There is no doubt that Alaska is the most strategically important place in the whole defense of this country that we have," commented Representative Ross A. Collins, D., of Mississippi, one of the seven subcommittee members.[14]

"I am getting to the place where I think perhaps we can get the base," responded Delegate Dimond.[15]

His optimism was short-lived. The bill was again reported without any Alaska item.

Again Dimond carried his fight to the floor, speaking fervently for his amendment which would appropriate enough to get the project near Fairbanks started. This time he was opposed by Representative David Lane Powers, R., of New Jersey, who saw no need for speedy action—in Alaska.

"I am hoping," said Powers, and I believe that the gentleman from Alaska eventually will see an air base in Alaska come into existence . . . but I do not wish to see the money appropriated at the present time." [16]

And so "the amendment was rejected." [17]

Appropriation—of $4,000,000—was finally made in the 1940 appropriation bill, and construction, not of a base, but of a "cold-weather testing station" for airplanes, begun near Fairbanks, which was to be named Ladd Field.[18]

The Navy, meantime, was proceeding in leisurely fashion—so far as Alaska was concerned.

Based on the so-called Hepburn Report, named after Admiral Arthur J. Hepburn, who headed a board charged with expanding naval aviation, fifteen new stations in the United States, its territories and possessions, were included in a bill which became law April 25, 1939 (53 Stat. 590). Among these were naval air stations at Sitka and Kodiak, for which $2,900,000 and $8,750,000, respectively, were authorized.

"My only apprehension," declared Delegate Dimond, "is that we are starting defensive measures too late and proceeding with them too feebly." It was only an authorization bill, he said, and proposed construction over several years.[19]

War had broken out in Europe on September 1, 1939. Hitler's *panzer* divisions had overrun Poland, and in the closing days of that conquest had been joined by Soviet forces moving across the Russo-Polish border. Across the Pacific the Japanese were pursuing their third year's effort to conquer China.

"As to the existing crisis abroad, we must face the facts. Any major developments there should be paralleled by added precautions in this country," began Chief of Staff George Catlett Marshall's presentation of the Army budget for the fiscal year 1941 before the Subcommittee on the War Department of the House Appropriations Committee, on February 23, 1940. "If Europe blazes in the late spring or summer, we must put our house in order before the sparks reach the Western Hemisphere." [20]

The budget proposed was relatively modest—in view of coming events. Including a supplemental estimate and as reduced by the Bureau of the Budget, it asked the Congress for $906,137,254.[21] It would be the last defense appropriation for years to come dealing only in millions—not billions—of dollars.

There was a new Alaska item in the proposed budget, an item authorized five years previously by the law of August 12, 1935.

"The establishment of an operating air base in Alaska is a project of major importance," testified General Marshall,[22] and he gave the justification for it—the first Army establishment in Alaska's history for national defense. It was to be located near Anchorage and $12,-734,000 was requested for its construction. Later in the hearings, Major General H. H. Arnold, chief of the Air Corps, and others testified to its necessity.[23]

The hearings were concluded on March 26th. When a few days later the subcommittee on the War Department reported the bill to the full Appropriations Committee the entire appropriation for the operating air base near Anchorage had been eliminated.

General Marshall promptly sought and obtained a hearing before the subcommittee and with Major General H. H. Arnold, Delegate Dimond and others pleaded for the restoration of this one item. The subcommittee was adamant in its refusal, and the House voted the appropriation bill on April 4th without the Alaska base.[24]

On April 9th Adolf Hitler invaded Norway and Denmark and in the ensuing weeks occupied those two countries. There was a different atmosphere when General Marshall and Major General Arnold appeared before the Subcommittee on the War Department of the Senate Appropriations Committee on April 30th and asked for the restoration of the Anchorage base item.[25] Before the Senate subcommittee had finished its hearings on May 17th, Goering's Luftwaffe had bombed Rotterdam without provocation or warning, Hitler's armies had seized the Netherlands, had swept through Belgium and had begun the invasion of France.

The Senate restored the Anchorage base. The House concurred. Thus Fort Richardson and its air establishment, Elmendorf Field, came to be. More bases for national defense in Alaska would follow.

But when the Japanese struck on December 7, 1941, without warning—as Alaska's delegate had prophesied six years earlier they would—not a military or naval base in Alaska was ready for action. Delegate Dimond's Cassandra-like warnings came further true, six months later, when the Japanese invaded the Aleutians, and occupied Attu and Kiska.

It is not within the scope of this volume to discuss the consequences of the neglect of Alaska's defenses against which Alaska's voteless delegate had inveighed in vain. Nor to do more than point out that while American forces were victorious on land, sea and air, and with their great triumph at Midway turned back the Japanese tide, the Aleutian campaign to drive the Japanese from Kiska and Attu, with its costly involvement of ships, material and men, and more important and more tragic, the loss of some 2,500 American lives, need never have taken place. Adequate defenses for Alaska, including the Aleutians, as requested by Alaska's delegate seven years before the outbreak of war, would have prevented the only invasion and occupation by the enemy in the Western Hemisphere and obviated the costly campaign to expel him.

Reserved for subsequent telling will likewise be the rejection by the War Department as late as April, 1941, eight months before Pearl Harbor, of the construction of the highway to Alaska, as "of no military value," and of a similar attitude during the summer and fall of that year by the joint American-Canadian Defense Commission. It required the outbreak of war itself to make these authorities change their minds—and then to build a highway in great haste, at a far greater cost, and over a route of dubious validity. So, also deferred, will be the story of the precipitate abandonment of Alaska's defenses immediately after V-J Day, in the face of a far greater menace looming up across Bering Strait.

For the purposes of this study we shall now outline the results in Alaska of America's entry into World War II.

For the Second World War brought to Alaska its first real airfields, its first radio range stations, utilized by both military and commercial aviation. It brought a multiplication of the mapping service of the Geological Survey, of the wire-dragging and coast-charting of the Coast and Geodetic Survey. It brought a road-construction program. First, the Glenn Highway, 190 miles in length, connected Anchorage and its small network of roads with the Richardson Highway, thus marking the beginning of an Alaskan road *system*. There had been only a few unconnected roads up to that time. Most important, it brought the Alaska Highway, first known as the Alcan, linking the forty-eight states with Alaska overland. It brought housing. It brought needed assistance, in the form of matching funds, for community utilities—water and sewer works and school buildings—in towns whose population had been materially increased by the war effort and subsequent defense undertakings.

In the course of the war some 300,000 young men in the uniforms of the Army, Navy and Air Force were stationed in Alaska. Not a few of them took a liking to Alaska, made up their minds to return there after the war and did so.

Governor John W. Troy, who had been in ill health, resigned his office in the summer of 1939. President Roosevelt appointed Ernest Gruening, the author of this book, as his successor. He had for the previous five years been Director of the Division of Territories and Island Possessions in the Department of the Interior. This was a new agency, created in 1934 to supervise the federal relations of the various territories and insular possessions. Up to that time Alaska and Hawaii had been in the office of the Department's chief clerk. Puerto Rico's affairs had been directed from the Insular Bureau of the War Department. The Virgin Islands, a few years previously, had been transferred from the Navy Department to the Interior Department.

In 1945 the territorial legislature established an Alaska Housing Authority, a Development Board, a territorial Department of Agriculture. It replaced the old Board of Health and its part-time commissioner with a department headed by a full-time executive and gave it the means with which to operate. At a special session, called shortly after the end of hostilities, when military hospitals could be made available for civilian use, the legislature made an initial appropriation to combat tuberculosis, which through long neglect had reached an incidence nine times that in the forty-eight states. At the same session in February of 1946, it passed the first veterans' act enacted by any state or territory. The law provided bonuses based on the length of service and loans up to $10,000 to enable veterans to acquire a home, a farm, a business or a fishing boat. The loans were financed by a $3,250,000 revolving fund raised through a temporary sales tax. The measure afforded Alaska's returning service men the best of opportunities to re-establish themselves in civilian life, and gave Alaska's economy a tremendous lift.

In 1949 the legislature completely overhauled the territory's obsolete and inadequate tax system. Under it, vast categories of businesses and individuals, deriving substantial profits in Alaska, were either paying no taxes or negligible ones. Among those which paid no taxes whatever to the territory were steamship companies, air lines, bus lines, lighterage companies, banks, motion-picture theatres, oil companies, construction companies, garages and service stations, radio stations, newspapers, logging operators. The canned-salmon industry was still paying a case tax based on the number of cases packed, that is, on the size and not on the value of the pack, a tax unfair both to the companies and to the public interest. A small pack with high prices might be more profitable to the canners than a large one at low prices, but the territory often received less revenue from the more profitable pack. The legislature corrected that longstanding fallacy with a tax based on the wholesale value of the pack. The 1949 legislature passed an income tax, uniquely geared to the federal, thus obviating the problem existing for taxpayers in states with income taxes of having to compute two totally different income taxes, and also facilitating checking and collecting. It enacted a property tax of 1 per cent, but credited against the municipal and school-district property taxes, so that there would be no duplication in property taxation. It supplied the act with business-incentive provisions providing for waiver of the tax for new enterprises. The legislature took over and amended the system of license taxes from the federal government which the latter had established in 1899, thus abolishing the Alaska fund, a measure requiring, because of the organic act, the subsequent approval of Congress before becoming effective.

As a result of these fiscal reforms the territory was able to meet its growing and important obligations in education, health, welfare, policing, highway, airport, and water-front construction, and other new committments in fisheries, agriculture, housing, economic development and tourist promotion, a National Guard and civilian defense.

The needed revenue measures were, according to custom, challenged by the shipping, canning and large mining interests, and the litigation traveled the usual routes through the district and circuit courts. While these actions somewhat impeded for a time the administration and collection of the new taxes, the tax laws were, with minor exceptions, upheld by judicial decisions.[26]

As a consequence of the above-mentioned and other constructive legislation and the increased activities on both federal and territorial fronts, the 1950 census showed a population of 128,000 and by July 1, 1953, of 182,000. These were by far the largest increases in Alaska's history. With them was born a new faith in Alaska's destiny and conviction that the last rediscovery of Alaska, incidental to international events, spelled permanence.

With this new confidence came a resurgence of the desire for self-government on the traditional American pattern—namely, statehood. For even full territorial government, so earnestly sought since 1912, had never been attained. The vital reforms which Alaskans had sought for nearly a half century were still wanting. *Not a single one of the basic requests which the first legislature had addressed to Congress and which subsequent legislatures had reiterated though resolutions and memorials had been granted.*

So as Alaska reached the historic "four score and seven years" after the fathers had brought forth its purchase on this continent, the following fundamental problems still confronted its people.

The land laws continued unsuitable and unworkable and impeded settlement, although their administration had improved somewhat.

The administration of justice and of law enforcement, retained by the Organic Act of 1912 under federal control, was gravely deficient.

Federal bureaucratic policies concerning the native population were creating new problems affecting not only it but all the people of Alaska.

Alaska's greatest natural resource, the Pacific salmon, retained under federal management over the unceasing protests of Alaskans, was being destroyed.

The four forms of transportation upon which Alaska depended—maritime, air-borne, highway and the Alaska Railroad—were suffering the restrictions of various kinds of long-range and absentee controls.

Government by consent of the governed Alaskans was still unattained by them. Their struggle for it was continuing.

These issues will be scrutinized in the following chapters.

ALASKA'S PENDING PROBLEMS

Land: The Unsatisfied Hunger

For eighty years various matters in Alaska, including public lands have been the subject of studies, recommendations, resolutions, petitions, and congressional hearings—directed at and dependent upon Washington for corrective action. In reviewing any sizable part of the accumulated record one is struck by the remarkable sameness in nature of observations made through the years. The pattern remains the same; the examples alone change. Repetition of the same grievances over a period of generations leads to the inescapable conclusion that distance and the political disadvantage of territorial status foster neglect. Alaska's pleas are easier shelved than acted upon. . . .

With the aid of free land the West was opened by a people for most of whom there was no turning back. Today, by contrast, daily transportation to the States is available to those who decide against settling in Alaska. Until the settlement process is simplified by adoption of lands-disposal legislation more in keeping with a frontier country, it will be a waste of time to seek to encourage widespread settlement of Alaska.

BURKE RILEY, 1947

THE story of land in Alaska is one of contrast between natural plenty and man-made restriction. It is a tale of continuous effort by Americans there to secure a small share of this abundant ground. It is, no less, a necrology of their legitimate and age-old aspirations through the thwarting by a distant government. Its full narration would become depressing. It begins in 1867, and in 1954 it is still "to be continued."

To start there was not in Alaska, as along other earlier American frontiers, a general pre-emption law, that is, a squatter's right, an individual "first-come-first-served" right to claim land on the pre-emption principle. In Alaska there was not merely *lack* of such law, but a definite prohibition. Less than a week after the flag was raised in Sitka, General Land Office Commissioner Joseph S. Wilson was citing, upon demand of his chief, Secretary of the Interior Orville H. Browning, an act of Congress of 1807 (2 Stat. 445) that even *attempts* by the people in Alaska to make claims and settlement were contrary to law. It was a strange law that in this special instance could indeed "keep a man from trying," something which Americans say can't be done. But that being the case, Secretary Browning had in turn to notify his cabinet colleague Seward, who had requested the information, that since such attempts at settlement were "in direct violation of the provisions of the laws of Congress applicable to the public domain secured to the United States by any treaty," military force might be used "to remove the intruders." [1]

Who were the intruders? They were the American counterparts—in Alaska—of the frontiersmen, pioneers, settlers, the advance guard who for a century and a half had been making the future United States. From the Old World to America's eastern shore, successively across the Appalachians, the Prairies and the Rockies and on to the Coast they came, recognized at the time and revered in retrospect, as the builders of a nation. But in the last lap—last in time and last in space—to the farthest west and farthest north, they had become "intruders."

It was no doubt painful for Secretary of State Seward, with his pride of achievement concerning Alaska and his vision for its future, to communicate these tidings to General Ulysses S. Grant, Acting Secretary of War, who in turn conveyed them to Major General Halleck, commanding the Department of the West at San Francisco, for further transmission to Alaska.[2]

That such a situation could long endure was obviously so unthinkable to Major General Halleck that three weeks later he wired the Adjutant General of the Army in Washington:

"It is understood that the best agricultural land in the newly acquired Territory of Alaska is to be found on the peninsula at Kenai, between Cook's Inlet and Prince William Sound. . . . It is proposed to establish a military post on this peninsula early next spring and no doubt settlers will follow as soon as they are certain of protection. I therefore respectfully suggest to the Department of the Interior that these lands be surveyed and brought into the market at as early a period as possible.[3]

No action was taken on General Halleck's suggestion. When Secretary Seward visited Alaska in the summer of 1869, he did not doubt that Congress would supply civil government for Alaska during the coming winter.

"It must do this," he said, in addressing the people of Sitka on

August 12th, "because our political system rejects alike anarchy and executive absolutism."

But eight Congresses, assembling for twenty-one regular sessions—in addition to eight special sessions of the Senate—did no such thing, and when after seventeen years of no government whatever, the national legislature conferred a weazened form thereof in 1884, it specifically provided that the general land laws of the United States should *not* apply to the District of Alaska.

Despite the reiterated protests of successive governors, of other federal officials in Alaska, of citizen mass meetings, general land legislation did not come till the turn of the century. When finally extended to Alaska it was not adapted to conditions there. But whatever its value, extension of the general land law was in effect nullified by lack of surveys. Its multiple defects were emphatically called to the attention of Congress in 1913 by the First Alaska Legislature whose right to legislate on land matters Congress had specifically foreclosed. One of the legislature's six memorials on the subject protested against the eighty-rod shore-space reservation established by the act of May 14, 1898, "extending the homestead laws." This strange provision reserved on all navigable waters a space eighty rods wide between all tracts which might be acquired by individuals. Since the shore frontage of those tracts was also limited to eighty rods—amended in 1903 to 160 rods—it meant that the government was reserving to itself first one-half, then one-third, of the sea and river frontage of Alaska.

Commissioner Clay Tallman of the General Land Office condemned the shore-space reservation exhaustively and unqualifiedly in his 1918 report. A bill pending before the Congress would repeal "the shore-space reserves and water-front restrictions in their entirety," and solve that long-standing difficulty, he wrote, by abolishing the reservations as to those lands to be classified and listed for entry by the Secretary of Agriculture under an act of June 11, 1906 (34 Stat. 233) and then, upon application, restored to entry, if the Secretary of the Interior saw fit to grant such application. In that form the bill became law June 5, 1920 (41 Stat. 1059).

It might as well not have been enacted. If the shore-space reservation was as objectionable as Commissioner Tallman pointed out—and on that score there was no disagreement—why not a straight repeal? The new law erected two new obstacles, namely, prior action by the Secretary of Agriculture as to certain lands, and prior action in every instance thereafter by the Secretary of the Interior. The law merely increased the already excessive red tape by adding steps which would-be claimants for shore lands had to take. For all the extra effort the result was little changed. Under few Secretaries of the Interior was an appreciable number of shore-space reservations waived. Under Harold L. Ickes, Secretary of the Interior from 1933 to 1946, it was a matter of undeclared policy not to waive them. Where Congress by legislation had opened a pleasing vista of facilitated land acquisition, arbitrary bureaucratic policy effectively blocked the prospect.[4]

Alaska fared no better under an amendment to the land laws relating to school lands passed by Congress in 1927. It will be recalled that on the last day of the Sixty-third Congress, March 3, 1915, it had passed an act not only establishing a land-grant college in Alaska, but reserving two sections out of every township for the support of the territory's common schools. But the measure included a largely vitiating feature. Sections 16 and 36 were to be available "when the public lands of the Territory of Alaska are surveyed under the direction of the Government of the United States." But surveys did not follow. The act had further provided that if these sections or any part thereof were of known mineral character the reservation of them would be ineffective, but the proceeds accruing from them to the United States would be set aside for the territory's schools. The same provision existed for the school sections reserved on public domain in the States. But experience had shown mineralization of such lands in the States to be almost negligible. The income derived by the federal government from mineral sections, to be turned over to state or territory, would therefore, at best, consist of the nominal payments by the patentee at the time patent was granted; but even these would not be forthcoming if the mineral claimant worked his claim, as he well might, to the point of exhaustion of its ores, without patent.

These considerations led to the enactment, January 25, 1927, of "An Act Confirming in States and Territories Title to Lands Granted by the United States" (44 Stat. 1026). It vested the title to schools' land sections mineral in character in the states. It was a beneficent move, making the best possible use out of a portion of the public domain, and was endorsed by such diverse organizations as the National Education Association, the Western Division of the American Mining Congress, the United States Chamber of Commerce, and the National Association of Attorneys-General.[5] Alaska—despite the presence of "territories" in the title and text of the act—was expressly excluded in the final draft, although the only one of the territories with any substantial mineral resources. This fact was—and is—an ironic revelation of Alaska's continuing plight. By the specific exclusion Alaska was denied an advantage obtained by the states from their public-school land grants. But Alaska, if included, would not have benefited because the sections in question had not been surveyed, as they had been in the States. So Alaska was again penalized by Congress for the long-standing failure of Congress to appropriate for surveys that would have made this act useful to Alaska if extended to it. Upon Alaska, in short, were visited the sins of the stepfather, even unto the third generation! [6]

A major aspect of Alaskans' grievances against the federal government's land policy was the great number of reservations and withdrawals. They too had begun in the early days of the district but were imprinted on the Alaskans' consciousness by the Tongass and Chugach National Forest reservations by President Theodore Roosevelt in the century's first decade. The presidential authority had been questioned, but was expressly affirmed by Congress on June 25, 1910 (36 Stat. 847).[7]

The First Alaska Legislature memorialized against reservations (S.J.R. 6), asked that they be revoked and "thrown open for the general use of the prospector, miner and settler."

The Chugach—originally some eleven million acres in extent, but gradually reduced to its present area of 4,800,000 acres—was a perpetual target of adverse criticism.

"No useful purpose is served by this reservation," declared Governor Strong in his 1916 report. His successor, Governor Riggs, likewise could see "little reason . . . for the existence of the Chugach Forest," adding in his 1918 report that if it were retained, there should be further elimination of non-forested areas.

Opposition to the Chugach reservation was repeatedly voiced in Congress with no congressional defenders.

"I look upon the making of that forest reserve as a great folly," stated Senator Knute Nelson.[8]

"The one great reservation," concerning which he had yet to hear "a word of justification," declared Senator Thomas J. Walsh. In a long speech he cited the law creating forest reserves, said that the Chugach did not meet a single one of its specifications and that it was costing the government over five times as much to operate as it was returning to the treasury. He followed with an account of the difficulties encountered in securing a homestead in the Chugach and quoted the pleas of Delegate Wickersham that it be abolished:

"Notwithstanding his prayer," continued the Montana senator, "the Chugach Forest Reserve remains. I addressed a communication to the Forest Service asking what it had done in reference to the matter, and was answered to the effect that they proposed to exclude from the reserve all of that region that is covered by the great glaciers and the tops of the mountains. That is the concession they are willing to make in the premises."

"Where no human beings live," adverted Senator Reed Smoot, R., of Utah.

"Where no one cares whether it is within a forest or not," responded Senator Walsh.

"They ask for land, and they are given ice," commented Senator Marcus Aurelius Smith, D., of Arizona.[9]

Bills to abolish the Chugach National Forest were on several occasions introduced, but their passage prevented by the opposition of the Forest Service.

The Chugach National Forest—still costing five times as much as it was producing in revenue[10]—came in for attention again in 1952, when the Army sought a withdrawal, for an anti-aircraft artillery range, of 86,570 acres in the lower Susitna Valley across Knik Arm from Anchorage. This withdrawal, witnesses pointed out at a hearing held in Anchorage August 1st, would complete the encirclement of that city and effectively prevent its expansion. As demonstrated by Mr. Robert B. Atwood, editor and publisher of the Anchorage Times, reservations—for trees, the Chugach National Forest, 4,800,-000 acres, to the east and south; for moose, the Kenai Moose Range (earlier a part of the Chugach Forest) 1,852,418 acres, to the southwest; for Indians, the Tyonic Reserve, 26,918 acres, to the west; and for railroad, military and a variety of other purposes, numbering fifty-eight in all in the city's surroundings—closed the ring on Anchorage. For good measure there were forty-one more within the city limits. Despite the unanimity of Anchorage's plea of "don't fence me in," the withdrawal was promptly approved by the Interior Department, the agency which makes the final determination on all reservations and withdrawals in Alaska, including those requested by other departments.

Large military withdrawals were inevitable incidental to World War II and the subsequent Cold War, and the Alaska public supported them until in its opinion military reserves went far beyond military requirements, some of the higher officers were confusing military needs with exclusive hunting and fishing opportunities, and the extent of some reservations was seriously impeding economic and population growth, likewise considered helpful to defense.[11]

One aspect of all withdrawals was that they were seldom returned to public domain, and only after every other federal agency was given a prior right to transfer the withdrawal to its own use.

At the hearing on the Susitna anti-aircraft range withdrawal on August 1, 1952, Ralph Browne, Assistant General Manager of the Alaska Development Board, testified that the military withdrawals in Alaska totaled fifty-two million acres as contrasted with a total of twenty million acres for the entire forty-eight states. Illustrative of the continuing nature of the withdrawals and reservations he pointed out that within the fourteen months between May 1, 1950 and June 30, 1951, a total of thirty-two withdrawals covering 284,461 acres had been made in Alaska. The armed forces accounted for fifteen of these, totaling 275,613 acres.

On May 3, 1,350 acres on Middleton Island were revoked as an air-navigation site. But these acres were immediately picked up by the Air Force.

On September 11th, 111,700 acres on St. Lawrence Island (already an Eskimo reservation) were withdrawn by the Air Force, followed on October 13th, by 14,825 acres on Kuskokwim Bay, and on November 9th, 21,500 acres near Fairbanks, by the same service.

On November 22nd, the Army released 1,460 acres near Fairbanks. The very same land order re-withdrew the land for the Air Force. On December 12, 3,827 more acres were withdrawn by the Air Force.

On February 2, 1951, 118,840 acres near Mount McKinley station were withdrawn for national defense purposes, service unspecified.

On April 25th, the Air Force withdrew 88,980 acres on Kaktoavik Island.

On May 4th, the Navy released five acres near Seward and the land was immediately re-withdrawn by the Army.

On May 24th, the Federal Communications Commission released 105 acres near Favorite Channel. The order making the revocation also re-withdrew the land for the Army.

On June 25th, the Air Force withdrew 6,400 acres on the Tatlina River. And there were other withdrawals ranging from one to eighty acres.

"The significant fact to emerge is that although a total of 257,613 acres were withdrawn during that period," Mr. Browne testified, "not one acre was restored to the public domain. As quickly as it was released it was snatched by another branch of the service." [12]

One basic objection on the part of Alaskans was that withdrawals and reservations usually put an immediate stop to all forms of economic activity, actual or in prospect. When Glacier Bay Monument was enlarged by executive order in 1937 by 1,132,534 acres, it put several dairy farmers and homesteaders out of business. The acreage added to the monument had been part of the Tongass National Forest for thirty years, and had had no value for forestry purposes, but was one of its few areas suitable for agriculture. With great difficulty several families had managed to establish themselves in it. Their endeavor to secure legitimate compensation for their loss was obstructed instead of being facilitated by the government agencies concerned. Such experiences were the rule rather than the exception. The transfer from national Forest Service to National Park Service added nothing to the scenic values of the monument which had been preserved in the 1,164,800 acres withdrawn eleven years earlier.

Alaskans had likewise learned that once land is withdrawn from public entry decades may pass before restoration orders are effected. The question has become even more acute with the large number of military withdrawals. At times these have been demanded by one commanding officer, and considered of little value by his successor, who requests still other withdrawals but without necessarily moving to return the previous withdrawal to public domain. In 1952 a prospective settler became interested in a tract of land near Port Chilkoot, a co-operative community of veterans who had bought the facilities of Chilkoot Barracks in 1947 when these were declared surplus by the Army. The settler found the land unavailable because it had been withdrawn in 1901 by the military to keep local citizens out of an area that was in line of fire of a rifle range at Fort Seward. Although the soldiery had long vanished, the tract was still reserved to protect the public from stray bullets.[13]

Despite the virtual unanimity and continuity of Alaskans' protests against reservations and withdrawals, they had continued. The process was accelerated after 1936 by a new policy inaugurated by Harold L. Ickes, Secretary of the Interior in President Franklin D. Roosevelt's cabinet, designed to place all Indians and Eskimos in Alaska on reservations. Reservations for Indians and Eskimos had been established earlier at long intervals in Alaska but only a few of substantial acreage, and then in remoter areas inhabited only by those for whom the reservations were created.[14] The Ickes program, in its purposed all-inclusiveness, coupled with the secretarial determination to achieve it regardless of the contrary wishes of virtually the entire population of Alaska, native as well as white, represented a new departure. It was suspended only in 1950 with the retirements from office of Secretary Ickes and his successor Secretary Julius A. Krug, who proclaimed three native reservations on his last day in office. Two of these, despite the efforts of Alaska personnel of the Office of Indian Affairs to persuade the natives of Shungnak and Barrow to accept this form of wardship, were rejected by them at an election, and the third reservation at Hydaburg was subsequently invalidated by decision of the United States District Court. But in the meanwhile not a few reservations had been created and great alarm engendered by the declared purpose further to blanket Alaska with them.[15] The consequences of this endeavor persist and will be fully treated elsewhere.

Reservations and withdrawals in Alaska had proceeded so far by the middle of the twentieth century that no authoritative information existed as to their extent, the origin of some, the validity for their continuation, the degree of their duplication and overlapping. Requests for this information led Oscar L. Chapman, after his appointment on December 1, 1949, by President Truman, as Secretary of the Interior, to order such a study. A preliminary report on June 30, 1951, indicated 543 reservations totaling 114,300,000 acres. The completed study in February, 1952, by the Bureau of Land Management, in the form of a sixty-page atlas, accompanied by a 117-page check list, reduced the total—because of duplicating and overlapping withdrawals—to 93,700,000 acres, an area equal to that of the nation's third largest state, Montana. The principal categories were military reservations, including the naval petroleum reserve, 52,400,000 acres; national forests, 20,700,000; wild-life refuges, 8,000,000; national parks and monuments, 6,900,000; native reservations, 3,500,000; withdrawals for classification and in aid of legislation 1,600,000; miscellaneous, 600,000. Two years later the atlas and check list were already out of date.

In the second session of the Eighty-second Congress, H.R. 80, a resolution to study and revise the nation's public-land laws, which had not been done since the Forty-fifth Congress, was adopted. The committee was authorized to spend $87,000, and the work of drafting new legislation designed to correct the defects of the old was to be completed not later than January 3, 1953, when the Eighty-third Congress would open—presumably ready for action.

A subcommittee, including Alaska's delegate, E. L. "Bob" Bartlett, and headed by Representative Lloyd M. Bentsen, D., of Texas, came to Alaska and held hearings at Anchorage and Juneau in September, 1952. There the long-standing problems passed in review. It was a friendly and sympathetic group. One of its members, Fred L. Crawford, R., of Michigan, with eighteen years of service on the committee, had headed a subcommittee that had held hearings in Alaska on statehood in 1947. Norris Poulson, R., of Los Angeles, had likewise visited Alaska before. Samuel Yorty, D., also of Los Angeles, had, like the others, been an active supporter of measures deemed beneficial to Alaska. They made no secret of their knowledge that suitable land legislation for Alaska was long, long overdue, and should be adapted to its needs through a special act, and not merely be included in a general revision of the nation's land laws. They indicated their belief that the tidelands—the lands between high and low water—which had been a problem in many cities because of the inability to secure title, should go at once to the territory, and not await statehood.

The committee heard that the shore-space reservations should be abolished; that anyone should be entitled to buy outright a small piece of land—one, two or five acres—of the public domain, something which cannot now be done; that a business enterprise ought to be allowed to purchase whatever acreage it legitimately requires—a bill permitting this, introduced by Delegate Bartlett, passed the

House, but the Senate reduced the maximum to 160 acres, an insufficient amount, and in that form it became law [Aug. 30, 1949. 63 Stat. 679]. That a non-profit organization, Boy or Girl Scouts, or a denominational group should be able to acquire fifty or a hundred acres for recreational purposes without obliging the Delegate each time to get a special bill passed. Delegate Bartlett had sponsored and secured action on some twenty-five such bills during the Seventy-ninth to the Eighty-third Congresses; a bill to obviate that cumbersome and time-consuming procedure had passed the House but had been pigeonholed in the Senate Interior Committee—the effort would be made again. That land not essential to forestry should be excluded from the national forests and made available for other uses. A small beginning had been made in the Tongass by returning a part of the suburban areas to public domain, thus facilitating town expansion, also making possible patenting of "special-use" sites, formerly rented on annual permit by the Forest Service; but that much forest land containing no commercial timber could be beneficially disposed of in similar ways, thus increasing private ownership. . . .

The committee heard the old complaints about the long delays in processing applications—years passing sometimes [16]—of the inability to get action on unsurveyed ground. It heard that the cultivation provisions should be removed from the homesteading requirements except on land clearly suited for agriculture, and the testimony of Ed Jarvi, homesteader, "The average homesteader can take anything that Alaska and its winters can bring. He cannot outfight the arbitrary and fickle rulings of the men who are supposed to help him." [17] But the committee also heard that the understaffed regional offices of the Bureau of Land Management were doing the best they could with the means at their disposal and despite difficulties issuing more patents every year.[18]

And finally the Congressmen learned that the total of surveyed land in Alaska was 2,470,960 acres—just a little under two-thirds of one per cent of Alaska's 375,000,000! [19] (At the rate the federal government had surveyed Alaska, members of Congress estimated it would take twelve thousand years to complete the job.)

But alas for Alaskans' hopes! The national elections of 1952 changed the control of the House of Representatives and with it the committee and subcommittee chairmanships. The new chairman had different ideas. The hearings in Alaska, in September of 1952, meticulously recorded by court reporters and illustrated with carefully prepared charts and graphs, were not even printed. The revision of the land laws—the special land legislation for Alaska to meet its special needs—was indefinitely postponed.[20]

Justice: The Failure of Law Enforcement

One can hardly expect in these distant regions that the law shall be greatly respected when the law has not shown sufficient respect for itself to provide respectable means for its enforcement.
SECRETARY OF COMMERCE WILLIAM C. REDFIELD, 1915

DEFICIENT law enforcement has been a condition in Alaska wherever the federal government has exercised exclusive sway. It began, as we have seen, with the total absence of any law in the first seventeen years of United States rule. It continued through the next sixteen years with the simulacrum of law conferred by the unworkable Oregon code, coupled with the non-purveyance by Congress of means to enforce such interpretation of legality as the lone federal district judge and his four far-flung commissioners might venture.

The belated adoption of civil and criminal codes for Alaska at the turn of the century improved this condition only slightly. The revised legal structure, with its amplified personnel, aggravated the shortcoming in one respect by eliminating even the modest part-time subsistence salary of $1,000 annually provided for the United States commissioners by the act of 1884, and making them thenceforth wholly dependent for their livelihood from the commissionerships on the fees they could collect, from the public chiefly, for their services. The stationing of troops at a half-dozen widely scattered posts was an awkward attempt by the federal authorities to compensate for the lack of adequate provision for law enforcement by the usual civil authorities. It was not a function the soldiery was qualified to assume, and the result, during the quarter-century maintenance of these "forts," was what might have been anticipated.

The generally law-abiding nature of Alaskans in the eighty-seven years of United States dominion has caused this serious, important and continuing problem to receive no more attention from the federal authorities than have other Alaskan needs. But it is a striking fact

that Alaska from its earliest days experienced almost none of the violence and vigilantism which was current in the West during the decades of frontier settlement there.

The "Soapy Smith" affair, which culminated in July, 1899, stands
out as the lone dramatic example of classic border banditry in Alaska.
Smith, an underworld character, had acquired his sobriquet on the
street corners of Western communities, by selling soap wrapped in a
greenback, when one of his accomplices in the crowd was the lucky
buyer. Smith followed the Klondike gold-rushers north. Shrewdly, he
stopped short of encounter with the effective Royal Canadian
Mounted Police by locating in Skagway. He and his confederates began by establishing shell games and other bunco gambling devices.
When they turned to waylaying miners, robbing them of their pokes,
and one miner was murdered, a citizens' committee—in the absence
of any effective governmental protection—was formed to act. Smith,
loaded Winchester repeater in hand, followed by a band of his hench-
men, proceeded down the long Skagway dock to break up a gathering
of townsmen at its far end. His approach was barred by their sentry,
Frank H. Reid, a former schoolteacher who had served as a voluntee1
in the Piute Indian War. Reid became a civil engineer and had laid
out the town plat of Skagway. When Reid denied Smith access to
the meeting, "Soapy" swung at Reid with his rifle. Reid grabbed
the rifle; in the struggle his opponent twisted the muzzle toward
Reid and fired. Reid fell, mortally wounded, but drew his revolver
and shot Smith through the heart. Smith's gang fled but was promptly
rounded up and shipped back to the States.

One other episode, a decade later, with all the elements of Western
melodrama, arose out of the contest for railway rights of way east
of Prince William Sound. The Alaska Syndicate had determined to
build its Copper River and Northwestern Railway from Cordova instead of Valdez, to the disappointment of the people of that town.
They then pinned their hopes on a prospective rival enterprise, the
Alaska Home Railway, promoted by H. B. Reynolds, whose undertaking had the support of former Governor Brady. A group of its workmen entered Keystone Canyon, north of Valdez, on the old Alaska
Syndicate right of way. There they encountered guards headed by a
man named Edward Hasey who had been sworn in as a deputy marshal by the United States Marshal of the Division. Assuming his role
to be that of protector of the Morgan-Guggenheim properties and re-

garding the workmen as trespassers, Hasey called upon them to retire. When they did not, Hasey fired, wounding one worker fatally and two others slightly. Hasey was tried twice and on the second occasion was convicted and sentenced to eighteen months' imprisonment. This fracas, with its bloody dénouement, increased the already high tension between the Guggenheim and anti-Guggenheim forces. "The Guggenheims" were charged with going to any lengths to prevent the construction of a rival railway over a route they had already decided to abandon. Aroused passions were further inflamed when jury-tampering was uncovered.

A bill for the entertainment of witnesses and jurors and payment of witnesses, rendered to John A. Carson, attorney for Hasey, was transmitted by Carson to Captain David H. Jarvis, an important official of the syndicate, and at that time treasurer of several of its affiliates. Carson's accompanying letter expressed his appreciation of the services rendered by one M. B. Morrisey, an accountant employed in the railroad construction, who was billing the Katalla Company, an affiliate, for his own expenses incidental to entertainment of witnesses and jurymen, as well as for the costs of the entertainment and cash payments. Carson wrote that Morrisey's "control" over "many of the government's witnesses" had enabled him "to be of the greatest possible service" to the defense, and asked Jarvis to "treat him in a very liberal manner." The voucher was approved by W. H. Bogle, the syndicate's general counsel in Seattle, and payment made. The letter and voucher had been taken from the syndicate's files by the company's auditor, H. J. Douglas, who had learned that he was about to be discharged from its employ. They were introduced into hearings of the House Committee on Territories by Delegate Wickersham.[1] Hasey's light sentence was attributed to powerful influences in his behalf, and allegations of political persecution against those who had helped convict him were given wide currency. Governor Hoggatt was involved in these charges. Jarvis, whose earlier public service in Alaska had shown great promise, committed suicide not long thereafter when he was named in an action by the federal government to recover for fraud in the sale of coal to Army posts in Alaska, for which two other company officials were convicted and given prison sentences. Indeed the rifle shot that first echoed against Keystone Canyon's walls, with its fatality, attendant circumstances and subsequent scandal, was to have wide reverberations in Alaska, which reached even the national capital. It became the territory's greatest sensation in the tumultuous years that marked the close of the century's first decade.

With these short-lived exceptions, Alaska has, amazingly enough, been the only American frontier without the turbulence, romantic in retrospect, which has become a great American legend, and is alluringly perpetuated today in the fiction of books, magazines, motion pictures, radio and video. No such typical "Westerns" other than as above noted are available from Alaskan source material.

Jack London's Alaskan short stories treated largely of conflict with isolation and the elements. The most famous character and hero of his longer Alaskan fiction was a "husky"—a sled dog named Buck, in *The Call of the Wild*. London's novel, *The Sea-Wolf*, dealt with the strife incident to pelagic sealing, which took place on the high seas. It was this marine lawlessness which gave rise to Kipling's "there's never a law of God or man runs north of Fifty-three," in his *Rhyme of the Three Sealers*, written in 1893, when fur-seal poaching was at its height. But this piracy of pelts scarcely reached the Alaskan main.

Rex Beach's *The Spoilers*, his best-known Alaskan novel, and for some years the most widely circulated of all book-length Alaskan fiction, dealt with a unique conspiracy to defraud the first gold discoverers in the Nome rush. The incident terminated, after the miners' appeals reached the United States Circuit Court at San Francisco, with the trial and removal of Judge Arthur H. Noyes, who, convicted merely of contempt of court, escaped appropriate punishment with only a $1,000 fine. His confederates, Alexander McKenzie, whom he had appointed receiver of the claimant's gold locations, and Joseph K. Wood, the United States District Attorney for Alaska's Second Judicial Division, received short jail sentences. But this notorious episode, totally devoid of physical violence, was an example of lawlessness not of Alaskans, a few of whom were for a time its victims, but of agents of the federal government who conceived the fraud even before their arrival in Alaska and perpetrated it promptly upon their advent there.

Until the vast defense-construction program, beginning in 1940, brought to the areas of its greatest intensity many undesirable camp followers of a great boom, the relatively slight incidence of crime in Alaska compared favorably with almost any part of the Union. The generally law-abiding character of Alaskans, as contrasted with other earlier frontier dwellers, may be attributed to various factors.

Apart from the antagonism engendered by the soldiery near their posts in the first decade after the purchase, and the occasional crime induced by "hoochenoo" among the primitive inhabitants, violent hostility between whites and Indians, incidental to the westward march of white settlement, did not exist in Alaska.[2] Unlike the redskin in the area of the forty-eight states, the Alaskan Indian was not driven from his ancestral habitats, but continues to reside in them. In Alaska aborigine and newcomer co-existed with a minimum of friction. While many whites brought their racial prejudices from the States and some earlier discrimination against the "native" resulted, interracial relations in Alaska were never stained as elsewhere in America by bloodshed.

Nor did the friendly and peaceable Eskimo nurse a burning personal sense of grievance against the whalers and walrus hunters of the eighteen seventies and eighties who destroyed much of his food supply, but, on the contrary, shared whatever he had with the white stranger when chance stranded him on the Arctic or Bering Sea coasts. In short, despite the early white Alaskans' apprehension of Indian uprisings, such as, with reason, alarmed the West through most of the nineteenth century, no massacre of whites by aborigines, and, conversely, no extermination or displacement of aborigines by whites, marred the history of Alaska.

As between white men, gold, fish and furs were the only material stakes over which they might battle. But in nineteenth-century Alaska, in the total absence of official "law and order," the gold-seekers early established a uniquely civilized and democratic form of self-government in the wild, which by meting out swift and just punishment to offenders against the miners' code, proved a great deterrent to evildoers. It was customary too, in the more settled communities, not to lock one's house or cabin in those days. It was unnecessary. Fur-seal poaching in the eighteen eighties and nineties, as has been pointed out, was not only confined to the high seas, but its illegality denied by those engaged in it, a view later sustained by international tribunal. Later, occasional fish piracy by robbing salmon from traps occurred, usually through the collusion of a trap watchman.

The other historic bases for Western lawlessness did not exist in Alaska. Land grabs could not take place because the only land ownership possible was that of the federal government. The desert battles over a water supply could likewise not occur in the absence of title and amid an abundance of rain and ground water. Cattle rustling was impossible because there were no cattle. Horse stealing—of the pack animals with whom the pioneers shared their burdens—was unthinkable: A monument on the White Pass to the Klondike commemorating the horses that died on the trail is a sentimental reminder of the comradeship between man and beast in the early Alaskan days, and of the code implicit therein.

Finally, the remoteness of Alaska which persisted until the end of the nineteen thirties, the obvious interdependence of the few people along the far-flung wilderness frontier, promoted a neighborliness, a friendly helpfulness and a generosity which persist today as widely prevailing Alaskan traits. Moreover, escape of one sought for a criminal act was difficult. Solitary exile in the northern wilds—for all but the most hardy—could be rigorous beyond the retribution of man-made justice. It generally ended in death or surrender.

Today a lone highway and air lines connect Alaska with the States, but they have been available for less than a decade and a half; and even over these recent escape routes fugitives could be easily watched and apprehended. Nor is escape by sea easily concealed.

Nevertheless such criminals as there were remained often unsought and unapprehended, and their crimes unpunished.[3] The failures of federal law enforcement have for seventy years been the subject of Alaskans' unremitting protest ever since the semblance of government provided by the organic act of 1884 at least gave rise to the hope, if it did not justify the assumption, that the protecting arm of the national government had been extended over Alaska. But as we have seen, the earnest attempts of the first four governors to bring Alaska's plight under that legislation to the attention of its congressional authors, and secure remedial action, were wholly in vain.

"The whole condition of Alaska, as far as the execution of the law is concerned, is a disgrace to our government, and I shall so report, but it will not do any good," wrote Robley D. Evans, later Admiral Evans, commanding a United States naval vessel in Alaskan waters in the middle nineties.[4]

After congressional enactment of the criminal and civil codes—1899-1900—criticism of the commissioner system, which they continued in amended form, was prompt, vigorous and unceasing. Indeed the voluminous literature on the subject which has accumulated in government files in over a half-century fails to reveal a dissenting defender amid the unanimity of protest. Objection was made to appointment by the United States district judges, but even more to the method of compensation by fees only. Governor Brady urged that commissioners be salaried and appointed by the Governor.[5]

President Theodore Roosevelt similarly recommended to Congress in his State of the Union Message on December 6, 1904, "that United States commissioners be appointed by the governor of the territory instead of by the judges, and that a fixed salary be provided for them to take the place of the discredited 'fee system,' which should be abolished in all offices. . . ."

President Roosevelt also recommended "that a mounted constabulary be created to police the territory outside the limits of incorporated towns—a vast section now wholly without police protection."

But Congress took no action on any of these presidential recommendations. The judges continued to appoint the commissioners, who continued to be unsalaried. A constabulary for Alaska was considered from time to time by the Congress and provision made for it in various bills. But they never reached enactment.[6]

Memorializing the Congress, the First Territorial Legislature in 1913 pointed out that more than three-fourths of the civil legislation in Alaska was disposed of by the United States commissioners acting as justices of the peace and probate judges; that practically all criminal litigation was either disposed of or initiated by the same officials acting as recorders, coroners or in other capacities; and that under the existing system they were "by far the most important functionaries in the territory, coming in their official capacity in closer, more frequent and more varied contact with the mass of our citizens than any other officials," and were thus "of more importance to the good order, peace and general well-being of the community than any other officials." The legislators declared that the fees collected in many precincts were "altogether insufficient to enable the commissioner to devote himself exclusively to his official duties for a livelihood," and that such a fee system afforded "constant temptation to the commissioners to encourage litigation and was therefore a menace to the conscientious discharge of their duties." And so the memorial (H.J.M. 2) asked Congress to enact a law to provide a salary of at least $2,000. At that time there were some forty commissioners. The total cost of the requested legislation would have been $80,000 annually, minus the fees collected, chiefly from the Alaskan public, which would have reverted to the federal treasury. Subsequent legislatures were to utter similar pleas with no more result.

The commissioner system was caustically described the following year, 1914, by the Reverend Hudson Stuck, Archdeacon of the Yukon, next to the Bishop the ranking Episcopalian clergyman in Alaska. Pointing out that as the unsalaried commissioners were compelled to "eke out a precarious and wretched existence on fees," it was "frequently impossible to get men of character and capacity to accept such offices." [7]

Bills to abolish the fee system and to salary the United States Commissioners in Alaska have been repeatedly introduced by Alaska's delegates. These have almost invariably had the endorsements of the federal departments concerned, the Department of Justice, which has the primary responsibility in this field, and the Department of the Interior, which has an over-all responsibility for Alaska. Such support, in the form of a favorable report on the delegate's bill, has usually been precipitated by word reaching Washington, of a scandal in one of the commissioners' courts. It may be one of the commoner forms of misconduct, such as intoxication on the bench. It may be the failure to make adequate accounting and transmission of fees— there have been a number of actual embezzlements; or it may even be complicity with litigants in dishonesty and fraud.[8]

"Commissioners are susceptible to the same temptations that beset other humans, and the Government is partly responsible if they succumb to some of them," wrote Mrs. Margaret Keenan Harrais, one of the outstanding women in Alaska, herself a United States commissioner at Valdez, and for many years a member of the territorial Board of Education, in a letter of testimony for a House hearing on a bill of Delegate Bartlett's, who introduced the communication into the record.[9]

"It is the business of government to make it easy to do right and hard to do wrong," continued Mrs. Harrais's letter. "In its treatment of commissioners, this order is reversed; it is made easy to do wrong and hard to do right. There is not sufficient income from the office for a living, so some have proceeded to get it otherwise—illicit dealing in liquor, wolf and coyote bounties and poisoned furs; appropriation of the assets of small estates; alliance with the underworld in protection of their nefarious activities.

"We can all recall U. S. commissioners who were utterly unfit to hold any position of responsibility. I recall an instance during prohibition days. No one in the community was willing to bother with the position for the meager income it yielded, so a man was sent in from another judicial division. He knew that the office did not yield an honest living, so he immediately wired for a boss bootlegger—a friend of his—to come. They both did well financially, to the disgrace of the Department of Justice and the breaking down of every vestige of respect for law in that community." [10]

The task of appointing commissioners—of finding in a given community a qualified person to make the necessary sacrifice—is the despair of Alaska's district judges. They often plead in vain with individuals whom they consider suitable, and are perforce driven to a less desirable selection. Or a commissionership remains vacant for a considerable period because no one can be found who is willing to accept the office.

In 1942 the Department of Justice, aroused by adverse comment on the administration of justice and law enforcement in Alaska, because it was made by one of the department's assistant attorney-generals, Norman M. Littell, after a visit there on other official business, the following year sent Mathias F. Correa, United States Attorney for the District of Southern New York, to investigate. Both made the time-honored recommendations for the abolition of the commissioner fee system, Littell urging a minimum annual salary of $2,400, "to raise the commissioner's office above the level of sheer poverty." [11] Based on those findings, Attorney-General Francis Biddle appointed a special assistant to the Attorney-General with the assignment to go into the matter more fully. He was Joseph W. Kehoe, long an Alaskan resident, then United States Attorney for the Third Division, who had been a United States commissioner, and would later become a United States District Judge in Alaska.

Mr. Kehoe's report on June 6, 1944, again made clear the essential nature of the commissionerships. The United States commissioner—in Alaska—was not only a committing magistrate as in the states, precinct recorder, justice of the peace, coroner and probate judge, but, since counties in Alaska were specifically prohibited by the organic act of 1912, the commissioner also took on the duties performed by the county recorder, county justice of the peace, county coroner, county probate officer and vital statistics officer.

There being few roads in Alaska and many communities therefore isolated, a commissioner was a necessity to them: "Without the United States commissioner," Mr. Kehoe reported, "minor crimes would go unpunished, no investigation would be made of deaths, no mining claims could be recorded, no primary or general elections held, no minor civil cases tried and no vital statistics kept." [12] And these were only a portion of a commissioner's duties.

But there was, the report disclosed, a marked disparity between the importance of the services rendered by these essential members of the judicial branch of our government and the compensation they received. In the three preceding years only in six cities had the commissioners collected fees in amount greater than the statutory $3,000 they were entitled to retain. These cities and amounts were: Anchorage, $10,357; Fairbanks, $9,348; Nome, $5,615; Juneau, $5,398; Ketchikan, $3,807; Seward, $3,201. In only two other cities, Sitka and Kodiak, did the fees total over $2,000. In eight towns, Bethel, Cordova, Innoko, Nenana, Palmer, Talkeetna, Valdez and Wrangell, they averaged between $1,000 and $1,500. In sixteen towns they ranged between $500 and $1,000. And in twenty-one towns the commissioners took in less than $500 annually. Of this last category eight commissionerships averaged less than $100 a year, and in five of these less than $50. Moreover with few exceptions commissioners furnished their own offices, typewriters and filing cabinets, and paid rent, this last in some cases in buildings owned by the federal government. The total of fees collected by all the commissioners in 1943 was $47,547.90. The greater portion of these fees was paid by the general public. The territorial government paid the fees in vital-statistics matters. The United States paid the fees only in criminal, coroners' and insanity cases.

In fact the administration of the lower courts in Alaska not only costs the United States nothing, but it actually makes a profit from them. The people of Alaska pay all federal income and other federal taxes that are paid by Americans in the forty-eight states. Yet they are compelled by the past action and subsequent inaction of Congress to pay also the costs of an admittedly defective court system, but have no voice in its management.

"The remedy for this deplorable situation is the passage of amendatory legislation by Congress providing for the payment of sufficient salaries to the United States commissioners to insure the selection of persons of ability and integrity," wrote George W. Folta, in 1943, when he was Counsel-at-large for the Department of the Interior in Alaska, in a memorandum to the Solicitor of the Department, which Mr. Kehoe quoted in his report. Mr. Folta, who had also had experience as United States attorney and was later to become a district judge, added that under the existing system the judges were "compelled to cajole or induce some person of questionable qualifications" to accept the commissionership in the smaller communities.

Mr. Kehoe recommended, as had all other commentators, the abolition of the fee system and in its stead a salary for commissioners. He suggested three categories of commissionerships depending upon the amount of work. The commissioners obviously had and have to depend on other sources of income to keep body and soul together.

Anthony J. Dimond, who served as delegate from 1933 through 1944, strove vainly, as had his predecessors, to secure favorable action on bills to make the commissionerships salaried posts. As District Judge—1945 to 1953—he faced the difficult task of securing qualified incumbents for the commissionerships in the Third Judicial Division.

His successor, Edward L. ("Bob") Bartlett, elected in 1944, promptly introduced a similar bill, H.R. 2262, on the convening of the Seventy-ninth Congress (January 3, 1945–August 2, 1946) which was unanimously endorsed by the Seventeenth Territorial Legislature.[13] Congress, however, took no action.

Bartlett introduced another bill, H.R. 1239, in the first session of the Eightieth Congress in 1947, amending existing law to provide a minimum salary of $200 a month for commissioners, and providing that they could retain fees to a maximum of $5,000 a year. The number of commissioners entitled to that minimum guarantee was limited to forty-six, so that the cost to the federal government would have been $110,400, minus the fees collected. The bill was endorsed by the Departments of Justice and Interior, and in a hearing before the House Committee on Public Lands was strongly supported by Mr. Henry P. Chandler, Director of the Administrative Office of the United States Courts, created in 1939, which had replaced the Attorney-General's office in its authority to establish the Alaska commissioners' fees (53 Stat. 1223). No testimony, written or oral, was presented in opposition. Nevertheless a member of the committee felt that the matter should be further investigated. (The issue had been before Congress only forty-seven years!) So a subcommittee of three was appointed. After some further inquiry the subcommittee met. Two of its members were favorable to reporting Delegate Bartlett's bill. But one member objected on the ground that the federal treasury would be subjected to unnecessary expense in the cases of those commissioners whose fees did not total an average of $200 a month. His objection prevailed. It was therefore agreed to compromise by raising the maximum that could be retained by a commissioner from the previous $3,000 to $5,000 annually (62 Stat. 80).

Delegate Bartlett again sought to put the commissioners on a minimum-salary basis in the Eighty-second Congress. The effort failed again. But Bartlett succeeded in increasing the amount that might be retained by a commissioner to $7,500 per annum (66 Stat. 592). Under the statute, however, commissioners are permitted to retain only the "net fees," which means that, prior to their computation, the commissioner is charged with all office expenses, including equipment, rental, telephone, light, stationery, etc.

A concomitant result of the delegate's efforts was also a revision of the schedule of fees, which had not been altered materially since the first schedule issued by Attorney-General Philander C. Knox in 1902. A new schedule, effective January 1, 1949, and revised slightly in 1950 and 1951, raised the fees which commissioners were entitled to charge for various services by about 50 per cent.

However, the legislation achieved after much earnest effort has benefited appreciably only a few commissioners. A survey made by the writer in 1953 showed that only four of them—in the principal cities—collect sufficient fees to retain the statutory maximum. Considering the importance of the commissionership in such cities as Ketchikan, Juneau, Anchorage and Fairbanks, and in view of the substantially higher living costs, especially in the last two, these emoluments, while an improvement over those preceding, are still scarcely adequate. But in the fifty-odd other commisionerships, the net compensation, despite the increase in fees, still remains utterly insufficient, and leaves the basic problem unsolved.[14]

Thus, after a half-century of unanimous protest by presidents, attorney-generals, secretaries of the interior, governors, judges, delegates, legislatures and others, the unsalaried commissionership persists. And so in Alaska, for want of willingness of Congress to appropriate what might by now amount to $200,000 annually, justice, cornerstone of a democracy, continues to be impaired.

Congress has also been derelict in its attention to the United States district judges. It was not till two years of the gold rush that Congress altered the existing single judicial district for all Alaska with headquarters at Sitka, by providing two more judgeships by the act of June 6, 1900. It was already apparent that the two newly created judicial divisions, encompassing all but southeastern Alaska, with their judges stationed at Eagle on the Yukon and at Nome on the Bering Sea, would not suffice for the great volume of litigation precipitated by mining claims and for the criminal cases. Within a few months it was more than clear that, given the lack of transportation and the heavy court calendars, the two additional judges could not take care of the multitudinous needs arising throughout the 560,000 square miles of central, northern and western Alaska. So demand for a fourth judicial division, for the vast Pacific Coast area and its hinterland up to the Alaska Range, was immediate. But nearly nine years elapsed, in the face of unremitting, urgent pleas from Alaska, before Congress would, on March 3, 1909, grant a fourth judicial division and a fourth judge.

Subsequent years show continuingly slow reactions by the Department of Justice and the Congress. Vacancies in Alaska judgeships are filled with a leisureliness which disregards the requirements of proper administration of justice. A lapse of months is the rule. The lapse of a year is not unusual.[15]

The ancient failings persist—to this day—and regardless of whether the administration is Democratic or Republican. When Judge Joseph W. Kehoe resigned his position as United States District Judge in the Second Judicial Division on September 12, 1951, his successor, J. Earl Cooper, was not appointed till July 17, 1952—ten months and five days later. As his was a recess appointment made by the Truman administration, it expired automatically at the end of the next session of Congress on August 3, 1953. Again the judgeship was vacant eight months. If the Eisenhower administration was not ready to name a Republican successor, it should have continued Judge Cooper, whose record on the bench had been excellent, with another recess appointment until it had determined on an appointee of its own. But the chronic inertia and indifference that have characterized the federal carrying out of its important responsibility in the administration of justice in Alaska were sufficient to suspend the operation of the Second Division court for an indefinite period.

An even more serious predicament resulted in the Third Judicial Division for which an additional judge has been vainly sought since 1947, the number of cases before that court having doubled between 1941 and 1947, and doubled again by 1953, reaching 1029 in that year. Judge Dimond, made ill by overwork, had tendered his resignation to take effect at the expiration of his second judicial term in February, 1953. The administration was thus fully apprised even before its inauguration on January 20th that the most heavily burdened of the four Alaska district judgeships was to be filled. Judge Dimond, who continued to carry out his duties until his successor should be appointed, died on May 28, 1953, his death hastened by overwork in the conscientious discharge of his duties. At that time 177 criminal and 1,053 civil cases were pending before the court. Yet the Eisenhower administration made no appointment till October 2, 1953— over four months later, when a recess appointment was given to J. L. McCarrey, who was confronted by a still further augmented litigious backlog.

For seven years a second judge for the Third Division has been sought in legislation. The additional judgeship is recommended by the Administrative Office of the Courts, whose function it is to expedite the judicial process. The legislation to satisfy this evident need follows a course to which Alaskans should be accustomed after eighty-seven years: A favorable report by the Judiciary Committee of one house of Congress; passage of the bill by that house; no action on the bill by the other house; or an amendment deleting the provision for an additional Alaska judge from a general bill providing more federal judges; the same performance with minor variations in the next Congress. And the next. In sum, no enactment.

On February 10, 1054, President Eisenhower signed a bill which had followed, as far as Alaska was concerned, the ancient routine. The Act (Public Law 294, 83C: 2s) created twenty-four more judgeships—three United States circuit and twenty-one district. Alaska was not included. Its sorely needed additional judgeship for the Third Division had been eliminated on the way to passage. At the time of enactment, 415 criminal and 1,370 civil cases were still pending before the United States District Court at Anchorage.

Justice deferred is often justice denied. The damage caused by the interminable delays; the actual denials of justice resulting in many instances—these would be less shameful if they were not so easily remediable. But they are not remediable by Alaskans.

For Alaska in its judicial framework and law enforcement is an anomaly under the Stars and Stripes, and in the past and contemporary treatment of American territories. It is distinct from the only other incorporated territory, Hawaii. In its organic act—enacted April 30, 1900—two years after annexation, Congress granted Hawaii a supreme court, circuit courts and "such inferior courts as the legislatures may from time to time establish." [16] The Supreme Court and Circuit Court judgeships are filled by presidential appointees subject to confirmation by the United States Senate, but their choice is confined to "citizens of the Territory of Hawaii." [17] The lower courts, unlike the commissioners' courts in Alaska, are created by the elected territorial legislature.

Alaska is likewise far less privileged than Puerto Rico, for fifty years an unincorporated territory, or "insular possession," elevated by Congress to commonwealth status in 1952. Under this unique and unprecedented political arrangement, made in response to and in accord with the expressed wishes of the people of Puerto Rico, the Supreme Court is appointed by the elective governor subject to confirmation by the Commonwealth Senate, and all other courts such as the legislature may determine.[18] (For good measure the lone United States district judge in Puerto Rico has since the inauguration of the commonwealth been a Puerto Rican appointed by the President on the recommendation of the Governor of Puerto Rico!)

Protection of life and property is the most elementary of the duties of government. Extremists at either end of the question of what functions government should or should not perform would find agreement there. Congress and the Department of Justice have been no less indifferent and negligent in that portion of their jurisdiction dealing with the apprehension and prosecution of criminals than they have in every other aspect of their responsibilities in the realm of justice in Alaska.

The Kehoe Report in 1944 also pointed out what has been known and condemned in Alaska for over a half-century concerning the marshals and their deputies. Their numbers are inadequate, their pay insufficient and their instructions hamstring them.[19]

In 1944 marshals and deputies for all Alaska numbered thirty-nine.

The chief deputy's salary in each judicial division was $3,300. The other deputies' salaries averaged $2,500 a year. This rate of pay was 50 per cent lower than that of the enforcement officers with comparable, but far less diverse or perilous, duties in the federal Fish and Wildlife Service. Outside the incorporated towns, each of which has its own police department and municipal magistrate, and where government on the local level functions with reasonable effectiveness, the marshals have been the only officials to whom appeal can be made when a crime is committed. Under their instructions, unchanged in over forty years, they are not permitted to investigate a crime without prior authorization, which often requires days. These conditions were not materially changed ten years later—in 1954.

With the great influx of personnel, construction workers, and, following them, the denizens of the underworld, who are attracted to the site of a boom, it was inevitable that, in the wake of war, crime should come to Alaska. The centers of greatest federal expenditure, the cities in the rail belt, Anchorage and Fairbanks, were hard hit. Within the cities, the municipal authorities have made a commendable effort to suppress crime, and have multiplied their police forces. But their jurisdiction ends at the city limits. It does not extend into the fast-growing suburbs and surrounding areas which furnish a refuge for nefarious characters in a no man's land where vice and crime enjoy a holiday.

In 1950 President Truman, apprised of this situation, requested the Department of Justice to make provision for a hundred additional deputy marshals in Alaska and to revise the instructions which so limited their effectiveness. The Department of Justice, however, was unable to secure from Congress an increased appropriation to pay even twenty-five additional marshals, to which figure it had pared down the President's request. Nor was any revision in the instructions to the marshals made.

To do its part in law enforcement outside the incorporated towns—despite the reservation of this function by the federal authorities to themselves—the Fifteenth Territorial Legislature in 1941 established a territorial highway patrol.[20] The force was steadily increased and in a decade numbered forty officers and patrolmen—of good character and high morale. The force served well and its services were greatly appreciated by Alaskans. The force's duties were subsequently extended beyond those of traffic control. Its scope was, however, severely restricted by the limited highway mileage in Alaska to which the patrol's services were necessarily confined.

Though the Alaska Highway Patrol was and is wholly supported by territorial appropriations, the fines levied in the commissioners' courts as a result of arrests by the patrol for traffic violations go into the federal treasury. To rectify this injustice Delegate Bartlett introduced a bill in the Eighty-second Congress to provide that such fines be deposited in the territorial treasury and be expended in the maintenance of the patrol.[21] No action was taken by the House Committee on Interior and Insular Affairs to which the bill was referred and it died there.

Crime continues rampant in the Anchorage area. Hardly a day passes that armed robbery, burglary, assault, or murder are not committed. What law enforcement there is, is supplied inside the city limits by the Anchorage city police which has coped with its problems with reasonable effectiveness. Outside of the city in its widely extended suburbs the problem is being tackled by the Territorial Highway Patrol, which the twenty-first legislature rechristened Territorial Police, giving it a mandate for the performance of every variety of police duty.[22] The contribution to the detection and pursuit of criminals rendered by the United States marshal's office in Anchorage, with its few deputies and unchanged policies, is negligible.

Across the border, eighty years previously—in 1873—the Dominion of Canada, six years after its formation, established the Royal Canadian Mounted Police. Its name has become inseparably associated with the reign of law in the most remote wilderness fastnesses. It has extended the Anglo-Saxon concept of law and order throughout the thinly settled northwestern provinces and territories. In neighboring Alaska, by contrast, the failure of the federal authorities to perform a similar duty has been and continues to be flagrant—and equally so under Democratic and Republican administrations.

Finally, the federal government's failure extends also to its provisions for United States attorneys, the agents of prosecution in all major criminal cases when malefactors have been apprehended and brought to the bar of justice.

The inadequate provision for these federal officials as well as the shortcomings of law enforcement through the marshals' offices were set forth by Judge Dimond in a letter to the Attorney-General of the United States on July 30, 1952, which in part is as follows:

Conditions intimately concerning the administration of justice and the enforcement of law in the Third Judicial Division of Alaska have become such as to compel, from a sense of duty, the writing of this letter.

. . . It is to be remembered that the United States Attorneys in Alaska prosecute all offenders for violation of all laws, local and Federal, and not merely those accused of violating the general laws of the United States; and that the United States Marshals and their deputies are not merely process servers but act also as law enforcement officers and perform the duties which are generally performed by sheriffs and their deputies in the several States. The whole life of law enforcement in Alaska depends upon the adequate and efficient organization and staffing of the courts, the offices of the United States Attorneys and the offices of the United States Marshals.

For years past, the office of the United States Attorney in this Division has been seriously understaffed. At the present moment, with the appointment of the former United States Attorney, Honorable J. Earl Cooper, to the office of the United States District Judge of the Second Judicial Division of Alaska, there is only one assistant United States Attorney, Mr. Seaborn J. Buckalew, here to carry on all the manifold and burdensome duties of the office. The office has never been adequately staffed since the beginning of my service here on January 3, 1945, and conditions have now become virtually intolerable. In my judgment, the office needs a personnel of at least four lawyers besides the secretaries and clerks, and in recent years it has never had more than the United States Attorney himself and two assistants. For many months past there has been only one assistant. . . . The time of one man in the office is largely taken up in interviewing people who wish to complain of what they believe to be the commission of crimes, some of them felonies. In addition to that, one assistant United States Attorney could and should devote a great deal of his time to preliminary hearings and trials in the office of the United States Commissioners and ex-officio Justice of the Peace for the Division, particularly the one at Anchorage. Many cases must be tried in the District Court and for that work the services of someone experienced in the trial of cases should, if possible, be availed of. Under present circumstances, some of those accused of crime are obliged to wait many months in jail before being afforded a trial. That has even happened in cases where the persons accused have waived grand jury presentation and consented that the government might proceed by information. This condition alone with respect to the office of the United States Attorney in some instances amounts to a grave denial of justice.

One reason for the understaffing of the office . . . is the meager compensation paid to assistant United States Attorneys. One of them who resigned the office after short tenure told me that he and his family could not live in Anchorage on that compensation. Although competent and diligent, he was obliged to resign in order to make enough money to support his wife and children and himself. I do not know how any married man can live on the pay allowed. While young men just out of law school may accept the jobs, ordinarily their tenure is short because they can make more money in private practice and therefore do not care to remain long as assistant United States Attorneys . . . I suggest that . . . the salaries of Assistant United States Attorneys be increased sufficiently to induce competent lawyers to undertake the work and stay with it for a reasonable period of time.

. . . As numerous as are the cases brought before the Court for trial it seems highly probable that many malefactors go unpunished because of lack of personnel for investigation . . . Because of lack of personnel in the offices of the United States Attorneys and United States Marshals, the commission of crime in this area cannot be adequately detected and offenders prosecuted. . . . We need at least three times as many deputy marshals as are now allotted to the office and their pay should be increased at least 50 per cent, if not more. Few reliable men will work for the salaries now given . . .

Judge Dimond's temperate indictment was seconded by Judge George W. Folta of the First Judicial Division, who on August 5, 1952, wrote the Attorney-General in part as follows:

. . . Because of the niggardly salaries paid the District Attorney and his assistants, inexperienced law school graduates are pitted against veterans who do their utmost, under our archaic system of criminal procedure, to perpetuate the sporting theory of justice in the trial of criminal cases. Their strategy is to make a farce of each trial, to run it off on a tangent; to try one collateral issue after another, in fact to try everything and everybody except the merits of the defendant. Manifestly in this process they commit numerous errors which would be reversible if the prosecution had the right of appeal. Since it does not, a great and undue burden is thrown on the Judge to keep the case from

getting out of bounds and see that each side is given a fair trial.
. . . All too often the prosecutor is unaware of what is taking
place. I need not remind you that it takes years of experience to
be able to give any formidable opposition to mouthpiece attorneys, and long before this experience is gained, the prosecutor
leaves for more lucrative fields. Anchorage and vicinity is so overrun with criminals because of the boom and the low state of law
enforcement that the prosecuting staff ought to be of the highest
caliber. . . . The proper remedy is adequate salaries. I should
like to urge, therefore, that the salaries of the United States Attorney and his assistants be increased by at least 50 per cent.

No corrective action on these requests—which were merely reitera-
tions of previously oft-made pleas—followed during the remaining
months of the retiring Democratic administration nor during the first
year of the succeeding Republican regime.

For eighty-seven years the administration of justice in Alaska, which
the federal government has insisted on reserving to itself, has been deficient. It has remained unrelievedly so despite the unceasing protests
of Alaskans. Its deficiency has steadily increased because in the last
forty-five years, during which the population of Alaska has tripled,
the number of judges, of United States attorneys and marshals has
remained stationary, while the number of deputy marshals has actually
been decreased. In the last decade its deficiency has been further increased by the criminal elements entering Alaska in the wake of the
extension of the national-defense program to the territory. While
erecting defenses against foreign gangsterism on America's western
front the national government has continued oblivious to the growing
menace of domestic aggression.

Native Claims:

Equality *versus* Wardship

It is the belief of the committee that all legislation dealing with Indian affairs should be directed to the ending of a segregated race set aside from other citizens. It is the recommended policy of this committee that the Indians be assimilated into the nation's social and economic life. The objectives, in bringing about the ending of Indian segregation to which the committee has worked and recommends, are: (1) The end of wardship or trust status as not acceptable to our American way of life, and (2) the assumption by individual Indians of all the duties, obligations and privileges of free citizens. The committee realizes that these objectives cannot be accomplished "overnight," but recommends a constant effort in that direction, with careful and earnest consideration always given to the rights of the Indians.

TOBY MORRIS, *Chairman*
REVA BECK BOSONE
WESLEY A. D'EWART
FRANK T. BOW
WAYNE N. ASPINALL[1]

FOR the first seventeen years of United States rule over Alaska, the aboriginal inhabitants, who constituted an overwhelming majority of its approximately thirty thousand souls, were as devoid of attention, or even mention, as was the population as a whole. They became, by virtue of the organic act of 1884, in one respect at least, a mildly privileged, or at least a less disadvantaged, group, as compared with subsequently arriving Americans.

For the act provided "that the Indians or other persons . . . shall not be disturbed in the possession of any lands actually in their use or occupation or now claimed by them." The natives' right of occupancy was, in other words, affirmed, while all later arrivals had to await the slow evolution of the land laws for even the assurance of the right to possess land.

"The terms under which such persons [the Indians or other persons]," continued the act, "may acquire title to such lands is reserved for future legislation by Congress."

Seventy years of future had passed by 1954 and the legislation by which the titles to Indians' lands could be acquired had not yet been enacted by Congress.

A later section (12) of the act provided that the Secretary of the Interior constitute a commission composed of the Governor and two other officers appointed under the act, "to examine into and report upon the condition of the Indians residing in said territory, what lands, if any, should be reserved for their use . . . what rights of occupation of settlers should be recognized, and all other facts that may be necessary to enable Congress to determine what limitations or conditions should be imposed when the land laws of the United States shall be extended to said district." Two thousand dollars was appropriated to defray the commission's expenses.

No commission, such as the act required the Secretary of the Interior to constitute, was constituted. No investigation, such as the commission was required by Congress to make, was made. There was not enough interest in the Department of the Interior to pursue the matter further, nor in the Congress to remind the department of its request. Besides, the $2,000 appropriated would scarcely have been adequate for the requested examination and report in a trackless wilderness of 586,000 square miles.

Still, when Benjamin Harrison succeeded to the Presidency in 1889, it might have been supposed that as the sponsor of the act of 1884, when he was Senator Harrison and Chairman of the Committee on Territories, he would have reminded the member of his cabinet whom he had appointed Secretary of the Interior of his duty in the premises. But there is no record of any interest in or action on the matter during the four-year term of Interior Secretary John W. Noble. Nor does the phrasing of the congressional instruction, or the history of congressional legislation for Alaska, suggest that had the report been made, Congress would have acted upon it, at least for twenty years or more, at which time any recommendations made in the middle eighties would probably have been obsolete and unserviceable.

President Arthur's administration was drawing to a close and the carrying out of the provisions of law in respect to examining and reporting on Indian lands would have fallen to Grover Cleveland's Secretary of the Interior, Lucius Q. C. Lamar. There is no mention of

Alaskan Indian lands investigation in any of his reports.[2] Such deviations of policy ofttimes accompany changes of administration, even under a presumed "government of laws, not of men."

In 1899, fifteen years after the congressional mandate in the act of 1884, the Department of the Interior published a 172-page printed volume "compiled under the direction of the Secretary of the Interior" entitled *Statistics of Indian Tribes, Indian Agencies and Indian Schools of Every Character.* It listed over three hundred tribes in the states and territories, a list complete from Apache to Yuma. But no mention whatever is made of Alaskan Indians. Technically, to be sure, there were no "tribes" in the legal sense in Alaska, and no Indian agencies or agents, although there were schools conducted by another agency of the Department of the Interior, the Bureau of Education. Alaska was also legally a district, not a territory. In any event the complete omission and ignoring of the existence of the Alaska aborigines in this official publication was symptomatic of the department's attitude toward those particular Alaskan charges. In that respect, however, it did not differ materially from the federal attitude toward Alaskans in general.

When, sixty years after the congressional instruction relating to Indians' lands, an effort was made in a portion of Alaska, namely, southeastern, to examine into "what lands if any should be reserved for their use," conditions had so changed that what might have been a relatively simple undertaking in 1884, when the population of Alaska was almost wholly aboriginal and primitive, and the penetration of white civilization scarcely begun, had become a difficult and complex undertaking. So difficult and complex, in fact, that its achievement in the form attempted was considered undesirable by nearly all concerned, including many of those who were presumably to be its beneficiaries, as well as nigh impossible of satisfactory realization. The effort was, moreover, preceded and accompanied by other administrative actions productive of alarm, confusion and opposition in Alaska.

Paradoxically, the federal neglect in a sense carried out at least a part of the mandate of Congress—by default. The Indians and other aborigines were *not* disturbed in the possession of any lands actually in their use, nor indeed have they been since. But they were gravely disturbed in what to them was more vital than land—the supply of the marine and terrestrial wild-life upon which they subsisted. The Eskimos' loss of a large part of their whale and walrus has already been mentioned. With the coming of the gold-seeking prospectors in 1898 the moose and caribou supply was likewise reduced. Both these losses were compensated for substantially by the introduction of reindeer. The sea otter upon which the Aleuts in particular depended for cash income was so nearly extinguished by commercial pursuit that it came under rigid protection in 1911 and in the subsequent forty-four years has not been restored to hunting. Elsewhere in Alaska commercial salmon fishing diminished the natives' supply. And while the coastal natives, particularly in southeastern Alaska, shared in part— as fishermen and cannery workers—the financial benefits of the commercial fishery, they were more adversely affected in this vocation than other workers, resident or transient, by seasonal failures, and by the steady decline of the salmon runs beginning in the middle nineteen thirties which reached disaster depths in 1953.

They were more adversely affected because they had fewer off-season earning possibilities, and had come to rely largely on the income during the fishing season for their whole year's livelihood.

In the years following the organic act's gesture toward the preservation of Indians' lands, secretaries of the interior under the administrations of Harrison, Cleveland and McKinley came and went. Although the Indians—and the term included Eskimos and Aleuts as well— were a special charge of the Department of the Interior, this responsibility was for a generation or more fulfilled only in the realm of education, in which, despite its inadequacy, more attention was paid to the natives than to the whites. This was a natural consequence of the missionary spirit and guidance of education in Alaska, inspired by Sheldon Jackson and John Brady. Some of the increasing white population viewed it as undue partiality, and shortly after the turn of the century the influence of the Presbyterian missionary group declined and vanished. The opposition to their efforts was poorly founded. Education of the natives, the effort to minimize the impact of the more untoward effects of the white invasion and to introduce the native to the more beneficent effects of what would be the dominant culture, was certainly the prior educational requirement. The whites, with their deeply ingrained educational traditions brought from the States, were bound to take care of their own school needs through local organization, and, as previously related, did so. Retrospectively the work of the early missionaries of all denominations is today appreciated in Alaska. To the extent of their endeavor they helped fill the void created by governmental nonfeasance.

In fact, much of the progress in assimilating the native to the white culture was due to the early missionary effort, transformed in part after 1884 into a federally conducted educational system, which, despite its chronic insufficiency of appropriations, represented till the end of the century the only evidence of governmental interest in the people of Alaska.

In the realm of health the federal government's participation was so insufficient as to be almost totally lacking. Yet such aid as it did render was extended exclusively to the natives. This likewise was fitting, since they were peculiarly the victims of diseases imported by the white man to which they were little resistant. Through the decades, smallpox, diphtheria, measles, influenza, the venereal diseases and tuberculosis repeatedly decimated the native population.

The most important single contribution made to the natives—or at least to a part of them—in the first half-century of United States rule was the importation of reindeer, which, during the period when their natural food supply had been greatly impaired, saved thousands of Eskimos from death by starvation.

With that exception the native subsistence economy and way of life were not greatly disturbed till the coming of substantial numbers of white men in the various gold rushes at the turn of the century.

Theodore Roosevelt was the first President to concern himself with the needs of Alaska's aborigines. He detailed an ethnologist, who, as a naval officer, had acquired special familiarity as well as deep sympathy with the natives of Alaska, to investigate. The report of Lieutenant George T. Emmons, U.S.N., retired, which the President submitted to Congress in January, 1905, remains a classic to this day.[3]

Emmons distinguished four principal groups, differing, ethnically, in their natural environment, in variations of contact with whites and degrees of adaptation to changing conditions, and in their consequently differing needs. For the practical purposes of governmental policy he divided the natives into two classes: those who were self-sustaining and needed only supervision, education and moral support; and those who had been deprived of their natural means of living "by the opening up of the country," and, in addition to the requirements of the first group, needed material assistance to bridge them over a period of transition and to teach them to provide for themselves under the changed conditions.

In the first group Emmons included the Tlingits, Haida and Tsimsheans—that is, the natives dwelling between the international boundary at latitude 54°40′, and the 141st meridian—in short, all in southeastern Alaska. Numbering about six thousand, they lived, he wrote, "in comparative comfort, in large, well-built villages along the coast and channel ways under very favorable conditions." Here the climate was mild and healthful, fish life abundant, and game more than sufficient for their wants. "They are intelligent, honest, good workers," Emmons reported, "an accumulative, thrifty people, quick to learn and anxious to improve their condition." The establishment of canneries, mines and lumber mills had given them an opportunity to add wages to their means; the products of civilization were within their reach.

"So today, wholly through their own exertions and industry, without any material assistance from the general government, they have established themselves as an independent self-supporting population, fully capable of rendering such labor as the conditions of the country demand."

However, these people had their limitations, and the fact that their improvement had come from within instead of from without, and that they had advanced their own interests unaided, Emmons warned, did not mean that they had no needs, and did not give the government "through persistent neglect, immunity from the fulfillment of its moral obligations."

These needs were the definition of the native's legal status to give him equality before the law and the full rights of citizenship: the right to file on a mining claim, to take up land, to get a mariner's license; the extension of educational facilities, so that he could acquire the English language and more technical knowledge through industrial training, upon both of which employment and wage increases depended. But the greatest need of all, Emmons insisted, was for hospitals and dispensaries.

"Anything looking toward land indemnity or money payment or tribal reservation would be the greatest mistake here," Emmons warned, "and would check the material advance already made."

As for the second group of natives—the Aleuts along the Alaska Peninsula and in the Aleutian Islands, the Athabascans throughout the interior, the Eskimos along the Bering and Arctic coasts and in the Kuskokwim, lower Yukon, Kobuk and Noatak valleys—they required, in addition to education and hospitals, protection of their basic food supplies.

President Roosevelt made some of Emmons's recommendations his own in his 1904 State of the Union Message to Congress (December 6).

Education, particularly industrial, to enable the natives to compete successfully in their changing environment; hospitals for the natives; the abolition of the fee system of which the unlettered natives were particularly the victims at the hands of unscrupulous commissioners; material relief to be extended by the government in periods of famine and in cases of extreme destitution. No recommendation was made in regard to lands or for the protection of resources for the natives, as such.

Federal action in the recommended endeavors was slow in coming. Educational facilities always lagged far behind need. Twenty years after the federal government had assumed that responsibility at least three-quarters of the native children were without schooling. One hundred and seventy-seven native villages with a school population of four thousand were unprovided with school facilities in 1905.[4] Yet the congressional appropriation of only $50,000 not only made it impossible to open the needed new schools, but compelled the closing of some already established.[5] Adult education—particularly needed in the circumstances—was undreamt of and the acquisition of the English language by the native population thereby postponed.

The health of the natives continued to be deplored by the governors and the need for hospitals echoed in the annual reports of the secretaries of the interior. Although the Bureau of Education—which continued in charge of all the natives' affairs till March 16, 1931, when its Alaska functions were transferred to the Bureau of Indian Affairs—had engaged in some earlier health activities, the first appropriation for medical assistance to the natives—$25,000—was not made till 1916. It was, as Governor Strong commented, "but a drop in the bucket." [6]

Constructive moves to validate natives' right to lands were made early in the century. On recommendation of Governor Brady, Secretary of the Interior Ethan Allen Hitchcock urged that the public-land laws be made applicable to them. Reminding that the organic act of

May 17, 1884, had provided that they should "not be disturbed in the possession of any lands actually in their use or occupation or claimed by them," he pointed out that they were not permitted to acquire title to such lands, as it had been held that they were "neither citizens nor aliens." [7] In fact they were not even classed as Indians. Some laws affecting Indians did not apply to Indians in Alaska, which though not a planned omission, was probably just as well. The natives' inability to secure title to lands in Alaska was of course shared by the whites because of the lack of surveys.

But now legal authorization for the natives to secure title to land was shortly forthcoming. In the first session of the Fifty-ninth Congress, Senator Nelson introduced a bill which passed both houses without debate and became law May 17, 1906 (41 Stat. 1059). By it the Secretary of the Interior was empowered in his discretion and under such rules as he might prescribe to allot no more than 160 acres of non-mineral land to any Indian or Eskimo of full or mixed blood, who was either the head of a family or twenty-one years of age. He was to have the preference right to secure thus the land he occupied. It was to be his and his heirs in perpetuity and inalienable and nontaxable until otherwise provided by Congress; and he was further advantaged by being relieved of the cultivation and other requirements of the homestead laws as applied to whites.

Such legislation, if carried into effect, might have gone far—certainly part way—to solve the problem of native land claims that was to haunt the territory forty years thereafter and to this day.

But a familiar obstacle interposed. Applications for such allotments were received, reported the Secretary of the Interior the next year, "but owing to the fact that there was no appropriation available for expenses of surveys, or for the necessary investigations into the merits of the claims, or for making or recording the allotments, it has not been practicable for the department to act favorably upon such applications." [8] An estimate, he added, would be submitted to Congress for an amount sufficient to carry the act into effect.

Congress did not make the appropriation, and the next year, another Secretary of the Interior, James R. Garfield, did not mention the matter in his annual report for 1907. But in 1908 he urged that the natives of Alaska be afforded the right to acquire public lands.[9] Actually they had the *right*—in some ways on even better terms than their white neighbors, being relieved of the usual homesteading requirements—but it was the Secretary of the Interior who had not been afforded the means to validate that right.

Little interest in making this legislation effective was shown either by subsequent secretaries of the Interior or by the Congress. Few of the intended allotments were able to overcome the joint executive and legislative inertia that rendered a potentially useful act largely a dead letter.

Apart from the acquisition of title to land the natives would have had an early opportunity to acquire citizenship under the General Allotment Act of February 8, 1887 (24 Stat. 388), which with modification appropriate to Alaska would have permitted individual land ownership with fee-simple title.[10]

Some Alaskan natives were enabled to acquire citizenship under an act passed by the 1915 territorial legislature (Chapter 24). The requirements followed the indications in the General Allotment Act for those who had "severed all tribal relationship and adopted the habits of a civilized life." To qualify they would have to pass an examination by a majority of the teachers at either a United States Government, territorial or municipal school, which would test the applicant's understanding of the obligations of suffrage and demonstrate his adoption of the "habits of a civilized life." His application also needed the endorsement of five white residents of Alaska. Application was then made for a certificate of citizenship to the district judge, who, after a hearing, would grant or deny it. By this method an increasing number of natives became citizens. The process was completed by the passage of federal legislation of June 2, 1924 (43 Stat. 253) extending citizenship to all Indians born within the territorial limits of the United States who had not yet received it. It was held to apply to Alaska.

Taking advantage of their citizenship, natives began voting in Alaska elections in the middle nineteen twenties, especially in southeastern Alaska. In 1926 they elected one of their number, William L. Paul, an attorney, to the House of Representatives from the First Judicial Division, re-electing him in 1928.

Legislation exempting Indians and Eskimos of full or mixed blood from all forms of taxation on town lots occupied or claimed by them was passed by Congress on May 25, 1926 (44 Stat. 629). The lots were inalienable and could not be sold by the native occupant or claimant except by permission of the Secretary of the Interior. Without such permission the occupant held what is known as a "restricted deed."

Far-reaching legislation known as the Indian Reorganization Act, or Wheeler-Howard Act, was passed by Congress on June 18, 1934 (48 Stat. 984). It provided new varieties of economic assistance to Indian tribes in the form of government loans to enable them through chartered corporations to set up their own industries. It made provision for individual loans for vocational training. These sections applied to Alaska. Other sections consonant with the existing reservation system in the United States, giving the Secretary of the Interior the power to create new reservations and to enlarge existing ones, did not apply to Alaska. Neither did Section 1, that thereafter no land on any Indian reservation should be allotted in severalty. In other words it provided for communal holding under government trusteeship and debarred individual ownership. Annual appropriations of ten and a half million dollars to carry out the purposes of the act were authorized.

Two years later the Department of the Interior sponsored supplementary legislation to extend the other provisions of the act to Alaska, including the power to set up reservations and the prohibition of ownership in severalty on all reservations, past, present or future. It authorized the Secretary of the Interior "to designate as an Indian reservation any area of land which has been reserved for the use and occupancy of the Indians and Eskimos by section 8 of the act of May 17, 1884 . . . or which has been heretofore reserved under any executive order and placed under the jurisdiction of the Department of the Interior or any bureau thereof, together with additional public lands adjacent thereto . . . or any other public lands which are actually occupied by Indians or Eskimos. . . ." The reservation, however, had to be ratified by a majority vote of not less than 30 per cent of the Indian or Eskimo residents at a special election called by the Secretary at thirty days' notice.

The legislation had been drafted in the Interior Department by Mr. Felix S. Cohen, a specialist in law dealing with Indians, and the author of a definitive compilation on the subject.[11] He was a firm believer in the reservation system and its communal land tenure under federal trusteeship for the American aborigine. Harold L. Ickes was in accord with this view. He had come east, with active membership in a "Republicans for Roosevelt" organization in the 1932 presidential campaign among his credentials, to seek the Commissionership of Indian Affairs. Unexpectedly made Secretary of the Interior when Senator Bronson Cutting was obliged for reasons of health to decline the appointment on the eve of inauguration, Ickes found himself in a powerful vantage point from which to execute his policies. John Collier, who for many years as a private citizen had been campaigning for a "new deal" for the Indians, was also in accord. As Ickes's Commissioner of Indian Affairs he likewise was in an effective position to put into practice his theories concerning the revival of the Amerindian culture and its preservation as nearly as possible in its pristine state. For him and his associates in the Interior Department preservation and reservation were one and inseparable.

Neither Secretary Ickes, nor Commissioner Collier, nor Mr. Felix Cohen in the Solicitor's Office had any first-hand knowledge of Alaska, having never even visited the territory when this legislation they projected for it was enacted. But all felt entitled to speak authoritatively on the needs of the Indians in the States. And they had no hesitation in assuming that what in their view was good for the Indians there must also be good for the Eskimos, Aleuts and Indians of Alaska.

There was nothing in the legislative history of the act to warn the people of Alaska that a major change was impending. On the contrary, Secretary Ickes's own testimony, contained in the customary departmental report on the bill, gave a different impression. In it he pointed out that the Wheeler-Howard Act of 1934 gave the Secretary of the Interior the power to issue charters of incorporation to a petitioning tribe. But Indian tribes did not exist in Alaska in the same sense as in the United States and the act had defined its proposed beneficiaries as "any Indian tribe, organized band, pueblo or the Indians residing on one reservation." But as, with few exceptions, the lands occupied by the natives of Alaska had not been designated as reservations, it was necessary, wrote Secretary Ickes, in order, therefore, to identify each native group with the land it was occupying and to conform with the language of the act, to call this a "reservation."

"In addition," wrote Secretary Ickes, "if native communities are to set up systems of local government, it will be necessary to stipulate the geographic limits of their jurisdiction. Reservations set up by the Secretary of the Interior will accomplish this." [12]

There was still a further reason for such reservations, continued the

Secretary's letter. It would enable the United States Government to fulfill its obligation under the act of 1884, "that the Indians . . . should [shall] not be disturbed in the possession of any lands actually in their use or occupation or now claimed by them." Such lands, Secretary Ickes pointed out, had not been segregated, and this could now be rectified. It sounded reasonable, and the bill was supported by Alaska's delegate Anthony J. Dimond, becoming law on May 1, 1936 (49 Stat. 1250).

Two years after the extension of the Wheeler-Howard Act to Alaska the Interior Department secured the enactment of another measure which authorized the Secretary in his discretion to withdraw and permanently reserve tracts not to exceed 640 acres each of the public domain for schools, hospitals and such other purposes as he might deem necessary in administering the affairs of the Indians, Eskimos and Aleuts of Alaska (May 31, 1938. 52 Stat. 593).

There already existed at that time 139 native school reservations. These had been made through the years since the first withdrawals for native schools in Sitka, Juneau and Douglas in 1890, whenever a school for natives was established. The greater number of these withdrawals, seventy-eight, were of forty acres apiece although a few were thirty times larger, twelve hundred acres or more, and others smaller. But they were presumed to take care of all the native school needs for land, and this had never been questioned, since additions to such reservations could be made easily by executive order. Withdrawals of the land on which the few hospitals or health centers for natives were located had also been made.

Since the native population dwelt in compact villages where it had since time immemorial, except in a few cases of voluntary abandonment, it was assumed in Alaska that the 640 acres, providing for withdrawals of the usual town-site dimensions, in the 1938 bill, would generally meet the requirements of the new Interior Department policies, especially since withdrawals for schools and hospitals had, as indicated previously, been long made, as needed. The Wheeler-Howard Act and its extension to Alaska provided for local government organization through a procedure which permitted the townsfolk to draw up a constitution and bylaws, and submit them for ratification by a majority of not less than 30 per cent of the citizens at an election to be called by the Secretary of the Interior. If ratified by the people, the constitution and bylaws had to be submitted to him for approval, and any subsequent change in either by popular vote had likewise to have his sanction.

Native villages had long before this been governed by local councils and other arrangements of their own design. The Wheeler-Howard Act spelled out the natives' wardship clearly. They had, of course, the alternative of existing federal and territorial legislation for incorporating, as had Alaska communities not merely that were wholly white, but others, such as Sitka, Juneau, Wrangell, Ketchikan and Haines, where a substantial proportion of the population was native. But since in the wholly native communities the essential services, particularly schooling, were defrayed by the federal government, the territorial form of incorporation, with its permissive municipal taxation for such services, as well as overhead costs, had been generally considered unnecessary, and up to this time most of the purely native communities, as also many of the smaller white and mixed communities, had remained unincorporated.

Nevertheless some native towns preferred the maximum of local autonomy, the authority to tax themselves for local improvements, the right to individual ownership in fee of town lots, that incorporation under territorial law afforded. Klawock and Hoonah, wholly native communities, had become incorporated cities in 1929 and 1946, respectively, and there were others.

News of the new type of reservations proposed under the Wheeler-Howard Act extension reached Alaska in 1943. They included the Venetie Reservation of 1,408,000 acres, just north of the Arctic Circle, for the benefit of some twenty-five Athabascan families. The great extent of the area was based on the assumption that this much land was needed to protect their hunting and trapping. What startled Alaskans was that this was announced to be only the first of one hundred similar reservations from which all but local native residents would be excluded. Such reservations would preclude mining and other activities by whites except by payment for the privilege to the resident natives, who had never had any interest in such mining. Natives of other villages were likewise excluded. Based on the Venetie acreage it was feared that from a third to a half of Alaska would be thus exclusively reserved. Moreover, as no hearings had preceded the Venetie Reservation proclamation, no one knew what land or whose land would be pre-empted by secretarial fiat. For although the act provided that it should not affect any valid existing claim, location or entry under the laws of the United States, or other purpose whatsoever, the Interior Department's contention was that "aboriginal rights" antedating even "possessory rights," were the basis of these reservations and that they superseded and invalidated all subsequent rights.

Public alarm was further increased by the announcement that investigations were under way to ascertain the extent of the claims made by the fourteen native communities of southeastern Alaska. They included the partially native populations of Juneau, Douglas, Haines, Sitka, Ketchikan, Wrangell and Craig, and the almost exclusively native populations of Yakutat, Klukwan, Hoonah, Angoon, Kake, Klawock and Saxman. Popular apprehension was based on what to Alaskans was a wholly new interpretation of lands "actually" in the possession or use of the descendants of the aborigines, concerning which there had never previously been the slightest controversy. Under a concept now being fostered by the Department of the Interior, such lands included any over which in the past any Indians might have hunted or picked berries, and the waters in which their ancestors had fished.[13] Such claims not only overlapped, as between various villages, but promised to include all southeastern Alaska.

The claims to exclusive fishing rights in the waters of southeastern Alaska—which were of more importance to the fishing economy of the natives than the land claims—were buttressed by an opinion issued under the name of Nathan R. Margold, Solicitor of the Department of the Interior, on February 13, 1942. This opinion written by Mr. Felix S. Cohen, then Assistant Solicitor, was given in answer to a question which he had himself propounded:

"Whether Indians of Alaska have any fishing rights which are violated by control of particular trap sites by non-Indians under departmental regulations, and whether such rights require or justify the closing down of certain trap sites or the allocations of trap sites to Indian groups or other remedial action by the Secretary of the Interior."

Mr. Cohen answered himself in the affirmative. The lengthy Margold opinion concluded "that original occupancy establishes possessory rights in Alaskan waters and submerged lands, and that such rights have not been extinguished by any treaty, statute or administrative action."[14]

Secretary Ickes approved the opinion on the same day that it was presented.

To hear the testimony for and against the claims in southeastern Alaska, particularly for the three villages of Kake, Klawock and Hydaburg, Secretary Ickes appointed R. H. Hanna, a former judge of the Supreme Court of New Mexico. The alleged validity of the procedure was based on Secretary Ickes's authority over the fisheries, which had been transferred from the Department of Commerce to the Department of the Interior in 1939. Specifically the hearings were to be on arguments for and against a proposed Fish and Wildlife Service regulation in 1944 that no fish trap could be located where "any Alaskan native or natives has or have any rights of fishery, by virtue of any grant or by virtue of aboriginal occupancy." The regulation was drafted by Mr. Felix S. Cohen, and Secretary Ickes ordered the Fish and Wildlife Service to include it in its proposed regulations.

The hearings embraced fifteen volumes of about 2,700 pages of transcript, and both petitioners and objectors were, according to Judge Hanna, represented by able counsel. Judge Hanna's report, issued on March 7, 1945, found a limited land occupancy, extending principally along the shores, and no basis for the claims of exclusive aboriginal possession of the waters.[15]

Secretary Ickes, however, reversed his chief investigator and decided otherwise. In a lengthy ruling, on July 27, 1945, prepared by Mr. Felix S. Cohen, he reaffirmed Mr. Cohen's view in the Margold opinion, further decided that public domain was both land and water, and that the submerged lands were susceptible to the claims of aboriginal possession. Secretary Ickes further ordered that land be reserved for the three villages to the extent of 101,000 acres for Hydaburg, 95,000 acres for Klawock, and 77,000 acres for Kake. But this was to be only a partial grant. Decision was reserved on areas totaling 2,008,000 acres, since there was a dispute about them between Kake and Klawock, and to give other Indian bands a chance to be heard. Nor did these adjudications "purport to settle the issue between the Indians and the United States resulting from past invasion of Indian property rights," Secretary Ickes decreed. Their only effect was "to advise the three petitioning Indian groups of the exact extent of the property rights which have not been taken from them or otherwise destroyed, and which they are still legally entitled to exercise and enjoy, and on the other hand to advise non-Indians of the areas in which homestead patents, mineral entries, fish-trap locations can be validly enjoyed. . . ." [16]

There were still further claims which, Secretary Ickes stated, remained for adjudication under another act. It was the Tlingit and Haida Jurisdictional Act of June 15, 1935 (49 Stat. 388), introduced by Delegate Dimond, which authorized the Tlingit and Haida Indians to bring suit in the United States Court of Claims for any claims they might have against the United States. A like bill had been introduced by Delegate Sutherland in the Seventy-first Congress, referred to the Committee on Claims, and not acted upon.[17] Similar bills were sponsored in the Seventy-second Congress by Senator Lynn J. Frazier, R., of North Dakota, and Delegate Wickersham. Adverse reports by Indian Commissioner Charles J. Rhoads were transmitted to the committee chairman by Secretary of the Interior Ray Lyman Wilbur.[18] Nevertheless a hearing on the Senate bill secured a unanimously favorable report from the Senate Committee on Indian Affairs of which Senator Frazier was chairman. In reply to a question how much land was involved in the claims, Delegate Wickersham replied: "Practically the whole of southeastern Alaska." [19] The bill passed the Senate without opposition. But in the House it was referred to the Committee on Indian Affairs, where it died. In the Seventy-third Congress companion bills presented by Delegate Dimond and Senator Frazier were not acted upon, and not until the Seventy-fourth Congress was the legislation, backed by the Interior Department's endorsement, enacted.

To date, however, it has proved a nullity. A suit entered under its provisions for the Tlingit claims only, to the extent of $35,000,000, "for the value of the land, hunting and fishing rights taken without compensation," was dismissed by the Court of Claims on the ground that the attorneys selected by the Tlingits had not been approved—as the act required—by the Secretary of the Interior (October 2, 1944. 102 C. of Cl. 209). Although the time for the filing of claims has several times expired and been extended by acts of Congress, the case has not yet been tried. Thus a quarter of a century has elapsed since the introduction of legislation to enable the natives of southeastern Alaska to obtain a judicial decision in the appropriate court on whether they have compensable rights—in consequence of executive orders such as that creating the Tongass National Forest, and other circumstances—and if so, to what amount. One difficulty, no doubt, arises from the problem of securing an attorney whom the Secretary of the Interior will approve, willing to take the case on the basis of the 10 per cent contingent fee as provided in the act. Congress could, of course, provide a solution by suitable amendatory legislation, and make such a determination of claims, long overdue, possible.

Commissioner John Collier retired in March, 1945. Secretary Ickes resigned from the Secretaryship of the Interior in February of 1946. Mr. Felix Cohen left government service in January, 1948, to practice law and particularly to represent Indian claimants. But their policies lived after them. The confusion caused by the Interior Department's approach to the question of Indian lands was soon to be pointed up in startling fashion.[20]

For forty years the people of Alaska had hoped for the establishment of a pulp and paper industry to utilize the virgin forests of southeastern Alaska, enclosed in the Tongass National Forest, a great resource of western hemlock, Sitka spruce, red and yellow cedar, largely going to waste, with its trees overripe and dying on the stump. Those hopes had been deferred for a variety of reasons, among them— for years—the contractual conditions required of prospective private enterprise by the Forest Service, although transportation costs and other factors played a part. American capital, meanwhile, was able repeatedly to establish mills in adjacent British Columbia, where both man-made and natural conditions were more favorable. In the nineteen forties, however, with the depletion of the northwestern forests, the shortages and rising costs of pulp and paper, the prospects for such undertaking in Alaska were immediate. Now, however, they were in danger of being shattered by the cloud of "aboriginal rights" over the title to all land in the Tongass National Forest—practically all of which had been claimed for or by the Indians—and, unless dispelled, would prevent any successful negotiations between the Forest Service and possible pulp and paper manufacturers.

The Eightieth Congress therefore considered a bill, H.J. Res. 205, which while permitting the Secretary of Agriculture to make contracts for the sale of the Tongass timber, provided that the receipts from all Tongass Forest sales should be put in a special fund in the Treasury Department which would not be disbursed until the issue of title had been settled. The measure stated that nothing in it either affirmed or denied the validity of the native claims. Agreement on an acceptable draft was beset with difficulties. There were wide divergencies of opinion not merely between the three governmental agencies concerned—Justice, Agriculture and Interior—but within this last department, where some officials of the Office of Indian Affairs (as it had been renamed) insisted on considering virtually all southeastern Alaska as Indian land.

The drafting of a bill that would reconcile these widely divergent views and stand a chance of passage in the hectic closing days of a Congress required unusual diplomacy and persistence, but was achieved through the untiring efforts of Warner Gardner, who had succeeded to the solicitorship of the Interior Department and then became one of its assistant secretaries. Testifying for it, he described the Alaska situation as "unmitigated chaos in land titles and land-claims." [21]

In transmitting the bill to Speaker Joseph W. Martin, Jr., Secretary Julius A. Krug, who had succeeded Ickes, alluded to the "tremendous uncertainty . . . and . . . thoroughgoing confusion" in Alaska among natives and whites alike concerning land titles, pointed to the bill as an imperatively needed interim solution, adding that it was "the expectation that suitable legislation to settle the matter would be recommended to the Congress very early in its next session." [22]

The need for this measure was great. Fishing under federal management had been declining steadily. The federal government, as a war measure, had closed down gold mining,[23] (although the neighboring Canadians took no such action) and with the greatly increased postwar costs it showed little prospect of resumption at previous levels. The Army in Alaska had, moreover, taken over much of the mining machinery, replacement costs of which had risen substantially in the meanwhile. Alaska was still handicapped by the seasonality of its economy. A substantial year-round pay roll, the considerable stable employment it would bring, the first important use of a great national resource previously going to waste—all combined to make this development of prime importance. It was warmly supported by all the federal departments concerned, by Alaska's Delegate Bartlett and other territorial authorities and by the Alaskan public. Given the vigorously expressed needs of the nation's newspaper publishers, it also had strong support in Congress. Despite this massive backing the bill barely passed in the closing quarter hour of the first session of the Eightieth Congress (August 8, 1947. 61 Stat. 920).

In his letter to Speaker Martin Secretary Krug had also written: "I have requested the Alaska Native Service [the name for the Office of Indian Affairs organization in Alaska] of this department to explain the proposals to the native villages and I am hopeful that there will be a general acceptance of this interim arrangement by those villages as well as by the other interests affected." [24]

In Alaska the officials of the Native Service explained the proposals as requested. However, they explained them in such a way that they aroused the previously negligible native opposition. In this they collaborated closely with the villages' attorney, Mr. James E. Curry. A former official of the Bureau of Indian Affairs, with which he maintained close contacts, Mr. Curry, a resident of Puerto Rico, had recently entered the promising field of Alaska Indian litigation and had secured a virtual monopoly of its representations, his contracts having all been approved by the Commissioner of Indian Affairs. Curry opposed the Tongass timber bill violently on the ground that the government, as a result of Secretary Ickes's decision, had already vested title in the Indians, stating "this land is theirs." He went even earlier and further than the Ickes findings, saying: "The Forest Service has these many years advertised and sold timber in the Tongass National Forest, pocketing the proceeds, without reference to who owned the timber." [25] The Forest Service, he maintained, would be continuing illegally to dispose of Indian property if it made arrangements after enactment of the proposed law to sell the timber. A campaign of assertion that the Indians were being robbed brought upon the Congress a barrage of letters from high-minded but misinformed sympathizers in the East who relied on what the Indians' attorney and his collaborators in and outside the Office of Indian Affairs were maintaining.

The opposition continued unabated after the bill had become law, and every effort was made to prevent its execution, interested pulp and paper companies being threatened with suit if they dealt with the Forest Service and not directly with the Indians, through their attorneys. Meanwhile attempts to achieve a permanent solution of the Indian land question were made in every successive session of Congress but without result. One of the rocks on which these efforts foundered was the definition of the word "actually" in the successive acts of 1884, 1891 and 1900 in reference to Indians' occupancy of land. The continued contention of the Indians' attorney and of offi-

cials in the Office of Indian Affairs was that Indian rights embraced
all the lands over which the aborigines had ever hunted, trapped, or
picked berries and the waters in which they had fished. The opposition pointed out that the Indians of southeastern Alaska had become
largely assimilated into modern life, and that such a solution was unrealistic and unattainable as well as undesirable from the very standpoint of its alleged beneficiaries.

The situation was only partially clarified by a decision of the Ninth
Circuit Court, February 11, 1947, in the case of Miller vs. United
States (159 Fed. 997). In September, 1942, the War Department,
pursuant to the Second War Powers Act of March 27th of that year
acquired by condemnation 10.95 acres of tidelands, including land
permanently under water, for the purpose of constructing a sub-port
of embarkation. These tidelands extended into the sea from the "Indian village" of Juneau. Miller and others, whose houses fronted on
these waters and had used them for launching their fishing boats,
claimed use from time immemorial and sought damages totaling $80,-
ooo. Their claim was rejected by Judge George F. Alexander in the
United States District Court of the First Judicial Division.

On appeal to the Circuit Court the judgment was reversed, the
right to compensation being upheld under the "possessory rights"
guaranteed by the act of 1884. On the other hand the court held that
"original Indian title," that is, "aboriginal rights," had been extinguished by the Treaty of Cession. The case was remanded to the District Court for further processings consistent with that decision. There
Judge George W. Folta found that the use or occupancy which the
Circuit Court had held to be compensable, "must be notorious, exclusive and continuous and of such a nature as to leave visible evidence thereof, so as to put strangers upon notice that the land is in
the use or occupancy of another, and the extent thereof must be reasonably apparent," but that these tests for compensable possessory
rights had not been met. So the court did now allow the claim for
damages.[26] The decision was not appealed.

No further executive, legislative or judicial action on lands followed
for several years. Other provisions of the Wheeler-Howard Act were
carried out. The chartered corporations purchased canneries for the
villages of Kake, Klawock, Hydaburg and Angoon through government loans at 1 per cent and proceeded to operate them for the benefit of these communities. These enterprises were free from federal and

territorial taxation. Plans for others were being made. Native cooperative stores, also financed by government loans both for the sale of consumer goods and the purchase of furs and native handicrafts for resale to the public, were organized in some thirty communities. Federal and territorial veterans' loans were of course also available to native as to white veterans.

A vocational boarding school of the highest type was established at Mt. Edgecumbe in Sitka harbor, using the buildings of the decommissioned Sitka naval air station. With an enrollment of over six hundred pupils, and a teaching and maintenance staff of 175, it became the largest and best-equipped educational institution in Alaska. In addition to a general education through junior college grades, every form of practical vocational training was afforded its pupils. The boys received training in house and boat building, as carpenters, machinists, plumbers, electricians, etc., the girls in every variety of office work, in nursing, domestic pursuits, etc.

There were other advantages which, applying to the native exclusively, assisted him in adjusting himself to a changing way of life. He was exempt from the requirement to buy hunting, trapping and fishing licenses. The federal government was at last coming to grips with his health problems and its six hospitals established for nearly two decades at Barrow, Bethel, Juneau, Kanakanak, Kotzebue and Tanana were for natives only. Now in the late nineteen forties a new two-hundred-bed hospital at Mt. Edgecumbe was further hospitalizing the tuberculous natives, and the best of surgery by an orthopedist of national repute provided for the restoration of those crippled by disease. A $6,000,000, four-hundred-bed hospital, for natives only, became available in Anchorage in 1953.

Restricted deeds were, however, creating a problem in a few of the older cities, such as Kodiak, where considerable real estate handed down through five or six generations and utilized for business was exempted from municipal and school-district taxation, and competing with enterprises not similarly privileged. To be sure, legislation had been enacted in the Eightieth Congress to permit the issuance of unrestricted deeds for town-site lands held by natives (February 26, 1948, 62 Stat. 35). But unrestricted deeds were available only if the owner of a restricted tax-free property petitioned for a change of status, and if the "Secretary of the Interior or his authorized representative" made a finding that the owner in question was competent to manage his own affairs. As the authorized representatives in the Office of Indian Affairs generally favored the perpetuation of restricted deeds, few unrestricted deeds were issued, although the restricted deed holders, in an increasing number of cases, were indistinguishable racially, culturally and in competence, from their "white" neighbors, and were enjoying the competitive advantage of being free from local taxation on their business properties and homes, and not contributing to the support of city government.

The issue created a new form of rift in the community. On the one hand was an elderly woman, clearly of Indian lineage, who resented the idea of not doing her part and insisted on regularly paying her taxes. She had vainly sought an unrestricted deed from the Department of the Interior. On the other hand some white men, taking advantage of marriage to women of slight Indian blood, were paying no taxes. The really unfortunate consequence, in the long-held view of Lee Bettinger, six times elected Kodiak's mayor, was the arousing of previously nonexistent racial antagonism. Said he in 1954:

"The majority of the people feel that they are victims of legalized discrimination. They resent that several score of local residents, some of whom only in a highly technical sense are 'Indians,' evade civic responsibilities they are amply able to assume, sending their children to the public schools and securing for free every other benefit and privilege paid for by their fellow-townsmen. This has caused, for the first time in the memory of living men, 'whites' and 'Indians' to be differentiated in the public mind. We should get rid of all caste and class distinctions."

On the territorial level there were important developments. In 1944 two Tlingit natives, Frank Peratrovich of Klawock and Andrew Hope of Sitka, had been elected to the House of Representatives. Although the native population in the First Judicial Division of approximately six thousand was only one-fourth that of the non-Indians, these two had run first and third in a field of sixteen competing for eight seats. In the subsequent election one of the two, Peratrovich, was elected to the Senate and another native, Frank G. Johnson of Kake, was elected to the House. Two years later Peratrovich was elected President of the Senate by unanimous vote. In 1948 Eskimos were elected to the legislature for the first time. These two, Percy Ipalook of Wales and William E. Beltz of Nome, two years later, were elected to the Senate, while two other Eskimos, James K. Wells of Noorvik and

Frank A. Degnan of Unalakleet, were elected to the House—all from the Second Division. In the 1951 legislature native representation reached a new high of seven—out of a total membership of forty— with three in the Senate and four in the House.

The 1945 session of the legislature had passed an anti-discrimination bill (Chapter 2). In a few Alaska restaurants, "We do not cater to native trade" or similar signs had indicated a racial prejudice on the part of the ownership. In Nome the only motion-picture theatre had established a practice of segregating whites and Eskimos on different sides of the center aisle. Exclusion from the U.S.O.'s of all native girls—although their brothers in uniform were admitted—had likewise been practiced in the early days of World War II with sanction of the Commanding General of the Alaska Command. These practices were now outlawed, with resulting im-proved native morale and better relationship between the races. Not an untoward incident was reported subsequent to the enactment of the "equal-treatment bill." Natives, moreover, were appointed to and served on major territorial boards; Alaska World War II Veterans Board, Alaska Housing Authority, Board of Public Welfare, Alaska Fisheries Board, Alaska Statehood Committee.

In southeastern Alaska the Native Service schools were closing and their children transferred to the territorial schools. The transfer for all the day schools, and the end of school segregation in them was sched-uled for completion by 1960.

In the closing hours of his last day in office on November 30, 1949, Secretary Krug signed an order creating three reservations—at Barrow and Shungnak in the Arctic and at Hydaburg in southeastern Alaska. The Barrow Reservation was of 480,000 acres for 385 Eskimos. The Shungnak Reservation was of 1,472,000 acres for 150 Eskimos. The Hydaburg Reservation was of 101,000 acres for 360 Haida Indians.

Testifying on the subject a year and a half earlier before a Senate committee Secretary Krug declared:

"I do not think we ought to set up reservations in southeastern Alaska." [27]

However, he had been persuaded to do so. The proclaiming of these reservations, Secretary Krug stated, had been recommended to him by Assistant Secretary William E. Warne, who had visited all three of the villages.[28]

When the new Ickesian reservation policies were promulgated in the early nineteen forties, there had been pretty general opposition to reservations among the native villagers.[29] Their petitions requesting the reservations were almost invariably solicited by the Alaska Native Service schoolteachers on orders from Juneau headquarters. The sentiment in many villages was that the reservation was a step backward and away from the full political, economic and social equality which their people desired. With elections announced the teachers were expected to preach the desirability of reservations, and various forms of persuasion were applied by some of the Native Service officialdom—although some of the teachers were extremely reluctant to pursue this policy. If despite previous indoctrination the election rejected the reservation, another election was scheduled and every effort made to reverse the earlier result. These practices preceded the elections on the Barrow, Shungnak and Hydaburg reservations.

Nevertheless the Barrow and Shungnak Eskimos voted down the reservations, Barrow, 231 to twenty-nine; Shungnak, fifty-one to twenty-five.

Strenuous efforts were made to convince the natives of Hydaburg where the election had been postponed till April 24th. Two months before the election the Native Service schoolteacher there reported that local sentiment appeared fairly evenly divided. However, in the weeks following, Mr. Curry visited the village and promised highly beneficial results. The Area Director for Alaska, Mr. Don C. Foster, also visited Hydaburg twice in the following weeks and presented strongly the case for the reservation. On the first occasion his meeting with the people lasted over six hours, and was followed by a straw vote. Had the election been held the next day, he reported to Washington, it would have been overwhelmingly favorable. But he took no chances and returned once more to Hydaburg before the election.

Mr. Felix Cohen likewise threw his influence into the scales. To an official of the Hydaburg Co-operative Association he wrote:

"If you accept the Reservation, the three traps that are within the Reservation area will belong to Hydaburg. . . . If you accept the Reservation, you will not lose any other area, in my opinion. You have already lost a large part of the land your ancestors once held. I do not think there is any chance of getting that land back, but I think there is a chance of recovering the value of that land in cash. Your right to secure a cash judgment for the land will not be affected in any way by your acceptance of the Reservation that is now offered."

There was considerable doubt that the people of Hydaburg wanted traps, however much the Office of Indian Affairs wanted them to want the traps it so temptingly proffered. Like all the other native people whose economy was based on fishing, the Hydaburgers had consistently opposed that form of stationary gear. They had voted for trap abolition by eighty-one to three a little over a year earlier (See Chapter XXVI). What they did want above all else was to have the traps in their accustomed fishing areas abolished so that the seine fishing which they practiced would stand a chance. In any event, the opportunity to get control of the objectionable traps, whether for use or abolition, and the intense electioneering to which the villagers had been subjected proved effective. Hydaburg voted ninety-five to twenty-nine for the reservation. If there were some among them who reversed their stand on trap ownership in view of the promised imminence of obtaining it, such inconsistency would not have been peculiar to Hydaburgers.[30]

The next few years were spent in efforts by the Office of Indian Affairs to assist the natives in taking over the traps—the real objective and prize in the Hydaburg reservation. The owner of one of the traps, Libby, McNeill and Libby, was requested by the Department of the Interior to vacate the waters which had been included in the reservation order or negotiate an agreement with respect to their future operations there. When the request was refused, suit was brought early in 1951 in the United States District Court in the name of the United States as sole plaintiff in its own behalf and in behalf of the natives of the Hydaburg Reservation.

The exhaustive opinion of Judge George W. Folta, delivered October 7, 1952 (107 Fed. Supp. 697), found that the reservation had not been validly created. It disqualified the case of the plaintiff—the United States—on a half-dozen counts, which if not reversed by a higher court would end the creating of reservations of the type proclaimed by Secretaries Ickes and Krug for the purpose of disposing of aboriginal or possessory claims. Nevertheless the Department of the Interior, which had originated and promoted the entire proceeding over a period of sixteen years, did not appeal from the District Court's decision and permitted the period within such appeal could be made to expire.

In addition to analyzing and rejecting the plaintiff's contentions one by one, Judge Folta gave vigorous expression to a view which, since it may be said to be widely prevalent in Alaska, justifies its quotation in part:

> At least since the discovery of gold in the Klondike, Congress has encouraged the settlement and development of Alaska, and since World War II, the importance of increased population to national defense has been stressed repeatedly in Congress, in military circles and by administrative spokesmen. In the ensuing fifty-four years the Indians of southeastern Alaska, and particularly the Haidas, have not only abandoned their primitive ways of life but are now fully capable of competing with the whites in every field of endeavor. Undoubtedly in the early days their rights were encroached upon and violated, for which perhaps no compensation would have been adequate. Now, after their assimilation in southeastern Alaska is an accomplished fact, an attempt is made to compensate not those who suffered under the impact of civilization, but their remote descendants, and this would be done at the expense of the whites who followed and had nothing to do with the exploitation of the Indians. It is a matter of common knowledge that today the Indians of southeastern Alaska prefer the white men's life despite all its evils and shortcomings.
>
> Viewing this controversy in historical perspective it is no exaggeration to say that nothing since the purchase of Alaska has engendered so much ill-feeling and resentment as the department's reservation policy and its encouragement of aboriginal claims, especially in the face of Miller v. United States . . . holding that aboriginal title was extinguished by the Treaty of Cession. Whatever may be said of reservations in the unsettled regions of Alaska, they are viewed as indefensible in southeastern Alaska, and generally condemned by whites and Indians alike as racial segregation and discrimination in their worst form. So far as the relations of the whites and Indians are concerned, racial discrimination is virtually nonexistent, and equality only awaits the emancipation of the Indian from wardship restrictions. Indians and Eskimos are found side by side in every walk of life, even in the legislative halls of the territory which would be beyond their reach without the votes of the whites.

While the $46,000,000 pulp mill just north of Ketchikan, made possible by the Timber Sales Act of 1947, was nearing production in

1954, a development beneficial to the people of Alaska, the issue underlying the legislative conflict remained. That the funds derived from the Tongass Forest receipts continued to accumulate in the federal treasury without benefit to the people of the area from which they were derived was only a minor aspect of the confusion created by Secretary Ickes's arbitrary and disingenuous efforts to impose his reactionary concepts upon the people of Alaska.

While it was probable that the considerable damage that he had inflicted on orderly democratic progress and to a growingly harmonious interracial relationship in Alaska would, for a time, persist, it was clear that, in fairness to all the people of Alaska, the flames into which an issue unresolved for seventy years had been needlessly fanned should be promptly extinguished. The issue needed to be resolved particularly in justice to the native people who had been led to believe that they had valid claims to extensive land or to compensation for it. Neither the ukase of a cabinet officer nor the opinion of a departmental solicitor, on the one hand, nor the decisions of a United States Circuit Court or of a United States District Court in specific suits, on the other hand, were conclusive. Congress could, if it would, provide to have that basic issue determined promptly, fairly— and finally.

And thereafter there were related and unresolved issues affecting the native people of Alaska which went far beyond land, or compensation therefor, to the building of full equality of economic and social opportunity without regard to race. It was an unresolved issue for all the people of Alaska, but one which they could come closer to solving if their federal overlords removed the obstacles they had created.

The Fisheries: Salmon in Disaster

Alaska has been cursed . . . with what in some of the old countries they called "absentee landlordism," where people who hold and control the resources of the country do not reside in the country and have no interest in it except to make as much money out of it as they can.

DELEGATE ANTHONY J. DIMOND, APRIL 11, 1934[1]

THE nearly third of a century which followed the White Act of 1924—hailed as the Magna Carta of fishery conservation by both federal and industry officials—was uncannily repetitive of what had gone before.

There were the repeated assurances by these two controlling powers that the resource was now amply protected.[2]

There was, paradoxically, the chronic—and justified—complaint by the regulatory officialdom, concurred in by industry spokesmen, and admitted by congressional authority, that Congress, despite increased appropriations, was providing insufficiently to conserve the resource.[3]

Regulation, such as it was, produced other abuses which bore heavily and exclusively on the fishermen. These abuses exemplified the continuing conflict between the resident and nonresident interest. Section 6 of the White Act provided that traps, boats and all fishing gear could be seized for violations and sold to satisfy the court's judgment if necessary. As interpreted and applied by the Bureau of Fisheries wardens, fishermen's boats and gear would be seized upon arrest for an alleged violation. The fisherman was then given the alternative of admitting guilt and agreeing on the spot to a fine, or awaiting trial, which with the customary "law's delay," meant losing most, and sometimes all, of the fishing season, and thus a whole year's livelihood. Eager wardens were arresting fishermen who considered themselves guiltless of the violation charged—and at times were. Guilty or innocent, they were effectively denied their day in court.

Specific examples of this abuse were detailed in a long letter to Delegate Dimond by Frank A. Boyle, a well-known and respected citizen, a former Register of the General Land Office, and an attorney who had been persuaded by the United States District Judge and fellow members of the bar to give up his private law practice to accept the United States commissionership at Juneau. His service there had brought him into direct contact with these practices. Boyle labeled them a "blackmailing procedure on the part of the government." [4]

Bills to end this abuse—and yet protect the government's interest if the arrested fisherman were convicted in court—had been introduced by Delegates Sutherland and Wickersham.[5] They continued to be introduced in Congress after Congress by Delegate Dimond,[6] who testified that the effect of the procedure in Alaska had been "baleful." [7] Boyle's testimony was corroborated by others, besides fishermen, including Joseph W. Kehoe, based on his experience as United States Commissioner at Ketchikan.

"As the law now stands," wrote Kehoe, "it gives the agents of the Bureau of Fisheries arbitrary power to rob a fisherman of the use of his boat and gear for a whole fishing season, whether he is guilty or not. . . . In my humble opinion a single instance of injustice should be sufficient to cause Congress to remedy the situation by the passage of your bill.[8]

Representative Schuyler Otis Bland, D., of Virginia, who was to continue in the chairmanship of the House Committee on Merchant Marine and Fisheries for fifteen out of his thirty-two years' service in Congress, declared that it looked "very much like a travesty on justice." [9]

Nevertheless the bills were not enacted. They never even got out of committee. Both the bureau and the industry were opposed.

Acting Commissioner of Fisheries Charles E. Jackson, in reporting adversely, declared that the measure would "handicap adequate enforcement of existing law and regulations," and "materially lessen the respect which has been created for such law and regulations." [10]

"A constantly recurring attempt on the part of law violators to obstruct effective law enforcement" was Edward W. Allen's and W. C. Arnold's joint view transmitted to the committee in opposition to H.R. 7542, Dimond's bill in the Seventy-sixth Congress to suspend boat and gear seizures before trial and conviction.[11]

So the "travesty on justice" continued—and continues to this day.

"Plead guilty, and you can go on fishing. Otherwise I'll take you in" was the formula of the Bureau of Fisheries warden, and is the

FISHERY PRODUCTION

MILLIONS OF
POUNDS OF
RAW PRODUCT   **WASHINGTON**

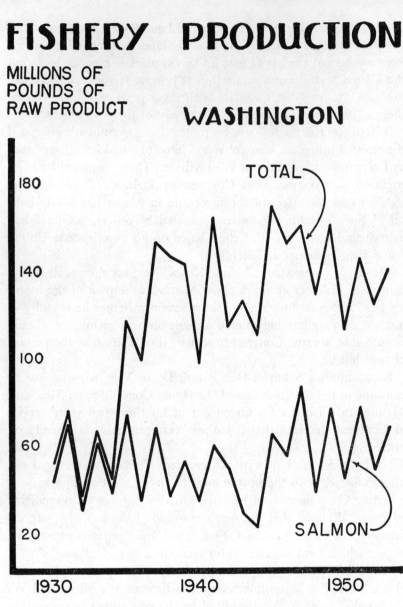

formula of the Fish and Wildlife Service warden, for the fisherman.[12]

An occasional fisherman fights the charge in court and secures acquittal—at the cost of most, if not all, of his season's fishing. If guiltless he loses either way.

The fish-trap operator encountered no such dilemma. When a trap was fishing illegally, that is, during one of the closed periods, a fine was imposed on the ownership—and sometimes also on the watchman, which the ownership paid—without more than a brief interruption, if any, in the trap's fishing. Nor is there any material record of trap confiscation after and because of conviction. On the contrary there is considerable evidence of harsher treatment accorded the fisherman than the trap operator.[13] But even identical fines would bear far more onerously on the person of the fisherman than on the ownership, whether corporate or individual (and the great majority were and are corporate) of the mechanism.

The difficulties of Alaskan toilers of the sea and shore were increased by the preferential treatment accorded nonresident fishermen and cannery workers—a story as old as the coming of the canned-salmon industry to Alaska in 1878. This discrimination against Alaskans, which originated with and was long continued by the industry alone, was reinforced, beginning in the late nineteen twenties, by the international labor unions with headquarters in Seattle and San Francisco. Alaskans soon discovered that despite paid-up membership their union card was at various times only a second-class ticket.

In the red-salmon area of Bristol Bay, from 1927 to 1938, members of the Alaska Fishermen's Union, coming from the States, received 4 cents more per fish than the members residing in Bristol Bay.[14] Due to the combined efforts of Delegate Dimond and the resident fishermen, who in 1935 formed a new union, The United Fishermen of Alaska, which soon gained membership throughout the territory, this discrimination ceased in 1938. But a new discrimination took its place. The union contracts drawn up in San Francisco provided that the first six and a half boats to every line of cannery machinery had to be manned by "outside" fishermen.[15]

"They must employ six and a half 'outside' boats [thirteen nonresidents] to a line before they can employ any residents at all; that is what it means," explained Mr. Edward Coffey, on that occasion spokesman for the fishermen.[16] "They use residents in Bristol Bay," he

FISHERY PRODUCTION

MILLIONS OF
POUNDS OF
RAW PRODUCT

ALASKA

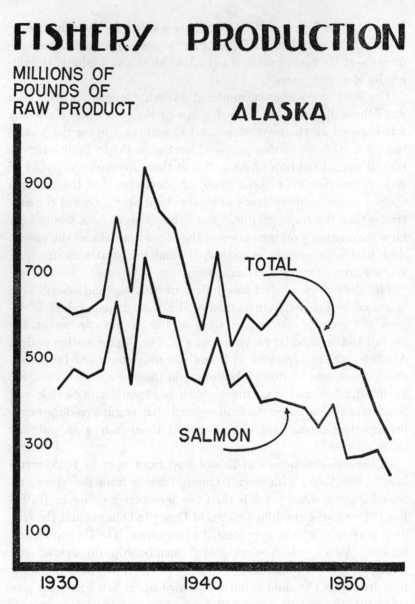

testified, concerning the cannery workers, "when they have a heavy
fish run. . . . There is no consideration given to the residents unless
they get short-handed, and then they will put a few of them to work
in the canneries." [17] The transportation for the "outside" fishermen,
Mr. Coffey further testified, was paid both ways from San Francisco.
Any Alaskan had to pay his own fare to and from the fishing
grounds.[18] His testimony was uncontradicted either by the representative of the industry, Mr. W. C. Arnold, who accompanied the committee, or by representatives of the Alaska Fishermen's Union who
testified subsequently.[19]

The Alaskans' grievance, which had existed for years and would
continue, was expressed by W. R. Wassenkari, President of the newly
formed United Fishermen of Alaska. When the season opened on the
morning of June 25, 1936, "approximately a hundred resident fishermen in the Bristol Bay area were left on the beach without a job." [20]

These men had been fishing in the bay for years; many had families
to support, and depended on the season's fishing for the year's livelihood; yet they were compelled to watch the fishing done by nonresidents.

"The nonresident fishermen are members of the Alaska Fishermen's Union," continued Mr. Wassenkari's statement, "with their
main office at 49 Clay Street, San Francisco. We resident fishermen of
Bristol Bay waters were fellow-members of this same union in the past,
but . . . were not accorded the protection nor given the rights and
privileges due us as fellow-members of the Alaska Fishermen's Union. Instead, we were exploited and discriminated against by these
nonresident brothers . . . we have even been threatened bodily violence."

Priority of employment for residents, to which they aspired, rather
than the posteriority, which they suffered, was sought by Delegate
Dimond in various bills which provided for gradually increasing quo-
tas of residents on the fishing grounds and in the canneries.[21] But
against the opposition of both the industry and the unions whose
headquarters and interest were "outside," and were supported by
their congressmen,[22] only a very slight measure of legislative relief
was obtainable. It provided that in the Bristol Bay area only commercial fishing with a stake net or set net, lesser forms of stationary gear,
could be performed only by those who had resided in that area for

FISHERY PRODUCTION

MILLIONS OF
POUNDS OF   **BRITISH**
RAW PRODUCT   **COLUMBIA**

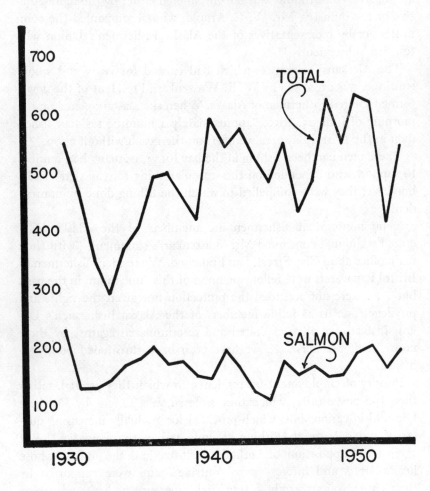

two years.[23] Stake and set netting encompassed only a minor part of the Bristol Bay fishery.

"Our people in Alaska must have these jobs if they are to live in Alaska," pleaded Delegate Dimond. "This is not to the same extent true of those who come into Alaska from the States. In fact, I am reliably informed that many members of the Alaska Fishermen's Union in San Francisco who fish in Alaska have other regular jobs in San Francisco which they quit in order to come to Alaska to fish because the fishing is more profitable than the other jobs. Alaskans are denied this opportunity; they have no other jobs and so they must fish or work in the fisheries if they are to live in the territory." [24]

Opposition to equality of treatment for Alaskans—let alone priority—was not limited to the legislative front. Representative Monrad C. Wallgren, who had both cannery operators and fishermen as constituents in his Second Washington Congressional District on the shore of Puget Sound, warned of "trouble" from another labor organization, the International Fishermen and Allied Workers of America, who "represent the important fisheries of Alaska." He also read into the record part of a letter dated January 8, 1940, from George Lane, whom he identified as secretary of the union, which served notice that "if the Alaska Fishermen's Union is expected to permit Alaskan residents to usurp their just proportion of jobs from the men in the States we will refuse to permit any fishing in the area." [25]

The discrimination in the fisheries against Alaskan residents by outside unions was not confined to the salmon industry. The contract between the herring packers with plants at Kodiak and on Prince William Sound and Local No. 14 of the Fish Reduction and Saltery Workers Union with headquarters in the Mutual Life Building, Seattle, provided:

"The company agrees to employ only members of the union and shall at the commencement of the season hire a full crew as herein agreed upon. Employees shall be cleared and accepted through the union at its headquarters in Seattle. It is further agreed if members cannot be obtained, then—

"The union agrees to permit bona-fide residents or natives of the Territory of Alaska for the purpose of replacement or extra help required and designated in this agreement, providing they are acceptable to the majority of the membership in the camp." [26]

Mr. Guy Alston, Secretary-treasurer of the union, declared his view that it was too much "to expect men who have followed the industry for a number of years to be good-hearted enough to say to an Alaskan, 'take my job, and I will stay down here.' " [27]

But if labor was being blamed, he asserted, "the burden . . . is being put in the wrong place. The place to put it is on the operators operating in that territory."

To which Delegate Dimond replied: "I suppose you know that these herring operators, when they are asked as to why they do not employ more Alaskans when there are literally hundreds of them available . . . who want jobs, say they want to hire Alaskans, but if they do, the Seattle union, your union, will tie up the plants." [28]

Mr. Alston testified that out of 367 men of his union working in Alaska 20 per cent were Alaskans.[29]

Mr. Conrad Espe, international representative of the Alaskan Cannery Workers' Union, with offices in the Arcade Building, Seattle, indicated that union and industry policy went hand in hand:

"As far as our union is concerned and the men involved are concerned, it has been the policy of the canned-salmon industry to hire nonresident labor. That labor in Alaska is no more foreign to Alaska than the canned-salmon industry itself. The vast majority of the owners of the canneries are nonresidents, both in residence and in the finances placed in the industry, as well as we are." [30]

Asked by territorial Senator Henry Roden, at a Seattle hearing: "Suppose a canner up in Alaska decides tomorrow that next season he will employ local labor only, and that local labor will join your organization, would there be any objection on your part down here then?" Mr. Espe replied:

"I think there would be, because we have made quite a study of the labor supply in most of these places, and . . . the nonresident membership has been narrowed down to actually experienced crews that are necessary for the operation of these canneries." [31]

Delegate Dimond expressed skepticism as to where the responsibility for the discrimination against Alaskans in the fisheries lay:

"Many of the operators now claim," he declared, "that they would prefer to employ residents of Alaska in fishing and in cannery work, but are prevented by the threat of strike, or the declaration of 'hot cargo,' by the nonresident unions. I am not able to say how much, if any, of such declaration is truth and how much is mere pretense. My doubt is based upon the fact that from the earliest days the operators at practically all times and under practically all circumstances declined to hire a resident of Alaska in any capacity in the fisheries if a nonresident worker were available. Ordinarily they hired residents only when they could not get nonresidents to do the work, and so now when they say they would hire residents if they were permitted to do so, I am still skeptical." [32]

Further basis for Delegate Dimond's skepticism seemed furnished by the support given over a decade later by the canned-salmon industry to the International Longshoremen's and Warehousemen's Union with headquarters in San Francisco, in the struggle with the Bristol Bay residents, now organized in a newly formed Bering Sea Fishermen's Union. It was another phase of the conflict begun over fifteen years earlier.

The intervening years had wrought great changes in union jurisdiction. World War II and the subsequently evident menace of communist imperialism had played a large part in these changes. The Congress of Industrial Organizations, previously with considerable membership in Alaska, had expelled its principal affiliates there engaged in shipping, longshoring, fishing and canning on the ground that they were communist-dominated. Uniting in the I.L.W.U. under Harry Bridges's leadership, that organization was in 1951 seeking to capture control in Bristol Bay. To achieve that end it undercut by a third the prices demanded from the canneries by the resident fishermen for their fish. The industry's acceptance would have spelled unemployment for the local residents or control by Bridges's union. A substantial number of Eskimos who had been brought in to work, if the industry did not sign up with the B.S.F.U., refused to accede to this arrangement which they regarded as strikebreaking. They were encouraged and supported by the resident clergy of various denominations and thus secured a victory in a long-standing and continuing conflict. A communist-controlled union on the shores of Bering Sea whose waters likewise lapped the not-distant coast of Soviet Siberia had other implications which the local residents and the Eskimos viewed with alarm.

Meanwhile the issue of conservation versus depletion continued to agitate at least the Alaskan residents engaged in the fisheries. Whereas industry and the federal regulatory agency saw no diminution and said so, fishermen thought otherwise and said so. In contrast with the afore-quoted pronouncements that fish were more plentiful than ever, that the White Act under federal administration had not only conserved but was increasingly building up the resource, the same hearings found many Alaskan fishermen in emphatic dissent.[33] Their understanding was all the more noteworthy in that the three preceding years had produced the largest, and the third and fourth largest annual packs, respectively, in Alaska's history, and the preceding five-year production was by far the largest of any other similar period with the sensational average of 6,905,843.6 cases.[34]

Depletion was associated principally in the minds of fishermen with the existence of traps. This continued increasingly to cause them to urge their abolition. At virtually every session of Congress bills were introduced by Alaska's delegates for their abolition as well as for transfer of the management of the fisheries to the territory. But in the face of both bureau and industry opposition these bills never got out of committee. On the other hand, the trap-operating members of the industry felt not wholly certain of the permanence of their trap control from year to year and continued to endeavor to secure it. Such an effort was made through a measure entitled, "A Bill to Assure Conservation and to Permit the Fullest Utilization of the Fisheries of Alaska," which reached the stage of a Senate Commerce Committee hearing in the second session of the Seventy-eighth Congress, January 20, 1944.

One of the curious aspects of Alaskan salmon traps was that the permit necessary to secure one was granted by the War Department under a Rivers and Harbors Act of March 3, 1899 (30 Stat. 1151). The War Department's sole interest in the matter was to make sure that the trap would not constitute an obstruction to navigation. In 1935 the Bureau of Fisheries, under the commissionership of Frank T. Bell, requested the War Department to grant no permit if in the bureau's view the trap would conflict with its fisheries regulations, and suggested that pending the securing of necessary legislation only one War Department permit should be issued for a trap site approved by the bureau.

By thus obviating the practice of "trap-jumping," which was prevalent at the time, the value of each permit was greatly increased. One interesting peculiarity of trap "holdings" was that while the trap was subject to sale, devise, lease, transfer or other disposal, it was not subject to attachment.[35]

The new procedure initiated by the Bureau of Fisheries was chal-

lenged by Delegate Dimond in 1939 on the grounds that it in effect
endowed each such permittee with proprietary rights and, apart from
his view that this was contrary to the public interest, that it violated
a provision in an amendment to the White Act (June 18, 1926, 44
Stat. 752) "that no exclusive or several right of fishery" should be
granted.[36]

The Fish and Wildlife Service which had now succeeded the Bureau of Fisheries in control of the Alaska fisheries receded from its
predecessor's arrangement because of its obviously questionable, if
not illegal, nature, and in regulations issued October 14, 1940, provided that a permit would be issued by the War Department for every
application, even if more than one were received for the same site.

This change in policy was protested by the canned-salmon industry and strong representations were made by it to restore the procedure followed during the previous five years. The Interior Department
thereupon proposed legislation that would clear up the confusion and
add other provisions that in its view would bring the Alaska fisheries
control law up to date. Such a measure was drawn up and given for
introduction to Monrad C. Wallgren, who had been elected to the
Senate in 1940, and was a member of the Subcommittee on Fisheries
of the Committee on Commerce which would pass on such legislation
in the upper house. Appearing before that committee Senator Wallgren explained that the bill, S. 930, he was now presenting differed "a
great deal" from the original bill (the draft prepared by the Fish and
Wildlife Service), and proposed that the amendments he had written
be accepted as committee amendments. He also called attention to a
number of persons present who desired to testify. Apart from Colonel
George R. Goethals, who had come to explain the War Department's
historic relation to fish traps, they were Mr. W. C. Arnold, Mr. Edward W. Allen, Mr. Nick Bez, Mr. F. J. Gunderson of Wrangell,
Alaska, an independent trap owner, and Mr. Bjorne Halling, of the
C.I.O. Maritime Committee.[37] All of them testified in favor of the
measure.[38]

Delegate Dimond on the other hand opposed the bill in every particular. Its very purpose was to grant an exclusive right of fishery in
the waters of Alaska and to legalize what, he declared, had been done
illegally at the instigation of the Bureau of Fisheries under a different
management; that it made certain that the trap owner would "be
able to occupy a piece of ground in the coastal waters of Alaska un-

til Kingdom come," unless the entire area was closed to fishing.[39]

"Everyone I know is opposed to it," said Delegate Dimond, adding that he had communications from fishermen's unions and others in Alaska declaring their opposition.

Senator Wallgren replied that he had been in touch with various fishermen's unions: "Of course, I understand a fishermen's union in Seattle and one in Alaska may be two very different institutions."

Delegate Dimond agreed that was so.

"They fish in Alaska, and I venture to say there are possibly a greater number that come up from Seattle and these other states to fish in these waters than come from Alaska itself," said Wallgren.

Delegate Dimond conceded it was true.

"And," said Senator Wallgren, "they are all agreeable to the legislation."

Delegate Dimond did not doubt that.

"I was very careful about that," said Senator Wallgren. "We had a meeting of almost everybody in the industry."

". . . Of everybody except Alaska," retorted Delegate Dimond. "This is an Alaska fisheries bill, but nobody in Alaska was consulted that I know of. Nobody even sent me a copy of the bill. I didn't know anything about it. Nobody asked my opinion. Nobody requested me to come here. I had to find out myself in order to come over and make my protest." [40]

The bill also created an advisory committee to be appointed by the Secretary of the Interior which was to meet once annually in Seattle. Said Dimond:

"We have fishermen in Alaska who cannot travel to Seattle. This is an Alaska industry and our fishermen are entitled to some consideration here. The packers can more easily go to Juneau than the fishermen with their small income can come to Seattle. I think it is an outrage." [41]

A deluge of protests from Alaska descended on the Senate committee. But it was Ira N. Gabrielson, Director of the Fish and Wildlife Service, who dealt what had become known as the Wallgren bill a death blow by declaring, "I don't believe anyone is entitled to a vested right in a natural resource." [42]

Without that provision the bill was no longer of interest to its proponents. Just so had their predecessors, thirty years previously, lost interest in a similar bill, designed for the same purpose, drawn up under corresponding auspices, when the highest regulatory authority at that time had likewise declared his opposition to granting a vested right in the same natural resource.[43]

Vested right or not, the traps continued, to the mounting distress of Alaska's fishermen, as effectively as if the Wallgren bill or one of its ancestral counterparts had been enacted. Trap ownership, likewise, was becoming more and more concentrated in a few of the largest canning companies. Of the 434 traps in operation in 1944, 396, or 91 per cent, were owned by nonresidents. Of these, 245, or 56 per cent, were owned by eight packing concerns. One of these had sixty, the next, fifty-eight. Thus two large absentee-owned companies held well over one-fourth of all of Alaska's traps.[44]

An effort was made in the seventeenth legislature in 1945 to bring about a gradual and evolutionary modification of this concentration by levying a moderate graduated tax on fish traps based on the number in one ownership. The measure which passed the territorial House of Representatives by a three to one majority was defeated in the Senate by a tie vote after the most intense opposition by the canned-salmon lobby.[45]

Two years later a fleeting vision of possible relief from the trap appeared to the people of Alaska. When the Eighteenth Territorial Legislature convened in January, 1947, a letter from Secretary of the Interior Julius A. Krug was received in the Governor's office stating that an early solution of the trap-regulation problem was desirable and that he felt the legislature should deal with the matter in the first instance. The legislators considered this—to them, astonishing—proposal, astonishing in that nothing in the previous attitude and actions of the Interior Department had indicated any willingness to relinquish its control of the regulation of the fisheries, of which fish-trap regulation was certainly an important part, and in that the department had opposed every bill designed either to abolish fish traps or to transfer the management of the resource to the territory.

Familiar, likewise, with the effectiveness of the canned-salmon lobby, the legislature resolved to present the vital issue of retention or abolition of fish traps to the people of Alaska. So a House bill provided for a referendum at the next general election in 1948 on whether traps should be retained or abolished over a period of five years. Unable, despite strenuous efforts, to defeat a bill which merely sought to sound out public opinion, the lobby concentrated on se-

curing an amendment lengthening the period of the proposed abolition to ten years. In this form the bill passed (Chapter 2, S.L.A.
1947). A memorial (H.J.M. 18) addressed to the Secretary of the Interior requested that no legislative action be initiated until the result
of the referendum should be known.

There were others, however, who did not desire to await the Alaskan people's verdict. Less than three months after the adjournment of
the legislature, the Department of the Interior had sent to Congress a
bill—"the result of a long series of discussions between this department and representatives speaking both for a group of the larger canners and for Alaska Salmon Industry, Inc., the industry trade
association," Secretary Krug wrote in transmitting it, which represented "an agreement of legislation that would be acceptable to the
department and to the salmon industry." He added that the bill was
"a compromise" but, he believed, "a good one." [46]

The bill, introduced on June 18th and sent to the Senate Committee on Interstate and Foreign Commerce, provided for the leasing
of salmon-trap sites to go into effect in 1948, with the proviso that
there be a percentage reduction in the number to be leased by those
then operating on more than twenty trap sites. This proposal would
have affected only the five largest companies. Based on their 1947
holdings, it would have reduced those of P. E. Harris Company from
sixty-four to forty-eight traps, Pacific American Fisheries from fifty-six
to forty-two traps, Libby, McNeill and Libby from thirty-five to
twenty-eight traps, Nakat Packing Company (the salmon branch of
the Great Atlantic and Pacific Tea Company) from twenty-seven to
twenty-four traps, and New England Fish Company from twenty-
three to twenty-one traps. Their remaining trap sites, and all others
numbering twenty or fewer under one operator, would be leased to
him for a period of fifteen years. There would be no provision for
their renewal or extension. The forty-two trap sites which the five companies were asked to relinquish were to be auctioned off upon sealed
bids by the Secretary of the Interior, with preference given to Alaskan
communities, which would likewise be given fifteen-year leases. This
provision, Secretary Krug stated, would afford "an opportunity to a
few native communities markedly to improve their economic conditions."

The bill also provided that a royalty of 5 per cent of the value of
the salmon taken by any trap and an additional 2 per cent on the

value in excess of $500,000 taken by any operator, be levied, half of which was to be paid into the national treasury. Thus it proposed, as had bills over thirty years previously, to take some of the established sources of revenue from the territory and give them to the federal government.

Nevertheless, the Interior Department's draft was not acceptable to the Alaska Salmon Industry, Inc., "without amendments which we consider fundamental and necessary," its Managing Director, Mr. W. C. Arnold, testified. They included extension of the term of the leases from fifteen to twenty years, and the elimination of the provision for no renewal at the end of that term. "We are not agreeable to signing a death warrant. . . ." said Arnold. Also, the five operators who were expected to surrender forty-two of their 205 trap sites sought a percentage formula that would permit them to relinquish fewer.[47]

"We have been called into consultation. We have taken part in the preparation of the bill," testified Mr. Philip D. Macbride, Chairman of the Board of Pacific American Fisheries. But it was "not our bill." It was inferior to the Wallgren bill of a few years earlier "in that the Wallgren bill recognized those who had the traps 100 per cent in their right to continue in possession." [48]

The proposed legislation—whose planned enactment for the fishing season of 1948 would have preceded the scheduled referendum by six months—provoked a storm of protest from Alaska. Its critics there saw that it would prevent any further reduction or abolition of fish traps for the duration of the leases.

Delegate Bartlett, testifying in opposition, revealed that he had not been invited to any of the conferences between the industry and the Department of the Interior during which the bill was formulated.[49]

"That is a matter in which we make very vital complaint—that the industry and the department agreed, but the people of Alaska were not consulted." [50]

Ralph J. Rivers, Attorney-General of Alaska, voiced the prevailing Alaskan opposition "to enactment of S. 1446 or any similar measure which would establish a vested interest in fish-trap sites and thereby in effect award to a favored few a major share of a natural resource which should be available to all." [51]

Most striking was the unanimity of protest from the native communities of southeastern Alaska to which it had been the Interior Department's purpose to allocate some of the surrendered traps. From Klawock, the President of the Alaska Native Brotherhood, Frank Peratrovich, wrote:

"It is recognized by the people of Alaska . . . this bill is the canned-salmon industry's bill. It is being pushed . . . by the powerful lobbyists of the industry . . . to legalize their methods of completely depleting our major resource of the territory. When this is accomplished they will move to greener pastures . . . and we, the people of the territory, will be left to carry on.

"Through a period of fifteen years the fishermen and residents . . . have come to realize that the fish trap must be completely eliminated if we are to maintain an average run of salmon and the agitation against the trap has increased within the past four years due to the fact that the decline in the run of salmon is directly traceable to this method of taking salmon. If this bill is allowed to pass, maybe the government will be willing to give Alaska to the Indians after the industry gets through with it. I hope this does not happen."[52]

The President of the Alaska Native Sisterhood, Mrs. Amy Hallingstad of Petersburg, and the presidents and secretaries of the A.N.B. and A.N.S. camps of Hydaburg, Ketchikan, Yakutat, Angoon, Haines, Juneau and Douglas all transmitted their opposition for the committee's record.[53]

No further action was taken on the bill.

The referendum taken in Alaska the following October 12th resulted in a vote of 19,712 to 2,624 for trap abolition. It was a demonstration that the people of Alaska, and not merely the fishermen, were against fish traps. Of the 22,336 who had voted, 88.7 per cent took that position. While the First and Third Divisions whose coasts harbored the fisheries gave the largest percentage vote against traps, the Second and Fourth, where there were no fish traps, returned majorities in excess of three to one and nine to one, respectively.[54] Again it was impressively shown that the Tlingit and Haida communities— to whom the bestowal of traps had been held out earlier in the same year by the Department of the Interior in its advocacy of the fish-trap leasing bill—were nevertheless wholly opposed, as they had been ever since the introduction of traps, and voted against them overwhelmingly and in ratios exceeding the votes of white communities: Angoon, forty-one to nine; Hoonah, 106 to eleven; Hydaburg, eighty-one to three; Kake, 123 to six; Kasaan, twenty-nine to nothing; Klawock, eighty-four to four; Yakutat, forty-six to three. Most striking of all was that Metlakatla, with seven traps belonging to the community, voted 112 to thirty-three for trap abolition.

"The overwhelming vote against fish traps . . . may mark the opening of a new chapter in the history of self-government and development," editorialized the Anchorage *Times*.[55]

House Joint Memorial No. 1, passed within a week after the assembling of the Nineteenth Territorial Legislature in January of 1949, pleaded for congressional action consistent with the expressed wishes of Alaska's people. It called attention to the abolition of fish traps in neighboring British Columbia and in the Pacific coastal states. It called attention to the "dangerous" depletion of Alaska's salmon fisheries "requiring immediate remedial action."

While there had been widespread dissatisfaction among the majority balloting for fish-trap abolition that they had been limited to a choice between retention and the protracted abolition over a ten-year period, they understood the necessity of Delegate Bartlett's H.R. 1515, promptly introduced in the Eighty-first Congress, to conform to the terms of the referendum provision and therefore calling for a 10 per cent annual trap reduction for a decade. But the public was surprised at the need of further extensive hearings on a subject that had been so thoroughly discussed not only in the campaign, but for years previously.[56]

The impact of *vox populi* upon the political and economic powers that ruled Alaska was to prove less than negligible. The referendum might as well not have taken place for any effect upon their performance.

Again, true to precedent, the Interior Department reported adversely on Bartlett's H.R. 1515 and proposed a substitute.

Again, the industry was united in opposition. This time it adopted the delaying tactic of "being unable to attend" the hearings which took place in Washington from March 30th to April 4th. By deferring their appearance till fall, the industry representatives would at least postpone any decisive action for a year. The chairman of the subcommittee, Representative Frank W. Boykin, D., of Alabama, was "glad to grant your request."[57]

Again a subcommittee of the House Committee on Merchant Marine and Fisheries journeyed north in the summertime. Again it held extensive hearings not only in Washington, but in Kodiak, Fairbanks,

Anchorage, Juneau, Petersburg, Wrangell, Ketchikan and Sitka. Again numerous witnesses (170) were heard and much other testimony recorded in two volumes totaling 772 printed pages. There was a slight departure from precedent. Whereas after the voluminous testimony collected by a similar subcommittee there had been a report—which arrived at few conclusions and produced no action[58]—ten years later, with the salmon supply steadily dwindling, the committee did not bother even to make any report.

Why were the fisheries declining? Had not the White Act guaranteed their preservation in perpetuity?

The fisheries were declining for several reasons.

First, the federal government had never appropriated and was not appropriating sufficiently to safeguard the resource.

"The enforcement of regulations is, for want of appropriations, dangerously inadequate," Interior Secretary Krug declared in June of 1947.[59]

Nevertheless, like Secretary Redfield thirty years earlier, and like all his cabinet predecessors, and successors, he did not wish to relinquish control of the bureau.

Second, the regulatory services were often in the dark on what to do to conserve the salmon. The fault was by no means wholly theirs. Denying funds even for proper enforcement, the Congress had never supplied the means for research which over the years would have accumulated a body of needed knowledge. One evidence of this lack of knowledge was revealed in Secretary Krug's admission of "dangerously inadequate appropriations" in a letter transmitting a proposal for legislation to Congress which could only have aggravated the salmon depletion.

Third, the regulatory decisions were by and large not freely made by the regulatory agency. Clamor against the annual regulations and the conservation measures they contained, in the hearings held after their issuance, was almost automatic and invariable from an industry gambling with a large investment and in quest of immediate profits. This clamor was reinforced, when necessary, by threats and political pressure at the top.

"I went to Secretary Roper and saw him right in his office. In 1936 I told him to take his regulations book and throw it in the Potomac River. . . ."[60] testified Nick Bez, a potent figure in the industry with ample political connections, as in fact all his fellow industry leaders had and have.

"Going over the head" of the fisheries commissioner or director, to the cabinet officer, invoking the friendly offices of one's senator to assist, if need be, was established, if not always successful, practice. "We'll get Gabrielson," was audible in the early nineteen forties when that director would not yield to pressure.

"We'll get Al Day," was said of his successor. And they did!

But there, too, arose the difficulty that the "experts" on whom the heads of the bureau depended were often operating "by guess and by God," and the industry and the fishermen and they themselves knew it. That in itself weakened official resistance to persuasion.

The heads of bureau or service had of course to depend on their field men. Frank T. Bell's appointment was political. Ira N. Gabrielson and Albert M. Day, his successors, were competent biologists and career men in the service but their experience in the Biological Survey had been with wild life; their training was as ornithologists and mammalogists and not as ichthyologists. They knew nothing of the fisheries—particularly the Alaska fisheries—when they assumed their important responsibilities.

Moreover, complaisant, as against intractable, "experts" had the prospect of security in their federal jobs, or even better, employment by the industry, at higher than a government salary, against the possible alternative of being unemployed after a change of administration, and even perhaps—in their specialty—unemployable.

Fourth, the desperation of the fishermen. Traditionally they had been the best of all conservationists—living the year round by the resource and cherishing it. Collectively—and sometimes individually —they were as well, if not better, informed on the fisheries as a distant federal officialdom, and their protests against official folly were compounded of both self-interest and first-hand knowledge. But the increasing monopolization of the fishing ground by untouchable and unassailable powers, and their decreasing opportunity to make a livelihood had tended to make them lawbreakers, breakers of laws and regulations which they consider profoundly unjust.

"A man who lives in Alaska and is starving to death during the summer," testified a fisherman, "and goes by a trap in a boat and sees fifty, sixty, seventy thousand fish in it, and then spends three or four

or five days looking for one fish to catch and cannot, is going to go to
the creek. He is driven to the creek. He has to go to survive."

The witness had two alternative solutions—unlike the congressional
committee whose responsibility lay in this field and reported after
weeks of investigation, "no remedy can be found."

"Either," said H. J. Lannen, "remove the traps from Alaska and
turn it over to her people, or I would say remove the people from
Alaska and turn it over to the traps. I do not believe there is any middle ground. I am serious, too, about that. It is getting worse all the
time." [61]

Fisherman Lannen was not the only one thinking along these lines.
Support for this evaluation of the Alaskan fisheries problem had
come two years earlier in the testimony of C. Howard Baltzo, then a
merchant of Wrangell, Alaska Fisheries Agent there, and President
of the Wrangell Chamber of Commerce.

"We are almost on the verge of disaster as far as the salmon industry
is concerned," he told a House committee visiting Alaska. Without
exception every one of the five species of salmon was going downhill
and many areas that were important had ceased to produce entirely.
As a result of the decline in fisheries the economy of southeastern
Alaska was "approaching a critical state."

Mr. Baltzo's views were not easily discountable. A graduate in
fisheries of the University of Washington, he had spent much of his
life in their conservation and was shortly to become the Assistant Director of the Fish and Wildlife Service's Alaska Fisheries.

"I think a lot of trouble," said Baltzo, "is caused by people who
make important decisions; who aren't there. The people who make
the most money and make the profits do not live in Alaska. They live
in Seattle. The fishermen never make enough money that they can
get out of here. These fishermen do not have the kind of money
that enables them to journey to Washington, D.C., and employ lobbyists who can present their case. The problem is plenty now but it
will be a lot more unless they are considered."

The great need, Baltzo felt, was properly managing and restoring
the fisheries. The federal government had never appropriated sufficient money for proper enforcement of the regulations, but "we
have to have the support of the fishermen." And he added, "I do
think that if we did have a state we would have better control over it
because all of these fishermen would be voters. They would vote for

the legislator who probably would not be able to overlook the needs of the fishermen as easily as the people in Washington, D.C., do at the present time."

"I think the point . . . is of great importance," interposed Delegate Bartlett. "In a concrete way what would you say was needed to make the fishermen respect the federal government's administration of the fisheries?"

Baltzo replied: "The fishermen are opposed to the fish traps for the reason that they consider the traps a vested interest taking an unreasonable portion of a natural resource which naturally does not belong to them. Statistics show that this district,[62] with something like two dozen traps, took over 60 per cent of the salmon caught, whereas the three hundred or four hundred fishing boats that fished during the same season caught less than 40 per cent. The traps belong to the people who make the money so that they can go back to Washington and continue to preserve the good thing they have. Therefore the fishermen feel there is no use supporting that authority that is condoning such a system." [63]

Further confirmation of this view came a year later in a letter from Milo Moore, Director of the State of Washington's fisheries. Based on his twenty-seven years' experience in fisheries and fifteen years after trap abolition there, he wrote:

"Our greatest menace involved in trap operations in the past was not merely the operation of an efficient appliance; rather, it was from the wealth produced from the operations which had certain adverse effects upon proper conservation of the fish. By the influence . . . of the wealth so produced, legislative and departmental regulations could not be effected to permit the desired yearly sustained yield from the fisheries resources. Today we are still suffering the ill effects of over-exploitation of our salmon runs; however, we have gained greatly in the past few years toward reinstating good populations of our salmon in Washington waters." [64]

By 1948 the Alaska fisheries had sunk to alarming depths. The pack had dropped to 3,968,521 cases. With one exception it had not been so small since the great slump of 1921, which had finally—after years of resistance—brought the legislative reform of the White Act. The diminution, as Baltzo had stated, a year earlier, was in all species. In southeastern Alaska pink salmon, the areas's principal dependence, had dropped below a two-million-case pack in every one of the preceding five years, which with one exception had not happened since the 1921 collapse. This deplorable deterioration deepened the region's economic depression, and in turn necessitated further curtailment, further shortening of the fishing season, further restrictions, and consequently still further injury to the fishermen's livelihood and to that of the entire Alaskan economy. Yet traps were not appreciably reduced in number during these years.

To meet this manifest decline, with which the federal authorities seemed unable to cope, the Nineteenth Territorial Legislature early in 1949 established a territorial Department of Fisheries. It was headed by an unpaid board appointed by the Governor and subject to confirmation by the legislature, and was to consist of three fishermen, a representative of the industry and a representative of the public. As its Executive Director the board chose a man widely experienced in the fisheries, taking him from the directorship of the state of Washington's Department of Fisheries which had made a notable restoration of that long overexploited and long dwindling resource.

The new department's function, while restricted by federal law, was to assist and supplement the work of the Fish and Wildlife Service in its task of propagating Alaska's fisheries. The department contributed its territorial funds to strengthen the undernourished federal enforcement by hiring additional stream watchers. It undertook the enlargement and improvement of depleted salmon-spawning areas. It engaged in long overdue research on the habits of the varieties of salmon. It began a program of stocking lakes and streams for sport fishing.

In addition to the material assistance it was intended to render the federal program, the new Department of Fisheries was—in the legislature's intent—to prepare for the management of the Alaskan fisheries in the event of statehood, or earlier transfer of the control from the Department of the Interior.

The territorial department performed useful service which was so recognized by the Alaskan public. Its appropriations were increased by the 1951 and 1953 legislatures. Its counsel was freely offered the federal agency, but its recommendations were, in the main, not accepted. It had no power in the field of regulation except to proffer advice.

And so the Alaskan fisheries continued to decline. By 1953 they had plummeted to the lowest point in thirty-two years with a pack of only 2,882,083 cases, a lower figure, except for 1921, than in any year since 1911.

Responding to the appeal of the territorial authorities, President Eisenhower declared Alaska to be a "disaster area," and federal relief funds were sent there.

Designation of a "disaster area" by the federal government customarily followed major calamities such as flood, drought, hurricane, tornado, earthquake, conflagration or pestilence, usually referred to as an "act of God." It was unique and unprecedented in the failure of a federally managed resource, attributable, rather, to the acts of man. But there was little question of the gravity of the disaster and of the need for help.

"18,000 TO LOSE JOBS" was the newspaper headline over the Associated Press dispatch from Seattle, disclosing that the Alaska Salmon Industry, Inc., was writing to that number of workers, addressing them as "former employees," expressing its inability to commit itself "to . . . any employment" for the following year. After citing "the disastrous season, just completed," the letter declared "the outlook for 1954 is equally bad." All union agreements were therefore canceled, beginning with the workers in Bristol Bay whose season was scheduled to begin and terminate earlier than the other Alaskan salmon fisheries.[65]

"However, industry and the federal officials did not agree . . . on steps to save the salmon. . . ." reported the Seattle *Post-Intelligencer*, of a three-day hearing called in Seattle in November. When Fish and Wildlife Service Director John L. Farley, newly appointed by Interior Secretary Douglas McKay to replace Albert M. Day, proposed a shortened season in southeastern Alaska, the proposal "drew heavy blasts from packers."[66]

A later proposal from Director Farley for a longer season but with sixty-hour weekly closed periods and a 50 per cent reduction in trap operation, was termed "unrealistic" by the assembled packers, who counterproposed far lesser curtailments. Mr. Seton Thompson, long connected with the Alaska federal fisheries organization, and chief of Alaska Fisheries of the Fish and Wildlife Service, "expressed doubts" whether the packers' plan "would be effective in rebuilding the pink-salmon run."[67]

A month later they were still more vigorous in opposing Mr. Farley's plan to close thirty-two specific traps and of the remaining two hundred to close enough to account for half of the 1953 catch. "Trap owners of southeast Alaska voiced vigorous objections here yesterday to 1954 fishing regulations proposed by the Fish and Wildlife Service," reported an Associated Press dispatch from Seattle, December 19th.[68]

For sixty-five years—ever since the first salmon-conservation legislation was passed by Congress in 1889—the Alaskan fisheries have been under the absolute management of federal bureaus and kept there by the Congress. The Treasury Department was succeeded by the Department of Commerce and Labor, which in turn was followed by Commerce without Labor, and then by the Department of the Interior.

Under all these regimes—under Republican and Democratic administrations alike—the story has been the same: inability to secure adequate appropriations from the Congress—a penny-wise ineptitude which arises within the departments where the budget proposals originate and are consistently set at inadequate levels. Inability to control the predatory human forces that have made for a great natural resource's destruction. Inability to carry out not only the primary conservation function but to understand and satisfy the important social and economic implications of the task.

Forty-two years ago, the Territory of Alaska, deprived, as no other territory had been, of the control and management of its fisheries, through the intrigue and political manipulations of the same forces that have helped destroy the resource, began to plead for that right of self-government. Again and again it has been pointed out to the Congress—by territorial legislatures, by the delegates, by the federally appointed governors and finally by the whole Alaskan people, who on a referendum in 1952[69] asked Congress by a vote of 20,544 to 3,479 to transfer the complete control of the fisheries to the territory —that the concern of Alaskans would necessarily be greater, their association closer, their knowledge more intimate, their understanding of the problem clearer, and their devotion to its solution more intense.

But an absentee industry, wealthy and politically potent, little concerned with the morrow of Alaska's resources, has been able to thwart this logical aspiration and long-overdue change, abetted by a bureaucracy equally unwilling to yield an iota of its perquisites.

"It is evident," declared one Alaskan fisherman, voicing a widely prevalent Alaskan view, "throughout the history of the regulation of the salmon fishery in Alaska by the Department of the Interior that the Department had considered first the interest of the Alaska salmon industry, second the conservation of the fishery, and third the interest of the people of Alaska." [70]

But that was no less true of every other federal government department entrusted with that responsibility.

Why does not the industry itself see the light?

Why in the presence of *disaster*—officially so declared by the nation's highest authority—is it not willing to relinquish its stranglehold on what was once Alaska's greatest natural resource, and perhaps the nation's greatest fishery resource? Is it because it prefers to retain its privileged position? Is it because it has found that often even a small pack with higher prices is more profitable than a big pack?

It is the fishermen and the people of Alaska who are the victims of the vanishment. But the whole nation is also the loser. Transfer of the fisheries to Alaska would spell the banishment of the fish traps by its people, who, being set free, would follow the example of their fellow-citizens of California, Oregon and Washington, and of their neighbors in British Columbia. For that reason only has the canned-salmon industry opposed the transfer as it opposed and opposes the territory's graduation into statehood, which would bring the transfer automatically. Meanwhile a great national resource is being destroyed.

Nothing in the history or prospect of joint control by federal bureau and absentee industry gives hope of its restoration under those auspices.

Transportation: Tangled
Life Lines

> . . . American transportation . . . has been the vital factor in the national development of the United States.
> ARCHER B. HULBERT, 1920 [1]

> . . . In the development of our great country, transportation necessarily preceded the people . . .

> Alaska presents a unique and distinct situation transportationwise . . . in the fact that the development and maintenance of all means of transportation are primarily the responsibility of the Federal Government. . . .
> REPRESENTATIVE CHARLES A. WOLVERTON, OF NEW JERSEY, FOR THE COMMITTEE ON INTERSTATE AND FOREIGN COMMERCE, 1948 [2]

THE transportation-mindedness of Americans, as well as manifest need, has been reflected in the ceaseless strivings of Alaskans to secure for the territory the various means of transport enjoyed by their fellow-citizens in the United States. Alaska's distances intensified the need. They urgently required for the territory's settlement and development the faster methods of locomotion conceived by nineteenth- and twentieth-century inventiveness. It was largely an American inventiveness, too, with Robert Fulton, originator of the steamboat, Henry Ford, genius of the "horseless carriage," and the Wright brothers, Orville and Wilbur, who developed the first heavier-than-air flying machine. The locomotive, the other invention in the tetrad of transportation, by an Englishman, George Stephenson, we rapidly adopted: steel rails soon spanned the continent, linking its east and west, and making the abstraction *e pluribus unum* a material reality. While the successful establishment of an American merchant marine has lagged, and not until 1952 did the S.S. *United States*, on her maiden voyage, recapture the "blue ribbon of the seas" from nautically superior Britannia, Americans have made the greatest utilization on earth of all other forms of transportation. Railways, highways and airways early surpassed the rest of the world in mileage and usage—in the forty-eight states. But Alaska, a territory of the United States, similarly challenging with vastness and newness, and requiring a similar linkage, has lagged far behind.

The lag in Alaska, as in all else, was due to factors beyond the reach and control of Alaskans. Their concern for the removal of distantly man-made obstacles, for the installation and improvement of those vital arteries through which the lifeblood of commerce would course, was expressed in their recurrent legislative memorials, far more of which were devoted to this one subject than to any other.

1. Shipping

Although physically a part of the North American continent, Alaska remains in effect an island, or two principal islands. For "the Panhandle" is barely connected with the main body of central and western Alaska by a narrow coastal fringe, rendered impassable by the great glaciers flowing into the sea from the towering Fairweather and St. Elias ranges. Actually hundreds of islands also compose Alaska. Indeed southeastern Alaska is predominantly the Alexander Archipelago; its numerous islands are more extensive than its mainland. On them are situated the cities of Ketchikan, Wrangell, Petersburg and Sitka, and the smaller communities of Craig, Klawock, Kake, Angoon and Hoonah. On islands, too, are dozens of salmon canneries—known to sea-borne commerce as "irregular ports." Across the Gulf of Alaska, Kodiak Island, as large as Puerto Rico, houses its growing city and navy base, headquarters of the Seventeenth Naval District. Beyond the tip of the Alaska Peninsula, sweeping westward in a nine-hundred-mile crescent, are the Aleutians. Excepting Fairbanks, every important Alaskan community is on salt water. Despite the vast interior, Alaskans are primarily a littoral people.

Maritime transportation, "Alaska's life line," was until 1940 the only link between the States and Alaska. It continues to be the essential conveyor of the freight which constitutes their commerce.

Its pattern was established by two words in the Maritime Act of 1920, which foreclosed the alternatives of shipment through Vancouver and Prince Rupert, both more economical for Alaskans, and made Seattle the port through which the Alaska trade would have to pass. At the same time that the monopoly for that city of the Alaska traffic was established by legislative enactment and judicial fiat, the mold of a maritime-transportation monopoly was likewise designedly cast. Before long the Alaska Steamship Line had absorbed the Pacific Steamship Line. In the absence of competition high rates rose higher and service deteriorated. Discriminatory tariffs continued to work further injury. All this was old in Alaska, almost as old, though not quite, as some of the ships on the Alaska run.[3]

The Fourteenth Territorial Assembly convened in January of 1939. It was the last legislature to function in an era of calm. That war would burst eight months later over Europe and before long extend to Alaska was undreamed of. Conditions in the territory appeared relatively prosperous. The fisheries had reached and for several years maintained an unprecedented volume, and their decline, though apprehended by fishermen, was not anticipated by the industry or the business community. Gold production, profiting by the price increase promulgated six years earlier, was rising steadily. Alaska, too, was reaping the benfits of various governmental innovations: the P.W.A. and W.P.A. were building works, great and small, and furnishing local employment. The C.C.C. was further taking care of locally needed projects, and affording young men a healthful livelihood. New homes financed by the Federal Housing Administration were under construction, supplying a growing need. Social security had been extended to Alaskans two years earlier. John W. Troy, old-time and beloved Alaskan, was Governor. In Washington Anthony J. Dimond was setting new high standards of solicitude for his constituents' wants, and was being regularly returned as Delegate to Congress, twice without opposition, by an appreciative electorate. There was little excitement in the political field. No important legislation which a territorial legislature might enact was in prospect.

Yet Alaska's reiterated requirements, and, by now, classic demands, had not abated one whit. The fourteenth legislature might not have much to legislate about, but in the fields where after twenty-six years it was still forbidden to tread, it was as deeply interested—and as vocal—as its predecessors.

The 1939 legislature adopted memorials urging the transfer of the fisheries and game management to the territory,[4] and for good measure a half-dozen additional memorials emphasizing the various shortcomings of federal control in these activities.[5]

It adopted a memorial against reservations and withdrawals in general.[6]

It adopted a specific memorial against fisheries reservations, against fisheries reservations exclusively for Indians, and against having commercial activities within these reservations specifically exempted from territorial taxation to which similar enterprises not on reservations were subject.[7]

It adopted an even more specfic memorial asking Congress not to withdraw Admiralty Island (one hundred miles long and twenty-five miles wide) as a bear refuge—a move seriously threatened by Secretary of the Interior Harold L. Ickes, who, thwarted in his effort to get the Forest Service transferred from Agriculture to Interior, contemplated this method of piecemeal annexation of that large area of the Tongass National Forest as a substitute.[8]

It protested against the terms of the Oil Leasing Act of February 25, 1920 (41 Stat. 447), which compelled prospectors to exchange their permits for leases before adequate time had been given for prospecting.[9]

It addressed memorials to the Secretary of Agriculture urging action to establish a pulp and paper industry in Alaska's national forests,[10] and that a similar effort be made to foster small wood-working industries.[11]

It adopted a memorial asking for additional hospital facilities to treat tuberculosis among the native population.[12]

And it adopted memorials dealing with all forms of transportation, highways, the Alaska Railroad, aviation and ocean shipping. For the moment we shall concern ourselves only with the last of these. They were two, one asking that the discriminatory provision against Alaska in the Jones Act be deleted by congressional amendment,[13] and the other requesting an investigation of maritime freight rates.[14]

"Freight tariffs," said the memorial, "have been increased to a point where they are now excessive and beyond the value of the service rendered," and that further anticipated increases would threaten "the entire economy and well-being of Alaska."

Substantial increases had been effected two years earlier, and 1939 offered the first legislative opportunity to protest against them.

Of the carriers operating between Puget Sound and Alaska at that time, first and foremost was the Alaska Steamship Company. It had been owned for nearly a third of a century by the Morgan-Guggenheim Alaska Syndicate. Its seventeen vessels—eleven combination passenger and cargo, and six cargo only, totaling 69,018 gross tons—served "all Alaska" from Ketchikan to Nome. Three lesser carriers were Northland Transportation Company, one-third owned by Gilbert W. Skinner of Seattle, one-third by his son David E. Skinner, having also canning interests in western Alaska, with five ships, three passenger and cargo, and two cargo, aggregating 14,405 tons; Alaska Transportation Company, serving southeastern Alaska only, with three freighters with a total tonnage of 3,675, principally owned by Norton Clapp, Tacoma capitalist, whose other Alaska interest centered in the fishery cold-storage activities of the newly created community of Pelican on Chichagof Island; and the Santa Anna Steamship Company, which had one freighter serving Goodnews Bay and the Kuskokwim.

The federal regulatory agency at that time was the United States Maritime Commission created in 1936 (49 Stat. 1985) which replaced a similar agency, the United States Shipping Board, established twenty years earlier (39 Stat. 728). Both bureaus were identical in being directed by a board or commission of five appointed by the President with the advice and consent of the Senate. The newer agency inherited and took over the operating officialdom from its predecessor.

The Maritime Commission, after considerable prodding, was persuaded to undertake the investigation requested by the legislature, and scheduled it for the summer of 1940. However, before the examination into the alleged excessiveness of the rates could take place, the carriers had sought and secured from the Maritime Commission an approximately 15 per cent increased schedule of passenger and freight rates, to become effective on May 20th of that year. The commission's action was a manifest contradiction of its purpose to investigate the previously existing rates. In answer to emphatic Alaskan protests, the commission on May 14th suspended the later increases, pending the results of its inquiry. But in answer to the carriers' plea that the higher tariff become effective—provided they would keep the increased revenues in a special account, and if denied increases, would refund the difference to the persons who had paid the May 20th tariff—the commission reversed itself on May 28,

1940, vacated the order of suspension, and allowed the increases to go into effect.[15]

The extreme complexity and costliness of refunding to hundreds of shippers and passengers who would travel or ship in the next eight or nine months was suggestive of the conviction on the part of both transportation companies and of the commission's officials that the increases would stand regardless of what the investigation might disclose.

The commission's investigators—accountants, rate experts and attorneys versed in their subject—held hearings in Alaska ports, questioned shippers, merchants and consumers, collected extensive data. They found that not only were the May increases not justified, but that certain of the previous charges were "unjust and unreasonable"; that some shippers were given lower rates than others for the same commodities from the same locality; and that undue preferential rates were given the canned-salmon industry, both in violation of the Shipping Act of 1916. They found that canned-salmon cases, southbound, and supplies and materials for the canneries, northbound, were receiving a substantially lower rate than other goods.[16]

The United States Maritime Commission, however, as its earlier action foreshadowed, disregarding the findings of its own investigators and allowed the increases virtually in toto.

As a result of the increases granted the carriers in 1940, the net earnings after taxes in 1941 increased by 14.8 per cent for the Alaska Steamship Company and 27.8 per cent for the Northland Transportation Company.[17]

On the next to last day of that year, December 30, 1941, and three weeks after the entry of the United States into World War II, the Alaska Steamship Company petitioned the Maritime Commission for permission to levy a 45 per cent surcharge on Alaska rates. The requested increase was granted without investigation or hearing on January 7th for all the carriers. The request was based and granted in anticipation that submarine warfare would take a heavy toll of ships on the Alaska run, and was designed to meet the increased costs of marine insurance and wage bonuses for perilous service. But submarine warfare did not materialize in Alaskan waters. In response to emphatic Alaskan protests the surcharge was reduced, three months later, to 25 per cent for southwestern Alaskan ports and 20 per cent for southeastern ports. The second surcharge was fixed as arbitrarily and as unscientifically as the first. It remained in effect long after Alaska had ceased to be a theatre of war operations. On April 1, 1944, the surcharge was fixed at 16 per cent and remained there.[18]

In 1944, the Alaska Steamship Company, after a distribution of $3,000,000 in dividends, was sold to the Skinner family for $4,290,-000. The Skinners now controlled both it and the Northland Transportation Company.[19]

During World War II the Alaska carriers had operated their ships under the control of the War Shipping Administration, which was none other than the United States Maritime Commission clothed with emergency powers. With the cessation of hostilities on August 14, 1945, and the prospective return to peacetime shipping operations, the Alaska carriers declared they would require a 108 per cent increase in rates. The Alaska public through its officials called for a demonstration of the necessity for such increase. Congressional hearings designed to seek a solution of the Alaska shipping problem were begun in the summer of 1946.[20]

These hearings developed, through Office of Price Administration studies, that Alaska steamship rates were already far higher than any others in the world. They were from two to three times higher on various commodities than rates charged by other American flag carriers for comparable distances between San Francisco and Honolulu.[21] Carrier representatives stressed the special difficulties surrounding Alaska shipping operations. But no explanation was made why rates to Ketchikan, 742 miles from Seattle, were 50 per cent, and more, higher than to Prince Rupert, on the same route, subject to identical conditions, and only ninety miles nearer to Seattle.[22]

The proportion of freight costs of building materials paid by Alaska retailers—that is, the percentage of increase of the landed cost in Alaska over the Seattle wholesale price—ranged, in some items, from well over 50 per cent in Juneau to over 100 per cent in Seward. In the case of one product the added landing cost was nearly 200 per cent in Juneau and nearly 300 per cent in Seward, viz. shingles, 53 per cent; cement, plaster, 68 per cent; drain tile, 70 per cent; sewer pipe, 187 per cent—in Juneau. The corresponding figures for Seward were: 108 per cent, 103 per cent, 100 per cent, 280 per cent.[23]

Comparison of the railroad freight costs from the points of origin in the United States and the additional costs by steamship from

Seattle to Alaskan ports emphasized, the O.P.A. reported, "rather strikingly the weight of the freight burden which Alaskans are required to pay for the ordinary necessities of life." [24]

To haul a crated davenport by rail from the factory in San Francisco to Seattle, a distance of 906 miles, cost $1.44. To carry the same davenport from Seattle to Juneau, a distance of 1,000 miles, cost $11.34; to Seward, a distance of 1,800 miles, cost $15.31. An enameled bathtub, crated, from Chicago to Seattle, a distance of 2,099 miles, cost $7.24; from Seattle to Juneau, $8.92, and to Seward $13.20. An electric refrigerator manufactured at Dayton, Ohio, 2,348 miles away, cost $7.33 to haul to Seattle, and $13.47 to carry from Seattle to Juneau. [25] Consignees in Anchorage or Fairbanks would pay the additional rail charges from Seward north.

Much corroborative and additional testimony came from Alaskans.

Mr. Al Anderson, Secretary of the Alaska Miners' Association, testified that "the mining industry cannot absorb the increase in freight rates and prosper and develop," and that "the mining industry feels it is already paying too much for what it gets as far as transportation is concerned." [26]

Mr. Homer Garvin, a furniture dealer, representing the Juneau Merchants' Association, testified as to some of the additional items of cost that the operations through the port of Seattle entailed. Owing to its lack of adequate warehouse facilities, trucks conveying furniture for shipment had to stand in line for hours, thereby quadrupling the cost of the drayage. To this were then added the actual steamer transportation costs. [27]

Mr. Charles E. Wortman, druggist, testified that on "many commodities and items," arriving at Sitka, which he represented at the hearings, "the freight rate actually exceeds the cost of the item." [28]

Representative Fred L. Crawford, R., of Michigan, cited testimony that the freight on a $29 baby carriage ordered from a mail-order house in the States, was $39. "Economic guillotining," he called it. [29]

Wilfred G. Stump, attorney, representing the Ketchikan Chamber of Commerce, touched on a deep-seated Alaskan grievance—the high interport rates—stressed at these and subsequent hearings. [30] These rates rendered it unprofitable for a local industry to ship its goods to nearby Alaskan ports, since those rates were as high as the rate from Seattle:

"There have been several times that a shingle mill has tried to start in Ketchikan and Wrangell, but the cost of shipping shingles from Ketchikan to Juneau is almost as much as shipping those shingles from Seattle to Juneau." [31]

The tariff, in other words, favored the Puget Sound shingle industry and limited the would-be Ketchikan manufacturer to local sales, as it favored other Seattle producers with whom Alaskan enterprises sought to compete within the territory. Thus American maritime policy, in regard to Alaska, was throttling territorial economic development in behalf of businesses in the steamship company's home port of Seattle.

Other preferential rates receiving criticism were those applying to southbound canned salmon as compared with northbound consumer goods. That the latter were paying more than their share of the total cost of steamship operation and that the salmon industry was thereby unduly favored at the expense of the Alaska public was the contention of the Office of Price Administration and of the territory's attorneys.[32] The Alaska Syndicate, the previous owner of the Alaska Steamship Company, had had both mining and canning interests in Alaska, and their tariffs had favored both of these.[33] The Skinner family, which succeeded to the ownership of the Alaska Steamship Company and to two-thirds of Northland Transportation Company, was also in the canned-salmon business with an interest in three canneries in western Alaska, as well as in the salmon-brokerage business in Seattle.[34] The charge that this practice was in violation of the Shipping Act of 1916 had been made in 1940 by United States Maritime Commission's own attorneys, Mr. David E. Scoll and Mr. Samuel D. Slade.[35] "The respondents' whole system of charges unduly favors the canneries," affirmed the commission's authorized legal representatives.[36]

The Maritime Commission ignored these charges. Questioned by the counsel of the House Merchant Marine Committee, Mr. Marvin J. Coles, about them, Mr. George E. Talmadge, representing the commission, replied:

"There were, in United States Maritime Commission Docket 651, allegations made and I believe some evidence offered that there was unjust discrimination or undue preference and privilege between the rates on canned salmon and the rates on consumer goods going to

Alaska. The Maritime Commission made no findings that there was such unlawfulness in the rates in its decisions dismissing the petition."

"MR. COLES: 'Was there a contrary finding that there was not such unlawfulness?'

"MR. TALMADGE: 'There was not.' "[37]

Faced with the necessity of re-establishing transportation on a peacetime basis, the Congress considered legislation making available to the private operators government ships at a charter hire of $1 a year and providing also for their marine insurance. The purpose of this subsidization, in the words of the bill's sponsor, Representative Henry M. Jackson, D., of Washington, was "in order that freight rates might be consistent with a healthy Alaska economy." [38] Impressed by the evidence of the burdensomeness of the Alaskan rates, the subcommittee hoped for their reduction through Public Law 12, which was enacted March 7, 1947 (61 Stat. 10). Nevertheless the carriers promptly demanded an over-all increase of 35 per cent. When Alaskans requested hearings in which to present their case, and ascertain the justification for the new demands, the steamship companies served notice that they would not continue service unless the increases were granted prior to any hearings.[39]

The Eighteenth Territorial Legislature, assembling in January of 1947, met the threat with the suggestion that other operators would be enlisted, possibly from Portland—which was beginning to show interest in the Alaska trade—that repeal of the Jones Act would be sought to permit Canadian vessels to serve Alaska if the Seattle ship companies would not, and concluded:

"Therefore your memorialist accepts the challenge laid down by the carriers, and directs its administrative officers to fight any increase in water-borne freight rates with every means at their disposal and hereby urges federal authorities to lend support to the Territory in this matter of national concern." [40]

Another memorial specifically requested repeal of the discriminatory language in the Jones Act, expressing the memorialists' feeling by declaring that "the discrimination of the Jones Act in favor of a few rundown Puget Sound ships is blocking movement of goods and passengers to Alaska in derogation of the territory's development and the national security," and further that "high freight rates had [have] obstructed Alaska's development for over thirty years, notwithstanding which substantial increases are proposed to bail out the present monopoly of the port of Seattle at the further expense of the industries and consumers of Alaska. . . ." [41]

Despite protests, the Maritime Commission granted, without a hearing and without modification, the increases requested.[42] They proved in reality to be far greater than the 35 per cent allegedly sought. In conjunction with the 16 per cent war surcharge, which remained in effect, the new tariffs increased the rate on fruits and vegetables 63.6 per cent above pre-war rates, 66.7 per cent on groceries, 71.4 per cent on furniture, 73.3 per cent on cement, 73.5 per cent on freight not otherwise specified, 74.2 per cent on meat, 77.8 per cent on lumber.[43]

The new schedule intensified the preferential treatment of the salmon industry as against the consuming public. The rate on canned salmon from Kodiak to Seattle which had been $7 a ton was increased to $12, while the rate on general merchandise between the same ports was increased from $16.50 a ton to $27. Other cannery items were similarly favored.[44]

In addition, the Maritime Commission gave three Alaska carriers (Alaska Steamship Co., Northland Transportation Co., Alaska Transportation Co.) exclusive contracts entitling them alone to the benefits of Public Law 12. Potential competitors from Portland, an independent operator who was seeking to enter the field, and any others who might be attracted by the unprecedented benefits made available by Congress, were debarred from the advantages of dollar-a-year ships and government-paid marine insurance.[45]

Besides confining the operation to Puget Sound operators, the commission further narrowed the field. The two companies controlled by Skinner and son were given twenty-one ships; their sole competitor, Alaska Transportation Company, was given only four, and despite its protests restricted to serving only southeastern Alaska.[46] Thus for the rest of Alaska was created a monopoly of one ownership.

Mr. Skinner, Senior, believed in monopoly in the Alaska shipping field, and said so:

". . . I do feel, and I have always felt," said he in reply to a question from Representative Thor Tollefson, R., of Washington, "that for the best interests of the territory a single operation of all the steamships is the most economical way to handle that trade." [47]

Mr. Skinner not only believed in monopoly but translated his beliefs into action. "Have you ever interfered, or particularly tried to keep other people from getting a charter under Public Law 12?" asked Senator Homer Capehart, R., of Indiana. Had Mr. Skinner, the Senator inquired further, ever tried to keep others "from operating ships into Alaska or establishing a new line?"

"MR. SKINNER: 'You mean other operators from Puget Sound, or other operators from—'

SENATOR CAPEHART: 'Either one.'

MR. SKINNER: 'We have used all of the influence we have to prevent that; yes, sir.' " [48]

Bills to repeal the discriminatory provision of the Jones Act by changing the word "excluding" to "including" and modifying earlier provisions of the Merchant Marine Act of June 19, 1886, were introduced in the Eightieth Congress by Delegate Bartlett in the House and by Senators Hugh Butler and Homer Capehart in the Senate. The former was then Chairman of the Committee on Interior and Insular Affairs which passed on all general legislation relating to Alaska, and the latter was chairman of the subcommittee on Alaska matters of the Committee on Interstate and Foreign Commerce to which legislation relating to all forms of transportation was referred. It was, to all appearances, a potent sponsorship. Senator Butler's presentation of his bill was vigorous and uncompromising. In a written communication to his colleague's subcommittee he referred to the speech he had made on the Senate floor, when introducing his bill on December 4, 1947, "on the discrimination against the Territory of Alaska in the present law, and of the need for the prompt removal of that discrimination if we are to demonstrate that we are in earnest in our determination to promote the development of Alaska."

The laudable purpose to build up the American merchant marine, Senator Butler continued, had not been achieved:

"Today, after twenty-seven years of operation under the Jones Act of 1920, the carriers have failed to establish satisfactory Alaskan service. The territory still is without adequate transportation to meet its needs.

"There are only six privately owned ships being operated in the Alaskan trade. Even these six are worn-out, antiquated vessels entirely unsuited to the present-day requirements of the Alaska trade." [49]

Turning to other reasons why the act of 1920 had "hindered and continues to greatly hinder, the development of Alaska," Senator Butler declared:

"Most Alaskan coastal towns are not connected with the continental United States, or with each other, by highway or rail. Accordingly, they have been at the mercy of a steamship monopoly of long duration. There could be no competition from rail or bus lines which would compel better services or lower rates. American steamship lines have not been able or willing to meet Alaska's transportation requirements. The service has been infrequent and the rates exorbitant."

After elaborating on the damaging effects on Alaska of the Jones Act and the fact that most of the "merchandise . . . food products and . . . other commodities" shipped to Alaska were "an exclusive Seattle prerogative," Senator Butler stated:

"The passage of this amendment to the Jones Act could well mean the difference between the slow, continued, strangulation of Alaska's economy, and the full development of the territory's vast potentialities."

He spoke of the discriminatory rates in favor of canned salmon, saying:

"The people of Alaska have long been subject to higher rates than has the salmon industry for general cargo. These higher rates are, in fact, a decree penalizing the resident Alaskan for living in Alaska; the lower rates are, in effect, a decree requiring the Alaska resident to make up for whatever deficits accrue from the costs of shipping canned salmon and salmon-cannery needs." And urging early and favorable action by the committee he concluded:

"The strangling provisions of the present laws would be eliminated by the enactment of S. 1834. The development of Alaska would be accelerated, and justice would be done to those permanent residents of our northwestern frontier who have, for so many years, struggled valiantly against discouraging circumstances to develop that area." [50]

Despite these brave words of a powerful committee chairman at a time when his party had a substantial majority in both houses of Congress, and when also the President of the United States, of the opposite party, officially supported the move,[51] Senator Butler's bill met the usual fate of legislation beneficial to Alaska when it conflicted with even a relatively minor stateside economic interest. Neither his nor Senator Capehart's similar measure even emerged from the committee. Nor did the subcommittee of which Senator Capehart was chairman so much as bother to report on his own or his colleague's bill after the two days of hearings thereon. Both were "sunk without trace" in the vasty deep which lies between a territory and a state.

Meanwhile Public Law 12 was due to expire on June 30, 1948. Should it be renewed? President Truman recommended its extension with modifications, saying that the "nominal-rate charters of surplus government vessels to private operators," had proved of "aid sufficient to keep shipping in the Alaska trade," but that it could "be administered to achieve even more desirable rate and service standards." "The modifications," he continued, "should prevent exclusive arrangements with any carriers and should provide financial incentives for efficient operations." [52]

The carriers let it be known that unless free ships and insurance continued the rates would have to be increased another 37.5 per cent, and supported various bills, which they had helped draft to complete the transition to peacetime operation. Delegate Bartlett introduced another, representing territorial desires and embodying the modifications President Truman had endorsed. Alaskans had been bitterly disappointed at the result—for them—of Public Law 12. They felt that some form of subsidy was justified, not merely because of the discrimination in the Jones Act, but because Alaskan shipping was held to be "coastwise," and therefore denied the substantial subsidies which all American flag lines engaged in overseas foreign trade received. Yet the Alaska trade vessels left port in the States and traveled seven hundred miles through open sea or within the coastal limits of a foreign nation before entering territorial waters. (The Virgin Islands, an insular possession of the United States, shortly after its transfer from the U. S. Navy to the civilian rule of the Department of the Interior, had, in order to assist its economy, been excluded, by specific legislation [49 Stat. 1207], amending the Maritime Act of 1920, from the restrictions of the coastwise laws.)

So Alaskans could see little advantage in extending this legislation, unless in return for the very generous benefits conferred on the carriers[53] such legislation forbade the exclusive contracts wrought by the Maritime Commission and thereby permitted competition; and unless, by the same token, it provided for the elimination of discriminatory rates, either in favor of one industry or penalizing Alaskan interport traffic. The carriers opposed these desired amendments which would have allowed more of the benefits of the subsidization to reach the Alaskan public.

Nor were some of the interested members of Congress pleased with the administration of Public Law 12. Its sponsor, Representative Henry M. Jackson, pointed out that the purpose of the act had been twofold: to give relief to the Alaska economy to the extent that free ships and insurance would achieve that end, and to provide a period of study for the Maritime Commission to work out a permanent solution. In furtherance of the latter objective the act required the commission to make various reports at not more than ninety-day intervals on the conduct of operations under the act. This, Representative Jackson informed Congress, the commission had not done:

"In my opinion, the commission did not comply fully with the letter and certainly not with the spirit of this provision of the law."

For a year or more Representative Jackson had been trying to get an audit of the companies' books and detailed accounting of their financial condition, but had been able to get only a preliminary report. This, however, revealed that the Alaska Steamship Company had made profits nearly twice as large as it had reported:

"It will be noted," said Representative Jackson, "that in the report the Alaska Steamship Company's statement shows a profit of $678,093 before federal income taxes, and the audit of the Maritime Commission shows a profit of $1,348,716.64—nearly a 100 per cent discrepancy." 54

The company had not included in its report on profits those made by the operation of its subsidiaries, the Alaska Terminal and Stevedoring Company and the Ketchikan Wharf Company. Through these it funneled ship repairs without competitive bidding at cost plus 20 per cent profit. These profits the Alaska Steamship Company did not allocate to ship operations.55

Representative Jackson asked that the matter be further and fully investigated. But the further and fuller investigation did not follow. What followed were further rate increases, granted without audit or investigation by the United States Maritime Commission, which in the absence of specific legislation continued to supply the carriers with ships at somewhat higher, but still moderate rates.

Before long the Alaska Transportation Company retired from the field. It had been hopelessly boxed by its more powerful and influential competitors.[56] With this smaller enterprise eliminated there was no longer the necessity for two lines under the same control, and Northland Transportation Company was merged into the Alaska Steamship Company.

However, other competition was coming without government assistance. Late in 1947, the experiment of freighting on large barges towed by tugs from Puget Sound to the rail belt was tried and proved feasible. The terminal port could be either Seward or war-born Whittier on Portage Bay, Prince William Sound. Whittier, a new port, had been promoted by Colonel Otto F. Ohlson, then General Superintendent of the Alaska Railroad, to save the time and cost of transportation over the steep grades on the also poorly maintained roadbed of the first sixty-three miles north from Seward. The Army, with its important headquarters base at Fort Richardson, and the conversion of Ladd Field into an operating base, required more port facilities and welcomed not only the additional dock space and shorter haul, but the additional security of two ports instead of one. It soon took over Whittier entirely and made it wholly a military port.

Some of the barging operations were short-lived. But a combination barge and trucking operation under the name of Alaska Freight Lines was developed successfully by a young Fairbanksian, Al Ghezzi, who had begun at age sixteen as a truck driver. His transportation service started with freight driven over the Alaska Highway, made available after the war to civilian traffic. This long haul proved unprofitable. Gradually he worked out a method by which trucks were driven from the warehouse to the dock at Seattle and Tacoma, motor and chassis then disconnected, and the truck body containing the freight lifted onto a barge. The barge was then towed to the Alaska terminal of Haines or Valdez—and later, when the highway connecting Seward with Anchorage was completed, to Seward. At these ports the truck body would be swung onto wheels, hitched to the motive power and driven to Anchorage, Fairbanks or intermediate points. Fairbanks was the chief beneficiary of this service, which could cut the costs of combined steamship and rail haul. It likewise eliminated one serious difficulty that had been encountered on the docks and on shipboard—pilferage of cargo.[57]

Another entrant into the Alaska maritime lists was the Coastwise Line, which, with cargoes originating in Los Angeles, San Francisco

and Portland, carried them principally to the rail-belt ports and Kodiak, and occasionally to Cordova and Valdez. These freighters were
able to save the steps, costly in the aggregate, of transporting goods
produced in or near Los Angeles, San Francisco and Portland, to the
railroad station, loading them onto freight cars, paying rail freight to
Seattle, unloading them there onto trucks and transferring them
across Seattle to the docks, again unloading them and loading them
onto the Alaskan-bound vessels. Thus for the first time two new types
of competition were introduced into the Alaska maritime trade,
one by a different and less costly method of transportation, the other
by traffic, also less costly, originating in different areas in the States,
and making the products of these regions in California and Oregon
directly available to Alaskans. Neither of these services was available
to southeastern or northwestern Alaska.

The competition, moreover, had beneficial effects on the practices
of the Alaska Steamship Company. In 1953 it introduced large metal
containers for the packaged cargo, thus protecting it against pilferage.
Early in 1954 it began trucking north from Valdez—in the same
manner as Alaska Freight Lines—the cargo destined for the air bases
at Eielson and Big Delta on the Richardson Highway.

Savings in costs, and greater assurance of delivery of merchandise,
were becoming, in the post-war years, of vital importance. For those
were years of frequent interruption in the shipping services due to
labor-management disputes, work stoppages, for one reason or another, and jurisdictional strikes.

Maritime workers before the nineteen thirties were underpaid,
wretchedly accommodated and highly insecure wage-earning members of society. They were blacklisted for trivial causes and their livelihood earned on what had been termed by an industry official a
"sweatship." Gradually, as a result of unionization, federal labor legislation and strikes, they achieved better pay and decent quarters on
shipboard. The exigencies of war, and the necessity to "keep the
ships running," enabled organized maritime labor at sea and on the
docks further to improve its economic status, and greatly to increase
its power. No leveling off, or moderation, came with the phenom-
enal betterment of its condition. Nor did increased power generate
a corresponding sense of responsibility.

The working day was steadily shortened—not in order to diminish
the physical strain of shipboard or longshore labor, which was in-

creasingly mechanized, but to move as rapidly as possible into "overtime" rates. Base pay on shipboard, where there are no living costs for the men, was, and is, in effect, merely a "retainer." All work, Saturdays and Sundays, on the high seas as well as in port, is "overtime." All work, weekdays, between 5 P.M. and 8 A.M. is also "overtime."

Analysis of the costs of a twenty-nine-day motorship voyage in 1951 from Seattle to Alaskan ports and return, of the *Coastal Monarch*, showed nine seamen receiving, in addition to $240.22 base pay, $649.39 overtime, a total of $889.61, while the master of the ship received $874.10. Under the increases granted by the 1953 scale, the seamen thereafter received for the same services $291.94 base pay and $782.30 overtime, a total for the voyage of $1,082.24, while the master received $1,142.67.[58]

"Featherbedding" practices have increased. One of the most flagrant is the payment of "penalty time" to sailors while they are idling, resting or sleeping below deck and others are working cargo. This payment, for what is known as "sack time," was instituted in 1947. The rate for not working has risen with the other increases. The 1953 agreement between the Pacific Maritime Association, the employers' agency, and the Sailors' Union of the Pacific, both with headquarters at San Francisco, provided as follows for the Alaska trade:

"*Section 133. Rest Period.*

"(a) In ports where sailors shall be required to work cargo, one full watch shall go below the second meal hour after cargo work starts and stay below until the following meal-hour period.

"Upon the watch below resuming work another watch shall go below for a rest period until the next meal hour, and this rotation shall continue until cargo operations are completed.

"The penalty rate of $1.95 per hour shall be paid deck-crew members on rest period as long as crew members continue to work cargo or until the cargo operations are completed." [59]

Since an Alaska voyage is generally not, as on many ship routes, from terminus to terminus, but includes a half-dozen or more ports, this burden is particularly heavy in that trade. All Alaskans work: there is no leisure class in Alaska. Their labor is paying—in increased transportation costs passed on in the price of every commodity—for the sailors while they loaf.

The operators' complaint has been directed not so much against the high wages, although they have made the Alaska trade crewmen virtually the highest paid unskilled and semi-skilled workers of our time, but at the steadily lessening amount of work performed per man, and the lengthening of the voyages thereby with consequently diminishing proceeds on ship and cargo.[60]

Alaskans have ever been acutely conscious of the direct relation between their cost of living and the cost of transportation. That consciousness was the natural result of being at the end of a long line, or a series of long lines. A cost-of-living study made by the Juneau local of the National Federation of Federal Employees in 1941 showed that costs rise proportionately to the distance of shipment from the States. Using the national capital as a basis of reference, the study showed that the cost of living was 35.52 per cent higher in Ketchikan than in Washington, D.C., 38.84 per cent higher in Petersburg, 49.40 per cent in Juneau, 59.82 per cent in Sitka. (Sitka demonstrates the point clearly; although nearer "as the crow flies" to Seattle, its maritime route was, and is, by way of Juneau.) In Seward the increased cost was 60.73 per cent, in Cordova, 75.59 per cent, in Anchorage 88.85 per cent, and in Fairbanks, 116.16 per cent.[61] (Cordova, although a hundred and fifty miles nearer to Seattle on the course to Seward, is not an exception to the rule, since some ships are routed there on the return journey.)

The testimony of Alaskans on the effect of high freight rates is overwhelming and unvarying.[62]

"Alaska must rely upon dependable water transportation at reasonable rates for its existence and development," stated George Sundborg, consultant and later manager of the Alaska Development Board. "High transportation rates are responsible, more than any other factor, for the economic backwardness of Alaska, and for a cost of living level so high as to discourage settlement, year-around residence, and industrial and other development." [63]

"You gentlemen, in your short stay in Fairbanks . . . have noticed the lack of modern homes . . . that you would see in communities in the United States that would have a comparable age," said Stanley Tatom, president of a machinery-distributing company, and at the time also President of the Fairbanks Chamber of Commerce, addressing a visiting congressional committee. "Also in the business district . . . there is a limited number of façade structures." The reason, he explained, was that concrete poured in the form was $30 a cubic yard in Fairbanks compared with $11.80 in Seattle.[64] The higher cost of cement and steel leads to continuation of the old practice of building with wood, and consequently higher fire-insurance rates—one of the numerous factors in the higher overheads for Alaska businessmen.

"Nothing . . . has prevented Alaska's growth as much as this lack of economical transportation," was the expressed belief of Edwin M. Suddock of Anchorage, President of Alaskan Merchandisers, a firm owned entirely by Alaskans.[65]

Shipping tie-ups damage Alaska incalculably and almost inconceivably, in the first instance, by skyrocketing costs. Alaskan communities do not have the freight-carrying alternatives that exist throughout the States: railways and trucks. Given Alaska's highly seasonal activity, an interruption for a few weeks at certain times often means the loss of a whole year for a construction project or business enterprise. Ship stoppages occurred with varying frequency in every year between 1946 and 1952. The Maritime Commission reported 127 days of no shipping in Alaska in 1946, but this by no means told the story, as the figure included only the general work stoppages, and not the innumerable single port "quickies" or "job actions," [66] often for the most trivial causes. But settlement of even a minor local dispute almost invariably was prolonged by the necessity of referral to either or both company and union executives from seven hundred to two thousand miles away in Seattle or San Francisco. Industry or union headquarters seldom delegate the authority to resolve locally a question that may involve only a few dollars to the presumably aggrieved parties, but before settlement may mean the loss of thousands of dollars to Alaskans.

In general tie-ups the actual number of days in which ships are idle conveys only a fraction of the extent of the interruption. Even after the vessels are permitted to resume service the accumulation on the docks at Seattle requires additional days for disposal. On top of that the steamship company notifies the railroads to embargo Alaska shipments until further notice, and the traffic jam extends back to the points of origin of the goods ordered for delivery in the territory.

Inter-union and even intra-union rivalries aggravate the difficulties. Many of the work stoppages originating variously with sailors, cooks and stewards, firemen and oilers, radiomen, even masters, mates and

pilots, or longshoremen and warehousemen, organized in some
twelve different unions, are due to the competitive struggle of A.F. of
L., I.L.W.U. and C.I.O West Coast leaders for power and the control of dues. One would suppose that having achieved what had become by mid-century an undeniably high standard of wage-income
and living on board ship, conditions which, for the work required,
surpass those in other fields of labor, some concern for the injury to
the people of Alaska, including their fellow-unionists there, would
temper the often irresponsible and ruthless performance of maritime-
union leadership in Seattle and San Francisco. Shipping stoppages
bring about the layoffs in Alaska of carpenters, plumbers, electricians, masons, painters, truck drivers—of labor, skilled and unskilled,
of all kinds—engaged in construction. But there has been little evidence that union solidarity in maritime labor headquartered in
Seattle or San Francisco, any more than in the fisheries, is not applied for its local self-interest first, last and only. The occasional
"relief ship" which the union bosses graciously consent to "release"
after long pleading, when dairy cows are being slaughtered in Alaska
for lack of feed, merely exemplifies the tyranny that distant men
exercise over Alaskans. Absentee government, absentee industry, and
absentee labor have been equally guilty.

One recurrent cause of trouble is the insistence of sailors resident
in Seattle to work cargo when boats are in Alaskan ports, to the exclusion, at least partially, of the local longshoremen. The dispute is
in essence jurisdictional, but, more importantly, it involves the basic
conflict between residents and nonresidents. The Alaska Steamship
Company, under pressure in its home port from union headquarters,
signs up with the sailors. Strife breaks out repeatedly when the ships
dock in Alaska, and the intermittently employed longshoremen there
are denied, or at least, limited in, the opportunity to work. It is another instance of discrimination against Alaskans wrought by absentee controls, by two of them, in this case, acting jointly. To the
sailors, already highly paid, unloading cargo in Alaskan ports merely
means additional income. To the Alaskan longshoremen it represents the only earnings they can get from their labor. It is argued
by the steamship company and the sailors that the number of longshoremen in each port is insufficient, which may be true of some
ports, though not of others, but their number is scarcely likely to
become sufficient under the exclusion imposed.[67]

One abuse, of multiple complicity, is the refusal, during a prolonged strike, to permit owners of personal property on the docks at Seattle to recover it for shipment to Alaska by air or truck. This happened to folks whose household goods, blankets and other articles they would need promptly on arrival were held as part of a program of pressure used by the parties to the controversy to compel the other to yield. The victims, however, were always Alaskans, who had no power to settle anything and were merely used as hostages. Then to add injury to injury, at the end of a long series of strikes, dock operators levied a demurrage penalty charge for every day that these goods had been held on the dock.[68]

A prolonged shipping blackout causes Alaskans, already heavily penalized by increased costs, to lose sight even of them, in their craving for delivery of essentials. Atrophy creeps into every walk of life when whole communities lack basic products for weeks. It is demonstrable that any prolonged interruption of maritime traffic, such as Alaska has repeatedly sustained, injures every Alaskan. At the very least it predicates an increased cost in the family budget in items that are unforegoable. In addition it sets up a chain reaction that reaches to the remotest corners of Alaska society. No comparable plight can exist in the forty-eight states.

It is almost impossible to enumerate the degrees and varieties of injury which repeated shipping tie-ups inflict on Alaskans. There is the ex-G.I. and his wife, come to start life in Alaska, who have invested their savings and the proceeds of a veteran's loan in a poultry farm and put their sweat and toil into it. The cost of air-flown feed is prohibitively high. The supply gives out; the chicks have to be slaughtered. Will these young folks, burdened with debt, have the heart to start all over again? Surely not, if they know that, after prodigious efforts and still greater sacrifice, the same crushing blow will descend upon them, and there is no prospect that it will not.[69]

Savings vanish, hopes are dashed, opportunities are destroyed. A small processor in the Anchorage area orders modern brick-making machinery from a manufacturer in North Carolina. Because of the uncertainties of the Alaska trade credit conditions are not comparable to those in the States. The purchaser's down payment has to be much larger—often for the full amount. When the machinery is ready for shipment, the railroad notifies the manufacturer that it has orders not to accept shipments because of the maritime tie-up.

After it ends the railroad still cannot accept the shipment "due to the accumulation and congestion at the port of Seattle." Before the railroad will accept, it requires a permit guaranteeing that the maritime carrier will also accept the freight. This the steamship company is often unable to do because of its own inability to forecast what one of the many unions concerned will do. Meanwhile the particular construction for which the brick is ordered can no longer be delayed. Arrangements are made for other materials and with other suppliers.[70]

Multiply these incidents a hundredfold with infinite variations, repeat them year after year, and the difficulties of building up the economy of Alaska at the end of so kinked a life line become clear.

The year 1952 was more than usually disastrous with tie-ups of eighty-six days' duration. A strike by the Sailors' Union of the Pacific against the Alaska Steamship Company only lasted from May 22nd to July 14th—normally Alaska's busiest season. An existing contract between the company and the S.U.P. was terminated by the latter, which demanded wage increases that the company refused to grant. All efforts at mediation and arbitration failed. The rail belt suffered less because of the Coastwise Line and Alaska Freight Lines which were not "struck." But hundreds of tourists from all parts of the United States arriving in Seattle, Alaska-bound, were obliged to cancel their vacation plans. Alaska lodge- and innkeepers, some of them opening up for the first time, others with their first prospect of a good season, having put all their savings and borrowings in the enterprise, were among the many who were severely hurt, if not ruined. A promising industry for Alaska—the tourist business—endeavoring to make its first real start after the creation by the 1951 legislature of the Alaska Visitors Association, partly financed by territorial appropriation and partly by public subscription, was nipped in the bud. The tourists who had journeyed from all parts of the United States to Seattle to take the uniquely beautiful "Inside Passage" trip to Alaska, which among American flag carriers was supplied only by the Alaska Steamship Company, had lost the first days of their vacation and the funds expended in reaching Seattle, for while their steamer fare was refunded—a total loss to the steamship company—plane accommodations to Alaska were not available, having already been booked to capacity.

Not only are these particular tourists unlikely to risk repetition of their disappointment and financial loss, but others will be deterred from coming, for the assurance of an Alaska voyage among travel agencies, booking prospective vacationists, has been nullified for some time to come. The reputation and prospect of Alaska as an ideal vacation resort, which it amply deserves, was thus injured immeasurably by distant factors wholly beyond the control of Alaskans.

In the fall of 1952 an intra-union fight involving only a few men in the dock foremen's union in Seattle tied up shipping for thirty-two days.

The recurring quarrels between steamship management and labor reach settlement—in which the Alaskans' interest is at best secondary, if not wholly disregarded—either before or after destructive suspension of a traffic essential primarily to Alaskans. The differences arising in Seattle or San Francisco, or referred there, are composed at constantly higher prices which Alaskans have to pay.[71] The national government which placed Alaska in its strait jacket is responsible in the first instance, and the industry and labor beneficiaries—both absentee to Alaska—resist any change which will diminish their sinecures, and are politically strong enough to prevail against the disenfranchised Alaskans.

Alaskans have hoped that with the vast amount of discussion of legislation designed to diminish industrial strife, the Congress would devise some measures which would recognize the great need—if not of Alaskans as people, then at least of the vast area which they occupy, in view of its national importance.

Interdiction of suspension in a vital industry, such as shipping is to Alaska; provision for compulsory arbitration; prohibition of jurisdictional strikes—all solutions which are opposed either by industry or labor, or both—would bring some improvement. But not one iota of permanent relief has been enacted into law, nor since the commendable congressional effort of Public Law 12, in 1947, even attempted.

The relation between maritime carriers and unions in the Alaska trade has been likened to two men—who, about to fight each other, settle their difference by turning on an innocent bystander and taking their quarrel out on him. The beaten-up bystander is Alaska. Alaska is a hostage, in the "protective custody" of those who firmly and jointly hold the other end of the life line. Alaskans have long been fearful that the already taut line may be pulled to the point of strangulation.

2. Air Transportation

"I thought I had seen and talked to air-minded people . . . but I had to come to Alaska to really find a place where air transportation is taken as a matter of course and has become a necessary adjunct to the economic life of the country," remarked Lieutenant-Colonel H. H. Arnold, commanding the first non-stop flight of Army airplanes to Alaska in 1934.[72]

That air transportation was already in full blast at the time of "Hap" Arnold's pioneering mission. It was intra-Alaskan aviation. It was wholly an Alaskan undertaking. Alaskan initiative and ingenuity had established internal communication through Alaska by air. Federal aid available under the Air Commerce Act of 1926 had not been forthcoming to Alaska as to other parts of the Union. But what the Alaskan bush pilots lacked in equipment and aids to aviation they made up in skill and courage. Commercial air contact with the outside world, on the other hand, which lay beyond the reach of Alaskans and required substantial capital and federal support, lagged far behind territorial enterprise.

Pan-American Airways had started its overseas service in 1927. By 1931 it had linked the United States with the Caribbean, Central and South America. In 1936 it established service across the Pacific. It was called "Pan-American" but the all-inclusive "Pan" did not include Alaska. Not until June, 1940, did it establish commercial service to Alaska, by clipper.[73] The first route from the outside world extended from Seattle to Ketchikan and Juneau, where it connected with services to Fairbanks, Nome and Bethel, previously established by Pan-American's purchase of the equipment and rights of Alaskan fliers and thereafter operated under the name of Pacific-Alaska Airways. It was a major event in Alaskan annals. It provided the first transportation link other than maritime with the States.

Alaskans promptly availed themselves of this new service, and the need and demand for more of the same followed forthwith. It was slow in coming. Six years later a visiting House Committee on Territories reported that while there were thirty-four air carriers operating within Alaska, but one air line was operating into the territory and its "fares are about three times those in the States." [74]

However, the war's ending stimulated action made possible by the

Civil Aeronautics Act of 1938 (52 Stat. 973). Military airports had come into being in Alaska and radio range stations were established. The Civil Aeronautics Board had under consideration the so-called Pacific Case, which would determine what routes should be flown across that ocean and by what carriers. Air-minded Alaskans, fully conscious that "North to the Orient" provided the shortest course along the Great Circle Route, were confident that for the first time in its history Alaska's geographic position would prove an asset, and inevitably be included importantly in any new pattern of westward flight. Their confidence seemed justified, moreover, when there emerged from the C.A.B. the report of its examiners, concurred in by the board's public counsel.

Their recommendations were threefold. Pan-American Airways was to be permitted to serve also Anchorage. A competitor was to be provided by a local carrier, Alaska Airlines. An entirely new airway was to be established over the Great Circle, connecting the eastern seaboard of the United States with the Far East by way of Chicago, the Twin Cities, Edmonton and Anchorage, the shortest possible route.

This solution seemed ideal to Alaskans, providing just what was needed. It gave the first outside carrier to serve Alaska access to the rapidly growing city of Anchorage, already on its way to becoming the territory's metropolis, connecting it directly with Seattle and obviating the awkward and delaying change of planes from Pan-American in Juneau to the two local carriers operating between Juneau and Anchorage—Alaska Airlines and Pacific Northern Airlines.

It provided competition for Pan-American, and, most important, competition from a local carrier, the one which had developed by far the largest intra-Alaskan air network. There had been a feeling among Alaskans that the large international carriers primarily regarded Alaska as a place to pass through in the establishment of global routes—a view that was confirmed by the testimony of Pan-American officials—[75] whereas a local carrier's interest would tend to insure distribution of air-borne goods and passengers from and to Alaska's remotest points, by tying its service with the "outside" directly into its intra-Alaskan network.

No less important to Alaska was the establishment of an entirely new overland route to the States, and—for the first time—to another part of the States. For Alaskan travelers to the Midwest or to the Atlantic seaboard and for the residents of these regions, it would provide service over the shortest distance and thus presumably the quickest and least expensive service, and would open up new contacts with new areas.

In short, Alaskans advisedly viewed the recommendations of the technically qualified experts, uninfluenced by political or special-interest pressures, but concerned only with the pertinent economic and logistical considerations, as a promise of a well-balanced air-transportation ration, which would provide the needed diversity of competition both between types of carriers and regions. Recommendation of which air line was to be the overland carrier was not made by the examiners.[76] That was left to higher authority.

Alaskans had rejoiced too soon. For hardly had the examiners' report seen the light of day than the Seattle Chamber of Commerce mobilized its Alaska Committee against the very concept of any commercial air service to or from Alaska—except by way of Seattle. The entire state of Washington congressional delegation lent its support. Given the great political strength inherent in a state delegation of two United States senators and six representatives, it was soon rumored that the overland route would be dropped from the finding in the Pacific Case.

Alaskans, after eighty years of experience, had learned to expect the discriminations they had suffered. But somehow when it came to air transportation, in which, within their limitations, they had pioneered and felt fully qualified to speak on, "enough was enough." Twenty-one Anchorage citizens chartered a plane and headed for Washington over the inland route which they had temptingly glimpsed in prospect and wanted to assure. On the way they stopped to plead their cause with the municipal authorities and chambers of commerce of Great Falls, Fargo, the Twin Cities, Milwaukee and Chicago. And they laid their case before President Truman in the White House.

Possibly as a result of this unprecedented action, a part, though a very small part, of the examiners' recommendations appeared to be salvaged. The Alaska carrier was eliminated. Pan-American was not permitted to go to Anchorage. The only new Alaska certifications were given to one carrier, Northwest Airlines, which was granted the northern route to the Orient and given both the Chicago–Edmonton–Anchorage overland, and the Chicago–Seattle–Anchorage certifications. Considering that there were seven applicants for any of these certifications, including, besides the Alaska carriers, such important American companies as United, T.W.A., Western and Pennsylvania Central (later Capital), the finding was, to say the least, unusual. (Pan-American was left with the central Pacific route, San Francisco and Los Angeles to the Orient via Honolulu.)

Before long it became apparent that the Seattle Chamber of Commerce and the Washington delegation had won their battle. A carrier does not compete with itself. Northwest Airlines established the same rates over the direct route, from Chicago overland to Anchorage of 2,874 miles, as over the Chicago–Seattle–Anchorage route, 325 miles longer. Moreover the equipment and service over the interior route was such as to discourage travel over it, a course suggested in the company's ticket offices. The service began with four flights a week contrasted with daily flights from Seattle, was reduced to three a week, and by 1953 to a single flight a week. The overland weekly flight was with a DC-4 as contrasted with daily Stratocruisers with pressurized cabins over the Midwest-Seattle-Anchorage route.

In the deterioration of the service over the inland route until it became a mere token, the interest of the eastern states, which coincided with Alaska's interest, was also sacrificed. Finding that in 1940, 74 per cent of the business in the Orient originated in the northeastern and middle eastern states, the board concluded:

"The data of record indicate quite clearly that a natural gateway to Oriental traffic in the United States is Chicago serving the eastern and central states. Seattle would serve the Northwest and Rocky Mountain regions.[77]

"The record shows a substantial community of interest between Alaska and the eastern portion of the United States, which would be served by a direct route from Chicago," [78] and so the board ordered:

"Northwest will be expected to provide service which not only fulfills the need of through traffic from the Chicago and Seattle gateways to the Orient, but also the needs of traffic between Chicago and Anchorage and between Seattle and Anchorage." [79]

The board's expectations were not fulfilled.

A new bureaucracy had been created by the Civil Aeronautics Act of 1938, and by amendments to it under Plan 4 of the Reorganization Act of 1939 (53 Stat. 561) which established the Civil Aeronautics Board on June 30, 1940. It was not surprising that these new agencies and Alaskans engaged in flying would soon come into conflict. Secton 401a of the act provided that no carrier could engage in air transportation unless a certificate of convenience and necessity had been issued to it. The provision itself was necessary as part of a program of control of a new and rapidly developing activity in the interest of safety for operators, passengers and public.

But the Washington officialdom, unaware of conditions in Alaska, and unmindful of the lack of other means of transportation and the dependence of small communities on air service, began interpreting the act as it would in densely settled portions of the United States provided with every other kind of transportation facility.

Less than nine months after the establishment of the C.A.B., the 1941 territorial legislature was voicing its protest against the manner in which certificates were being denied some operators and granted to others under restrictive conditions which prescribed and defined the area of each one's service. The legislature asked that "the privilege of engaging in air transportation as generally carried on in Alaska" be not denied, and pointed out how unworkable some of the allocations of routes had proved. It requested that "in that part of Alaska west of the Yukon Territory," certain modifications be made until such time as recommendations could be presented to the board, which would "more adequately reflect what is required from the public convenience and necessity in the western portion of Alaska and for the welfare of what had heretofore been a thriving industry which the territory cannot afford to have jeopardized." [80]

By stressing the area west of Yukon Territory, the memorialists excluded southeastern Alaska. The problem did not exist there. Southeastern Alaska was being adequately served by two well-managed companies, Ellis Airlines in Ketchikan and Alaska Coastal Airlines in Juneau, which were developing the largest seaplane operations in the world, wholly financed and conducted by local talent.

The lack of sufficient scheduled freight and passenger air service between Alaska and the States brought into action a great number of "non-scheds." Some twenty-six of these were operating toward the close of the war, bringing down the cost of air cargo and serving remote and isolated communities.

"The unscheduled air services have served tremendously to solve the transportation problems . . ." reported the House Committee on Territories in 1946.[81]

For a brief period the federal authorities appeared to have some understanding of Alaska's needs. In a "Notice of Proposed Rule-Making" on November 20, 1947, the Civil Aeronautics Board found a "need for a greater volume of air transportation of cargo between the continental United States and the Territory of Alaska," and declared that "the air carriers certificated for the Alaska–States service apparently are not able to supply the facilities necessary to satisfy the present demand for cargo service."

The board therefore proposed to grant exemptions not only to eleven Alaskan air carriers which held certificates for operation within Alaska, but to other carriers which had operated at least six round trips between Alaska and the States in the three months preceding October 31st of that year.[82]

The proposed order was "heartily endorsed" by the Navy Department[83] and by the Interior Department. In a long letter of commendation Interior Secretary Julius A. Krug said he had no doubt that the board's proposed action would "have the enthusiastic support of all Alaskans." [84]

However, Alaskans were not given the opportunity to vouchsafe their support. The larger carriers objected.[85] On March 10, 1948, by a simple press release, the board announced that "after further consideration . . . it had determined that the proposed action was not in the public interest."

The board's interpretation of "the public interest" thenceforth was increasingly not that of Alaskans as voiced by their elected representatives. For the board began cracking down on the non-scheduled operators, imposing restrictions which made their continuation more and more difficult. Although nothing had occurred to refute the board's publicly expressed view that the scheduled carriers it had certificated for service between Alaska and the states were not able to supply the facilities necessary to satisfy the demand, it was now accepting the view of those carriers. The Civil Aeronautics Act gave the board the power (under Section 416 b) to grant exemptions to non-scheduled carriers, but despite Alaskans' pleas it refused to do so.

In vain did the 1949 legislature in a memorial addressed to the C.A.B. point out that the alternative means of transportation available throughout the States, such as railways, trucks and bus lines did not exist in Alaska except in very limited areas, that the scheduled air lines had "never provided the type of service required in Alaska at rates which Alaska business and industry can afford to pay . . ." [86]

In vain did the delegate and other territorial officials protest: "It has been very hard to deal with the C.A.B.," Delegate Bartlett testified. "No progress at all has been made. One member in the privacy of his office said he did not care what Alaska wants." [87]

One by one the "non-scheds" were being extinguished. The 1951 legislature made another attempt to save them. It pleaded "that due consideration be given to the necessity of adequate air service for the territory and that the needs and wishes of the people of Alaska be respected." [88] But even while the legislative memorial was on its way to passage on March 17, 1951, the board was delivering the coup de grâce. On March 2nd it had amended its economic regulations to limit the non-scheds to three round-trip flights per month over major traffic segments and eight round trips between all other points—conditions under which none could operate profitably. The order was effective April 6th.

By great effort some interest was aroused in the Congress. A subcommittee of a Select Committee on Small Business of the United States Senate scheduled hearings both for Alaskan complaints and from non-scheduled carriers in the States, which, however, had by no means been annihilated.

Miss Sally Carrighar, a naturalist of standing and a well-known writer who had been living in Alaska, testifying to the value of the "non-sched" services, and the damaging effects in areas where they had been forced out of business, reported:

"The regional director for Alaska boasted to me that he had reduced the non-scheds from twenty-eight to four and that all the four are on the way out." [89]

Other testimony was that the scheduled carriers between Alaska and the States were not providing adequate service and that for a whole month Northwest Airlines had had to embargo all air freight to Anchorage. With coincident suspension of shipping the embargo was doubly serious. Air freight in that crisis had been carried by the last of the non-scheduled carriers.[90]

The subcommittee, headed by Senator John Sparkman, D., of Alabama, recommended:

"The board should act promptly to relieve the hardships it is imposing on Alaska through its restriction of flights from the United States. The board should recognize the special need for cargo transportation to Alaska and the lack of alternative forms of low-cost passenger service." [91]

The board did not act promptly, or indeed at all. It did not recognize Alaska's "special need."

While the last surviving "non-sched," Aircoach Transport Associates, was conducting—in the courts—a losing fight for life, the 1953 Alaska legislature repeated its predecessors' oft-reiterated pleas that Alaska needed non-scheduled flying and expressed the hope that the board would take some affirmative action in the pending States–Alaska Case. [92]

The States–Alaska Case which the Civil Aeronautics Board was considering in 1954 was a sequel to the United States–Alaska Service Case of 1951, which followed the Pacific Case of 1946. The judgment of the board in that earliest case, as far as the northern route across the Pacific and service to Alaska were concerned, had scarcely been vindicated, as the board's own comment revealed. Additional service to Alaska was clearly overdue. The board sought to supply it by adding a single Alaska carrier, Pacific Northern Airlines, to the service between Alaska and the States. The board in its previous decision had granted exclusive certification to that carrier for the Anchorage–Juneau run. In its decision of September 29, 1950, it gave P.N.A. also a certificate to fly between Anchorage and Seattle, either direct, or by way of Juneau. Ketchikan continued to be served by only one carrier, Pan-American, as was Fairbanks.

Five years earlier such a certification of an Alaska carrier would have greatly diminished the inadequacy of the Board's Pacific Case decision. But much had happened in the meantime. The territory's population had almost doubled, and despite all handicaps Alaska was burgeoning with new life which foreshadowed a steadily accelerating growth.

Cognizant of this situation, President Truman ordered a substantial addition to the board's certification, a power reserved for the chief executive by Section 801 of the Civil Aeronautics Act, which makes all board decisions relating to certification subject to his approval.

On May 18, 1951, the President ordered the certification also of another carrier, Alaska Airlines, to operate from Fairbanks, and established both for it and Pacific Northern that Portland, Oregon, should be a co-terminus with Seattle. Both these additions spelled important gains in service to Alaska. They meant that the two international carriers, Northwest, operating to Anchorage, and Pan-American, operating to Fairbanks, would each have competition to Seattle, and in both cases the competition of an Alaska carrier.

Both these certificates were made temporary, to expire in 1953, when the seven-year certification granted Northwest would also expire, thus enabling the board to appraise and determine—at one time —the requirements over the northern route to the Orient and of the States–Alaska traffic.[93]

Testimony at the hearings fully justified the President's amendments. It brought out that the resulting competition had kept the freight rates at reasonable levels, had actually reduced the passenger rates, and greatly improved the service.[94]

Making Portland a co-terminus with Seattle was not merely an acknowledgment of the nearness of these two cities to each other, and of Portland's revived interest in the Alaska trade, evidenced by the entry into the maritime-transportation field of the Coastwise Line. It would also benefit Alaska!

Seattle representatives, however, fought hard against the proposal itself and against the equal freight and passenger fares for both cities to and from Alaska, which were implicit in the co-terminal arrangement.

"It is the position of the Seattle Chamber of Commerce and the Seattle Traffic Association that we strongly oppose the common rating of Portland with Seattle," testified Mr. J. D. Paul, who represented both. To grant such equality ". . . with respect to air freight rates to and from Anchorage, Fairbanks and other points in Alaska . . . removes Seattle's natural geographic advantage." [95]

"The growth and development of Seattle and Alaska have been synonymous," Mr. Paul stressed subsequently. ". . . Seattle's economy is geared to the economy of Alaska . . . Alaska is Seattle's best customer and Seattle is Alaska's best supplier." [96]

Alaskans did not agree; Fairbanks and Anchorage witnesses supported making Portland a co-terminus.[97]

Oregon's weight, thrown on the scales with Alaska's, perhaps helped determine the outcome. The Civil Aeronautics Board upheld the equality of freight rates for the co-termini Seattle and Portland. "The elimination of Portland as a competitive source of supply for Alaska," the board held, "would have an adverse effect upon the economy of Alaska." [98]

Upon an appeal from this decision by Seattle representatives, the C.A.B. rejected their contention that it had "no statutory authority to consider what the effect upon the economic situation in Alaska might be." [99]

Seattle, however, remained victorious in the passenger field. The board did not sanction a corresponding equality of passenger fares, but permitted a higher rate to and from Portland to Alaska points based on the 129-mile difference in air distance between the co-termini. The issue had not been raised by Seattle or Portland in the case of their co-terminal position for flights to and from Hawaii, in which Seattle was the more distant terminus, but whose passengers paid the same rate on both Pan-American World Airways and Northwest Airlines to and from the other Pacific territory, and incurring no additional charge for their first 129 miles outbound, or their last 129 miles inbound. Nor had the issue been raised on the service between both coastal cities and Chicago rendered by United Airlines in which Seattle was the more distant terminus.[100]

As the States–Alaska Case hearings adjourned in March, 1954, Alaskans were seriously worried that the Eisenhower administration's retrenchment program would bring about no increased States–Alaska service, which they felt needed by both contemporary requirements and imminent growth. There was even apprehension in some quarters that the service might be diminished—by cuts in air-mail pay and subsidies which all scheduled Alaska carriers received.

Anchorage, lying on the Great Circle Route from Chicago to the Orient—but not on the Great Circle Route from Seattle to the Orient—was particularly fearful that with the virtual abandonment by Northwest Airlines of the inland route, the Seattle–Orient service would attempt to overcome the distance handicap by following the Great Circle Course south of Anchorage through the Aleutians and thus by-pass Anchorage completely.

"Continued neglect is scheduled for the inland air route from Anchorage to the Middle West, under latest plans of Northwest Airlines," warned the Anchorage *Times* editorially. "This is the air route that Anchorage residents worked especially hard to get. It is the one that precipitated a long battle against Seattle where efforts were made to kill it. It is the air route that made the North Pacific route the shortest way of travel from New York to the Orient." [101]

Returning to the theme, three days later, the Anchorage daily declared:

"Northwest was given the certificate for the purpose of pioneering the route which extends through Canada to Anchorage to Tokyo. . . . Northwest should be made to perform adequately on the inland route, or else be pushed aside so some other air line can do so."

In other words the people of Anchorage were wondering whether the C.A.B. would consider applicable the provision of the Civil Aeronautics Act (Sec. 404 a) which declared it "the duty of every air carrier to provide . . . upon reasonable request . . . reasonable through service . . . and adequate service." It was clear that their journalistic spokesman did not consider a DC-4 once a week "reasonable" or "adequate," especially when Super-Constellations had been announced for other of the company's routes.

The people of Anchorage had a just right to be concerned. Airwise their city ranked seventh in 1953 among all the cities in the nation, with 252,896 airplane operations. Of these 175,131 were from Merrill Field, and 77,761 from the International Airport.[102] Anchorage was exceeded in flight operations only by Chicago, Cleveland, Detroit, Los Angeles, New York and Miami. Nor did Anchorage's figures include the very substantial number of seaplane departures and arrivals at Lake Hood, which are not recorded in the Civil Aeronautics Authority's compilation.[103]

If the inland route through Anchorage continued in its state of near-desuetude, Alaska—in effect—might be by-passed on the Seattle–Orient route, since Adak in the Aleutians, a possible refueling stop on that route, was not a civilian population center but merely a military base. In that event, Anchorage, which in 1954 had grown fivefold since 1946 and with its hinterland contained one-third of Alaska's population, would have less air service than it had had then, service its people considered had become insufficient at the end of the eight-year period since the Pacific Case, even with the one-carrier additional certification of Pacific Northern Airlines to Seattle-Portland provided in the United States–Alaska Service Case of 1951.

And the people of central and northern Alaska whose goods were distributed through Fairbanks—also a growing city—wanted the continuation of the improved, competitive air services they had enjoyed for three years as a result of President Truman's intervention.

3. Highways

"The principal reason for the failure of Congress to extend the provisions of that act [The Federal Aid Highway Act] has probably been that the vast area of Alaska would entitle it to an unduly large share of the total appropriation made under the act," reported the House Committee on Territories in 1946, whose chairman, Hugh Peterson, D., of Georgia, was likewise a member of the House Committee on Roads.[104]

This official pronouncement confirmed what Alaskans had long known and had long vainly sought to change, with legislature after legislature memorializing Congress and Alaska's delegates introducing bills in each Congress for that purpose. The members of Congress were willing to share with Hawaii, Puerto Rico and the District of Columbia, since their area was small, the hundreds of millions of dollars appropriated for annual expenditure as highway aid, but not with Alaska. Alaska's area was too vast! That its needs were correspondingly vast was not considered.

The 1939 legislature, referred to earlier in relation to its memorials dealing with all the territory's forms of transportation, in addition to the usual request for Alaska's inclusion under the Federal Aid Highway Act, touched on two other highway problems particular to Alaskans living in communities within the boundaries of Alaska's two national forests.

It was the belief of many of these Alaskans that the federal agency charged with highway construction and maintenance in those forest areas, the Bureau of Public Roads, followed long-standing practices developed in the forty-eight states which were unsuitable to Alaska. This agency's program was to improve gradually, at great cost, the almost negligible mileage in the Tongass National Forest. This mileage, which afforded the only land outlet for the cities of Ketchikan, Wrangell, Petersburg, Sitka and Juneau, extended out of town for short stretches and stopped. Development likewise stopped at that point, although some hardy and enterprising Alaskans would with great exertions carry building materials on their backs to a choice site in the forest stillness beyond road's end, build there, and carry their daily supplies by hand, hoping always for the road's extension past their habitations. Alaskans wanted more highway and not the very little available under standards appropriate for the heavily traveled highways of the United States. House Joint Memorial 9 requested that "a lower standard or standards for Forest Highways in Alaska be made available."

Related to this situation was another complaint which had been voiced for over a quarter of a century, namely, that road construction in Alaska was under three agencies, two of them federal, namely, the aforesaid Bureau of Public Roads, long in the Department of Agriculture, then briefly within the Public Works Administration, and subsequently transferred to the Department of Commerce. Under all these, however, the same bureaucracy maintained the same policies and their consequences remained the same for Alaska: a minimum of highway of high quality at high cost. Alaskans subject to the bureau's performance considered it highly wasteful. They wanted to go places which this program would in no foreseeable future permit them to reach. Senate Joint Memorial 4 of 1939 expressed the view that a single agency "would function more efficiently and more economically," and further, "that the people of Alaska should rightfully have a voice in the planning and building of all roads within the territory."

The people of Alaska had had no such voice. In the national forest areas, the decision would be made on the recommendation of the regional forester to the Bureau of Public Roads in Washington, without public hearings or ascertainment of the Alaskan public's desires. The situation was without parallel in the States where the national forests were wilderness areas and did not enclose cities. But in Alaska the forest extended to the limits of every city whose avenues of ingress and egress were determined by bureaucrats whose primary consideration was forest management, rather than the people's needs. This attitude, coupled with the permanent reduction by Congress in the early nineteen thirties of Alaska forest-highway appropriations, left southeastern Alaska, half a century after its blanketing by the Tongass National Forest, with only short stubs of roads leading nowhere and dead-ending after a few miles.

The territorial agency, the Board of Road Commissioners, consisting from 1931 to 1953 of two elected officials, the highway engineer and the treasurer, and the federally appointed governor, had no voice in the expenditure of the Alaska taxpayers' money, deposited until 1950 in the Alaska fund. They could, to be sure, prescribe where they wanted the road funds appropriated biennially by the legislature expended, but these funds would go unmatched in the national forests if the project did not meet with the approval of the federal officials in charge, or, if matched, would have to conform to B.P.R. standards, which meant that there would be little mileage to show for the expenditure.

However in 1950, the Congress, following a visit in 1948 of a Subcommittee on Newsprint and Paper Shortages of a Senate Special Committee to Study Problems of American Small Business, which was interested in the development of newsprint in Alaska,[105] made a special appropriation of $7,000,000 (64 Stat. 786) for the "extension and improvement" of the highway system in the Tongass National Forest. The money was expended under a program determined by the Regional Forester, which, according to custom, produced a minimum of extension but the highly costly improvement of a small extent of existing mileage. Suggestions from the public for the use of these funds for greater highway extension were not welcomed, and the attempt of the territorial Board of Road Commissioners to participate in the planning rebuffed. Only seven miles of new highway resulted from the $7,000,000 and that mileage's location was viewed with small favor by the public.

As a further aggravation, the Bureau of Public Roads, when engaged in its elaborate and costly improvement, rendered the highways virtually impassable during such reconstruction, a disservice to the public without parallel either in the States or in those other parts of Alaska where the Alaska Road Commission had responsibility. The consequence was either denial of access for substantial periods of time to householders beyond or along the stretches being reconstructed, or badly damaged and at times even wrecked automobiles for those who were, of necessity, compelled to use those only available arteries of travel to their homes or businesses. A "the public be damned" attitude had long been that Bureau's practice in Alaska and continued to be so despite that public's pleas and protests, which were totally ignored.

Most of the territorially appropriated road funds therefore went to co-operative projects with the Alaska Road Commission, under the Interior Department since 1932, which had charge of all road construction outside of the national forests. But for the first ten years after its transfer from the War Department, this agency received virtually no funds for new construction, but only for maintenance.

Attempts by Alaska's delegates to secure inclusion under the Federal Aid Highway Act having been unsuccessful for thirty years, Delegate Bartlett in 1948 attempted a new approach.[106] Under his H.R. 4574, the matching formula would be based on only one-half of Alaska's land area and thus reduce Alaska's share substantially. In exchange for this considerable reduction, the federal and territorial matching funds were to be available for maintenance as well as new construction. But the Congress refused even to consider this formula under which Alaska would secure only partially the benefits extended to the forty-eight states, Hawaii, Puerto Rico and the District of Columbia.

The legislative memorialists of 1939, whose pleas for inclusion of Alaska in the Federal Aid Highway Act provisions, and for a voice in their road programming, were to be repeated in 1941,[107] had pointed out that the territory had contributed liberally in the past toward the construction of roads, and would continue to do so to the limit of their financial ability.

Actually the people of Alaska had contributed more to the federal road-building program than the people of some states. In the forty years since 1905 when the Alaska Road Commission, as an agency of the War Department, had begun the first road construction, until June 30, 1945, when World War II was drawing to a close, Alaskans had contributed 23 per cent of the total of $39,298,489 spent in that period. By contrast Nevada's participation under the Federal Aid Highway Act was 12.5 per cent.[108] Nevada's participation, the lowest of any state, was based on 87 per cent of its land being in public domain.

However, the menace of Soviet aggression in the late nineteen forties was to bring a "new look" to at least a part of Alaska's highway needs.

"The War Department is deeply concerned over the lack of roads . . . in mainland Alaska," testified Major-General W. H. Arnold, Deputy Director of the Plans and Operations Division of the General Staff, early in 1947. "The support of military bases in Alaska and the development of new sources of strategic raw materials are vital requirements of national defense." [109] He listed as highly desirable the extension of highways in several directions: from Anchorage southward to the Kenai Peninsula, westward from the Richardson Highway to Mount McKinley Park, northward from Fairbanks in several directions.

No action on the matter was taken by the Eightieth Congress in that session. After its adjournment, the Secretary of the Army, Kenneth C. Royall, communicated his department's view to Secretary of the Interior, Julius A. Krug, that the deficiencies of the existing road system in mainland Alaska jeopardized the mission of national defense.

"The support of military bases in Alaska and the development of new sources of strategic raw materials are vital requirements of national defense," he continued.[110] He listed the road projects he deemed of major importance. Some were not merely of military value only; they were useful also for general development, and the Department of Defense did not hesitate to approve and justify this dual beneficiality.

"Any economic improvement of Alaska will aid the mission of national defense, particularly as such development tends to make Alaska self-sufficient economically," testified Lieutenant-General Howard Craig, Commander-in-Chief of the Alaska Command from 1946 to 1948, in behalf of the needed appropriations.[111]

The second session of the Eightieth Congress began to appropriate for the new program. Alaska Road Commission appropriations, which had averaged $2,348,661 in the six years 1941 to 1946, and had increased to slightly above $4,000,000 in 1947 and 1948, now rose to $15,734,413 in 1949. The Interior Department placed an Army Engineer, Colonel John R. Noyes, in charge of the A.R.C., with the new title of Commissioner of Roads.

The 1950 appropriations, including both new construction and maintenance, was $24,363,708, and in 1951 rose to a new high of $30,597,479. A five-year program provided for (1) a highway from Anchorage down the Kenai Peninsula to Homer, opening up an important agricultural and homesteading area, and giving access to proposed auxiliary defense establishments; (2) connection of this highway with the road from Seward to Hope and linking Seward to Anchorage; (3) a highway from Tanacross on the Alaska Highway northward to Eagle on the Yukon through a mining area where it was hoped the search for gold would be succeeeded by the discovery of strategic minerals; (4) and for an east–west highway from the Richardson Highway at Paxson's to Mount McKinley Park, passing through a heavily mineralized area, making Mount McKinley Park accessible by highway from the States; (5) the black-topping of the Glenn, Richardson and Alaska highways.

It was assumed by Alaskans, by the Alaska military command of that period and by the Interior Department that this would be a continuing program, and that one new major construction project would be initiated each year.

But while Alaska's long overdue and barely initiated highway program was soon to be afflicted with recurrence of a chronic malady which Alaskans had long suffered—"appropriation anemia"—it was seized by an acute attack of another familiar ailment, locally referred to as "bureaucratic bursitis." No sooner had the incipient highways stimulated construction of roadhouses, tourist lodges, filling stations and settlers' cabins, than the Interior Department so broadened the highways' rights of way as to greatly impede such development.

In 1947 the department had established a field committee in Alaska. It consisted of the heads of the various Interior Department agencies stationed in Alaska: The Alaska Road Commission, the Alaska Railroad, the Bureau of Land Management, the Fish and Wildlife Service, the Alaska Native Service, the National Park Service, the Bureau of Mines, the Geological Survey, the Bureau of Reclamation, and for a time, the Governor's office. The Field Committee was supposed to co-ordinate Interior's activities in Alaska, to formulate a development program, and to serve in an advisory capacity to the department.

The committee had been asked to render its opinion on the widths for rights of way on Alaska highways, so that the department could be properly advised. With only one member dissenting, the committee recommended three hundred feet for the Alaska Highway, two hundred feet for principal roads and one hundred feet for lesser roads, which would have reserved approximately 135 feet on either side of the Alaska Highway, some eighty-five feet on either side of the other principal roads, and some forty feet on each side of the lesser roads. However, from the Interior Department came an order overruling the committee, establishing six hundred feet of right of way for the Alaska Highway, three hundred feet for the other primary roads, two hundred feet for secondary roads and one hundred feet for feeder roads. Delegate Bartlett termed the proposal "fantastic." In a letter of protest to Secretary Krug, he declared that "it would push the would-be settler back as if he were not wanted in Alaska. It would in many cases push him up a mountain, over a cliff or into a stream or lake. It would multiply the difficulties which for him are very considerable already."

Delegate Bartlett proceeded to enumerate these difficulties. There would be problems in driveway construction, maintenance, snow clearance, and in the obtaining of driveway clearance through the right of way. "Don't try to tell any Alaskan who has had dealings with the department that there would not be red tape and delay in connection with that. And for what?" Bartlett asked. "I confess I am unable to think of a good reason for tying up all this territory right where we want people, accommodations for travelers, service facilities, etc."

The delegate reported that he had driven over the Alaska Highway the preceding summer and was willing to testify that, even from the standpoint of appearance and interest to the traveler, development along the road was exactly what was needed. He gave his idea that a reasonable right-of-way reservation, which would amply protect all the interests of the federal government, would be two hundred feet for the Alaska Highway and other primary roads and one hundred feet for lesser roads.[112]

Delegate Bartlett was expressing a view that was emphatically shared by virtually all Alaskans. The members of the Field Committee who recommended more considerable dimensions, perhaps not uninfluenced by a knowledge of departmental tendencies, were officials of various lengths of residence in Alaska, entrusted by the department with the highest responsibilities in their respective fields. But their judgment, rendered after many hours of discussion and deliberation, was arbitrarily overruled in Washington by the nonresident assistant secretary whom Secretary Krug had placed "in charge of Alaska." (He was William E. Warne.)

And his decision prevailed, to the serious damage of those enterprising Alaskans who had moved quickly to do their part in developing Alaska, for they were trespassers without title and without chance to obtain it, with a choice of either removing their buildings or continuing with the uncertainties of a "permit," subject to future changes of policy wrought by the whim of some distant and unseen federal official. And beyond these individual hardships was the discouragement of development by others which the highways under normal conditions would stimulate.

By 1952 the highway appropriations began to decline. They averaged under $21,000,000 for 1952 and 1953. For 1954 the Truman-approved budget retained the appropriation at the slightly higher level of $21,000,000, but the Eisenhower administration reduced it to $17,600,000. For 1955 it was fixed by the House at $10,000,000 of which $7,000,000 was for new construction and the rest for maintenance.

These reductions were in fact greater than appeared. Continuing inflation had increased construction costs. The new mileage entailed additional maintenance expense. Many lesser farm and suburban roads had been added.

In consequence of these reductions one of the five projects programmed five years earlier was far from completed—the Richardson Highway-Mount McKinley Park Road. But what seemed ominous to Alaskans was that for three years no new highway construction had been projected, and that the program of developmental construction aiding the mission of national defense was slowing down to a halt.

The extremely important Copper River Highway, sought for fifteen years, had, after tremendous efforts by Delegate Bartlett, finally received, in 1952, the unusually friendly treatment of a $100,000 appropriation by Congress after the Bureau of the Budget had failed to include it, and the next year an additional $550,000. For the fiscal year 1954, $2,400,000 was transferred to it from the Mount McKinley Park Road by the A.R.C. in order to make a start possible. This highway, to be built over the water-level roadbed of the Copper River and Northwestern Railroad, abandoned in 1938, whose steel bridges were still standing, would link Cordova, the principal community and only seaport in central Alaska still unconnected with the highway system to it, would thereby provide an additional and excellent harbor and gateway in case of emergency, would open up a heavily mineralized area and give access to the region of greatest scenic splendor in Alaska, the Chitina Valley. From every aspect it was a more needed and useful highway than two of the five which had received earlier military endorsement, and Alaska public opinion so deemed it decisively. Its estimated cost was around $12,000,000.

But despite every effort, the House in the 1955 appropriation bill allowed only $700,000 for it, and that only to permit the road's extension to the edge of the Katalla-Yakataga oil fields, extensive drilling of which was in prospect.

Considering Alaska's great road needs, a substantial portion of which may justly be classed as in the interest of national defense, and the long neglect of them, the five-year construction program initiated as a military requirement but apparently destined for quiet evanescence represents just another of those occasional flurries raising Alaskan hopes only to dash them by distant decision. Had Alaska not been excluded from the Federal Aid Highway program since its enactment in 1916, the territory's share would have exceeded $350,000,-000, and Alaska's past contributions would have come pretty close to equaling the matching required. In any event the difference could have been made up by Alaskans. True, Alaskan legislatures had been criticized in Congress in the early nineteen fifties for failing to increase the territorial fuel tax above 2 cents a gallon.[113] Doubtless a higher tax, earmarked for highway construction of that portion derived from highway users, would have been the better part of wisdom. But the 2-cent Alaska tax applied to all forms of liquid fuel, including that used by the fishing fleet, and was not diminished by refunds to other than automotive usage that in 1954 existed in all but two states, and were extensive in some. Moreover the crude federal discrimination persisting also for forest-road funds, if it did not justify the Alaskans' frugality, at least made it understandable.

Were Congress to reconsider its ostracism of Alaska and come to appreciate the importance of helping to create a real highway system there, a $50,000,000 annual construction and maintenance program for at least ten years should be forthcoming, although more than that amount could be profitably invested for the national interest. Such investment would at the end of that period bring Alaska close to if not wholly abreast of the sums that have been denied to this one area under the flag, while it has been subject to all the taxes—including the 2-cent federal gas tax—which the beneficiaries of the federal-aid legislation pay.

For Alaska that federal highway system has been a one-way street for the safe-conduct of Alaskans' tax dollars to the federal treasury in aid of all the rest.

In the first week of April, 1954, when the House of Representatives had cut Alaska's roads funds for 1955 to the lowest point in six years and to less than half of the average appropriation during that period, the Senate passed by voice vote and sent to the House for conference a billion-dollar Federal Aid Highway authorization—the largest in history—for the benefit of all the other areas under the flag.[114]

4. The Railroad

With war clouds shadowing the Pacific horizon, the Alaska Railroad became an adjunct of defense. Previously, despite the incompletion of its construction, the shortcomings of its earlier operation, its high fares, and the neglect of its potentialities because of insufficient feeder roads, its value in opening up interior Alaska was considerable. But to the military program initiated in 1940 it was absolutely essential. To make it even more useful for defense and more secure against attack, a new port, Whittier, was established and became wholly an Army operation. At that time the Richardson Highway was still not much more than a wagon road from Valdez to Fairbanks. The Glenn Highway, which was to connect it with the military establishment near Anchorage and thus provide a thoroughfare from the command headquarters to the interior, was not built. The railroad was the only means by which matériel, equipment and supplies could be transported northward.

But vital as the railroad proved in the Second World War, it would be even more so in the protection of Alaska—and of the nation—against the threat or in the event of a Third. For World War II in Alaska early moved away from the military bases at Anchorage and Fairbanks and the naval base at Kodiak to the Aleutians. Port Heiden, Cold Bay on the Alaska Peninsula, Dutch Harbor, Umnak, Adak, Amchitka and Shemya on "the chain," were successively developed as bases from which Army, Navy and Air Force attacks would be launched, first at the invader on Kiska and Attu, and later against the enemy's northern outposts in his homeland. With the dawning of a new and greater threat from nearby Siberia, the character of Alaskan defenses changed. The "heartland" concept emerged, under which the Aleutians were virtually abandoned, the perimeter of Alaska considered expendable, and defense and offense concentrated along a line running from Kodiak through Anchorage to Fairbanks, with depth provided by additional bases at Eielson and Big Delta. For this concept the railroad became indispensable. In its rickety condition it was inadequate to serve the national need. The aforementioned military pleas for road construction, beginning in 1947, were no less emphatic on the need for railroad rehabilitation.

"The War Department," Major-General W. H. Arnold testified, was also "deeply concerned over . . . the critical condition of the Alaska Railroad." It was, he said, the Army's "primary all-season line of communication." He "strongly" urged its rehabilitation "within the ensuing three years." [115]

Despite the urgency, the first session of the Eightieth Congress adjourned without action, and the attack was renewed in the next session, with Army Secretary Royall firing the opening salvo. "The limited capacity of the railroad," he wrote, jeopardized "the mission of defense." [116]

"The Alaska Railroad is the only high-tonnage line of communication from tidewater to the interior of the Alaskan mainland," testified Lieutenant-General Craig. "As such, it is a prime strategic asset. The military development program for Alaska contemplates the construction of major bases in the interior—north of the Alaska Range. The movement of construction materials and equipment and of the supplies required by the military forces must be accomplished over this single line of communications. . . . We consider the rapid accomplishment of the rehabilitation program and re-equipping of the Alaska Railroad as essential to the progress of the military . . . program, and as primary requisites for the security of Alaska." [117]

So the rehabilitation of the railroad was begun in 1949. It proceeded slowly, as every year a strenuous contest had to be waged in Washington to secure the appropriation to carry the program further. In the Eighty-second Congress funds to rehabilitate the sixty-three miles between Seward and Portage were denied despite the vigorous testimony as to its necessity of Lieutenant-General William E. Kepner, who flew to Washington twice to appear before both House and Senate appropriation committees, and the supporting testimony of Assistant Secretary of the Army Karl R. Bendetsen. In 1954 this mileage was still not rehabilitated. Without waiting for the slow-going attempts to secure funds through the Interior Department, the

Army had in 1948 built a twenty-six mile extension southeastward from Fairbanks to the new air base at Camp Eielson.

However the 476 miles north from Portage, where the twelve-mile branch to Whittier diverged, were in better condition than they ever had been, and the railroad, in the words of one military leader, was the aorta of heartland defense.

Indeed during the nineteen forties two-thirds of the freight was for military or related governmental purposes. Private enterprise found little encouragement to use the railroad because of high rates, and as far as possible patronized the truck lines from Valdez to Fairbanks.

"Part of this extremely high charge," a senatorial "task force" of a Subcommittee on Preparedness of the Armed Services Committee reported in 1951, was due to the railroad's being "required to operate many services at a loss to meet the military requirements within the territory."

The Senators—Lester C. Hunt, D., of Wyoming, Leverett Saltonstall, R., of Massachusetts, and Wayne Morse, R., of Oregon—called attention to a similar situation on the government-owned railroad in the Panama Canal Zone, where relief had been granted the commercial users by making the appropriate charges against national defense, und suggested "that the same pattern should be followed in connection with the operation of the Alaska Railroad." It should, they felt, "be reflected in decreased costs to the consumers of material transported over the railroad." [118]

But three years later the senatorial recommendation had not been followed. Alaskans, in addition to all federal taxes, were paying a part of the cost of national defense through the higher freight rates to which they were subject, because the government railroad was carrying the military cargo at a loss.

The high freight rates, it will be recalled, had been the object of Alaskan protests for a decade before the military use of the Alaska Railroad. In 1939, before the military construction had begun, the legislature had addressed to the President, Secretary of the Interior and appropriate congressional committees a memorial pointing out that under existing policies the railroad was "failing to realize the objective for which the road was originally constructed." The tariffs were "so economically oppressive as to reduce tonnage and stifle development," a situation aggravated by the continuing "unjust and unfair practice of imposing tolls" in order to force shippers to use the railroad.[119]

Secretary Ickes, who, in Alaska, operated under what a nationally known newspaper columnist, Marquis Childs, termed the " 'Papa knows best' theory of government," paid no attention to the legislators' request. The tolls on the Richardson Highway were lifted only when this specimen of bureaucratic high-handedness conflicted with incoming defense constructors, and the underequipped railroad was unable to handle the unexpected load.

"The entire rate structure on such transportation facilities as now exist—railway, steamship, airways and highways—is now entirely too high for their proper use in developing Alaska," was the judgment of the House Committee on Territories which visited Alaska in 1945.[120] The air-line rates in 1954 had, on some routes, by virtue of competition, been reduced below the high 1945 levels, although there was no assurance that the Civil Aeronautics Board would permit that competition so valuable to Alaska to continue. But in other forms of transportation the charges had risen steadily to points far above those which a congressional committee nine years earlier had declared entirely too high.

The remedies lay far beyond the reach of the people of Alaska. They were in the hands of the Congress and the federal bureaus:

In the case of maritime transportation—the Congress, which continued the unique discrimination against Alaska in the Merchant Marine Act of 1920; and the Federal Maritime Board, which, like its predecessors, approved every carrier-requested rate increase without audit to ascertain to what extent such increase was or was not needed.

In air transportation—the Civil Aeronautics Board, whose decisions often disregarded Alaska's greater dependence on airways, and but for President Truman's overruling action would have left the Alaska-U.S. service to interior Alaska wholly inadequate.

In highway transportation—the Congress, which denied Alaska, uniquely, inclusion in the Federal Aid Highway Act, and arbitrarily reduced, for the benefit of other areas, Alaska's rightful share of forest-highway funds; the Interior Department, which imposed its whimsical and inappropriate ideas on the widths of highway rights of way; and the Bureau of Public Roads, which in the domain under its jurisdiction showed little regard for the wishes and needs of Alaskans.

In the case of the railroad—the Department of the Interior, which despite congressional counsel maintained freight rates punitive to Alaskan private enterprise.

5. A Railroad between the States and Alaska

The uncertainties and limitations of the three forms of transportation between the forty-eight states and Alaska—shipping, air lines and highway—led, at mid-century, in the face of the unabated Russian menace, to interest in a fourth means of communication: a railroad. A bill providing for negotiation with the Dominion of Canada for agreement to procure a location survey for a standard-gauge railroad extending from the railway system terminating at Prince George, British Columbia, to Fairbanks, was sponsored by Representative Henry M. Jackson of Washington. It passed the House of Representatives by unanimous vote on August 24, 1949. Speaking for the measure, Mr. Jackson declared:

"The development of Alaska, both from a strategic and from an economic point of view, is dependent largely on the reliability of surface transportation to and from the territory. . . . The water transportation is, for the most part, highly vulnerable in the event of conflict. And should the water routes be cut off, the highway alone would not be sufficient.[121]

Two weeks later, General J. Lawton Collins, Army Chief of Staff, at a press conference in Anchorage, scouted the idea. Under the heading, "General Collins Holds Alaska Railroad Link Unnecessary," he was quoted by the Associated Press as saying: "Alaska can be defended from the States without a railroad. Steamships, highways and planes are able to bring enough men to defend the territory." [122]

Nevertheless the bill passed the Senate unanimously on October 17 and became law on October 26 (63 Stat. 908).

The military's adverse view having been given, no action as sought by the legislation followed.

A review of the similar military disapproval, for some time before and on to the eve and outbreak of World War II, of the highway to Alaska, is pertinent.

As early as January 8, 1934, Delegate Anthony J. Dimond had introduced a bill, H.R. 6538, for construction of a highway between the United States and Alaska. The War Department's report expressed the view that the highway was feasible from an engineering stand-point but rendered no opinion either as to its military or economic value.

Four years later, in 1938, the War Plans Division of the General Staff was queried on the military value of such a road, and a resulting opinion by the Chief of Staff, General Malin Craig, declared, "The military value of the proposed Alaska highway is so slight as to be negligible." [123]

Two years later, on August 2, 1940, six weeks after France had fallen and the Battle of Britain was under way, a report on another bill of Delegate Dimond's, H.R. 10064,[124] signed by Henry L. Stimson, Secretary of War, declared, "The value of the proposed highway as a defense measure is negligible." [125]

Ten months before the United States' entry into the war, Delegate Dimond again introduced a bill to construct a highway to Alaska.[126] It was referred to the Committee on Roads as the previous bills had been. A report requested from the War Department was not transmitted until eight months later.

Meanwhile other efforts were being made to secure action on such a highway. The Alaskan International Highway Commission, created May 31, 1938 (50 Stat. 390), under legislation sponsored by Representative Warren G. Magnuson, had rendered a favorable report which President Roosevelt transmitted to Congress.[127]

Following this report conversations were initiated in the fall of 1940 by the State Department with the Dominion Government, whose commission had also rendered its report. It developed that the Canadians were unwilling to authorize the necessary right of way unless the United States would affirm that the proposed highway had military value; the only agency which could so assert authoritatively was the War Department. In an endeavor to secure such an expression, the Chairman of the Commission, Representative Magnuson, submitted to the Secretary of War an analysis of the two routes under consideration. The more westerly, or A route, through Prince George and Whitehorse to Fairbanks, was favored by the American commission; the B route, through Prince George, Watson Lake, Dawson and thence to Fairbanks, was favored by the Canadian commissioners.

The War Department was asked to indicate which of the two routes it considered preferable from a military standpoint. A reply dated April 22, 1941, signed by Henry L. Stimson, Secretary of War, drafted in the General Staff, stated:

"The War Department considers that the construction of such a highway cannot be justified on the basis of military necessity. Because of this view, it is believed that it would be inappropriate to comment upon the relative merits of the two suggested routes." [128]

Notwithstanding, Delegate Dimond insisted on August 4th: "The immediate construction of a highway to Alaska is not only economically justified, but is demanded by considerations of national defense." [129]

On October 6, 1941, the War Department's report on Delegate Dimond's bill introduced on February 5th, signed by Secretary Stimson, declared that "from an evaluation of the trend in international affairs the construction of this highway now appears desirable as a long-range defense measure." [130]

The enemy, however, operated at close range, and two months later attacked Pearl Harbor without warning. The highway was built in great haste, at great cost, and over a previously unsurveyed route, after the United States was at war.[131]

The episode demonstrated anew that Alaska's civilian delegate was far more alert to the military needs of the nation and to the value of Alaska as its bulwark of defense than the military experts, and that his foresight was superior to their hindsight. Nor was Delegate Dimond alone—among Alaskans—in his prescience. Nearly three years before the outbreak of the war, Alaska's twenty-four legislators, foregathered in Juneau for the Fourteenth Territorial Assembly, had urged upon Congress the construction of the highway, citing among other reasons that "the interests of national defense would be greatly served by this project." [132]

History is said to teach only the lesson that it teaches no lessons. But if ever a cogent precedent would indicate the need of constructing a railroad to Alaska it may be found in the stubborn refusal of the military experts to approve the Alaska Highway in the face of repeated promptings.

Despite the categorical disapproval of a railroad to Alaska by the Army Chief of Staff, J. Lawton Collins, in 1949, the briefing of the senatorial task force at the Alaska Command Headquarters in the fall of 1950 contained this suggestive warning:

". . . In an emergency, if the sea lanes were denied us, the highway system would require extensive improvement, including all-weather paving and heavier bridges * * * (Delected for security reasons)." [133]

One of the secrets that penetrated from behind the Iron Curtain was that the Union of Soviet Socialist Republics had in 1954 a tremendous fleet of submarines of the most modern design, which left little doubt that in the event of hostilities the sea lanes would be "denied us" between Alaska and the United States. That one gravel-surfaced highway, twenty-five hundred miles in length from the northern Montana boundary to the Alaskan border, requiring "extensive improvement, including all-weather paving and heavier bridges," could be readied for useful service after war had begun, was scarcely admissible, or that even after being so readied it would suffice. In the absence of shipping only a railroad could effectively transport the heavy matériel that modern warfare requires.

These considerations prompted Senator Warren G. Magnuson, on February 18, 1953, to introduce S.J. Res. 46, calling for the establishment of an Alaska International Rail and Highway Commission, to be appointed by the President to make a complete study of the most feasible rail and highway transportation routes between the United States and Alaska, and to co-operate with a corresponding commission appointed for such purpose by the Dominion of Canada or the Province of British Columbia. The proposal was similar to that which Mr. Magnuson as Representative sponsored for the highway in 1938.

Alaskans naturally wished that a more tangible result in behalf of a railroad might be secured—in time of peace—than was achieved by the earlier commission. It would hardly be possible, they knew, to construct in a year's time, after the outbreak of hostilities—as with the Alaska Highway—the far more elaborate railway, especially under the vastly different conditions of the total war which sanity would seek to avert by adequate defense planning. Such planning would include the railway as essential to the successful defense of Alaska, or its maintenance for offense.

But no action was taken on Magnuson's legislative approach to the railroad during the Eighty-third Congress.

Self-Government: The Quest for Statehood

> Adventure has nurtured men of spirit, who have built the world for those who lacked spirit. In Alaska are men of spirit who stand ready to build a great state.
> SENATOR CLINTON P. ANDERSON OF NEW MEXICO,
> MARCH 9, 1954

THE attempts to achieve full territorial government, begun immediately after the enactment of the organic act of 1912, were destined to get nowhere. Every Alaska delegate, every territorial legislature, Governors Strong, Riggs and Troy, countless organizations in Alaska, repeatedly urged action on measures by which Congress would increase Alaskans' autonomy and bring their government at least up to equivalence with that of every other earlier territory. Despite these efforts, no extension whatever of the powers of self-government was obtained. Every significant amendment—and at least one was introduced in every session of Congress—was pigeonholed. Of the six amendments enacted in forty-two years, the first five merely corrected minor defects or wrought perfunctory changes.[1]

In the sixth amendment enacted November 13, 1942 (56 Stat. 1016), Congress made a partial response to an attempt by Delegate Dimond to reform the deficient system of representation in the territorial legislature which Congress had lazily imposed on Alaska thirty years earlier. He sought to establish proportionate representation in both houses and to increase the number of senators.

Proportionate representation had for some time been sought in Alaska. It was first attempted in 1924 through a bill introduced by Delegate Sutherland with the backing chiefly of First Division voters who felt that its larger population entitled them to more than the existing equal representation in the legislature.[2]

The American Legion, Department of Alaska, in annual convention at Seward in 1935, called for "proportionate representative government." Its resolution, passed by unanimous vote, declared Alaska to be the only territory in which that principle had been disregarded in the establishment of a legislature. It also pointed out that much legislation had been defeated by the votes of four senators.

Delegate Dimond considered it wise to await the next census returns in order to have a current basis for reapportionment. They showed: First Division, 25,241; Second Division, 11,877; Third Division, 19,312; Fourth Division, 16,094.

With more than twice as many people in the First as in the Second Division, and the population of all divisions, except the Second, increasing, it was apparent, testified Delegate Dimond, "that the Alaska legislature, under present population trends and under the existing setup, is becoming less and less responsive to the actual population and citizenship of the territory." [3]

His bill proposed proportional representation by electing one member to the Senate and one to the House for every four thousand persons or major fraction thereof, in each division, and provided for reapportionment after every decennial census. This reform, Delegate Dimond was convinced, was supported by 80 per cent of the people of Alaska.[4] Four senators, he urged, could defeat the will of the twenty other legislators, and if those four came from the Second and Fourth Divisions, representation of only a little over a third of the population would nullify the wishes of the majority: "We are truly subject in Alaska, so far as the legislature is concerned, to government by the minority." [5]

Twenty-four unsolicited messages and resolutions of support were placed in the record. They came from the service clubs, fraternal, labor, fishermen's and women's organizations, from the chambers of commerce of the smaller communities, from individuals. Opponents sent six messages which included the larger cities' chambers of commerce (except Ketchikan). Asked from what source the opposition came, Delegate Dimond replied:

"Mostly from a few of the chambers of commerce of Alaska. It is inspired pretty largely, in my judgment, by what we might call the 'absentee landlords.' " [6]

Commenting on the Fairbanks chamber's resolution in opposition, Frank S. Gordon, Fairbanks merchant and Fourth Division Representative, wrote . . . "the chamber ran along with the mining and steamships interests." [7]

The isotherms above, showing lines of equal average temperature for winter months, reveal more strikingly than words the facts about Alaska's climate. Due to the Japan Current, which skirts the entire Pacific coastal area, its cities and towns, containing the greater part of Alaska's population, enjoy milder winters than the northern parts of the United States. Ketchikan's and Sitka's winter temperatures approximate those of Washington and Philadelphia, respectively, Juneau's those of New York City, and are higher than those of Boston, Detroit, Chicago, Omaha and Denver. The winter temperatures of the Anchorage area are higher than those of northern New England, Wisconsin, Minnesota, the Dakotas, Wyoming and Montana. Even Nome, less than a hundred miles below the Arctic Circle, has winter temperatures higher than those of the provincial capitals of Winnipeg and Regina just north of the United States-Canada boundary. Fairbanks, with its environs, is the only substantially populated area with temperatures which occasionally drop to the fifties and sixties below zero. But at such times there is no wind, and the ice-fog stillness that invariably prevails makes these weather conditions more endurable than the sub-zero temperatures of our northern prairie states with their prevailing wind velocities, which are not abated by low temperatures.

Two members of the House committee, Hugh Peterson, D., of Georgia and Nat Patton, D., of Texas, objected to proportional representation in the Senate. They argued from the analogy of Congress and of their states that senators represented an area, whereas representatives represented population. Delegate Dimond contended that the analogy did not apply to Alaska, that Alaska's four "divisions were established and their boundaries fixed upon supposed convenience in the administration of justice and . . . there had been no thought that they would be used later as election districts." [8] But when the Congress nevertheless had made them such it had made the unprecedented disposition of identical areas as both senatorial and representative districts.

The committee disregarded Delegate Dimond's desires and followed those of two of its voting members. As enacted the bill provided for proportional representation in the House only, increasing the number of representatives to twenty-four, and also doubling the number of senators.

The following census, that of 1950, would show the disparity in representation still further increased: First Division, 28,203; Second Division, 12,272; Third Division, 59,518; Fourth Division, 28,650. In consequence the House of Representatives in the Twentieth Territorial Assembly in 1951 had six members from the First Division, three from the Second, ten from the Third, and five from the Fourth. But now *less* than a third of the population had half the representation in the Senate and an effective veto power on all legislation.

It was another illustration of long-range government, as Delegate Dimond viewed it. Here was a bill which concerned Alaska only. It clashed with no stateside interests (except those of the lobbyists who found the original setup easier to manipulate). It embodied a reform which the great majority of the people of Alaska wanted, and as such was presented to the committee by its one member who had knowledge—profound knowledge—of Alaska. Yet it was denied Alaskans by the opposition of two members who at that time had no first-hand acquaintance with Alaska, but, having votes, were able to prevail.

A year later, on December 2, 1943, Delegate Dimond introduced his first statehood bill. While he had no hope of securing favorable action, his eleven years in Congress had convinced him that the territory would never progress substantially until it had statehood, and that statehood would be no more difficult to obtain than full territorial government by the piecemeal efforts which had failed for thirty years. Delegate Wickersham had arrived at the same conclusion twenty-eight years earlier when he introduced Alaska's first statehood bill.

Delegate Dimond's statehood bill, H.R. 7368, 78 C: 1 s, was referred to the House Committee on Territories, where no action was taken upon it. A companion bill, S. 951, sponsored by Senator William Langer, R., of North Dakota, and Senator Pat McCarran, D., of Nevada, met a similar end in the Senate Committee on Territorial and Insular Affairs.

Delegate Bartlett, upon succeeding Delegate Dimond, introduced a statehood bill in the first session of the Seventy-ninth Congress.[10] It provided that excepting national parks and monuments, lands actually in the use of the United States, lands reserved for schools and the university, or for Indians, Aleuts and Eskimos, the new state was to have "all vacant and unappropriated lands, including lands reserved or withdrawn from entry." In this respect the bill went far beyond some of its predecessors which followed an earlier practice of transferring to the state only two numbered sections, 16 and 36, out of each township.

The statehood movement was to be given a new impetus by the Seventeenth Territorial Legislature, meeting in 1945. A memorial requesting the admission of Alaska as the forty-ninth state, the first such memorial from an Alaska legislature, introduced early in the session by Representatives Stanley J. McCutcheon, D., of Anchorage, and Frederick G. Hanford, D., of Wrangell, passed the House by unanimous vote and the Senate twelve to four.[11] Following this, a bill sponsored by Senator Norman R. Walker, D., of Ketchikan, provided for a referendum at the next territorial election on October 8, 1946 to ascertain the will of the people of Alaska on statehood.[12]

The vote was 9,630 for and 6,822 against. It was the first test; those voting against doubted whether Alaska could support statehood. That minority view was understandable since at that time Alaska had no comprehensive tax system. The principal journalistic supporters of statehood were the Anchorage *Times* and the Ketchikan *Chronicle*. Opposed were the *Alaska Daily Empire* of Juneau, which since the death of its former editor and owner, John W. Troy, had receded from its advocacy of full territorial government; the Ketchikan *Fishing News,* whose outlook coincided with that of the canned-salmon industry, and the Fairbanks *News-Miner,* organ of Austin E. Lathrop, whose view was that statehood would increase taxation, and was shortly to assist in converting into a daily the weekly Anchorage *News,* for the purpose of fighting the *Times* of that city on the statehood issue.

The following year would see one of the numerous federal actions which brought home to Alaskans their disadvantaged position in the national family, and would increase the sentiment for statehood. In 1939 Alaska was made a Coast Guard District with headquarters at Ketchikan. This move was overdue. Alaska had long been a part of the Thirteenth Coast Guard District with headquarters at Seattle, which had responsibility not only for the Oregon and Washington coasts, but across a seven-hundred-mile gap of foreign territorial waters and high seas, of Alaska's multiple marine assignments.

"The Coast Guard's function is to assist everyone," testified Commander Harry G. Hamlet, concerning his service's role in Alaska.[13] Besides its time-honored life-saving mission, to which government reorganization had added the lighthouse service, steamboat inspection, Loran (long-range aid to navigation) and air-sea rescue, the Coast Guard had long rendered special services in Alaskan waters. There was the Bering Sea Patrol with its transportation of doctors and nurses to remote villages and the evacuation of the sick and stranded; the annual court cruise along the Alaska Peninsula and the Aleutians where the Third Division Judge would dispense justice; the convoying of the seals to the Pribilofs to prevent pelagic sealing; and a great variety of acts of co-operation with communities.

But in its dependence on the Coast Guard for succoring fishermen and others in storm and distress lay the appreciation of a people two-thirds of whom derived their livelihood from the sea. So unlike some other federal agencies, with which Alaskans had come in conflict, the Coast Guard was highly popular, and in no state of the Union did it play so important a part.[14]

Yet in 1947 the Alaska Coast Guard District was suddenly abolished, and the headquarters moved back to Seattle. Congress, at war's end, had made a drastic slash in the over-all Coast Guard appropriations and left it to that agency to decide where it should make the enforced economies. An attempt by its authorities to consolidate the

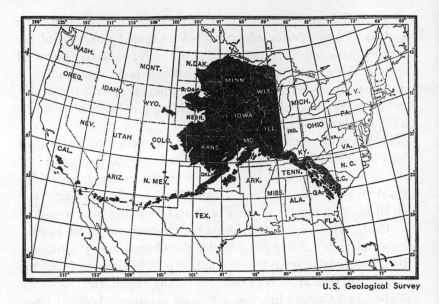

U.S. Geological Survey

Superimposed map shows relative size of Alaska and the United States.

two California districts with headquarters at San Francisco and Long
Beach—the latter responsible for only the southern three hundred
miles of California's coast—was promptly squelched by the state's
two United States senators. Alaskan protests, promptly and unceas-
ingly delivered, somehow lacked the necessary weight! However, a
study by a private management concern of the Coast Guard's "administrative, management and fiscal policies" with a view to promoting their efficiency, resulted in recommendations for other district
consolidations, including the two California districts, and for the restoration of the Alaska District.[15] After three years the Alaska District
was restored, the headquarters being established at Juneau. The incident—as Wickersham disclosed twenty years previously—illustrated
the need of an Alaska delegate to add to his normally extensive duties
by being ever ready "to prevent something from happening," or "to
try to undo something already done."

Help from an unexpected quarter was to come to the statehood
cause. In his very first State of the Union Message, delivered to the
second session of the Seventy-ninth Congress on January 21, 1946,
President Truman urged "that the Congress promptly accede to the

wishes of the people of Hawaii that the territory be admitted to statehood in our Union, and that similar action be taken with respect to Alaska as soon as it is certain that this is the desire of the people of that great territory."

President Truman's support of statehood for Alaska preceded by over eight months the referendum's recording of the popular desire for it there. Thereafter he was to miss no opportunity to espouse the statehood causes of both the incorporated territories. He was the first President of the United States to do so for either.

The next statehood bill, H.R. 206, was introduced by Delegate Bartlett on the opening day of the Eightieth Congress, January 3, 1947. Hearings were begun in Washington and continued in Alaska. The bill was supported by the Department of the Interior, Secretary Julius A. Krug, the first witness, testifying:

"Alaska has suffered for many years under what is virtually a colonial system that has encouraged absentee exploitation of its natural resources without leaving enough social and economic benefits for the territory. If Alaska is granted statehood, its people will have more to say about their economic as well as their political destiny. Absentee interests, working for their special ends, will find it more difficult to dominate the economy of the area. This type of financial control will continue just as long as the Alaskan people find it necessary to travel six thousand miles to Washington in order to obtain the legislative action which they need to deal with their problems." [16]

The department, however, objected to the transfer of all the public lands, provided, with certain noted exceptions, in this, as it had been in Delegate Bartlett's previous, bill. It recommended that instead some 22,000,000 acres in numbered sections be transferred.[17]

Another statehood bill, H.R. 1808, was introduced by Representative Homer D. Angell, R., of Oregon, who had visited Alaska twice and declared it "a striking example of taxation without representation," that its "period of pupilage should be ended," and that Alaska had "grown up and should discard its knee pants." He also submitted for the record an endorsement of Alaska statehood from the Portland Chamber of Commerce.[18]

The first hearings ever to be held on statehood recorded the testimony of 150 witnesses, among whom some twelve registered their opposition to statehood "at this time."

Among the supporters was found General of the Air Force H. H.

Arnold, who had written an article for a special statehood edition of
the Ketchikan *Chronicle*, saying:

"In this world of tomorrow, Alaska is assured a position of great importance. Upon Alaska our future may well rest. What, then, would
be better; what would insure a greater provision for our future than
to recognize that most important area and make it a state, equal to our
forty-eight States?" [19]

Elmer E. Rasmuson, Alaska-born Anchorage banker, asked:
"Should it not be a matter of national chagrin to have had Alaska
eighty years now and yet there is a question as to whether Alaska is
ready for statehood?" [20]

Francis C. Bowden, pharmacist and Mayor of Anchorage, called attention to "the restrictions which often impede, delay and obstruct
the proper administration of municipal affairs in Alaska." These restrictions, he stated, "are the result of remote controls over Alaska
held by the federal government at Washington." He detailed the delays attendant upon getting congressional legislation permitting the
city to bond itself for necessary improvements. "Alaskans generally,
and especially the people of Anchorage," he concluded, "do not like
their present status as eunuchs among the citizens of the United
States. They don't like to look to Congress for authority to transact
the ordinary affairs of life, which citizens elsewhere handle themselves.
They want local autonomy not only in their municipal government
but in their state as well." [21]

George Sundborg, Manager of the Alaska Development Board,
urged that Alaska, in addition to the advantages of statehood, needed
the responsibilities of statehood:

"We will never amount to much or go very far toward developing
this country until we have a form of government which places a primary responsibility with the people who live here." [22]

Referring to the criticism leveled by opponents of statehood at the
territory's failure to enact sufficient revenue measures (an accusation
that was fully justified before the 1949 legislative session) Sundborg
said:

"Those who have complained to the committee that Alaska has
never taxed itself adequately to support even a good territorial government are the very people who are responsible for that condition.
Those who say we are not ready for statehood are those who have

been working hardest at session after session of our legislature to keep us from being ready." [23] (Likewise a true statement.)

Evangeline Atwood, born in Alaska, member of the territorial Board of Public Welfare, testified:

"As long as we remain a territory we will lack that feeling of loyalty and pride which comes from possessing something over which we have complete control. That is why throughout the past eighty years our citizens, when they have accumulated considerable wealth, move outside, investing their money in the States instead of reinvesting it in the land from which they extracted it. . . . The same lack of loyalty and pride is reflected in our territorial legislature where our legislators are willing and ready to sell themselves out to the big absentee interests with the result that they are willing to see millions of dollars earned here and not a penny of tax levied upon them. . . . There are many of us younger Alaskans who are thoroughly ashamed of this state of affairs but we can understand why such a condition exists. We want to do something about it and basically we believe a change in political status is fundamental." [24]

Speaking in opposition to the bill, Herbert L. Faulkner, attorney, of Juneau, and at various times lobbyist for mining and canning interests, said he was not opposed to statehood but that he felt the time for it had not arrived and gave the reasons extensively.[25]

Richard F. Lewis, of Piedmont, California, owner of a water-distribution system in Juneau and of mining interests in Alaska, felt that the issue was whether the people of Alaska could afford the additional cost of state government. He thought it would be too great for the number of people there.[26]

Clarence Moriarty, executive for a large stateside construction firm, declared: "Statehood for Alaska at this time is little short of suicide, and can only result in failure and disappointment for all the people of Alaska, as well as shame before the world for having undertaken so foolhardy an expedition." [27]

Norman Stines, mining promoter, of Fairbanks, resident of California, testified that statehood "would be a calamity." [28]

Al Anderson, Executive Secretary of the Alaska Miners Association and its lobbyist, felt that "the talk of Alaska's vast resources" was "greatly exaggerated, so that the resources to run the new state are limited indeed. . . ." [29]

W. C. Arnold, Managing Director of the Alaska Salmon Industry, Inc., who generally followed congressional committees coming to Alaska, closely, testified three times; at Fairbanks, September 4th, at Juneau, September 9th, and at Ketchikan, September 12th.[30] Nowhere in his testimony did Mr. Arnold oppose statehood but argued that the territory could never develop "until some stable transportation system is effected where goods can move into and out of this territory . . . at a reasonable rate. We do not have such a system now." He thought that statehood discussion was "not untimely," that now was "the time to approach it . . . and the approach ought to be about putting our house in order by solving the problems which confront us and which would enable us to develop the territory and statehood to come as a natural development. I do not advocate delaying the statehood question. I advocate the solution of the basic problems which prevent the development of this territory." [31]

As the hearings drew to a close in Ketchikan, September 12th, a charge of attempted coercion by canned-salmon industry officials was presented to the committee. The complainant was James A. Wooten, President of Alaska Airlines, who had previously testified in favor of statehood.[32] He interpreted the company officials' statements to him as threats that if he did not desist from advocating statehood he would lose the companies' business of transporting cannery workers and fishermen to their places of work. Mr. Wooten's letter was given to the press by the subcommittee chairman, Representative Fred L. Crawford, R., of Michigan. It was published in the Ketchikan *Chronicle* on September 13th.[33]

The subcommittee reported the statehood bill favorably by unanimous vote. Its basis for the finding was in part as follows:

"About one-third of the voters of Alaska are opposed to statehood. Opponents argue that the population of the territory is too small at the present time; that the expense of statehood is too great for Alaska to bear, since the sources of revenues for Alaska as a state are uncertain; that federal reservations would deprive the state of revenue from, and jurisdiction over, vast areas; that Alaska, as a noncontiguous area, is too far removed from the United States to have the same interests and develop the same problems as the states; that the federal government now carries on many activities in Alaska which would cease with statehood to Alaska's disadvantage.

"However on the basis of the record and findings of fact, the subcommittee concludes that Alaska should be admitted to statehood. Alaska has served a long period of tutelage in a territorial status. . . . The desirable development of Alaska and its resources can best be brought about by an increase in its permanent population, in the investment capital available, and by the establishment of new industries. These in turn will be induced most rapidly by statehood." [34]

However the subcommittee accepted the Interior Department's views on the amount of public land the state of Alaska should have and a substitute bill, H.R. 5666, giving Alaska numbered sections 2, 16, 32, and 36 for schools and 33 for the university, a provision similar to that obtained by the last three states admitted to the Union, was submitted to the full committee.

In that form it received the unanimous approval of its twenty-five voting members, which, given the diversity implicit in that number, was considered a remarkable showing.[35] It was reported to the House April 14, 1948.

However, the House leadership had different views. It was a Republican Congress, made so by the 1946 election, and though the Republicans on the committee outnumbered the Democrats fourteen to ten and obviously disregarded party considerations in their finding, the Speaker, Joseph W. Martin Jr., R., of Massachusetts, decided that Hawaii was likely to send Republicans to Congress, and Alaska Democrats. So Hawaii in the Eightieth Congress received his blessing and thereby "a rule" from the Rules Committee, which meant authorization to have its statehood bill brought up and voted upon. Hawaii's bill, H.R. 49, passed the House on June 30, 1947, while the opportunity for a similar test was denied Alaska's bill. This was the beginning of a partisanship in relation to the two territories that henceforth motivated certain powerfully placed officials, while others in Congress, contrariwise, believed the issue should be above partisan considerations, and acted accordingly.

Had Alaska's statehood bill been granted a rule in the House, it would, given the committee's favorable report, undoubtedly have passed that body. Yet it would not have been enacted into law. For in the Senate it would have encountered the opposition of Hugh Butler, R., of Nebraska, Chairman of the Committee on Interior and Insular Affairs, who opposed statehood for Alaska. But Hawaii fared no better. For Senator Butler likewise opposed its statehood. Had he favored it Hawaii would have become a state before mid-century. For there was much sentiment for Hawaiian statehood in the Eightieth Congress. So much support was there that a group of senators headed by William Knowland, R., of California, even tried the unusual procedure of seeking to discharge the committee in order to allow the Senate to vote on the measure. After waiting vainly for over ten months for a report he introduced a resolution to discharge the committee.[35]*

"One Senator from one state," said Knowland when the resolution came up for debate, "is keeping ninety-five senators, representing forty-eight States, from even having a chance to pass on this major matter of national policy. . . . Unless my motion prevails statehood is dead for this session." [36]

Given the Senate's respect for its customs and traditions (and every senator may some day be a committee chairman!) the move was bound to fail. Yet it mustered twenty votes, including that of the greatly respected Arthur H. Vandenberg, R., of Michigan, himself chairman of a committee—that on Foreign Relations. The power of an individual in a system of representative government—that of Speaker of the House, and that of the chairman of a congressional committee—was thus illustrated.

President Truman was continuing his battle for both statehood bills.[37] The day after the unsuccessful attempt to bring the Hawaii statehood bill to the Senate floor, he sent a special message to Congress "relative to the enactment of necessary legislation to admit Alaska to statehood at the earliest possible date." After calling for prompt action on the statehood bill "unanimously recommended by the Committee on Public Lands" [H.R. 5666], and making specific proposals for improvement of the transportation system, the extension of the temporary shipping subsidy, the rehabilitation of the Alaska Railroad, a long-range highway-building program, the construction of housing and community facilities, and the development of Alaska's hydroelectric power, the President concluded his detailed message thus:

"With imagination and farseeing effort by the people of Alaska and the government, the resources of Alaska can play a growing role in our national economy and can provide a sound livelihood for the people now there and many thousands will join them.

"In the long view, the most important action the government can take to assure this end is to permit Alaska to become a state." [38]

With a fuller and more understanding consideration of Alaskan problems and needs than had ever been given by an American President, it was the most important message concerning Alaska to emanate from the White House since the purchase.

The Democratic leadership in the Eighty-first Congress permitted both Hawaii and Alaska statehood bills to come to the floor, the power of the Rules Committee having been curtailed earlier in the first session by action of the entire House. After receiving a favorable committee report—this time with one dissenter—the Alaska statehood bill, H.R. 331, passed the House on March 3, 1950 by 186 to 146. The Hawaii bill passed shortly thereafter.[39]

Senate hearings on H.R. 331 and a companion bill, S. 2036, sponsored by Senator Estes Kefauver, D., of Tennessee, and others, began April 24. Some fifty witnesses were heard, and with exhibits and communications, the report covered 531 printed pages.

The hearings disclosed the growing support of statehood both in Alaska and in the nation. In the States it had secured the endorsement of the large national organizations—business, labor, patriotic, fraternal. They included the United States Chamber of Commerce, the Junior Chambers of Commerce, the American Federation of Labor, the C.I.O., the twenty organizations comprising the Railway Labor Executives Association, The American Legion, the Veterans of Foreign Wars, the Amvets, the Catholic War Veterans, The National Grange, The General Federation of Women's Clubs, the Dames of the Loyal Legion, the Congress of Home Missions, comprising some thirty Protestant denominations, the National Association of Attorneys General, the Kiwanis and Lions Internationals, the Loyal Order of Moose, and beginning in 1947, the National Governors' Conference. Governor Earl Warren of California flew to the hearings to testify for Alaskan statehood on the opening day, adding testimony for Hawaii's case. Governor Alfred E. Driscoll of New Jersey likewise appeared in person. Governors John W. Bonner of Montana, Vail Pittman of Nevada and J. Bracken Lee of Utah sent endorsements. Statehood had the almost unanimous support of the American press.

The military gave the cause strong backing. Robert P. Patterson, former Secretary of War, wrote at length to sustain his conviction that statehood would "strengthen the national defense." [40] Lieutenant General Nathan F. Twining, Commander in Chief of the Alaska Command, so testified.[41] The National Committee for Alaskan Statehood listed the names of General of the Army Douglas MacArthur,

General of the Air Force H. H. Arnold, Fleet Admiral Chester W. Nimitz, Vice Admiral Harry G. Hamlet of the Coast Guard, Rear Admiral Richard E. Byrd.[42]

The opposition was directed wholly at the bill and no longer against statehood itself! The case against the bill was effectively presented with a corroborating array of maps, graphs and charts by W. C. Arnold, who declared:

"By this bill Alaska would be relegated to the status of a mendicant state; a poor and distant relative. . . . Knowingly or unknowingly, the advocates of the passage of H.R. 331, in their anxiety to reach their objective, have perpetrated a great hoax on the people of Alaska and the nation. . . .[43] This bill would make Alaska a state in name only and would doom the new state to perpetual pauperism and bureaucratic control." [44]

The view was echoed by telegrams from Alaska, from thirty-four individuals most of whom had opposed statehood as such.[45] The same view was supported throughout the hearings by the committee's ranking minority member, Senator Hugh Butler.

While granting that any bill was capable of improvement and of greater generosity in its terms, its supporters—and no Alaskan appeared in person in opposition—felt it was better to have even a fair bill than no bill, which they feared would likely be the alternative.

"The amount of public land that the state would acquire is of great interest to Alaskans. We would like to acquire as much as we can," testified Robert E. Ellis, Ketchikan air-line executive and the city's former mayor. "If we try to drive too hard a bargain, we are likely to lose the whole deal. We think that the terms that are carried in this bill before us are equitable to both the federal government and to the new state." [46]

"We would be less than human if we did not want all the land that we can get," testified Edward V. Davis, attorney, representing the Anchorage Chamber of Commerce. "If it comes to the question as to whether we get statehood now without more land than the bill provides as against the question of no statehood now with more land some day 'maybe,' we would certainly choose statehood now without any hesitation at all."

Voicing the fear that statehood opponents were seeking to make the bill so generous that the executive departments would oppose it and cause Congress to defeat it, Davis said: "In your effort to help us, we ask that you don't overdo it. In your desire to give us a perfect state, we ask that you don't risk the probability of defeating statehood entirely." [47]

A similar stand was taken by Gunnard Engebreth, President of the Territorial Senate and President of the Anchorage Republican Club, which he represented at the hearings:

"Some . . . Republicans . . . and Democrats in Alaska are opposed to statehood. . . . They are smart enough to know that you cannot be opposed to statehood in principle, so they have to use some other means for defeating it. . . ." Those who opposed statehood in general were now concentrating on decrying the particular bill, H.R. 331, he said, but that he believed it "satisfactory to the great majority of Alaskans," and "that the proposed amendments which would provide unprecedented land grants to the new state wear all the badges of sabotage, designed to kill or delay statehood." [48]

The Reverend G. Edgar Gallant, the first priest ever ordained in Alaska, and with the Reverend Paul C. O'Connor, authorized by the Right Reverend Francis D. Gleeson, Roman Catholic Bishop of Alaska, to present their views on statehood, testified that the telegrams opposing H.R. 331 resulted from propaganda against the bill in Alaska to the effect that it was not the same bill originally introduced, and seeking to spread the belief "that we are not getting anything at all at this time." Having compared the drafts, Fr. Gallant rejected that contention. Most of the people of Alaska, he said, were favorable to statehood and were the kind who would "make the best of any deal they get." [49]

To refute the contention that statehood would be helpful to national defense—for which there had been substantial testimony from the highest ranking military men—the canned-salmon industry produced a retired Rear Admiral, Ralph N. Wood. During the latter part of World War II he had been commandant of the Seventeenth Naval District, which comprised Alaska. Mr. Arnold introduced him as a witness "to make a statement, expressing his views on the relationship between statehood and national defense," adding:

"Rear Admiral Wood comes here at my request and at the expense of the Alaska Salmon Industry, Inc." [50]

The admiral's statement was:

"It has been stated that statehood for Alaska is now going to bolster somehow the national defense. In my opinion it makes no difference whether Alaska is a state or a territory as far as national defense is concerned." [51]

The hearings were concluded on April 29th and the committee reported H. 331 out by a vote of eight to two on June 29th. The report contained a letter from President Truman supporting both H.R. 331 and H.R. 49, the Hawaii statehood bill, as well as Senator Butler's minority views.[52]

But as summer dragged on, with a press of important business, the war in Korea, action on the statehood bills seemed less and less likely. A motion to bring up the Hawaii bill on the consent calendar on August 8th was objected to by Senator McCarran, who made similar objection to the Alaska bill, and both "went over."

At this point Majority Leader Scott Lucas, D., of Illinois, declared that he considered the Alaska bill of extraordinary importance in view of what was "going on at the present time throughout the world." Senator Knowland arose to say that he favored both Alaska and Hawaii statehood and hoped both would be considered. Senator Lucas assured him that was his purpose.[53]

Motions to bring both up failed again on September 13th through objections by Senator Walter F. George, D., of Georgia. The session adjourned on September 23rd to reconvene on "a day certain," November 27th, and the prospect for serious consideration of the statehood bills was obviously slight.

The reconvening Senate received a long letter from President Truman addressed to the presiding officer, Vice-President Alben W. Barkley, expressing the "hope that at this session the Senate will approve the bills now before it for the admission . . . of Hawaii and Alaska as states," and urging that the Senate "give the highest priority to the statehood measures." [54]

Majority Leader Lucas asked that the Senate proceed to consider them. The ensuing debate, led by Senator Joseph C. O'Mahoney, D., of Wyoming, Chairman of the Interior and Insular Affairs Committee, dealt with the Alaska bill. The opponents of statehood objected to its consideration. They included Senators Butler, Stennis, D., of Mississippi, McClellan, D., of Arkansas, Russell, D., of Georgia, Hoey, D., of North Carolina. And while the motion to take up the Alaska bill failed, some discussion of Alaskan statehood took place— for the first time—on the Senate floor.

Senator Stennis, principal spokesman for the opposition, declared:

"We have the shocking fact—and it is a shocking fact—that of all the great area of Alaska, which is as large as the combined areas of Texas, California, and Montana . . . the government owns 99.7 per cent. In other words, in the eighty-three years Alaska has been under the control of the federal government, only three-tenths of 1 per cent of all that vast area has found its way into private hands. . . ." This would amount to only fifteen hundred square miles and the "shocking fact" was that it was "actually seriously proposed" that it "be given two seats on the floor of the Senate of the United States." [55]

Only the gold rush and government programs caused Alaska's population to increase, said Senator Stennis, and the decline between 1900 and 1930 was "due to the extreme climate and the hazardous living conditions. Congress cannot change the climate . . . the basic factors which have been holding back Alaska are ones which we cannot change." [56]

Quoting from an article by Hanson W. Baldwin in the New York *Times:* "It is a land of great distances, of sparse populations, of towering peaks, of barren tundras, of untrodden wildernesses and of relentless winters. Wintertime temperatures range down to 65 degrees below. Brief exposure can mean death," Senator Stennis continued:

"There is a region which has not been developed. Its lack of development is not due to the lack of a flag flying over it or a lack of protection by the federal government. The lack of development of Alaska does not arise because of any lack of law or order, but the explanation is to be found in that short sentence which I have read . . . 'Brief exposure can mean death.' " [57]

If Alaska is admitted, Senator Stennis asked, would we then "admit Hawaii? And then are we going to admit the Virgin Islands? Are we going to admit Puerto Rico? Are we going to admit Guam? Okinawa? " [58]

Senator Clyde R. Hoey of North Carolina said:
"When we come to think about . . . the resources of Alaska, we find that they have not been developed because people do not want to stay there in the extremes of climate which are found there." [59]

Kenneth McKellar, D., of Tennessee, said that he had served for many years on the Appropriations Committee and as far as he could recall "we have never turned down a request looking to the aid and betterment and upbuilding of the Territory of Alaska."

"Looking at the matter solely from the standpoint of the Territory of Alaska, the land and the people," Senator McKellar continued, "I doubt if there would be as good a government there, if statehood were granted, as now exists, because our whole country seems to feel that we should look after the people there and help them, and we do that."

Senator Hoey concurred that what "the very able Chairman of the Committee on Appropriations . . . says is absolutely accurate." [60]

Senator Butler declared: "The Territory of Alaska has always received fair and equitable treatment from the National Congress and from federal territorial officials under its present form of government. At least any problems it has had in its relations with the federal government cannot be fairly laid to its territorial status." [61]

Senators O'Mahoney, Lehman, D., of New York, Anderson, D., of New Mexico, Cordon, R., of Oregon, Morse, R., of Oregon, Thye, R., of Minnesota and Ecton, R., of Montana, spoke for the motion.

Senator Cordon regretted that those who were in deep opposition to the bills, "will—and they have frankly so stated—take advantage of every parliamentary situation in their favor to delay action or to defeat the motion." [62] And he summed up his own position as follows: "If taxation without representation was tyranny in 1776 it is tyranny today. If the right of people to govern themselves, to participate in their government, was so dear to those giants of old who gathered and promulgated the Declaration of Independence, that they were willing to pledge their lives, their fortunes and their sacred honor, in support of that proposition, it is just as dear today." [63]

"Give to Alaska statehood and Alaska will take care of the rest." [64]

Senator Morse, who a few weeks earlier had visited Alaska as a member of the Armed Services Committee, said:

"We have tried to make clear throughout our history that we do not look with favor upon a policy of colonialism, because a policy of colonialism inevitably, as history shows, is inclined to lead to taking advantage of the subjects of the colony. It is inclined to lead to a pattern of exploitation of people who are not given a voting voice in self-government.

"One cannot travel through Alaska . . . without recognizing that Alaska suffers from the great evil of absentee ownership. Absentee ownership and the evils that inevitably go along with it can thrive best when self-government is denied." [65]

To the much controverted question whether statehood would or would not strengthen national defense, Senator Morse, just back from an official mission to ascertain the exact state of Alaska's military preparedness, brought new and expert testimony:

"The defenses of Alaska," he concluded, "would never have reached the weakened condition into which they were permitted to get following World War II, if the Territory of Alaska had had voting representation in the House of Representatives and in the Senate." It "would have brought . . . the evidence and arguments which would have prevented Congress from figuratively sticking its head in the sand while the great defenses of Alaska were permitted to become so weakened," thereby jeopardizing "the security . . . of 160,000,000 American citizens . . ."[66]

After three days given partially to the debate, Senator Lucas, who the preceding month had been defeated for re-election, gave up—far too quickly and easily, some statehood supporters felt—and moved on to other business.[67] The opponents of statehood had, in Senator Morse's words, "thrown up a parliamentary barricade to prevent a vote upon the statehood measures." [68] It was assumed by their supporters that, if voted upon, the bills would have stood a good chance of passage, and with their previous approval by the House would have become law. Motions to consider them were made once more on December 15th, and were objected to, the *Congressional Record* disclosed, by "several senators." The Eighty-first Congress expired shortly thereafter and the efforts to secure enactment of statehood legislation had to be undertaken anew.

The leadership of the Eighty-second Congress decided that since the House had passed statehood bills on which the Senate had not acted, the Senate should now be tried first. S. 50, the Alaska bill, started promisingly with nineteen sponsors.[69] However a controversy arose within the committee—whose composition had been substantially changed—the opponents of Alaskan statehood requesting further hearings. This, Chairman O'Mahoney and six other members felt, would cause delay sufficient to preclude action in the Eighty-second Congress; they considered the preceding April's hearings sufficient, and reported the bill out, seven to six, on April 3, 1951. The Hawaiian bill, S. 49, had been reported previously.[70]

The committee's report summarized the evidence for and against statehood, noting that in the hearings "no resident of the territory appeared in opposition, but that the burden was carried by representatives of the fish-packing industry with headquarters in the States." [71]

Several paragraphs refuted ancient and persisting allegations that Alaska's climate presented insuperable obstacles—to settlement, development, and, therefore, to statehood.[72]

The committee made one modification in the land provisions. Instead of the four numbered sections, following the previous practice for new states, Alaska would receive some 23,000,000 acres of its own choosing. This would obviate the inclusion of mountain top, tundra or otherwise worthless land. It would transfer from the public domain to the new state an area larger than Maine or West Virginia, giving it more land than was possessed in 1951 by four Western public-land states: Arizona, Idaho, Utah and Nevada.[73]

The minority report repeated the "Minority Views of Senator Butler" of the previous session and added some derogatory material which reflected the views which Senator Butler had previously expressed on the floor of the Senate.[74] A sixty-four-page printed "Analysis and Refutation of Minority Views on S. 50," published by the Alaska Statehood Committee,[75] and written for it by Dr. George W. Rogers, an economist of standing thoroughly familiar with Alaska, characterized some of the "Minority Views" as "distortion of general truth," "the most unfortunate kind of misstatement," and others as "based upon smear literature produced by the malicious fringe of one of our major political parties during the 1950 election campaigns and recognized at the outset by most Alaskans of all political affiliations as a low form of partisan slander, since amply answered and refuted." [76]

"As presented by the report of the Minority," the "Analysis and Refutation" declared, "this material does not merit further discussion beyond calling attention to the deplorable practice of introducing such maliciously false propaganda into what is represented to be an objective study." [77]

Four efforts to bring up the statehood bills during the remainder of the first session of the Eighty-second Congress were thwarted by objectors.[78] The bills were made the order of business early in the second session, Senator Ernest W. McFarland, D., of Arizona, the majority leader, bringing up the Alaska bill January 31, 1952.

Even before the debate it was known that an opposition consisting of "Taft Republicans" and "Southern Democrats" had combined to recommit the bill, a well-known method of killing a measure without actually voting against it. Three elements composed this opposition. There were those Republicans who viewed statehood largely from a partisan angle and Alaska as a state that would probably send Democrats to Congress: there were the Southerners deeply concerned about federal fair-employment-practices legislation and fearing the admission of senators who might not share those views. There was a third group partially overlapping the first two, composed of senators susceptible to all the traditional arguments used repeatedly against the admission of new states: dilution of the Senate by bringing in states with a relatively small population; inadequate resources to support a state; remoteness, to which in the case of Alaska and Hawaii was added the new wrinkle of noncontiguity, a heaven-sent oratorical weapon to the opponents! And there were some who had been led to doubt the equitableness of the Alaska bill. The coalition leaders believed they had a ten-vote margin for recommittal.

The nature of the Southern opposition was not too freely admitted. Nor did it include all the South's senators. It had been touched upon tactfully by Senator Cordon toward the close of the Eighty-first Congress in what was in effect an appeal to the southerners not to carry their views on civil rights as they would affect their own states to the extent of blocking the admission of two new states.[79]

However the attitude was definitely explained by one Southern senator, well regarded for his cultural attainments. When asked by a cabinet member whether he would not support Alaskan statehood, he replied:

"I'm sorry, but a group of us are committed to oppose the admissions of any states whose senators are not likely to support our stand on cloture. The merits of the statehood issue won't play any part in our decision."

This group was unalterably opposed to federal F.E.P.C. legislation which President Truman had vigorously sponsored, insisting that the matter should be left to the states. But fearing a senatorial majority might enact the legislation, they were prepared to filibuster indefinitely to prevent it. Under existing rules sixty-four senators, or two-thirds of the Senate, were needed to impose cloture—that is, to shut off debate. The addition of four senators whose views were of necessity unknown might weaken the anti-cloture forces. Hence the opposition to statehood.

"We have carried . . . political and economic freedom steadily west across the North American continent," declared Senator O'Mahoney in opening the debate,[80] "but now Alaska is held back because it does not have the statehood this bill would grant. People who enjoy political and economic freedom are loath to move into a territory where their activities are controlled from beyond their borders . . . by government bureaus in Washington. . . . Without statehood it will be impossible to develop the vast treasures of this great territory as they should be." [81]

Senator Spessard L. Holland, D., of Florida, stressed the development of his state after statehood had been granted and its lack of progress before that time.[82]

Senator Lester C. Hunt, D., of Wyoming, said that he had returned from Alaska two years earlier convinced that Alaska was ready for statehood. A terrific injustice was being done its people every day they were kept outside the Union. New industry would not establish itself there until it could count on stable tax laws.[83]

Senator Magnuson said that he knew that industry had refused to go to Alaska "because of the bureaucratic instability." [84]

Senator Dennis Chavez, D., of New Mexico, felt that "as a matter of right and as a matter of policy we should not have any territories under our dominion." [85]

Senator Herbert H. Lehman, D., of New York, thought "that the granting of statehood would be a ten-strike in the contest for freedom the world over." [86] He called attention to "the gap which often exists between public sentiment and congressional action as illustrated by the fight over statehood for Hawaii and Alaska" by citing the Gallup poll—public sentiment favoring Alaska by nine to one and Hawaii by six to one.[87]

Senator Knowland rejected the opposition's contention that admission of Alaska and Hawaii would set a precedent, but affirmed that on the contrary it would fulfill one. He adverted to the reasons for Southern opposition by introducing an editorial from the New York *Herald Tribune* entitled: "What Blocks Alaskan Statehood?" [88]

Senator Fred A. Seaton, R., of Nebraska, gave a detailed account of the arguments similar to those against Alaskan statehood in the debates on the admission to statehood of "practically every territory." "Experience," he said, "has proved them false." [89]

Speaking for recommittal Senator Butler declared: "Under the pending bill, Alaska would be relegated to the status of a poor and distant relation of the Federal Union.[90]

"Another suggestion which I have made in the past," said Nebraska's senior senator, "and which I think is perfectly logical, is to attach a territory to the state which is nearest to it. I understand that Montana or Washington would be very glad to have the territory attached to its domain and made a part of either state." [91]

"In all fairness to the great bulk of the Alaskan populace," he said, "the Senate should conduct hearings on statehood within Alaska itself, to give both opponents and proponents equal opportunity to state their case. . . . It has been two years since hearings have been held on this question. And the Senate has never held hearings on the issue in Alaska." [92]

The opposition to statehood was conducted principally by Senator George Smathers, D., of Florida, the committee member most insistent on further hearings, who made the motion to recommit the bill, and by Senator Stennis. The Mississippi senator marshaled his arguments with great skill but always with generosity toward Alaskans. His thesis was that they faced unsurmountable handicaps in their effort to support a state. But apart from that hardy perennial of congressional debates on Alaska—the calamitous climate—most of the Alaskans' difficulties cited were those which they had vainly implored Congress to rectify:

There was the "fact that only six-tenths of 1 per cent of that great area has ever even been surveyed," [93] that "only three-tenths of one per cent of privately owned land" existed, "the rest of it belongs to the Government of the United States." [94] There were "the problems of transportation." [95] There were no counties in Alaska!

"The county is the great training ground" for citizenship, said Senator Stennis. "With all deference to the fine people of Alaska the main essential training element for American citizenship would be totally lacking." [96]

Finally, should the United States embark on "a new policy . . . namely . . . whether we shall take a disconnected area, whether it be in the Pacific, in South America, in Africa, or anywhere else . . . into the bosom of our nation? We are changing the pattern of our Union once we launch out on this program." [97]

Twenty-five pros and cons of Alaskan statehood were painstakingly set forth by Senator O'Mahoney.[98] The arguments advanced against it in the debate were answered one by one by Senator Cordon.[99]

"If Alaska at the moment is perhaps at an economic disadvantage, it is not the fault of Alaska," declared Oregon's senior senator. The fault rests with the United States Government which has never given to Alaska its birthright or any hope for the future.

"Mr. President, Congress is responsible for that situation. . . . Congress can remedy it. The laws will be changed if the people of Alaska are given a voice in Congress, and their representatives can stand in the halls of Congress on an equality with the rest of us and insist on their rights. Then they can plead for the things we should have given them without their plea, and they can demand the things which the law gives them, but which administrative interpretation has withheld from them." [100]

Replying to the attacks on statehood by the effort to discredit the bill conferring it, Senator Cordon said:

"I do not undertake to say that the bill now pending is a complete answer to the economic needs of a new state in Alaska. . . . But . . . that is wholly beside the point. . . . If it is not enough, the Congress that grants statehood and grants aids to relieve economic necessity can add to them. No argument can be made against statehood based upon any shortcomings in this bill. There is a finality, true, in the granting of statehood, but there is no finality with respect to the aid which may be granted to a new state . . . to assist it in overcoming its economic handicaps of the moment." [101]

The vote on February 27, 1952, gave forty-five for and forty-four against recommittal. The outcome was in doubt until the last vote was cast. The great interest in the measure was demonstrated by the presence of eighty-nine senators, with six others paired and only one not recorded. The parties were evenly divided, twenty-five Democrats and twenty Republicans voting for recommittal; twenty-four Democrats and twenty Republicans against. The first full-blown debate on Alaskan statehood had occupied a large part of eleven days over a period of four weeks. Considering the circumstances surrounding Alaska's first test in the upper house of Congress and the one-vote margin of defeat, it represented a long step forward on the tortuous road to self-government.

There were hopeful portents. The Republican National Convention meeting in July changed the "eventual statehood for Hawaii, Alaska . . ." of its 1948 platform to "immediate statehood for Hawaii," and for Alaska, "statehood under an equitable enabling act."

Political considerations played the major role in that change. Senator Butler's opposition to Hawaiian statehood, so vigorously expressed in his "Minority Views" on S. 49, the bill awaiting Senate action after the Alaska bill had been recommitted, was unaltered.[102] That is, until Senator Taft, viewing the eight Hawaiian delegates as badly needed in his campaign for the nomination, persuaded Senator Butler, on the eve of the convention, to support the "immediate statehood" plank.[103] The Alaskan plank, favoring statehood under an equitable enabling act, was also a step from "eventually" to "now." It accommodated itself to Senator Butler's attacks on the previous Alaska legislation and appeared like a commitment to produce, and then support, a bill which the Republican leadership would consider "equitable."

The Democratic National Convention meeting in Chicago a week later readopted its 1948 planks for immediate statehood for Alaska and Hawaii. As a unique evidence of good will and good faith the convention gave the two territories, for the first time in history, their alphabetical place in the roll of states, lifting them from their previous position at the bottom of the list. Alaska thus became second in the roll call in the 1952 convention, immediately following Alabama, a position of more than sentimental value. Hawaii followed Georgia and preceded Idaho.

Senator Taft failed to achieve the nomination. But the November elections, which, despite victory, gave the Republicans only a tenuous majority of one in the Senate, caused Senator Butler further to perceive the advantages of admitting Hawaii promptly to statehood. The Hawaiians had had the foresight, even before congressional approval of statehood, to call a constitutional convention, draw up a constitution and have it ratified by popular vote.[104]

Were Hawaii to be admitted to statehood in the Eighty-third Congress, it could elect two senators in 1954, and, Senator Butler told the President-elect when they met in Honolulu after Eisenhower's trip to Korea, he hoped and expected they would be Republicans. Alaska, even if admitted to statehood in the Eighty-third Congress, could not comply with the requirements for a constitutional convention and a popular vote on a constitution before 1956.

Both Alaskans and Hawaiians had reason to be hopeful about the prospects for statehood under the incoming administration. Besides the platform commitments—the first time that both major parties had pledged statehood to both territories—was the publicly recorded support of President Eisenhower. Speaking at Denver in September, 1950, as President of Columbia University, he had been reported by the Denver *Post* as follows:[105]

ALASKA, HAWAII STATEHOOD SEEN
AS SIGN TO WORLD

Quick admission of Alaska and Hawaii to statehood will show the world that "America practices what it preaches," Gen. Dwight D. Eisenhower said Saturday in a brief talk to 1,500 Denverites gathered at the freedom bell.

The famed war and peacetime leader declared admission of the two territories is "in conformity with the American way of life," granting them self-government and equal voice in national affairs.

PRACTICAL SYMBOL

Alaskan and Hawaiian statehood will serve to the people of the world as a "practical symbol that America practices what it preaches," Eisenhower said. He said he hopes Congress would soon pass admission legislation now before it.

It came, therefore, as a great shock to Alaskans, when in his State-of-the-Union Message on February 2, 1953, President Eisenhower endorsed statehood for Hawaii, but omitted any mention of Alaska. Moreover, he urged that Hawaii be granted statehood "promptly with the first election in 1954." [106]

The emphasis on the 1954 election indicated to observers that the President had been alerted to the usefulness of improving, at the first opportunity, the G.O.P.'s hair-line majority in the Senate.

The Twenty-first Alaska Legislature, which had assembled in Juneau less than a week earlier, was heavily Republican, the October, 1952, election having produced majorities of eleven to five in the Senate and twenty to four in the House, thus maintaining Alaska's repute of accurately forecasting the national electoral results. The legislators immediately telegraphed a protest to President Eisenhower at the omission of Alaskan statehood from his message. They followed this up with a memorial alluding to the statehood "prospect . . . of our sister Territory of Hawaii," and requested like consideration for Alaska.[107] The memorial passed by the unanimous vote of both houses.

But no declaration of a change in attitude was forthcoming from the White House. Indeed President Eisenhower subsequently explained his new stand on Alaskan statehood at press conferences by saying he thought Alaska was not ready for it. (The population of Alaska had been recorded as 182,000 on August 1, 1953, or 54,000 greater than when President Eisenhower endorsed statehood four years earlier.) But his reversal from his earlier position, generally attributed to his political advisors, was seen by Alaskans, in view of the all-out presidential support of Hawaiian statehood, as just another discrimination against Alaska. It strengthened the statehood sentiment in Alaska. On February 27, 1954, the Fairbanks *News-Miner*, long opposed to statehood, came out strongly for "Statehood Now." [108]

Meanwhile there was renewed action on the legislative front. In the House of Representatives hearings on five statehood bills under the chairmanship of John P. Saylor, R., of Pennsylvania, resulted in his bill, H.R. 2982, being reported by a vote of nineteen to five.[109] It provided 40,000,000 acres of land for the new state and $50,000,000 for road construction, public buildings and land surveys, thus seeking to compensate in part for the long federal neglect in these activities.[110]

In the Senate the majority of the Committee on Interior and Insular Affairs was preparing to vote out the Hawaiian statehood bill, S. 49, but not the Alaskan bill, S. 50. To prevent this discrimination, Senator Clinton Anderson moved that the bills be joined and hearings ordered on both. The motion carried eight to seven, one Republican, George W. Malone, joining the seven Democrats. Malone made no secret of the fact that he was opposed to statehood for either territory, but felt that if one was to be voted on, the other should not be denied the same opportunity. Planning to secure action on Hawaiian statehood alone, Chairman Butler had not even attempted to draw up the "equitable enabling act" which the Republican platform had promised.

Although a year earlier Senator Butler had called for hearings in Alaska "in all fairness to the bulk of the Alaskan populace," he now opposed them. But he had been outvoted. When he learned that committee members would go to Alaska to hold hearings, even if he did not, he decided to go. He ruled, however, that none who had previously come to Washington to testify would be heard again. He had repeatedly indicated his view that the "little people" of Alaska had not been heard and that they should be.

The "little people" were heard—120 of them at hearings in Ketchikan, Juneau, Fairbanks and Anchorage, from August 17th to August
25th, before six committee members.[111] One hundred and ten testified
for statehood, ten against. The committee appeared deeply impressed
with the enthusiasm and sincerity behind Alaska's statehood cause.
Even Senator Butler in a press interview indicated his belief that the
chances for statehood were "not bad."

To the amazement of Alaskans, Senator Butler, upon his return
to Omaha, was reported by the Associated Press as saying that he
thought he had convinced "the rank and file in Alaska that statehood
should not come at this time.

" 'Most of the clamor for statehood is coming from politicians who
want to run for office' he declared in an interview Saturday.

" 'When we pointed out the obstacles, most of the people agreed
they should wait awhile,' Butler said.

"Statehood would hurt rather than help Alaska because of the tax
load the citizens would have to bear, the Senator said. Most of the
land is owned by the federal government and 'this means there isn't
enough land on the tax rolls to pay for a state government,' he
added." [112]

"Statements attributed to Senator Butler on Alaska statehood in
an Omaha interview are at such variance with the facts that it is impossible to understand how they could be made," editorialized the
Anchorage *Times*.[113]

An investigation of the mystery by that newspaper resulted in an
Associated Press report that Senator Butler had said he had been
quoted correctly but that his remarks had been misinterpreted. But
as he did not make clear how he expected his correctly reported remarks to be interpreted, the mystery remained.[114]

With the convening of the second session of the Eighty-third Congress, a Subcommittee of the Senate Committee on Interior and Insular Affairs under the chairmanship of Senator Cordon went to work
to draft a bill which would satisfy all hands of its equitableness.
Hearings from January 20th to February 24th produced a bill which
would give Alaska one hundred million acres of its own selection
from the unreserved public lands, plus 400,000 acres of the national
forests, plus 2,750,000 acres for institutional and other purposes. It
also authorized the appropriation of $48,000,000 for road construc-

tion over a period of six years, and $30,000,000 for road maintenance over a period of thirty years.[115]

This time a motion to tie the Hawaii and Alaska bills together failed in the committee, because one of the seven Democrats favored reporting Hawaii separately, but it was agreed that now S. 50, the Alaska bill, would be reported after the Hawaii bill, and it was, by a committee vote of fourteen to one.

On February 26th, Senator Anderson submitted an amendment to add S. 50 as title II to S. 49.[116] His stated reason for the action was that it was the only way that Alaskan statehood could secure consideration in the Eighty-third Congress. In the House, Representative Saylor's bill, H.R. 2982, reported out nine months earlier, had been "on ice before the Rules Committee" with no prospect of its release.[117] Introducing a theme new in the statehood debates, Senator Anderson cited the precedents of states which had come into the Union in pairs: Vermont and Kentucky, Indiana and Mississippi, Illinois and Alabama, Maine and Missouri, Arkansas and Michigan, Iowa and Florida.

Senator Jackson pointed out that in the previous Congresses the bills had been handled separately because there was an assurance that President Truman would sign both bills, if passed, but that there was no assurance that President Eisenhower might not veto the Alaska statehood bill. Both Senators Anderson and Jackson made clear that if the move to unite the statehood bills failed they would vote for Hawaii, a position taken generally by Northern Democrats.[118]

Politics is said to make strange bedfellows. Uniting to vote for combining the bills were senators who favored statehood for both territories and others who opposed statehood for either. The former supported their combination because they were outraged by the administration's partisanship on the issue, felt that Alaska had every right to be voted on, and believed that this end could be attained only by uniting the measures. The latter felt that there was a better chance to defeat both bills if they were tied together.

The issues were again debated. Senator Murray declared that before his visit to Alaska he had been informed "that a siren song was being sung in Washington by Alaskans advocating statehood who did not fairly represent the attitudes of their fellow-citizens . . . that on arrival we would find, on the part of the substantial people, as well as the little men, a reluctance to assume the responsibility of statehood. What we actually discovered was a stirring demonstration that the pioneer spirit, the spirit that cries out for political freedom is as alive in Alaska today as it was in other areas of our great country where such freedom was denied. . . . We failed to find any genuine opposition to statehood . . . among the Alaskan people." [119]

"I know where the opposition comes from. . . . Much of it comes from my home town of Seattle," interposed Senator Magnuson, with noteworthy courage. "Many of the persons who oppose Alaskan statehood are friends of mine, personally and politically. Many of them have gone to Alaska and made a great deal of money there. I know why they are afraid to have Alaska admitted. They are afraid they may have to assume some of the responsibilities of statehood. . . . But I know who works up the propaganda in opposition to statehood. It comes from about nine hundred miles south of Alaska." [120]

The debate was on S. 49, and centered chiefly on Hawaii, which bore the brunt of attacks, as Alaska had two years earlier. The Senate leadership opposed the joining of the two bills, and was supported by a statement from President Eisenhower who opposed their being joined. Nevertheless Senator Anderson's motion to combine them prevailed, forty-six to forty-three. [121] The vote followed party lines. All but two of the Democrats voted for the motion, and all but two of the Republicans against it.

The following day Senator Butler of Nebraska asked that a statement of his entitled "A New Approach to Alaska Statehood" be printed in the Record. [122] The gist of it was that he now favored statehood for Alaska because the Alaska bill was in his opinion "an equitable enabling act."

Senator Butler's professed conversion to Alaskan statehood neither alarmed the interests opposed to it and with which he had worked closely, nor gave substantial encouragement to many Alaskan statehood supporters. Those familiar with the committee chairman's mental processes suspected it to be a stratagem to weaken the Democratic resistance to enacting the Hawaiian bill alone.

Those opposed to both bills now came forward with a new proposal: "commonwealth status" for the two territories. It was sponsored by Senator A. S. Mike Monroney, D., of Oklahoma, and co-sponsored by Senators James W. Fulbright, D., of Arkansas, Price Daniel, D., of Texas, and Smathers. [123] Although merely a general declaration of purpose and unspecific in commitment, it held out the prospect of application of the Puerto Rican formula by which Alaska and Hawaii would be relieved of federal taxes but denied voting representation in Congress and its citizens denied the vote in national elections. The proposal was promptly and emphatically denounced by Delegates Farrington and Bartlett. It received virtually no public support.[124]

Senator Fulbright found useful examples in the contrasting experiences of Great Britain and France:

While "France attempted to incorporate into her continental area" —as American statehood advocates wish to do here—"territories lying beyond the boundaries of France, it has not been satisfactory. I think most of us are familiar with the difficulties which France today is encountering in her territories in Africa.

"Such a policy is in contrast with the policy followed by the United Kingdom in its creation of a commonwealth when and if a territory achieved a certain maturity, which entitled it, in the opinion of Great Britain, to self-government. The latter system has been the most satisfactory one for the evolution of backward people the world has ever seen." [125]

The Senate's commonwealth advocates were recommending Britain's policy for the United States with respect to Alaska and Hawaii.

The proposal was given its quietus by Senator Clinton Anderson. To diminish the status of an incorporated territory to that of an unincorporated commonwealth, he made clear, was unconstitutional. So was the corollary proposal to relieve an incorporated territory of federal taxation.[126] Opponents of statehood had counseled caution in conferring statehood because statehood was "irrevocable." The status of an incorporated territory, Senator Anderson advised them, was no less irrevocable.[127]

Senator Cordon concurred on the question of the proposal's unconstitutionality: "It is the ultimate answer to questions that have been raised here." [128]

The commonwealth amendment was defeated sixty to twenty-four.

The combined statehood bills passed by a vote of fifty-seven to twenty-eight. The majority was made up of thirty-three Republicans, twenty-three Democrats and one Independent. The minority consisted of nine Republicans and nineteen Democrats.[129]

The passage for the first time by the Senate of the two statehood

bills by a more than two-to-one majority was viewed by their supporters as a triumph. The ultimate fate of the bills, requiring House
concurrence, was uncertain. Their enactment, it was generally assumed, would depend upon whether President Eisenhower would
give them wholehearted support. If he did not, it was deemed probable that neither would pass in the Eighty-third Congress.

Alaskans had stood too much, too long, to be discouraged or other
than determined to fight on to validate the most basic of American
principles—government by consent of the governed. Apart from their
own perpetual frustrations they knew that the interest of all the American people was being sacrificed by the non-utilization of Alaska, its
extensive area beckoning for settlement, its underdeveloped resources
needed by the entire nation. They knew that under their colonial
status Alaska's greatest potential would remain unrealized—that of a
populous, prospering, self-reliant society erecting in America's farthest
north and farthest west a citadel of spiritual as well as of material
strength, a far-advanced firm front of our democratic idea. It could
long since have been, they knew, it could be now, a bulwark for the
western world, not merely of arms, but even more important, a shin-
ing demonstration, for the whole world to see, of what free men could
accomplish in those latitudes long ignored by other Americans. They
knew that the history of Alaska, as once under Russian dominion, and
its geography, in its juxtaposition to the Soviet police state, uniquely
qualified them for that challenging role. But they also knew that they
could not assume that part, however great their eagerness to play it,
until they were themselves free and equal, as other Americans long
had been. They had seen their colonialism actually intensified in the
years 1953-1954. And so they knew through unchanging experience
that the state of Alaska would not improve appreciably till the State
of Alaska came into being.

THE FORTY-NINTH STATE

The Achievement of Statehood

The whole form and fabric of our free government is based on the
assumption that people can govern themselves in better fashion
than they can be governed by anyone else.
DELEGATE ANTHONY J. DIMOND
DECEMBER 1, 1943

BY 1955 ALASKANS were becoming impatient. Although ten years
had passed since the 1945 Territorial Legislature had enacted a pro-
statehood resolution and provided for a referendum at the 1946 election at which the people of Alaska had wholeheartedly expressed their
support of statehood, Congress continued to ignore their wishes.

One achievement of note between 1954 and 1958 was an act of
Congress which brought the treatment of Alaska's mentally ill from
the Middle Ages into the twentieth century. The move to end the
barbaric treatment of the mentally ill in Alaska, who were tried by
juries like criminals and held in jail until they could be sent to Morningside Hospital in Portland, Oregon, began in 1948 when the American Medical Association conducted the first field study of mental
health in Alaska. In 1949 the Department of the Interior appointed
a committee headed by Dr. Winfred Overholser, superintendent of
St. Elizabeth's Hospital, Washington, D.C., which on February 10,
1950, recommended a model mental health program for Alaska and
drafted proposed legislation to transfer responsibility for mental health
to the territory. In February and March, 1955, Delegate Bartlett and
Representative Edith Green, D., of Oregon, each introduced bills designed to establish a modern mental health program and to construct
a hospital for the mentally ill in Alaska. The House Subcommittee on
Territories and Insular Affairs began hearings on April 21. Subcommittee Chairman Leo O'Brien, D., of New York, on May 18 introduced H.R. 6334, which incorporated amendments suggested by
administration witnesses, who had made clear their desire to turn over
care of the mentally ill to the territory. Because it was generally felt
that the legislation would have to be sponsored by an Oregon representative—the loss of revenue to Morningside Hospital in Portland

would be substantial—Representative Edith Green on June 15 introduced H.R. 6376, which was identical with O'Brien's bill. It was an act of rare political courage on Mrs. Green's part. Three weeks of hearings were held in Alaska in July, and on January 18, 1956, the House passed H.R. 6376 by voice vote. As enacted by the House, the bill transferred responsibility for the mentally ill from the federal government to Alaska; modernized commitment and hospitalization procedures; authorized $6.5 million for construction of facilities in Alaska for the mentally ill; a ten-year program of $6 million in grants-in-aid to the territory; and provided for a land grant of one million acres to the territory to assist in the long-term support of a mental health program.

Senate consideration of the bill was greeted by a small, noisy minority opposing the legislation. Various misguided individuals and organizations seized on the fact that one million acres of land in Alaska were being set aside for mental health purposes as an indication that some huge tract of land would be fenced in so that persons adjudged mentally ill not only in Alaska but throughout the United States could be confined in a sort of "Siberia in Alaska." It was even suggested that governors of various states would be selecting political and personal enemies and exiling them to confinement in Alaska. While there was never the slightest validity to these allegations, as the Senate hearings clearly demonstrated, the canard has persisted, leading to occasional inquiries even to this day from people led astray by false reports and suspicions.[1]

The bill passed the Senate on June 27 with an amendment to permit the state to draw up its own commitment procedures. House and Senate conferees accepted the Senate version with minor changes, and the measure finally passed both House and Senate and became P.L. 84-830. As a result, the State of Alaska now had the Alaska Psychiatric Institute at Anchorage and its custodial facility at Valdez.

Otherwise, Congressional indifference to Alaska continued. The reasons were political. Previous voting records indicated that, if admitted, Alaska would elect Democrats to Congress, and Hawaii Republicans. President Eisenhower's proclaimed partiality toward statehood for Hawaii and his opposition to statehood for Alaska caused pro-Alaska sponsors of statehood legislation to introduce a joint Alaska-Hawaii statehood bill in the Eighty-third Congress in 1953. They reasoned that the President would not veto statehood for Alaska at the expense of Hawaii. Although the Senate passed this joint bill, the opposition of the President and the Republican leadership in the House could not be overcome.

Equally disheartening to most Alaskans was the lack of action in the Eighty-fourth Congress. Senator James E. Murray, D., of Montana, introduced a joint statehood bill in the Senate, which took no action in the belief that it was now the House's duty to act first. In the House for the first time a joint statehood bill was favorably reported, but on May 10, 1955, it was recommitted on a motion by Representative John R. Pillion, R., of New York, by a vote of 218 to 170. Thus, while the authorized committees of both houses of Congress had uniformly produced reports favoring statehood for Alaska and Hawaii, the indispensable enactment of any statehood bill *by both houses in the same Congress* had not followed.

Events and people in Alaska, however, had already gathered enough momentum to create a moral and political force destined to overcome the obstructionism of Congress. On January 24, 1955, the Territorial Legislature passed a bill to establish a constitutional convention to draft a constitution for the future state. The bill, accompanied by a House Joint Memorial, which under suspension of the rules passed by a vote of 22 to 0, also appropriated $300,000 for the convention's expenses. The inspiration for this far-sighted and audacious move originated with Wendell P. Kay, an Anchorage attorney who was speaker of the House. In the previous 1953 legislature he had sponsored such a measure with the co-sponsorship of the three other Democrats in the heavily Republican House. Kay's bill was referred to a special House Committee on Statehood, where it was promptly interred with a "Do not pass" verdict by its five Republican members.[2] However, the 1954 election had reversed the political composition of the 1955 legislature, which, as a result, had a 12 to 4 Democratic preponderance in the Senate and a 21 to 3 margin in the House. Kay's bill, therefore, was enacted. Co-sponsored by all twenty-one House Democrats, it passed by a vote of 23 to 1 in the House and by a unanimous vote of all sixteen senators.

In this overture for statehood the legislators rejected the inept judicial-political divisions established in the Organic Act of 1912 and instituted an unprecedented system of election for the delegates to the convention. The territory was divided into twenty-two election districts, of which sixteen had but one representative; included among these were the recording districts containing the six principal cities.

The old four judicial divisions were allotted delegates in a number roughly proportionate to their population who were elected at large. Finally, seven delegates were elected at large from the whole territory. These three categories were specifically designed to encourage the candidacies of purely local representatives, the candidacies of men or women known throughout their long-established voting areas (namely, the judicial divisions), and figures known state-wide. Thus, an aspirant from Juneau, for example, could compete for the one place in that city, or be among the seven running from the First Division (southeastern Alaska), or he could be one of seven running territory-wide. This effort to create the most diverse, widest, and fairest representation, and to include the outlying, sparsely settled and relatively neglected areas of the territory, brought to the convention and its product, the state constitution, an interest and support it could not otherwise have secured.

The election of delegates was held on September 13, 1955. They numbered fifty-five, the same number that had gathered in Philadelphia in 1787 to frame the Constitution of the United States.[3] The candidates, who were nominated by petition, were elected without reference to party. As it turned out, thirty-six were Democrats, fourteen Republicans, and five without any known political affiliation. The widespread interest in the election was demonstrated by the filing of some fifty candidates for the seven at-large positions. On November 9, 1955, the delegates gathered on the campus of the University of Alaska, near Fairbanks, where they were to remain for seventy-five days with one recess to enable them to report to and exchange views with their constituents. Former Governor Gruening delivered the keynote address. It was entitled "Let Us End American Colonialism." The result of the convention's deliberations was a state charter rightfully hailed by political scientists as a model of clarity and efficiency.

The outstanding characteristic of the Alaska constitution was the concentration of power in the state's chief executive. Except for the governor and the Secretary of State, who would be elected with him, as in the case of the President and Vice President of the United States, all offices were to be appointive, with their incumbents serving at the governor's pleasure. The governor was given the power to veto items in appropriations bills, a power denied many state governors as well as the President of the United States,[4] and these vetoes could only be overridden by three-fourths of the members of the legislature.

Other vetoes required only a two-thirds majority. The governor's term was fixed at four years, with one reelection permitted. He was allowed to run again after an intervening four years.

This concentration of power in the governorship reflected the frustration of territorial executives against whom had been erected a cushion of federally appointed administrative boards, which in turn appointed departmental executives. The delegates were resolved to do away with such boards. They felt that, since their governor was elected by the people of Alaska, he should be permitted to perform with a minimum of hindrance and be subject to their approval or rejection only at the quadrennial elections. The only major check against his power was that his major appointments required confirmation by both houses of the legislature in joint session.

The legislative apportionment for the new state carried on in the spirit of the provisions for election of the delegates to the constitutional convention. Provisions were made for the representation of the outlying areas, subject to reapportionment after every census. A senate of twenty and a house of forty members were established.

The judicial system was based on the so-called Missouri plan. A judicial council composed of three lawyers appointed by the State Bar Association and three lay members appointed by the governor would supply the governor with at least two names for every judicial position from which he could appoint supreme and superior court judges. These would be subject to ratification by the voters after a term of years on the bench. The chief judge of the supreme court would be chairman of the judicial council.

The Territory of Alaska had been prohibited from establishing counties, and the question of political subdivisions proved a thorny problem. The convention avoided the somewhat discredited "county" nomenclature and called the larger local units other than municipalities "boroughs." By 1968, nine boroughs had been established in population centers throughout the state.

An unanticipated but momentous act was the convention's adoption of what soon came to be called the "Alaska-Tennessee" plan. An enterprising, public-spirited New Orleans businessman by the name of George H. Lehleitner had, in his study of American history, discovered that a number of territories had successfully dispensed with the ordinary procedures for achieving statehood. The first was Tennessee. The

territory lying west of the Carolinas—then called Franklin—anxious
to achieve statehood and envious of Kentucky's admission in 1792,
called a constitutional convention, drafted a constitution, and elected
two "senators," who in 1796 went to Philadelphia, then the nation's
capital, to present the case for statehood. They returned victorious
four months later. Although six other territories pursued similar procedures,[5] the plan had been lost in history and forgotten.

Lehleitner had been unable to interest Hawaiians, who mistakenly
counted on the support of Speaker Joseph W. Martin. The Alaska
Constitutional Convention, however, accepted Lehleitner's proposal
and at the territorial election held on April 24, 1956, when the proposed constitution was presented to the voters, adoption of the
"Alaska-Tennessee" plan was also on the ballot. Alaskans voted overwhelmingly to adopt both the constitution and the Alaska-Tennessee
plan.

Too late for primaries, the parties nominated their candidates for
the Congressional offices at conventions. For the Republicans, John
Butrovich, of Fairbanks, an insurance man and a territorial senator,
was nominated for the six-year Senate term; Robert B. Atwood, editor
and publisher of the Anchorage *Times*, who had been in the forefront
of the statehood movement, for the four-year term; and Charles
Burdick, retired assistant regional forester and a resident of Juneau,
for the House. The Democrats nominated Ernest Gruening, William
A. Egan, veteran territorial legislator, and Ralph J. Rivers, of Fairbanks, who had held a variety of public offices, including the attorney-
generalcy of the territory.

The three Democrats were elected. Upon arrival in Washington on
January 7, 1957, they were immediately told they would not be allowed the privileges of the floor, although the Tennessee delegation
had had such privileges, and were also promptly told that they would
have to run again for election if statehood was approved.

From the delegation's Washington office went forth a stream of
communications—particularly Gruening's keynote address to the constitutional convention—to journalists, political scientists, industry executives, and to every member of Congress. During the two sessions
of the Eighty-fifth Congress the delegation called on each member of
Congress personally. The greatest obstacles to be overcome were noncontiguity and the smallness of Alaska's population. Typical of

Congressional reaction was that of a friendly senator, later converted, who said:

> I am sympathetic with your desire for statehood. I understand why you want it and I think your desires are fully justified. But how can I justify giving this handful of people [and invariably the reference would be to the 1950 census, which gave Alaska only 127,000 people, although its population by this time had increased to nearly 200,000] two Senators when the great State of New York, with 15,000,000 people, has only two.

The delegation answered by pointing out that if this argument had prevailed in the early days of the republic, the United States of America would still number only thirteen states, since the subsequent states west of the Appalachians invariably had far fewer people than those already in the Union, and second, that Alaska's population would not grow substantially until statehood was achieved. One unalterably opposed senator would analyze Alaska's population, based again on the 1950 census; he would throw out the natives as not being civilized, the military and their dependents as not being part of the permanent population, the government employees as being transients, and come up with figures that indicated that Alaska had virtually no population at all! In any event, in the Eighty-fifth Congress, commencing in 1957, bills proposing statehood for Alaska had once again been introduced.

President Eisenhower had fully revealed in September 1956 his ideas on statehood for Alaska. In an interview with Frank Hewlett, Washington correspondent of the Honolulu *Star-Bulletin*, he said:

> Well, I think I have talked about that subject . . . time and again. As far as Hawaii is concerned, there is no question. I not only approved of it in the '52 platform, but time and again I brought it before the Congress in the terms of recommendations. Now, Alaska is a very great area and there are very few people in it, and they are confined almost exclusively to the southeastern corner. Could there be a way worked out where the defense requirements could be retained, I mean the areas necessary to defense requirements could be retained under Federal control in the great outlying regions and a State made of that portion in which the population is concentrated, it would seem to me to be a good solution to the problem. But the great and vast area is

completely dependent upon the United States for protection and it is necessary to us in our defense arrangements.

The President was mistaken in thinking that the majority of Alaskans lived in the southeast. The majority of Alaskans were by that time living in the Railbelt, which extends from Seward in south central Alaska to Fairbanks. Some 80,000 people dwelt in the Seward-Kenai-Anchorage-Palmer region, a greater population by far than in all southeastern Alaska. Eisenhower's idea had apparently originated two years earlier with Governor Frank Heintzleman, who took the view that only the south and southeastern portions of the territory were economically viable and that the new state should not be burdened with the other more sparsely populated northern and western regions. For Eisenhower, however, the crux of the matter lay in the nation's "defense needs"; in 1955 Defense Secretary Charles Wilson had voiced the administration's opposition to statehood for Alaska in testimony given before the Senate Committee on Interior and Insular Affairs on the ground that statehood would handicap national defense. Senator Henry M. Jackson, D., of Washington, pointed out that under the Truman administration the Department of Defense had not raised such objections and that it was apparent that the Defense Department's position under Eisenhower was based more on politics than on national security. In testimony given during the Eighty-fifth Congress, however, the administration gradually put forth a proposal that an area equal to roughly one-half of Alaska north of the Yukon and Kuskokwim rivers be reserved for defense purposes. Acceptance of such an amendment would be required to secure Eisenhower's approval of statehood.

However, a single event which helped change the course of Alaska's history occurred when Secretary of the Interior Douglas McKay was persuaded by the President to resign from the Interior Department to run against Senator Wayne Morse of Oregon. Eisenhower appointed former Nebraska Senator Fred Seaton as his replacement. On February 20, 1952, Seaton, as a senator from Nebraska, had delivered his sole speech on the floor of the Senate in which he supported statehood for Alaska and noted that his own state had failed to fulfill the procedural requirements for statehood. At Seaton's confirmation hearing before the Senate Committee on Interior and Insular Affairs, Chairman James E. Murray placed his speech in the hearing record and asked Seaton if he still felt the same way. Seaton said that he did.

As a result of numerous hearings and with Seaton's support, it soon became clear that the whole of Alaska could become a state without hindering the President's ability to withdraw land for defense. A face-saving amendment was added to the statehood-bill drafts which gave the President the power to make such withdrawals within the northern half of Alaska. It remained, and was of no significance.

In the meantime, with each successive Congress the drafts of the statehood bill had become more generous. In the Eighty-fourth Congress land to be granted the state of Alaska had been increased to 102,950,000 acres from the vacant unreserved and unappropriated lands of the public domain, plus 400,000 acres from the national forest lands in Alaska. Seventy percent of the net proceeds of the Pribilof seal industry would go to the state. Most helpful was the provision that 90 percent of the royalties and net profits from oil, gas and mineral leases on the public domain would go to the State of Alaska. This unique benefit not enjoyed by other western states was granted in part in compensation for Alaska's not being—as they were—under the Reclamation Act.

By the second session of the Eighty-fifth Congress sentiment for Alaskan statehood was growing throughout the country. A Gallup Poll showed that the overwhelming majority of the American people supported statehood. The publication in March 1958 of Edna Ferber's novel *Ice Palace* helped so much to arouse public support for Alaska's cause that it was called the *Uncle Tom's Cabin* of Alaskan statehood.

House action on the Alaskan-statehood bill, H.R. 7999, was delayed in the Rules Committee by the opposition of its chairman, Representative Howard Smith, D., of Virginia. When the bill was finally brought up on May 21, 1958, as a privileged bill by Representative Wayne Aspinall, D., of Colorado, chairman of the House Interior Committee, several points of order were raised against it by Representative Clarence Cannon, D., Missouri, considered to be the leading parliamentarian in the House of Representatives. But Democratic Speaker Sam Rayburn had made a study of the governing precedents in anticipation of such moves and overruled all points of order. The motion to bring up the bill prevailed by a vote of 217 to 172.

The debate lasted three days. The statehood case was presented by Representative Leo W. O'Brien, D., of New York, chairman of the Subcommittee on Territories. Leading the opposition was Representative Arthur Lewis Miller, R., of Nebraska. On May 28 the bill passed by a vote of 210 to 166, and the first hurdle had been overcome. In the Senate the bill came up on June 23, and debate went on intermittently for a week. On June 30 various attempts to defeat the bill by amendment and other tactical moves had been defeated, and it was clear that statehood proponents had an overwhelming majority. When the final vote came, several who had sought to defeat or sidetrack the bill switched to support it in view of the historic import of their vote, and the vote on passage on June 30, 1958 was 64 to 20. There was resounding applause in the galleries which was only mildly rebuked by the presiding officer, Senator Richard Neuberger of Oregon, himself a long and vigorous statehood supporter, where members of the delegation and others from Alaska viewed the crowning episode in their long struggle.

One obstacle remained. A last-ditch effort by the opposition had provided that at the primary election on the following August 26, when the two political parties would nominate their candidates for office, the people of Alaska should also vote on three propositions: (1) Shall Alaska be admitted to the Union as a state? (2) Shall the boundaries of the new state, as prescribed by the statehood act, be approved? (3) Shall all the other provisions of the act be approved? All three propositions were overwhelmingly supported by the voters of Alaska. And so Alaska became the forty-ninth state. The final act was the signing of the statehood proclamation by President Eisenhower at the White House on January 3, 1959.[6]

The general election in November 1958 saw national political figures enter the lists in support of candidates for statewide office in Alaska. Democrats Frank Church and John F. Kennedy and Republicans Richard Nixon and Secretary of the Interior Seaton campaigned for their respective parties. When the final count was made, the Democrats had made a clean sweep. Gruening and Bartlett won seats in the United States Senate and Ralph Rivers gained Alaska's lone seat in the House of Representatives. William A. Egan was the state's first elected governor. The Democrats captured control of both houses of the first legislature. There were eighteen Democrats and two Republicans in the Senate, thirty-four Democrats and six Republicans in the House.

The Democratic landslide victory was only a temporary harbinger of the future of party politics in Alaska. In 1960, although Richard

Nixon won Alaska's three electoral votes by a slender margin over John F. Kennedy, the Democrats retained a substantial majority in both houses of the state legislature. In 1962 Egan won a second term over Republican Mike Stepovich, although his margin of victory was considerably less than it had been in 1958. The membership of the state House of Representatives was evenly divided between the two parties; the Republicans, with the support of a few Democrats, succeeded in electing a Republican speaker and in organizing the House. Control of the Senate remained in Democratic hands. In 1964 Alaskans followed the national example and overwhelmingly disapproved of Barry Goldwater's bid for the Presidency. The Democrats regained their firm hand over affairs in both houses of the legislature. Only Democratic Congressman Ralph Rivers, who had run successfully three times, was hard pressed to win over his Republican opponent.

In 1966, however, the Republican Party toppled the Democrats from their position of predominance in Alaska politics. The question would naturally arise to puzzle future historians why, after the landslide Democratic victory in the first state election, the political complexion of the state was so completely changed after a single two-term gubernatorial incumbency.

It was pretty generally conceded that William A. Egan had been a dedicated, conscientious and able governor. His integrity and his devotion to his task were beyond question. His public experience had given him unusual preparation for his office. He had served in the legislature continuously since 1941, with only one interruption for war service, first as a member of the territorial House of Representatives and then as a territorial Senator. He was elected president of the Constitutional Convention, with a resulting familiarity with the problems of transition from territorialism to statehood.

Alaska, on the eve of the 1966 election, was prospering. The salmon fisheries, depleted almost to the vanishing point under federal mismanagement in territorial days, were being restored under the able direction of the state Department of Fish and Game. A great new marine product, Alaska king crab, had added an important economic resource to the fisheries. Oil and natural gas were bidding fair to outstrip all other Alaskan natural resources in their favorable impact on the state's economy. A part of these resources were being converted into urea and liquefied gas for export, thus marking the arrival of

Alaska's first major industries (except for two wood pulp mills). Trade with Japan—a unique example of a state developing commerce with a foreign nation—was opening up undreamed-of economic potentials. The ferry system inaugurated after statehood with gubernatorial, legislative and popular support—all without federal subsidy—was bringing a partial solution to one of the hitherto-unsolved problems of transportation. Finally, every one of the seven bond issues requested by Governor Egan and approved by the legislature would be ratified at the very election in which Governor Egan was defeated by 1,081 votes and both houses of the legislature captured by the Republicans. The approval of the voters of the bond issues was a clear manifestation of support of Governor Egan's policies and *public* record.[7]

Why, then, was there so great a political reversal?

The explanation undoubtedly lay in certain political mistakes made by Governor Egan. First, he decided to run for a third term. While the constitution provided that a governor could serve only two consecutive terms and then another term after an interval of four years, it was provided that if a governor had not served two full terms, the two-term restriction did not apply. Governor Egan had actually served only 331 days in his first term, and that term, therefore, fell short of a full term by 34 days. The constitution provided that he was eligible under the circumstances to run for a third term. Nevertheless, there was a substantial feeling that his running for a third term, even though he was technically eligible to do so, was a violation of the spirit of the constitution. This issue was raised by his opponent in the Democratic primary, Wendell P. Kay, an Anchorage attorney, who had served with distinction in the legislature and had been speaker of the House in 1953. Kay was defeated, but the issue was again raised by Republican gubernatorial candidate Walter J. Hickel, a self-made Anchorage entrepreneur.

However, this would in no wise have accounted for Egan's defeat. A far more pertinent reason had to do with the question of reapportionment.

Under the United States Supreme Court decisions of "one man—one vote"[8] it was clear that Alaska's Senate did not fulfill these requirements and the section of Alaska's constitution providing for the Senate's apportionment was now unconstitutional. The attorney-general of Alaska[9] had given the governor an opinion that he could reapportion the Senate. Governor Egan had appointed a commission to study reapportionment and with some modifications of its proposal issued a proclamation on September 3, 1965, putting it into effect for the 1966 primary and general elections. This formula meant that one-half of the Senate incumbents who had been elected in 1964 for four-year terms would have to run again in 1966. Fifteen of the Senate's twenty members were Democrats. They objected not only to this reapportionment formula which, they foresaw, would retire a substantial number of them but also to Governor Egan's determination to do this for the 1966 elections. Senate and House concurrent resolutions denounced the proposal.[10] The United States Supreme Court had not required such speedy action. When the governor refused to yield to the legislators' pleas, the fifteen Democratic senators took the matter to court.[11] A brief designed to void the governor's proposition which was prepared by a Juneau attorney, Avrum Gross, pointed out that the state's constitution did not give the governor the power to reapportion the Senate, although it had given him the power to reapportion the House. The plea was sustained in the verdict rendered by Judge James von der Heydt in the Superior Court of the First Judicial District. The judge found that Alaska's constitution did not give the Governor the power to redistrict the Senate; ordered the 1966 election to proceed under the existing provisions and proposed that the state constitution's provision for Senate election be changed by a modification of the state's constitution, which could be done either by the legislature or by a constitutional convention. The court fixed December 1, 1967 as a reasonable date for enactment of a valid constitutional amendment.

The Democratic senators and party followers generally breathed a sigh of relief. A political disaster had obviously been averted. Then, to their amazement, Governor Egan decided to appeal the Superior Court's decision to the State Supreme Court. It was, however, generally assumed that the Supreme Court would sustain Judge von der Heydt.

The Supreme Court's opinion, written by Chief Justice Buell Nesbett, admitted that the Alaska constitution did not give the governor the power to reapportion the Senate but concluded that had the delegates to Alaska's Constitutional Convention anticipated the U.S. Supreme Court's decision they *would* have provided the governor with that power! So Judge von der Heydt's decision was reversed, and the election based on the governor's formula ordered for 1966.[12]

The consequences of this decision were politically disastrous. In the south central area (Anchorage) the Republicans placed seven strong candidates in the field, and four in the central area (Fairbanks). These men not only brought their friends to the polls but secured their votes both for themselves and for the entire ticket, which the Republican gubernatorial candidate, Walter J. Hickel, headed. In the election, the Democrats got only one of these seven seats in the south central area, and none in the central area. In southeast Alaska two of the five Democratic senators were eliminated and were understandably bitter. In the northwest area, three out of four Democrats were eliminated. It was obvious that these men "sat on their hands" in the election, as the returns from the areas demonstrated. One of them was so bitter that he supported Hickel and made a substantial contribution to his campaign. These circumstances alone would more than explain the turn of the political tide in the 1966 election.

Egan, Rivers, and other Democratic candidates were unable to counter the well-financed Republican campaign mounted by Hickel and Congressional candidate Howard W. Pollock, a state legislator from Anchorage. The November 8, 1966 election resulted in a Republican victory. Hickel and Pollock won their races and led their party to a substantial majority in both houses of the state legislature. Only Senator Bartlett, a consistently great vote-getter, who had retained his Senate seat in the 1960 election, as had Gruening in the election of 1962, was able to withstand the Republican onslaught.

Transition

Frequently we have heard, as we still hear, that ours is a government of laws, and not of men. I have never fully agreed with that theory. Ours is a government of laws and of men. Without men, we could have no laws, because men must enact the laws. Without men, the laws could not be interpreted, because it is necessary to interpret the laws. Without men, the laws could not be enforced. . . . So I do not, in any sense, concur in the view that ours is a government either of laws or of men, separately; I contend that it is a government of laws and of men. Men must interpret the laws; otherwise, they would be dead letters on our statute books.
SENATOR ALBEN W. BARKLEY,
MARCH 2, 1956

DURING the first year of statehood both federal and state efforts were directed toward making the transformation from territorial status. The Congressional delegation in Washington recognized that the first and most important item of business was to ensure that federal assistance to Alaska to ease the burdens of transition be as generous as possible. On March 28, 1959, legislation for this purpose was introduced. The Alaska Omnibus Bill, S. 1541, was the result of a seven months' study by the Bureau of the Budget, to determine what legislative steps would be needed to assist the new state. As introduced, the bill authorized $27.5 million in transitional grants, which were to be disbursed to the state over a five-year period. Funds under the bill would be used for lengthening the runways at the Anchorage and Fairbanks airports—which were to be transferred from federal to state control—for programs of mental and general health, and for operating recreational facilities formerly under the jurisdiction of the Bureau of Land Management of the Department of the Interior. The bill established full participation for Alaska in the Federal Aid Highway Act and removed the previous arbitrary ceiling on federal expenditures in Alaska under the act. It amended numerous federal grant-in-aid statutes to permit Alaskan participation and allowed the Federal District Court to hold sessions in Ketchikan as well as Juneau, Anchorage, Fairbanks, and Nome. The Ninth Circuit U.S. Court of

Appeals was given authority to hold annual sessions in Anchorage. Federal property no longer needed by the federal government was transferred to the state government. The bill passed substantially as introduced.

One early transitional crisis arose in connection with the Federal Aid Airport Act of 1959. Congress reluctantly and hastily voted a reduced amount of funds for the program in the face of President Eisenhower's threatened veto of the larger authorization previously voted. The reduction seriously jeopardized Alaska's ability to handle its need to extend the runways of the Fairbanks and Anchorage airports—the transitional grants under the Omnibus Act provided only a portion of the necessary financing. More serious, the act continued to treat Alaska as a territory and gave it less than the share it would have had if its new status had been recognized. To meet the crisis, Bartlett and Gruening introduced S. 2208, which, as finally passed and signed into law, enabled the forty-ninth state to receive certain discretionary funds from the administrator of the Federal Aviation Agency for exceptional airport projects which had not been funded. The next Congress amended the act to allow Alaska to participate in the program on an equal basis with other states.

In the meantime, the new state government in Alaska had moved, not without incident, to organize itself. The first governor of the state, William Egan, took the oath of office on January 3. A formal inauguration ceremony and parade were planned to precede the convening of the first state legislature. However, a dramatic and near-tragic set of circumstances shattered these plans. On the same day he was sworn in, Egan was rushed, seriously ill, to a Juneau hospital. On January 19 he was flown to a Seattle clinic in a condition near death from a pancreatic ailment. He was not to resume office until April 20. Secretary of State Hugh Wade, acting governor in Egan's absence, assumed the responsibility of preparing a budget, presenting the governor's message to the legislature, and presiding over the operation of the executive departments.

Neither the executive nor the legislative branch of the new state government was entirely new, since the base of the previous territorial government already existed. Moreover, Alaska's citizens had had the foresight to prepare for the transition. The Alaska Statehood Committee, under the chairmanship of Anchorage newspaper publisher Robert B. Atwood, had arranged for studies of transitional problems by the

Public Administration Service of Chicago. Work on the studies had begun in the spring of 1958. In addition, the 1957 territorial legislature had directed its legislative council to study ways and means of transition and its report was forwarded to the Public Administration Service. Both reports were substantially in accord and both were in the hands of the new state legislators when they convened in January.

The major work of the first session of the legislature was the reorganization of the executive branch in accordance with the new state constitution. The recommendations of the reorganization studies were in the main followed. As finally approved by the legislature, the state government consisted of twelve departments,[1] ten of which were headed by commissioners who served at the pleasure of the governor. Two exceptions were the Departments of Education and Fish and Game, around which centered most of the controversy of the first session. A small group of Alaskans—supported by outside interests—felt that education and the management of fish and wildlife resources should, because of their special nature, be independent of the governor, and efforts were made to establish independent boards to govern these activities. However, the final decision resulted in the establishment of advisory Boards of Education and Fish and Game whose members would be appointed by the governor.

Legislative reorganization was less difficult. The legislature established uniform rules of procedure for both houses and the number and names of the two houses' committees were standardized. The major problem—and it continued to be a perennial political issue—arose with the Legislative Council's recommendation that members should receive an annual salary of $3,000 and a per diem allowance of $40. The compromise finally reached set the salary at $2,500 and the per diem at $35. In 1966 the annual salary was raised to $6,000.

By the terms of the Statehood Act the state judiciary system was allowed three years to organize itself in preparation for the assumption of jurisdiction. Until then the federal courts would continue to function. However, before the first session of the legislature had adjourned, the Ninth Circuit U.S. Court of Appeals declared itself to be without jurisdiction to hear appeals from the U.S. District Court in Alaska. The judicial council was then hastily activated, and it proceeded to consider nominations for the Supreme Court. The governor announced his appointments on July 29. By early October the court had organized and announced it was ready to receive appeals. In mid-

November the governor announced his appointments of the superior court judgeships, and the system went into operation in early 1960.

With the close of the first session of the first state legislature, and the first year of Congressional representation in Washington, Alaskans were ready to move on to the pending and pressing problems that lay ahead. By far the most urgent—which encompassed many others— was how to develop the economy of the new state. But to tap Alaska's resources, the tangled lifelines of transportation, some of which had strangled the Territory, had first to be made straight.

31

Transportation: Life
Lines Untangling

What is to be the future of the Forty-ninth State? Of one thing her
citizens can be certain: skyrocketing world population and transportation breakthroughs will mean that Alaska's greatest handicap, her
geographic location, will become a diminishing liability.
TED C. HINCKLEY,
JUNE 9, 1967

1. Water Transportation

WHEN ALASKA became a state, the high cost of water transportation to Alaska remained as one of its most serious economic problems.
The Alaska Steamship Company continued to exercise its long accustomed monopoly. It was, to all intents and purposes, the only
regular carrier in the trade, and its unchallenged control of water transportation to Alaska was, as before, characterized by the highest water-
freight rates in the domestic commerce of the United States. Repeated
efforts to relieve Alaska's plight by alterations in the membership,
policies, and practices of the maritime regulatory agencies had been
unavailing. Indeed, the Federal Maritime Board served as the protector rather than as the regulator of the steamship company and
Alaska continued to be the victim.

Yet, five years after statehood, changes began to occur. Alaska
Steam, while still the largest Alaska carrier, no longer monopolized the
trade to the railbelt. Although the southeastern and western ports
were still almost completely dependent upon that carrier, and although it still provided service to the railbelt, other carriers with more
modern equipment providing better or, at least, equivalent service
were at last challenging Alaska Steam's monopoly. In 1959 it had been
virtually the sole carrier to the railbelt; but in 1964 its share of the
trade had been reduced to less than one-third of the total tonnage delivered to Alaska's south central ports, which received 60 percent of

the total traffic to Alaska. Altogether, in 1964 Alaska Steam carried only approximately 54 percent of the one million tons of dry cargo moved to Alaska.

Puget Sound–Alaska Van Lines came into the trade first in 1960, offering containerized service via tug and barge. However, competition really began with the entrance into the railbelt trade of the Canadian National Railroad in 1962. This carrier revolutionized water-transportation methods to Alaska by introducing hydrotrain service—cargo carried in rail cars was rolled onto rail barges at Prince Rupert, British Columbia, and loaded onto Alaska Railroad trains at Whittier.

From the time the Canadian National Railroad announced its plans to operate in the Alaska trade with American-built rail barges (thus eliminating any question as to compliance with American cabotage laws) the Alaska Steamship Company and the American transcontinental railroads voiced their fears about the threat of lower-cost Canadian service, and various arrangements were proposed to meet the new competition. An ingenious plan, the joint creation of Alaska Steam and the railroads, emerged in the spring of 1962. In the Eighty-seventh Congress Senator Bartlett introduced S. 3115 to authorize American registry of the Japanese-built, Liberian-registered *City of New Orleans*, which Alaska Steam had the option to purchase. The *City of New Orleans* was a large, fast steamship equipped to carry fifty-six rail freight cars which could be rolled off and on connecting rail carriers without expensive cargo handling. Once the foreign-built ship had been blessed with American registry—thus allowing operation between Seattle and Alaskan ports—the railroads would file with the steamship company single factor rates allowing through shipments of cargo to Alaska from all points in the United States. The establishment of "solid through rates" would match the Canadians'.

Also, the enormous size of the ship, which would be the largest in the trade, would give its owners effective control over cargo movements to the railbelt. The possibility of the entry of the *City of New Orleans*, with its large capacity, posed a serious threat to the developing plans of Puget Sound–Alaska Van Lines to increase its fleet and provide additional, competitive service to the state. Not only was Puget Sound–Alaska Van Lines threatened but the possibility of any other carrier competing with Alaska Steam virtually vanished.

The originators of the plan did not count on the opposition of domestic shipbuilders and unions, to say nothing of that of Puget Sound–Alaska Van Lines, to the conversion of the Japanese ship to American registry. Although the Senate Commerce Committee reported favorably on the bill, it got no further during the Eighty-seventh Congress.

In the Eighty-eighth Congress Senator Bartlett introduced S. 534 for the same purpose. This time the opposition was stronger. It was one of the few occasions in their otherwise close working relationship that the two Alaska senators differed on an Alaska issue. On June 13, 1963, the surprising result was announced: the committee had rejected S. 534 by a vote of 8 to 7, and Alaska Steam's growing competitors had an opportunity, which would otherwise have been lost, during the 1963 season to provide Alaskans a competitive choice of carriers.

Unable to obtain Congressional blessing for the *City of New Orleans*, the Alaska Steamship Company changed her name to the *Alaska* and went back to work with the railroads to devise another plan to beat the competition to the railbelt ports. A new company, the Alaska Trainship Corporation, was formed to operate the *Alaska*. It built thirty-three miles of railroad from the U.S.-Canadian border and a new port facility it called Delta Alaska, near New Westminster, British Columbia, to accommodate the shipment of cargo to Whittier. In the summer of 1964, the *Alaska* finally got underway, free from any regulatory controls of the United States but at an obvious disadvantage with respect to diverting shipments from Seattle-based competitors and the Canadian National Railway.

In the spring of 1964 yet another significant contender for railbelt service entered the trade. Sea-Land Service, Incorporated, a worldwide transportation service, selected Anchorage as its terminal point for cargo loaded at Seattle. This choice gave a welcome impetus to the Port of Anchorage, which was in grave danger of failing as an investment because it had not attracted the trade expected when the city issued bonds for its construction. Other carriers had kept away on the assumption that Cook Inlet, with its floating ice, would not be navigable in winter. Sea-Land vessels proved the contrary. By 1965 Sea-Land was an established carrier from Seattle to Anchorage and had begun operations to Kodiak as well. This marked another landmark change in transportation patterns for Alaska since Kodiak had in the past been almost completely dependent upon Alaska Steam.

Meanwhile, the State of Alaska had acted vigorously to provide

Alaska with a system of surface transportation in southeast Alaska, where highways are impossible because that area is part archipelago and its mainland coast is cleft by deep fiords. The new state launched a singularly imaginative system of marine highways for which a fleet of ocean-going ferries was constructed. In the summer of 1963 three of the new ferries went into operation providing accommodations for passengers, their motor cars, and for commercial vehicles. Service was established between Prince Rupert, British Columbia, and Ketchikan, Wrangell, Petersburg, Juneau, Haines, Skagway and Sitka on a regular schedule at published tariffs. In August 1964 the ferry system was extended to south central Alaska, linking Cordova and Valdez, and farther west, Anchorage, Seward and Kodiak. As a transportation service and as a tourist attraction the ferry system proved to be enormously popular.

The changes in transportation patterns were accompanied by important changes in the form of regulation of these services. The first sign of revision of federal regulatory policy came in 1961, when President Kennedy decided to reorganize the maritime regulatory agencies. For many years knowledgeable observers in the maritime industry and in the federal government had strongly objected to the arrangement whereby the chairman of the Federal Maritime Board also acted as administrator of the Maritime Administration. This dual responsibility placed the chairman-administrator in the position of attempting to regulate, as chairman of the Board, the same industry he was required to promote as Maritime administrator. In 1961 adoption of Reorganization Plan Number Seven established a new Federal Maritime Commission of five members and separated the promotional functions of the Maritime administrator from the regulatory agency.

The first action of the new commission affecting Alaskans was to rehear the 10 percent increase filed by Alaska Steam in December 1959 and firmly embedded in the Alaskan economy before the state was a year old. Although the earlier board had, as usual, rubber-stamped the rate increase, Alaskans had cause for hope when the new commission tied on its vote on whether to overrule the earlier decision to allow the increase. (Only four of the five members voted since a new member had not been serving when the case was heard.) Although the result of the final decision confirmed the earlier one, it was significant that the new chairman, Admiral John Harllee, and the vice chairman, James V. Day, sustained the state's every contention that the increase should be denied.

In another case before the new commission, Alaska Steam requested a 10 percent increase on seasonal cargo to western Alaska, a 20 percent increase on cannery cargo and a 10 percent increase on south-bound canned salmon. For the first time in the history of the regulation of Alaska freight rates, the increase was denied.

The Alaska carriers responded with alacrity to the apparent threat of a regulatory agency showing signs of transformation from a household pet to a potent watchdog of its former masters. The remedy, it appeared, since escape from some form of control was not politically feasible, was to find some agency other than the Federal Maritime Commission to perform the expected service of automatic approval of rate increases, with no unpleasant questions asked.

The carriers turned to the Interstate Commerce Commission, which emerged as an increasingly significant factor in regulation of the trade. (Ironically, except for opposition of the Alaska Steamship Company at the time of the Statehood Act, the ICC would have automatically assumed regulatory responsibility for the Alaska trade. A specific amendment to the Statehood Act required retention of regulation by the Federal Maritime Board.)

Maneuvers of the carriers to escape effective regulation began with support for enactment in the Eighty-seventh Congress of Public Law 87-595, legislation enacted for the ostensible purpose of allowing the filing with the ICC of joint rates and through routes to Alaska by motor and water carriers regulated by ICC with water carriers regulated by the Federal Maritime Commission. The announced purpose was to give the public the benefit of lowered costs resulting from filing single factor rates combining transcontinental carrier rates with Alaska water tariffs.

In the fall of 1967 when Alaska Steamship Company and Sea-Land filed a cancellation of their tariffs with the Federal Maritime Commission, it became apparent that the carriers intended to use the joint-rate, through-route procedures of Public Law 87-595 to claim ICC jurisdiction on the grounds that incidental pick-up and delivery service within the port area of Seattle and transfers of cargo to and from the Alaska Ferry System constituted service not subject to FMC jurisdiction. The Federal Maritime Commission ruled against this contention and asserted that its authority over the carriers was not diminished. However, the matter would not be settled until the carriers had exhausted judicial remedies.

An easier way to escape regulation appeared with the issuance by President Kennedy of Executive Order 11107 on April 25, 1963, which in theory applied certain provisions of the Interstate Commerce Act to the Alaska Railroad. The purpose was to provide a façade of ICC regulation of the Railroad, thus allowing the Railroad to file joint rates and through routes with the water carriers—a practice not accepted by the ICC in the past because it had no authority over the Railroad. As a matter of fact, virtually the only provisions of the Interstate Commerce Act effectively invoked by the order were those allowing joint filings. So many essential regulatory provisions were not made applicable to the Railroad that the order was useless as a forum of control of the carriers. Its only value was to the water carriers, which rushed to take advantage of the order by causing the Alaska Railroad to file joint rates with the ICC as soon as possible after the order was issued. The result was that by the fall of 1964 most of the traffic of Alaska Steamship Company and Puget Sound–Alaska Van Lines was not subject to FMC regulation, nor, to all intents and purposes, subject to ICC controls.

The "forum shopping" of the water carriers from FMC to ICC in a purposeful effort to avoid regulatory controls was yet another obstacle to lowering freight rates. The diffused and overlapping regulatory pattern cancelled many of the potential improvements that were hoped for when the Federal Maritime Board was reorganized in 1961. For the time being, effective regulation was impossible.

Meanwhile the Alaska Steamship Company, throughout the time it was bending its efforts to eliminate regulation in any form, decreased its service to southeast Alaska, where it still controlled the waters. Petersburg, although formerly served directly by the Alaska Steamship Company, now had to depend on transfers via the Alaska Ferry System from Ketchikan. Wrangell and Sitka were served directly only on certain weeks and were dependent on transfers via the Ferry System for alternating deliveries.

In March, 1967, the Federal Maritime Commission issued its long-awaited study of Alaska trade, which had been promised in the wake of its October 1964 decision to uphold the 10 percent rate increase announced by Alaska Steam in December 1959 and allowed to go into effect on January 10, 1960. The study was an effort to look at the causes of Alaska's high shipping costs and, more important, to determine what could be done to remedy the situation.[1]

The report confirmed what many Alaskans had come to know: that in the regions where competition existed, costs were significantly lower than in the areas served exclusively by Alaska Steam. South central Alaska, comprising the ports of Seward, Whittier, Kodiak and Anchorage and serving the largest part of the state's population, was enjoying lower freight rates and more efficient service than the rest of the state. It was hardly coincidental that this was the only area of Alaska where Alaska Steam's monopoly had been broken.

What was the effect of Alaska Steam's monopoly on the cost of living and the economy? The commission reported:

> If merchants at Juneau order food products from Seattle, transportation costs on apples, lettuce, flour and potatoes would raise f.o.b. prices 29, 41, 29, and 22 percent respectively. Transportation charges on lumber and cement would raise prices on these items 71 and 100 percent respectively.

In northwest Alaska, ocean transportation, including lighterage costs, increased Seattle f.o.b. prices on some food and construction items even more, and combined with the merchant's markup, raised prices approximately 60 percent. The differences between areas served by Alaska Steam and those where there was competition was striking:

> For instance, the carload rates to Anchorage [of Alaska Steamship Company] which cover the water and rail haul and motor delivery on bakery goods, building materials, fresh fruits and vegetables, household goods, radios, liquor, boxes, cigarettes, empty cans and other commodities are lower than Alaska Steam's rates that apply on approximately equal volume shipments to Juneau.

There were some qualifications. The commission found some truth in some Alaskans' contention that "it is not the freight rates but merchants who mark up the prices that cause such high retail prices." But the basic reason for high costs remained.

In addition to Alaska Steam's high freight rates, costs were increased by its antiquated and slow equipment. Alaska Steam's dock facilities at Ketchikan and Juneau operated by an agent at Sitka and Petersburg were inefficient and inadequate. At Ketchikan and Juneau, wharfage and handling costs exceeded those of Seattle by 185 percent; at Petersburg the disparity was found to be 251 percent.

The commission called for a long-overdue investigation of Alaska Steam's costs of handling and shipping freight. It recommended that the carrier's efficiency of performance be a consideration in rate-making. It recommended legislation to authorize improved control of terminal rates and charges. Most important, it recommended that the jungle of overlapping regulatory systems seeking to control surface transportation to and within Alaska be defoliated; the ICC, FMC, and CAB were urged to coordinate their efforts for the good of the people of Alaska. The Federal Maritime Commission's report was a landmark in the history of Alaska's water transportation. The nine years of statehood had brought increased competition and lower costs to the area which were of such vital importance to the well-being of the Alaskan economy. By exposing how much Alaska had benefited from the breaking up of the previous monopoly, the commission gave hope that the future would be more favorable for the people of Alaska.

2. Highways

IN 1916 CONGRESS enacted the Federal Aid Highway Act, one of the most important acts of Congress in the nation's history. It ushered in an entirely new era and revolutionized American life by making the automobile available as a new instrument of travel. It gave Americans increased mobility. It gave "suburbia" new vast dimensions. Typical of the discrimination that Alaska suffered as a territory was total exclusion from participation in the act.

The act provided 50-50 federal matching with the understanding that in exchange for this subsidy the highways would be built to a high standard set by the federal government. But the western states, with large areas of federally owned "public domain" which could not be taxed by the state and hence produced no revenue, received a formula more favorable than the dollar-for-dollar matching. This formula was based on the total area of the state, the proportion of public domain to the total area, the state's population, and the existing post road mileage. Contemplating Alaska's vast area and the proportion of public domain (virtually total), Congress shuddered and refused to include Alaska. For forty years—from 1916 to 1956— Alaska's voteless delegates would hopefully seek to amend the Federal Aid Highway Legislation to include Alaska. Their bills never even got out of committee. Other outlying areas, such as Hawaii and Puerto Rico, were subsequently permitted to share in the program, but not Alaska. Yet during these forty long years Alaska was paying all federal taxes while continuing to suffer taxation without representation.

In 1956 a further discrimination took place. Congress approved President Eisenhower's proposal for a vastly improved highway system with the stipulation that it be financed not through the long-term bonding proposed by the President, but through a pay-as-you-go system created by additional taxes on tires, trucks, trailers and gasoline. Although the method of financing the proposed system had been the subject of a sharp dispute between Congress and the Executive, in one respect both branches agreed that Alaska should be excluded from the benefits of this monumental road-expansion program but should pay the additional taxes on gasoline, tires, trucks, and trailers! So Alaskans were paying these additional levies to improve highways in the forty-eight states, but not in Alaska.

Senator Richard Neuberger of Oregon, aroused by this forty-year-old discrimination against Alaska, and the further discrimination of the 1956 amended Highway Aid Act, proposed an amendment to it to provide that Alaska would receive one-half of the amount it would have been entitled to under the prescribed Federal Aid Highway Act formula for the public domain states. Congress reduced his proposal to one-third of Alaska's entitlement. So, for the next three years until statehood, Alaska shared moderately in federal highway aid to the extent of about $13 million a year.

As a result, Alaska entered the Union in the unique situation of having not merely a few, but a majority, of its communities unconnected with any other, either by highway or by rail—a situation unthinkable in the forty-eight states. It seemed to Senator Gruening that the proper procedure to remedy the situation would be to authorize and appropriate federal funds to compensate for the nearly half-century of omission from federal highway assistance and enable Alaska to catch up with the rest of the nation. Undersecretary of Commerce Dan Martin, in charge of transportation, was sympathetic and pledged the administration to support rectifying legislation. But he insisted that before legislation to secure additional funds was introduced there should first be a highway study of Alaska to determine the exact nature of its needs. This seemed wholly unnecessary to Alaska's delegation, but it yielded reluctantly in view of the promise of administration support. An appropriation of $400,000 for the study was approved during the Eighty-seventh Congress.

By terms of the resolution authorizing the study which was enacted as Section 13 of the Federal Aid Highway Act of 1962, the report was due on May 15, 1964, but it soon became evident there was small prospect that it would be completed by the statutory deadline. The date for completion of the report was moved a year ahead to May 15, 1965. However, that date came and went and no report was available. For two years after the statutory deadline for the report, the Department of Commerce was beseeched by letter, telegram, phone call and personal interview to produce the promised executive-branch recommendation for Alaska highway legislation. The matter was lost in the maze of bureaucracy, shuttling from the Bureau of Public Roads, to Commerce, back to BPR, back to Commerce, then to the Bureau of the Budget, then back to Commerce.

As the date for hearings on the Federal Aid Highway Act of 1966 approached, additional efforts were made to obtain the scheduled Commerce Department report. Finally, it was extricated from the bureaucratic morass at 5:45 P.M., Tuesday, May 10, 1966, the day before Senator Gruening was scheduled to testify on the amendment he had introduced to provide funds for highways in Alaska.

The report of the department was disappointing. It gave half-hearted recognition to the need for some specialized approach to the unique problem of constructing and maintaining the missing highways in Alaska. However, the proposal which appeared after the promise of administration support, followed by the two years of study, recommendation, review, restudy, revision and consideration, would merely have allowed Alaska the use of funds to which it was already entitled under the Federal Aid Highway Act for construction of certain access roads and ferry equipment and, also, use of Federal Aid Highway funds for highway maintenance for a period of five years. The amount to be authorized in each case was recommended as 10 percent of the annual federal-aid apportionment.

The Bureau of the Budget, which contributed a covering letter to the report, was even less favorable in its recommendations. The bureau flatly rejected the recommendation that Alaska obtain additional funds for highways. Its only suggestion was that Alaska be authorized to utilize the excess of its already authorized funds not required for construction during a particular fiscal year for highway maintenance. It further recommended that the authorization be reduced progressively over a five-year period. Obviously, the entirely deficient recommendations of the executive branch were completely inadequate to meet the state's real needs. Unfortunately for Alaska, Dan Martin, the high executive official who had promised administration support to rectify the long-standing discrimination in the matter of highway construction had left the government service. The legislative branch would have to proceed unaided.

Therefore, Gruening introduced an amendment to S. 3155, the Federal Aid Highway Act of 1966, to allow the state to use Federal Aid Highway funds for road maintenance, to allow use of Federal Aid Highway funds for access and development roads crucially needed for exploration and resource development, and to provide for the authorization of $10 million annually for ten years out of the Highway Trust Fund beyond sums then allocated under existing law for Alaska. The justification for such legislation was obvious. In 1959 it was estimated by the Bureau of Public Roads that Alaska would have received $575 million in Federal Aid Highway funds had it not been excluded from the act. By 1966 in all the 586,400 square miles of Alaska only 4,609 miles of highways and streets had been constructed. The roadlessness of Alaska was largely attributable to its forty-year pre-statehood exclusion from participation in the Federal Aid Highway legislation.

Most of Alaska's road mileage had resulted from upgrading and hard-surfacing of the meager military-road system which was a legacy of the Second World War. However, the design standards of this system had been compromised to meet the limits of appropriations. A primary network of hard-surfaced roads, later to become Alaska's Federal Aid Primary System was completed in 1955. By the time Alaska became a state, many of the primary highways were in a severe state of disrepair and one of the first tasks facing the state was the need to rebuild nearly the entire primary system to adequate design and traffic standards.

In some instances, the cost of highway construction in Alaska was twice that of other states. For each cubic yard of earth moved in Alaska, two yards could be moved in Colorado for the same cost. To meet these burdensome costs, Alaskans taxed themselves and appropriated funds for the construction and maintenance of highways on a scale unmatched by any other state. Although state and local highway revenues were double those of the average state on a per vehicle basis and exceeded the average on a per capita basis by more than two-thirds, they fell short of meeting requirements and had been regularly supplemented by appropriations from the general fund. In the five years from 1959 through 1963 road-user revenues averaged approximately $6 million annually, while appropriations from the general fund averaged $6.9 million. In addition, an average of $5 million was expended by cities on roads and streets off the state system. The ratio between road-user and general funds was found in no other state and the result was that Alaska's general-fund appropriations equaled about one-eighth of the entire state budget. Considering Alaska's needs in other sectors, this was a potentially dangerous situation.

Further support was now elicited from the Congress because, in addition to other handicaps, Alaska faced exceptionally difficult road-maintenance problems stemming from its climate and geography. Even the Department of Commerce in its highway study of Alaska recognized the extremely high cost of highway maintenance in subarctic and arctic areas. Extensive ground ice formations—"permafrost" —and the damage resulting from alternate freezing and thawing actions on its highways, roads and streets created special problems for road construction in Alaska.

The Senate heard the pleas of Alaskans for special assistance and passed Gruening's amendment intact. The House of Representatives, however, was adamant in its refusal to allow use of the Highway Trust Fund for additional highway assistance to Alaska because it was prospectively overdrawn. As finally passed by Congress and signed into law by the President, the amendment authorized an additional $14 million annually for five years, to be appropriated from the general fund of the Treasury.

3. Airways

AIR TRANSPORTATION, in contrast with water and land transportation, has been an outstanding success in Alaska. This was due in large part to the pioneering spirit of Alaskans and to the absence of highways which automatically led them to resort to the only alternative method of getting around—namely, flying.

Before World War II Alaska had no airports worthy of the name, no radio range stations, no aids to navigation. The Alaskan bush pilot, a unique and intrepid figure, merely held up a moistened finger to the breeze and took off. His landing fields would be beaches, sand bars in rivers, tiny clearings in the wooded wilderness, on pontoons on lakes, rivers and coastal waters and, in winter, on skis on the snow-covered tundra.

World War II saw the beginning of airports as necessary adjuncts to defense. It brought the international airports at Anchorage and Fairbanks. Alaska's commercial aviation had all been developed by bush pilots who transformed their individual "puddle-jumping" operations into successful airlines. The Wien brothers, Noel and Sigurd, developed Wien Airlines in the northern parts of Alaska; Ray Petersen developed Northern Consolidated and with it the facilities at Katmai National Monument. Art Woodley created Pacific Northern. Sheldon Simmons and Robert Ellis, developed Alaska Coastal and Ellis Airways, respectively, operating out of Juneau and Ketchikan till they were consolidated. Merle Smith fathered Cordova Airways. A series of bush pilots put together what became Alaska Airlines. Bob Reeve developed Reeve-Aleutian Airlines, which served from Anchorage points westward along the Alaska Peninsula and the Aleutian Islands. Several smaller local airlines came into being. These air services were competitive, and Alaskans and the traveling public were the beneficiaries.

Pan-American was among the first Alaskan air trailblazers, utilizing the know-how of Juan Trippe and Charles Lindbergh. The first connecting flights between the lower forty-eight states and Alaska—by Pan-Am Clippers—took place in June 1940.

Subsequently Alaskan aviation developed rapidly. Jet planes cut the flying time. Perhaps the most important development was the inauguration of trans-polar flights, with Anchorage as a midway stop between Europe and Asia.

Thus, in the middle sixties, Anchorage became the air crossways of the northern hemisphere utilized by international carriers[2] from France, the Netherlands, the Scandinavian countries, Germany and Japan, as well as by Northwest Airlines which inaugurated flights from the eastern seaboard of the United States to the Orient and return by way of Anchorage.

In 1967 and 1968, important consolidations bade fair to further improve Alaska's air transportation. Alaska Airlines absorbed Alaska Coastal and Cordova Airways; Wien and Northern Consolidated merged, and Western Airlines acquired Pacific Northern, furnishing daily flights between Californian cities, Seattle and Anchorage. Alaska Airlines had regular flights between Alaskan communities and Seattle-Tacoma and had applied for certification between Anchorage and Hawaii and from Hawaii to Seattle, thus furnishing a triangular route which would link the two Pacific states and thus maintain and furnish a new outlet for European travelers who would pass through Anchorage and enjoy the diverse climates and scenery of the forty-ninth and fiftieth states.

32

Developing the Economy

> But I see the Alaska of the future . . . I see an Alaska that is the
> storehouse of our Nation, a great depository for minerals and lumber
> and fish, rich in waterpower and rich in the things that make life
> abundant for those of us who live in this great Republic.
> JOHN F. KENNEDY,
> SEPTEMBER 3, 1960

1. The Role of the Federal Government

AS ALASKA ended its first century of life under the American flag,
its economy bore many of the marks of that of one of the emerging
nations of Latin America or Asia. A special Presidential study group
reported in 1964 that Alaska resembled such a nation in its chronic
shortage of capital for development; that its economy was narrowly
based and dependent on extractive industry; that it had a serious
import imbalance in its trade relations; that selective inflation was a
problem; that modern managerial and marketing methods were relatively unused; and that social-overhead-capital expenditures were
needed to help create a climate for development. In other respects,
Alaska differed from the emerging nations: it was underpopulated; it
had a transient population; *it was part of the republic.*[1] Unfortunately,
it was probably easier for India to convince the American government
of its need than it was for the governor of Alaska and the Congressional delegation to persuade the executive and legislative branches
of the federal government that Alaska had a unique and pressing need
for assistance after years of deprivation and neglect as a territory and
that development of its largely unutilized resources would be beneficial
not only to Alaska but to the entire nation.

Nevertheless, statehood enabled Alaska to present its case much
more effectively to the powers in Washington, if only because it now
had two senators and a representative who were members of Congressional committees dealing with much of the legislation affecting
Alaska and whom the executive branch was forced to reckon with
before making decisions of consequence with regard to Alaska. The

federal government played an indispensable role in Alaska's economic development since statehood at the same time that, following the colonialist policy of territorial days, it imposed arbitrary restrictions and impediments in the young state's paths. Throughout the first few years of statehood, government accounted for a significant portion of economic activity in Alaska; in 1965 the federal government alone was responsible for one-third of personal income in Alaska, as compared with a national average of 5.2 percent. Although salaries and wages comprised the major portion of the government's contribution to the economy, and although military expenditures had little if any developmental impact, the federal government—as in other states—spent millions of dollars on social-overhead-capital investments, such as highways, airports, and harbor facilities. Statehood meant full participation in the Federal Aid Highway Act, plus special federal assistance for highway construction in Alaska. In fiscal year 1967 the federal government allocated more than $31 million for Alaskan highways. In the same year almost $4 million was allotted to Alaska under the federal airport development program. The U.S. Army Corps of Engineers helped to build flood control and navigation projects; in 1967 almost $2.8 million was let in prime contracts. The year 1967 also saw the beginning of the previously almost totally neglected hydroelectric power development with the construction of the Snettisham power project near Juneau and the establishment of the Alaska Power Administration. At the same time Secretary of the Interior Stewart Udall made an adverse report on the Rampart Dam project on the Yukon River, the nation's greatest potential power site, on which the U.S. Army Corps of Engineers had expended $1 million in studies. Since risk capital was almost impossible to find in Alaska, the Small Business Administration stepped into the gap and provided a much-needed link between private enterprise and federal money. The Economic Development Administration financed projects to establish a viable economic base in a number of Alaskan communities. Alaska also shared in the great body of recent federal legislation in the fields of health, education and welfare as it never would have as a territory. The Congressional delegation succeeded in amending a number of programs, such as the Elementary and Secondary Education Act, veterans benefits, and Federal Housing Administration programs, to allow for Alaska's higher costs and thus provide more equitable treatment for the residents of the forty-ninth state.

Higher education in Alaska improved immeasurably after statehood. Before Alaska became a state, the University of Alaska—a land-grant institution—had suffered years of deprivation resulting, in part, from Alaska's territorial status and from the restrictions imposed by the absentees' control of legislatures. The territory lacked the will and the federal government lacked the interest to provide financial support for higher education.

In 1958, the last year of territorialism, enrollment at the main campus of the University totaled 847; by 1967, 1,828 students were enrolled at the main campus and approximately 3,000 others were attending community colleges and evening and off-campus courses. The budget for 1966-1967 was $16 million, 45 percent of which came from the state and 40 percent from the federal government. In addition to operating six community colleges throughout the state, the university directed ten research units, including the Arctic Research Laboratory at Barrow, the Institute of Social, Economic, and Government Research, and the Institute of Arctic Biology. Part of the reason for the dynamic growth of the university lay in the leadership of President William R. Wood, who assumed office in 1960, as well as the changed attitude of the legislatures since statehood. Moreover, increased federal support for what was now a state university was a factor. Most important, the people of Alaska consistently recognized their responsibility toward educating their children and on three occasions voted capital-improvement bond issues totaling $24.9 million.

The first four-year private university in Alaska opened in 1960. Alaska Methodist University resulted from the efforts of the Division of National Missions of the Methodist Church which, with the advice of its Academic Advisory Council, chose Anchorage as the site for the new university. The university retained the services of architect Edward Durrell Stone to oversee the development of its constantly growing new physical plant. Under the presidency of Dr. Frederick P. McGinnis it received accreditation in 1964 and, along with Sheldon Jackson Junior College in Sitka, a Presbyterian institution, Alaska Methodist University provided a useful alternative for young Alaskans wishing to pursue their higher education in their home state.

The best example of Alaska's new status in Washington was the response of the federal government to the disaster of the Good Friday earthquake in 1964. On March 27, 1964, one of the severest earthquakes ever recorded on the Richter scale struck south central Alaska, in an area extending 500 miles from east to west and 300 miles north to south. The damage to the new state was of catastrophic proportions. Fortunately, the disaster struck at an hour—5:35 P.M.—when schools were empty and business areas uncrowded, and the death toll was limited to 115. However, estimates of property damage exceeded $400 million. In some areas, land masses were thrust up as high as thirty-three feet; in other places the land sank as much as eight feet. Navigable waterways and harbors and rail and auto routes along the coastline were seriously disrupted. Large underwater slides carried away many port facilities in several communities. The earthquake triggered numerous rockslides, snow avalanches and landslides throughout southern Alaska. The earthquake-generated waterwaves, or tsunamis, struck with devastating force along the coast between Kodiak and Cordova. The disaster area contained 60 percent of Alaska's population, produced over 55 percent of the state's revenues, and contained the state's key transportation complex. "In a state with a broader-based economy, such a blow would have been awesome. For Alaska, it was calamitous."[2]

Shortly after midnight of March 27 President Johnson communicated with the Alaska Congressional delegation and made arrangements to have the members flown immediately to Anchorage in his own presidential jet, accompanied by Ed McDermott, the director of the Office of Emergency Planning, for a first-hand look at the damage. Within five days the President had appointed a Federal Reconstruction and Development Planning Commission for Alaska under the chairmanship of Senator Clinton P. Anderson, D., of New Mexico. On April 6 the House and Senate acted within hours of each other in passing a special $50 million appropriation requested by President Johnson for the federal disaster relief fund out of which the Office of Emergency Planning could draw to provide for Alaskan relief costs. On April 25 President Johnson recommended an increase of $22.5 million in the transitional grants to the state previously authorized by the Statehood Act; Congress passed legislation authorizing $23.5 million.

On May 25 the Reconstruction Commission proposed additional legislation which the President recommended to Congress in the form of amendments to the Alaska Omnibus Act. In the proposed legislation, S. 2881 and H.R. 11438, the President asked for an increase in the federal share (from 50 to 94.9 percent) of the cost of repairing and reconstructing the non-forest federal-aid highways damaged by the earthquake. Further, the Farmers Home Administration and Rural Electrification Administration would adjust the indebtedness of some of their borrowers to enable them to overcome earthquake losses and the Housing and Home Finance Administrator would provide federal assistance to the state in marketing up to $25 million in state bonds for public works programs to help the state receive a favorable interest rate and thereby restore its credit rating. The Small Business Administration was to be allowed to increase maximum terms on disaster loans from twenty to thirty years, and the Corps of Engineers would make modifications in previously authorized civil works projects to overcome adverse effects of the earthquake. The Housing and Home Finance Agency would enter into contracts for urban renewal projects in Alaska up to a maximum of $25 million on a 75 to 25 matching basis and the HHFA would be permitted to compromise or release any portion of any FHA-insured mortgage held by the agency as the agency would find necessary because of the loss or damage due to the earthquake.

Congress amended the legislation in three ways. The federal share of urban renewal projects was increased from 75 percent to 90 percent; HHFA was authorized to purchase (as part of the $25 million bond authorization provision) up to $7.2 million in State of Alaska bonds for completing state capital-improvements programs, which had been approved prior to the earthquake but not issued; and a program of grants to retire outstanding mortgage obligations on one- to four-family dwellings destroyed or severely damaged in the earthquake was authorized to be financed on a 50-50 matching basis by the federal and state governments.

On August 28, 1967, President Johnson reported to Congress that federal recovery assistance to Alaska had totaled more than $350 million. The Department of Housing and Urban Development had purchased over $15 million in state bonds and had distributed more than $9 million in urban renewal projects in Kodiak, Anchorage, Valdez, and Seldovia, with a further $16 million approved and awaiting disbursal. The Small Business Administration had made over $92 million in disaster and small business loans. More than $5 million in federal funds had been used to finance twenty-three highway-reconstruction projects. The sum of $51 million from the President's disaster-relief fund financed the repair of public buildings, streets, bridges, schools and utilities. It was highly doubtful that the federal response to disaster in the Territory of Alaska would have been quite so speedy and generous as it was to the State of Alaska. In August 1967, Fairbanks experienced a devastating flood, to which the federal government responded with equal alacrity.

The earthquake and its aftermath proved to be a turning point in the federal government's relationship with Alaska. Federal and state officials worked together toward rebuilding Alaska in a way that would contribute to the long-term economic development of the state. As a result of this experience, the Federal Reconstruction and Planning Commission recommended that a joint federal-state planning committee to plan the long-range economic and resource development of Alaska be established. On October 2, 1964, President Johnson issued an executive order creating the Federal Field Committee for Development Planning in Alaska, thereby recognizing the responsibility and stake of the federal government in the forty-ninth state. The committee was composed of representatives of the principal federal agencies in Alaska and was charged with planning the orderly development of the natural resources of Alaska in the national interest. The Ninetieth Congress extended the life of the committee until June 30, 1970.

2. The Fishing Industry

THE FISHERIES had long been Alaska's most important industrial activity. The very existence of a number of coastal communities depended on them, and even in the interior a cash economy was maintained to a great extent by the wages paid to cannery workers who traveled to the coastal areas to work each summer. From a 1936 high of 8.5 million cases of salmon, a persistent decline set in, so that by 1959, the last year of federal management of the fisheries, fewer than 1.7 million cases were packed. Among the reasons for the decline, absentee ownership and absentee federal management played the major part in the depletion of one of the state's greatest natural resources and in producing a major conservation fiasco.

The Statehood Act established that the new state would not obtain control of fish and wildlife resources until January 4, 1960, a full year after the state government assumed jurisdiction over Alaska. In the meantime, the issue of fish traps—the territory's most visible psychological and physical symbol of outside control—descended as a legacy of territorial history. In a 1956 referendum Alaskans had voted to abolish fish traps. In a campaign promise in the election of 1958, Secretary of the Interior Seaton had gone on record as saying that the Department of the Interior's 1959 regulations would abolish fish traps. Moreover, on the day Governor Egan assumed office he announced that fish traps would no longer be legal, basing his edict on the fact that the state had authority over the tidelands where they were located. The legal question of whether Egan or Seaton had jurisdiction became moot when on March 9 the Department of the Interior's regulations confirmed Seaton's promise. Fish traps were at last abolished.[3] The outcry expectedly was one of approval among Alaskans—whose interest had finally been consulted—and dismay among Seattle cannery associations, which brought an unsuccessful court action to stay the order.

The results clearly demonstrated the wisdom of permitting Alaskans to control their own resources. The 1964 salmon pack exceeded 3.6 million cases, the largest in fifteen years. In 1966 the total value of all production was $174 million, as opposed to the 1959 figure of $72 million. In 1967, however, the poorest season since 1959 left fishermen and entire villages destitute to the point that the Department of Agriculture's surplus-food program was put into operation and the Bureau of Indian Affairs was forced to consider requesting a supplemental appropriation to support its welfare activities in the villages. The state's Board of Fish and Game was led to study the possibility of limiting the number of fishermen allowed in the Bristol Bay area. Although statehood meant a marked improvement in the productivity of the fisheries, the 1967 season was a grim reminder that all was not well in the industry.

Dependence upon the salmon, historically the foundation of the industry, prevented the fisheries from becoming a stable base for the economy of Alaska. The cyclical nature of the salmon and the seasonal nature of the work meant that those who depended on salmon fishing were largely at the mercy of nature. Moreover, it was unfortunate that the salmon fisherman was equally dependent upon the whim of the American housewife. Americans preferred tuna to salmon. In 1940 the average American ate 2.0 pounds of salmon and 0.6 pounds of tuna. By 1963 he had almost completely reversed his eating habits and consumed 2.0 pounds of tuna and only 0.9 pounds of salmon. The tuna industry profited from aggressive packaging, marketing and advertising techniques, which the salmon producers ignored.

Moreover, the fishing industry in Alaska and in the rest of the United States was slow to tap unused resources and modernize its production techniques. The President's Review Committee for Development Planning in Alaska noted that "the actual potential afforded by the fishing banks off the coast of Alaska is virtually untapped, with foreign fleets harvesting far more than is harvested by American interests."[4] In the North Pacific region as a whole the United States caught less than one billion pounds annually out of an estimated potential catch of ten billion pounds. Expansion into year-round products, such as shrimp and bottomfish, appeared to be a necessity. The burgeoning king-crab industry in Alaska provided a good example of the potential of fisheries resources other than salmon. In 1966, barely twenty years after commercial exploitation of king crab was begun in earnest, the king-crab industry accounted for 19 percent of the wholesale value of fisheries production in Alaska. At the same time, Americans lagged far behind Scandinavia, Japan and the Soviet Union in production and processing techniques; in 1964 alone, Soviet publications described 137 new units of fish processing equipment.

Finally, American fishermen lacked consistent protection from their government. The Eighty-eighth Congress passed a bill introduced by Representative Ralph Rivers and Senator Bartlett which prohibited fishing in the territorial waters of the United States and certain other areas by persons other than U.S. nationals or inhabitants. Violators could be fined, imprisoned, and their gear and catch forfeited. The Eighty-ninth Congress further extended protection by passing Bartlett's bill to establish exclusive rights to fishing in a nine-mile zone beyond the three-mile limit. Yet in 1967 alone there were three violations of American waters off the coast of Alaska by Soviet fishing vessels. The captain of the first vessel seized on March 2 was fined only $5,000. On March 22 a second Soviet vessel was captured and its captain was fined $10,000. The third violation occurred on August 3 and involved the same vessel that had been seized on March 22, although the captain was different. In this instance the U.S. attorney in Anchorage dismissed the charge against the captain of the ship and libeled the vessel's gear, which was redeemed for $20,000. The Department of State, in a misguided attempt to calm international tensions, virtually dictated the extent of prosecution to the Department of Justice. It was clear that until the Department of State made up its mind that the national interest demanded that the domestic fisheries of the United States be protected from foreign encroachment, efforts to develop the fisheries would be in vain.

3. Minerals and Forests

AT THE BEGINNING of 1968 Alaska was fast approaching becoming the tenth largest oil-producing state in the country. Alaska had ninety wells producing an astonishing per-well average of more than 1,600 barrels a day. The average well in Louisiana, the second-ranking producer, produced 56.2 barrels a day.

Alaska entered the oil industry on July 19, 1957, when the Richfield Oil Company struck oil in the Swanson River field on the Kenai Peninsula. Sixty years before, the cry had been "Gold!" and thousands of individual adventurers had made their way north and reminded Americans of the existence of Alaska. Now the adventurers were sophisticated multibillion dollar industrial complexes whose "grubstake" was provided by thousands of stockholders, who gambled on the profitability of investing millions of dollars in high-cost exploratory activities in Alaska. The gamble paid off spectacularly for all concerned. In 1955 no petroleum was produced commercially in Alaska. By 1966 oil and natural gas accounted for almost 60 percent of the mineral production of Alaska, and the State of Alaska received in the same year $19 million in oil and gas lease rentals and royalty payments.

Companies interested in prospecting and drilling for oil had to overcome the opposition of conservation groups which predicted the destruction of the moose in the Kenai Moose Range. In 1940 Ira Gabrielson, director of the newly created Fish and Wildlife Service had recommended to Secretary of the Interior Ickes that two million acres be reserved in Alaska for moose. And so the two-million acre Kenai Moose Range was created—without the benefit of public hearings. It was the same Ira Gabrielson who, as president of the Wildlife Management Institute, led the fight against oil exploration in that federal preserve. Hearings were held in the Department of the Interior on December 9 and 10, 1957. Conservationists, with a saner view on the alleged imperilment of wildlife and aware of the needs of human beings, favored oil exploration and extraction, and won the support of Senator Joseph C. O'Mahoney of Wyoming, one of the most influential members of the Senate, who had been the floor manager of one of the statehood bills and was himself an ardent conservationist. As a result, Secretary of the Interior Seaton issued an order permitting oil exploration and drilling in the northern half of the Moose Range. A great new industry had been brought to Alaska, saving the state from bankruptcy. Furthermore, far from diminishing, the moose multiplied, ranging over Alaska into areas where they had never been seen before.

The gold-mining industry continued to decline after statehood. The average value of production in the years 1957 to 1961 was $6 million; by 1966 it had dropped below $1 million, with the physical volume of production registering the lowest mark since 1886. The reason for the decline was simple. Costs continued to rise while the price of gold remained fixed by law at $35 an ounce. Since the Eightieth Congress there were more than 125 legislative attempts to assist the ailing American gold-mining industry. All were opposed by the Treasury Department on the ground that increasing the price of gold or subsidizing its production would undermine the international monetary system, which rested on the dollar, which in turn rested on gold pegged at a price of $35 an ounce. However, despite administration opposition, in the Ninetieth Congress, the Senate Committee on Interior and Insular Affairs favorably reported to the Senate S. 49, Gruening's bill to revitalize the industry. The bill would establish a domestic program administered by the Secretary of the Interior for payments to American producers based on the differences in the costs of gold production in the last quarter of 1939 (1940 was the industry's peak production year), and current costs of production on an individual gold-mine basis. New gold-mining enterprises, and other gold mines with no history of production in the last quarter of 1939 could qualify for similar aid through establishment of constructive costs, taking into account production costs of gold mining in the same or adjacent mining districts.

However, in March, 1968, responding to the dollar crisis, following Britain's devaluation of the pound, the Treasury Department announced new regulations which permitted the free sale of gold at the market price to licensed users in the United States and free exports to foreign buyers by domestic producers without restrictions. At the same time the Treasury Department stated that it would no longer purchase gold in the private market or sell gold for professional, industrial, or artistic purposes. While the effect of this new policy on domestic gold production was not immediately clear, the Treasury's long-existing restraint against buying and selling gold at a price higher than $35 an ounce was removed.

The coal industry in Alaska, which depended largely on purchases by the Department of Defense, suffered a severe setback in 1967, when Fort Richardson and Elmendorf Air Force Base converted from coal to gas as a source of power. The future of the industry was, at best, uncertain.

Alaska was also blessed with significant deposits of copper, iron ore, beryllium, mercury, and platinum, and there was also substantial production of sand and gravel. Yet, although in the neighboring Yukon Territory and in the upper third of British Columbia, smaller in extent than Alaska and presumably with similar geology, there were forty-nine major active mining projects—in Alaska there were only seven. One reason for this marked difference was the more enlightened mining incentive policies of the dominion and provincial governments of Canada. The Congress of the United States in 1966 took a step in the direction of assisting minerals exploration when it passed a bill introduced by Senator Gruening to liberalize tax-deduction provisions for mining exploration expenditures (PL 89-570). The new law allowed mining companies to take as current income tax deductions all costs of minerals exploration without limitation. Previously deductions had been limited to $100,000 annually or a total of $400,000, regardless of the mine operator's expense. The measure included the provision that, when a mine became productive, the operator would forgo depletion allowances equal to the amount previously deducted as an expense or include as income for the year production reached an amount equivalent to the deduction. However, it was also apparent that minerals development in Alaska would probably also need better transportation and low-cost power, both of which, across the border in Canada, were part of its incentive program.

The announcement in early 1968 that the U.S. Forest Service had completed the sale of 8.75 billion board-feet of timber to U.S. Plywood-Champion Papers, Incorporated, indicated that the future of the forest industry in Alaska was bright. Most of the industry's operations were located in southeastern Alaska, with major pulp mills near Ketchikan and Sitka.

The Japanese, who also displayed significant interest in the petroleum products of Alaska, controlled the pulp mill at Sitka, in addition to a sawmill at Wrangell. The Japanese first entered Alaska in 1954, when a Japanese consortium invested in the Wrangell sawmill. The same company then proceeded to finance the pulp mill at Sitka, which by 1967 was exporting $40 million a year in lumber and pulp to Japan. In 1967 the Tokyo Gas Company and Tokyo Electric Power Company signed a fifteen-year contract to purchase liquefied natural gas from Phillips Petroleum and Marathon Oil, which began construction of a $100 million plant at Port Nikiski on the Kenai Peninsula for this purpose. Port Nikiski was also the site of a $50 million fertilizer complex to be owned by Japan Gas–Chemical Company and Collier Carbon and Chemical Company. Alaskco, a group of Japanese oil companies, was planning to search for oil in Alaska in a joint venture with Gulf Oil. The Japanese also had substantial financial interests in seafood-processing plants in Anchorage and Cordova. Alaska's position on the rim of the Pacific made it a prime source of raw materials for Japan. So important was Japan to the future of Alaska that the State of Alaska opened an office in Tokyo to represent its interests in that country.

4. Power

THE FIRST appropriation of funds to study the feasibility of building the proposed Rampart Dam, located approximately a hundred miles northwest of Fairbanks along the Yukon River, was made during 1959, the first year Alaska had voting representation in Congress. Rampart would have an installed capacity of 5.04 million kilowatts, which could produce 34.2 billion kilowatt hours of firm energy a year, deliverable at tidewater locations in Alaska at a cost of from two to three mills per kilowatt hour. Rampart would provide power for the industrial base now lacking in Alaska and would help the nation meet a critical power shortage in the future. Besides its economic necessity for the state, Rampart would have significant recreational value. The site of the proposed dam was a wasteland; the man-made lake created by construction of Rampart would give Alaskans an unprecedented opportunity for water sports and for fresh-water fishing.

Opposition to Rampart came from some conservationists who reacted almost hysterically to the supposed destruction of wildlife which they alleged Rampart would bring about; but they disregarded the economic needs of the species *Homo sapiens,* who needed the wherewithal to make use of the natural resources of the earth to ensure his survival.

In June 1967 Secretary of the Interior Udall announced that the department had recommended against construction of Rampart. The secretary declared in justification: "We cannot afford to antagonize the sportsmen." A far-flung campaign against Rampart had been organized by opposing conservationists through articles appearing in a number of periodicals. The nature of the attack was best characterized by an article by Paul Brooks entitled "The Plot to Drown Alaska," which appeared in the May 1965 issue of the *Atlantic Monthly.* This was rebutted by Ernest Gruening in an article in the same magazine the following July entitled "The Plot to Strangle Alaska." It remained for the U.S. Army Corps of Engineers to make a final decision on the project which was vitally needed by the State of Alaska.

At the same time, Secretary Udall issued an executive order establishing the Alaska Power Administration and appointed Gus Norwood, long-time executive secretary of the Northwest Public Power Association, as its first administrator. In 1968 Norwood, on behalf of the secretary, recommended to Congress construction of the Lake Grace hydroelectric power project near Ketchikan and the Takatz Creek Project near Sitka. This development, along with the commencement of construction of the Snettisham project near Juneau in 1967, gave evidence that Alaska's vast hydroelectric power potential would at last be tapped.

The Natives—and the Still-Unsatisfied Hunger for Land

> Until the full force of national policy is brought to bear on the problem, there will be no hope of widespread improvement for the native peoples in western and Arctic Alaska.
>
> FEDERAL FIELD COMMITTEE
> FOR DEVELOPMENT PLANNING IN ALASKA, 1966

THE GREAT unresolved question and conflict of the sixties was the method of disposition of the claims to great tracts of land in Alaska made by the natives[1] of Alaska. The Organic Act of 1884, which gave Alaska an unworkable modicum of civil government, provided that "Indians or other persons in said district shall not be disturbed in the possession of any lands actually in their use or occupation or now claimed by them, but the terms under which such persons may acquire title to such lands is reserved for future legislation." That "future legislation" was never passed by Congress. The Statehood Act gave the state authority to select 103 million acres of land to provide itself with a viable economic base, but at the same time said that "the state and its people do agree and declare that they forever disclaim all right and title . . . to any lands or other property (including fishing rights), the right or title to which may be held by any Indians, Eskimos, or Aleuts." Congress in the years after statehood still did not decide what lands the natives could rightfully claim. Efforts by the Congressional delegation to secure action from the Interior Department in the shape of proposed legislation which would have administration approval proved unavailing. Impatient over this protracted inaction, the natives of Alaska began, in 1961, to organize themselves into groups and associations, which commenced to lay claim to blocks of land in earnest. The State of Alaska continued to select lands under the Statehood Act. Confronted by a threatened chaotic situation, due largely to the department's procrastination, Secretary of the Interior Udall, who had halted approval of state-land selections and other public-land transactions pending resolution of the natives' claims, finally in late 1966 submitted the draft of a bill. It proved wholly unsatisfactory to the natives as well as to Senator Gruening, who introduced it "by request." Their objection and his to S. 1964 was that it vested complete power in the Secretary of the Interior over the disposal of the lands and funds provided by the legislation, thus perpetuating the near century of control over their lives by the Interior Department.

Demonstrating their opposition, the Alaska Federation of Natives drafted another bill, which provided that their claims to land be referred to, and settled by, the United States Court of Claims. This bill, S. 2020, was likewise introduced by Senator Gruening on June 26, 1967.

Upon further consideration, the native groups felt that this approach would entail long delays. Also evident was that the Interior Department would oppose it.

Thereupon, a native task force, appointed by Governor Hickel, which included widespread representation from nearly every part of Alaska drafted a third bill. This bill involved a departure in that it proposed to take funds from the receipts of oil exploration on Alaska's continental shelf to satisfy the natives' financial claims. This idea had been suggested by Secretary Udall himself on a trip to Alaska. It likewise called for corresponding action by the state legislature to make funds from Alaskan land acquisitions available. Senator Gruening arranged that hearings be held by the full Interior Committee—instead of by its Subcommittee on Indian Affairs—and for hearings to be held in Anchorage, at the earliest possible moment. The Interior Committee met for three days: February 8, 9 and 10. Senators present were Henry M. Jackson (D., of Washington), Lee Metcalf (D., of Montana), Paul Fannin (R., of Arizona) and Ernest Gruening (D., of Alaska). The committee established new senatorial precedents as to hours, convening on successive days at 8, 7 and 6 A.M. Witnesses from all parts of Alaska were heard, and all who desired to testify were given the opportunity. Never before had so wide a representation of natives and other supporters assembled to plead their cause, but some opposition to the legislation was also voiced.[2]

The natives' plight was repeatedly and movingly expounded. Emil Notti, an Athapascan, resident of Anchorage, and president of the Alaska Federation of Natives, summed up their case clearly, saying in part:

The native people who for centuries have made their living off the land can no longer do so. The decline of game animals due to increased pressures of hunting from the urban areas and by trophy hunters has made it difficult for natives to make a living by subsistence hunting. The native people who for 10,000 years made a living off of the land by subsistence hunting are now prevented from doing so because of artificial game regulations that are foreign to the native people and the penalties for breaking these regulations are severe in terms of money fines.

The needs for a quick settlement are many and overwhelming. The human needs, the suffering and deprivations that exist in the villages are beyond description and are as bad as the worst conditions anywhere in the world. The native people in many areas face a daily crisis just to exist. They need attention and action now. We cannot wait for more federal studies. The situation has been documented by many of the major federal agencies. The conditions that exist are well known, but nothing is done about them.

The decline of hunting and the encroaching civilization would not be so bad if it brought with it a means to offset the loss of the subsistence way of life, but unfortunately this is not the case. The Federal Field Committee for Development Planning in Alaska found in a study published in 1967 that there was 60 percent unemployment among the native people in Alaska. This unemployment is a crisis of major proportions to us and should prompt immediate action to correct the situation.

But, unfortunately, it has not. Another facet of the native method for subsistence living has hit an all-time low. That is the salmon fishing industry. The responsibility for the ruin of the fishing industry lies with the federal government. . . . Furthermore, the ruin of the industry was done against the will of the people of Alaska, who by referendum voted to abolish the cause of the ruin, the fishtrap. The Alaska salmon industry was the world's greatest salmon industry, but it was ruined under federal control and the industry that was a major employer of the Alaska native has been ruined to the point that the state is seriously considering closing the salmon season to commercial fishing. Salmon industries and fishing boats employed many hundreds of native Alaskans. Canneries that ran to capacities are now running with skeleton crews and many have closed their doors. . . . The ruining of the industry has put many natives out of work and has not been replaced by other means of making a living.

As the Interior Department voiced no objection to the legislation under consideration, it was assumed that its report on this legislation would be favorable. It came, therefore, as a great surprise and shock when, some three months later, Secretary Udall's Interior Department reported adversely on S. 2906 and presented an entirely new administration bill which had some of the objectionable features of his first bill, S. 1964. It abandoned the idea he had proposed earlier of using revenues from the continental shelf and provided instead a cash appropriation of $180 million of which each native recipient would be entitled to $3,000.

Meanwhile, valuable time had been lost. Senator Gruening, who had committed himself to S. 2906, declined to sponsor this bill but had it introduced by Chairman Henry M. Jackson "by request." He introduced S. 3586 on June 4, 1968.

It was feared that because of the long delay caused by Secretary Udall's reversal and the complexity of the subject, plus the difficulty of getting a direct appropriation from the Congress during an era of drastic retrenchment caused by the war in Southeast Asia, that no action would be taken by both houses during the Ninetieth Congress and that action would have to wait until the Ninety-first Congress. This was a great disappointment to all who hoped for speedy action on this long-overdue legislation.

The natives saw the land-claims issue as the key to bringing an end to their disadvantaged status. The Eskimo, Indian, and Aleut, who at the time of statehood comprised approximately 20 percent of the population of Alaska, had long since ceased to suffer legal discrimination. A public accommodations law, sponsored by Governor Gruening and which made discrimination on the basis of race illegal, had been placed on the statute books of the Territory of Alaska in 1945, far in advance of various other states of the Union. But for reasons of history, economics, geography, and culture, the Alaska native in western and northern Alaska continued to labor under a much more subtle form of economic discrimination, which proved all the more difficult to eradicate. "This is a land without a foothold in the twentieth century," reported Joseph H. FitzGerald, chairman of the Federal Field Committee for Development Planning in Alaska, referring to the vast area inhabited by Athapascan Indians, Eskimos and Aleuts.

In 1966 the per capita income of the native village of Grayling, Alaska, for example, was $350; 45 percent of this was in the form of welfare and unemployment compensation. In 1964, 80 percent of those on the state's welfare rolls were natives. At the time of statehood, the average native had barely finished the sixth grade. The tuberculosis rate, which showed marked improvement since statehood, in 1966 was still ten times the national average. The infant mortality rate was among the highest in the world. When Alaska became a state the Alaska native could look forward to a life expectancy of 34.7 years, while his fellow Alaskan who happened to be white could expect to live for 70 years.

Underneath the statistics lay a human profile of what it was like to live as a native. Despite the infant mortality rate, the head of a family was usually responsible for a large number of children. He lived in a village with a population ranging from fifty to several hundred and which in the winter might be accessible only by air or dog sled. (In many areas the dog began to give way to the internal combustion engine, and the dog sled was being replaced by the snowmobile.) Along the Yukon-Kuskokwim rivers, for example, in the beginning of summer he would begin his efforts to lay up enough fish, principally salmon, to see him and his family through the winter. Despite the growing incidence of employment for cash wages, his economy was essentially of a subsistence nature.

But his society was nevertheless replete with contradictions. A few years ago his requirements for goods had been limited to a few staples, such as sugar and salt. With a growing dependence on a cash economy and with the stores in the villages carrying such goods as rifles and snowmobiles, his expectations were rising and the need to define his place in society was growing. It would have been untrue, therefore, to overemphasize the primitiveness of his way of life since it was a mixture of hundreds of years of tradition and modern technology. The incredible growth of air transportation put the native within hours of metropolitan centers. Radio and even television informed him of current events. With the formation of native associations and groups, his political power grew. Most important, education widened his horizons. Thousands of young native children were forced to attend boarding schools operated by the Bureau of Indian Affairs far from their homes. Many went on to college or technical institutions. The result was a growing proportion of natives who saw and experienced for themselves how, for better or for worse, how the rest of the world lived.

The role of government in the development of the native was substantial, well-meaning, but not always effective. The Bureau of Indian Affairs remained responsible for the Alaska native from the cradle to the grave, and it was clear that until the bureau's paternalistic attitude was changed and until the native was taught to help himself, his lot would not be improved.

One of the most significnt actions with regard to the status of the Alaska native on the federal level was the successful introduction of legislation authorizing a housing program for natives by Senator Bartlett in the Eighty-ninth Congress. Although 97 percent of the natives were living in what was officially described as substandard housing, none of the existing federal housing programs fitted their situation in Alaska. The Farmers Home Administration loan program was beyond their incomes. The Housing Assistance Authority's self-help program could not work because of the absence of the electricity, sewer, and water requirements (except in Metlakatla and Hoonah). Any homes within their financial means could not meet Federal Housing Administration requirements for financing.

In the Eighty-ninth Congress Bartlett introduced S. 1915, by which the Department of Housing and Urban Development would be permitted to make loans and grants to the State of Alaska for housing for natives. The federal government's share would be 75 percent of up to $7,500 per unit. To put the program into operation $10 million would be authorized. Bartlett succeeded in having the bill made an amendment to the Demonstration Cities and Metropolitan Development Act of 1966. Unfortunately, appropriations for the program were not immediately forthcoming. The President in 1967 requested $1 million for fiscal year 1968, which was deleted by the House, restored by the Senate, and lost in conference. The incidence of disease, such as respiratory infections caused by crowding in unsanitary conditions, made it imperative that the program be implemented.

The federal government was not altogether oblivious to the plight of the native. Sargent Shriver, head of the Office of Economic Opportunity, made his first trip to Alaska in the summer of 1967. What he saw shocked him. The day after he returned to Washington he told a Senate committee that the conditions among the Alaska natives were among the worst he had seen in the United States.[3] Shriver was led to set up a task force within the Office of Economic Opportunity to study Alaska's unique problems and furnish recommendations for action. OEO's financial support of a cooperative effort to electrify sixty-seven villages in Alaska by 1970 gave evidence that the federal government's commitment to the Alaska native was firm.

But whatever the impact of federal programs upon the natives' way of life, as Alaska ended its first decade of statehood, it was clear that how Congress would resolve the land-claims issue would, in no small degree, determine the future not only of the natives of Alaska, but of the State of Alaska as well.

Beginning the Second Century

The first hundred years are the hardest.

ANONYMOUS

THE CENTENNIAL YEAR, 1967, was highlighted by a far-reaching, varied, all-embracing activity to celebrate the anniversary of Alaska's acquisition by the United States. Begun in the administration of Governor William A. Egan and carried forward under that of Governor Walter J. Hickel, the Alaska Purchase Centennial Commission[1] with the cooperation of other committees and numerous individuals, both within and outside of Alaska, state-appointed and federal, enacted a program of construction, pageantry, recognition of historic sites, collecting and collating historic memorabilia, appropriate creative expression in the arts—painting, sculpture, drama, music and literature— that reached to the remotest areas of Alaska's vastness and enlisted a galaxy of talent in a prodigious accomplishment.

The scope and effectiveness of the centennial celebration was increased by the Eighty-ninth Congress, which passed a bill introduced by Senators Bartlett and Gruening and Congressman Rivers which provided $4.6 million in federal funds for the Centennial. The Senate approved $3.6 million, but Rivers persuaded the House to raise the figure to $4.6 million, an amount subsequently agreed to by the Senate in conference. The bill (PL 89-375) authorized the federal government to use $4 million for matching grants to finance industrial, agricultural, educational, research, and commercial projects which would contribute to Alaska's economic development. It also authorized expenditure of $600,000 for federal participation in centennial ceremonies and exhibits.

The focal point of centennial projects was the "Alaska 67" exposition at Fairbanks, the official Alaska Purchase Centennial Exhibition Site. It consisted of a gold-rush town, a native village, a "mining valley," where Alaska gold mining was demonstrated, the renovated stern-wheeler *Nenana,* and an amusement park. It housed a magnificent collection of paintings by "Rusty" Heurlin, one of Alaska's great artists, picturing the gold rush of the 1890's and especially executed for the Centennial. A tasteful and happy combination of Disneyland and Williamsburg, "Alaska 67" was expected to serve as a permanent attraction for the increasing number of tourists to Alaska.

Twenty-eight other Alaskan communities received federal assistance for projects to mark the Centennial. In Anchorage, projects included an aviation museum, a museum of fine arts, and a native arts-and-crafts center at Anchorage International Airport. The English fort built at Fort Yukon in 1842 was restored, and at Homer a new museum was constructed. Residents of Juneau agreed to a voluntary sales tax to help finance a new Alaska State Museum. At Kenai the centennial celebration featured the restoration of Fort Kenay, and in Ketchikan a building was constructed to house municipal offices and the Tongass Historical Society. Sitka was the site of a beautiful new convention hall.[2]

Throughout the year special programs were organized to celebrate the first century of American rule, including a visit by Mrs. William Henry Seward, III, the widow of the last of Seward's descendants, who dedicated the Seward Memorial in Anchorage which was sculpted by Gerald Conaway from a single Alaska marble slab weighing several tons. Other artistic efforts included an original musical play, a traveling art show (in addition to a show at the Alaska 67 site), an international drama festival, and various books published jointly by the University of Alaska and the Centennial Commission.[3]

These far-flung activities, pursued with enthusiasm and devotion, went far to diminish sectionalism, to promote the Alaskans' sense of unity, to strengthen their consciousness of Alaska's rich and diverse heritage, to instill awareness of its unique place in the contemporary world, and to inspire their rededication to constructing in the continent's farthest north and west, an example of all that was best in the American tradition and avowed purpose. Their centennial achievement demonstrated that they could come close to attaining, in the century ahead, whatever goals their hearts and minds would set.

Bibliographical Note

The history of Alaska since its acquisition by the United States is, to a degree greater than in other American political entities, found in government documents, published and unpublished. This arises inevitably from the federal dominance in Alaskan affairs.

During the earlier years the studies of ethnologists, biologists and other natural scientists of the Smithsonian Institution, the Bureau of Fisheries, the Biological Survey, etc., and later the geographic and geologic investigations of the Geological Survey, as well as the explorations of Army and Revenue-Marine officers—issued from the Government Printing Office.

The meager documentation in the field of political science during the nineteenth century reflects the scant interest that Alaska had awakened in federal legislative or executive circles. Few records were made of congressional hearings on Alaska matters before the turn of the century and none was printed. Yet from reports of the executive branches, particularly of the various agencies of the Treasury, which played the principal federal role in Alaska, considerable material may be winnowed.

During the twentieth century government publications are increasingly valuable sources—reflecting the increased government surveillance of Alaska. In the annual departmental reports, and in congressional hearings, reports and debates may be found much that illuminates Alaska's history. Since 1884 there have also been the annual governors' reports, and since 1913 the territorial legislatures' session laws, Senate and House journals, and the biennial reports of territorial departments. Since early days the Alaska press has been varyingly valuable as a reflector of the feelings and habits of Alaskans, and as a recorder of their actions.

Alaska still represents a relatively unexplored field for the historian. Hubert Howe Bancroft dealt fully with the Russian period, concluding with the organic act of 1884. F. A. Golder subsequently added much to our knowledge from his distillation of previously unavailable material from the Russian archives. Victor J. Farrar has revealed the circumstances surrounding the purchase. Jeannette Paddock Nichols has made the only comprehensive study of political relations and economic influences up to the Second Organic Act in 1912. Since then Henry Wadsworth Clark in 1930, Clarence Leroy Andrews in 1931, Stuart Ramsay Tompkins in 1945 and Clarence C. Hulley in 1953 have successively brought the general history of Alaska up to date.

There is very considerable descriptive, travel, adventure, hunting and personal-experience literature about Alaska, some of which contains nuggets of fine gold for the historiographer. There has been very little about the economic factors that have shaped Alaska's destiny and of their interaction with political forces. The "unseen" in Alaska's past has been also unwritten.

The material in this volume is derived chiefly from readily accessible governmental sources. These are cited in what the writer sought to make a minimum of footnoting, and therefore only (1) in the case of a direct quotation, (2) when the subject matter required the citation of its authority, (3) when collateral material, in the writer's judgment, was of interest, yet was better omitted from the narrative as a diversion from its flow.

The writer desires to express his deep appreciation to Mrs. Ruth Coffin Allman for giving him access to the forty volumes (1900-1939) of the unpublished diary of James Wickersham; to Edward L. Keithahn, curator of the Territorial Museum and Library for facilitating the use of its valuable material; to Miss Mary Lee Council and Mrs. Margery Goding Smith of Delegate Bartlett's office for assistance in securing government reports and other data; to Gerald Fitzgerald, Chief Topographic Engineer of the United States Geological Survey, for co-operation in the preparation of maps; to Clarence L. Anderson, Director of the Territorial Department of Fisheries, for the charts on the fisheries, for data relating to the national forests in Alaska to Arthur W. Greeley, regional forester, who recently succeeded B. Frank Heintzleman, for sixteen years regional forester in Alaska, when the latter was appointed Governor of Alaska by President Eisenhower in 1953, to other federal and territorial officials and others who have generously responded to requests for information, and to Katherine T. Alexander for typing and other devoted assistance.

Given the necessary footnote citations it has seemed like needless duplication to re-list the great number of reports and hearings consulted, especially since such a bibliography would be tediously repetitious, with hearings after hearings dealing with the same subject before corresponding congressional committees with only the years and the numbers on the bills changed.

The repetitiveness which the reader will thus be spared, cannot, unfortunately, be wholly avoided in the text. Nor should it be. For it is the most constant of all characteristics in the near-century of United States rule. Alaska's history's *leitmotif* is the Alaskans' efforts to achieve political and economic self-determination. It has been "again and again and again," to adopt a phrase made famous by President Franklin D. Roosevelt.

Reviewing these efforts, a pessimist might be inclined to summarize their results with the Gallicism, *"Plus ça change plus c'est la même chose."* But the frontier, especially "the last frontier," breeds optimists.

Notes

CHAPTER 1

[1] It has been variously spelled, *viz.*, Aliaska, Aliaksa, Aliaksha, Alakshak, etc.

CHAPTER 2

[1] Stejneger, Leonhard, *Georg Wilhelm Steller*, p. 90.
[2] *Diary*, in Golder, F. A., *Bering's Voyages*, Vol. II, p. 221.

CHAPTER 3

[1] Cook, James, *Voyage to the Pacific Ocean*, p. xxxi.
[2] Willson, Beckles, *The Great Company*, pp. 50-1, 274, 515-26.
[3] Raymond, Charles P., *Reconnaissance up the Yukon River*.
[4] June 23, 1899. Willson, *op. cit.*, p. xii.

CHAPTER 4

[1] 40 C: 2 s, H. of R. *Ex. Doc.* 177.
[2] *Ibid.*
[3] *Ibid.*
[4] April 5, 1867.
[5] Report of Commissioner Rousseau to Secretary Seward. 40 C: 2 s, H. of R. *Ex. Doc.* 125.
[6] 40 C: 2 s, H. of R. *Ex. Doc.* 177.
[7] Article 3 of the treaty was as follows: The inhabitants of the ceded territory, according to their choice, reserving their natural allegiance, may return to Russia within three years, but if they should prefer to remain in the ceded territory, they, with the exception of uncivilized native tribes, shall be admitted to the enjoyment of all the rights, advantages and immunities of citizens of the United States, and shall be maintained and protected in the free enjoyment of their liberty, property and religion. The uncivilized tribes will be subject to such laws and regulations as the United States may, from time to time, adopt in regard to aboriginal tribes of that country.
[8] Speech of Rep. Wm. Loughridge, R., of Iowa, June 30, 1868. 40 C: 2 s, *Cong. Globe*, p. 3621.
[9] April 1, 1867.
[10] April 9, 1867. The New York *Tribune* on April 11, 1867, declared: "We simply obtain by the treaty the nominal possession of impassable deserts of snow, vast tracts of dwarf timbers, inaccessible mountain ranges, with a few islands where the climate is more moderate, and a scanty population supported by fishing and trading with the Indians. Virtually we get, by an expenditure of seven millions in gold, Sitka and the Prince of Wales Islands. All the rest is waste territory, and no energy of the American people will be sufficient to make mining speculations in the 60th degree north latitude profitable, or to reclaim wildernesses which border on the Arctic Ocean. We may make a treaty with Russia but we cannot make a treaty with the North Wind or the Snow King. . . . Ninety-nine hundredths of Russian America are absolutely useless; the remaining hundredth may be of some value, but is certainly not worth seven million dollars to a nation already possessed of more territory than it can decently govern, and burdened with debt. . . . The expense and trouble of a territorial government . . . in this distant and uninhabitable land would far outweigh any advantage from its codfish or bearskins. To Russia it was an encumbrance, to us it

would be an embarrassment, and by
the next session of Congress we trust
the folly of the purchase will be made
so plain that the House will refuse to
make the necessary appropriation."
Quoted in Virginia Hancock Reid,
The Purchase of Alaska. On the other
hand, newspapers favoring the treaty
included The New York *Times*, the
Baltimore *Sun*, the Chicago *Evening
Journal*, the Portland *Oregonian*, the
San Francisco *Evening Bulletin* and
the Sacramento *Daily Union*.

[11] 40 C: 2 s, H. of R. *Rept.* 37.
[12] 40 C: 2 s, July 1, 1868, *Cong. Globe*,
pp. 3668-9.
[13] *Ibid.*, p. 3807.
[14] *Ibid.*
[15] *Ibid.*, 3808.
[16] 40 C: 2 s, July 1, 1868, *Cong. Globe*,
pp. 3663-8.
[17] 40 C: 2 s, July 7, 1868, *App. Cong.
Globe*, pp. 400-2.

CHAPTER 5

[1] 40 C: 1 s, Sen. *Ex. Doc.* 17.
[2] May 22, 1867. 40 C: 2 s, H. of R.
Ex. Doc. 177. In notifying Brigadier
General Jefferson C. Davis of his command and giving him detailed instructions, Halleck wrote, on September 6,
1867: "Notwithstanding the most be-
nevolent intentions of the Emperor
toward his American colonies, their
immense distance from the metropolitan government, and the delay and
difficulties of communication, have
probably heretofore prevented the application to them of the same fostering care which they would otherwise
have received; they have been too far
from the heart of a vast empire to feel
the warmth of the life current and
enjoy the vitality of the government
of a common country. Hence the
trade of these colonies has languished,
their agriculture has been neglected,
and their general progress almost im-
perceptible. Perhaps these facts have
constituted the moving causes which
induced his Imperial Majesty to consent to the cession of this territory,
and the transfer of the allegiance of
its inhabitants to the United States,

as a government more capable from
its proximity, of promoting its interests and supplying its wants.

"But, henceforth, the citizens of
that territory . . . will be entitled to
all the rights, privileges, and immunities guaranteed by the Constitution of
the United States to all the inhabitants of our republic. They will be
under the care and protection of our
government."

After outlining the resulting economic benefits General Halleck concluded that, "with these facilities for
trade and commerce with other parts
of the world, this new territory must
soon become what nature intended it
to be . . . 'the New England of the
Pacific.'" *Ibid.*, pp. 101-2.

On the same day, September 6,
1867, Assistant Adjutant General
James B. Fry likewise wrote General
Davis that as it was "probable that
during the next session Congress
would organize a territorial government" the buildings that the military
were to occupy in Sitka might be required by the civil government and
suggested that under those circumstances the military establishment
should be transferred to Japan Island
[Japonski] in the bay of Sitka. *Ibid.*
[3] In Philadelphia there had been
formed "The Pioneer Association for
the Civilization of the lately acquired
Russian Territory," and its officers,
headed by Captain Nathaniel R. Harris, wrote Secretary Seward on April
21, 1867, to inquire "what arrangements could be effected between the
government and the parties which are
anxious to emigrate to that country."
40 C: 2 s, H. of R. *Ex. Doc.* 177.
[4] In response to a letter of inquiry from
Secretary of State Seward, Secretary
of the Interior O. H. Browning transmitted the reply of Commissioner
Joseph S. Wilson of the General
Land Office that, under the act of
March 3, 1807, any citizens of the
United States attempting to make
claims and settlements under the
town-site or pre-emption laws, in the
absence of specific legislation by Congress for Alaska to organize land districts and to extend the system of

surveys, were acting "not only without the sanction of law," but "in direct violation of the provisions of the laws of Congress applicable to public domain secured to the United States by any treaty made with a foreign nation." "If necessary . . . military force may be used to remove the intruders," added Secretary Browning. Seward felt obliged to transmit these painful tidings to the Acting Secretary of War, Ulysses S. Grant, with the request that appropriate orders to that effect be telegraphed to Major General Halleck, commanding the Department of the Pacific, who in turn was to transmit them to the U. S. Army commander in Sitka.

[5] 40 C: 2 s, *Sen. 619.*

[6] In September, 1867, General Halleck, desiring to prevent the sale of whisky to Indians, requested the Secretary of War to ask President Johnson to declare Alaska "Indian Territory." The President took the matter under advisement, but did not act. On February 4, 1870, President Grant, in pursuance of the authority vested in him by the provisions of the 2nd section of the act approved July 27, 1868 (sec. 1955 U.S. Rev. stat.), issued a proclamation prohibiting the importation of distilled spirits into the District of Alaska and the Secretary of the Treasury, George S. Boutwell, issued a circular ordering customs collectors to carry out the terms of the proclamation. In March, 1873, the act of 1868 was amended by adding to it two sections, *viz.*, sections 20 and 21 of the act of 1834 which forbade the sales of liquor to Indians, and prohibited the setting up of distilleries. 43 C: 1 s, *Ex. Doc. 71.*

[7] 41 C: 2 s, S. 32 (16 Stat. 180). However, the seal-islands legislation was amended four times by Congress in the years between 1869 and 1874.

[8] This was of course not the fault of the military. Major General O. O. Howard, who visited Alaska on an official inspection trip in June, 1875, reported:

". . . I could not fail to see that our government has not carried out in good faith the treaty stipulations made at the time of the purchase of the territory. Good civil government, as well as religious and secular teaching, is nowhere in heathendom more needed than in Alaska; and yet up to the present there is none." Elsewhere in the report he wrote: I wish to renew my earnest recommendation that by proper and speedy legislation, Alaska be attached as a county to Washington territory, or in some other way be furnished with such a government as the treaty with Russia in the transfer plainly contemplated." *Compilation of Narratives of Explorations in Alaska,* pp. 47-8.

[9] "Previous to the arrival of the military its manufacture was unknown to the Indians, but no sooner had the soldiers made their appearance in Alaska than the detestable traffic commenced," wrote William Gouverneur Morris, Special Agent of the Treasury Department, after two years of especial study of Alaska matters. "One of the evil effects of this detestable vice has been the debauchery and degradation of the native women by a licentious soldiery. . . . A whole race of prostitutes has been created, and the *morbus indecens* of the Latins, is found in full feather. . . . Today there is not a single surgeon or physician in Southeastern Alaska, and when a victim becomes infected with the *lues venerea,* his fate can be predicted. Syphilitic diseases are the bane of the country." 45 C: 1 s, *Sen. Doc. 59.*

Collector of Customs William S. Dodge wrote Special Indian Commissioner Vincent Colyer: "Many has been the night when soldiers have taken possession of a Russian house and frightened and browbeaten the women into compliance with their lustful passions. Many is the night I have been called upon after midnight by men and women, Russian and Aleutian, in their night-clothes, to protect them against the malice of the soldiers. . . . The conduct of some of the officers has been so demoralizing that it was next to impossible to keep discipline among the soldiers. . . . Officers have carried on with the same high hand among the Russian people; and were the testimony of citizens to be taken, many instances of real infamy and wrongs would come to light. For a long time some of the officers drank immoderately . . . and one or two of them have been drunk for a week at a time. The soldiers saw this, the Indians saw it; and as 'ayas tyhus' or 'big chiefs,' as they called the officers, drank, they thought they too must get intoxicated. Then came the distrust of American justice when they found themselves in the guard-house, but never saw the officers in when in like condition." 41 C: 2 s, *Report of Secy. of Int.*

I. C. Dennis, Deputy Collector of Customs at Wrangell and for eight years a resident, wrote to the *Puget Sound Argus:* "I have known many soldiers while here make a business of manufacturing liquor and selling it to the Indians. Even in the company's quarters stills were erected that produced the famous 'hoochenoo.' . . . The future welfare of this country and the best interests of the people in it demand that we have no more military rule, but that instead civil authority, judicial power and law be tried." 45 C: 1 s, *S. Doc. 59.*

Wrote John G. Brady, Presbyterian missionary and later Governor of Alaska: "The sending of the soldiers to this country was the greatest piece of folly of which a government could be guilty. It will require twenty years to wipe out the evils which were brought to the natives. They knew nothing of syphilis, nor did they know how to make an intoxicating liquor from molasses; but now they are dying from these two things." Letter to W. G. Morris, May 6, 1878. 45 C: 1 s, *S. Doc. 58.*

E. J. Baily, Surgeon, United States Army, Medical Director of the Department of Alaska, wrote Vincent Colyer, Commissioner of Indian Affairs, October 25, 1869: "A greater mistake could not have been committed than placing the troops in their [the Indians'] midst. They mutually debauch each other, and sink into that degree of degradation in which it is impossible to reach each other through moral or religious influences.

"Whisky has been sold in the streets by Government officials at public auctions, and examples of drunkenness are set before them almost daily, so in fact the principal teaching they at present are receiving is that drunkenness and debauchery are held by us not as criminal and unbecoming a Christian people, but as indications of our advanced and superior civilization.

"These Indians are a civil and well-behaved people; they do not want bayonets to keep them in subjection. . . . I look upon the different military posts in this department as disastrous and destructive to their well-being; they are not and can never be, of the least possible use; they are only so many whisky fonts, from whence it is spread all over the country. If we ever have trouble with them and become involved in war, it will be found to arise from these causes." *Ibid.,* p. 78.

In 1869 an Indian crossing the parade ground at Sitka was shot and killed by a sentry acting under an order that had been revoked, but the sentry was unaware of that through the neglect of a drunken officer to promulgate the order of revocation. The military command declined to take any punitive action or to compensate the victim's family. The victim's brother then killed two white men, which was in keeping with the Indians' code of atonement of that time and place. His identity was revealed only sixteen years later through his confession. Swineford, Governor Alfred P., *2nd Annual Report,* October 1, 1886.

Bancroft is caustic in his condemnation of military misconduct and does not spare the Commanding General, Jefferson C. Davis. Quoting the Reverend William Duncan's statement: " 'If the United States Government did but know half, I am sure they would shrink from being identified with such abominations that cause so much misery. I hope and pray that . . . the soldiers will be moved away,'" Bancroft comments: "It is unnecessary to detail all the outrages that called for this well-deserved remark." He does, nevertheless, devote twenty pages to detailing them. He holds the military responsible for arousing the otherwise peaceable Indians to violence, and gives his view that "it is probable that many lives would have been saved if no United States soldier had ever set foot in the Territory." Bancroft, Hubert Howe, *History of Alaska*, pp. 606-626.

10 By General Orders No. 1 issued April 23, 1877, "the companies of the Fourth Artillery garrisoning Sitka and Fort Wrangell will be withdrawn by the first steamer arriving from Portland . . . upon the departure of the troops, Sitka and Fort Wrangell will be discontinued as military posts, and all control of the military department over affairs in Alaska will cease." 45 C: 1 s, *S. Doc.* 59.

11 *Ibid.*

12 July 23, 1877. Morris's letter reported: "In a conversation had yesterday with Captain Charles Thorne, master of the steamer *California*, he expressed to me grave fears of a general uprising of the Sitka Indians. . . . About 1,000 are now absent engaged in fishing. Sitka Jack, a noted chief, informed Captain Thorne that . . . when they returned they intended to seize all the government buildings and other valuable property at Sitka; that the country and everything in it belonged to his tribe.

"Captain Thorne further states, the Indians, contrary to when Sitka was garrisoned by troops, thronged his vessel while at the dock, and were generally haughty, insolent, and overbearing in their manner; that the citizens had a ball in the house known as the 'Castle,' and during the festivities the Indians entered the stockade and obtruded themselves upon those present, rendering themselves peculiarly disagreeable and obnoxious. It is his opinion, and that of the officers of his ship, that an outbreak is not far distant, which will result in the destruc-

tion and plunder of private property, and if the whites make any demonstration of resistance, a wholesale massacre will ensue. The Russian priest has already sent his family to Nanaimo, in British Columbia, and general consternation and terror prevails among the whole white inhabitants."

13 Morris's report to John Sherman, Secretary of the Treasury, dated November 25, 1878, occupies the first 142, and with appendices, the first 163, pages of Senate Document 59, Forty-fifth Congress, first session, and is included in Vol. IV of House Report No. 495 entitled *Seal and Salmon Fisheries and General Resources of Alaska*, authorized in 1896 and published by the Government Printing Office in 1898. Morris begins his narrative and compilation by stating: "For the past two years or more I have made Alaska matters my especial study and have devoted much time and patient attention to gathering all available information relating to that unexplored region."

14 *Ibid.*

15 *Ibid.*

16 45 C: 2 s, *Ibid.*

17 "The Indians carry on a large smuggling trade in blankets, liquors, etc., from the adjacent province of British Columbia" reported Morris on November 25, 1878. *Ibid.*

"In the fur trade everything has been suffered to slip away from our own people, and to be gobbled up by smugglers from the line along the Northern coast of British Columbia . . . chiefly through the want of facilities on the part of the customs officers for stopping the business," testified Collector M. D. Ball, February 21, 1880, before a U.S. Senate subcommittee. 47 C: 1 s, *S. Rept.* 457.

18 Morris reported this, stating "the Russian and American charts are entirely unreliable" and that "the Coast Survey chart of 1868 is of no practical value for inland navigation, because it has not one fortieth part of the rocks and shoals on it, and several of the channels and courses indicated on it cannot be steered."

A confirmatory condemnation was contained in a letter to the Quartermaster Department of the U.S. Army from W. Freeman, Jr., commanding the U.S. quartermaster steamer *Newbern*, who stated that had he depended on the only available American chart, issued by the Coast Survey in 1868, he would have lost his ship on Middleton Island, an island ten miles long and five miles wide in the Gulf of Alaska, which was totally missing from the U. S. map, but which was on the British charts, taken chiefly from Vancouver's survey in 1792.

Morris lists fifteen vessels that had been wrecked in inland waters of southeastern Alaska, most of which had struck uncharted rocks. *Ibid.*

Commander L. A. Beardslee, who was shortly to be the ranking naval officer in Alaskan waters, reported in his first communication to the Secretary of the Navy after arriving in Sitka, June 23, 1879: "We found great difficulties in entering the harbor, on account of incorrect sailing directions and charts" [46 C: 2 s, *Ex. Doc.* 105] and "were forced . . . to give up our attempts to reconcile the actual positions of various islands and reefs with those assigned upon our charts, and to identify the same by our sailing directions, for both charts and directions were very erroneous." 47 C: 1 s, *Ex. Doc.* 71.

The concluding paragraph of Senator Charles Sumner's speech on Alaska, April 9, 1867, had said: "An object of immediate practical interest will be the survey of the extended and indented coasts by our own officers, bringing it all within the domain of science and assuring to navigation much needed assistance, while the republic is honored by a continuation of national charts, where execution vies with science, and the art of engraving is the beautiful handmaid. Associated with this survey, and scarcely inferior in value, will be the examination of the country by scientific explorers, so that its geological structure may become known by its various products, vegetable and min-

eral. But your best work and most important endowment will be the republican government, which, looking to a long future, you will organize, with schools free to all and with equal laws, before which every citizen will stand erect in the consciousness of manhood."

But, as is well known, "no Congress can bind its successors," nor is the invocation of a senator, even a committee chairman, binding on his colleagues. Eleven and a half years later Special Agent Morris was reporting: "Since the acquisition of the Territory . . . no adequate steps have been taken by the Government to properly acquire any definite knowledge of its geography, topography, ethnology, or natural resources." 45 C: 1 s, *S. Doc. 59.*

No "adequate steps" were to be taken for several more decades.

[19] *Ibid.*
[20] *Ibid.*, pp. 16-17.
[21] Quoted by Nichols, Jeannette Paddock, *Alaska, A History of its administration . . . under the rule of the United States*, p. 60.
[22] 47 C: 1 s, *Ex. Doc. 71.*
[23] *Ibid.*
[24] 46 C: 2 s, *Exc. Doc. 105.*
[25] 45 C: 1 s, *S. Doc. 59.*
[26] 46 C: 2 s, *Sen. Ex. Doc. 105.*
[27] "I am satisfied," Beardslee reported to the Secretary of the Navy eight days after his arrival, "that both the local Indians and the Chilcats have friendly feelings toward the whites, and that there is no danger of any premeditated attack upon the settlement . . ."

"The two settlements have existed in juxtaposition for many years, and it is exceedingly creditable to both that, with no law to govern, they have both governed themselves that outrages and disorder are uncommon. There is, however, a terrible danger to which the whites are exposed, and it is far from an imaginary one. When intoxicated with the vile hoochenoo, like all drunken men, the Indians are liable to commit outrages which the whites are powerless to prevent, and to resent which would draw upon them the vengeance of the entire family to which the culprit belonged." *Ibid.*

[28] 47 C: 1 s, *Sen. Ex. Doc. 71.*

[29] Letter from Attorney General Devens to Secretary of Treasury John Sherman September 24, 1878. *Ibid.*

[30] *Ibid.* Beardslee transmitted this further view to the Navy: "At the date of the proclamation of General Grant [forbidding the sale of liquor to the Indians] it was wise and timely; the Indians had not learned the secret of hoochenoo making, and thus its provisions covered the case, and prevented them from getting liquor. Now the Indians do not want whisky; it is too high priced, and not strong enough; molasses of which they can have all they want, they prefer."

[31] *Ibid.*

[32] *Ibid.*

[33] *Ibid.* Beardslee's first efforts were made within a few weeks after his arrival. Six months later he wrote again: "The land here should be surveyed and existing titles perfected and protected, and it made possible to transfer real estate. The government owns much land and a number of buildings (the latter going to ruin) which could be sold at good prices. Dilapidated as they are, many of the buildings are now rented by the collector, and they are eagerly sought. The development of Alaska would be greatly advanced if the public land could be thrown open to pre-emption . . ." January 22, 1880.

[34] In the first years after the purchase, a school was established in Sitka whose teacher was paid by voluntary subscriptions. It was discontinued for want of support.

[35] *Ibid.*

[36] 47 C: 1 s, *H. of R. Ex. Doc. 81.* The proclamation was as follows: "Notice is hereby given that considering the absence of any form of civil government in the Territory of Alaska, and the liability that acts of violence threatening the safety of the lives and property of citizens may occur at any time, and also considering the necessity of preventing such acts, I, Henry Glass, a commander in the United States Navy, and senior United States

officer in the Territory, do announce that until instructions to the contrary are received from the President of the United States, the military authority will be the only government recognized and all residents of the Territory will be governed in accordance with military law." Another paragraph stated that "any local mining laws properly established, not in conflict with the laws of the United States" would not be affected.

[37] Letter of Secretary of the Navy William H. Hunt to Commander Henry Glass July 11, 1881. 47 C: 1 s, *Sen. Rept. 457,* p. 5.

[38] 47 C: 2 s, *H. of R. Ex. Doc. 17.*

[39] 48 C: 2 s, *H. of R. Ex. Doc. 227.*

CHAPTER 6

[1] Italics in original memorial.

[2] 47 C: 1 s, *H. of R. Rept. 560, pts 1 & 2.*

[3] Hayes: *3rd message,* Dec. 1, 1879; *4th message,* Dec. 6, 1880. Arthur, *1st message,* Dec. 6, 1881; *2nd message,* Dec. 4, 1882; *3rd message,* Dec. 4, 1883.

[4] Hayes, *3rd message.* In his longer treatment a year later, Hayes said:

"The recommendation of the Secretary of the Navy that provision be made for the establishment of some form of civil government for the people of Alaska is approved. At present there is no protection of persons or property in that Territory except such as is afforded by the officers of the United States ship *Jamestown.* This vessel was dispatched to Sitka because of the fear that without the immediate presence of the national authority there was impending danger of anarchy. The steps taken to restore order have been accepted in good faith by both white and Indian inhabitants, and the necessity for this method of restraint does not, in my opinion, now exist. If, however, the *Jamestown* should be withdrawn, leaving the people, as at present, without the ordinary judicial and administrative authority of organized local government, serious consequences might ensue.

"The laws provide only for the collection of revenue, the protection of public property, and the transmission of the mails. The problem is to supply a local rule for a population so scattered and so peculiar in its origin and condition. The natives are reported to be teachable and self-supporting, and if properly instructed doubtless would advance rapidly in civilization, and a new factor of prosperity would be added to the national life. I therefore recommend the requisite legislation upon this subject." Hayes, *4th message*, Dec. 6, 1880.

President Arthur in his first annual message declared:

"I regret to state that the people of Alaska have reason to complain that they are as yet unprovided with any form of government by which life or property can be protected. . . ."

A year later he reiterated:

"Alaska is still without any form of civil government. If means were provided for the education of its people and for the protection of their lives and property, the immense resources of the region would invite permanent settlements and open new fields for industry and enterprise."

And for the third time the year following he urged:

"I trust that Congress will not fail at its present session to put Alaska under the protection of law. Its people have repeatedly remonstrated against our neglect to afford them the maintenance and protection expressly guaranteed by the terms of the treaty whereby that Territory was ceded to the United States. For sixteen years they have pleaded in vain for that which they should have received without the asking.

"They have no law for the collection of debts, the support of education, the conveyance of property, the administration of estates, or the enforcement of contracts; none, indeed for the punishment of criminals, except such as offend certain customs, commerce and navigation acts.

"The resources of Alaska, especially in fur, mines and lumber, are considerable in extent and capable of large development, while its geographical situation is one of political and commercial importance.

"The promptings of interest, therefore, as well as considerations of honor and good faith, demand the immediate establishment of civil government in that Territory." *3rd message*, Dec. 4, 1883.

[5] Referring to the pledge in the Treaty of Cession "that the inhabitants . . . shall be admitted to all the *rights, advantages and immunities* of citizens of the United States, and *shall be maintained and protected in the free enjoyment of their liberty, property, and religion*," Senator Matthew Calbraith Butler, D., of South Carolina, Chairman of the Committee on Territories, reported for the Committee: "These are the solemn stipulations and guarantees of this government . . . and yet . . . for fifteen years . . . our citizens . . . have been wholly without 'maintenance' or 'protection' . . . It will not do, in reply . . . to say that the number of inhabitants is too small, or the territory too remote and unprofitable or unproductive to justify the expense and trouble of giving them the protection of law . . . It is not a safe rule to measure the performance of national guarantees in affording protection of law by the *number* of people to be thus protected, but rather by the *right* of every single citizen, however remote or insignificant he may be, to that protection. But it will be found that neither the numbers of its inhabitants, nor the extent of its domain, nor the value of its productions, nor its capabilities for development, are insignificant." 47 C: 1 s, *Sen. Rept. 457* (italics in original report).

Quoting the same section of the treaty, the minority report of the Committee on Elections, which had considered the seating of M.D. Ball as delegate, declared: "But the 4th of July, 1881, saw no act of fulfillment of this pledge, and on that anniversary the men of a large mining settlement, stood with folded arms, above the rich veins of ore, eager to develop them, but lacking all the forms of law essential to that end. Not only so, but lacking also every accessory safeguard of citizenship; the constitutional guarantees of speedy trial and the *habeas corpus* denied them; their property unprotected, their personal liberties held at the arbitrary will of armed military power . . ." 47 C: 1 s, H. of R. *Rept. 560.*

⁶ Sen. Comm. on Territories substitute for S. 1153. 47 C: 1 s, *Sen. Rept. 457,* April 21, 1882. Sen. M.C. Butler, Chairman, signed the report for the committee.

⁷ 48 C: 1 s, Jan. 21, 1884. *Cong. Rec.,* p. 529.

⁸ 48 C: 1 s, Jan. 23, 1884. *Cong. Rec.,* p. 597.

CHAPTER 7

¹ The historian Andrews is authority for the statement that mining law was denied Alaska until California interests secured the Treadwell Mine in Douglas in the early eighteen eighties. Clarence L. Andrews, *The Story of Alaska,* p. 164. A partner in the Treadwell also was the powerful Senator John P. Jones of the mining state of Nevada, who was elected to the Forty-third Congress and served through the Fifty-seventh, from 1873 to 1903.

² Such education as there had been since the purchase had been carried on by American missionaries, with the exception of a school that was supported by private subscription in the first five years in Sitka; the schools maintained on the Pribilof Islands as part of the contract with the U. S. Government, an Anglican mission on the Upper Yukon sent out from Canada, and the few Russian church schools which gave principally religious instruction.

³ Kinkead was born in Smithfield, Pennsylvania, in 1826, and educated in the schools of Zanesville and Lancaster, Ohio. He engaged in the mer-

cantile business successively in St. Louis, Salt Lake City, California and Nevada. He was treasurer of Nevada Territory and a member of the constitutional convention that drew up the constitution under which Nevada became a state in 1864.

"In the summer of 1867," he later wrote, "I found myself 'out of a job' and ready for almost any adventure. The purchase of Alaska had been completed and all San Francisco was agog with the possibilities of this new addition to Uncle Sam's farm. . . . The boom naturally caught me and I determined to look at the new 'Promised Land.' Soon after, Mr. Conness, then U.S. Senator from California, telegraphed a mutual friend that he was anxious to nominate the first federal officer for the new Territory." Sitka *Alaskan,* May 30, 1891.

Kinkead was named postmaster, that being the only available position, at a salary of $12 a year. He stayed in Sitka for three years, established a trading post, was for a time elected "mayor" by the townspeople, and then returned to Nevada where the outlook seemed more promising. He was subsequently elected Governor of Nevada, serving from 1879 to 1883. After his brief term as Governor of Alaska he returned to Nevada.

⁴ *2nd Rept.,* 1886.

⁵ *3rd Rept.,* 1887.

⁶ *4th Rept.,* 1888.

⁷ Sitka *Alaskan,* June 12, 1886.

⁸ *Ibid.,* June 26, 1886.

⁹ *Ibid.,* May 7, 1887.

¹⁰ *Ibid.,* October 22, 1887. This "last straw" caused the Sitka *Alaskan* to comment bitterly on "indifferent Congressmen and callous Senators" and to plead: "Surely the exertions made by the pioneers of this vast outlying portion of the Union . . . are worthy of some recognition from the federal government."

¹¹ "Creoles," as used in Russian America and in early Alaskan parlance, were the offspring of Russian fathers and native women.

¹² Sitka *Alaskan,* July 17, 1886.

¹³ *Ibid.,* September 24, 1886.

[14] *2nd Rept.*, 1886.
[15] *1st Rept.*, 1885.
[16] *2nd Rept.*, 1886.
[17] *Eleventh Census Report*, 1890, pp. 258-9.
[18] *1st Rept.*, 1885.
[19] *4th Rept.*, 1888.
[20] Sitka *Alaskan*, July 31, 1886.
[21] *1st Rept.*, 1885.
[22] *2nd Rept.*, 1886
[23] *2nd Rept.*, 1886
[24] *4th Rept.*, 1888
[25] *4th Rept.*, 1888
[26] Thomas Henry Carter, compiler of *Carter's Code*, embracing all the laws of Alaska up to 1900, United States Senator from Montana, 1895-1901, and again, 1905-1911, testified to this in the Senate debates as an argument for the revision of Alaska's civil and criminal codes. 55 C: 3 s, *Cong. Rec.*, pp. 1888, 1937-8.
[27] *1st Rept.*
[28] *3rd Rept.*
[29] Sitka *Alaskan*, November 14, 1885.
[30] *Rept. of General Agent of Education in Alaska*, May 2, 1887, in *Rept. of Commissioner of Education*, 1887, p. 750.
[31] *Rept. of the Commissioner of Education*, 1887. In 50 C: 1 s, *H. of R. Ex. Doc. 1*, Pt. 5, p. 1228.
[32] *Rept. of General Agent*, June 30, 1887.
[33] Sen. Res. of February 15, 1886.
[34] *Ibid.*
[35] *Rept. to the Secy of the Interior of the Visit to Alaska of Hon. N.H.R. Dawson*, Comm. of Education, Oct. 1, 1887. 40 C: 1 s, *H. of R. Ex. Doc. 1*, Pt. 5, p. 1220.
[36] The Juneau City *Mining Record* expressed itself as follows: "At the last meeting . . . the salaries of the government teachers were reduced to $80 per month under the instructions of the U. S. Commissioner of Education, who issues his edicts under the name of N.H.R. Dawson. This gentleman paid a visit of several weeks to Alaska, stopping at Sitka as the guest of the people at the Mission Home. During his stay he . . . devoted considerable time in writing glowing letters East relative to Alaska and the cheapness of living in this far-off land, taking probably as his standard his expenses as a guest of other people. Since his return to Washington he apparently has used every effort to reduce the salaries of government teachers and has finally succeeded. Last year the salaries of the Juneau teachers were reduced by the aid of a member of the board who has high-priced ideas for anything he does, but low-priced ones for labor performed by others.
"In California, where . . . the price of living is very little compared with . . . Alaska, teachers in country districts receive from $80 to $100 per month. In Alaska, where everything is expensive, and we are denied the various luxuries enjoyed elsewhere . . . teachers are compelled to labor for . . . less." June 27, 1889.
[37] *2nd Rept.*
Again Swineford contrasted the Russian regime with the American. Under the former "schools were not only established and maintained in all the principal settlements . . . but hospitals and dispensaries were likewise maintained for their benefit, at Sitka, Kodiak, Unalaska and the Hot Springs, in which, in 1860, no less than 14,450 patients were entered, of whom only thirty-four died. These hospitals were maintained up to the time of the transfer . . ."
"The want of a hospital at Alaska's capital was never more apparent than at the present moment, when erysipelas, consumption and other maladies are carrying off the natives at such an alarming rate," commented the Sitka *Alaskan*. "The reports from Juneau announce a similar state of affairs, funerals there being almost a daily occurrence. . . . While the general government is expending hundreds of thousands of dollars annually in caring for the American aborigines scattered throughout the vast domain of the Union, it is utterly indifferent to the pressing necessities of the Alaska native." February 4, 1888.
[38] Petroff, p. 33.
[39] *Ibid.*, p. 77; Swineford, *1st Rept.*, 1885.
[40] *3rd Rept.*, 1887.

[41] Sitka *Alaskan*. February 27, March 13, 1886.

[42] Sitka *Alaskan*. February 13, February 27, 1886.

[43] Before a Select Committee of the U.S. Senate holding hearings in San Francisco in May, 1889, on "Relations with Canada," Charles Goodall of the firm of Goodall, Perkins, & Co., General Agents for the Pacific Coast Steamship Co., testified that the shipments of "lumber, powder and all sorts of products for consumption" were the elements in a great increase in the Alaska trade. Ten years earlier when they had bought the line it consisted of "one little steamer." Now they were "running three regularly and one excursion steamer five trips a season." 51 C: 1 s, *Sen. Rept. 1530, Pt. 1, pp. 24-5, 42.*

The shipments of lumber from Pacific Coast ports to Alaska showed an extraordinary increase after 1884. It is striking how much the relative increase in lumber shipments during these years exceeds the increase in the value of total products shipped. (*Commercial Alaska, 1867-1903.* Dept. of Commerce and Labor, 1903, p. 114.)

Value of total merchandise	Year	Lumber (board feet)
$ 615,000	1884	384,980
$ 853,000	1885	407,058
$ 874,000	1886	634,446
$1,134,000	1887	945,678
$1,487,000	1888	1,607,792
$1,686,000	1889	5,578,368
$1,897,000	1890	6,972,960

Subsequently in the hearings while questioning Captain James Carroll of the Pacific Coast Steamship Co., Senator Joseph N. Dolph, R., of Oregon, expressed his awareness of the Alaskans' inability to obtain their own timber. He had, he said, introduced a provision in a bill at the previous session of Congress concerning the homestead and pre-emption law, providing for extending the townsite law over Alaska and also providing for the survey and sale of land for purposes of trade. These provisions did not, however, alter the restrictions on timber use on the public domain. In any event his provisions were not enacted into law. *Ibid.*, pp. 363-4.

When Senator Eugene Hale, R., of Maine, was questioning Mr. Goodall the following colloquy took place:

"Q. Is there any feature outside of the increase of population or the increase of any branch of business in Alaska, that leads to the increase of trade? A. Oh, yes; the establishment of more canneries and the going up there of more coal miners, and then there are more explorations in the country by men who are looking after other mines and discovering other mines. This place called Juneau is the headquarters of the mining country there. There is a great Douglas mine, on an island where gold is worked by stamps.

"Q. Is that American country? A. American country, yes; and the mines are owned by men residing here principally." *Ibid.*, pp. 42-3.

[44] Sitka *Alaskan*, January 4, 1890.

[45] *Annual Report*, 1889.

[46] *4th Rept.*, 1888.

[47] *Ibid.*

[48] *Ibid.*

[49] When Frederick Schwatka, then a lieutenant in the United States Army, sought to organize an expedition in 1881 to explore the still-unknown Yukon River, it was his hope to be accompanied by qualified scientists whose observations would be of value to the nation. But the request for funds was disapproved by both the commanding general of the army and the Secretary of War. Two years later, however, Schwatka, with scant funds, with six other Army men, including a surgeon, engineer, topographer and photographer and a civilian, managed to go, rafted down the mighty river from its source to its mouth and brought back much valuable information.

[50] Two years after the transfer, Special Agent H. H. McIntyre in a report to Secretary of the Treasury George S. Boutwell reckoned that at 6 per cent

compound interest added to the purchase price, Alaska in twenty-five
years would cost $30,901,792, which,
plus $500,000 a year for military and
naval establishments, would bring the
cost up to $43,401,792. "As a finan-
cial measure," he concluded, "it
might not be the worst policy to
abandon the territory for the present . . ." November 30, 1869 41 C:
2 s, *Ex. Doc. 32.*

[51] The requests were itemized as follows: "For salaries of governor, judge,
attorney, marshal, clerk, four commissioners, and four deputy marshals,
$20,000. Contingent expenses, fuel,
lights etc., to be expended under the
direction of the governor, $3,000.
Actual and necessary expenses of
judge, marshal and attorney, while
traveling in discharge of their duties,
$1,500. Rent for office of marshal,
fuel, books, stationery and other incidental expenses, $1,000." The seal-
islands items were: "To enable the
Secretary of the Treasury to use revenue steamers for the protection of
the interests of the government on
the seal islands and sea-otter hunting
grounds, $30,000. For salaries and
expenses of agents at seal fisheries,
$13,350." Education in Alaska re-
ceived $40,000, divided into $25,000
for education of children without
reference to race, and $15,000 for the
support and education of Indian children. There was also a $4,000 con-
struction item for a log courthouse
and jail at Sitka.

The item appropriating for the two
revenue cutters caused the Sitka
Alaskan to say editorially: "All the
legislation that has been enacted in
regard to Alaska up to the passage of
the act providing a civil government
and a semblance of law for the territory, has been exclusively in the interest of the [Alaska Commercial]
Company. And, even in a more
marked degree than in the legislation,
have they been favored in the 'protection' of the Treasury and other
departments. Through those long,
dark years when the civilized whites
of southeastern Alaska were imploring
the help of the government in vain,

to save them from Indian violence
. . . and the precipitation of which
was finally prevented only by a miracle
and a magnanimous English officer,
when not even a revenue cutter could
be spared to indicate . . . that the
United States had not utterly abandoned the people it had solemnly
pledged itself to protect, every summer, one and sometimes two vessels
would be sent away to the West, to
make good the warranty of their
grand monopoly to the Alaska Commercial Company . . . In fact the
government departments have seemed
actually to think that all there was of
Alaska consisted in two seal islands,
against which all the powers of dark-
ness were directed, and which alone
required their consideration." April
24, 1886.

[52] 48 C: 1 s, Jan. 22, 1884. *Cong. Rec.*
p. 566.

[53] This was Louis Sloss, who was to be
first President of the Alaska Commercial Company, 1868-1870, and again
from 1887-1892.

[54] *Annual Rep. of Treasury, 1868.* In
*Seal and Salmon Fisheries and Gen-
eral Resources of Alaska,* Vol. 1, p. 5.

He also had a "left bower" in
Governor H.H. Haight of California
who had written to Secretary Seward:
"A firm of gentlemen here, Messrs.
Hutchinson, Kohl & Co., composed
of six highly respectable merchants,
have purchased the assets and rights
of the American-Russian Commercial
Company, and succeeded to all their
relations with the Russian Government, and assumed all the obligations
of that company. Of course these
gentlemen did not for a moment suppose that their large investment would
be prejudiced by any exclusive privileges granted by the government of
the United States to others, having
in all respects inferior claims to the
successors of the Russian Company.
. . . It is quite manifest that the citizens of the Pacific states would not
regard with complacency the exclusion of their merchants from
legitimate business pursuits in a
neighboring territory, by reason of
grants of exclusive privileges to per-

sons on the other side of the continent." April 13, 1868. 40 C: 2 s, *H. of R. Misc. Doc. 130*. (The persons on the other side of the continent alluded to were Williams, Havens, & Co., of New London, Conn., who were actively pursuing Alaska's fur seal prospects.)

[55] Dall, William H., *Alaska and its Resources*, p. 240.

[56] The thirteen bids as well as the terms of the lease are found in A. L. Belden, *The Fur Trade of America*, pp. 130-1.

[57] Some of the Treasury officials were also concurrently serving the interests of the company. It hired a number of them, a familiar method of reciprocating for a previously complaisant attitude, though not necessarily evidence of improper favors previously rendered. Such episodes were far from uncommon during the Grant administration—and have been known since. A bitter attack on the Alaska Commercial Company's performances as viewed by the unsuccessful bidders, *A History of the Wrongs of Alaska*, a 43-page pamphlet, was published by "The Anti-Monopoly Association of the Pacific Coast," in San Francisco in 1875. A subsequent vindication was given the company, as well as the Treasury officials responsible for the lease, by a Committee of the House of Representatives. 44 C: 1 s, *H. of R. Rept. 623*.

[58] *Op. cit.*, p. 4.

[59] 47 C: 1 s, *Sen. Rept. 457*.

[60] *Ibid.*, p. 41.

[61] *Ibid.*, p. 13.

[62] In a report to the Secretary of the Treasury in November, 1874, he recommended the following governmental program for Alaska "always excepting the Pribilof Group of Seal Islands which are well provided for by Special Acts of Congress . . ." 1. Withdrawal of troops from Alaska. 2. A collector of customs stationed at Kodiak. 3. A small revenue steamer which would cruise around the territory and every two or three months pick up the mail at Tongass (the southernmost tip of Alaska) from another revenue steamer that would bring up mail from the states every two or three months. 4. Cancellation of the existing "subsidized" mail service between the states and southeastern Alaska. 5. Appointment of an agent who would travel on the steamer and keep the government informed. 6. Extension of the jurisdiction of the Washington and Oregon courts over Alaska to which people charged with crime and arrested should be sent. (He made no provision for marshals or deputies to arrest such, for means of detention or transportation.) 7. Extension of the mining laws to Alaska. He was opposed to the establishment of any schools by the government. Elliott, Henry W. *Rept. upon the Condition of Affairs in the Territory of Alaska*. There appears to be little doubt of Elliott's influence on Congress through the years.

[63] In *Harper's Monthly*, in November 1877, Elliott wrote: "Though we know that Alaska never will be, in all human probability, the land for us, yet we have one great comfort in its contemplation, for we shall never be obliged to maintain costly mail routes or appoint the ubiquitous postmaster there. We shall never be asked by its people for a territorial form of government, with its attendant Federal expenses; and much as the coast looms on the map, we shall never have to provide lighthouses for its vacant harbors. No, the revenue annually derived from the seal islands alone is in itself six times greater every year than the sole outlay required at the hands of the government in the regular employment of a revenue steamer for the protection of the seal islands, the sea-otter hunters, and the prohibition of whisky, which tends to debauch and demoralize the Christian natives especially. And so, though Alaska makes no offer of any art or industry or invitation suited to our people, yet she annually pays into the Treasury far more than she asks in return for her protection and support; and in this respect she gives us less ground for fault-finding than do many of our

long-settled States that have natural advantages which this unhappy country never has had, and never can have, in our day at least."

[64] "Clothed by the Government with a monopoly of the seal fur trade by which it has profited to the extent of many millions, it has, octopus-like, thrown out its great tentacles and gathered to itself about all there is of value in the fur trade of the whole Territory. It has, by the power of its great wealth, driven away all competition and reduced the native population to a condition of helpless dependence, if not one of absolute and abject slavery. Unhampered by a healthy competition, it offers and compels acceptance by the natives, on pain of starvation, such beggarly prices for their peltry that it manages invariably to keep them in its debt and at its mercy. Its insatiable greed is such that it is not content with robbing the poor native in the price it sets upon the product of his dangerous toil, but it robs him also in the exorbitant prices it exacts for the goods given in exchange. And there is no appeal; no alternative. There are no other trading stations in that vast section, and the natives must pay the price asked and accept that which is offered—the first, a hundred per cent advance on the amount at which the same goods are sold to the whites, and the last, low enough to add still another hundred per cent to the company's profit. As, for instance, there is no timber on the Aleutian Islands, and the native who goes out to hunt the sea otter has no time to provide himself with fuel by gathering driftwood from the shores, as many are able to do. He must have fuel for the winter, and the company generously takes his sea-otter skins at half their real cash value and pays him in coal at $40 per ton—coal of the same quality as that which it sells to the few white residents for $20. . . .

With all this, and much more is true concerning its treatment of the native people, instances are not lacking where it has boycotted and driven away from the islands Government officials, who, intent upon the honest, faithful discharge of their duties have incurred the displeasure or refused to do the bidding of its agents. . . . Its paid agents and lobbyists are kept at the national capital to oppose any and every effort that may be made to promote the welfare of Alaska through such legislation as will encourage immigration and the enlistment of capital in the development of the natural wealth hidden away, in her forests, streams and mountains; its every aim and effort is in the direction of prolonging its existence and strengthening its tyrannical hold by a blocking of the wheels of progress; and to its pernicious influence is due the fact that Alaska is not today largely populated with an industrious, enterprising, prosperous people; that millions where there are now only hundreds, have not long ere this been invested in the developments of her many varied and . . . incomparably great natural resources."

[65] *4th Rept.*

CHAPTER 8

[1] "A monthly mail service for seven months in the year has been inaugurated between Sitka and some points in western Alaska, with Kodiak as one of the ports of call. The compensation for this service is very small, and the vessel employed to carry the mail is a small steamer of but thirty-five tons, without any passenger accommodations. As no postmasters have been appointed at ports of call, much confusion and irregularity prevails, and the bulk of a voluminous mail from western Alaska is still carried by private parties directly to San Francisco. . . . For all practical purposes the people of this section are not much better off than they were previous to the establishment of the mail route." *Eleventh Census Report*, p. 76.

[2] "The arrival of the steam schooner *Elsie* inaugurated a new era in the meagre history of the Alaska mail service. . . . A good deal of surprise

and chagrin were expressed by everyone in Sitka at the smallness of the schooner and her lack of passenger accommodations. There were at least a dozen people awaiting this vessel's arrival at Sitka for the purpose of securing transportation to various western points and their disappointment at not being able to secure passage was manifest. The *Alaskan* had hoped that the letting of this mail contract would tend to open up some of the dormant resources which are known to exist at the westward, and it . . . believes that with adequate carrying facilities a large business could be created in the transportation of freight and passengers at reasonable rates. The policy of simply distributing mail bags at western post offices in the Territory and virtually debarring people from visiting their correspondents for either business or pleasure, savors very much of a desire to perpetuate those monopolies with large capital which have so long controlled the commerce of that section of Alaska, to the exclusion of that very desirable class of determined and energetic pioneers who have in all our history been the heralds announcing the growth of virgin territory into wealthy and populous communities." Sitka *Alaskan*, July 11, 1891.

³ "To the great annoyance of the North American Commercial Co., the western portion of Alaska is attracting considerable attention on account of its immense deposits of coal and its recent discoveries of gold and silver mines. Such things have a tendency to cause the hardy and adventurous miner and prospector to go to the new fields and this company . . . does not want any there but its employees and . . . will be monarch of that section if money and power will prevail." Juneau City *Mining Record*, July 30, 1891.

⁴ There were eight bidders, and the bid of the North American Commercial Company was substantially higher than that of any of its competitors. However the lease was less attractive than it had been, as the seal herd had been greatly reduced because of pelagic sealing, and the number of seals to be taken was not fixed in the contract, but left to the determination of the Secretary of the Treasury. For the first year, ending May, 1891, the number was fixed at 60,000. Belden, *op. cit.*, pp. 131-2. See also text of contract signed December, 1889, between Wm. Windom, Sec'y of Treasury, and I. Liebes, Pres't. No. Am. Commercial Co. 62 C: 1 s, *Hearings on H.R. 73*, pp. 83-4.

⁵ Take, for example, the village of Belkofsky on the Alaska Peninsula in the early nineties as described in the *Eleventh Census Report*: "Nearly all the houses . . . are neat frame cottages, erected for the natives by trading companies when sea otters were plentiful. They are generally painted in white or light colors, and are set off in pleasing contrast by the green mountain slope behind them. Even now, in its decadence, Belkofsky contains 185 people, among them a few white men, sea-otter hunters, who make this their permanent home. Less than a decade since the sea-otter pelts collected at this station numbered in the thousands, and there were three large rival stores bidding for the precious peltry, wheedling and coaxing the lucky hunter to sell his skins, then stimulating him to the most reckless extravagance, and finally hurrying him off again with an outfit given on credit to face the whistling gale and raging sea in search of more furs. In those days the storekeeper would keep only the most expensive wares . . . the families of absent hunters feasted upon canned meats and preserved delicacies. . . . During these flush times the natives made gifts of valuable peltry to the church for the purpose of erecting a fine building, which, together with a handsome parsonage, now forms the chief ornament of the settlement. In our days the glory of Belkofsky has departed . . . poverty and strict economy have taken the place of affluence and extravagance. The rival stores stand vacant, and even the shelves of the only surviving place of

business are but thinly stocked with inexpensive wares . . . and the luxuries of former days are but a pleasant memory." p. 87.

[6] Petroff, 45 C: 1 s, *Sen. Doc.* 59, p. 194. *Eleventh Census Report*, p. 79.

[7] A few of the youngsters of that day were still living in Juneau sixty-four years later.

[8] Chap. 415, Rev. Stat.

[9] The native population was subdivided into Eskimo, 14,012; Athabascan, 3,439; Tlingit, 4,737; Haida, 391; and Tsimshean, 952. The Eskimo were scattered from Bristol Bay to Demarcation Point, along the Kuskokwim, lower Yukon, Noatak and Kobuk rivers; the Athabascans through interior Alaska. The Tlingits occupied all but the lower part of southeastern Alaska and as far west as Yakutat; the Haida were on Prince of Wales Island, and the Tsimsheans were the Indians whom the Reverend William Duncan had brought from British Columbia and established at Metlakatla on Annette Island. The classification of Aleut, which had appeared in Petroff's census, numbering 2,145, did not appear in the *Eleventh Census Report*. In diminished numbers they were included among the 1,823 "mixed."

[10] *Eleventh Census Report*, p. 179.

[11] The Pacific Coast Steamship Company reported the following increase in excursion tickets to Alaska: 1884, 1,650; 1885, 1,871; 1886, 2,753; 1887, 3,889; 1888, 4,446; 1889, 5,432; 1890, 5,007. *Eleventh Census Report*, p. 250.

[12] "No man through his own explorations has added more to a geographic knowledge of Alaska than Lieutenant Allen," wrote Alfred H. Brooks in 1906.

[13] *Eleventh Census Report*, p. 42.

[14] *Ibid.*, p. 218.

[15] *Ibid.*, p. 218.

[16] *Ibid.*, p. 218.

CHAPTER 9

[1] Editorials in Juneau City *Mining Record*, February 7, May 16, July 25,

1889. The revenues from the seal fisheries made Alaska's annual contribution to the federal treasury larger than that of any territory.

[2] *First annual message*, Dec. 3, 1889.

[3] "The people of S.E. Alaska have at last taken the initiatory steps to insure recognition by Congress of their inalienable rights as U.S. citizens," editorialized the Sitka *Alaskan* optimistically, Oct. 18, 1890.

[4] March 3, 1891. (26 Stat. 1095).

[5] Sitka *Alaskan*, August 8, 1889.

[6] Nichols, *op. cit.*, p. 83.

[7] One Sitka weekly's comment—among many—on these two officials and of the commissioner at Juneau, was: "Competency is a word that will be searched for in vain in the vocabulary of Judge (God save the mark) McAllister's legal attainments. He is no more fit . . . to sit as a judge on the bench of a United States court, than is the Oregon rascal who so briefly held after him, by reason of his abilities as a forger and a swindler, to join the angel throng above." Sitka *Alaskan*, March 6, 1886. "The appointment of the official next in importance, namely, the Commissioner at Juneau, whereby far the largest amount of legal business surpasses even that of the dishonest judge. . . . Under such officials it is not strange that the so-called dispensation of justice has hitherto borne fruit only in mischief, mockery and maladministration." *Ibid.*, March 20, 1886.

[8] May 23, 1889.

[9] *Ibid.*, December 31, 1891.

[10] February 25, 1892.

[11] February 4, 1892.

[12] *Ibid.*, November 5, 1891.

[13] It will be recalled that President Hayes in his fourth message applied the term "peculiar" to Alaska's population. Alaskans' sensitiveness to this term, however, had not then developed.

[14] Henry E. Haydon, in Sitka *Alaskan*, September 19, 1891.

[15] A senatorial committee visited Alaska in the summer of 1889 aboard the U.S. Fish Commissioner's steamer *Albatross*. It was composed of Senator

Henry L. Dawes, R., Mass., Chairman, Senator James K. Jones, D., Ark., Senator Charles F. Manderson, R., Neb., and their wives, Senator Francis B. Stockbridge, R., Mich., and six other members of the party. After their visit to the capital, Sitka, they were interviewed. As reported by the Sitka *Alaskan*, July 20, 1889, "Senator Dawes . . . wondered why the civil officials had not been able to urge successfully upon the authorities at Washington the needs of some additional legislation being enacted in compliance with the wishes of the people. Senator Jones expressed the opinion that it was discreditable that such a state of affairs should exist that a bona-fide resident, could not, under the law, cut timber and erect a dwelling for himself. The law, now in force, makes it necessary for a man to construct his own coffin before he dies, as the cutting of timber for other than mere personal use is distinctly prohibited. Senator Manderson admitted that the interests of the people of Alaska had been long neglected and that Congress was primarily responsible. But the truth was that the time of the House of Representatives was so taken up with the consideration of private bills that it was impossible for the body to devote the attention which it should to matters of public importance. . . ."

"The outcome of the visit cannot be otherwise than advantageous to the interests of Alaska and its people," the Sitka *Alaskan* editorialized hopefully.

[16] Sitka *Alaskan*, September 12, 1891.
[17] June 14, 1890.
[18] September 26, 1889.
[19] *Ibid.*, August 13, 1891.
[20] February 4, 1892.
[21] "The merchants and others of the state of Washington will naturally conceive a great interest in Alaska's affairs and seek to obtain most of the trade. The merchants . . . and others . . . should . . . transfer their patronage from Oregon to Washington. It may be . . . 'out of the frying pan into the fire.' But when we contemplate the hardships and abuse to which we have been so long subjected under Oregon rule it will certainly be worth the risk . . . to change our allegiance from Oregon to Washington and interest the senators of that state to take up our cudgels as against the malign influence of Oregon senators who have so long oppressed us and opposed any remedies for our unfortunate condition." Juneau City *Mining Record*, February 4, 1892.
[22] Juneau City *Mining Record*, July 7, 1892.
[23] *3rd Annual Rept.*, 1891.
[24] President Cleveland's fourth annual message in his first term, President Harrison's second, third and fourth annual messages, and all four of President Cleveland's annual messages in his second term, dealt with the preservation of the fur-seal resources of the Pribilof Islands and the controversies surrounding it.
[25] *Seal and Salmon Fisheries*, Vol. I, p. 291.
[26] In his opinion Judge Dawson declared:

"The purchase of Alaska was unquestionably made with a view to the revenues to be derived from the taking of fur seal in the waters of Bering Sea . . . The industry and consequent revenues would be hopeless without the residuary power of the United States to protect and regulate the taking of fur-bearing animals in that part of the domain. The effort of the United States to seize and drive out the illicit piratical craft that have been navigating those waters for years, indiscriminately slaughtering fur-bearing animals . . . is a legitimate exercise of the powers of sovereignty under the law of nations, with which no nation can lawfully interfere." Dawson, Judge Lafayette, *List of Cases Reported from the District Court of Alaska. March 13, 1886 to August 25, 1888. Alaskan Reports*, Vol. I, p. 61.
[27] Stuart Ramsay Tompkins avers that the Canadian case was strengthened by the revelation "that the seizures in Bering Sea had been inspired by the Alaska Commercial Company

who were active lobbyists in Washington. Moreover, one of their agents at Sitka had coached the judge in his handling of the case." *Promyshlennik and Sourdough*, p. 208.

[28] Moore, John Bassett, *International Law Digest*. Vol. I, pp. 890-929.

[29] The pelagic seal take reached its greatest height after the *modus vivendi* was agreed upon in 1891 and renewed the following year. It was 61,858 in 1892, 121,618 in 1893, 119,980 in 1894, 104,724 in 1895. From then it diminished steadily. 62 C: 1 s, *Hearings on H.R. 73*, p. 32.

[30] Belden, *op. cit.*, pp. 31-2. After paying Hutchinson, Kohl & Co. $1,729,-000 for its stock in trade, vessels and other assets, and making substantial additional capital expenditures, the company was able to declare a $200,-000 dividend in January, 1872, on its 20,000 shares, held at that time by sixteen stockholders. This dividend was based on the profits of a one-year catch of 101,425 skins in 1871, since regular sealing operations did not start in 1870, when only 3,473 skins were taken, the lease being signed on August 3rd of that year. *Alaska Commercial Company*, 1868-1940, pp. 7, 15, 17.

[31] *Seal & Salmon Fisheries*, Vol. II, pp. 294-300. McIntyre had visited the Pribilof Islands as a Treasury Special Agent, had been hired by the Alaska Commercial Company, and had been with it during the entire period of the lease.

[32] Belden, *op. cit.*, pp. 31-2.

[33] Nevertheless the North American Commercial Company did not fare too badly. Although its twenty-year catch of 343,365 seals was approximately one-sixth of the Alaska Commercial Company's twenty-year take of 1,856,224, higher prices gave it an estimated net profit of nearly five million dollars during its lease, which contrasted with the federal government's loss on the operation during that period. 62 C: 1 s, *Hearings on H.R. 73*, p. 964.

[34] 62 C: 1 s, *Hearings before the Committee on Expenditures in the Department of Commerce and Labor on*

H.R. 73, pp. 83-4.

[35] *Ibid.*, p. 32.

[36] Rept. of Agent-in-Charge Charles J. Goff to William Windom, Secretary of the Treasury, July 31, 1890. *Seal and Salmon Fisheries*, Vol. II, pp. 230-6.

[37] *Seal and Salmon Fisheries*, Vol. I, pp. 222-231.

[38] Elliott, *op. cit.*

[39] Rept. to Sec'y of Treasury, John Sherman, *Seal and Salmon Fisheries*, Vol. I, p. 119.

[40] *Ibid.*, Vol. I, p. 185.

[41] Rept. of First Asst. Agent Joseph Murray to Charles J. Goff, Agent in Charge, July 31, 1890. Vol. I, p. 237.

[42] *Ibid.*, p. 135.

[43] Murray to Goff, 1890, *Ibid.*, p. 236.

[44] Asst. Treasury Agent S. R. Nettleton to Goff, 1890. *Ibid.*, p. 265

[45] *Seal and Salmon Fisheries*, Vol. I, Rept. 1893. Murray to Agent in Charge Joseph B. Crowley, p. 427.

[46] Secy. of Treasury Charles Foster to Agent W. H. Williams. May 27, 1891. *Ibid.*, pp. 267-271.

[47] *Ibid.*, p. 277.

[48] 171 U.S. 110. May 31, 1898.

[49] 62 C: 1 s, *H.R. 73*, p. 61.

[50] December 15, 1892.

[51] *3rd Rept.*, 1895.

[52] *3rd & 4th Repts.*, 1895, 1896.

[53] Rept. to J. G. Carlisle, Secy. of Treasury, March 1, 1895. *Seal & Salmon Fisheries*, Vol. I, p. 452.

[54] This was nothing new. It had been recurring since the inauguration of civil government under the act of 1884. In April 1889, the District Judge, John H. Keatley, gave public notice that he had been obliged to cancel his May term of court at Juneau. He found that there were not sufficient funds on hand "to pay the expenses of the extraordinary number of jurors and witnesses absolutely required by law to try several important criminal cases—one for murder—awaiting trial." Juneau City *Mining Record*, May 2, 1889.

[55] Rev. stat., Chapt. 387, June 9, 1896.

[56] *1st Rept.* He reiterated these criticisms in his 2nd and 3rd annual reports.

[57] *1st Rept.*, 1897.

CHAPTER 10

[1] ". . . the major portion of this session will undoubtedly be consumed . . . on the bill [H.5975, Homesteads and Right of Way in Alaska], at least one third of the membership of the Senate, and probably an equal representation in the other branch of Congress being constantly importuned to secure some action upon the measure," declared Senator Thomas H. Carter, R., of Montana, February 24, 1898. 55 C: 2 s, *Cong. Rec.*, p. 2119.

". . . there are 20,000 people now in the city of Seattle in my state waiting to go to Alaska . . . all of whom are vitally interested in legislation under which land titles may be procured . . ." said Senator George Turner, R., of Washington, March 3, 1898. *Ibid.*, *Cong. Rec.*, p. 2412.

"The Alaska bill is certainly of paramount importance . . . 50,000 people are at this hour waiting for the action of the Congress . . ." said Senator Henry Clay Hansbrough, R., of North Dakota. *Ibid.*, *Cong Rec.*, p. 2411.

[2] Except an act providing four additional commissioners and four deputy marshals (June 4, 1897) and an act appointing a surveyor general for the District of Alaska, at a salary of $2,000 per annum, replacing the marshal who performed this function, ex-officio, under the act of 1884.

[3] May 14, 1898. 30 Stat. 409.
[4] 55 C: 2 s, *Cong. Rec.*, p. 2467.
[5] *Ibid.*, p. 2278. The senator was the Perkins of Goodall, Perkins & Co.
[6] Delaney, Arthur K., *Government in Alaska*, p. 13.
[7] *2nd Rept.*, 1898.
[8] 55 C: 2 s, *Cong. Rec.*, p. 2277.
[9] *2nd Rept.*, 1898.
[10] March 3, 1899. 30 Stat. 1253.
[11] "The Committee on Territories," said its chairman, Senator George L. Shoup, R., of Idaho, "have prepared certain licenses which . . . will create a revenue sufficient to defray all the expenses of the government . . . of Alaska. . . . They are licenses peculiar to the condition of affairs in the Territory of Alaska . . . Not a dollar of taxes is raised on any kind of property there."

"MR. CHANDLER. 'Then I understand that the commercial and business conditions in Alaska being peculiar, a special code of license taxes has been devised.'

"MR. SHOUP. 'That is correct.'" 55 C: 3 s, *Cong. Rec.*, p. 2235. February 23, 1899.
[12] 55 C: 3 s, *Cong. Rec.*, p. 383.
[13] *Ibid.*, p. 578.
[14] *Ibid.*, p. 2705.
[15] This provision, taken without much consideration from the Oregon code, was to prove a severe handicap when the construction of railroads in Alaska was undertaken a few years later. The British-owned White Pass and Yukon R.R., the first to be constructed, could well afford to pay the $2,000 annually on the twenty miles within Alaska.
[16] 55 C: 2 s, *Cong. Rec.*, p. 1886.
[17] *Ibid.*, p. 1886.
[18] *Ibid.*, p. 1890.
[19] *Ibid.*, p. 1888.
[20] *Ibid.*, pp. 1937-8.
[21] 55 C: 3 s, *Cong. Rec.*, p. 2904.
[22] *Ibid.*
[23] 55 C: 2 s, *Cong. Rec.*, p. 3132.
[24] *Ibid.*, p. 3358.
[25] 56 C: 1 s, *Cong. Rec.*, p. 4217.
[26] One reasonably industrious lawyer, traveling about in a revenue cutter could do all the work, said Vest, and he ought to be glad to do it, for if there was any country on earth "where a man ought to be employed in order to escape suicide and insanity" it was Alaska. 55 C: 2 s, March 22, 1898. *Cong. Rec.*, pp. 3084-5.
[27] 55 C: 2 s, March 3, 1898, *Cong. Rec.*, pp. 2417-8.
[28] 55 C: 2 s, *Cong. Rec.*, p. 3083.
[29] 55 C: 2 s, *Cong. Rec.*, p. 3083. An increase in the Governor's duties was a provision authorizing him, with the approval of the Secretary of the Interior, to make a contract with one or more asylums west of the Rocky Mountains for the care of the insane. This function was, however, taken away from the Governor four years later and transferred wholly to the Secretary of the Interior (April 28, 1904. 33 Stat. 526). The year after,

per contra, the Governor was made ex-officio superintendent of public instruction for the district (January 27, 1905. 33 Stat. 616).

Another new duty assigned the Governor was the disbursal of a fund to be known as the District Historical Library Fund. This was to be made up of the notarial fees and the ten-dollar fees paid by members of the bar to the clerk of court for a certificate to practice law. The fund was to be used to establish and maintain an historical library and museum. It was to contain copies of all laws relating to the district, all papers and periodicals published within it, and such curios relating to the aborigines and settlers as the Governor deemed of historical importance. The collection thus made was to be described by the Governor in his annual report to the Secretary of the Interior.

[30] Act of 1884, Secs. 5 and 9.

[31] 55 C: 2 s, *Cong. Rec.*, p. 3084.

[32] March 3, 1901. 31 Stat. 1438.

[33] The Juneau and Valdez chambers of commerce in a petition to the President and Congress, pointed out that as Alaska had no delegate the people could express themselves only through petitions. They requested that all the license moneys be returned to the towns. "The people have since 1899 paid a large amount of money into the national treasury in the shape of license taxes, and they are not unmindful of the slogan of their ancestors, 'No taxation without representation.' . . . Our people respectfully ask how long the cities of New York and Boston would submit to the turning over one-half of all the liquor and license taxes collected in said cities to the Treasury of the United States." The petition also requested that Congress authorize a delegate. 57 C: 1 s, *Sen. Doc. 238*.

[34] April 28, 1904. 33 Stat. 529.

[35] Brooks, Alfred H., *The Investigation of Alaska's Mineral Wealth. Governor's Rept.*, 1904.

[36] *Investigation of Coal and Gold Resources in Alaska.* 54 C: 2 s, H. of R. Doc. 171.

[37] The names of those early geologists as

well as of their colleagues in the Coast and Geodetic Survey were properly preserved in the names of peaks, glaciers and other landmarks: *viz.* Mts. Marcus Baker, Brooks, Dall, Gerdine, Hayes, Hess, Spurr; Barnard, Mendenhall, Muldrow, Spencer, glaciers; Nelson Island, Thomas Bay; to name only a few.

[38] Brooks, Alfred H., *The Geography and Geology of Alaska*, p. 132.

[39] In the order of size they were the Alaska Commercial Co., the North American Transportation & Trading Co., financed by the Cudahy family of Chicago, the Seattle Yukon Transportation Co., the Alaska Exploration Co., and the Empire Transportation Co.

[40] *Report on the Operations of the U.S. Revenue Steamer Nunivak*, pp. 280-1.

[41] H.R. 5763, June 6, 1900. 31 Stat. 658. The Senate Committee on Public Lands however deleted from the House bill the extension of the general land laws relating to homesteads. 56 C: 1 s, *Sen. Rept. 1210*.

[42] This was the first of many requests in ensuing decades asking that Alaska be detached from other established districts whose headquarters at San Francisco, Portland or Seattle tended to give Alaska's needs secondary consideration. These requests went long unheeded.

[43] 58 C: 2 s, *Rept. 282, Conditions in Alaska*.

[44] "Alaska in her salmon industries alone adds annually to the world's wealth about $8,000,000, but the district derives but trifling benefits from the industry. It is to a large extent controlled by corporations and carried on through operatives who are brought from San Francisco and other outside ports in the spring and return in the autumn. Only a small portion of the wages paid them is expended in Alaska." The committee recommended an increase of the tax from 4 cents to 10. *Ibid.*, pp. 5, 6, 16.

[45] "Assessment work" is the annual work upon an unpatented mining claim on the public domain, necessary under U.S. laws for the maintenance of title.

[46] Senator Hansbrough of the Senate Committee on Public Lands and Representative John F. Lacey, R., of Iowa, of the House Committee on Public Lands in identical reports requested amendment of the earlier legislation because "owing to the rules and regulations, and on account of the construction put upon these laws by the Land Department, they have in fact been inoperative, because they only provide for the location and entry of surveyed lands. The public surveys have been extended by law to Alaska, but owing to the great expense of such surveys there has been but little done, and it is necessary, in order to render the coal available, that some method of special surveys should be provided for as applicable to coal lands." 57 C: 2 s, *Sen. Rept.* 3287 and *H. of R. Rept.* 3541.

[47] April 28, 1904. 33 Stat. 525.

[48] March 3, 1903. 32 Stat. 1028.

[49] 56 C: 1 s, *H. of R. H.R.* 9294; *Rept.* 570. *H.R.* 9295, *Rept.* 572; *H.R.* 9310, *Rept.* 566. 56 C: 2 s, *Sen. Doc.* 69; *S.* 5589, *Rept.* 2414.

[50] 58 C: 2 s, *Sen. Rept.* 282.

[51] 61 C: 2 s, August 1, 1912.

[52] 58 C: 2 s, *Rept.* 282, Pt. 2, *Conditions in Alaska.*

CHAPTER 11

[1] 57 C: 1 s, December 3, 1901. The Philippines were mentioned nine times, Puerto Rico five times, Hawaii twice. In the case of each, President Roosevelt recommended legislation which he considered beneficial for them.

[2] December 2, 1902.

[3] December 7, 1903. 58 C: 2 s.

[4] December 6, 1904.

[5] The difficulties were frequently discussed in congressional committees and in debates on the floor, viz. Senate Debate on Army Appropriation bill, April 18, 1904. 58 C: 2 s, *Cong. Rec.*, pp. 4995-9.

[6] 33 Stat. 61.

[7] The Senate Committee report drafted by Senator Nelson said: ". . . It is unfair and unjust to the people of Alaska, who are our kith and kin, to impose upon them these burdensome taxes without giving them the direct benefit of the same. In all the organized territories of the United States the expenses of the civil government; that is to say the salaries of the judges, marshals, district attorneys, clerks of court . . . and other public functionaries, are all paid out of the general funds of the United States, to which fund the people of such territories have never been required to contribute . . ." 58 C: 2 s, *Sen. Rept.* 744.

[8] 58 C: 3 s, *Rept. of the Board of Road Commissioners for 1905, H. of R. Doc.* 192.

[9] *Ibid.*

[10] "Sourdough," the Alaskan for "oldtimer" is derived from the practice of the early Alaskan prospectors of making bread or flapjacks with flour and water fermented without yeast. The opposite of "sourdough" in Alaskan (the equivalent of the "tenderfoot" of the West) is "cheechako," pronounced *cheechawker*, derived from a word in the Chinook jargon meaning "newly arrived."

[11] Twenty-four states contributed to a total gold production of 4,703,000 ounces in 1906. Of this Colorado produced 1,122,814 ounces valued at $23,210,629, and Alaska 1,066,029 valued at $22,036,794. California was third with 906,182 ounces worth $18,732,452.

[12] *Governor's Rept.*, 1907.

[13] This was perhaps a discreet attempt by a government executive agency to call attention to a situation for which Congress was responsible without inviting congressional wrath.

[14] Brooks, Alfred H. and others, *Mineral Resources of Alaska*, 1910.

[15] The withdrawal was alleged to be temporary. So Theodore Roosevelt declared at the time: "It is not wise that the Nation should alienate its remaining coal lands. I have temporarily withdrawn from settlement all the lands which the Geological Survey has indicated as containing, or in all probability, containing, coal. The question can be properly settled only

by legislation." But the "temporary" withdrawal was to last eight years.

[16] Taking issue with the statement of Alaska's first delegate, Frank H. Waskey, who had written President Roosevelt November 28, 1906, that "the most important matter politically is that of home government," Hoggatt, who was likewise in Washington at the time, wrote the President two days later:

"It is the consensus of opinion of the conservative businessmen of Alaska, almost without exception . . . that the time is inopportune for this form of government . . ." 59 C: 2 s, *Sen. Doc. 14.*

[17] Except the smaller Seward Peninsula mining railways and the Copper River and Northwestern R.R. which had not carried out the original purpose to reach the Yukon and had become merely a mining railroad supplying the Kennecott mines and exporting their ore to tidewater.

[18] Brooks, *The Mining Industry in 1912. Bulletin* 542 of the U. S. Geological Survey.

[19] *Ibid.,* 1911. *Bulletin* 520.

[20] U.S. Geological Survey, 1912. *Bulletin* 542.

[21] *Ibid.*

[22] 47 C: 1 s, *H. of R. Rept. 1106, Pt. 2.* May 11, 1882.

[23] 50 C: 1 s, *H. of R. Rept. 1318.* March 26, 1888.

[24] 54 C: 1 s, *H. of R. Rept. 751.* March 12, 1896.

[25] 59 C: 1 s, *H. of R. Hearings before House Comm. on Territories,* February 5, 1906.

[26] Later at the same hearing on February 23rd, former Governor Swineford testified that in the first election of Nebraska's delegate only 954 votes had been cast. At the first election for an Alaskan delegate on August 14, 1906, 8,673 ballots were cast for the short-term delegate and 9,236 for the long term.

[27] John W. Troy, editor of the Skagway *Daily Alaskan* under the heading "Wasting Time" declared that the passage of Representative Francis W. Cushman's bill for an elected delegate was "a foolish expenditure of energy.

. . . The bill would please nobody. It is not wanted by Alaskans. The people of this district are on record clearly and unequivocally for a full territorial government, with a legislature of their own." March 7, 1904. Troy pointed out that three conventions held in Nome, one Democratic and two Republican, had endorsed territorial government, and that a nonpartisan convention in Juneau had done likewise. He endorsed a bill providing full territorial government sponsored by Representative William Sulzer of New York, who had spent considerable time in Alaska.

[28] 58 C: 2 s, *H. of R. Rep.* 1300, March 2, 1904.

[29] 58 C: 3 s, *Sen. Doc. 110.*

[30] 58 C: 2 s, March 10, 1904. *Cong. Rec.,* p. 3092.

[31] December 4, 1906. 59 C: 2 s.

[32] December 8, 1908. 60 C: 2 s.

[33] In that same decade, 1900-1910, the population of Arizona Territory increased from 122,931 to 204,354, or 66.2 per cent; Idaho, from 161,772 to 325,594, or 102 per cent; Montana, from 243,329 to 376,053, or 54.5 per cent; Nevada, from 42,335 to 81,875, or 93.3 per cent; New Mexico Territory, from 195,310 to 327,301, or 67 per cent; Washington, from 518,103 to 1,141,990, or 120.4 per cent.

[34] Governor Walter E. Clark, replying to Senator William Alden Smith of Michigan. 62 C: 2 s, *Hearing on Conditions in Alaska,* February 23, 1912.

CHAPTER 12

[1] 61 C: 2 s, December 7, 1909.

[2] 61 C: 3 s, December 6, 1910.

[3] A typical Alaskan reaction was the editorial in the Seward *Daily Gateway,* entitled "No Commission Wanted."

"President Taft could hardly have chosen a more direct way in which to call forth the criticism of Alaskans than by his proposal to appoint a commission to govern the Territory. The people of Alaska have suffered much from the lack of proper laws

and from unwise legislation that has
been enacted by . . . Congress . . .
which, in some instances, has been
densely ignorant of the needs of the
people who are developing the country, and in others grossly indifferent.
There is a feeling, however, that they
would rather bear the ills they have
than to take the chances of greater
ones growing out of a government by
a commission. A commission has been
tried on the Filipinos, but the intelligent Alaskan very much objects to
being classed with those people and
being subjected to a paternal, not to
say, infernal, kind of government that
might possibly have some advantages
for the untutored savage." December
11, 1909.
[4] *Governor's Rept.*, 1911.
[5] 62 C: 2 s, *Hearing before the Senate
Committee on Territories, on General
Conditions in Alaska.* February 23,
1912.
[6] Clark, in his four-times-annually-re-
peated pleas, had brought about no
change, and his successor Governor
J. F. A. Strong would plead similarly:
    "With a constantly increasing de-
mand for coal, not only for domestic
use, but for industrial purposes as
well, the vast coal-bearing areas are
still withheld from development. . . .
To say that the industrial development of Alaska on a scale commen-
surate with the extent and variety of
its resources, depends on the development of the coal fields, is but stating
a fact that is exceedingly trite. With
practically unlimited quantities of
. . . coals within the Territory, for
many years its people have been compelled to import nearly all the coal
needed for domestic fuel and for industrial purposes from British Columbia, and not infrequently from Japan
and Australia. During the past summer the not altogether edifying spec-
tacle of a foreign ship discharging foreign coal for the use of the United
States Government was witnessed at
Unalaska. A strike of coal miners in
British Columbia, which has been in
existence for nearly two years past,
has caused the coal-supply situation
to become acute in some sections of

Alaska, which are dependent upon
that country for coal.
    "From an economic and industrial
standpoint it may also be pointed out
that if the coal areas of Alaska were
developed a tremendous impetus
would be given to quartz mining in
nearly every section of Alaska. . . .
In Alaska are immense deposits of
metalliferous ores . . . which can
only be worked profitably if coal and
coke are available at reasonable prices.
The cost of both these products is
now so great that development of
many of these ore bodies is out of
the question. Given a cheap fuel supply, smelters would be built and the
ore treated at home with coal mined
and coke manufactured within Alaska;
mining would be stimulated vastly
and trade and commerce would be
greatly extended; prosperous industrial
communities would be created and
the population of the Territory would
increase rapidly." *Governor's Rept.*,
1913.
[7] The Congress in this and in many
other instances was oblivious to whatever public opinion there was on the
subject. Under the title "Pencil Miners" the Seattle *Post-Intelligencer* editorialized as follows:
    "A dispatch from Fairbanks . . .
speaks anew of an abuse which has
existed since the first discoveries of
gold in that Territory, which has not
a single defender among the people
of Alaska, which Congress has been
urged for a dozen years to abolish, but
which still exists, and which is likely
to exist until something can be done
to overcome the inertia of the National Legislature.
    "That abuse is the 'pencil miner.'
The mining laws not only permit an
individual to locate claims for himself, but permit him to locate,
through powers of attorney, other
claims for as many persons as he
can get to provide him with powers
for the purpose.
    "In the latest instance of this abuse
. . . in the Big Delta country, where
important new discoveries have been
made, the curse of the 'pencil miner'
is largely in evidence . . . An act of

Congress ten lines long would end this abuse." February 1, 1912.

[8] February 6, 1912. 62 C: 1 s, *Hearings before the House Committee on Territories on Conditions in Alaska.*
February 23, 1912. 62 C: 1 s, *Hearings before the Senate Committee on Territories on Conditions in Alaska.*

[9] "The available funds have been found altogether too small to meet the popular demand for more roads."

"The establishment of lighthouses and other aids to navigation is of the highest importance. Several considerations . . . emphasize the necessity for more liberal provisions for these safeguards." *Governor's Rept.*, 1910.

"Unless an increase in appropriations is made, the new mileage from year to year may be expected to decrease gradually, since the cost of maintenance is naturally raised as the amount of road to be repaired grows larger. . . . It is earnestly recommended . . . that the total funds to be provided for this work next year be not less than $500,000."

"Although more aids to navigation have been installed . . . than in the whole history of the Territory heretofore, the number of these aids . . . is still woefully small. . . . It is earnestly urged that appropriations at least four times as large . . . be authorized." *Governor's Rept.*, 1911.

There were in 1912 but three first-class lighthouses in Alaska, according to the testimony of former Senator John L. Wilson of Washington, at that time the publisher of the Seattle *Post-Intelligencer.* Appearing before the House Committee on Territories to urge Congress to speed aids to navigation in Alaskan waters, he testified that during the previous fifteen years vessels to Alaska had carried cargoes valued at $31,000,000, exclusive of coal, which amounted to $18,000,000. In that period there had been seventy-seven wrecks, for which marine insurance companies paid $6,-300,000. As a consequence insurance rates on vessels sailing those waters had advanced from 5 to 15 per cent. 62 C: 2 s, H. of R. *Hearings on Con-*

ditions in Alaska. February 8, 1912.
[10] *Governor's Rept.*, 1911.
[11] Hawaii had a full-fledged elective legislature under its organic act of 1900 and a delegate to Congress. Puerto Rico, under its organic act of 1900, had a legislative assembly, the upper house of which was appointed by the President of the United States with confirmation by the United States Senate and a lower House of Delegates elected by popular vote. Puerto Rico was under the same act given the right to elect a non-voting member of the United States House of Representatives, termed a Resident Commissioner. The Philippines, under an act of Congress passed in 1902, were entitled to two non-voting representatives in the lower House of the United States Congress, entitled Resident Commissioners.
[12] 61 C: 2 s, *Statements on S. 5436 To Create a Legislative Council in the District of Alaska.* January 20, 1910.
[13] The message was based on the first annual report of Secretary of the Interior Walter L. Fisher whom Taft had appointed following Secretary Ballinger's resignation.
[14] Figures to demonstrate this were cited by Rep. Flood and Rep. Jefferson M. Levy, D., of New York. Levy gave $35,816,674 as the total amount expended by the federal government, including the purchase price, between 1867 and 1911, and placed the total of tax receipts plus the value of minerals, fisheries and furs at $446,640,-984, leaving a balance in Alaska's favor of $410,824,310. 62 C: 2 s, *Cong. Rec.*, p. 4933, and Appendix, pp. 114-117.
[15] It included the well-known "Alaska to Uncle Sam" by Sam Dunham, published in 1901, which has done valiant service before and since:
"Sitting on my greatest glacier,
    with my feet in Bering Sea,
I am thinking, cold and lonely,
    of the way you've treated me.
Three and thirty years of silence!
    Through ten thousand sleeping nights
I've been praying for your coming,
    for the dawn of civil rights.

When you took me, young and
trusting,
from the growling Russian Bear,
Loud you swore before the Nation
I should have the Eagle's care.
Never yet has wing of Eagle
cast a shadow on my peaks,
But I've watched the flight of buz-
zards,
and I've felt their busy beaks."
[16] 62 C: 1 s, *H. of R. Rept.* 163. August 21, 1911.

CHAPTER 13

[1] September 21, 1912.
[2] Cordova *Daily Alaskan,* September
23rd.
[3] Ketchikan *Miner,* October 11, 1912.
[4] September 3, 1912.
[5] September 14th.
[6] *Ibid.*
[7] *House Journal of the First Legislative
Assembly of the Territory of Alaska,*
pp. 4, 5.
[8] November 16, 1912.
[9] *Senate Journal of the First Legislature
of the Territory of Alaska,* pp. 8-17.
[10] House Joint Memorials Nos. 3, 4, 6,
7, 15; Senate Joint Resolution No. 6.
[11] Under an act of Congress passed in
1907 the clerks of the district courts
at Nome and Fairbanks were to act as
ex-officio registers, the U.S. marshals
at those places as ex-officio receivers.
Neither had the time or the training
to attend to these Land Office duties.
This was an economy which defeated
the purpose of the legislation.
[12] S.J.R. 6.
[13] S.J.M. 26.
[14] H.J.M. 2.
[15] S.J.M. 16.
[16] S.J.M. 31.
[17] S.J.M. 9. It said in part: "From the
earliest settlement of our country this
Government has encouraged the forward movement and the opening of
new territory, and it has always had
within its borders the blood and
brawn of the pioneers; and as they,
single handed and alone, and in small
groups have blazed their way and advanced into the unknown, their faces
ever westward, combatting not only

wild nature but often wilder men, the
strong arm of the Government has
followed the pioneer and made it possible to still follow with more civilized
modes of life, even going to the extent of donating hundreds of millions
of value in lands in aid of transportation. The Government has given millions in money for the aid of brown
men of the Philippine Islands, and
has given Cuba millions in money and
lives of brave men. We would respectfully ask, are the Cubans, the Filipinos, or the Puerto Ricans more valuable to this great country of ours
than the hardy, brave, intelligent pioneers of Alaska, every one of whom,
from sixteen to seventy years of age
are willing to fight for their country
and flag? . . . We believe that the
time has come for just consideration
of our great needs by those in authority and power, to relieve and assist in
the development of our great territory."
[18] Annual message, 1915.
[19] December 25, 1913.
[20] 63 C: 2 s, *H. of R. Hearings before
the Committee on Territories on H.R.
11740.*
[21] *Ibid.,* p. 5.
[22] The word applied by Henry F. Fort-
mann, President, Alaska Packers' Association. *Ibid.,* p. 8.
[23] So stated in telegram of Frank B.
Peterson, President, Red Salmon Canning Co., of San Francisco. *Ibid.,* p. 7.
[24] *Ibid.,* pp. 27-8.
[25] It appeared from the testimony at
this hearing that the efforts on the
part of the canned-salmon industry to
write into the organic act of 1912 a
definitive prohibition of the Alaska
legislature's right to tax the fisheries
had miscarried through lack of co-
ordination of these efforts in the two
houses of Congress. After the act of
1912 had passed the House, Mr. John
S. Webb, representing a group of
Seattle salmon canners operating in
Alaska, according to his testimony,
had called the attention of Senator
Wesley L. Jones of Washington to a
speech of Delegate Wickersham declaring the delegate's intention to secure for the territorial legislature the

right to tax the fisheries. The Senator, according to Mr. Webb, agreed that that would not be right and introduced an amendment in the Senate inserting the word "fish" between the words "game" and "fur seal," to exclude fish from the field of legislation upon which the legislature could act, presuming it would debar also the right to tax. However, when the bill went to conference Wickersham persuaded the House conferees to add the sentence to permit the legislature to impose "other and additional licenses and taxes." *Ibid.*, pp. 28-9.

[26] *Ibid.*, p. 29.

[27] *Ibid.*, p. 10.

[28] *Governor's Rept.*, 1914, p. 91.

[29] *Senate Journal*, 1913, p. 283.

[30] *Senate Journal*, 1913, pp. 347,350, 354-5.

[31] In view of the overwhelming popular opposition to traps the arguments of those favoring them should be cited: "MR. BOWER [Ward T. Bower of the Bureau of Fisheries]: 'The trap is not the menace to the salmon industry that the purse seine is. Undoubtedly the purse seine is the most destructive agency employed in the salmon industry in Alaska today.'" May 24, 1912. 62 C: 2 s, *Hearings on S. 5856.*, p. 388.
"MR. DORR [Charles W. Dorr of Seattle, Wash., representing certain salmon packers operating in Alaska, with headquarters on Puget Sound]: 'This fight against the trap has been going on . . . for twenty years, and whenever it has been analyzed . . . it has always been found to be a labor question. A trap fishes in the night when the man sleeps; it employs less men than other kinds of gear; it is a labor-saving device, and this is the real reason why traps are assailed.'" *Ibid.*, p. 389.
"DR. EVERMANN [Barton W. Evermann, Chief, Division of Alaska Fisheries]: '. . . the purpose of any fishing apparatus is to catch fish, and we must provide and permit that sort of apparatus which will catch fish in reasonable quantity and at a minimum cost . . . a trap properly handled—and as it will be handled by

any cannery man who is not hampered—is not destructive to fish, because it catches practically no fish but salmon. . . . Traps, as compared with purse seines or gill nets or haul seines, are really the fairest method of catching fish, provided the trap has no jigger. . . . A trap has a definite location. It can be inspected. Its method of catching fish can be determined; whether it is being operated in accordance with law and the regulations can be determined. But a purse seine is a movable apparatus which can be paid out any place, make a try for the fish in a certain place, and if that is not found to be a satisfactory place, try another and another. If the fish are moving along the purse seine can follow them up. It is the same with haul seines and gill nets to some extent. So it seems to me, of these four kinds of apparatus, the fairest one for the fish, and in many places the most economical one for the operators, is the stationary trap; and the worst of all is the purse seine, because it is virtually a movable trap and difficult to keep track of by the inspectors.'" *Ibid.*, pp. 458-9.

Twelve years later Mr. E. S. McCord, representing Pacific-American Fisheries, Libby, McNeill and Libby and others, gave his view that:

"The discovery of a location for fish traps is somewhat similar to the discovery of a mine upon the public lands of the United States. After the discovery of the mine and the demonstration of the existence of mineral therein the Government permits the discoverer or locator of the mine to acquire title to it. . . . Most of these locations or sites have been purchased by the present occupants. In many instances they were discovered by other locators—many of them residents of Alaska—and sold to the packers who now occupy them. The present occupants have in many instances paid thousands of dollars for a single location or site . . . we have paid as high as $10,000, $25,000 and $50,000 for a bare possessory right." *Hearings on H.R. 2714*, pp. 103, 142.

"If the packers must depend upon seine fish entirely the chances of putting up the contemplated pack is very greatly diminished. Bankers will advance the packers who own traps the necessary money for their operations. Without the traps the capital is more timid and the bankers more reluctant to supply the cost of outfitting." *Ibid.*, p. 146.

[32] "This hatchery provision, that is in the present law, which was passed in 1906, was proposed by me," Mr. Dorr testified before a U.S. Senate Subcommittee, detailing the reasons for it. *Alaska Fisheries. Hearings before the Subcommittee of the Committee on Fisheries of the U.S. Senate on S. 5856, 62 C: 2 s, A Bill to Amend an Act for the Protection and Regulation of the Fisheries of Alaska,* pp. 38-9. April 26, 1912.

[33] "SENATOR NELSON: 'Jarvis lobbied a bill through here amending the fishery by which they escaped the canning tax they had to pay before. They can do it by putting in what they call a special fry and giving a certificate that they put in so many fry and turning that in in lieu of taxes. They have robbed one third of our Alaskan fund by just that trick.'" January 20, 1910. 61 C: 2 s, *Statements on S. 5436* before Sen. Comm. on Territories. Nelson repeated the charge even more extensively two years later. February 23, 1912. 62 C: 2 s, *Conditions in Alaska. Hearings before Sen. Comm. on Territories.*

[34] *Hearings on H.R. 9528,* p. 104. 64 C: 1 s, H. of R.

[35] *Ibid.*

[36] George W. George, Vice-President of the Columbia River Packers' Association, with a cannery on the Nushagak River and one at Chignik Bay, wrote Senator George E. Chamberlain:

"But few private hatcheries have been operated, and these few have been on streams where those operating hatcheries benefitted almost exclusively by the increased outputs from those streams, due to the hatcheries. Rebate certificates in the past have been issued at the rate of 40 cents for each thousand young fry liberated from the hatcheries. This does not seem large, and yet it is no doubt true that some of the largest packers in Alaska, who have operated hatcheries on a few streams from which they have had the exclusive benefit of increased production have practically been relieved of all taxation on their Alaska pack. . . . It is manifestly unfair that if one packer has a hatchery on a certain stream, from which practically all the benefits accrue to him, that he should be released from taxation on his pack on other streams where there are no hatcheries." 64 C: 2 s, *Hearings on S. 5856,* p. 103.

[37] "MR. CURRY [Rep. Charles F. Curry, R., of California]: 'The Government has two hatcheries up there. I believe the canneries would be pleased to turn their hatcheries over . . . without compensation or condemnation of proceedings.'

"MR. BRITTON: 'Speaking for the Alaska Packers' Association, they have taken the position that they would prefer to operate hatcheries.' He added that they would be willing to surrender them if the Government desired but expected to be compensated on a fair valuation.

"MR. CURRY: 'I believe it costs the packers a good deal more to run the hatcheries than any rebate they get from the Government.'

"MR. BRITTON: 'It costs them 42 cents per thousand, whereas they get 40; it is expensive for them to run hatcheries.'" 64 C: 1 s, *Hearings on H.R. 9528,* pp. 31-2.

[38] Under an act of Congress of June 30, 1906 (34 Stat. 684) 10 per cent of the receipts from a national forest during any fiscal year were to be paid at the end of such year to the state in which the national forest is situated to be expended as the state legislature may prescribe for the benefit of public schools and public roads in the county or counties in which such national forest is situated. An act of May 23, 1908 (35 Stat. 260), raised the percentage to 25. No payments were made to the District of Alaska from

the receipts of the Tongass and Chugach National Forests. A request for these funds was rejected by the "auditor for state and other departments" who ruled that the act applied to states and the Territory of Hawaii, which was organized, while Alaska was not an "organized" territory, and moreover had no counties. This conclusion was concurred in by the Comptroller of the Treasury (Sept. 14, 1908. 13 Comp. Dec. 219). The First Alaska Legislature near the close of its session in 1913 passed an act (Chapter 83) directing the territorial Treasurer to apply for moneys due from the forest-reserve fund. The request was refused by the Treasury Dept. Delegate Wickersham's diary contains the following notation, June 27, 1914:

"Preparing brief on appeal to the Comptroller of the Treasury . . . in an effort to secure payment of about $40,000 from the Forest Reserve Fund—being 25 per cent given to the territory by law but denied by a mere technicality. Decision against the territory but I am trying to get it reversed on appeal to the Comptroller. A hard job!"

Wickersham's reasoning prevailed. Another Comptroller of the Treasury, George E. Downey, reversed the previous rulings and allowed Alaska the amount due, retroactive to the enactment of the legislation, amounting to $31,164.75 (July 30, 1914, 21 Comp. December 27).

[39] S.J.M. 2.
[40] S.J.M. 16.
[41] H.J.M. 13.
[42] H.J.M. 4.
[43] H.J.M. 15.
[44] H.J.M. 23.
[45] H.J.M. 12.
[46] S.J.M. 13.
[47] S.J.M. 14.

CHAPTER 14

[1] December 2, 1913. 63 C: 2 s, *Cong. Rec.*, p. 45.
[2] *Railway Routes in Alaska.* Message from the President of the United States transmitting Report of the Alaska Railroad Commission. 62 C: 3 s, *H. of R. Doc. 1346.*
[3] *Construction of Railroads in Alaska. Hearings before the Committee on Territories on S. 48,* a Bill to Authorize the President of the United States to Locate, Construct, and Operate Railroads in the Territory of Alaska, and S. 133, a Bill to Provide for the Construction of Railroads in Alaska. 63 C: 1 s, pp. 267-86.
[4] *Ibid.*, p. 356.
[5] *Sen. Rept. 65.* 63 C: 1 s, *Cong. Rec.*, pp. 2018, 2130-1.
[6] 63 C: 1 s, *Cong. Rec.*, p. 2131. In opening the debate Senator Chamberlain stated: ". . . Alaska has been knocking at the doors of Congress for the last fifteen years, asking for the enactment of some laws that would be practical for the development of her coal mines and to protect those mines from monopolistic control, but Congress has not done anything. Congress has practically refused to do anything. The delegate from Alaska ever since he has been here has had some bill for the relief of Alaska, seeking to have some safe and sane legislation adopted for the development of the mineral resources of that country; and yet we have not done anything." 63 C: 2 s, *Cong. Rec.*, p. 1515.
[7] *Ibid., Cong. Rec.*, p. 1707.
[8] *Ibid.*, p. 1640.
[9] *Ibid.*, p. 1964.
[10] *Ibid.*, p. 2094.
[11] *Ibid.*, p. 2099.
[12] *Ibid.*, p. 2109.
[13] *Ibid.*, p. 2040.
[14] *Ibid.*, p. 1910.
[15] *Ibid.*, p. 2103.
[16] *Ibid.*
[17] *Ibid.*, pp. 2100-1.
[18] *Ibid.*, p. 2156.
[19] *Ibid.*, pp. 2163-4.
[20] 63 C: 2 s, *Cong. Rec.*, p. 1078.
[21] *Ibid.*, pp. 1078-84.
[22] *Ibid.*, p. 2953.
[23] *Ibid.*, p. 2965.
[24] *Ibid.*, p. 2986.
[25] *Ibid.*, p. 3338.
[26] *Ibid.*, p. 161.
[27] *Ibid.*, pp. 3625-6.

[28] *Ibid.*, p. 3627.

[29] *Ibid.*, p. 164.

[30] *Ibid.*, p. 2958. Rainey quoted Webster as follows:

"What do we want with this vast worthless area, this region of savages and wild beasts, of deserts, of shifting sands and whirlwinds of dust, of cactus and prairie dogs? To what use could we ever hope to put these great deserts or these endless mountain ranges, impenetrable and covered to their base with eternal snow? What can we ever hope to do with the western coast, a coast of three thousand miles, rockbound, cheerless, and uninviting, and not a harbor on it. What use have we for such a country? Mr. President, I will never vote one cent from the Public Treasury to place the Pacific Coast one inch nearer to Boston than it is now."

[31] *Ibid.*, p. 2969.

[32] *Ibid.*, p. 1688.

[33] *Ibid.*, p. 2981.

[34] *Ibid.*, p. 2988.

[35] *Ibid.*, p. 3623.

[36] *Ibid.*, pp. 3646-7.

[37] *Ibid.*, p. 1647.

[38] *Ibid.*, p. 1671.

[39] *Ibid.*, pp. 14,482-4.

[40] *Ibid.*, p. 14,488.

[41] Said Senator Borah: "It is my opinion that if this leasing system works at all . . . it will not be . . . the man of small means or of limited means, but it will be the man of vast wealth against whom we are supposed to be legislating." September 24, 1914. *Ibid.*, p. 15,624.

[42] *Ibid.*, pp. 14,483-4, 15,532.

[43] 63 C: 3 s, *Cong. Rec.*, pp. 3927-8, 4543-5, 5485-8, 5507. Delegate Wickersham, in his address at the laying of the cornerstone of the college, July 4, 1915, declared that Falconer's opposition was due to the interest of a constituent, a Seattle real-estate man, in another town site in Alaska. In his diary (February 24th and March 5, 1915) Wickersham identified the man as John E. Ballaine, who had acquired most of the Seward town site, and further alleged that Ballaine had sold Falconer some lots there. Ballaine had been one of the promoters of the Alaska Central Railroad, and at the various railroad hearings made no secret of his interest in Seward, which he had been instrumental in founding. He had hoped to sell his holdings to the government for the use of the railroad, but the authorities instead decided to locate its headquarters and car shops at Anchorage. Wickersham gave credit to Senator Thomas Sterling, R., of South Dakota, and to Speaker Champ Clark, D., of Missouri, for making the college bill's passage possible in their respective chambers.

CHAPTER 15

[1] 236 Fed. Nos. 2709, 2713, 2720, 2731, September 5, 1916. The opinion of the Ninth Circuit Court was delivered by Judges William B. Gilbert and Erskine M. Ross concurring. The territory was represented by its chief counsel, John H. Cobb, appointed by Governor Strong. The case for the canners was presented by Hellenthal and Hellenthal and Z. R. Cheney of Juneau, Warren Gregory and Curtis H. Lindley of San Francisco, E. S. McCord and W. H. Bogle of Seattle.

[2] January 15, 1917. 242 U.S. 648.

[3] March 3, 1919. 249 U.S. 47.

[4] *Hearings on H.R. 9527*, p. 80.

[5] *Hearings on H.R. 9528*, pp. 3-9.

[6] *Hearings on H.R. 9528*, p. 15.

[7] *Hearings on H.R. 9527*, pp. 38-46.

[8] *Ibid.*, p. 40.

[9] *Ibid.*, p. 38.

[10] *Hearings on H.R. 9528*, p. 36.

[11] *Ibid.*, p. 201.

[12] *Ibid.*, p. 241.

[13] *Hearings on H.R. 9527*, pp. 39-47.

[14] *Hearings on H.R. 9528*, p. 15.

[15] *Hearings on H.R. 9527*, pp. 28-9.

[16] *Hearings on H.R. 9528*, p. 41.

[17] *Ibid.*, p. 42.

[18] *Ibid.*, p. 342.

[19] *Hearings on H.R. 9527*, pp. 82-3. The principal debtors to the territory and the amounts owed for 1913-15, were Alaska Packers' Association, $75,018.-31; Booth Fisheries Co., $25,471.82; Libby, McNeill and Libby, $13,-

299.56; Alaska-Portland Packers' Association, $6,468.86. *Hearings on H.R. 9528*, pp. 322-3.

[20] On action brought against the Alaska Mexican Gold Mining Co., a Treadwell affiliate, the territory was sustained in both the United States District and Circuit Courts. The action was to recover the taxes due on a net income of $59,655 for the second half of 1913 and of $119,953, for 1914, the amount due, after exemptions, being $846.31. The company had been paying the federal government an annual tax of $360— $3 on each of its 120 stamps. 236 Fed. Reporter, 64-70.

[21] *Hearings on H.R. 9527*, pp. 79, 85.

[22] Wickersham's diary on February 26, 1915 records: "Personally delivered to Tumulty [President Wilson's secretary] letter dated February 25th presenting my views of Alaska salmon fisheries question."

[23] 64 C: 1 s, *Cong. Rec. App.*, pp. 1518-23.

[11] *Ibid.*, p. 264.
[12] *Ibid.*, pp. 386-7.
[13] *Ibid.*, p. 596.
[14] *Ibid.*, p. 369.
[15] *Ibid.*
[16] *Hearings on H.R. 6056*, A Bill to Amend an Act entitled "An Act to Create a Legislative Assembly in the Territory of Alaska, to Confer Legislative Power Thereon and for Other Purposes" approved August 24, 1912. Pp. 19-21, February 19, 1916, 64 C: 1 s.
[17] *Hearings on H.R. 6954*, p. 285.
[18] *Ibid.*, pp. 585-590.
[19] *Ibid.*, p. 591.
[20] *Ibid.*, p. 411.
[21] *Ibid.*, pp. 511-13.
[22] *Ibid.*, p. 352.
[23] *Ibid.*, p. 353.
[24] *Ibid.*, p. 451.
[25] *Ibid.*, pp. 451-2.
[26] *Supplemental Hearings on H.R. 5694*, p. 83.

CHAPTER 16

[1] Reprinted in *Hearings on H.R. 5694*, 67 C: 1 s, pp. 110-142.

[2] Some twenty-five years later President Franklin D. Roosevelt asked the writer: "If a bear belonging to the Department of Commerce mates with a bear belonging to the Department of Agriculture, to whom does the offspring belong?" The answer, he said, was "Congress."

[3] 63 C: 2 s, February 2, 1914, *Cong. Rec.*, p. 2722.

[4] *Hearings on H.R. 5694*, "To Provide for the Administration of National Property and Interests in the Territory of Alaska," pp. 1, 3.

[5] *Ibid.*, p. 176.

[6] *Supplemental Hearings on H.R. 5694*, p. 129.

[7] *Hearings on H.R. 5694*, p. 610.

[8] *Ibid.*, pp. 385-6.

[9] *Supplementary hearings on H. R. 5694*, pp. 129-30.

[10] *Ibid.*, p. 130. *Hearings on H.R. 5964*, p. 263.

CHAPTER 17

[1] For several years previously, Congress had recognized the necessity of the Geological Survey's making its plans for the Alaskan investigations well in advance of the opening of the field season, whose average length is 110 days, by including them in the first appropriation bill and thereby making the funds available by the middle of February. But in 1912 the appropriation was not made till August 24th, and was moreover cut from $100,000 to $90,000, and in 1913 it was not made till June 23rd. A total of one year's work was lost by the delays, and a substantial part of the money wasted. Brooks, Alfred H., *Mineral Resources of Alaska*, 1912, 1913, 1914.

[2] *Ibid.*, 1914. A similar forecast of the establishment on Prince William Sound of "one or more smelters capable of smelting the copper ores which are now being mined" immediately after the opening of the Alaska coal mines, was made by Secretary of Interior Walter L. Fisher

in an address on Alaskan problems before the American Mining Congress, October 27, 1911.

[3] Brooks, Alfred H., *Mineral Resources of Alaska*, 1916.

[4] *Ibid.*, 1920.

[5] Gregory, Homer, and Barnes, Kathleen, *North Pacific Fisheries With Special Reference to Alaska Salmon*, p. 310. Alaska Dept. of Fisheries, *Annual Rept. No. 1*, pp. 25-26.

[6] *Annual Rept. No. 1*, Alaska Dept. of Fisheries, p. 25.

[7] *Governor's Rept.*, 1919.

[8] *Rept. of the Federal Trade Commission on Canned Salmon*, December, 1918.

[9] Governor Strong in 1916 took direct issue with the Bureau of Fisheries which had furnished him with a statement to be used in his annual report, rejecting the idea that salmon were being depleted in Alaska, and repeated his warning in his 1917 report, a warning that was re-echoed by his successor, Governor Thomas Riggs, Jr., in his 1919 report.

[10] *Governor's Rept.*, 1919.

[11] Information furnished by Bureau of Fisheries, *Governor's Rept.*, 1919.

[12] Chapt. 75.

[13] *Repts. of the Secretary of the Interior*, 1917, 1918.

[14] *Hearings on H.R. 5694*, p. 267, 67 C: 1 s.

[15] *Governor's Rept.*, 1919.

[16] Representative Charles F. Curry, R., of California, who served in Congress for seventeen years, and after 1918 became Chairman of the House Committee on Territories in which position he became well versed in Alaskan matters, discussed Forest Service policies repeatedly:

"There was an organization at San Francisco, a corporation, that wanted to start a paper-pulp industry on the Alaska coast, and they . . . were not permitted to go ahead. . . . The department wanted to give them a twenty year franchise . . . and have the fixing of the cost in the hands of the department itself, without the people who had their money invested having a word to say about it; and having it refixed every three or five years, according to the judgment of the department.

"Now, it would cost from $10,000,-000 to $17,000,000 to go up into Alaska and put up a town for the employees, construct the buildings and the plant . . . get the light and power and the water. These people could not stand for that; but they have invested $17,000,000 in a similar plant in Canada. That is on account of our so-called conservation policy. It is not conservation at all. I believe in conservation and use." July 23, 1919. 66 C: 1 s, *Hearings on H.R. 7417*, p. 84.

Five years later Curry said: ". . . Under the law no timber or products of timber can be exported from Alaska. It cannot be sent to Washington, California or anywhere else. The only way that logs, lumber, or timber may be exported from Alaska is under a rider that is attached every year to the Agricultural appropriation bill permitting the Secretary of Agriculture at his discretion to permit, during that one year, the export of timber, lumber or the products thereof.

"Last year there was exported about $100,000 worth and the year before $60,000 under the authorization of that rider attached to the appropriation bill. Most of that went to Australia and Japan. Of course there can be no development of the timber industry in Alaska until the Department of Agriculture—the Forest Service—is willing that that act be repealed. They promised several years in succession that they would make that recommendation to Congress and it has not yet been made. So there is no inducement for capital to go into the Panhandle of Alaska and develop those forest resources. There is enough timber in that Panhandle to supply in perpetuity at least one-third of the paper that is used by the newspapers in the United States. . . . They could open up that Panhandle and there could be pulp plants and paper manufacturing plants in there at a cost of from $12,000,000 to $14,000,000 to

establish each plant. They have not
done it and they will not do it.
Therefore, so far as the timber resources of Alaska are concerned, they
do not and will not amount to
anything until that act is repealed."
March 27, 1924. 68 C: 1 s, *Hearings
on H.R. 8114*, p. 10.
[17] 67 C: 1 s, *Hearings on H.R. 5694*,
p. 27.
[18] Chapter 5.
[19] Chapter 28.
[20] Chapter 64.
[21] *Rept. of the Alaska Road Comm.*,
1919.
[22] July 11, 1916. 39 Stat. 355.
[23] The Federal Aid Highway Act (Nov.
9, 1921, 42 Stat. 212) provides a
complicated formula for state participation. First, each state designates,
after each federal highway act appropriation, a system of primary roads
that it desires to have built which
shall not exceed in mileage 7 per cent
of its existing total mileage. These
highways shall not exceed three-
sevenths of the total mileage receiving federal aid. For them each state
or participating territory is entitled to
receive 50 per cent of the total cost
of construction, plus an amount
based on a percentage of that cost
equal to one half the percentage
which the area within the state of
unappropriated public lands bears to
the state's entire area. Under this
part of the formula, the Western
states—the public-land states—receive
a proportionately larger amount of
federal funds, and Alaska's potential
share with its vast extent of unappropriated public domain, would be
the largest of all, though reduced in
its beginnings because, having a
negligibly small road system, it could
obtain federal aid for construction of
only 7 per cent of that existing mileage. The other approximately two-
sevenths of the total amount available, after a deduction of not to
exceed 2.5 per cent for the federal
agency to cover administrative costs,
is distributed to the states on a three-
part formula: One-third in the ratio
which the state's area bears to the
total area of the states; one-third in

the ratio which the state's population
bears to the total population of the
states; one-third in the ratio which
the state's mileage of rural-delivery
routes and star routes bears to total
of such routes in all the states. Under
this part of the formula Alaska would
also fare well, since under the first of
the three parts, based on area, it
would receive approximately one-fifth
of the total. While Hawaii, Puerto
Rico and the District of Columbia
were by special acts included,
Congress, despite the repeated efforts
of Alaska's delegates, refused to extend the act to Alaska.
[24] From unpublished copies of collectors of customs' correspondence with
Treasury Department in Alaska Historical Library, Juneau. In the same
letter Dodge also recommended:
"A lighthouse should be erected
here suitable for harbor purposes; a
fixed light of the ordinary character
will suffice and ought not to cost
much money. Somewhere near Mount
Edgecumbe however, the department
will find it necessary ere long to erect
a light of the 1st or 2nd order."
Neither of these recommendations
was acted upon.
Dodge was attempting to furnish
his government light in an abstract
sense as well—with no greater success. On January 16, 1868, he wrote
his chief McCulloch:
"The great need of this country is
the organization of a civil government
with a generous code of legislation. It
is full of wealth and under proper
management bands of hardy adventurers, the pioneers of our civilization,
will rapidly develop its resources, and
in a few years repay tenfold the cost
of the purchase, besides extending
well toward the coast of Asia the
genius of Republican institutions."
Ibid.
[25] *Ibid.* The record is silent on whether
Dodge was finally paid, and when.
[26] Morris, *op. cit.*, pp. 22-3, 56-8.
[27] Brady, John G., "Alaska: Its Resources and Needs." *The Independent*, January 18, 1900.
[28] *Rept. of the U.S. Lighthouse Board*,
1899.

²⁹ 56 C: 1 s, *H. of R. Doc.* 271.
³⁰ 57 C: 1 s, *H. of R. Doc.* 441.
³¹ *Repts. of the Lighthouse Board*, 1905-1910. *Rept. of the Secy of Commerce and Labor*, 1910.
³² Feb. 11, 1915. 63 C: 3 s, *Cong. Rec.*, pp. 3580-5.
³³ April 6, 1916. *Centennial Celebration of the United States Coast and Geodetic Survey*, p. 132.

"In Tongass Narrows alone are found the Potter Rock, the Ohio Rock, the Idaho Rock, and the California Rock," Representative Humphrey had told the Congress a year earlier. "Each of these rocks is a gravestone . . . a costly monument proclaiming the ignorance, the indifference, and the neglect of Congress." 63 C: 3 s, *Cong. Rec.*, p. 3581.

Other coastal landmarks named after sunken vessels in Alaskan waters are City of Topeka Rock, Colorado Reef, Fortuna Strait, Mariposa Rock, Orizaba Reef, Sennett Point, Tahoma Reef, Wayanda Ledge, Yukon Reef. (Names furnished by U.S. Coast and Geodetic Survey with the statement "numerous other examples could be cited." September 1, 1953.)
³⁴ 67 C: 1 s, *Hearings on H.R.* 5694, p. 298.
³⁵ *Ibid.*, p. 299.
³⁶ *Ibid.*, p. 299.
³⁷ *Ibid.*, p. 297.
³⁸ *Ibid.*, p. 350.
³⁹ *Ibid.*, p. 300. Sample contrasting rates were: Insurance on hulls, Seattle to Alaskan ports, 12 to 15 per cent; Seattle to other Pacific and foreign ports, 6 per cent. On merchandise: to Ketchikan, 742 miles, .5 per cent; to Cordova, 1,404 miles, .63 per cent; to Nome, 2,621 miles, .75 per cent; to Fairbanks, 3,524 miles, .25 per cent. To San Francisco, 800 miles, .2 per cent; to San Diego, 1,200 miles, .25 per cent; to London, England, 9,621 miles, .5 per cent.
⁴⁰ *Ibid.*, p. 338. May 9, 1921.
⁴¹ 63 C: 3 s, *Cong. Rec.*, p. 3676.
⁴² *Ibid.*, p. 3677.
⁴³ 66 C: 1 s, *Hearings on H.R.* 7417, pp. 5, 167-8, 183-6.

⁴⁴ 67 C: 1 s, H.R. 8442.
⁴⁵ 67 C: 1 s, *Cong. Rec.*, p. 7211.
⁴⁶ Governor George A. Parks in his 1925 report wrote: "July 7, 1924, Mr. Noel W. Smith was appointed Special Assistant to the Secretary of the Interior, and was sent to Alaska to study the operation of the Alaska Railroad and to make recommendations to the Secretary as to the future policy of the road and an estimate of the cost of completion. . . . It is estimated that to complete the Alaska Railroad, furnish it with the necessary facilities and equipment for performing its proper function as a transportation agency, that an expenditure of $11,-878,781 will be necessary. This expenditure for completion is due to the fact that in the original construction the early completion of the line was considered important, and it was found necessary to adopt many expedients, such as construction of wooden trestles from hastily cut and prepared native piling, the building of bridges on pile foundation without the proper quantity of ballast under the ties, construction of cuts and fills with only sufficient width to allow of laying the track, and similar methods of construction. The result of this character of construction is that the costs of maintenance are entirely out of proportion to what they will be when the railroad is completed, as the road as it is now constructed requires constant repairing to keep it in safe condition. . . . It is believed that such completion will return adequate interest on the money invested in the decreased maintenance and operation costs.
⁴⁷ In the second session of the Fifty-eighth Congress, when Senator Beveridge sought action on Senator Nelson's bill, S. 3339, which had been favorably reported by the Committee on Territories, Senator Foraker, collaborating with Senator Platt, succeeded in supplanting consideration thereof by a motion to proceed to executive business (March 10, 1904. 58 C: 2 s, *Cong. Rec.*, pp. 3087-94). The delegate bill was not brought up again in the second session, and when

it came up in regular order on January 10, 1905, in the third ("lame duck") session, it was passed over again on motion of Senator Platt. When it again recovered its place on the calendar on February 17th, it was recommitted to committee—a common procedure for defeating a measure—on motion of Senator Thomas R. Bard, R., of California, who, incidentally, had been defeated for re-election the previous November (58 C: 3 s, *Cong. Rec.*, pp. 625, 2771). Foraker, who had served two terms in the Senate, failed of renomination in 1908, owing to publication of correspondence between him and John D. Archbold, Vice-President of the Standard Oil Company, which revealed that Foraker had been the recipient of thousands of dollars from the company while serving in the Senate. Foraker defended his actions on the ground that these sums were in payment for legitimate legal services rendered the company, but his public career was nevertheless ended thereby. The Ohio Republican caucus in his stead nominated Theodore E. Burton, who was elected to the Senate by the Ohio legislature. In a subsequent attempt to return to the Senate in 1914, after popular election of Senators had been provided by constitutional amendment, Foraker was again defeated in the primary by Warren G. Harding. (Everett Walters, *Joseph Benson Foraker, An Uncompromising Republican*, pp. 273-293.)

[48] Information furnished by Board of Geographic Names, Dept. of the Interior, September 3, 1953. See also Frederick Cook, *To the Top of the Continent*, p. 73. (The Board of Geographic Names has no knowledge who "Miss A.F. Hunter of Newport" is. Letter of October 23, 1953, to the writer)

[49] Brooks, Alfred H. *The Alaska Mining Industry in 1920*, p. 31.

[50] 67 C: 1 s, *Hearings on H.R. 5694*, pp. 57-9, 333.

[51] *Ibid.*, p. 239.

[52] Two years later Alfred H. Brooks wrote: "Alaska has not yet recovered from the interdict placed on the development of mineral fuels by the withdrawal from entry of the coal lands in 1906 and of the oil lands in 1910. The leasing law . . . opened up the coal fields, but some of its provisions appear to be not liberal enough to encourage large developments." Brooks, Alfred H. and others, *Mineral Resources of Alaska, 1919*, p. 60.

[53] Letter of Asst. Commr. C. M. Bruce of General Land Office to Rep. James S. Davenport, dated December 16, 1913. The same letter revealed the total of all other varieties of patents issued in Alaska: Mineral, 311; mission sites, 12; town sites, 7; coal, 2; cemetery sites, 1. 63 C: 2 s, *Cong. Rec.* pp. 1100-1. The last item created some congressional mirth, Representative Davenport declaring that it was "one of the most useful things in the world for the farmer who goes to Alaska a poor man and undertakes to make a farm," thereby providing a cemetery in which he might be buried.

[54] 67 C: 1 s, *Hearings on H.R. 9654*, p. 178.

[55] *Ibid.*, p. 108.

[56] *Ibid.*, p. 178.

[57] *Ibid.*, p. 56.

[58] The opening comments on Hawaii of Secretary of the Interior Walter L. Fisher, in his one annual report, in 1912, may have a pertinence:

"The jurisdiction of the Department of the Interior over Hawaii is extremely limited. While the governor and some other territorial officials are appointed by the President, the islands are largely self-governing, under authority and limitations contained in the acts of Congress. Under the joint resolution of July 7, 1898, providing for annexing the Hawaiian Islands to the United States, Congress provided that the existing laws of the United States relative to the public lands should not apply to such lands in the Hawaiian Islands, but that special laws for their management and disposition should be enacted by Congress. . . . It has been held . . . that there is no appellate jurisdiction

in regard to the public lands, and the department has never been called upon to administer those laws."
[59] 67 C: 1 s, *Hearings on H.R. 5694*, pp. 296-7.
[60] May 12, 1921. 67 C: 1 s, *Hearings on H.R. 5694*, p. 502.

CHAPTER 18

[1] S.J.M. 28, 1913; S.J.M. 16, 1915; H.J.M. 13, 1921.
[2] S.J.M. 9, 1915.
[3] H.J.M. 12, 1921.
[4] S.J.M. 10, 1923.
[5] Sitka *Alaskan*, June 19, 1886.
[6] Juneau City *Mining Record*, November 22, 1888.
[7] January 24, 1889. Editorials also of June 6, 1889 and August 18, 1892.
[8] February 28, 1892.
[9] An "Alaska Advisory Committee" appointed by Secretary of the Interior John Barton Payne, consisting of representatives of Interior, Agriculture, Post Office and Shipping Board, reported: "It was the opinion of practically every person appearing before the committee that money could not be attracted to Alaska, industries dependent on transportation by regular lines started, or general development go forward under existing rates, and this was the conclusion reached by the Committee." June 11, 1920. 67 C: 1 s, *Hearings on H.R. 5694*, p. 76. This committee to investigate Alaska conditions did not visit Alaska but came to Seattle and held hearings there. *Ibid.*, p. 174.
[10] May 9, 1921. *Ibid.*, p. 294.
[11] *Ibid.*, p. 607.
[12] 63 C: 1 s, *Supplemental Hearings on H.R. 5694*, p. 134.
[13] Martin, C.G., *Mineral Resources of Alaska*, 1918. Brooks, Alfred H. *Mineral Resources of Alaska*, 1919. *Governor's Rept.*, 1919.
[14] *Governor's Rept.*, 1918.
[15] Rustgard, John, *A Statement Relative to Steamship Transportation Between Puget Sound and Alaska*. 67 C: 1 s, *Supplemental Hearings on H.R. 5694*, pp. 132-3.
[16] *Governor's Rept.*, 1919.

[17] *Ibid.*
[18] *Ibid.*
[19] 62 C: 2 s, *Hearings before the Committee on Commerce relative to S. 4012*.
[20] March 22, 1920, *Ibid.*, p. 81.
[21] Senate Concurrent Resolution 5.
[22] S.J.M. 10.
[23] H.J.M. 6.
[24] *Alaska vs. Troy*, 258 U.S. 101. February 27, 1922.
[25] 67 C: 1 s, *Hearings on H.R. 5694*, p. 608.
[26] *Ibid.*, p. 609.
[27] *Ibid.*, pp. 135-8.

CHAPTER 19

[1] Bean, Tarleton H., *Report on the Salmon and Salmon Rivers of Alaska, with Notes on the Conditions, Methods and Needs of the Salmon Fisheries*, in Bulletin of the U.S. Fish Commission for 1889, p. 167.
[2] March 2, 1889. 25 Stat. 1009.
[3] After the passage of the act of March 3, 1889, Samuel Elmore, a salmon canner of Astoria, testified: "Unless the government enforces the law, they will fast diminish the packing there." Asked "What particular provision of the law?" he replied: "The dam, the weir, that is placed across small streams, and as fast as the fish come in they are taken out and not allowed to go to their spawning grounds at all. The law prohibits them leaving these dams in, but it has got to be enforced." 51 C: 1 s, *Sen. Rept.* 1530. p. 246.
Henry D. Woolfe, who had visited the salmon operations at Karluk, asked by Senator Dolph as to the salmon supply in Alaska, answered that there was no lack at present, but that there would be within five years: "I believe these people will kill the goose that lays the golden egg. . . . If . . . restriction is not put upon the fishing business up there the quantity of fish will be greatly less-ened in a few years." *Ibid.*, p. 138.
Governor Knapp, in his second report (Oct. 1, 1890): "The import-ance of protecting the fishing busi-

ness in Alaska by effective legislation is more and more apparent every year. In many places the salmon fishing is overdone, and in many more, unwise and destructive methods are employed."

[4] Some of these factors were interestingly revealed in the salmon circular for 1888 issued by the Johnson-Locke Mercantile Co. of Portland:

"The Columbia River season opened at very high figures. One or two large operators secured a small quantity of fish at $1.45 to $1.55. The market rapidly advanced to $1.65 and for favorite brands . . . reached $1.80. . . .

"The position of Columbia River fish is very seriously threatened by the Alaska product, for with the curtailed pack on the Columbia, and the consequent high price of fish, Alaska is becoming a prime favorite, and especially so as it is being sold at 60 cents to $1 a case under the Columbia River fish. There is no danger to be apprehended from the increased Alaska production, for it must be recollected that as the Alaska pack increased, the Columbia River pack decreased in a corresponding ratio. This is evidenced by the fact that notwithstanding exertions that were made by canners from Alaska to the Sacramento River this year to put up a large pack, they only succeeded in increasing the general output some 70,000 cases more than last year. This increase is not felt and salmon today is ruling at higher prices than at any corresponding time within the last seven or eight years.

"The outlook for next year is very promising. While there will be five or six more canneries probably in Alaska, it must be borne in mind that these canneries will be near well-known locations, side by side with canneries that are already started, and the new ones will necessarily decrease the supply of fish of the old ones, and therefore not materially increasing the pack. This rule has held good wherever salmon canneries have been established. The Columbia River will undoubtedly show a decrease in pack

of 50,000 to 100,000 cases under last year. This decrease has been noticeable right straight along. Many fall streams have been fished out. The Sacramento as a canning river is a thing of the past, and it is fair to presume that not more than 1,100,-000 cases of fish will be the total output of the coast next season; and the probabilities are, if anything unforeseen occurs, such as a strike or trouble with the fishermen, the pack may be decreased. Increased cost of raw fish on the Columbia River, with a marked increase in the price of Chinese labor, brought about by the restriction act, with the limited stocks that now prevail throughout the world, lead us to believe that the price of canned salmon will be maintained for twelve months hence in any event, with a possibility of a still longer duration of prosperity. But for twelve months, or during the next canning season, high prices may be confidently looked for." 51 C: 1 s, *Sen. Rept.*, 1530, Pt. 1, pp. 49-50.

[5] "Upon careful inspection of the salmon-fishing industry at Karluk, on the island of Kadiak, the principal site of the canning industries of Alaska, and of many other canneries scattered over the territory, I am satisfied that the salmon are rapidly decreasing because of the incessant and indiscriminate fishing and the illegal use of weirs, nets, etc., thus obstructing the streams," Hamlin reported. *Seal and Salmon Fisheries of Alaska*, Vol. I, p. 452.

[6] "An Act to Amend an Act entitled 'An Act to Provide for the Protection of the Salmon Fisheries of Alaska.'" 54 C: 1 s, June 9, 1896. 29 Stat. 316.

[7] *Governor's Rept.*, 1897.

[8] H.R. 13543, 59 C: 1 s, *Hearings on S. 5856.* 62 C: 2 s, pp. 332, 363-70.

[9] *Hearings on H.R. 2714*, 68 C: 1 s, pp. 49-51.

[10] 34 Stat. 263.

[11] April 2, 1914. 63 C: 2 s, *Hearings on H.R. 11740*, Pt. 3, p. 7.

[12] *Ibid.*, p. 56. Kings had increased from $3.78 a case in 1906, to $6.48 in 1911; reds from $3.77 to $6.33; cohos from $3.63 to $5.67; pinks from $3.

to $3.94; chums from $2.87 to $3.72.

[13] *Ibid.*, p. 60.

[14] *Hearings on S. 5856, 62 C: 2 s*, pp. 74, 424.

[15] *Ibid.*, p. 75.

[16] *Ibid.*, p. 76.

[17] *Ibid.*, p. 80.

[18] *Ibid.*, pp. 79-80.

[19] *Ibid.*, p. 83.

[20] *Ibid.*, p. 391.

[21] *Ibid.*, p. 89.

[22] *Ibid.*, pp. 402-3.

[23] *Ibid.*, p. 408.

[24] *Ibid.*, p. 409.

[25] *Ibid.*, pp. 132-4.

[26] *Ibid.*, p. 270.

[27] *Ibid.*, p. 491. At a subsequent hearing Delegate Wickersham testified: "In 1869 those people took over the first fur-seal lease from the United States, and Sloss and Liebes, and that group of men, had the fur-seal fisheries of Alaska for twenty years. In 1890, when their lease expired, they had discovered a better thing, and they formed the Alaska Packers Association, to put up salmon in Alaska, and became the first great Alaska Salmon Trust. They have been engaged in that business ever since and they have made enormous fortunes out of it." *64 C: 1 s, Hearings on H.R. 9528,* p. 276.

[28] *Ibid.*, p. 162.

[29] *Ibid.*, p. 166.

[30] *Ibid.*, p. 238.

[31] *Ibid.*, p. 242.

[32] *Ibid.*, p. 247.

[33] *Ibid.*, p. 261.

[34] *Ibid.*, p. 248. Governor Clark had also testified to the need of further fisheries conservation measures; he did not believe in the abolition of fish traps, but that the jigger should go. *Ibid.*, pp. 29-33.

[35] *Ibid.*, p. 421.

[36] *Ibid.*, p. 454.

[37] *Ibid.*, p. 458.

[38] *Ibid.*, p. 455.

[39] *Ibid.*, pp. 467-8.

[40] *Ibid.*, p. 468.

[41] *Ibid.*

[42] Pp. 449-50.

[43] *Hearings on H.R. 9528, 64 C: 1 s,* pp. 9-15.

[44] *Ibid.*, p. 41.

[45] *Ibid.*, p. 50.

[46] *Ibid.*, p. 61.

[47] *Ibid.*, p. 63.

[48] *Ibid.*, pp. 65-75.

[49] *Ibid.*, p. 77.

[50] *Hearings on S. 5856,* p. 83.

[51] *Ibid.*, p. 394.

[52] *Hearings on H.R. 9528,* p. 230.

[53] *Ibid.*, p. 291.

[54] *Ibid.*, pp. 284-5.

[55] *Ibid.*, p. 209.

[56] After a field investigation in the summer of 1919 Gilbert and O'Malley of the Bureau of Fisheries reported to the Commissioner their conviction "that the industry has now reached a critical period in which the salmon supply of Alaska is threatened with virtual extinction, unless a radically new administrative policy be substituted for one now in force." September 20, 1919. *68 C: 1 s, Hearings on H.R. 2714,* p. 284.

The *Bulletin* of the Alaska Bureau of Publicity, published under the authority of the Governor's office, in its issue of December 10, 1919, declared: "That the future of Alaska's greatest industry and her greatest source of revenue, that of fishing, is threatened, there is no gainsaying. The falling off is not due to fewer concerns engaged in the business, but to fewer fish returning from the mighty ocean to the spawning grounds, which condition has been brought about by the inordinate greed of trappers, seiners and trollers who for years have plied their methods for taking fish so close to the mouths of spawning streams . . . until depletion is not only threatened but imminent." *66 C: 2 s, Hearings on H.R. 13334,* p. 27.

[57] *Hearings on H.R. 2394,* p. 4.

[58] *Ibid.*, p. 46.

[59] *Ibid.*, p. 6.

[60] *Ibid.*, p. 7.

[61] *Ibid.*, p. 48.

[62] *Ibid.*, p. 68.

[63] The language in controversy was: "Any right of possession and occupancy to a fishing site or location now lawfully held by any occupant thereof shall not be lost by nonuse thereof when such nonuse is caused by an order closing, limiting, or prohibiting

fishing in the waters where such locations are situated." Sutherland's contention was that this was recognition of a title, and that the area of the trap location was therefore reserved to the individual or company, saying: "We will assume that the section is closed for five or even ten years, until the streams are replenished. When the area is reopened fishermen wish to participate in the fishing there. They are told they can't. The area is reserved. The fact is it belongs to the men Mr. McCord represents." *Ibid.*, p. 51.

[64] *Ibid., Hearings on H.R.* 2714, p. 2.

[65] *Hearings on H.R.* 2714, p. 4.

[66] Confirmation of Delegate Sutherland's charge may be found in the testimony three years earlier of E. Lester Jones, for many years in the Bureau of Fisheries, its Deputy-Commissioner till 1915, when he became Director of the Coast and Geodetic Survey in the same department. On salmon fisheries he said: "I don't believe in so many canneries being licensed, but it is pretty hard to stop them unless a law is passed. I wired from Alaska that the Copper River should not be fished. Pressure was brought to bear through the Secretary of Commerce on the Bureau of Fisheries and he overrode my recommendation. What has happened? The supply of salmon is being reduced. I knew there was going to be trouble. Now, Copper River is going to be closed, but it should never have been opened." May 10, 1921, 67 C: 1 s, *Hearings on H.R.* 5694, p. 364.

[67] *Ibid.*, pp. 21-99.

[68] *Ibid.*, pp. 53-5.

[69] *Ibid.*, p. 84.

[70] Senator Wesley L. Jones and Representative Lindley H. Hadley of Bellingham, Washington, accompanied Commissioner O'Malley on his two months' inspection trip to Alaska in the summer of 1923. *Bureau of Fisheries Document No.* 973, p. 50.

[71] *Hearings on H.R.* 2174, pp. 27-8.

[72] *Ibid.*, p. 120.

[73] *Ibid.*, p. 116. Dec. 21, 1922.

[74] *Ibid.*, pp. 246-8.

[75] *Ibid.*, p. 85.

[76] 68 C: 1 s, *Cong. Rec.*, p. 5451.

[77] *Ibid.*

[78] *Ibid.*, p. 5969.

[79] *Ibid.*, pp. 5972-3.

[80] *Ibid.*, p. 5977.

[81] *Ibid.*, p. 5979.

[82] *Ibid.*, p. 5978.

[83] *Ibid.*, p. 5980.

[84] *Ibid.*

[85] *Ibid.*, pp. 9519-20.

[86] *Ibid.*, p. 9687.

[87] Under the heading "Alaska Fisheries Policy Established," the *Pacific Fisherman* editorialized:

"The passage of the Alaska Fisheries Act brings to a successful conclusion an effort extending over many years on the part of those interested in the perpetuation of the fisheries. It means the final establishment of a definite policy by the federal government for the protection of this great resource, and provides means whereby the salmon runs may be permanently maintained as the basis of a productive industry and a source of profit to the community." June, 1924. Vol. XXII, No. 6.

[88] Gregory, Homer E., and Barnes, Kathleen. *North Pacific Fisheries with Special Reference to Alaska Salmon*, p. 48.

[89] *Hearings on H.R.* 2714, p. 98.

[90] *Alaska Fishery and Fur-Seal Industries in 1924*, pp. 91-2.

CHAPTER 20

[1] May 10, 1921. Testimony of Col. E. Lester Jones. *Hearings on H.R.* 5694, p. 352.

[2] In a letter to Delegate Sutherland, January 27, 1923. *Hearings on H.R.* 2714, p. 35.

[3] This was the opening sentence in his first annual report, September 7, 1922. Governor Riggs had written the 1921 report.

[4] *Governor's Rept.*, 1923.

[5] *Ibid.*

[6] *Rept. of the Secretary of the Interior*, 1925.

[7] *National Spectator*, quoted in *Cong. Rec.* March 5, 1926, 69 C: 1 s, p. 5126.

[8] July 27, 1923.

[9] *Rept.*, 1925.

[10] Reprinted in *Governor's Rept.*, 1922.

[11] *Message to Seventh Territorial Legislature*, March 4, 1925.

[12] December 8, 1925.

[13] January 6, 1926, 69 C: 1 s, *Cong. Rec.*, p. 1584.

[14] *Ibid.*

[15] *Hearings on H.R.* 5694, p. 171.

[16] 66 C: 1 s, S. R. 329. *Sen. Doc.* 252.

[17] Letter from Acting Secretary of the Interior Alexander T. Vogelsang to President of the Senate. *Hearings on H.R.* 5694, p. 172.

[18] 71 C: 2 s, S. R. 298.

[19] 71 C: 3 s, S. *Rept.* 1230, January 5, 1931.

[20] December 11, 1931. *Hearings before Subcomm. of House Comm. on Appns. on Interior Dept. Appn. bill for 1933*, pp. 1015-17.

[21] From an interview printed in magazine *Labor*. Quoted in *Diary*, April 21, 1931.

[22] Before a House Appropriations subcommittee Mr. Ebert K. Burlew, for many years budget officer of the Department of the Interior, expressed "the Secretary's view about this toll, which is that the Richardson Highway was built up by the government. The taxpayers in Alaska did not contribute toward it, and it is being maintained exclusively by government money." To this Delegate Dimond, who was present, retorted that "up to June, 1932, the territory paid 27.4 per cent of all the cost of building and maintaining roads in the Territory of Alaska." January 28, 1935. 74 C: 1 s, *Hearings on Interior Dept. Appropriation bill, 1936*, pp. 473-4.

[23] In view of Governor Parks's expertness in this field and its importance, his further comment is valuable:

"The survey of the public domain should proceed in a logical manner, and the first step should be the extension of first-order triangulation along certain routes in the interior of Alaska. This will furnish the framework on which the rectangular surveys can be arranged, and the result will be that the principal meridians and base lines will be properly co-ordinated in the rectangular net.

"The rectangular system of surveying public lands in the United States is the best that has ever been devised. . . . In the extension of this system it is necessary to adopt new reference points in various localities. An accurate determination of the geodetic position of these reference points is of utmost importance if the surveys that are subsequently referred to them are properly placed with reference to other surveys in the territory, hence the triangulation stations established by the Coast and Geodetic Survey should be available before the subdivisional surveys are attempted.

"The permanent development of the public domain depends primarily on placing title to the agricultural lands of the territory in individuals who will utilize them. However, before the government can be divested of this title, the land must be surveyed, and, as shown above, the logical way to make the survey is first to provide an accurate control by a system of triangulation; hence the continuation of the surveying work is a necessary step in the development of the territory."

[24] 72 C: 1 s, *Hearings before a Subcommittee of the Committee on Appropriations, U.S. Senate, on H.R.* 8397, *Interior Appropriation bill for 1933*, p. 10.

[25] 72 C: 2 s, *Hearings on H.R.* 13710 *before a Subcommittee of the Committee on Appropriations, U.S. Senate*, pp. 1-9.

[26] Letter of Secretary of the Interior Ray Lyman Wilbur to Representative Edward T. Taylor, Chairman, Subcommittee on Interior Appropriations, January 3, 1932. *Hearings on Interior Department Appropriation Bill, 1933*, pp. 1009-10, 72 C: 1 s.

[27] Letter from E. K. Burlew to Senator Wesley L. Jones, Chairman, Senate Committee on Appropriations, February 24, 1932. *Hearings on H.R.* 8397, *Interior Dept., Appropriation Bill for 1933*, pp. 288-9. 72 C: 1 s.

[28] *Rept. of the Secretary of the Interior*, 1924.

[29] *Governor's Rept.*, 1928.

[30] November 4, 1921. Ex. Order 3574.

[31] January 22, 1925. Ex. Order 4131.

[32] 69 C: 1 s, H. *of R. Doc. 432.*

[33] *Annual Rept., 1926.* Governor Parks further stated: "Apparently little effort was made to enforce the law in some of the important districts. Last year the Second Judicial Division was without a game warden, the Yukon River districts were not given adequate protection, and no provision was made for a warden on the Kuskokwim River. The traders complain about the many reports that are demanded from them and also of the unsuppressed traffic in contraband furs in certain districts which militates against those who abide by the law. The taxes imposed by the game law on residents of the territory should be repealed. The territorial legislature imposes a similar tax and the duplication is unnecessary and unjust."

[34] In view of this negative record and the limited accomplishments as contrasted with promises of the Wilson administrations, the national party platforms during this period are of some interest.

The 1920 Republican platform made no mention of Alaska.

The 1920 Democratic platform: "We commend the Democratic administration for inaugurating a new policy as to Alaska, as evidenced by the construction of the Alaska Railroad, and opening of the coal and oil-fields.

"We declare for the modification of the existing coal-land law, to promote development without disturbing the features intended to prevent monopoly.

"For such changes in the policy of forestry control as will permit the immediate initiation of the paper pulp industry.

"For relieving the territory from the evils of long-distance government by arbitrary and interlocking bureaucratic regulation, and to that end we urge the speedy passage of the Lane-Curry bill now pending, co-ordinating and consolidating all federal control of natural resources under one department to be administered by a non-partisan board permanently resident in the territory.

"For the fullest measure of territorial self-government with the view of ultimate statehood, with jurisdiction over all matters not of purely federal concern, including fisheries and game, and for an intelligent administration of federal control we believe that all officials appointed should be qualified by previous bona-fide residence in the territory.

"For a comprehensive system of road construction with increased appropriations and the full extension of the Federal Road Aid Act to Alaska.

"For the extension to Alaska of the Federal Farm Loan Act."

The 1924 Republican platform: "We endorse the policy of the present administration with reference to Alaska and favor a continuance of the constructive development of the territory."

The 1924 Democratic platform: "The maladministration of Alaskan affairs is a matter of concern to all our people.

"Under the Republican administration of Alaska development has ceased, and the fishing industry has been seriously impaired.

"We pledge ourselves to correct the evils which have grown up in the administration of that rich domain.

"An adequate form of local self-government for Alaska must be provided, and to that end we favor the establishment of a full territorial government for the territory similar to that enjoyed by all the territories except Alaska during the last century of American history."

The 1928 Republican platform repeated the language of four years previously.

The 1928 Democratic platform: "We favor the development of Alaska and Hawaii in the traditional American way, through self-government. We favor the appointment of only bona-fide residents to office in the territories. We favor the extension and improvement of the mail, air mail, telegraph and radio, agricultural experimenting, highway construction, and other necessary federal activities in the territories."

[35] "The failure of Congress to provide funds for the administration of Mount McKinley National Park has again prevented the National Park Service from taking possession of that area. Already the Interior Department has twice submitted estimates for a ranger force, the park having been created as an emergency measure to prevent the slaughter of its game. A third estimate, in amount of $10,000, is being submitted to Congress with a request for an appropriation for purely protective and administrative purposes, and it is sincerely hoped that it may receive favorable attention when the next sundry civil bill is prepared." *Rept. of the Secretary of the Interior*, 1918.

"Although Mount McKinley National Park was established in February, 1917, as an emergency step in the preservation of the great herds of wild animals in that region, Congress has not yet provided any funds for carrying out the provisions of the . . . act." *Rept. of the Secretary of the Interior*, 1919.

[36] *Gov. Rept.* 1923.

[37] January 6, 1926. 69 C: 1 s, *Cong. Rec.*, p. 1605.

[38] In 1925, a typical year, the industry employed 27,685. Of these 15,996 were classed as whites, 4,607 natives and 7,082 "orientals," divided into Chinese, 1,278; Japanese, 1,548; Filipinos, 2,246; Mexicans, 1,510; Negroes, 255; Puerto Ricans, 150; Miscellaneous, 95. There is no breakdown to show how many of the whites were brought in, but from Sutherland's figures it may be inferred that most of them were. *Governor's Repts.* 1924-1928.

[39] Mr. R. E. Robertson, of Juneau, testified that he was attorney for a hundred corporations, and that "so far as the majority of these corporations are concerned, unfortunately, both for the territory, and, as I think, from the point of view of the corporations, very few of them have any bona-fide residence in Alaska. They are not even voters. In fact, a large number of them in the winter time, in the voting time, have only a watchman in Alaska." March 27, 1924. *Reapportionment of the Alaska Legislature.* 68 C: 1 s, *Hearings on H.R. 8114*, p. 7. *Ibid.*, p. 11.

[40] By the same approach the work of the Board of Fish Commissioners, begun in 1919, which with a biennial appropriation of some $80,000 had been operating hatcheries at Ketchikan, Cordova and Seward, removing obstacles to spawning from salmon streams and destroying hair seals and other predators on salmon, was eliminated by the 1927 legislature. It was argued of course that this was a federal function and adequately provided for. The canned-salmon industry, besides objecting to the territorial expenditure, also viewed this as a remaining entering wedge for territorial management of the fisheries.

[41] April 30, 1927.

[42] Potter, Jean, *The Flying North*, p. vii.

[43] *Ibid.*, p. 115.

CHAPTER 21

[1] July 24, 1925.

[2] The major party platforms were unusually devoid of commitments during this period. The Democratic platform contained no allusion to Alaska either in 1932 or 1936. In 1940 it declared:

"We favor a larger measure of self-government leading to statehood for Alaska, Hawaii and Puerto Rico. We favor the appointments of residents to office, and equal treatment of the citizens of each of these three territories. We favor the prompt determination and payment of any just claims by Indian and Eskimo citizens of Alaska against the United States."

The Republican platform of 1932 declared:

"We favor the policy of giving to the people of Alaska the widest possible territorial self-government and the selection as far as possible of bona-fide residents for positions in that territory and the placing of its citizens on an equality with those in the several states."

The Republican platforms of 1936 and 1940 made no mention of Alaska.

[3] In the eight years 1933-1940 inclusive the average annual appropriation was $509,597. To this were added relief appropriations which averaged $452,-246 for the same period. The Alaska fund's share averaged $152,311. Just over a million dollars a year—$1,001,-143—was available for Alaska's highway program, exclusive of the national forest areas during that period. (Data supplied by Alaska Road Commission, July 20, 1953.)

[4] Provisions of the act were extended to Hawaii July 1, 1924, Puerto Rico July 1, 1937 and District of Columbia July 1, 1939.

[5] 75 C: 1 s, *Hearings before the Subcommittee of the Committee on Appropriations on the Agricultural Department Appropriation bill for 1938*, pp. 1504-5. Testimony of Delegate Anthony J. Dimond, April 1, 1937.

[6] *Ibid.*, pp. 1507-10.

[7] Federal Highway Act of 1940. *Hearings before the Committee on Roads on H.R. 7891*, pp. 390-2. 76 C: 3 s, H. of R.

[8] April 9, 1937. 75 C: 1 s, *Hearings before the Subcommittee of the Committee on Appropriations, U.S. Senate, on H.R. 5779*.

[9] Discrimination against Alaska's interest in the certification of such carriers between the United States and Alaska will be fully treated subsequently.

[10] Hearings before subcommittee of House committee Interior Dept. appropriation bill for 1935. 73 C: 2 s, pp. 704-7.

[11] For operation and maintenance of one-teacher schools, $350 more a year was allowed in the States than in Alaska; $1,200 more for a two-teacher school; $1,850 more for a three-teacher school; $1,500 more for a four-teacher school; $3,750 more for a five-teacher school. The annual discrimination against Alaska amounted in a given year when the Office of Indian Affairs operated one hundred

day schools and two boarding schools in Alaska, 1939, to $73,500. In the items for repair of schools there were corresponding differences amounting to $24,600 to Alaska's disadvantage. February 15, 1939. 76 C: 1 s, *Hearings before the Subcommittee of the Committee on Appropriations of the Interior Department Appropriation bill for 1940*, Pt. II, pp. 731-3.

[12] Figures supplied by Director, Alaska Agricultural Experiment station, January 12, 1953.

[13] A thoughtful and authoritative analysis of Alaska agriculture's needs, problems and present status, is found in Johnson, Hugh A., and Irwin, Don L., *The Position of Agriculture in Alaska's Current Economy*, 1953, published jointly by the University of Alaska and the Agricultural Research Administration of the U.S. Dept. of Agriculture, who write:

"Throughout Alaska's history, no real official interest was taken in agricultural development prior to 1935. Even the motives behind the founding of the Matanuska Colony were conducive to a peasant-type subsistence economy rather than to commercial agriculture. Individual effort in the Matanuska Valley brought about the commercial agriculture—not the funds spent on the Colony. Small tracts were combined into economic-size units by individuals through purchase, trade or lease.

"The first real, concrete, forward-looking effort to encourage commercial agriculture in Alaska occurred in 1946 when the Task Force was sent here to prescribe for the agricultural ills of the community. Following their report, the Congress in 1947 began appropriating funds for agricultural research to encourage development in the territory. . . .

"Work under way in soils, in agricultural engineering, in entomology, in pathology and in economics has progressed only to the exploratory stages. Work on nutrition and on the effect of the light factor, for example, is needed desperately by all sections of agricultural research—but there is no money and no facilities. In spite of the seemingly generous sums being spent on agricultural research, they are inadequate for a balanced program. We are trying to do too much too fast with too little. Agriculture's research problems cannot be settled in a year or five years. They cannot be settled without adequate financial support. . . .

". . . there are no adequate agricultural statistics in the territory . . .

"Research is necessary! But it is not enough. Would-be farmers must have personal or procurable capital available if they are to develop commercial farms from woodland in a short time. This capital has not been available in Alaska. Production has been increasing in recent years, but not so rapidly as the demand for locally grown food. . . . A rapid expansion of production will require an entire new program of financing adapted to Alaskan conditions. Land settlement and development in Alaska must be divorced from the antiquated Homestead Laws and from the ill-advised limitations of the Veterans Preference Acts."

CHAPTER 22

[1] 73 C: 2 s, *Cong. Rec.*, p. 2754.
[2] 74 C: 1 s, *Cong. Rec.*, pp. 3242-7, February 20, 1935.
[3] *Ibid.*
[4] *Hearings . . . on H.R. 6621 and H.R. 4130.* 74 C: 1 s, pp. 17, 21, 86.
[5] *Ibid.*, p. 61.
[6] *Ibid.*, pp. 120-1.
[7] *Ibid.*, pp. 22-3.
[8] *Ibid.*, pp. 30-1.
[9] April 29, 1937. 75 C: 1 s, *Cong. Rec.*, p. 4014.
[10] April 30, 1937. *Ibid.*, p. 4056.
[11] *Ibid.*
[12] 75 C: 3 s, *Hearings . . . on Interior Dept. App'n Bill for 1939*, pp. 912-13.
[13] February 18, 1938. 75 C: 3 s, *Hearings on Military Establishment App'n Bill for 1939*, p. 765.
[14] *Ibid.*, p. 766.
[15] *Ibid.*

[16] March 28, 1938. 75 C: 3 s, *Cong. Rec.*, pp. 4168, 4245.
[17] *Ibid.*, p. 4247. Both Dockweiler and Powers were members of the Subcommittee on the War Department of the House Appropriations Committee, which made their opposition virtually insuperable.
[18] "Unfortunately the name air base has been applied to the Fairbanks installation. Fairbanks is not a base. It was never intended for a base . . ." testified Brigadier General George V. Strong, Assistant Chief of Staff, War Plans Division, explaining that "that cold-weather experiment station was put in primarily to find out what the operation of planes and engines was going to be under extreme temperature conditions; to find out how fuel would act; how the electrical installation would stand up, and how communications matters would work . . ." *Hearings . . . on H.R. 9209.* 76 C. 3 s, p. 212.
[19] 76 C: 1 s, *Cong. Rec.*, p. 1773.
[20] *Hearings . . . on Military Establishment Appropriation Bill for 1941*, p. 3. 76 C: 3 s.
[21] *Ibid.*, p. 261.
[22] *Ibid.*, p. 23.
[23] *Ibid.*, pp. 485-6, 826-36.
[24] Delegate Dimond made one more attempt from the floor to have the Anchorage base re-inserted. "It is evident," he began his prolonged plea, "that the proposed air base is out of the bill. This may be called economy by annihilation." April 3, 1940. 76 C: 3 s, *Cong. Rec.*, p. 3949.
[25] *Hearings . . . on H.R. 9209, Military Establishment Appropriation Bill for 1941*, pp. 23-6. 76 C: 3 s.
[26] This executive, legislative and judicial conflict will be treated fully in a subsequent volume.

CHAPTER 23

[1] October 24, 1867. Morris, *op. cit.*, pp. 120-1.
[2] October 28, 1867. Morris, *op. cit.*, p. 121. The text of this memorable letter is as follows:

"General: In the absence of specific legislation by Congress for the organization of land districts in Alaska, claims of pre-emption and settlements are not only without the sanction of law, but are in direct violation of laws applicable to the public domain. Military force may be used to remove intruders, if necessary. Will you have the goodness to instruct Major General Halleck to this effect by telegraph, and request him to communicate the instruction to Major General Rousseau at Sitka."

³ November 19, 1867. *Hearings on H.R. 5694, p. 159.*

⁴ Four years earlier the same issue— that of conveying power to the Secretary of the Interior, "to prescribe rules and regulations," and "to exercise his discretion," and thereby perhaps nullifying the intent of Congress —had been fought out in other legislation.

A bill (H.R. 14775, 64 C: 1 s) to establish Mount McKinley National Park was introduced by Delegate Wickersham at the request of the Department of the Interior. Sections 2, 3 and 4 continued all previously existing mining rights. Section 5 placed the park under the control of the Secretary of the Interior and gave him authority to issue rules and regulations concerning its management. Section 6 was as follows:

"That the said park shall be, and is hereby, established as a game refuge, and no person shall kill any game in said park except under an order from the Secretary of the Interior for the protection of persons or to protect or prevent the extermination of other animals or birds: Provided, That prospectors and miners engaged in prospecting and mining in said park may take and kill therein so much game or birds as may be needed for their actual necessities when short of food; but in no case shall animals or birds be killed in said park for sale or removal therefrom, or wantonly."

When the House hearing opened (May 4, 1916) Sub-committee Chairman James V. McClintic, D., of Oklahoma, read a letter from Secretary Lane to Chairman Scott Ferris of the Public Lands Committee, making the department's report on the bill which read in part:

"The measure . . . is satisfactory except as to section 6, the proviso . . . authorizing prospectors . . . to . . . kill . . . game . . . when short of food, etc. Under this language some question might arise as to who are prospectors or miners, and in order that there may be no uncertainty on this point it is best that provision be made for the issuance of permits in such cases. This may best be provided for . . . by inserting after the word 'may' . . . the words 'under such regulations and restrictions as may be prescribed by the Secretary of the Interior . . .'

"If the bill be amended as suggested, it has my approval . . ."

Wickersham objected: "It gives the Secretary of the Interior power to make rules and regulations in regard to prospectors killing game. I am very much opposed to it. If you put that in you might as well leave the rest out. He could make rules and regulations the next day which would be of such a character that no prospector could have any benefit of the law. I object to Alaska being controlled by rules and regulations made by some bureau official. We have suffered from that more than any other one thing in the Territory of Alaska. It has done more to retard the development of the territory than any other one thing."

"MR. TIMBERLAKE [Charles B. Timberlake, R., of Colorado]: 'As a representative from the West, I indorse that statement, but you recognize also that without something of that kind in the bill to conform to the best wishes of the department, that it will be very hard to get the legislation enacted.' "

"MR. WICKERSHAM: 'Well, I think the time has come when Congress has got to stand up and pass laws without any control from the departments in these matters.' "

Wickersham argued that the proposed amendment was a violation of the principles which Secretary Lane had espoused when he wrote "Red Tape in Alaska," and that Section 6, which he himself had written was clear and ample.

Chairman McClintic was fearful that unless the Secretary's wishes prevailed the bill would fail of passage.

At the Senate Territories Committee hearing on the companion bill (S. 5716) Wickersham said he had been inclined to be against the bill but that his objections had been overcome because of its extension of the mineral laws to what might be a great quartz mining area, but that Secretary Lane's amendment destroyed "the very certainty of the law that I wished in respect to miners and prospectors. It all resolves itself now into rules and regulations to be prepared by the Secretary of the Interior . . ."

"THE CHAIRMAN [Sen. Key Pittman]: 'I entertain about the same view that Judge Wickersham does about red tape. I have suffered from it myself. . . . It is a benefit to the prospector to have some kind of a game refuge and the real prospector . . . does all he can to protect it.'

"MR. WICKERSHAM. 'You have now so many restrictions upon the development of the territory that I regret very much to see another large area withdrawn and regulations adopted which will by their severity exclude the miners. A miner can not carry a very large amount of food supplies with him when he goes into the mountains. If he cannot get game he cannot go. All of the strikes in that interior region have been made by men prospecting under those circumstances who had to depend upon the country as they went along. . . .'

"SENATOR HARDING [Warren G. Harding, R., of Ohio]: 'Would it be practicable for the prospector who goes out there to have a regularly issued permit to do that?'

"MR. WICKERSHAM. 'That is utterly impracticable. He is out in the mountains somewhere, and he wants to go into the park boundaries prospecting, but he is one hundred miles from Fairbanks, and when he goes to Fairbanks, which is the capital of that region, he is several thousand miles from Washington, and the official who issues the permit is in Washington, with many other things to do.' "

Senator Harding then asked why there wouldn't be a park authority to do that. Wickersham pointed out that it was not provided in the bill and Belmore Browne, one of the advocates of the legislation creating the park, who was present, said there would be prospectors coming in at the western end of the park and that they would be "hundreds of miles" from park headquarters.

Wickersham declared flatly that he would not favor the bill with the amendment—and won out. Section 6 was not amended.

Wickersham was not present (although subsequently declared elected) in the Sixty-fifth and Sixty-sixth Congresses when the shore-space legislation with discretionary powers vested in the Secretary of the Interior was introduced and passed. Had he been seated, Wickersham might conceivably have been equally successful in preserving within that legislation the obvious intent of Congress, which would have coincided with his own desires and Alaska's interest. His feat in the Mount McKinley Park bill was rare. It is related merely because of its pertinence to a long-standing and continuing conflict, and that is its chief importance. For the special provision, allowing prospectors to take game in the park for their own use, was later repealed, and, in the writer's opinion, in view of changed circumstances, wisely.

⁵ Riley, Burke, *Federal Land Policy and Its Effect on Development and Settlement in Alaska*, p. 32.

⁶ 1927, it may be noted, was the sixtieth year since the purchase, and the year after even the triangulation surveys in Alaska had been suspended.

⁷ The act provided: "The President may, at any time in his discretion, temporarily withdraw from settlement, location, sale or entry any of

the public lands of the United States, including Alaska, and reserve the same for water-power sites, irrigation, classification of lands, or other public purposes to be specified in the orders of withdrawals, and such withdrawals or reservations shall remain in force until revoked by him or by an act of Congress."

[8] May 23, 1911. 62 C: 1 s, *Civil Government in Alaska. Hearings on S. 1647.*

[9] January 15, 1914. 63 C: 2 s, *Cong. Rec.*, pp. 1698-9.

[10] The following tables show expenses and receipts of the two national forests in Alaska for the last eight years. It will be noted that neither is self-supporting but the Tongass far more nearly so than the Chugach. In addition to the operational costs for each are the expenses of the regional office which manages both areas. The receipts from the Tongass are expected to improve materially when Alaska's first pulp mill, near Ketchikan, begins operations in 1954. (Data supplied by U.S. Forest Service.)

EXPENSES FOR MANAGEMENT AND DEVELOPMENT OF THE NATIONAL FORESTS IN ALASKA:

Fiscal Year	Regional Office	Tongass Forest	Chugach Forest	Total
1946	$116,786	$191,489	$ 45,137	$353,412
1947	122,593	342,385	60,819	525,777
1948	131,006	257,523	70,998	483,527
1949	138,365	317,050	81,006	536,421
1950	164,327	344,718	116,669	625,714
1951	147,246	271,327	96,311	514,884
1952	203,812	276,673	85,330	565,815
1953	199,336	262,104	144,550	605,990

FOREST RECEIPTS:

Fiscal Year	Tongass	Chugach	Total
1946	$ 45,411.88	$11,639.33	$ 57,051.21
1947	142,655.36	13,909.52	156,564.88
1948	166,804.24	12,795.67	179,599.91
1949	143,111.99	12,966.49	156,078.48
1950	95,212.58	12,362.98	107,575.56
1951	157,792.64	12,698.79	170,491.43
1952	255,564.71	19,527.83	275,092.54
1953	215,723.74	18,681.25	234,404.99

[11] Brigadier General Richard G. Prather, Chief of Staff of the Alaska Command, in a written statement, presented, September 26, 1952, to a subcommittee of the House Interior and Insular Affairs Committee investigating Alaska land problems, gave the Command's view that "A settled Alaska is more easily defended because military economy is greatly influenced by the local economy." 82 C: 2 s, *Transcript of Hearings before subcommittee on the Revision of the Public Land Laws of the House Committee on Interior and Insular Affairs, sequent to H.R.* Unpublished.

[12] Transcript of Hearing, August 1, 1952, at Anchorage on request of the Army for the withdrawal of approximately 86,000 acres in the vicinity of Anchorage. (Unpublished, in possession of Bureau of Land Management.)

[13] Testimony of Ralph Browne. Hearing, August 1, 1952.

[14] The larger reservations, prior to Sec

retary Ickes, were Annette Island (Metlakatla), 86,741 acres, March 3, 1891; St. Lawrence Island, 1,250,000 acres, January 7, 1903; Kobuk River Reservation, including the village of Noorvik, 144,000 acres, November 21, 1914; Norton Bay, 316,000 acres, October 12, 1929—the last three principally in connection with reindeer grazing for the Eskimos—and Tetlin, 786,000 acres, June 10, 1930. Except for the first of these established by act of Congress, they were created by executive—that is to say, presidential—order, in contrast with those created after 1936 which, under the legislation extending the Wheeler-Howard Act (48 Stat. 986) to Alaska (49 Stat. 1250) were by secretarial order.

[15] A sample protest was Senate Joint Memorial No. 1 of the Seventeenth Territorial Legislature in 1945 which passed the Senate unanimously and the House with but one dissenting vote. It was as follows:

TO THE HONORABLE THE CONGRESS OF THE UNITED STATES:

Your Memorialist, the Legislature of the Territory of Alaska in the Seventeenth Regular Session assembled, does most respectfully submit that:

WHEREAS, this legislature now convened is facing the task of devising ways and means of safeguarding the territory's population and welfare during the present conflict, and of planning for a broader economic development that will insure a sound future for our own returning veterans and thousands of others in the armed forces and large numbers of civilians, all of whom are looking forward to a home in the northern frontier; and

WHEREAS, the area of the Territory of Alaska is 378,165,760 acres and of this 20,850,000 acres is in the national forests; 6,706,938 in national parks and monuments; 214,-471 acres reserved for power sites and withdrawn for power site classification; 32,370 acres reserved for air navigation sites; 23,000,000 acres in military and naval reserves; 48,000,-000 acres in the northern Alaska

Petroleum Reserve; 15,000 acres in lighthouse reservations; 2,339,950 acres in Indian and native reservations; 13,800,840 in game and bird refuges; 9,000,000 acres in highway and railway reservations; 253,440 acres in the Matanuska colonization project; 270,000 acres patented under various public land laws; and

WHEREAS, there is a total of 151,-482,909 acres of reserved land in the Territory of Alaska with plans underway for further withdrawals at the direction of the Secretary of the Interior; and

WHEREAS, the Secretary of the Interior while publicly voicing a desire to aid and assist in populating the territory and developing its resources has, notwithstanding, followed a persistent course to the contrary, and through questionable interpretation of his powers has withdrawn vast areas of land and water from the public domain and prohibited their use and development and the welfare of its people; and

WHEREAS, a continuation of such a policy will lead to placing most of Alaska in reservations and curb its development and the welfare of its people; and

WHEREAS, it has been through the years the announced policy in connection with public lands in the nation to make them available to the people, thus building a great and virile nation of strong and independent people; and

WHEREAS, the actions of the present Secretary of the Interior, the Honorable Harold L. Ickes, are in direct conflict with this policy;

NOW, THEREFORE, your Memorialist, the Legislature of the Territory of Alaska in Seventeenth regular session assembled, respectfully petitions the Congress of the United States through its proper committee to immediately investigate the policies of the Secretary of the Interior relating to land withdrawals in Alaska that relief may be granted from the ever-growing burden resulting from his policies, and that copies of this memorial be sent to the President of the Senate, the Speaker of the House of Representatives, the Honorable E. L. Bartlett, Delegate to Congress from Alaska; the Public Lands and Surveys Committee of the Senate and the Public Lands Committee of the House of Representatives.

AND YOUR MEMORIALIST WILL EVER PRAY.

Passed by the Senate, February 13, 1945.

Passed by the House, March 15, 1945.

Session Laws of Alaska, 1945, pp. 188-9.

[16] Senator Hugh Butler, R., of Nebraska, Chairman of the Senate Committee on Interior and Insular Affairs in the Eightieth and Eighty-third Congresses, and its ranking minority member in the Eighty-first and Eighty-second, after visiting Alaska with a subcommittee in the summer of 1947, reported:

". . . Nearly every place we went in Alaska were cases where individuals had been trying to get title to land anywhere from twenty to thirty-five years, and they had not yet secured it." Feb. 24, 1948. 80 C: 2 s, *Sen.*

Hearings before Subcommittee of Committee on Interior and Insular Affairs on S. 2037 and H.J. Res. 162, p. 187.

[17] Detailed examples of homesteaders' and other would-be land-users' difficulties with "arbitrary and fickle rulings" are found in the testimony, October 28, 1949, of Charles Herning, Joseph C. Kruger and Carl Lindstrand, all of Steel Creek Road in the Fairbanks area, and of Earl N. Ohmer, of Petersburg, November 4, 1949, in *Hearings . . . on H.R. 1515*, Pt. 2, 81 C: 1 s, pp. 172-77, 177-79, 188-89 and 454-55.

[18] In the fiscal year 1953 the bureau's two Alaska offices at Anchorage and Fairbanks issued a total of 760 patents. They included 177 homesteads, 292 "small tracts" and the remainder under a variety of acts. As of June 30, 1953, 2,406 "small tract" leases were in effect, thirty-five grazing leases totalling 811,463 acres, 1,053 unperfected homestead entries covering 159,750 acres. The extensive suburban development of Anchorage has in the last ten years passed from public domain into private ownership.

[19] The total of U.S. Land Surveys is made up as follows:

Rectangular surveys.	
Public land	1,637,331.25 acres
Coal land	286,476.54
Coal land within Chugach National Forest	35,301.92
Chugach National Forest exclusive of coal lands	4,881.63
Tongass National Forest	185,487.96
* Reservations	174,401.95
Glacier Bay National Monument	8,979.96
Special surveys	
* Reserved land	81,530.95
** Public land	74,568.65
	2,470,960.80

* Does not include land grants to schools.
** Does not include Mount McKinley National Park or Forest elimination surveys.

[20] In the Eighty-third Congress the House took no action on general land legislation and the Senate Committee on Interior and Insular Affairs failed to act on two land bills for Alaska which had passed the House. The Anchorage *Times*, under the heading, "Congress Neglects Alaska" on August 10, 1953 editorialized as follows:

"One of the factors that makes statehood for Alaska an everlasting issue that will not die, is the continual failure of Congress to meet its responsibilities under the territorial relationship. . . .

"For the last eighty-five years the United States has tried unsuccessfully to administer the territory from Washington. History shows that it has been ineffective. There is no indication that the situation will improve.

"While Senators are expressing concern over whether Alaska is ready for statehood, Alaskans have good reason to be concerned with whether the United States is ready to govern the territory.

"Congress fails repeatedly in providing the legislation necessary for Alaskans to live under the American system. The Congress that adjourned last week was no exception. . . .

"Two dismaying instances in which the neglect of Alaska was demonstrated are in the files of the Senate Interior Committee. That group allowed two land bills to lie dormant that would have aided immeasurably in meeting current problems.

"One bill would have extended the Small Tract Act to unsurveyed lands. The committee failed to allow the measure to go to the Senate floor for enactment.

"Existing law provides for the sale of five-acre tracts from surveyed lands in the public domain. There is no authority for the sale or lease of unsurveyed lands. The proposed law would have authorized the Interior Department to negotiate leases for homes, cabins, camps, health, convalescent, recreational or business sites in unsurveyed areas.

"Rep. Miller of Nebraska, Chairman of the House committee that recommended enactment, declared that the existing law 'is of little practical application since most of Alaska is unsurveyed.' He also noted that the new law would involve no expenditure of federal funds.

"During the final days of Congress, Alaska's delegate appeared before the committee urging that the measure be taken to the floor of the Senate for enactment. It had already passed the House.

"The Senators listened to the delegate's plea. There was no opposition to the measure. But they did nothing.

"Another piece of legislation got the same treatment from the same committee. It would have authorized the Interior Department to negotiate for the sale of certain lands to organizations such as churches and Boy Scouts. This bill had no opposition. It would have eliminated the necessity for Congress to pass a special law for each such sale. . . .'"

CHAPTER 24

[1] February 21, 1911. Copper River and Northwestern Railway. 61 C: 3 s, H. of R. *Hearings before Comm. on Terr.*, pp. 57-8.

[2] An outstanding exception was the bombardment and destruction of three Indian villages in southeastern Alaska by the U.S.S. *Saginaw*, under orders by Brigadier General Jefferson C. Davis. It followed the killing by Kake Indians of two prospectors in atonement for the unpunished killing of two tribesmen by U.S. Army sentries. There were no further casualties, the Indians having fled at the warship's approach.

[3] Typical was the statement in 1890 of John Gardner, a trader in the Shumagin Islands and a resident of western Alaska since 1871, who had come to Sitka as a grand-jury witness. Gardner recounted in detail the murder of one John Brown, a worker in a cod fishery at Unga by a man known as "Russian Pete." The murderer continued to work on Unga Island as a coal digger. No effort had been made to arrest him, although Gardner reported the crime to every United States official that he met and "even pointed out the miscreant." Gardner reported that four other murders had been committed along the Aleutian chain during the ten previous years for which no one had

been arrested. Sitka *Alaskan*, November 15, 1890.

The difficulties of law enforcement were revealed in an interview with a long-time Alaskan resident, Edward H. Brown, as follows:

". . . Under the organic act . . . the judicial officers of this vast territory are a United States judge, marshal, clerk of court and United States attorney, all stationed at Sitka; a United States commissioner at Sitka, Juneau, Wrangell and Ounalaska. With this vast army of officers crime was . . . to be wiped out in Alaska. But something seemed lacking. A murder is committed at Kodiak. A month or two later a sailing vessel arrives. The murder is reported and on its return to San Francisco word is sent to the deputy marshal at Ounalaska, also by sailing vessel, or possibly a revenue cutter or steamer of the Alaska Commercial Company, which makes semi-annual trips. He then reports to his chief at Sitka, via San Francisco, and if the vessels are not lost in the course of a year or so, he may get a warrant for the arrest of the malefactor. If he is in haste to arrest him, he will take the first vessel for San Francisco, thence to Kodiak—as this is the shortest and usually the only route between the ports. If he is lucky enough to find the man still alive he will arrest him; and by this time the last vessel for the season having probably sailed, he and his prisoner will wait quietly another six months, when by schooner and steamer by way of San Francisco and Puget Sound, prisoner and marshal may arrive at Sitka to find that in the three or four years there has been a change of administration, the case forgotten, and the deputy marshal salted for all his expenses. . . ." Sitka *Alaskan*, December 27, 1890.

[4] Evans, Robley D., *A Sailor's Log: Recollections of Forty Years of Naval Life*, p. 341.

[5] Under the heading "United States Commissioners," Governor Brady's 1904 report declared:

"These officers in Alaska . . . can sit as committing magistrates; as justices of the peace to try civil cases where the amount involved is $1,000 or less; can try criminal cases, and . . . sentence to a year's imprisonment; they are clothed with full authority as probate judges; they act as coroners,, notaries, and recorders of precincts; they are appointed by the judges and receive fees for compensation. There is, really, no appeal from a commissioner's court to the district court, for the judge usually appoints some particular protégé, and feels bound to sustain his man. It is noticed that the appointments to nearly all the places which pay best are filled by persons who are peculiarly related, socially or politically, to the judge. The attorneys and their clients understand this and say: What is the use to appeal? There is a way out of this, by providing that the governor may appoint these officers. The judge cannot then be suspected of anxiety to sustain the wrong or arbitrary doings of a commissioner. The officer will know that his acts are liable to be reviewed at any time by a judge who has no particular concern for him.

"The fee system, as it is practiced in the commissioners' courts, is an abomination. It works against the public peace and welfare to clothe an officer with such great authority and have him depend on fees for compensation. Unless there is trouble how can he live? Trouble breeders are really the welcomed visitors at his court. The judiciary committees of both Houses of Congress should take up the matter of commissioners for Alaska and amend the law for their appointment and compensation. The fees are too high for the services rendered. The good of the community will be better served by placing commissioners and deputy marshals on salaries. One commissioner in the Kayak district was not content to charge the high legal rate for recording but charged a flat rate of $5 for nearly every kind of instrument. His extortion amounted to thousands of dollars, for the locations for coal and oil lands have been very numerous.

While this officer has been removed from the commissionership he has not been made to disgorge the amount taken illegally, and still more wonderful he has been appointed assistant United States attorney at that place."

[6] In the Fifty-eighth Congress a constabulary was included in S. 6383, a bill providing for a part appointive, part elective governing board for Alaska. In reporting the bill favorably for the Committee on Territories, Senator Charles H. Dietrich, R., of Nebraska, wrote: "The bill also provided that there shall be established a constabulary to be patterned largely after the Canadian mounted police. . . . No better or more efficient body of men can be found in the world, and such a system ought to be put in operation in Alaska." The bill, however, failed to pass either house.

[7] Stuck, Hudson, *Ten Thousand Miles with a Dog Sled*, p. 364. Archdeacon Stuck's further comment is as applicable today as it was forty years ago: "One would have supposed that among all the legislating that has been done for and about Alaska in the last year or two, one crying evil that the attention of successive administrations has been called to . . . would have been remedied. That evil is the unpaid magistrate and the vicious fee system by which he must make a living. It is a system that has been abolished in nearly all civilized countries; a system that lends itself to all sorts of abuse; a system that no one pretends to defend. No greater single step in advance could be made in the government of Alaska, no measure could be enacted that would tend to bring about in greater degree respect for the law than the abolition of the unpaid magistracy and the setting up of a body of stipendiaries of character and ability. . . . The district court is compelled to wink at irregularities of life and conduct in its commissioners because it cannot get men of a higher stamp to accept its appointments."

[8] A flagrant example was that of the United States Commissioner at Kotzebue who in 1946 co-operated with two locally well-known white businessmen to defraud an Eskimo of his jade mining claims, in which as a means of carrying out their purpose, the Eskimo was further victimized by being arrested, falsely charged with stealing property, improperly convicted, and sentenced to jail in the Commissioner's court. The conspiracy was investigated by George W. Folta, then Counsel-at-large for the Department of the Interior, and fully reported to it under the heading: "Report on Arrest and Prosecution of Charlie Sheldon."

These men sought also to "frame" an Army officer, Major Marvin R. Marston, to make him appear guilty of larceny of a piece of jade, because apprised of the attempt to defraud other Eskimos of their jade claims, he had vigorously espoused their cause. The commissioner was removed from office by Judge Kehoe of the Second Judicial Division as soon as the facts were brought to his attention.

Folta pointed out that these businessmen were in the habit of ingratiating themselves with any new appointee to the office of deputy U. S. marshal or commissioner by extending favors of various kinds. "Since there are very few white people in a town like Kotzebue," reported Folta, "it is not difficult for a lonely United States commissioner, depending on fees for compensation, or for a United States deputy marshal, to find themselves under obligations to and under the influence of these men." Folta's reports, dated July 30 and 31, 1946, are printed in *Hearings on S. 2037*, 80 C: 2 s, pp. 215-221.

The mulcting of Indians in southeastern Alaska by United States commissioners, who built up their incomes by levying heavy fines for offenses either negligible or nonexistent, had been detailed over forty years earlier by Lt. George T. Emmons, U.S.N. His report, transmitted to Congress by President Theodore Roosevelt in January, 1905, was printed as a Senate document. (*Doc. 106 58 C: 3 s.*)

[9] 80 C: 1 s, H. of R. *Hearing before*

Subcommittee on Territorial and In-sular Possessions of Committee on Public Lands on H.R. 1239, May 12, 1947.

[10] Some of Mrs. Harrais's further comments merit repeating:

"The importance of having men of integrity to hold government positions in the far-flung nuclei of civilization in our Alaska wildernesses cannot be emphasized too strongly. Often there is only one officer to uphold law and order and advance civilization. In the local eyes *he is the government*. If honest men cannot hold the position and make a living it does not take a prophet to tell us that the service will not be good. It will either be a sideline for someone who is pushing his own private business, or fall into the hands of incompetents, or crooks. You do not get something for nothing very long in any business relation. Why expect it from the Commissioner's office?

"I have been a U. S. commissioner for two and a half years. During that time I have listened to about every phase of human relationships. People come into the office and usually begin, 'I do not know whether anything can be done.' Right there the office may be a peacemaker or a trouble breeder. The stories told are usually of neighbors' misunderstandings and disagreements. Nine times out of ten these disagreements can be ironed out amicably, but by so doing, the Commissioner talks himself out of a fee—no trouble, no fees. The temptation is obvious. I am alone, so it is not so hard to teach them that a soft answer turneth away wrath and send them home to settle their differences without litigation; but if you have a family to fend for, if you are facing another Alaskan winter and last winter's coal bill is yet unpaid, if your wife needs a new coat and Johnnie's tonsils should be removed, what would you do? You would either jump the job, or decide to wait until next spring to begin the role of peacemaker.

"The fee system is pernicious from every angle. I do not see how its psychology could be worse. All the other federal and territorial officers are provided with salaries, office rooms and expenses. We must provide our own office and pay for its heating and lighting (no small item in Alaska), rustle our own compensation 'catch as catch can,' and do a great deal of work for both federal and territorial governments for which we receive no compensation at all, and pay for the stationery and stamps with which to do it. The Commissioner has not even franking privilege for official business. . . ."

[11] Report of Assistant Attorney-General Norman M. Littell to Attorney-General. If carried out at that time Mr. Littell's recommendation would have cost the federal government $139,200 annually, minus the amount of the fees collected.

[12] *Rept. of Special Assistant to the Attorney General, Joseph W. Kehoe, to the Attorney General.*

[13] S.J.M. 21, February 19, 1945.

[14] In all but the few larger cities, the survey revealed, the commissioners are perforce compelled to seek other income, or take on the commissionership as a side line to employment sufficiently remunerative for a livelihood. A few already have other sources of income when they accept the commissionership.

One commissioner, whose fees are about $250 a year, draws a monthly World War II veteran's disability pension of $31.50; cuts and hauls wood; does a little mining, and receives financial help from brothers and sisters in the East.

Another commissioner combines that duty with the postmastership; draws U. S. Army retirement pay; tags beaver skins at 10 cents each.

Another "gets by" because he is an automotive mechanic at a nearby air base which employs him five days a week. He holds court evenings and week-ends.

Various commissioners are not only postmaster but also agents for the Territorial Department of Taxation, for the Department of Public Welfare, and for the Fish and Wildlife Service which also pay on a fee basis. One, a woman whose income from the commissionership is about $1,500 a year, finds these multiple duties so time-consuming that her husband is occasionally appointed Special Commissioner, but works for nothing, his regular income being derived from operating a bulldozer.

One, in a precinct where the commissionership is a full-time job, makes more as a fisherman than as a commissioner, although his fishing earnings are reduced by the time required by his federal duties. Several commissioners depend on fishing for extra income.

Some commissioners write insurance but are conscious that that may conflict with the proper performance of their official duties. One commissioner writes a policy when requested, but feels he cannot solicit the business since the purchaser might consider that the commissioner was under obligation to him—an embarrassing situation should he be haled before the court for some minor offense or be party to a suit in the commissioner's court.

Some commissioners are storekeepers who derive their livelihood from that source, and take on the commissionership only from a sense of public obligation. Civic duty needs to be a strong motive with commissioners because they are consulted concerning such varied subjects as selective service, income tax, civilian defense, fisheries regulations, game laws and any and all governmental matters generally. Not the least of the problems on which advice is sought are personal. All of these services they are expected to render gratis.

"Most of the home folks expect their local justice to have the time and the common sense to help them settle difficulties, which if not settled at home would lead to long, expensive cases in our already overcrowded District Court," writes a highly respected commissioner in a small coastal community.

"It is after all the only connection that any of the people have with the judiciary," writes another, "and I am sorry to say it is not always the quality the people have a right to expect."

While the majority of commissioners are devoted, and imbued with a sense of public responsibility, their own personal financial problems pose a real difficulty. One, whose income from the commissionership is about $1,600 annually, is stopped from securing steady additional income because of the need to be available when people want him. So he is limited to part-time labor jobs near home.

With one exception every commissioner heard from believed that a salary or a minimum guarantee should be substituted for the present system. The exception—a commissioner with other "steady income"—felt that fees actually earned for services rendered constituted a fair basis of compensation, but suggested that the way to increase the compensation was to increase the fees. A number of commissioners, however, felt that the present scale of fees was already unduly high and constitute burdensome charges against the public.

Many commissioners cite that they have to pay out of their own pockets for their office equipment, files, typewriter, stationery, and stamps, as well as heat and light for their offices. These, in some cases, total more than their fees. One states that the position today in his village is "actually the butt of local jokes," and that "up to the present time every yokel in town has been the commissioner."

One commissioner is the teacher in a village where the preceding teachers have also been the commissioners. Here the school janitor gets $50 a month, common labor $1.75 an hour, but the average earning of the commissioner for work requiring two full evenings a week, is about $5 monthly. He points out that as teachers change frequently, the commissionership is handled by inexperienced newcomers.

One of the troublesome consequences of the commissioner system with its frequent changes of incumbents and the resulting lack of experience is the faultiness of the records.

"A poor commissioner can work havoc in the real-property records, and to correct his mistakes is extremely costly to the property owners," writes one.

Some commissioners with a bent for detail and accuracy often uncover scores of errors made by predecessors. One who happened to be in office for a number of years had found and corrected over a hundred. In other offices errors go uncorrected with unfortunate results years afterwards when an estate is probated or a sale of property is undertaken.

"A working knowledge of real-property law is essential to proper recording of an instrument," comments one commissioner. But few commissioners have such knowledge either about real-estate law or any other law. While legal training should be a prerequisite to appointment under a proper conception of a judicial system, it is not required and is clearly unattainable under the fee system."

"Considering the actual time one spends at this work," writes one commissioner, "the compensation would average 5 cents an hour."

One outstanding commissioner whose precinct covers several thousand square miles relates chartering a boat to travel a hundred miles by water to conduct an inquest, an inescapable duty where there is a presumption of foul play:

"I . . . took with me a physician, a deputy marshal and a stenographer. The boat owner received $35 per day; the physician $5 per day; jurymen, $4 for about two hours of their time; witnesses, $2 for about twenty minutes of their time; I spent three days on the trip and an entire day of office work, for which I received the government fee of $8—$2 per day. Even the roustabout on the boat received two and a half times as much as the commissioner."

[15] "Judge Harding's appointment was confirmed today by the Senate, and we have a judge again after nearly a year's delay," Wickersham noted in his diary, January 15, 1929, concern-

ing the First Division judgeship.

[16] Organic Act of Hawaii, Sec. 81.

[17] *Ibid.*, Sec. 82. Hawaii also has two United States District Judges who try cases that are purely federal, as in the forty-eight states.

[18] Constitution of the Commonwealth of Puerto Rico. Art. V, Secs. 1, 2, 8.

[19] Governor Strong reported this situation in 1916 and 1917. In the latter report he wrote:

"In the annual report of this office for the fiscal year 1916 reference was made to the commission of capital crimes, especially in the remote regions of the territory, and it was stated that in many cases the perpetrators have never been apprehended, due in part at least to the lack of funds to investigate such cases, the United States marshals' offices having no moneys at their command which can be used in ferreting out crime and bringing the offenders to the bar of justice. Under the system which prevails, should the United States marshal's office hear of a crime committed at any distance from the courthouse, an investigation can not be made until someone has filed an information and a warrant has been issued. Only then can expenses which must be incurred be authorized. Because of this many murders committed in the past few years are still unsolved mysteries."

[20] Chap. 65, S.L.A., 1941.

[21] 82 C: 1 s, H.R. 5135.

[22] Chapter 144, S. L. A. 1953.

CHAPTER 25

[1] Subcommittee of House Committee on Interior and Insular Affairs, *Rept.* 2503, pursuant to H.R. 698, 82 C: 2 s, December 15, 1952.

[2] However, the thirty-five pages devoted to Indians out of his 91-page 1885 report reveal a striking contrast between the peaceableness of the Alaskan aborigines—who are not mentioned—and those in the West, *viz:*

"On the 17th of last May Indian agent Ford telegraphed this department that fifty Chiricahua bucks from among those under exclusive military control . . . had broken away and left the reservation. . . . This band of Indians, which altogether is reported at less than two hundred, including men, women and children, escaped to the neighboring mountains and thence to Mexico without being overtaken by the United States troops who were sent to capture them. Their track was marked by murder, rapine, burning of homes, and horrible cruelties upon defenseless women and children. Not less than seventeen persons were killed in Arizona and New Mexico from the beginning of the outbreak. . . ."

However there were other disturbances of different origin, *viz.*:

"Another exception to the general order and peace among the Indians arose in the case of the Southern Utes almost simultaneously with the occurrences just referred to. The cause of the disturbance, upon investigation, was found to be the oft-recurring one of short rations. No game is on the reservation, and to prevent starvation the agent had given several small parties permission to go to the mountains to hunt. A camp of eleven of these Indians reached a point forty miles north of their reservation, where about daylight on the morning of the 19th of June, they were attacked by a party of about twenty white men, who killed six Indians (three males, two squaws and one child) and wounded two other Indians."

Next the Secretary's report dealt with the Cheyennes:

"The Cheyenne Indians, whose reservations, with the Arapahoes, lie in the western portion of Indian Territory, have for a year manifested a restless and turbulent temper, which threatened for a time to develop into open hostilities. . . ." Pp. 4, 5, 6.

There is no mention of Alaskan Indians in the 1886 report, but Secretary Lamar stated his belief that "the desired policy of the government in reference to our Indian population . . . the incorporation of the Indian race into our political and social system as citizens," cannot be attained

without "some radical changes in our Indian policy." He listed three essential changes: "First, installation of a system of individual property holding; second, education . . . in English, in the daily affairs of life, mechanical arts among the males, and domestic arts among the females; third, a system of law and order among them." P. 4.

[3] *Condition and Needs of the Natives of Alaska,* 58 C: 3 s, Sen. Doc. 106.

[4] *Rept. of the Secretary of the Interior,* 1905.

[5] *Ibid.*

[6] *Governor's Rept.,* 1915.

[7] *Rept. of the Secretary of the Interior,* 1905.

[8] *Rept. of Secy. of the Interior,* 1906.

[9] *Ibid.,* 1908.

[10] Wickersham's diary contains the following notation: "Attended Alaska Native Brotherhood meeting . . . and spoke for an hour on the civil rights of the Indians. I denounced Indian reservations and urged them to become citizens of the United States under the Indian Severalty Act of 1887 [General Allotment Act] as soon as possible. It seems the leaders of the Brotherhood are much opposed to reservations, while the Bureau of Education . . . favor reservations because reservations mean officials and jobs while the other plan means independent citizenship which the Indians want. My talk last night was simply a plain statement of the law and the road that leads to becoming a citizen of the U.S. and seemed very satisfactory to the Indian men. The officials tried to heckle me with questions and to muddy the waters—but with no success." November 20, 1921.

[11] Cohen, Felix S., A *Handbook of Indian Law,* 1941.

[12] *Letter of Secretary of the Interior Harold L. Ickes to Hon. Will Rogers, Chairman, House Committee on Indian Affairs, March 14, 1936.* 74 C: 2 s, H. of R. *Rept.* 2244.

[13] An excellent study of the earlier and present uses of land, water and their resources by the people of three southeastern communities, Kake, Klawaock and Hydaburg, made in connection

with these claims, is Goldschmidt, Dr. Walter R., and Haas, Theodore H. *Possessory Rights of the Natives of Southeastern Alaska*, made as a report to the Commissioner of Indian Affairs, October 3, 1946.

[14] The Margold opinion (M. 31,634) is found in *Hearings . . . on S. 2037 . . . and H.J. Res. 162*, pp. 415-26.

[15] *Hearings . . . on S. 2037*, pp. 426-33.

[16] *Ibid.*, pp. 434-9.

[17] H.R. 6301, January 8, 1930.

[18] March 11, 1932. *Hearing . . . on S. 1196*, 72 C: 1 s, pp. 13-15.

[19] *Ibid.*, p. 4. Wickersham's testimony, March 23, 1932, pp. 4-13, presents an exhaustive justification of the case for compensation of the natives of southeastern Alaska.

[20] The divergence between the policies which Secretary Ickes had declared he would follow when he was seeking congressional approval of the act of May 1, 1936, and the policies he then inaugurated, was repeatedly called to his attention in memoranda by the writer. Ickes's policies and performance in this field and in other relations to Alaska can be only briefly alluded to in this work for lack of space, but will be fully treated in a subsequent volume dealing in more detail with the last twenty years of United States rule in Alaska.

[21] *Hearings on H.J. Res. 205*, p. 8. May 26, 1947. 80 C: 1 s, H. of R.

[22] *Ibid.*, p. 2.

[23] War Production Board order L–208, October 8, 1942. It remained in effect till July 1, 1945, when it was rescinded.

[24] *Hearings . . . on H.J. Res. 205*, p. 3.

[25] June 14, 1947. *Ibid.*, pp. 67, 81.

[26] U.S. vs. 10.95 acres of land. No. 4090 A. March 11, 1948. 75 F. Supp. 841.

[27] March 5, 1948. *Hearings . . . on S. 2037 . . . and S.J. Res. 162*. 80 C: 2 s, p. 509.

[28] Press Releases, Dept. of the Interior Information Service, November 30, 1949.

[29] In 1945 Frank Peratrovich, probably the outstanding leader among the native people of southeastern Alaska, for years an officer of the Alaska Native Brotherhood, and subsequently elected its president, the first native to be elected to the territorial senate, and at that time President of the Alaska Purse Seiners' Union, testified:

"I made a statement at the last session of the legislature that I was against any form of reservation. . . . I don't think that is the solution to our problems here in Alaska; and by Alaska, I'm not only speaking for the native population; I'm speaking for everyone who has seen fit to adopt this country for his home. And I maintain, as far as the First and Third Divisions are concerned, that the solution to the problem of the existing conditions is the elimination of fish traps," adding subsequently, "I'd like to stress the point again that I think the solution to everything here, the problems of the Indians as well as the others, is dependent on fishing." Ketchikan, August 4, 1945. *Hearings before the Committee on Territories of the House of Representatives, pursuant to H.Res. 236*, 79 C: 1 s, pp. 33-4, 37.

[30] In fact, four years earlier, on February 23, 1946, at hearings in the Department of the Interior on a proposed amendment to the fishing regulations to limit any one company's holdings to twenty traps, which would have compelled the larger companies to give up more than half of theirs, and their top executives appeared in force to protest, an owner of a cannery which had no traps who had been brought on from Seattle as a star witness, testified against the proposal. When asked whether he would accept one of the traps of which the larger companies might have to divest themselves, he declared emphatically that the procedure would be un-American and against the principles he had fought for on Iwo Jima and Tarawa. Red faces followed the production by a department official of a letter which the witness had written Secretary Ickes two weeks earlier asking that some of the trap sites to be redistributed be allocated to him.

CHAPTER 26

[1] *Hearings . . . on H.R. 5205, 73 C: 2 s*, p. 11.

[2] "Since the adoption of the White Law of June 6, 1924, there has been steady and unmistakable progress in true conservation of the fisheries of Alaska. The most ardent critic is forced to concede that excellent results have been achieved in building up the runs of salmon in various parts of the territory. It will be my purpose to faithfully continue a policy of conservation which will mean the fullest possible use and development of the fisheries of Alaska consistent with their continuance in perpetuity." Frank T. Bell, Commissioner of Fisheries, April 11, 1934 in memorandum transmitted by Assistant Secretary of Commerce. *Hearings . . . on H.R. 5205, A bill to Transfer the Jurisdiction over the Alaska Fisheries to the Territory of Alaska.* 73 C: 2 s, p. 3.

"Wise regulations to meet conservation needs have been promulgated, and the fisheries have reached and are maintaining a high level of productivity. Continuation of this control will mean adequate protection and conservation of the fisheries and will add to the wealth and prosperity of Alaska and the people residing there." Ward T. Bower, Chief, Division of Alaska Fisheries, Bureau of Fisheries, April 11, 1934. *Ibid.*, p. 66.

"The fisheries of Alaska are in fine condition." Frank T. Bell, Commissioner of Fisheries, February 4, 1935, in letter to Secretary of Commerce Daniel C. Roper. *Hearings . . . on H.R. 4254 and H.R. 8213, Bills to Abolish Fish Traps and Limit the Lengths of Seines.* 74 C: 1 s and 2 s, p. 3.

"I think I made it clear that as a result of the White Act in 1924, the bureau was given further and more effective control, and the conservation angle has been accomplished, and they get a larger production without any harm to the streams, or the future runs." J. M. Gilbert, of Seattle, representing the Alaska-Pacific Salmon

Co. (owning eleven canneries in Alaska), January 16, 1936. *Ibid.*, p. 128.

". . . there are more fish on Prince William Sound, more pink salmon on Prince William Sound than there were in the days before commercial fishing was commenced here. It is also true of every salmon-producing area in the Territory of Alaska." W. C. Arnold, representing Alaska Salmon Canners, September 6, 1939. *Hearings . . . on H.Res. 162, A Resolution Authorizing a Study of the Fisheries of Alaska*, p. 332. 76 C: 1 s.

"But the fact of the matter is salmon in Alaskan waters are more plentiful than they were before the introduction of fish traps thirty years ago. The annual runs are stabilizing, and generally speaking, on an upward trend." Edward W. Allen, of Allen, Froude & Hilen, of Seattle, and W. C. Arnold, in brief "on behalf of 95 per cent of the Alaska Salmon Canners," September 14, 1929. *Ibid.*, p. 894.

". . . when the White bill became a law and went into effect right away we raised the dickens. We said we are going to have a man that is going to tell us when and where to start fishing and when it is to end. We all thought that was terrible. I, for one, was against it. As time went on we discovered as we learned more about it that the White bill was our savior. I truthfully can say today if the White bill did not become a law in 1924 today we would hardly have any commercial fishing in Alaska." Nick Bez, of Seattle, cannery operator. January 21, 1944. *Hearings . . . on S. 930, A Bill to Assure Conservation of and to Permit the Fullest Utilization of the Fisheries of Alaska*, p. 102. 78 C: 2 s.

[3] "I want to emphasize . . . that much more money could have been spent wisely in the proper policing of the fisheries than we were able to spend. We did the best we could with the funds available." Ward T. Bower, April 11, 1934. *Hearings . . . on H.R. 5205.* 73 C: 2 s, p. 66.

"The Bureau of Fisheries should receive additional appropriations so that it may provide for more effective patrol and that it may conduct adequate research upon which to base its regulatory service." Allen, Froude & Hilen, and W. C. Arnold, October 11, 1939. Brief, preliminary summary, October 11, 1939, *Hearings . . . on H. Res. 162*, 76 C: 1 s, p. 887.

"The Bureau of Fisheries must of necessity have a larger appropriation in order to enforce regulations for the conservation of the salmon runs." Carl A. Sutter, President, Fidalgo Island Packing Co., October 13, 1939. *Hearings . . . on H. Res. 162*, p. 928.

". . . if we had the patrol facilities, the boats and personnel for adequately patrolling the fisheries of Alaska, the chances of illegally operating either fixed or mobile gear would be greatly reduced." Dr. Frederick Davidson, Director of Seattle Laboratory, Bureau of Fisheries, January 10, 1940. *Ibid.*, p. 1086.

"As is known very well to you, Mr. Chairman, the Bureau of Fisheries is handicapped on account of lack of finances." Nick Bez, cannery and trap operator, September 2, 1939. *Ibid.*, p. 146.

"THE CHAIRMAN. 'Yes; that is true.'" *Ibid.*, p. 147.

"It is true, we have never been able to get sufficient appropriations for the Bureau of Fisheries." Schuyler Otis Bland, Chairman, House Committee on Merchant Marine and Fisheries, September 11, 1939. *Ibid.*, p. 687.

". . . there is a pressing need for increased funds with which the Bureau of Fisheries can carry on its scientific work and administer the laws of the United States with respect to the Alaskan fisheries. . . . It is difficult to appreciate the volume and value of the fisheries of this immense territory. . . . The economic foundation of the territory is laid upon the productivity of its fisheries; but this is a natural resource. Proper scientific knowledge, as a basis for a sound conservation policy, and the welfare of the territory and its residents must precede profits, or coming generations will point to a vanished industry even as those of our day look with regret upon the once thriving fisheries of many of our coastal states which have now utterly disappeared, leaving the bitter memory of a penny wise and pound foolish policy." Subcommittee on Alaskan Fisheries of House Committee on Merchant Marine and Fisheries. June 5, 1940, *H. Rept. 2379*, 76 C: 3 s.

[4] Boyle's letter, dated January 29, 1934, but describing events in 1927, 1928 and 1929, was read into the record of the *Hearings . . . on H.R. 6175 and H.R. 7523*, February 21, 1936. 73 C: 2 s, pp. 11-14.

[5] H.R. 253, 71 C: 1 s, and H.R. 495, 72 C: 1 s.

[6] H.R. 3824, 73 C: 1 s; H.R. 7523, 73 C: 2 s; H.R. 156, 74 C: 1 s; H.R. 1565, 75 C: 1 s; H.R. 7542, 76 C: 2 s; H.R. 3960, 78 C: 2 s.

[7] *Hearings . . . on H.R. 7523*, February 21, 1934, p. 16. 73 C: 2 s.

[8] *Hearings . . . on H.R. 7542*, March 12, 1940, pp. 28-9. 76 C: 3 s.

[9] *Ibid.*, p. 35.

[10] *Hearings . . . on H.R. 7523*, pp. 8, 9. A different view on "the respect which has been created for such law and regulations" was expressed by George B. Case of Wrangell, President of the Alaska Salmon Purse Seiners Union:

"Fishing is our life. When the salmon come in the spring, they bring with them the promise of food and clothing for the winter. They buy our fuel. They fill our people with a bustling activity and make our communities thrive. They are our life, yet they are controlled by an outsider who, when he takes his position, knows nothing about them, and must learn from the ground up. His position is given him, not for his ability in this field, but for some reason better known to men in politics. His power is absolute. His every whim is law. He can control our progress; make or break our prosperity with a word. The spirit of any free people rebels at the thought. In any case where laws are made without the consent of the governed they breed contempt for themselves. A respect for laws as well as for people cannot be demanded; it must be inspired." September 10, 1939, *Hearings . . . on H.Res. 162*, pp. 554-5.

[11] *Hearings . . . on H.Res. 162*, p. 887.

[12] The regulatory power over Alaska's fisheries was transferred from the Department of Commerce to the Department of the Interior, July 1, 1939 (53 Stat. 1431). Amalgamation of what had been the Bureau of Fisheries of the Department of Commerce and what had been the Biological Survey of the Department of Agriculture under the name of Fish and Wildlife Service took place June 30, 1940 (54 Stat. 230).

[13] Testimony as to nominal fines imposed on the larger canning companies for illegal trap fishing was introduced by Delegate Sutherland in *Hearings . . . on H.R. 2714*, 68 C: 1 s, p. 77.

Contrast between the heavier penalty imposed on two fishermen whose guilt was more than doubtful and who maintained their innocence, and the nominal fine imposed on an admittedly illegal trap operation is found in a communication to Delegate Dimond from Paul Jones, President, and Nick Zonick, Secretary, of the Alaska Seiners Association in *Hearings . . . on H.R. 7542*, 76 C: 3 s, pp. 31-2.

[14] Mr. Edward Coffey of Anchorage, a former fisherman, in 1939 a member of the Territorial legislature, so testified September 1, 1939. *Hearings . . . on H.J.Res. 162*, pp. 25-33. Mr. W. C. Arnold, representing the industry, confirmed this, stating that "the Alaska Fishermen's Union of San Francisco forced the operators to pay a penalty of one-third of the cost of the fish at that time. At that time it was 12 cents . . . and the operators had to pay a penalty of 4 cents a fish to the Alaska Fishermen's union of San Francisco for every fish caught by a resident." He condemned this practice as "certainly not a very ethical thing." *Ibid.*, p. 55.

[15] *Ibid.*, p. 25. A "line" of cannery machinery is the equivalent of the assembly line in an automobile factory. By it the whole raw fish brought in by a conveyor belt are processed into the final canned product. Canneries have from one to five lines.

[16] *Ibid.*, p. 36.

[17] *Ibid.*, p. 30.

[18] *Ibid.*, p. 44. Similar discrimination against Alaskans desiring employment in the construction of Alaskan naval bases, beginning in 1939, was established by a contract drawn up between thirty-one Seattle American Federation of Labor building trades unions and Puget Sound contractors with the sanction of the United States Navy Department. The attendant circumstances and the struggle to remove this discrimination will be treated in a subsequent volume.

[19] The extensive investigation of Alaska fisheries, conducted in 1939-40 by a special Subcommittee on Alaskan fisheries of the House Committee on Merchant Marine and Fisheries, before which the above and subsequently cited testimony was given, originated in House Concurrent Resolution No. 1 of the 1939 territorial legislature which requested an investigation of the fisheries by a congressional committee, to be accompanied by a standing committee of the legislature. The resolution appropriated $10,000 to cover the expenses of the territorial committee. Delegate Dimond thereupon secured the passage of H. Res. 162 in the first session of the Seventy-sixth Congress. Hearings in Anchorage, Kodiak, Sitka, Juneau, Petersburg, Wrangell, Craig, Ketchikan, Seattle and Washington recorded the testimony of 164 witnesses and depositions, affidavits, briefs from others, which filled 1136 printed pages. A lengthy report (*H. Rept.* 2379, 76 C: 3 s) was issued June 5, 1940. (It was reprinted in *Hearings . . . on H. Res. 38*, pp. 71-113. 79 C: 3 s.)

The report consisted largely of summaries of the testimony and a few recommendations either on noncontroversial matters or couched in noncommittal terms. The committee's overall conclusion was:

"The problems affecting the industry are perplexing and no specific remedy can be found for them."

On fish traps, which the text of H. Res. 162 had named as the first subject of "special reference" to be investigated, and had consumed, the committee reported, "75 to 90 per cent of the time," the recommendation began as follows:

"Your committee believes that a review of the evidence and arguments submitted, and a casual perusal of the testimony, will demonstrate that it is impossible for your committee after a study of a few weeks, to say definitely that all traps should be abolished, the time and manner of abolition, or which traps should go, if some but not all should be abolished.

"We feel it would be great temerity on our part to recommend total abolition immediately or by any prescribed program. The matter is one for scientific study and for administrative effort to reconcile conflicting interests. It will require far more time and facilities than have been at our disposal to prescribe a remedy. . . ."

There were six more paragraphs of the same tenor. The closest approach to specific recommendations on this subject were:

"Your committee feels that trap sites should not be assignable or transferable, and traps should be removable at any time for failure to comply with the regulations, to obey the law, or to follow conditions imposed by the permit."

(No action to validate the committee's feeling in any of these respects followed. Traps continued to be assignable and transferable, and were not removed for violations.)

On fishermen's gear seizure before trial, the committee recommended:

"We agree that some better procedure should be provided, and invitation will be extended to the Department of Justice to join with the Bureau of Fisheries and with our committee in framing legislation which will serve to enforce the law in a fair, just and equitable manner, and will

not punish first and try later."

(No action followed even to the extent of the joint drafting of such legislation.)

The committee concluded with: "Your committee is confident that the information obtained on its visit to Alaska will form the basis of improved conditions in the fisheries of Alaska. All who went on that trip have a better knowledge and clearer comprehension of the problem than ever before." The committee added that the report was preliminary and that at least one more report would be made. But none was made.

The result of the elaborate, time-consuming and costly investigation was therefore nil. It did not in any degree meet the hopes of the territorial memorialists who had initiated it, and did not correct what they termed the "unjustifiable and discriminatory policy employed by the Bureau of Fisheries officials," or the "evils and wrongs to which our people have been subjected on account of the maladministration of our fisheries by the bureau," or the "autocratic and dictatorial power" which those officials had "arrogated to themselves . . . not contemplated by the laws, to the detriment and irreparable injury of Alaska and her fisheries" and the consequent "intense and unnecessary privation and suffering among the fishing population and business people of Alaska." (H.C.R. No. 1, S.L.A. 1939, pp. 247-8.)

Nor was the committee's confidence that "improved conditions in the fisheries of Alaska" would be formed on the basis of the information it had obtained, borne out by the steady decline of that resource thenceforward.

[20] Reprinted in *Ibid.*, pp. 81-83, under the heading "Nonresident Fishermen Attempting to Starve Out Bristol Bay Fishermen," as it originally appeared in the Valdez *Miner*, July 17, 1936.

[21] H.R. 7987, H.R. 7988, and H.R. 8115. 76 C: 3 s, among others.

[22] Testimony of Representative Albert E. Carter, R., of Oakland, California, in *Hearings . . . on H.R. 7987, H.R. 7988 and H.R. 8155*, pp. 65-69, 76

C: 3 s, and protests inserted by Representative Richard J. Welch, R., of San Francisco, California, and Representative Monrad C. Wallgren, D., of Everett, Washington, pp. 138-42.

[23] April 7, 1938 (52 Stat. 208).

[24] *Hearings . . . on H.R.* 7987 *etc.*, p. 89.

[25] *Hearings . . . on H. Res.* 162, p. 1090.

[26] *Ibid.*, p. 846.

[27] *Ibid.*, p. 847.

[28] *Ibid.*, p. 848.

[29] *Ibid.*, p. 849.

[30] September 14, 1939. *Ibid.*, p. 862.

[31] *Ibid.*, p. 870.

[32] March 14, 1940. *Hearings . . . on H.R.* 7987, *etc.*, p. 87.

[33] The following fishermen testified to specific depletion in 1939. (The number after each name refers to the page in the printed testimony on H. Res. 162 where their testimony may be found: Harley Sharp, Shumagin Island, 124; Fred Kelm, Anchorage, 144; Peter Wolkoff, Kodiak, 241; Karl Brunstad, Kodiak (on herring depletion), 253; Mike Babic, Cordova, 280, 322-3; Louis Giska, Cordova, 285; J. R. Webber, Cordova, 288-9, 352-4; H. J. Lannen, Cordova, 291; Otto Tiedeman, Cordova, 298-9; Oscar Donaldson, Cordova, 299-302; Joseph Bernard, Cordova, 385; J. F. Krause, Ketchikan, 645; Roderick Davis, Metlakatla, 653; George Keegan, Ketchikan, 664; Frank G. Johnson, Kake, 678.

[34] The case packs for those years were: 1934, 7,481,830; 1935, 5,133,122; 1936, 8,437,603; 1937, 6,669,665; 1938, 6,806,998. Excepting 1935, the other four years had higher packs than any year previously.

[35] This peculiarity was discussed at a subsequent hearing:

"MR. GARDNER [Warner Gardner, Solicitor and later Assistant Secretary of the Department of the Interior]: 'To round out "property rights," which have grown up by custom and tradition around—property rights, I should add, should be in quotation marks—around the trap site, which have grown up by custom and tradition, these trap sites which are after all simply the right to use the public waters, can be sold and have frequently been sold, the average price in recent years being about $10,000 a site. An exceedingly good trap site has some years ago sold for as much as $100,000 which is, to our way of thinking, a large sum of money to pay somebody else for the privilege of using the public-domain property.

" 'They pass by inheritance. They cannot, however, as I understand the operating law of the territory, be reached by one's creditors, so they are on the whole a rather desirable form—'

"SENATOR MAGNUSON [Warren G. Magnuson, D., of Washington] 'In other words, you cannot slap a lien on a trap site?'

"MR. GARDNER. 'I understand a marshal once tried to levy on a trap site and was not allowed to do so. So it seems to be a property with all the advantages of property and none of the disadvantages.' " *Hearings . . . on S.1446,* 80 C: 1 s, p. 10.

[36] Elsewhere that year Delegate Dimond had fully stated the reasons for his opposition to salmon traps in Alaska, based on several grounds, but "the first and . . . the most powerful objection" lay in the fact "that they constitute a species of special privilege."

"The frame of a fixed or standing trap consists of piles driven into the ground underlying the shallow coastal waters. A floating trap is placed in such waters and is securely anchored to the bottom. In either case the operator of the trap has the special and exclusive privilege of fishing permanently for the entire season on the site so occupied. Every other fisherman is excluded therefrom. Since the power thus exercised is exclusive in its nature and cannot be secured by any other fisherman during the season and since the structure exclusively occupies and in fact seizes upon possession of a definite area of the sea, which should be open to the use of all fishermen, it is indeed a special privilege within the true definition of the term."

Since all existing sites for traps were already occupied and no citizen or other person could secure one, Delegate Dimond continued, he considered it a violation of the provision of the White Act forbidding granting exclusive rights. *Hearing . . . on H. Res. 162*, p. 12, 76 C: 1 s, September 1, 1939.

[37] *Hearings . . . on S.930*, 78 C: 2 s, pp. 9-17.

[38] *Ibid.*, pp. 62-85, 101-5.

[39] *Ibid.*, pp. 31-38.

[40] *Ibid.*, p. 39.

[41] *Ibid.*, p. 42.

[42] *Ibid.*, p. 87.

[43] See p. 393. Two bills with the same title and designed to achieve the trap objectives of S. 930 in their original draft had been previously introduced by Senator Wallgren, S. 1915 and S. 2227, in the first and second sessions of the Seventy-seventh Congress, but no hearings were held on them in view of the known attitude of the new director of the Fish and Wildlife Service, Ira N. Gabrielson. With the translation of Mr. Wallgren from House to Senate, bills of this character became Senate bills, being entrusted to him by his interested constituents. His role in this respect was similar to that of Senator Wesley L. Jones of Washington in earlier years.

[44] *Governor's message*, 1945.

[45] The activities of the canned-salmon lobby on this and other occasions will be treated fully in a subsequent volume.

[46] Letter of Secretary of the Interior Julius A. Krug to Hon. Arthur H. Vandenberg, President *pro tempore* of the Senate. *Hearings . . . on S. 1446*, 80 C: 1 s.

[47] *Hearings . . . on S. 1446 and H.R. 3859*, 80 C: 2 s, pp. 52-4.

[48] *Ibid.*, p. 28.

[49] *Ibid.*, pp. 98-9.

[50] *Ibid.*, p. 116.

[51] *Ibid.*, p. 218.

[52] *Ibid.*, pp. 210-11.

[53] *Ibid.*, pp. 209-13.

[54] The divisional votes were: First, 7,179 for abolition. 1,113 against; Second,

1,821 for, 521 against; Third, 8,454 for, 522 against; Fourth, 4,213 for, 438 against. Out of a total of 225 precincts only ten showed a majority favoring trap retention, while in thirty-one not a single vote was cast for retention.

[55] October 15, 1948.

[56] At *Hearing on H.R. 4254 and H.R. 8213*, 74 C: 2 s, bills introduced by Delegate Dimond to abolish traps and limit the length of purse seines held January 15 and 16, 1936, Harry Stuhr, Cordova fisherman, said, "There has been so much said about fish-traps that not much more can be said." P. 66. Acting Secretary of Commerce John Dickinson and Secretary of Commerce Daniel C. Roper reported adversely on these bills, transmitting the adverse recommendations of Commissioner Frank T. Bell. The hearings, however, produced a volume of 288 printed pages.

Ten years later Mr. W. C. Arnold stated that fish-traps had "been the subject of dispute at every session of the legislature" from 1913 to 1946, and that there had been numerous hearings before congressional committees and that nothing had been said "in these hearings and no point . . . made that was not previously made." August 6, 1946. *Hearings . . . on H. Res. 38*, 79 C: 2 s, p. 166.

Two years later Mr. Arnold again testifying on fish-traps said: "There has not been anything new said on the question for 20 years. It is simply a repetition of known facts." January 28, 1948. *Hearings . . . on S.1446 and H.R. 3859*. 80 C: 2 s, p. 94.

[57] *Hearings . . . on H.R. 1515*, 81 C: 1 s, pp. 116-7. Industry representatives alleged they were busy getting ready for the Alaska fishing season. The year previously Warren G. Magnuson, the senior Senator from the state of Washington stated:

"I have been around here thirteen years, and I have never failed, during the month of January, having all the salmon people down here from Seattle. I like to see them, *but they are here all the time*, and I would like it to be possible for them to stay *there* sometimes." *Hearings . . . on S. 1446 and H.R. 3859*, 80 C: 2 s, p. 84. (Italics supplied by author.)

[58] See note 19, pp. 557-8.

[59] *Letter to Senator Vandenberg, Op. cit. Hearings . . . on S. 1446*, 8 C: 1 s, p. 15.

[60] September 2, 1939. *Hearings . . . on H. Res. 162*, pp. 145-6.

[61] Testimony of H. J. Lannen of Cordova, March 31, 1949. *Hearings . . . on H.R. 1515*, 81 C: 1 s, p. 75.

[32] For purposes of regulation Alaska is divided into fishing districts.

[63] September 10, 1947. *Hearings . . . on H. Res. 93*, 80 C: 1 s, pp. 326-8.

[64] July 13, 1948. *Hearings . . . on H.R. 1515*, 81 C: 1 s, p. 472.

[65] Anchorage *Times*, October 20, 1953.

[66] November 5, 1953.

[67] Anchorage *Times*, November 23, 1953.

[68] Juneau *Alaska Daily Empire*, December 19, 1953.

[69] Provided by the Twenty-first Territorial Legislature, Chapter 89, S.L.A. 1951.

[70] Testimony of W. O. Smith. *Hearings . . . on H.R. 1515*, 81 C: 1 s, p. 515.

CHAPTER 27

[1] *The Highways of Commerce*, by Archer Butler Hulbert, Yale University Press, 1920, p. vii.

[2] *Rept. No. 1272.* 80 C: 2 s, H. of R., pursuant to H.R. 318, 79 C and H.R. 153, 80 C, January 27, 1948.

[3] The Alaska S.S. Co.'s *Victoria*, used through the nineteen-forties, was built in 1870.

[4] H.J.M. 36, S.J.M. 10.

[5] S.C.R. 1, S.J.M. 2, H.C.R. 1, H.J.M. 21, 28, 31, 40.

[6] S.J.M. 3.

[7] S.J.M. 6.

[8] S.J.M. 16. Secretary Ickes was dissuaded from seeking an executive order, or failing that, sponsoring legislation to create Admiralty Island National Monument as a reservation for brown bear, by Director Ira N. Gabrielson of the Fish and Wildlife Service, who pointed out that the bear were increasing rapidly under existing game-management policies, and that with total protection they would multiply so fast as soon to reach a point of deterioration. Dr. Gabrielson, as the head of two combined agencies which had just been annexed by the Department of the Interior, had unusual influence with Secretary Ickes who up to that time had publicly excoriated his National Park Service Officials for daring to register their dissent from his proposal for the same reason that Gabrielson had advanced, as well as the additional reason that Admiralty Island had no scenic features that justified its being made a National Monument.

[9] S.M. 1.

[10] H.J.M. 7.

[11] H.J.M. 10.

[12] H.J.M. 35.

[13] H.J.M. 1.

[14] S.J.M. 7.

[15] Dockets 571, 572, U.S.M.C., 1940, pp. 1, 2.

[16] *Ibid.* The fifty-nine-page printed brief dated December 30, 1940, was signed by David E. Scoll and Samuel D. Slade, Attorneys, United States Maritime Commission.

[17] Testimony of Mr. Gilbert Skinner in *Hearings before a Subcommittee of the Committee on Merchant Marine and Fisheries pursuant to H. Res. 38*, 79 C: 2 s, p. 80.

[18] *Ibid.*, pp. 5, 80-1.

[19] *Ibid.*, pp. 91, 97, 180.

[20] The hearings were conducted under the authority of H. Res. 38, 79 C: 2 s, giving the House Committee on Merchant Marine and Fisheries authority to investigate various Alaska matters, including water transportation, fisheries and Coast Guard operation.

[21] O.P.A. exhibit No. 22. *Hearings . . . pursuant to H. Res. 38*, p. 86.

[22] *Ibid.*, p. 86. The comparative figures in O.P.A. exhibit No. 23 were as follows:

Classification	Seattle to Prince Rupert (short ton)	Seattle to Ketchikan (short ton)	Percentage Difference
Freight (n.o.s.)	$ 8.78	$13.17	50.0
Canned goods (car lot)	7.65	11.52	50.5
Meat (fresh or frozen)	22.50	37.24	65.5
Salt (car lot)	6.75	10.94	62.0
Potatoes, onions (car lot)	8.10	12.88	59.0
Beer (car lot)	9.00	14.38	59.7

[23] *Ibid.*, p. 86.

[24] *Ibid.*, p. 85.

[25] *Ibid.*, O.P.A. exhibit No. 21.

[26] *Ibid.*, p. 69. August 5, 1946.

[27] *Ibid.*, pp. 54-56. "I have here a bill from the Merchants Transfer and Storage Co. of Seattle, whom we employ for the handling of merchandise," Mr. Garvin testified by specific example, "one item on which, drayage, is $9.90, and on which the driver of the truck has six hours stand-by time at $3 an hour or $18, and his extra man at $1.50 an hour or $9. So in order to deliver one little shipment on which the drayage is $9.90, we pay $27 to the driver and teamster who hauled that down." Asked by Representative Christian Herter, R., of Massachusetts, whether this was a regular occurrence, Mr. Garvin replied, "Yes, it is."

[28] *Ibid.*, p. 164.

[29] *Ibid.*, p. 425.

[30] *Hearings before a Subcommittee of the Committee on Interstate and Foreign Commerce, United States Senate, 80 C: 2 s, on S. 1834, S. 2092, S.J. Res, 218, and S.J. Res. 222.* Pp. 131, 192-3.

[31] *Hearings . . . on H. Res. 38*, p. 61.

[32] *Ibid.*, p. 87. O.P.A. exhibits 18 and 19, pp. 638-9.

[33] *Alaskan Rates, Dockets 571 and 572,* United States Maritime Commission, 1940. Pp. 16, 19, 23, 24, 37.

[34] Testimony of Mr. Gilbert W. Skinner, *Hearings . . . on S. 1834, etc.*, p. 74.

[35] Dockets 571, 572. *Op. cit.*, p. 37.

[36] *Ibid.*, p. 23. The attorneys also found that rates on commodities used in the cannery business were increased less than rates on the same commodities destined for the public. (P. 16.)

They likewise reported that the Alaska Steamship Company was giving preferential rates to the Siems-Drake-Puget Sound Company engaged in construction for the Navy at Sitka and Kodiak, supplying general merchandise, furniture, automobiles, etc., at markedly lower rates than were imposed on these same goods for other purchasers in those two communities. This preferential schedule, they asserted, was "in clear violation of Section 16 of the Shipping Act of 1916," and furnished the beneficiaries with "rate advantages . . . which no other member of the shipping public in the same locality enjoyed," and were therefore "unjustly discriminatory." Pp. 27-8.

[37] July 24, 1947. *Hearings on H. Res. 38. 80 C: 1 s,* pp. 374-5.

[38] 81 C: 1 s, *Cong. Rec.*, p. 7117.

[39] *Hearings . . . on H. Res. 38*, p. 463.

[40] S.J.M. No. 1, S.L.A., 1947.

[41] H.J.M. 4, S.L.A., 1947.

[42] The increases went into effect May 21, 1947.

[43] *Hearings . . . on H. Res. 38*, p. 466.

[44] *Ibid.*, p. 465.

[45] *Ibid.*, pp. 464-5.

[46] "It is our position, the position of our company that we can accomplish a lot by a real competitive service out of Puget Sound," testified Mr. Norton Clapp, President of Alaska Transportation Company. "That is what we have endeavored to do . . . despite the fact that we have been held down largely to southeastern Alaska."

"SENATOR CAPEHART: 'Would you like to service other than southeastern Alaska?'

MR. CLAPP: 'Yes, sir; we would, sir.'

SENATOR CAPEHART: 'But you are prohibited from doing that on account of this agreement?'

MR. CLAPP: 'Yes . . . We . . . were the only outfit that was entirely free and independent . . . we felt that the only way there could be competition in the westward area would be for our company to be out there. . . . It is our position that there should be more competition in Alaska than there is today.' " *Hearings . . . on S. 1834, etc.*, pp. 82-4.

[47] *Hearings . . . on H. Res. 38*, p. 433, November 21, 1947.

[48] *Hearings . . . on S. 1834, etc.*, p. 75, April 14, 1948.

[49] Of the twenty-six ships in the Alaska trade prior to World War II, the majority had been sold, and several lost.

[50] *Ibid.*, pp. 16-18. Senator Butler's statement was read at the first hearing of the subcommittee by the committee clerk, Edward Jarrett, April 14, 1948.

[51] In a special message to Congress, May 21, 1948, dealing wholly with Alaska, President Truman, after full exposition of the need "of developing a satisfactory transportation system" there, recommended "that our transportation laws be amended to remove the present bar to shipping goods in bond between the United States and Alaska by Canadian rail, port and shipping facilities. This bar does not apply between any of our states, and there is no reason thus to discriminate against Alaska. Furthermore, Canadian ships should be permitted to transport passengers and freight between Alaska ports in order to provide more adequate service. These recommendations are also in accord with the mutual interest which we will continue to have with our Canadian neighbors in the development of the great northwest territory of this continent." 80 C: 2 s, *Sen. Doc. 159.*

[52] *Ibid.*

[53] Under the Merchant Ship Sales Act of 1946 (60 Stat. 41) ships might be chartered by American operators at 15 per cent annually of their value. The C-1-MAV-1 ships worth about $2,000,000 new, and valued by the U.S.M.C. at $700,000 for sale or charter, made available to the Alaska carriers at $1, represented therefore a saving of $105,000 per ship. The twenty-one ships chartered to the Alaska Steamship and Northland Transportation companies thus spelled a subsidy of $2,205,000, plus the saving on hull insurance which at the then current 9 per cent rate added $198,450, making a total subsidy of $2,403,450 per annum to the one ownership. *Hearings . . . on S. 1834, etc.*, pp. 244-5.

[54] May 27, 1949, 81 C: 1 s, Cong. Rec., pp. 7115-6.

[55] *Ibid.*

[56] Midway in the operation of Public Law 12, Mr. Norton Clapp, President of Alaska Transportation Company, testified:

"Today there is a monopoly in Alaska. We have spent the last two days explaining to our bosses, the Maritime Commission, how this interim plan worked out. . . . Since the war the situation is somewhat different than before the war, and the records are replete again with the fact that now Alaska Steamship Co. and Northland Transportation Co. are under common control.

"Under the interim plan, the ratio of ships they have as against the ships we have is approximately 6 to 1. We have no passenger ships and we are not allowed to handle anything commercially outside of southeastern Alaska. The result is that there is a monopoly in southwestern Alaska and an overwhelming competition in southeastern Alaska. We have asked that the interim plan be modified. That is in the hands of the commission for their consideration . . . we are going to ask for the right to serve all of Alaska. We feel that it is in the public interest that there be separate carriers serving all of Alaska—more than one. We regard the other two companies as one company, and we feel that if that is one company, we should

be the other." November 21, 1947.
*Hearings . . . pursuant . . . to H.
Res.* 38, 80 C: 1 s, p. 446.

The Maritime Commission did not
modify the interim plan. Alaska
Transportation Co. was handicapped
by the ability of Alaska Steamship
Co. to arrange with salmon companies operating canneries in southwestern Alaska to carry their salmon
cargo provided they would let Northland Transportation Co. take the
salmon from their canneries in southeastern Alaska. That was an important part of the competition which
Mr. Clapp termed "overwhelming."
[57] Pilferage claims against the Alaska
Steamship Co., in one year, 1945,
amounted to $41,942. *Hearings . . .
pursuant . . . to H. Res.* 38, 80 C:
1 s, p. 197.
[58] Figures supplied by the Alaska
Steamship Company.
[59] *Agreement between Pacific Maritime
Association and the Sailors' Union of
the Pacific. Covering the Intercoastal,
Offshore and Alaska Trades, Dated
October 1, 1953*, p. 29.
[60] S. J. Swanson, General Manager of
the Alaska Transportation Company,
testified: "No one here has any
objection to high wages. What they
do object to is this. In comparing
1941 with 1945, we find that the
overtime rate of pay has increased
only 19 per cent. However we find
that because of make-work practices,
featherbedding and other labor practices, the money paid out has increased 95 per cent. . . . It is possible for a crew member in the Alaska
trade to earn twenty-eight hours of
overtime in one day. You will sit
there and say there are only twenty-
four hours in one day, but it is still
possible to add up to not only this
daily pay in the form of monthly
wages but in addition twenty-eight
hours overtime." August 5, 1946.
Hearings . . . pursuant . . . to H. Res.
38, pp. 117, 119.
[61] *Hearings before the Committee on
Territories, H. of R.* 79 C: 1 s, *pursuant to H. Res.* 236, *"to Conduct
a Study and Investigation of the
Various Questions and Problems Relating to the Territory of Alaska*,
p. 124.
[62] An exception should be made of
some in Alaska employed by the
maritime carriers. They may cite by
way of anecdotal refutation the Fairbanks barber who explained the $2
price of a haircut to a startled newcomer by saying: "It's the freight!"
Obviously it is not the freight on
his brushes, combs and hair tonics,
but on the necessities he requires as
a consumer.
[63] October 28, 1949. *Hearings . . . on*
H.R. 1515, 81 C: 1 s, p. 185.
[64] A cement plant in the rail belt was
contemplated in the late nineteen
forties for which the necessary materials were available near by. It
would have saved millions of dollars
in military and civilian construction
costs, but met with various obstacles,
the first of which was the opposition
of the National Park Service, of the
Department of the Interior, to permit the quarrying of the necessary
limestone from the southeast corner
of Mount McKinley National Park
which is skirted by the Alaska Railroad, although the area is wholly
unrelated to the scenic, wild-life and
other values of the park. Twelve
years earlier in Puerto Rico, the
Puerto Rico Reconstruction Administration, a federal agency, built a
cement plant, the cost of which was
fully repaid with interest to the government in a few years, and stimulated the erection of another, by
private capital and enterprise. Both
have been steadily productive ever
since to the great benefit of the
Puerto Rican economy.
[65] *Hearings . . . pursuant to H. Res.*
93, p. 73.
[66] "Job action" is viewed as a device to
violate the terms of existing collec-
tive-bargaining contracts, and to by-
pass arbitration machinery, thereby
attempting to impose the union
members' own interpretation of the
contract.
[67] The repeated dock workers' strikes
in Seward from that cause to the
detriment of the population of the
entire rail belt, were described by

Edwin M. Suddock, August 31, 1947, in *Hearings before the Subcommittee on Territorial and Insular Possession of the Committee on Public Lands, H. of R. 80 C: 1 s, pursuant to H. Res. 93,* pp. 66-75.

[68] *Hearings . . . on Reducing Industrial Strife in the United States . . .* before the Committee on Labor and Public Welfare, U.S. Senate. 80 C: 1 s, pp. 2171-2178.

[69] This incident and a detailed account of the maritime tie-ups as of April 29, 1953, are found in *Hearings before the Committee on Labor and Public Welfare, U.S. Senate, 83 C: 1 s, on Proposed Revisions of the Labor-Management Relations Act of 1947,* pp. 2311-26.

[70] *Ibid.,* p. 2317.

[71] The year following the dock foremen's tie-up of the port of Seattle was followed by over a year of waterfront peace, an interlude attributed in part to the efforts of a "Mayor's Maritime Advisory Committee" which succeeded an "Alaska Life Line Committee" formed during the interruptions of 1952, and which celebrated a fourteen months' cessation of strife with a banquet in Seattle attended by some four hundred persons on February 15, 1954.

The previous month the Alaska Steamship Company requested a ten per cent rate increase. Delegate Bartlett requested hearings, pointing out that no examination of the company's books and no audit had ever preceded the granting of the increases demanded, and that while these might be justified, there was every reason why their validity should be demonstrated. The Federal Maritime Board, which succeeded the U.S. Maritime Commission in 1950, did not accede to the delegate's request and granted a 7½ per cent increase to both the Alaska Steamship Company and the Coastwise Line.

The Federal Maritime Board was established under the Reorganization Act of June 20, 1949 (63 Stat. 206). It created a Board of three commissioners appointed by the President subject to confirmation by the Senate, and placed the agency within the Department of Commerce, while leaving the board independent in the field of regulation. The agency inherited and took over the operating personnel from its predecessor.

[72] Quoted by Robert B. Atwood in *Hearings before the Committee on Interstate and Foreign Commerce on H.R. 3509 and 3510. 80 C: 1 s,* p. 5.

[73] "World" was legally incorporated in the company's name in 1950, although the title "Pan-American World Airways" had been used eight years before that.

[74] February 15, 1946. *Rept. 1583, pursuant to H. Res. 236, 79 C: 2 s,* pp. 9, 27.

[75] The intra-Alaskan routes which Pan-American had acquired in 1932 and improved and operated thereafter established "a position in Alaska which would be of tremendous assistance in the extension of such service . . . to the Orient," Vice-President Harold N. Bixby testified in 1943. The Fairbanks to Nome run would be the first leg in an airway across Siberia; the Fairbanks-Bethel route the first link in an airway to Tokyo. By securing these routes in Alaska, the company established "grandfather" rights on potential certifications to Asia. *Docket No. 458, Mail Rates for Pacific-Alaska Airways and Pan-American Airways, Transcript of Hearings,* August 23, 1943, pp. 44, 74, 75.

In the States-Alaska case, Howard Hamstra, counsel for Pan-American Airways, stipulated that one reason for Pan-American's going to Alaska was to secure "a gateway to the Orient." February 9, 1954. *Transcript,* pp. 4866-7.

[76] The examiners were Ross Newmann and Lawrence Kosters. The public counsel were Rock Grundman, Merle P. Lyon and Russell Bernhard.

[77] C.A.B. *Docket 547,* June 20, 1946, pp. 13, 14.

[78] *Ibid.,* p. 27.

[79] *Ibid.,* p. 28.

[80] H.J.M. 20, S.L.A., 1941.

[81] *H. Rept. 1583, 79 C: 2 s, pursuant*

to *H. Res. 236*, p. 23. February 15,
1946.
[82] *Economic Regulations Draft Release
No. 24*, November 20, 1947.
[83] Letter of John Nicholas Brown, Asst.
Sec'y. of the Navy for Air, to James
M. Landis, Chairman of the C.A.B.,
December 30, 1947.
[84] In his letter, dated December 26,
1947, to Chairman Landis, Secretary
Krug said in part: "There is indeed
a present need for a greater volume
of air transportation of cargo between the States and the territory.
. . . Shipping facilities to the territory have been unsatisfactory in the
extreme. There has been . . . a
virtual monopoly of service, rates
have been fixed and kept at high
levels. Alaskans have seen the cost
of food and other essentials go
higher and higher, as the retail prices
of the goods they buy reflect the increases in freight rates."
[85] The carriers registering opposition,
either by written presentation or
orally at a hearing, to the granting
of exemptions to additional carriers
for service between Alaska and the
States were Pan-American, Northwest, Pacific Northern and United,
although the last was not serving
Alaska. Alaska Airlines supported the
proposed exemption order.
[86] H.M. 2, S.L.A., 1949.
[87] October 29, 1949. *Hearings . . . on
H.R. 1515. 81 C*: 1 s, p. 200.
[88] H.M. 52, S.L.A., 1951.
[89] April 27, 1951. *Hearings before a
Subcommittee of the Select Committee on Small Business, U. S.
Senate, 82 C*: 1 s, on *Role of Irregular Airlines in United States and Air
Transportation Industry*, p. 117.
[90] *Ibid.*, pp. 123-4.
[91] *Report on Role of Irregular Airlines
in United States Air Transportation
Industry by the Select Committee on
Small Business, U.S. Senate*, July 10,
1951, *82 C*: 1 s. The other members
of the subcommittee were Lester C.
Hunt, D., of Wyoming, Charles W.
Tobey, R., of New Hampshire and
James H. Duff, R., of Pennsylvania.
[92] Committee Substitute for H.M. 7,
S.L.A., 1953.

[93] *United States-Alaska Service Case,
Docket No. 3286 et al. Supplemental
opinion and order*, adopted by C.A.B.
May 24, 1951.
[94] Philip A. Anderson, President of the
Fairbanks Chamber of Commerce,
testified in detail concerning the improvement brought about by the two
certifications to and from Fairbanks.
Included was his statement: "I personally know that before Alaska Airlines came into the picture you could
not consistently expect to get air-
freight service on Pan-American."
States-Alaska Case, Docket No. 5756
et al., October 20, 1953. *Transcript*,
pp. 196-200.
    Asked whether or not it was a fact
"that up until Alaska [Airlines]
started its States–Fairbanks service,
Pan-American had been charging a
fare of $105 and that it reduced its
fare from $105 to $90 in order to
meet the reduced fare charged by
Alaska Airlines," Mr. Alvin P.
Adams, Vice-President of Pan-American World Airways, replied: "I think
that is correct." *Ibid.*, February 4,
1954. *Transcript*, pp. 4406-7.
[95] *Pacific-Northwest-Alaska Tariff Investigation*, Docket No. 5067, p. 834.
August 25, 1952.
[96] *Ibid.*, p. 851.
[97] Undoubtedly the majority of Alaskans—excepting only those with ties
of pecuniary self-interest to the
Seattle business world—favored the
widest diversity of trade opportunity
and therefore welcomed Portland's
participation. They would have been
inclined to disagree with Mr. J. D.
Paul's view that "Seattle's natural
geographic advantage" should preclude other cities as competitors, and
to consider that the "natural" advantage had been increased by artificial means, such as the special interest legislation within the Jones
Act, with the consequent maintenance in Seattle of higher charges
uniquely discriminatory against
Alaska; or the use of influence on a
federal executive agency to exclude
other than Puget Sound carriers
from participation in government
subsidy under Public Law 12 in

1947—an act, let it be noted, sponsored by a state of Washington legislator for the benefit of Alaska as well as for his state; or by political pressure to attempt the elimination of the inland air route to Alaska.

Nor would these Alaskans have been apt to agree with Mr. Paul that "the growth and development of Seattle and Alaska have been synonymous," but rather that the growth and development of Seattle had been synchronous with a period of arrested growth and development in Alaska. These Alaskans would have agreed that the greater part of the wealth derived from Alaska during those years had built up Seattle, but that Seattle interests and influences exercised in governmental circles had prevented a larger share of that wealth from being plowed back for the growth and development of Alaska. This view was publicly expressed at an earlier hearing by Alaska's Attorney-General Ralph J. Rivers:

"The Alaska Department of the Seattle Chamber of Commerce has issued reams of assurances to Alaskans that Seattle was the territory's best friend and that constructive measures were being taken to put Alaska on the map. It was never mentioned that Alaska was in 'protective custody' so to speak." August 5, 1946. *Hearings . . . pursuant to H. Res.* 38, 79 C: 2 s, pp. 45-49.

The fact was that the relations of "Seattle" with Alaska, which could and should have been wholly neighborly and friendly, had been seriously—and needlessly—impaired by a relatively few individuals with large business interests in Alaska who viewed Alaska in the first half of the twentieth century much as King George III and his ministers viewed the Thirteen Colonies in the eighteenth. The potent figures who dominated the so-called "Alaska Department" or "Alaska Committee" of the Seattle Chamber of Commerce were chiefly responsible for the restrictive moves in regard to Alaska. Seattle's half-million people,

who were in no wise responsible for these tactics, were also injured by them. Actually Seattle would inevitably be the principal beneficiary of any growth and development in Alaska, and diversification and expansion of the territory's commercial ties would speed that development.

The underlying conflict represented merely an historic swing of the pendulum. In the second half of the nineteenth century San Francisco and Portland enterprisers dominated Alaska and some of their actions and similar attitudes toward Alaskans' efforts to establish themselves aroused a corresponding resentment among the latter. The transfer of absentee Alaskan activities to Seattle and the domination of Alaskan affairs from within that city began in the twentieth century's first decade.

[98] *Pacific Northwest-Alaska Investigation, Docket No.* 5067. *Order No.* E-7732. September 15, 1953.

[99] *Ibid., Supplemental Opinion and Order on Reconsideration, Order No.* E-8154. March 5, 1954.

[100] The *Official Airline Guide* for March, 1954, gave the fare between Chicago and Portland–Seattle at $114.75. P. 438.

[101] March 3, 1954.

[102] The International Airports near Anchorage and Fairbanks were constructed by the federal government, beginning in 1949, when the military authorities decided that for reasons of national security the States–Alaska commercial services could no longer use Elmendorf and Ladd Fields. It was considered inadvisable by the C.A.A. to enlarge the existing airports—Merrill at Anchorage and Weeks at Fairbanks—because of their proximity to Elmendorf and Ladd military air bases. *Hearings before a Subcommittee of the Committee on Interstate and Foreign Commerce, U.S. Senate,* 80 C: 2 s, on S. 1371, S. 1396, H.R. 3510 and S. 2451, p. 6.

[103] It has been estimated that Lake Hood accommodates 10 per cent of all the privately owned sea-planes in the nation.

[104] *H. Rept. No. 1583 on H. Res. 236.* 79 C: 2 s, p. 25.

[105] Pursuant to S. Res. 20, 80 C: 2 s.

[106] In 1945 a Subcommittee to Investigate the Alaska Highway, of the House Committee on Roads, five of whose members visited Alaska, recommended the extension of the Federal Aid Highway Act to Alaska. They were J. W. Robinson, D., of Utah, Jennings Randolph, D., of West Virginia, Hugh Peterson, D., of Georgia, Paul Cunningham, R., of Iowa and J. Glenn Beall, of Maryland. *H. Rept. No. 1705, 79 C: 2 s, on H. Res. 255,* p. 71. Their recommendation was not accepted by the full committee.

[107] H.J.M. 8, 1941.

[108] Testimony of Thomas H. MacDonald, Commissioner, Public Roads Administration, April 6, 1948. *Hearings . . . on H.R. 4574,* 80 C: 2 s, p. 18.

[109] January 27, 1947. *Hearings on Interior Dept. Appropriation Bill for 1948,* pp. 334-5.

[110] October 28, 1947. *Hearings on Interior Dept. Appropriation Bill for 1949,* pp. 968-9.

[111] February 19, 1948. *Ibid.,* p. 954.

[112] Delegate Bartlett's letter, dated February 22, 1949, was printed in *Hearings on H.R. 331,* 81 C: 2 s, p. 97.

[113] The principal critic was Representative Ben F. Jensen, R., of Iowa, a member for many years of the subcommittee on the Interior Department of the Appropriations Committee and its chairman in the 83rd Congress, who had repeatedly shown his interest in Alaska and sympathetic understanding of its problems.

[114] S. 3184, April 7.

[115] January 27, 1947. *Hearings . . . on Interior Dept. Appropriation Bill for 1948,* H. of R. 80 C: 1 s, pp. 334-5.

[116] Letter to Secretary of the Interior Julius A. Krug, October 28, 1947. In *Hearings . . . on Interior Dept. Appropriation Bill for 1949,* H. of R. 80 C: 2 s, pp. 960-70.

[117] *Ibid.,* February 23, 1948, pp. 954-5.

[118] *Doc. 10, Seventh Rept. . . . under the authority of S. 18.* 82 C: 1 s, p. 33.

[119] S.J.M. 5, 1939.

[120] *House Rept. No. 1583,* Pursuant to . . . H. Res. 236. 79 C: 2 s, p. 28.

[121] 81 C: 1 s, *Cong. Rec.,* p. 12188.

[122] Seattle *Post-Intelligencer,* September 8, 1949.

[123] *House Rept. 1705,* 79 C: 2 s, p. 6.

[124] June 11, 1940, 76 C: 3 s.

[125] *House Rept. 1705,* 79 C: 2 s, p. 6.

[126] February 5, 1941. H.R. 3095, 77 C: 1 s.

[127] April 26, 1940. *House Doc. 711,* 76 C: 3 s.

[128] Representative Magnuson's letter was dated April 12, 1941. Correspondence in his files.

[129] *Cong. Rec.,* p. A3750, 77 C: 1 s.

[130] *House Rept. 1705,* 79 C: 2 s, p. 8.

[131] The route selected for the Alaska Highway followed the recommendations of neither the United States nor the Canadian commission, but began at Dawson Creek, just west of the Alberta boundary, four hundred miles northwest of Edmonton, from which a low-grade road already existed, thence to Whitehorse and Fairbanks. This route was disappointing to Alaskans who hoped for one nearer the coast which would ultimately permit connecting roads with the coastal cities of Juneau and Ketchikan and possibly down the Stikhine Valley to the neighborhood of Wrangell and Petersburg. The justification for the belated choice was that it connected the airports built in 1941 at Fort St. John, Fort Nelson and Watson Lake, and facilitated their supply. The choice was made by the Permanent Joint Board of Defense—United States-Canada, composed of military and civilian members which had recommended the construction of those airports in November, 1940, but—no more than the General Staff—had sensed the necessity of connecting them by highway until February, 1942.

[132] H.J.M. 17, S.L.A., 1939.

[133] Briefing by Brigadier General Elmer J. Rogers, Director of Plans and Operations, Alaskan Command. *Doc. 10. S. Res. 18.* 82 C: 1 s, p. 49.

CHAPTER 28

[1] The amendment of August 29, 1914 (38 Stat. 710), permitted federal officials to fulfill certain duties for the territory. That of March 3, 1917 (39 Stat. 1131), permitted the territory (as distinct from incorporated towns) to conduct schools and appropriate for the purpose. That of March 26, 1934 (48 Stat. 465), changed the date for convening the legislature from the first Monday in March to the second Monday in January, and changed the date of the territorial election from the first Tuesday after the first Monday in November to the second Tuesday in September, also giving the legislature the power to change that date again. That of April 13, 1934 (48 Stat. 583), repealed prohibition for the territory, following the repeal of national prohibition. That of April 18, 1940 (54 Stat. 111), again changed the date of the convening of the legislature to the fourth Monday in January.

[2] H.R. 8114, 68 C: 1 s.

[3] *Hearings before the Committee on Territories, H. of R. 77 C: 1 s, on H.R. 4397, To Amend the Organic Act of Alaska*, p. 5.

[4] *Ibid.*, p. 2.

[5] *Ibid.*, p. 5.

[6] *Ibid.*, p. 37.

[7] *Ibid.*, p. 25.

[8] *Ibid.*, p. 3.

[9] March 30, 1916. H.R. 13978, 64 C: 1 s.

[10] H.R. 3898, 79 C: 1 s.

[11] H.J.M. 7, S.L.A., 1945.

[12] Chapter 24, S.L.A., 1945.

[13] Hearings on H.R. 5694, 67 C: 1 s. Hamlet later became Commandant of the Coast Guard. The relations of the Coast Guard to Alaska are worthy of much fuller treatment than can be accorded here. An excellent summary is found in Chapter IX of *The United States Coast Guard, A Definitive History*, by Stephen H. Evans, published by the United States Naval Institute, 1949, and *The Contribution of the Coast Guard to the Development of Alaska,* by B. L. Reed, in U.S. Naval Institute Proceedings, May, 1929.

[14] Another popular federal agency was the Alaska Communication System operated by the Signal Corps of the U.S. Army. The A.C.S. originated in the gold-rush days and continued to be the telegraph service between points within Alaska and with the States.

[15] *Hearings before the Subcommittee of the Committee on Appropriations on the Supplemental Treasury and Post Officer Appropriations Bill for 1949*, H. of R. 80 C: 1 s, pp. 131, 179, 195, 217.

[16] April 16, 1947. *Statehood for Alaska. Hearings before the Subcommittee on Territorial and Insular Possessions of the Committee on Public Lands.* H. of R. 80 C: 1 s, on H.R. 206 and H.R. 1808, p. 8.

[17] Letter of Acting Secretary of the Interior Warner W. Gardner to Chairman Richard J. Welch of House Public Lands Committee, April 14, 1947. *Ibid.*, pp. 11-13.

[18] *Ibid.*, pp. 49-50.

[19] *Ibid.*, p. 120.

[20] *Hearings . . . on H. Res.* 93, p. 79.

[21] *Ibid.*, pp. 4, 6.

[22] *Ibid.*, p. 362.

[23] *Ibid.*, p. 364.

[24] *Ibid.*, pp. 39-40.

[25] *Hearings on H.R. 206 and H.R. 1808*, pp. 185-200.

[26] *Ibid.*, pp. 73-8, 121-185.

[27] *Hearings on H. Res.* 93, p. 138.

[28] *Ibid.*, p. 125.

[29] *Ibid.*, p. 130.

[30] *Ibid.*, pp. 155-169, 282-299, 355-6.

[31] *Ibid.*, pp. 156-7.

[32] On August 30. *Ibid.*, pp. 8-17.

[33] The text of the letter was as follows:

Seattle, Washington
September 9, 1947

Dear Congressman Crawford:

Following my testimony before your committee, concerning the matter of statehood for Alaska, I was approached by six different individuals, over a period of three days and advised that it was very dangerous for me to take a position as firmly in the interest of statehood, as I did. The question was asked of me, did you not know the canned-salmon industry is entirely against your position and that your aggressiveness in this matter will very seriously injure your position with this industry. One of my newly made acquaintances advised me that in all probability they would not even consider our air line for next season's travel. The revenue which we realized this summer was in excess of $400,000. I paid little heed to these statements and charged them merely to gossip and wild conjecture, until just prior to my appearance before Senator Butler's committee, I was approached by Judge Arnold, where he in the course of casual conversation most definitely implied that my position was most unwise. One, because I was a newcomer to Alaska and not well informed, and two, because I might have some interest in serving the canned-salmon industry. His statements were made to me personally and there were no witnesses. I definitely interpreted them as a threat, as I am sure that is the way he intended them.

I have deliberated seriously reporting this matter to you but since arriving in Seattle last night, I was advised by Doug Sherrif of Alaska Packers Association and Loren Daley, Jr., of Bristol Bay Packing company that, "You're sticking your neck out a mile and if you expect to get any of the canned-salmon industry business, you sure in hell had better change your position and keep your mouth shut."

These statements have been coming so thick and fast, I am ready to make an affidavit concerning these incidents, if in your opinion you think this is necessary or would assist the cause. . . .

Very truly yours,
ALASKA AIRLINES, INC.
J. A. WOOTEN

Alaska Airlines did not obtain the companies' business the following year: it went to a competitor. The Ketchikan *Chronicle* was likewise penalized, its editor and publisher,

Mr. William L. Baker, informed the writer, for publishing Mr. Wooten's letter, by the diminished advertising of a local department store, one of whose principal stockholders was a large salmon-cannery owner. The other Ketchikan daily, the *Fishing News*, did not publish Mr. Wooten's letter.

[34] The subcommittee's report is in the committee's files. The full committee's report was No. 1731 to accompany H.R. 5666, 80 C: 2 s, H. of R.

[35] The membership merits recording. Republicans, Richard J. Welch, California, Chairman, Fred L. Crawford, Michigan, Robert F. Rockwell, Colorado, William Lemke, North Dakota, Frank A. Barrett, Wyoming, Dean P. Taylor, New York, Jay LeFevre, New York, A. L. Miller, Nebraska, Wesley A. D'Ewart, Montana, Norris Poulson, California, Charles H. Russell, Nevada, John Sanborn, Idaho, Edward H. Jenison, Illinois, William A. Dawson, Utah; Democrats, Andrew L. Somers, New York, J. Hardin Peterson, Florida, C. Jasper Bell, Missouri, John R. Murdock, Arizona, Antonio M. Fernandez, New Mexico, Clair Engle, California, E. H. Hedrick, West Virginia, Preston E. Peden, Oklahoma, Monroe M. Redden, North Carolina, John A. Carroll, Colorado.

The full committee's report said in part: "If statehood were granted to Alaska, it would benefit not merely the people of Alaska. Actually, statehood would be as much, if not more, in the interests of the people of the United States. . . . Surely in the present uneasy state of world affairs it is to the advantage of the United States to have Alaska fully developed and populated. Because it was not, at the time of World War II, the United States was required to spend about twenty-five times the amount originally paid for Alaska, for defense purposes alone.

"Alaska's importance to the United States does not rest alone on military considerations. Its vast resources are far from fully developed. . . .

"Admitting Alaska to statehood will have great significance from an international standpoint, as indicating that the United States practices what it preaches about self-determination. . . .

"Alaskans are the spiritual descendants of the early pioneers, courageous and individualistic. We should be proud to welcome them into the Union on an equal footing with the people of the continental United States."

[35]* S. 232, 80 C. 2 s, May 10, 1948.

[36] May 20, 1948. 80 C. 2 s, *Cong. Rec.*, p. 6163.

[37] On February 2, 1948 in a message to Congress the President had declared:

"The present political status of our territories and possessions impairs the enjoyment of civil rights by their residents. I have in the past recommended legislation granting statehood to Alaska and Hawaii and organic acts for Guam and Samoa. I repeat these recommendations.

"Furthermore, the residents of the Virgin Islands should be granted an increasing measure of self-government, and the people of Puerto Rico should be allowed to choose the form of government and their ultimate status with respect to the United States." 80 C: 2 s, *Cong. Rec.*, p. 929.

[38] May 21, 1948. 80 C: 2 s, *Sen. Doc.* 159.

[39] The 1948 Democratic platform urged "immediate statehood for Hawaii and Alaska." The 1948 Republican platform favored "eventual statehood" for both.

[40] *Hearings before the Committee on Interior and Insular Affairs, U.S. Senate*, 81 C: 2 s, on H.R. 331 and S. 2036, pp. 489-90.

[41] *Ibid.*, p. 60.

[42] *Ibid.*, p. 495.

[43] *Ibid.*, p. 204.

[44] *Ibid.*, p. 211.

[45] For example, Emery Tobin, of Ketchikan, editor of the Alaska *Sportsman*, who had consistently been opposed to statehood in general. On April 25, 1950, he wired Senator Joseph C. O'Mahoney:

"Although would very much like to see Alaska have vote in Congress am opposed statehood now as proposed House Resolution 331." *Ibid.*, p. 268.

Three years earlier, on September 12, 1947, before the subcommittee on Territorial and Insular Affairs of the House Committee on Public Lands, Mr. Tobin had testified:

". . . it is my personal opinion that it would be unwise for the people of Alaska to accept statehood at this time." *Hearings . . . on H.R. 93*, 80 C: 1 s, p. 371.

Three years later, on August 17, 1953, before the Senate Committee on Interior and Insular Affairs, Mr. Tobin testified:

". . . I say we are not ready yet for statehood." *Hearings . . . on S. 50 . . . and S. 224.* 83 C: 1 s, p. 61, and "I think if you are going to add the costs of statehood which would be 50 to 100 per cent greater than taxes are now, you would hinder the development of Alaska." *Ibid.*, p. 62.

[46] *Ibid.*, p. 81.

[47] *Ibid.*, pp. 157, 159.

[48] *Ibid.*, p. 173.

[49] *Ibid.*, pp. 147-8.

[50] *Ibid.*, p. 369.

[51] *Ibid.*, p. 370.

[52] 81 C: 2 s, *Sen. Rept.* 1929. President Truman's letter concluded with:

"America justly takes pride in its record of fulfilling to the letter its obligations to foreign nations. We should be no less scrupulous in carrying out the promises made to our citizens in Alaska and Hawaii. The case for statehood rests on both legal and moral grounds.

"These are troubled times. I know of few better ways in which we can demonstrate to the world our deep faith in democracy and the principle of self-government than by admitting Alaska and Hawaii to the Union as the forty-ninth and fiftieth states."

Senator Butler's minority report

was in part:

"Statehood for Alaska at this time might well spell financial ruin. . . .

"Instead of strengthening national defense as its proponents claim, passage of H.R. 331, by bringing economic chaos to an important, strategic area, might in fact weaken our military position.

"No military authority has at any time held that Alaska statehood is necessary for defense. I refer you to the testimony of Rear Admiral Ralph Wood . . . He said . . . [Admiral Wood's afore-cited testimony was quoted.]

"The failure of Alaska to develop more rapidly is due to a combination of climatic and geographic handicaps, plus a gigantic superstructure of stifling regulations and restrictions upon the use of its resources by various bureaus of the federal government. . . . Foremost among these restrictions is the federal policy of withdrawing vast areas of Alaska's most promising resources from development and use. . . .

"To grant statehood at this time is to put the cart before the horse. Alaska's great problem is the development of its resources. Rather than pass this bill, we could best help Alaska's development by investigating thoroughly the restrictive policies now hampering the exploitation of Alaska and insisting they be removed."

Under the heading "Alternative," Senator Butler's report concluded:

"It is my belief, however, that the Congress should do everything possible to further the development of the political institutions of Alaska and to broaden the opportunities for self-government. The people of Alaska are competent to manage their own local affairs. There is no reason why the governor should be selected by Washington or why the Alaskans should have to come to Washington every time they want some change in their basic law. I propose, therefore, that, as a substitute for statehood, the people of Alaska should be given the right im-

mediately to select their own governor and other territorial officials. . . . If such legislation is enacted, we will be following the pattern already set for Puerto Rico. In the case of Alaska, however, the right of selection of a governor might well be a step toward full statehood at a later date."

[53] 81 C: 2 s, *Cong. Rec.*, p. 11984.

[54] *Cong. Rec.*, pp. 15772-3.

[55] 81 C: 2 s, *Cong. Rec.*, p. 15931.

[56] *Ibid.*, p. 15933.

[57] *Ibid.*, p. 15936.

[58] *Ibid.*, p. 15937.

[59] *Ibid.*, p. 15978.

[60] *Ibid.*

[61] *Ibid.*, p. 15923. Senator Butler had apparently forgotten his statement printed in his minority views attributing Alaska's "failure to develop" in part to "a gigantic superstructure of stifling regulations and restrictions . . . by various bureaus of the federal government."

[62] *Ibid.*, p. 16030.

[63] *Ibid.*, p. 16029.

[64] *Ibid.*, p. 16030.

[65] *Ibid.*, p. 16032.

[66] *Ibid.*, p. 16033. Senator Morse gave this as his personal opinion, but Alaskans knew he was speaking "by the card," having observed the previous unsuccessful efforts of Delegate Dimond to secure adequate defenses for Alaska before the outbreak of World War II, and learning thereby that even in matters of the gravest national concern a voteless delegate's exhortation, no matter how fortified by logic and truth, does not register as does the presentation by two United States senators and a representative. The belated post-war restoration at mid-century of Alaska's defenses to whose weakened condition Senator Morse referred, was due to the support of the northwestern states' congressional delegations when their own interest was aroused by the threatened removal of the Boeing aircraft plant from Seattle to Wichita, which was actually initiated by the U.S. Air Force in 1949.

[67] Senator Lucas's motion to proceed to the consideration of H.R. 331 was

made on November 27th (*Cong. Rec.*, p. 15779). The debate began November 28th (*Cong. Rec.*, p. 15919). On Thursday, November 30th, Senator Lucas said: ". . . It is quite apparent there will not be a vote on the statehood bills. In other words, it is impossible to obtain . . . agreement . . . even for the Senate to vote on the motion to consider the bill providing for statehood for Alaska." He therefore asked for unanimous consent to bring up the railway labor bill, the following Monday, December 4th (*Cong. Rec.*, p. 15987). While there were further speeches on statehood, the next day, December 1st, the majority leader actually capitulated on the third day of debate.

On December 5th, Senator Robert C. Hendrickson, R., of New Jersey, introduced into the *Congressional Record* an editorial from the Newark *Evening News* of December 2nd, entitled "Filibuster Against Justice," which charged that statehood for Alaska and Hawaii was being blocked by a threatened filibuster of Southern Democrats and Republicans under the leadership of Senator Butler who "opposes statehood for Alaska on the ground that the bill is an administration attempt to bring two left-wing Democratic Senators to the Congress to offset the effects of the November 7th general election, which reduced the Democratic margin of control to two seats (*Cong. Rec.*, p. 16104)."

Whatever may have been the intentions of the statehood opponents on that occasion, the evidence of three days' speeches, all germane to the subject of statehood, scarcely warranted the allegation of filibuster. It did warrant the charge of unwillingness of statehood opponents to allow the matter to come up for a vote.

[68] *Cong. Rec.*, p. 16032.
[69] They were Anderson, Benton, Chavez, Douglas, Gillette, Holland, Humphrey, Hunt, Lehman, Magnuson, Murray, Neely, O'Mahoney, Democrats, and Knowland, Morse,

Nixon, H. Alexander Smith, Mrs. Margaret Chase Smith and Thye, Republicans.
[70] The numbers of the statehood bills, S. 49 for Hawaii, and S. 50 for Alaska, were intended to symbolize their admission as the forty-ninth and fiftieth states.
[71] 82 C: 1 s, *Sen. Rept.* 315, p. 9.
[72] The report stated: "*Climate.*— Alaska is so large that almost any kind of climate and topography can be found, but the popular conception of Alaska as a land of snow and ice is incorrect. The average annual temperature varies from 45° above zero at Ketchikan to a low of 9.9° above zero at Point Barrow. The January mean temperature of 20° above zero in Anchorage compares to that in Concord, N. H. The January mean of 33.6° at Ketchikan is about the same as Denver and New York. Ketchikan's record low of 8° below zero approximates record low temperatures for Washington, D.C. and is considerably warmer than the record cold in such cities as Chicago and Boston. Ketchikan's all-time high is 96; Juneau, 89; and Fairbanks, 99. The temperature at Fort Yukon, 20 miles above the Arctic Circle, has often reached heights of 100° above zero. The temperature also has been known to drop below minus 70 during the winter in that community.

"The average annual precipitation varies from a high of 176.9 inches at Latouche to a low of 4.34 inches at Barrow. Precipitation in Alaska in its present agricultural areas is 11.71 inches in the Tanana Valley, 15.45 inches in the Matanuska Valley, and 32.59 inches on the Kenai Peninsula.

"The only pronounced climatic difference between a large part of Alaska and much of the northern and western portion of the United States is the long hours of summer daylight and, conversely, the short winter days. The average growing season varies from about 170 days in southeastern Alaska to ninety days in the northern interior.

"Despite the fact that Alaskan

waters are hundreds of miles to the north, there are . . . more frozen rivers and harbors in the United States than there are from the Aleutians to the southern tip of the Alaska Panhandle. This is largely due to the influence of the Japanese current, which skirts the Alaska coast." *Ibid.*, p. 17.

[73] Arizona's land ownership was 19,327,927 acres; Idaho's 19,269,006; Utah's, 14,803,363; Nevada's, 8,894,920.

[74] November 28, 1950. 81 C: 2 s. *Cong. Rec.*, pp. 15923-30. Some of Senator Butler's allegations were answered by Senator Clinton Anderson, November 29, 1950. *Ibid.*, pp. 15955-60.

[75] The Alaska Statehood Committee, with an original appropriation of $80,000, was created by the Nineteenth Territorial Legislature (Chap. 108, S.L.A., 1949) "in recognition of near attainment of statehood for Alaska," and was continued by the two succeeding legislatures. It was composed of eleven members not more than six of whom could belong to the same political party, appointed by the Governor, and subject to confirmation by the legislature, plus ex-officio, the Delegate, his immediate predecessor, and the Governor.

[76] *ALASKA STATEHOOD. Analysis and Refutation of Minority Views on S. 50 (Senate Report No. 315, 82 C: 1 s).* Alaska Statehood Committee, January 1952, pp. 14-15.

[77] *Ibid.*, p. 16.

[78] On May 17th by Senator Ellender (*Cong. Rec.*, p. 5427); June 21st, by Senator McCarran (*Ibid.*, p. 6847); July 23rd, by Senator Ellender (*Ibid.*, p. 8634); October 11th, by Senator Russell (*Ibid.*, p. 12942).

[79] December 1, 1950. 81 C: 2 s, *Cong. Rec.*, p. 16030.

[80] *Ibid.*, p. 763.

[81] *Ibid.*, p. 764.

[82] *Ibid.*, pp. 767-8.

[83] *Ibid.*, pp. 760-70.

[84] *Ibid.*, p. 775.

[85] *Ibid.*, p. 776.

[86] *Ibid.*, p. 970.

[87] *Ibid.*, p. 1135.

[88] *Ibid.*, p. 1097. The editorial said in part: "It has become clear that . . . the fear that four new senators from regions which do not share the Southern point of view, will lead to an end of the South's ability to block cloture on debate. . . . The question of admitting any territory as a new state is a serious one and deserves consideration on the highest plane. . . . Cloture is a technical matter of much concern to the Senate. . . . But to attempt to maintain a defense against it by permanently keeping thousands of Americans in a status of second-class citizenship is in itself indefensible. Every Senator should search his conscience this week and determine whether he can ethically lend aid and comfort to such a device."

[89] *Ibid.*, pp. 1217-21.

[90] *Ibid.*, p. 1528.

[91] *Ibid.*, p. 1527. Both of Montana's senators, James E. Murray, D., and Zales N. Ecton, R., and both of Washington's senators, Warren G. Magnuson, D., and Harry P. Cain, R., were supporting Alaskan statehood and voted against recommittal.

[92] *Ibid.*, pp. 1526-7. Senator Butler apparently had forgotten that he himself had held hearings as chairman of a Subcommittee of the Committee on Public Lands, as it was then called, in the late summer of 1947. Accompanying him were Senators Arthur V. Watkins, R., of Utah, Ecton and McFarland. Senator Watkins was taken ill early in their visit to Alaska and forced to return to the States, but Senator Butler and his other two committee members held hearings in Ketchikan, Wrangell, Petersburg, Juneau, Skagway, Haines, Anchorage and Fairbanks. After his departure Senator Butler, in a press interview, was quoted as saying that Alaska would attain statehood in from three to five years, and certainly in eight years, and that Alaska would have had it sooner if it had had a basic tax program. The basic tax program was enacted by the Nineteenth Territorial Legislature in 1949.

[93] *Ibid.*, p. 1148.
[94] *Ibid.*, p. 1138.
[95] *Ibid.*, pp. 1142, 1147.
[96] *Ibid.*, p. 1143.
[97] *Ibid.*, p. 1137. There was considerable repetitiveness in the arguments for and against statehood. Rear Admiral Ralph N. Wood, Retired, rendered service far beyond the call of duty, being quoted by statehood opponents not less than four times, twice by Senator Stennis (*Ibid.*, pp. 1140, 1142) and twice by Senator Smathers (*Ibid.*, pp. 1211, 1545). Senator O'Mahoney finally read the testimony at the hearing of W. C. Arnold: "Rear-Admiral Wood comes here at my request and at the expense of the Alaska Salmon Industry, Inc."

"The Alaska Salmon Industry, Inc." continued Senator O'Mahoney, "is the industry under the directorship of Mr. Arnold which financed the campaign against statehood because it wants to impose absentee landlordship upon the people of . . . Alaska." (*Ibid.*, p. 1547.)

In the 1950 debate Senator Anderson had contrasted Senator Stennis's quotation from "an obscure rear-admiral who was brought in to testify . . ." with that of five-star generals who had endorsed statehood for Alaska. 81 C: 2 s, *Cong. Rec.*, p. 15958.
[98] *Ibid.*, pp. 1351-53.
[99] *Ibid.*, pp. 1416-19.
[100] *Ibid.*, p. 1407.
[101] *Ibid.*, p. 1408.
[102] 82 C: 1 s, *Sen. Rept.* 314, pp. 66-69.
[103] The information of Senator Butler's change of heart was conveyed to Delegate Joseph R. Farrington by the Senator in a letter of June 26th, and broadcast by the Delegate July 3rd. A dispatch to the Honolulu *Star-Bulletin* from the Convention Hall at Chicago, July 8th, stated:

"Taft has removed one of the most persistent sources of opposition to statehood by getting Senator Butler of Nebraska to drop his hitherto implacable animosity toward statehood legislation."

Senator Butler was a strong supporter of Taft's candidacy and in his letter to Delegate Farrington expressed the belief that Taft would be President.
[104] Hawaii's state constitution was adopted November 7, 1950, by a vote of 82,788 for to 27,109 against.
[105] September 17, 1950.
[106] 83 C: 1 s, *H. Doc. 75, Cong. Rec.*, p. 751. Speaking of resource conservation, President Eisenhower continued: ". . . these particular resource problems pertain to the Department of the Interior. Another of its major concerns is our country's island possessions. Here one matter deserves attention. The platforms of both political parties promise immediate statehood to Hawaii. The people of that territory have earned that status. Statehood should be granted promptly with the first election scheduled for 1954."
[107] H.J.M. 17. S.L.A. 1953.
[108] After the death of the newspaper's owner Austin E. Lathrop, it was sold to C. W. Snedden, and John Joseph Ryan became its editor. Its changed attitude was expressed editorially, in part, as follows:

"Here in Alaska we live at the whim of federal agencies and exist according to the will of Congress. We are disfranchised, helpless American citizens, living under a form of oppression almost as disheartening and tyrannical as that which brought about the Boston Tea Party and the glorious American Revolution of 1776.

"The *News-Miner* has long advocated that we should try to build industry and develop the resources of Alaska before taking the long step to statehood. But we are disheartened with this waiting and waiting, while our destinies are twisted this way and that way by threats of filibusters, the whims of federal agencies and the uncomprehending attitude taken by many Congressmen. . . .

"Alaska has a great destiny. We are going to be a prosperous, valued State of the Union some day, through the toil, foresight and enterprise of our citizens here in the north. But . . . we are not going to

make substantial progress toward this
destiny . . . living under the supervision of a Congress that does not
understand our problems or realize
our possibilities.

"We say, turn Alaska loose from
this deadly federal embrace. Give
Americans in Alaska the full privileges of American citizenship. Turn
Alaska's destiny over to Alaskans.
. . . Alaskan citizens can meet the
challenges of statehood, and they are
eager to do so. Alaskans should demand statehood, now."

[109] June 26, 1953. *H. Rept. on H.R.
2982, 83 C: 1 s.*
[110] *Hearings before the Subcommittee
on Territories and Insular Possessions
of the Committee on Interior and
Insular Affairs, 83 C: 1 s, pp. 30-37.*
[111] *Alaska Statehood and Elective Governorship. Hearings before the Committee on Interior and Insular Affairs,
U.S. Senate on S. 50 and S. 224.
83 C: 1 s.* The committee members
attending the hearings were Butler,
Barrett, Murray, Anderson, Clements
and Jackson.
[112] As reported in the *Alaska Daily
Empire,* September 8, 1953.
[113] September 8, 1953, in an editorial
entitled "The Tragedy of 1953."
[114] The contradictory aspects of the
episode were set forth in an Anchorage *Times* editorial, September 28,
1953, entitled "Abracadabra in Statehood."
[115] *Alaska Statehood. Hearings before
the Committee on Interior and
Insular Affairs, U.S. Senate, 83 C:
2 s,* on S. 50, pp. 329-39.
[116] March 9, 1954. 83 C: 2 s, *Cong.
Rec.,* p. 2745.
[117] *Ibid.,* p. 2749.
[118] *Ibid.,* p. 2755.
[119] *Ibid.,* pp. 2886-8.
[120] *Ibid.,* p. 2888.
[121] March 11, *Ibid.,* p. 2910.
[122] March 12, *Ibid.,* pp. 2978-9.
[123] *Ibid.,* p. 3297.
[124] Except for an article by Walter
Lippmann in his syndicated column
which appeared in the Washington
Post, March 16th. It was effectively
answered in the Scripps-Howard
newspapers by Douglas Smith, whose

article appeared in the Washington
Daily News, March 18th.
[125] *Cong. Rec.,* p. 4078.
[126] *Ibid.,* p. 4072.
[127] *Ibid.,* p. 4081.
[128] *Ibid.,* 192. April 1, 1954. *Ibid.,* p.
4090.

CHAPTER 29

[1] For a full treatment of this incredible
propaganda campaign, the reader is
directed to an article by Dr. Marjorie
Shearon, which was placed in the
Congressional Record of August 3,
1966, p. 17223, by Senator E. L.
Bartlett.
[2] They were Howard W. Pollock, William K. Boardman, Carl T. Rentsch-
ler, John B. Coghill, and Frederick
O. Eastaugh.
[3] The members of the Constitutional
Convention of Alaska were Rev. R.
Rolland Armstrong, Juneau, Presbyterian minister (later president of
Sheldon Jackson Junior College in
Sitka; Miss Dorothy J. Awes, Palmer,
lawyer; Frank Barr, Fairbanks, bush
pilot, territorial legislator; John C.
Boswell, Fairbanks, manager of operations of the U.S. Smelting, Refining
and Mining Company; Seaborn J.
Buckalew, Jr., Anchorage, lawyer,
territorial legislator; John B. Coghill,
Nenana, merchant, territorial legislator; George D. Cooper, Fairbanks,
owner of a ready-mix concrete business; John M. Cross, Kotzebue, bush
pilot; Edward V. Davis, Anchorage,
lawyer; James P. Doogan, Fairbanks,
trucker and mover; William A. Egan,
Valdez, merchant, territorial legislator
(later governor of Alaska); Truman
C. Emberg, Dillingham, commercial
fisherman and union official; Mrs.
Helen Fischer, Anchorage, housewife
and Democratic Party official; Victor
Fischer, Anchorage, city planner;
Douglas Gray, Juneau, former Fish
and Wildlife Service agent, hotel
manager, territorial legislator; Thomas
C. Harris, Valdez, businessman; Mrs.
Mildred R. Hermann, Juneau, law-
yer, Alaska Director of the Office of
Price Administration during World

War II; Herb Hilscher, Anchorage, author; Jack Hinckel, Kodiak, land consignee for Union Oil Company; James Hurley, Palmer, manager of Alaska Rural Rehabilitation Corporation; Maurice T. Johnson, Fairbanks, lawyer, territorial legislator; Yule F. Kilcher, Homer, homesteader and rancher; Leonard H. King, Haines, merchant; William W. Knight, Sitka, former superintendent of the Alaska Pioneers' Home; W. W. Laws, Nome, chief of police, territorial legislator; Eldor R. Lee, Petersburg, commercial fisherman; Rev. Maynard D. Londborg, Unalakleet; Steve McCutcheon, Anchorage, photo-shop owner, territorial legislator; George M. McLaughin, Anchorage, lawyer; Robert J. McNealy, Fairbanks, lawyer, territorial legislator; John A. McNees, Nome, businessman, territorial legislator; M. R. Marston, Anchorage, realtor; organizer of Alaska territorial Guard; Irwin L. Metcalf, Seward, merchant; Leslie Nerland, Fairbanks, merchants; James Nolan, Wrangell, druggist, territorial legislator; Mrs. Katerine D. Nordale, Juneau, bank employee, former collector of customs for Alaska; Frank Peratrovich, Klawock, merchant and fisherman, territorial legislator; Chris Poulsen, Anchorage, theater owner; Peter L. Reader, Nome, businessman; Burke Riley, Haines, lawyer, former administrative assistant to the governor, and territorial legislator; Ralph J. Rivers, Fairbanks, lawyer, former U.S. Attorney, territorial legislator, territorial attorney general, Mayor of Fairbanks, member of Unemployment Compensation Commission, later member of U.S. House of Representatives; Victor C. Rivers, Anchorage, architect and engineer, territorial legislator; R. E. Robertson, Juneau, lawyer; John H. Rosswog, Cordova, druggist; B. D. Stewart, Sitka, retired territorial Commissioner of Mines; W. O. Smith, Ketchikan, commercial fisherman; George Sundborg, Juneau, newspaper editor, former executive assistant to the governor and general manager of the Alaska Development Board; Mrs.

Dora M. Sweeney, Juneau, housewife, territorial legislator; Warren A. Taylor, Fairbanks, lawyer, territorial legislator; H. R. Vander Leest, Juneau, retired druggist; M. J. Walsh, Nome, miner and businessman; Barrie M. White, Anchorage, businessman; Mrs. Ada B. Wien, Fairbanks, housewife.

[4] However, the President of the United States in recent years has exercised similar power by impounding funds appropriated by Congress and refusing to spend them, as in the case of the ill-fated B-70 bomber.

[5] They were Michigan in 1835; Iowa in 1846; California in 1850; Minnesota in 1858; Oregon in 1859; and Kansas in 1861.

[6] A fuller account of "The Battle for Alaska Statehood" appears in a book with that title by the author published by the University of Alaska and the Alaskan Centennial Commission in 1967.

[7] The bond issues were: $15.5 million for two new ferries and related ferry-landing facilities; $16.9 million for construction at the University of Alaska and for construction of buildings for community colleges in Juneau and Anchorage; $10.5 million for state matching funds for highway construction; $11.5 million for airport improvements; $5 million for regional high schools in rural areas of the state; $2.2 million for elementary and high school construction; and $900,000 for state matching funds for state parks and campgrounds.

[8] Baker v. Carr, 369 U.S., 186, Reynolds v. Sims, 377 U.S. 533.

[9] Warren Colver.

[10] S. Con. Res. 9, H. Con. Res. 27.

[11] The senators were: Robert R. Blodgett, Howard Bradshaw, Neal W. Foster, John B. Hall, Harold Z. Hansen, David C. Harrison, Eben Hopson, Yule F. Kilcher, Robert J. McNealy, James Nolan, Alfred Owen, Grant H. Pearson, Frank Peratrovich, Pearse M. Walsh, Robert H. Ziegler.

[12] Shortly after the reversal of his decision on reapportionment, Judge von der Heydt was selected from a number of qualified members of the

Alaska bench and bar and was nominated for a U.S. district judgeship in Alaska, succeeding Judge Walter Hodge, who was retiring.

CHAPTER 30

[1] They were the Departments of Administration, Law, Revenue, Health and Welfare, Labor, Public Safety, Commerce, Natural Resources, Public Works, and Military Affairs. The Departments of Education and Fish and Game were headed by boards appointed by the governor. In 1962 Egan created a separate Department of Highways by executive order. The 1962 legislature created a Department of Economic Development and Planning, which in 1966 became the Department of Economic Development.

CHAPTER 31

[1] *Alaska Trade Study*, Federal Maritime Commission, Washington, D.C., July 1967.
[2] These lines were Air France, Lufthansa, KLM, SAS, and Japan Airlines.

CHAPTER 32

[1] *Economic Development in Alaska*, Federal Field Committee for Development Planning in Alaska, Washington, D.C., August 1966, p. 6.
[2] *Response to Disaster*, Federal Reconstruction and Development Planning Commission for Alaska, Washington, D.C., September 1964, p. 1.
[3] Except in the Indian community of Metlakatla, which the Secretary of the Interior exempted from the fishtrap ban. The State of Alaska took the matter to court and eventually in 1962 the Supreme Court of the United States decided that the Secretary did have such authority over Metlakatla because of its legal status as a reservation.

However, similar exemptions for Angoon and Kake were struck down by the Court in a companion decision. (*Metlakatla Indian Community v. Egan* and *Organized Village of Kake and Angoon Community Association v. Egan*).
[4] *Economic Development in Alaska*, Federal Field Committee, p. 22.

CHAPTER 33

[1] In Alaska, according to established usage, *natives* means Indians, Eskimos and Aleuts.
[2] Testimony was presented by the following at the Senate Interior Committee hearings on Native Land Claims at Anchorage, Alaska, February 8, 9 and 10, 1968: Alaska Sportsmen's Council; Amedias, Frank, Bethel Native Association; Anderson, Ralph, Chugiak, Alaska; Bailey, Eben, G., resident of Alaska; Begich, Nick, Alaska State senator; Bellringer, Edward A., president, Alaska Sportsmen's Council; Boddy, A. W. "Bud," executive director, Alaska Sportsmen's Council; Borbridge, John, Jr., president, Central Council of Tlingit and Haida Indians; Boyko, Edgar Paul, attorney general of Alaska; Bradley, J. B., president, Juneau Bar Association; Bradley, Waring, geologist, Anchorage, Alaska; Brenwick, Lucy, Copper Center, Alaska; Brewer, Dr. Max, director, Arctic Research Bureau; Charley, Walter, Ahtna Tannoh Ninnah Association, Copper River Indians; Chichenoff, Katherine, Kodiak Area Native Association; Connor, Roger, attorney, Aleut League; Christiansen, Raymond C., Alaska State senator; Deacon, John, Grayling, Alaska; Dean, S. Bobo, attorney for Metlakatla Indians; Degnan, Frank, Unalakleet, Alaska; Delkittie, Mike, Nondalton-Lime Hills Indian group; Demientieff, Claude, Galena, Alaska; Demaski, Andrew, chairman, Council of Nulato; Evanoff, Bill, Nondalton-Lime Hills Indian group; Floresta, Helen, Nondalton-Lime Hills Indian group; Frank, Richard, president, Fairbanks Native Association; Franz, Charlie, president, Alaska Peninsula Native Association; Fritz, Dr. Milo, member, Alaska House of

Representatives; Goodlataw, Joe, chief, Copper River Tribe; Gordon, Rt. Rev. William, J., Episcopal missionary, district of Alaska; Groh, Clifford, lawyer, Anchorage, Alaska; Groves, Meredith A., superintendent, Alaska mission, Methodist Church; Guess, Gene, minority whip, Alaska House of Representatives; Hays, Rev. Walter, Jr., president, Alaska Council of Churches; Hensley, William L., a representative in the Alaska Legislature; Hickel, Gov. Walter J., Alaska; Holdsworth, Phil, Alaska Miners Association; Hopson, Alfred, Arctic Slope Native Association; Hopson, Eben, Arctic Slope Native Association; Isaacs, Andrew, chief, village of Tanacross; Jackson, Barry W., attorney for a number of Indian organizations; John, Peter, spokesman for Minto village; Johnson, John J., resident of Alaska; Katchatag, Stanton, Anchorage, Alaska; Kelly, Phil, president, THEATA; Kelly, Thomas E., commissioner, department of natural resources; Kelly, Walter, Bethel Native Association; Ketzler, Alfred R., spokesman from Nenana, Alaska; Kignak, Ernest, Arctic Slope Native Association; King, George, Nunivak Island, Alaska; Klashinoff, John, Cordova, Alaska; Kvasnikoff, Sarjus, English Bay, Alaska; Laumoff, Ewen Moses, Kodiak Area Native Association; Lekanof, Flore, president, Aleut League; Lovely, Lum, geologist, Anchorage, Alaska; McCabe, David, Anchorage, Alaska; McCutcheon, Stanley, lawyer, Anchorage, Alaska; Mallot, Byron I., president of Five Chiefs of Yakutat; Marston, Col. Muktuk, Alaska National Guard; Matfay, Larry, Kodiak Area Native Association; Meganack, Walter, Port Graham, Alaska; Metcalf, Hon. Lee, a U.S. Senator from the State of Montana; Miller, Dave, first vice president, Takotna-McGrath Native Association; Mizak, Ivan, Bethel Native Association; Moerlein, George, chairman, Land Use Committee, Alaska Miners Association; Mueller, Jay C., president, Alaska Big Game Trophy Club, Inc.; Naanes, Elva, secretary, Alaska Fed-

eration of Natives; Nicholls, Hugh, first vice president, Arctic Slope Native Association; Northway, Walter, chief, Ajunk Northway village; Notti, Emil, president, Alaska Federation of Natives; Nylin, Ernest, Seward Peninsula Native Association; Ondola, George, chairman, Village Council of Eklutna; Oquilluk, William, Seward Peninsula Native Association; Oskolkoff, Larry, president, Kenai Peninsula Native Association; Oskolkoff, Father Simeon, Orthodox priest, Tyonek village; Paneak, Simon, Arctic Slope Native Association; Paul, Frederick, Arctic Slope Association; Paul, William, Sr., representing Tlingit, Haida, and Arctic Slope Natives; Paukan, Moses, president, Association of Village Council Presidents of the Lower Kuskokwim and Yukon villages; Peacock, J. C., Washington, D.C.; Peratrovich, Frank, Alaska Native Brotherhood; Pillifant, Thomas H., Eklutna, Alaska; Pollock, Hon. Howard W., a U.S. Representative in Congress from the State of Alaska; Rader, John, former state senator and attorney general; Rasmuson, Elmer, former mayor of Anchorage; Rexford, Herman, chief, Village Council of Kartovik, Alaska; Rothstein, Joe, executive editor, Anchorage Daily News; Sackett, John, Huslia, Alaska; Samuelson, Harold Harvey, Akiakhak, Alaska; Schroeder, Herman, Dillingham, Alaska; Semple (Simple), Peter, spokesman from Fort Yukon; Seton, Joe, Bethel Native Association; Severson, George, Nondalton-Lime Hills Indian group; Shadura, Alex, Kenai, Alaska; Smith, William de Ville, Nondalton-Lime Hills Indian group; Soboleff, Rev. Walter, president of Alaska Native Brotherhood; Stevens, Ted, majority leader, Alaska House of Representatives; Stick, Edna, Kenai Peninsula Native Organization; Tallman, James K., attorney, Nondalton-Lime Hills Indian group; Tansy, Ruby, spokesman for Cantwell village; Thiele, Mrs. Flora, Kenai Peninsula Native Association; Topsekok, Frank, Seward Peninsula Native Association; Trigg, Jerome, Seward Peninsula Native Association; Weissbrodt, I. S. attorney, Tlingit and Haida Indians; Westdah, John, Alaska State representative; Wilcox, Donald, secretary-director, Alaska Miners Association; Wilson, Alexander, Kenai, Alaska; Woodman, Betzi, Anchorage, Alaska; Wright, Donald R., president, Cook Inlet Native Association; Zabriskie, Father Alexander, Episcopal Church of Anchorage; Zaegel, William, Anchorage, Alaska.

[2] *Hearings before the Subcommittee on Employment, Manpower, and Poverty of Committee on Labor and Public Welfare, U.S. Senate,* "Hunger and Malnutrition in America," July 11–12, 1967, p. 188.

CHAPTER 34

[1] Its members were Claire O. Banks, Anchorage; C. M. Binkley, Fairbanks; William R. Cashen, College; William E. Feero, Skagway; Vernon D. Forbes, Fairbanks; Mrs. Genevieve F. Harmon, Juneau; Mrs. Alice A. Harrigan, Sitka; Robert K. Herman, Nome; Milton A. McRae, Kodiak; Jack R. Peck, Anchorage; Robert L. Powell, Anchorage; Mrs. Doris Volzke, Ketchikan; Arthur F. Waldron, Anchorage; Edward M. Wolden, Anchorage; Frank P. Young, Fairbanks.

[2] The other communities were Barrow, Bethel, Cordova, Gambell, Haines, Hydaburg, Klawock, Kodiak, Kotzebue, Matanuska-Susitna Borough, Ninilchik, Nome, Petersburg, Point Hope, Savoonga, Seldovia, Seward, Skagway, Soldotna, Valdez, Wrangell.

[3] These included: *The Purchase of Alaska,* by Archie Shiels; *100 Years of Alaskan Poetry,* edited by Carol Beery Davis; and *The Battle for Alaska Statehood,* by Ernest Gruening. The Centennial also stimulated the publication of other books, although not officially sponsored by the commission, which greatly enriched existing Alaskana. Among them are *Lost Heritage of Alaska,* by Polly and Leon Gordon Miller; *William Henry Seward,* by Glyndon G. Van Deusen; *Mt. McKinley (The Pioneer Climbs),* by Terris Moore; "U.S. Army in Alaska 100 Years"; "An Alaskan Reader" edited by Ernest Gruening; *The Alaska Railroad,* by Edwin M. Fitch; *Sourdough Sagas,* edited by Herbert L. Heller; *Eskimos of the Nushagak River,* by James W. Van Stone; *Account of the Russian Discoveries between Asia and America* (first published in 1787), by William Coxe; *People of the Noatak,* by Clare Fejes; and *Alaska and Its History,* edited by Morgan Sherwood.

INDEX

ABOUT THE AUTHOR

ERNEST GRUENING gave up a career in medicine to go into journalism. He began his apprenticeship in Boston, serving as reporter, rewrite man, copy-desk editor, editorial writer, city editor and managing editor on the Boston *American*, the Boston *Herald*, the Boston *Traveler* and the Boston *Journal*. Later he served as managing editor of the New York *Tribune* and as managing editor of the New York *Post*, as well as managing editor of *The Nation*.

His interest in Latin-American affairs led him to journalistic campaigns to withdraw U. S. marines from Haiti, Santo Domingo and Nicaragua, and to go to Mexico and report on conditions there following the Mexican revolution which had begun in 1910. A book, *Mexico and Its Heritage*, in 1928, resulted from his studies and travels in Mexico. His knowledge in this field led to his appointment in 1933 as the adviser to the United States delegation at the 7th Inter-American conference in Montevideo.

In 1934 President Roosevelt invited Gruening to head a new agency, the Division of Territories and Island Possessions under the Department of the Interior. This agency was to have supervision of the federal relations of Hawaii, Alaska, Puerto Rico, the Virgin Islands, the Equatorial Islands and, later, until their independence, of the Philippines. This agency likewise assisted in the organization of the United States Antarctic Service, which sent the first government expedition to the world's farthest south.

In his five years as director of the Division of Territories, Gruening paid two visits to Alaska and became familiar with its problems. In 1939 he was appointed governor of Alaska and served until April 1953. His service of thirteen years and four months was the longest of any governor in Alaska's history. It included appointment for three four-year terms by the President and confirmation by the United States Senate which was granted each time unanimously. He was, therefore, the war governor of Alaska. As chairman of the Alaska War Council, he brought about the organization of Alaska's National Guard and when this was federalized on the eve of World War II, a Territorial Guard.

After his retirement from the governorship he devoted his efforts to advancing the cause of Alaskan statehood. This book, published in 1954, was a part of that effort. In 1955 Gruening was asked to deliver the keynote address to the Alaska Constitutional Convention whose fifty-seven delegates assembled on the campus of the University of Alaska. The address was entitled "Let us End American Colonialism." In 1956 Gruening was elected a United States senator under the so-called Alaska-Tennessee Plan, which had been approved by Alaska's voters at the same election at which they ratified the proposed constitution for the hoped-for state. Along with William A. Egan, also elected as senator, and Ralph J. Rivers, elected as representative, the Alaska Congressional delegation went to Washington to present their credentials to Congress. They were not seated as had been other earlier delegations from states adopting the Tennessee plan, and were informed that in the event of statehood they would have to run again for their respective offices, to which they cheerfully assented. They spent the next two years lobbying the members of the Eighty-fifth Congress, which enacted the desired statehood bill. Gruening was then elected to the United States Senate in 1958 and re-elected in 1962.

In 1914 Ernest had married Dorothy Elizabeth Smith of Norwood, Massachusetts. They had three sons, Ernest, Jr., Huntington Sanders and Peter Brown. Ernest, Jr., died in 1931, aged fifteen, and Peter in 1955. At the time of his death at age thirty-two, Peter, who had been a fighter pilot in World War II, was the general manager of the United Press for Australia and New Zealand.

While living in the Governor's House, Dorothy and Ernest built their Alaska home at Eagle River Landing, twenty-four miles north of Juneau.

Their son, Huntington, was a pilot in the Eighth Air Force during World War II, came to Alaska after his military service, began flying as a commercial pilot, and became operations manager and vice-president of Alaska Coastal Airlines, where he continued his duties after its merger in 1968 with Alaska Airlines. The Hunt Gruenings have five children: Clark, who is studying law at George Washington University; Bradford, who volunteered for military service in 1967 and became a paratrooper in Vietnam; Winthrop, who is at the Air Force Academy at Colorado Springs; Kimberley Louise and Peter Sather, who are living with their parents in Juneau.